P9-CAJ-590

American Casebook Series
Hornbook Series and Basic Legal Texts
Black Letter Series and Nutshell Series

of

WEST PUBLISHING COMPANY
P.O. Box 64526
St. Paul, Minnesota 55164-0526

Accounting

FARIS' ACCOUNTING AND LAW IN A NUTSHELL, 377 pages, 1984. Softcover. (Text)

FIFLIS, KRIPKE AND FOSTER'S TEACHING MATERIALS ON ACCOUNTING FOR BUSINESS LAWYERS, Third Edition, 838 pages, 1984. (Casebook)

SIEGEL AND SIEGEL'S ACCOUNTING AND FINANCIAL DISCLOSURE: A GUIDE TO BASIC CONCEPTS, 259 pages, 1983. Softcover. (Text)

Administrative Law

BONFIELD AND ASIMOW'S STATE AND FEDERAL ADMINISTRATIVE LAW, 826 pages, 1989. Teacher's Manual available. (Casebook)

GELLHORN AND LEVIN'S ADMINISTRATIVE LAW AND PROCESS IN A NUTSHELL, Third Edition, approximately 420 pages, 1990. Softcover. (Text)

MASHAW AND MERRILL'S CASES AND MATERIALS ON ADMINISTRATIVE LAW—THE AMERICAN PUBLIC LAW SYSTEM, Second Edition, 976 pages, 1985. (Casebook) 1989 Supplement.

ROBINSON, GELLHORN AND BRUFF'S THE ADMINISTRATIVE PROCESS, Third Edition, 978 pages, 1986. (Casebook)

Admiralty

HEALY AND SHARPE'S CASES AND MATERIALS ON ADMIRALTY, Second Edition, 876 pages, 1986. (Casebook)

MARAIST'S ADMIRALTY IN A NUTSHELL, Second Edition, 379 pages, 1988. Softcover. (Text)

SCHOENBAUM'S HORNBOOK ON ADMIRALTY AND MARITIME LAW, Student Edition, 692 pages, 1987 with 1989 pocket part. (Text)

Agency—Partnership

FESSLER'S ALTERNATIVES TO INCORPORATION FOR PERSONS IN QUEST OF PROFIT, Second Edition, 326 pages, 1986. Softcover. Teacher's Manual available. (Casebook)

HENN'S CASES AND MATERIALS ON AGENCY, PARTNERSHIP AND OTHER UNINCORPORATED BUSINESS ENTERPRISES, Second Edition, 733 pages, 1985. Teacher's Manual available. (Casebook)

REUSCHLEIN AND GREGORY'S HORNBOOK ON THE LAW OF AGENCY AND PARTNERSHIP, Second Edition, 683 pages, 1990. (Text)

SELECTED CORPORATION AND PARTNERSHIP STATUTES, RULES AND FORMS. Softcover. 727 pages, 1989.

STEFFEN AND KERR'S CASES ON AGENCY-PARTNERSHIP, Fourth Edition, 859 pages, 1980. (Casebook)

STEFFEN'S AGENCY-PARTNERSHIP IN A NUTSHELL, 364 pages, 1977. Softcover. (Text)

Agricultural Law

MEYER, PEDERSEN, THORSON AND DAVIDSON'S AGRICULTURAL LAW: CASES AND MATERIALS, 931 pages, 1985. Teacher's Manual available. (Casebook)

Alternative Dispute Resolution

KANOWITZ' CASES AND MATERIALS ON ALTERNATIVE DISPUTE RESOLUTION, 1024 pages,

---

List current as of July, 1990

Alternative Dispute Resolution—Cont'd

1986. Teacher's Manual available. (Casebook) 1990 Supplement.

RISKIN AND WESTBROOK'S DISPUTE RESOLUTION AND LAWYERS, 468 pages, 1987. Teacher's Manual available. (Casebook)

RISKIN AND WESTBROOK'S DISPUTE RESOLUTION AND LAWYERS, Abridged Edition, 223 pages, 1987. Softcover. Teacher's Manual available. (Casebook)

American Indian Law

CANBY'S AMERICAN INDIAN LAW IN A NUTSHELL, Second Edition, 336 pages, 1988. Softcover. (Text)

GETCHES AND WILKINSON'S CASES AND MATERIALS ON FEDERAL INDIAN LAW, Second Edition, 880 pages, 1986. (Casebook)

Antitrust—see also Regulated Industries, Trade Regulation

FOX AND SULLIVAN'S CASES AND MATERIALS ON ANTITRUST, 935 pages, 1989. Teacher's Manual available. (Casebook)

GELLHORN'S ANTITRUST LAW AND ECONOMICS IN A NUTSHELL, Third Edition, 472 pages, 1986. Softcover. (Text)

HOVENKAMP'S BLACK LETTER ON ANTITRUST, 323 pages, 1986. Softcover. (Review)

HOVENKAMP'S HORNBOOK ON ECONOMICS AND FEDERAL ANTITRUST LAW, Student Edition, 414 pages, 1985. (Text)

OPPENHEIM, WESTON AND MCCARTHY'S CASES AND COMMENTS ON FEDERAL ANTITRUST LAWS, Fourth Edition, 1168 pages, 1981. (Casebook) 1985 Supplement.

POSNER AND EASTERBROOK'S CASES AND ECONOMIC NOTES ON ANTITRUST, Second Edition, 1077 pages, 1981. (Casebook) 1984–85 Supplement.

SULLIVAN'S HORNBOOK OF THE LAW OF ANTITRUST, 886 pages, 1977. (Text)

Appellate Advocacy—see Trial and Appellate Advocacy

Architecture and Engineering Law

SWEET'S LEGAL ASPECTS OF ARCHITECTURE, ENGINEERING AND THE CONSTRUCTION PROCESS, Fourth Edition, 889 pages, 1989. Teacher's Manual available. (Casebook)

Art Law

DUBOFF'S ART LAW IN A NUTSHELL, 335 pages, 1984. Softcover. (Text)

Banking Law

LOVETT'S BANKING AND FINANCIAL INSTITUTIONS LAW IN A NUTSHELL, Second Edition, 464 pages, 1988. Softcover. (Text)

SYMONS AND WHITE'S TEACHING MATERIALS ON BANKING LAW, Second Edition, 993 pages, 1984. Teacher's Manual available. (Casebook) 1987 Supplement.

Business Planning—see also Corporate Finance

PAINTER'S PROBLEMS AND MATERIALS IN BUSINESS PLANNING, Second Edition, 1008 pages, 1984. (Casebook) 1990 Supplement.

Statutory Supplement. *See Selected Corporation and Partnership*

SELECTED CORPORATION AND PARTNERSHIP STATUTES, RULES AND FORMS. 727 pages, 1989. Softcover.

Civil Procedure—see also Federal Jurisdiction and Procedure

AMERICAN BAR ASSOCIATION SECTION OF LITIGATION—READINGS ON ADVERSARIAL JUSTICE: THE AMERICAN APPROACH TO ADJUDICATION, 217 pages, 1988. Softcover. (Coursebook)

CLERMONT'S BLACK LETTER ON CIVIL PROCEDURE, Second Edition, 332 pages, 1988. Softcover. (Review)

COUND, FRIEDENTHAL, MILLER AND SEXTON'S CASES AND MATERIALS ON CIVIL PROCEDURE, Fifth Edition, 1284 pages, 1989. Teacher's Manual available. (Casebook)

COUND, FRIEDENTHAL, MILLER AND SEXTON'S CIVIL PROCEDURE SUPPLEMENT. Approximately 450 pages, 1990. Softcover. (Casebook Supplement)

FEDERAL RULES OF CIVIL PROCEDURE—EDUCATIONAL EDITION. Softcover. Approximately 635 pages, 1990.

FRIEDENTHAL, KANE AND MILLER'S HORNBOOK ON CIVIL PROCEDURE, 876 pages, 1985. (Text)

KANE AND LEVINE'S CIVIL PROCEDURE IN CALIFORNIA: STATE AND FEDERAL 498 pages, 1989. Softcover. (Casebook Supplement)

Civil Procedure—Cont'd

KANE'S CIVIL PROCEDURE IN A NUTSHELL, Second Edition, 306 pages, 1986. Softcover. (Text)

KOFFLER AND REPPY'S HORNBOOK ON COMMON LAW PLEADING, 663 pages, 1969. (Text)

MARCUS, REDISH AND SHERMAN'S CIVIL PROCEDURE: A MODERN APPROACH, 1027 pages, 1989. Teacher's Manual available. (Casebook)

MARCUS AND SHERMAN'S COMPLEX LITIGATION–CASES AND MATERIALS ON ADVANCED CIVIL PROCEDURE, 846 pages, 1985. Teacher's Manual available. (Casebook) 1989 Supplement.

PARK'S COMPUTER-AIDED EXERCISES ON CIVIL PROCEDURE, Second Edition, 167 pages, 1983. Softcover. (Coursebook)

SIEGEL'S HORNBOOK ON NEW YORK PRACTICE, 1011 pages, 1978, with 1987 pocket part. (Text)

Commercial Law

BAILEY AND HAGEDORN'S SECURED TRANSACTIONS IN A NUTSHELL, Third Edition, 390 pages, 1988. Softcover. (Text)

EPSTEIN, MARTIN, HENNING AND NICKLES' BASIC UNIFORM COMMERCIAL CODE TEACHING MATERIALS, Third Edition, 704 pages, 1988. Teacher's Manual available. (Casebook)

HENSON'S HORNBOOK ON SECURED TRANSACTIONS UNDER THE U.C.C., Second Edition, 504 pages, 1979, with 1979 pocket part. (Text)

MURRAY'S COMMERCIAL LAW, PROBLEMS AND MATERIALS, 366 pages, 1975. Teacher's Manual available. Softcover. (Coursebook)

NICKLES' BLACK LETTER ON COMMERCIAL PAPER, 450 pages, 1988. Softcover. (Review)

NICKLES, MATHESON AND DOLAN'S MATERIALS FOR UNDERSTANDING CREDIT AND PAYMENT SYSTEMS, 923 pages, 1987. Teacher's Manual available. (Casebook)

NORDSTROM, MURRAY AND CLOVIS' PROBLEMS AND MATERIALS ON SALES, 515 pages, 1982. (Casebook)

NORDSTROM, MURRAY AND CLOVIS' PROBLEMS AND MATERIALS ON SECURED TRANSACTIONS, 594 pages, 1987. (Casebook)

RUBIN AND COOTER'S THE PAYMENT SYSTEM: CASES, MATERIALS AND ISSUES, 885 pages, 1989. (Casebook)

SELECTED COMMERCIAL STATUTES. Softcover. Approximately 1650 pages, 1990.

SPEIDEL'S BLACK LETTER ON SALES AND SALES FINANCING, 363 pages, 1984. Softcover. (Review)

SPEIDEL, SUMMERS AND WHITE'S COMMERCIAL LAW: TEACHING MATERIALS, Fourth Edition, 1448 pages, 1987. Teacher's Manual available. (Casebook)

SPEIDEL, SUMMERS AND WHITE'S COMMERCIAL PAPER: TEACHING MATERIALS, Fourth Edition, 578 pages, 1987. Reprint from Speidel et al., Commercial Law, Fourth Edition. Teacher's Manual available. (Casebook)

SPEIDEL, SUMMERS AND WHITE'S SALES: TEACHING MATERIALS, Fourth Edition, 804 pages, 1987. Reprint from Speidel et al., Commercial Law, Fourth Edition. Teacher's Manual available. (Casebook)

SPEIDEL, SUMMERS AND WHITE'S SECURED TRANSACTIONS: TEACHING MATERIALS, Fourth Edition, 485 pages, 1987. Reprint from Speidel et al., Commercial Law, Fourth Edition. Teacher's Manual available. (Casebook)

STOCKTON'S SALES IN A NUTSHELL, Second Edition, 370 pages, 1981. Softcover. (Text)

STONE'S UNIFORM COMMERCIAL CODE IN A NUTSHELL, Third Edition, 580 pages, 1989. Softcover. (Text)

WEBER AND SPEIDEL'S COMMERCIAL PAPER IN A NUTSHELL, Third Edition, 404 pages, 1982. Softcover. (Text)

WHITE AND SUMMERS' HORNBOOK ON THE UNIFORM COMMERCIAL CODE, Third Edition, Student Edition, 1386 pages, 1988. (Text)

Community Property

MENNELL AND BOYKOFF'S COMMUNITY PROPERTY IN A NUTSHELL, Second Edition, 432 pages, 1988. Softcover. (Text)

VERRALL AND BIRD'S CASES AND MATERIALS

Community Property—Cont'd

ON CALIFORNIA COMMUNITY PROPERTY, Fifth Edition, 604 pages, 1988. (Casebook)

Comparative Law

BARTON, GIBBS, LI AND MERRYMAN'S LAW IN RADICALLY DIFFERENT CULTURES, 960 pages, 1983. (Casebook)

GLENDON, GORDON AND OSAKWE'S COMPARATIVE LEGAL TRADITIONS: TEXT, MATERIALS AND CASES ON THE CIVIL LAW, COMMON LAW AND SOCIALIST LAW TRADITIONS, 1091 pages, 1985. (Casebook)

GLENDON, GORDON AND OSAKWE'S COMPARATIVE LEGAL TRADITIONS IN A NUTSHELL. 402 pages, 1982. Softcover. (Text)

LANGBEIN'S COMPARATIVE CRIMINAL PROCEDURE: GERMANY, 172 pages, 1977. Softcover. (Casebook)

Computers and Law

MAGGS AND SPROWL'S COMPUTER APPLICATIONS IN THE LAW, 316 pages, 1987. (Coursebook)

MASON'S USING COMPUTERS IN THE LAW: AN INTRODUCTION AND PRACTICAL GUIDE, Second Edition, 288 pages, 1988. Softcover. (Coursebook)

Conflict of Laws

CRAMTON, CURRIE AND KAY'S CASES—COMMENTS—QUESTIONS ON CONFLICT OF LAWS, Fourth Edition, 876 pages, 1987. (Casebook)

HAY'S BLACK LETTER ON CONFLICT OF LAWS, 330 pages, 1989. Softcover. (Review)

SCOLES ANL HAY'S HORNBOOK ON CONFLICT OF LAWS, Student Edition, 1085 pages, 1982, with 1988–89 pocket part. (Text)

SEIGEL'S CONFLICTS IN A NUTSHELL, 470 pages, 1982. Softcover. (Text)

Constitutional Law—Civil Rights—see also Foreign Relations and National Security Law

ABERNATHY'S CASES AND MATERIALS ON CIVIL RIGHTS, 660 pages, 1980. (Casebook)

BARRON AND DIENES' BLACK LETTER ON CONSTITUTIONAL LAW, Second Edition, 310 pages, 1987. Softcover. (Review)

BARRON AND DIENES' CONSTITUTIONAL LAW IN A NUTSHELL, 389 pages, 1986. Softcover. (Text)

ENGDAHL'S CONSTITUTIONAL FEDERALISM IN A NUTSHELL, Second Edition, 411 pages, 1987. Softcover. (Text)

FARBER AND SHERRY'S HISTORY OF THE AMERICAN CONSTITUTION, 458 pages, 1990. Softcover. Teacher's Manual available. (Text)

GARVEY AND ALEINIKOFF'S MODERN CONSTITUTIONAL THEORY: A READER, 494 pages, 1989. Softcover. (Reader)

LOCKHART, KAMISAR, CHOPER AND SHIFFRIN'S CONSTITUTIONAL LAW: CASES—COMMENTS—QUESTIONS, Sixth Edition, 1601 pages, 1986. (Casebook) 1990 Supplement.

LOCKHART, KAMISAR, CHOPER AND SHIFFRIN'S THE AMERICAN CONSTITUTION: CASES AND MATERIALS, Sixth Edition, 1260 pages, 1986. Abridged version of Lockhart, et al., Constitutional Law: Cases—Comments—Questions, Sixth Edition. (Casebook) 1990 Supplement.

LOCKHART, KAMISAR, CHOPER AND SHIFFRIN'S CONSTITUTIONAL RIGHTS AND LIBERTIES: CASES AND MATERIALS, Sixth Edition, 1266 pages, 1986. Reprint from Lockhart, et al., Constitutional Law: Cases—Comments—Questions, Sixth Edition. (Casebook) 1990 Supplement.

MARKS AND COOPER'S STATE CONSTITUTIONAL LAW IN A NUTSHELL, 329 pages, 1988. Softcover. (Text)

NOWAK, ROTUNDA AND YOUNG'S HORNBOOK ON CONSTITUTIONAL LAW, Third Edition, 1191 pages, 1986 with 1988 pocket part. (Text)

ROTUNDA'S MODERN CONSTITUTIONAL LAW: CASES AND NOTES, Third Edition, 1085 pages, 1989. (Casebook) 1990 Supplement.

VIEIRA'S CONSTITUTIONAL CIVIL RIGHTS IN A NUTSHELL, Second Edition, 322 pages, 1990. Softcover. (Text)

WILLIAMS' CONSTITUTIONAL ANALYSIS IN A NUTSHELL, 388 pages, 1979. Softcover. (Text)

Consumer Law—see also Commercial Law

EPSTEIN AND NICKLES' CONSUMER LAW IN A NUTSHELL, Second Edition, 418 pages,

Consumer Law—Cont'd

1981. Softcover. (Text)

SELECTED COMMERCIAL STATUTES. Softcover. Approximately 1650 pages, 1990.

SPANOGLE AND ROHNER'S CASES AND MATERIALS ON CONSUMER LAW, 693 pages, 1979. Teacher's Manual available. (Casebook) 1982 Supplement.

Contracts

CALAMARI AND PERILLO'S BLACK LETTER ON CONTRACTS, Second Edition, approximately 450 pages, 1990. Softcover. (Review)

CALAMARI AND PERILLO'S HORNBOOK ON CONTRACTS, Third Edition, 1049 pages, 1987. (Text)

CALAMARI, PERILLO AND BENDER'S CASES AND PROBLEMS ON CONTRACTS, Second Edition, 905 pages, 1989. Teacher's Manual Available. (Casebook)

CORBIN'S TEXT ON CONTRACTS, One Volume Student Edition, 1224 pages, 1952. (Text)

FESSLER AND LOISEAUX'S CASES AND MATERIALS ON CONTRACTS—MORALITY, ECONOMICS AND THE MARKET PLACE, 837 pages, 1982. Teacher's Manual available. (Casebook)

FRIEDMAN'S CONTRACT REMEDIES IN A NUTSHELL, 323 pages, 1981. Softcover. (Text)

FULLER AND EISENBERG'S CASES ON BASIC CONTRACT LAW, Fifth Edition, approximately 1100 pages, 1990. (Casebook)

HAMILTON, RAU AND WEINTRAUB'S CASES AND MATERIALS ON CONTRACTS, 830 pages, 1984. (Casebook)

JACKSON AND BOLLINGER'S CASES ON CONTRACT LAW IN MODERN SOCIETY, Second Edition, 1329 pages, 1980. Teacher's Manual available. (Casebook)

KEYES' GOVERNMENT CONTRACTS IN A NUTSHELL, Second Edition, approximately 530 pages, 1990. Softcover. (Text)

SCHABER AND ROHWER'S CONTRACTS IN A NUTSHELL, Third Edition, approximately 438 pages, 1990. Softcover. (Text)

SUMMERS AND HILLMAN'S CONTRACT AND RELATED OBLIGATION: THEORY, DOCTRINE AND PRACTICE, 1074 pages, 1987. Teacher's Manual available. (Casebook)

Copyright—see Patent and Copyright Law

Corporate Finance

HAMILTON'S CASES AND MATERIALS ON CORPORATION FINANCE, Second Edition, 1221 pages, 1989. (Casebook)

Corporations

HAMILTON'S BLACK LETTER ON CORPORATIONS, Second Edition, 513 pages, 1986. Softcover. (Review)

HAMILTON'S CASES AND MATERIALS ON CORPORATIONS—INCLUDING PARTNERSHIPS AND LIMITED PARTNERSHIPS, Fourth Edition, approximately 1250 pages, 1990. (Casebook) 1990 Statutory Supplement.

HAMILTON'S THE LAW OF CORPORATIONS IN A NUTSHELL, Second Edition, 515 pages, 1987. Softcover. (Text)

HENN'S TEACHING MATERIALS ON THE LAW OF CORPORATIONS, Second Edition, 1204 pages, 1986. Teacher's Manual available. (Casebook)

Statutory Supplement. *See Selected Corporation and Partnership*

HENN AND ALEXANDER'S HORNBOOK ON LAWS OF CORPORATIONS, Third Edition, Student Edition, 1371 pages, 1983, with 1986 pocket part. (Text)

SELECTED CORPORATION AND PARTNERSHIP STATUTES, RULES AND FORMS. Softcover. 727 pages, 1989.

SOLOMON, SCHWARTZ AND BAUMAN'S MATERIALS AND PROBLEMS ON CORPORATIONS: LAW AND POLICY, Second Edition, 1391 pages, 1988. Teacher's Manual available. (Casebook) 1990 Supplement.

Statutory Supplement. *See Selected Corporation and Partnership*

Corrections

KRANTZ' CASES AND MATERIALS ON THE LAW OF CORRECTIONS AND PRISONERS' RIGHTS, Third Edition, 855 pages, 1986. (Casebook) 1988 Supplement.

KRANTZ' THE LAW OF CORRECTIONS AND PRISONERS' RIGHTS IN A NUTSHELL, Third Edition, 407 pages, 1988. Softcover. (Text)

ROBBINS' CASES AND MATERIALS ON POST-CONVICTION REMEDIES, 506 pages, 1982. (Casebook)

Creditors' Rights

BANKRUPTCY CODE, RULES AND OFFICIAL FORMS, LAW SCHOOL EDITION. Approximately 875 pages, 1990. Softcover.

EPSTEIN'S DEBTOR-CREDITOR RELATIONS IN A NUTSHELL, Third Edition, 383 pages, 1986. Softcover. (Text)

EPSTEIN, LANDERS AND NICKLES' CASES AND MATERIALS ON DEBTORS AND CREDITORS, Third Edition, 1059 pages, 1987. Teacher's Manual available. (Casebook)

LOPUCKI'S PLAYER'S MANUAL FOR THE DEBTOR-CREDITOR GAME, 123 pages, 1985. Softcover. (Coursebook)

NICKLES AND EPSTEIN'S BLACK LETTER ON CREDITORS' RIGHTS AND BANKRUPTCY, 576 pages, 1989. (Review)

RIESENFELD'S CASES AND MATERIALS ON CREDITORS' REMEDIES AND DEBTORS' PROTECTION, Fourth Edition, 914 pages, 1987. (Casebook) 1990 Supplement.

WHITE'S CASES AND MATERIALS ON BANKRUPTCY AND CREDITORS' RIGHTS, 812 pages, 1985. Teacher's Manual available. (Casebook) 1987 Supplement.

Criminal Law and Criminal Procedure—see also Corrections, Juvenile Justice

ABRAMS' FEDERAL CRIMINAL LAW AND ITS ENFORCEMENT, 866 pages, 1986. (Casebook) 1988 Supplement.

AMERICAN CRIMINAL JUSTICE PROCESS: SELECTED RULES, STATUTES AND GUIDELINES. 723 pages, 1989. Softcover.

CARLSON'S ADJUDICATION OF CRIMINAL JUSTICE: PROBLEMS AND REFERENCES, 130 pages, 1986. Softcover. (Casebook)

DIX AND SHARLOT'S CASES AND MATERIALS ON CRIMINAL LAW, Third Edition, 846 pages, 1987. (Casebook)

GRANO'S PROBLEMS IN CRIMINAL PROCEDURE, Second Edition, 176 pages, 1981. Teacher's Manual available. Softcover. (Coursebook)

HEYMANN AND KENETY'S THE MURDER TRIAL OF WILBUR JACKSON: A HOMICIDE IN THE FAMILY, Second Edition, 347 pages, 1985. (Coursebook)

ISRAEL, KAMISAR AND LAFAVE'S CRIMINAL PROCEDURE AND THE CONSTITUTION: LEADING SUPREME COURT CASES AND INTRODUCTORY TEXT. Approximately 725 pages, 1990 Edition. Softcover. (Casebook)

ISRAEL AND LAFAVE'S CRIMINAL PROCEDURE—CONSTITUTIONAL LIMITATIONS IN A NUTSHELL, Fourth Edition, 461 pages, 1988. Softcover. (Text)

JOHNSON'S CASES, MATERIALS AND TEXT ON CRIMINAL LAW, Fourth Edition, approximately 790 pages, 1990. Teacher's Manual available. (Casebook)

JOHNSON'S CASES AND MATERIALS ON CRIMINAL PROCEDURE, 859 pages, 1988. (Casebook) 1990 Supplement.

KAMISAR, LAFAVE AND ISRAEL'S MODERN CRIMINAL PROCEDURE: CASES, COMMENTS AND QUESTIONS, Seventh Edition, 1593 pages, 1990. (Casebook) 1990 Supplement.

KAMISAR, LAFAVE AND ISRAEL'S BASIC CRIMINAL PROCEDURE: CASES, COMMENTS AND QUESTIONS, Seventh Edition, 792 pages, 1990. Softcover reprint from Kamisar, et al., Modern Criminal Procedure: Cases, Comments and Questions, Seventh Edition. (Casebook) 1990 Supplement.

LAFAVE'S MODERN CRIMINAL LAW: CASES, COMMENTS AND QUESTIONS, Second Edition, 903 pages, 1988. (Casebook)

LAFAVE AND ISRAEL'S HORNBOOK ON CRIMINAL PROCEDURE, Student Edition, 1142 pages, 1985, with 1989 pocket part. (Text)

LAFAVE AND SCOTT'S HORNBOOK ON CRIMINAL LAW, Second Edition, 918 pages, 1986. (Text)

LANGBEIN'S COMPARATIVE CRIMINAL PROCEDURE: GERMANY, 172 pages, 1977. Softcover. (Casebook)

LOEWY'S CRIMINAL LAW IN A NUTSHELL, Second Edition, 321 pages, 1987. Softcover. (Text)

LOW'S BLACK LETTER ON CRIMINAL LAW, Revised First Edition, approximately 430 pages, 1990. Softcover. (Review)

SALTZBURG'S CASES AND COMMENTARY ON AMERICAN CRIMINAL PROCEDURE, Third Edition, 1302 pages, 1988. Teacher's Manual available. (Casebook) 1990 Supplement.

Criminal Law and Criminal Procedure—Cont'd

UVILLER'S THE PROCESSES OF CRIMINAL JUSTICE: INVESTIGATION AND ADJUDICATION, Second Edition, 1384 pages, 1979. (Casebook) 1979 Statutory Supplement. 1986 Update.

VORENBERG'S CASES ON CRIMINAL LAW AND PROCEDURE, Second Edition, 1088 pages, 1981. Teacher's Manual available. (Casebook) 1990 Supplement.

Decedents' Estates—see Trusts and Estates

Domestic Relations

CLARK'S HORNBOOK ON DOMESTIC RELATIONS, Second Edition, Student Edition, 1050 pages, 1988. (Text)

CLARK AND GLOWINSKY'S CASES AND PROBLEMS ON DOMESTIC RELATIONS, Fourth Edition. Approximately 1125 pages, 1990. Teacher's Manual available. (Casebook)

KRAUSE'S BLACK LETTER ON FAMILY LAW, 314 pages, 1988. Softcover. (Review)

KRAUSE'S CASES, COMMENTS AND QUESTIONS ON FAMILY LAW, Third Edition, 1433 pages, 1990. (Casebook)

KRAUSE'S FAMILY LAW IN A NUTSHELL, Second Edition, 444 pages, 1986. Softcover. (Text)

KRAUSKOPF'S CASES ON PROPERTY DIVISION AT MARRIAGE DISSOLUTION, 250 pages, 1984. Softcover. (Casebook)

Economics, Law and—see also Antitrust, Regulated Industries

GOETZ' CASES AND MATERIALS ON LAW AND ECONOMICS, 547 pages, 1984. (Casebook)

MALLOY'S LAW AND ECONOMICS: A COMPARATIVE APPROACH TO THEORY AND PRACTICE, Approximately 152 pages, 1990. Softcover. (Text)

Education Law

ALEXANDER AND ALEXANDER'S THE LAW OF SCHOOLS, STUDENTS AND TEACHERS IN A NUTSHELL, 409 pages, 1984. Softcover. (Text)

Employment Discrimination—see also Women and the Law

ESTREICHER AND HARPER'S CASES AND MATERIALS ON THE LAW GOVERNING THE EMPLOYMENT RELATIONSHIP, 962 pages, 1990. Teacher's Manual available. (Casebook) Statutory Supplement.

JONES, MURPHY AND BELTON'S CASES AND MATERIALS ON DISCRIMINATION IN EMPLOYMENT, (The Labor Law Group). Fifth Edition, 1116 pages, 1987. (Casebook) 1990 Supplement.

PLAYER'S FEDERAL LAW OF EMPLOYMENT DISCRIMINATION IN A NUTSHELL, Second Edition, 402 pages, 1981. Softcover. (Text)

PLAYER'S HORNBOOK ON EMPLOYMENT DISCRIMINATION LAW, Student Edition, 708 pages, 1988. (Text)

PLAYER, SHOBEN AND LIEBERWITZ' CASES AND MATERIALS ON EMPLOYMENT DISCRIMINATION LAW, Approximately 810 pages, 1990. (Casebook)

Energy and Natural Resources Law—see also Oil and Gas

LAITOS' CASES AND MATERIALS ON NATURAL RESOURCES LAW, 938 pages, 1985. Teacher's Manual available. (Casebook)

SELECTED ENVIRONMENTAL LAW STATUTES—EDUCATIONAL EDITION. Softcover. Approximately 1040 pages, 1990.

Environmental Law—see also Energy and Natural Resources Law; Sea, Law of

BONINE AND MCGARITY'S THE LAW OF ENVIRONMENTAL PROTECTION: CASES—LEGISLATION—POLICIES, 1076 pages, 1984. Teacher's Manual available. (Casebook)

FINDLEY AND FARBER'S CASES AND MATERIALS ON ENVIRONMENTAL LAW, Second Edition, 813 pages, 1985. (Casebook) 1988 Supplement.

FINDLEY AND FARBER'S ENVIRONMENTAL LAW IN A NUTSHELL, Second Edition, 367 pages, 1988. Softcover. (Text)

RODGERS' HORNBOOK ON ENVIRONMENTAL LAW, 956 pages, 1977, with 1984 pocket part. (Text)

SELECTED ENVIRONMENTAL LAW STATUTES—EDUCATIONAL EDITION. Softcover. Approximately 1040 pages, 1990.

Equity—see Remedies

Estate Planning—see also Trusts and Estates; Taxation—Estate and Gift

LYNN'S AN INTRODUCTION TO ESTATE PLANNING IN A NUTSHELL, Third Edition, 370 pages, 1983. Softcover. (Text)

Evidence

BROUN AND BLAKEY'S BLACK LETTER ON EVIDENCE, 269 pages, 1984. Softcover. (Review)

BROUN, MEISENHOLDER, STRONG AND MOSTELLER'S PROBLEMS IN EVIDENCE, Third Edition, 238 pages, 1988. Teacher's Manual available. Softcover. (Coursebook)

CLEARY, STRONG, BROUN AND MOSTELLER'S CASES AND MATERIALS ON EVIDENCE, Fourth Edition, 1060 pages, 1988. (Casebook)

FEDERAL RULES OF EVIDENCE FOR UNITED STATES COURTS AND MAGISTRATES. Softcover. Approximately 380 pages, 1990.

GRAHAM'S FEDERAL RULES OF EVIDENCE IN A NUTSHELL, Second Edition, 473 pages, 1987. Softcover. (Text)

LEMPERT AND SALTZBURG'S A MODERN APPROACH TO EVIDENCE: TEXT, PROBLEMS, TRANSCRIPTS AND CASES, Second Edition, 1232 pages, 1983. Teacher's Manual available. (Casebook)

LILLY'S AN INTRODUCTION TO THE LAW OF EVIDENCE, Second Edition, 585 pages, 1987. (Text)

MCCORMICK, SUTTON AND WELLBORN'S CASES AND MATERIALS ON EVIDENCE, Sixth Edition, 1067 pages, 1987. (Casebook)

MCCORMICK'S HORNBOOK ON EVIDENCE, Third Edition, Student Edition, 1156 pages, 1984, with 1987 pocket part. (Text)

ROTHSTEIN'S EVIDENCE IN A NUTSHELL: STATE AND FEDERAL RULES, Second Edition, 514 pages, 1981. Softcover. (Text)

Federal Jurisdiction and Procedure

CURRIE'S CASES AND MATERIALS ON FEDERAL COURTS, Fourth Edition, approximately 1125 pages, 1990. (Casebook)

CURRIE'S FEDERAL JURISDICTION IN A NUTSHELL, Third Edition, approximately 260 pages, 1990. Softcover. (Text)

FEDERAL RULES OF CIVIL PROCEDURE—EDUCATIONAL EDITION. Softcover. Approximately 635 pages, 1990.

REDISH'S BLACK LETTER ON FEDERAL JURISDICTION, 219 pages, 1985. Softcover. (Review)

REDISH'S CASES, COMMENTS AND QUESTIONS ON FEDERAL COURTS, Second Edition, 1122 pages, 1989. (Casebook) 1990 Supplement.

VETRI AND MERRILL'S FEDERAL COURTS PROBLEMS AND MATERIALS, Second Edition, 232 pages, 1984. Softcover. (Coursebook)

WRIGHT'S HORNBOOK ON FEDERAL COURTS, Fourth Edition, Student Edition, 870 pages, 1983. (Text)

Foreign Relations and National Security Law

FRANCK AND GLENNON'S FOREIGN RELATIONS AND NATIONAL SECURITY LAW, 941 pages, 1987. (Casebook)

Future Interests—see Trusts and Estates

Health Law—see Medicine, Law and

Human Rights—see International Law

Immigration Law

ALEINIKOFF AND MARTIN'S IMMIGRATION PROCESS AND POLICY, Second Edition, approximately 1100 pages, October, 1990 (Casebook)

Statutory Supplement. *See Immigration and Nationality Laws*

IMMIGRATION AND NATIONALITY LAWS OF THE UNITED STATES: SELECTED STATUTES, REGULATIONS AND FORMS. Softcover. Approximately 400 pages, 1990.

WEISSBRODT'S IMMIGRATION LAW AND PROCEDURE IN A NUTSHELL, Second Edition, 438 pages, 1989, Softcover. (Text)

Indian Law—see American Indian Law

Insurance Law

DEVINE AND TERRY'S PROBLEMS IN INSURANCE LAW, 240 pages, 1989. Softcover. Teacher's Manual available. (Course book)

DOBBYN'S INSURANCE LAW IN A NUTSHELL, Second Edition, 316 pages, 1989. Softcover. (Text)

KEETON'S CASES ON BASIC INSURANCE LAW,

Insurance Law—Cont'd

Second Edition, 1086 pages, 1977. Teacher's Manual available. (Casebook)

KEETON'S COMPUTER-AIDED AND WORKBOOK EXERCISES ON INSURANCE LAW, 255 pages, 1990. Softcover. (Coursebook)

KEETON AND WIDISS' INSURANCE LAW, Student Edition, 1359 pages, 1988. (Text)

WIDISS AND KEETON'S COURSE SUPPLEMENT TO KEETON AND WIDISS' INSURANCE LAW, 502 pages, 1988. Softcover. (Casebook)

WIDISS' INSURANCE: MATERIALS ON FUNDAMENTAL PRINCIPLES, LEGAL DOCTRINES AND REGULATORY ACTS, 1186 pages, 1989. (Casebook)

YORK AND WHELAN'S CASES, MATERIALS AND PROBLEMS ON GENERAL PRACTICE INSURANCE LAW, Second Edition, 787 pages, 1988. Teacher's Manual available. (Casebook)

International Law—see also Sea, Law of

BUERGENTHAL'S INTERNATIONAL HUMAN RIGHTS IN A NUTSHELL, 283 pages, 1988. Softcover. (Text)

BUERGENTHAL AND MAIER'S PUBLIC INTERNATIONAL LAW IN A NUTSHELL, Second Edition, 275 pages, 1990. Softcover. (Text)

FOLSOM, GORDON AND SPANOGLE'S INTERNATIONAL BUSINESS TRANSACTIONS—A PROBLEM-ORIENTED COURSEBOOK, 1160 pages, 1986. Teacher's Manual available. (Casebook) 1989 Documents Supplement.

FOLSOM, GORDON AND SPANOGLE'S INTERNATIONAL BUSINESS TRANSACTIONS IN A NUTSHELL, Third Edition, 509 pages, 1988. Softcover. (Text)

HENKIN, PUGH, SCHACHTER AND SMIT'S CASES AND MATERIALS ON INTERNATIONAL LAW, Second Edition, 1517 pages, 1987. (Casebook) Documents Supplement.

JACKSON AND DAVEY'S CASES, MATERIALS AND TEXT ON LEGAL PROBLEMS OF INTERNATIONAL ECONOMIC RELATIONS, Second Edition, 1269 pages, 1986. (Casebook) 1989 Documents Supplement.

KIRGIS' INTERNATIONAL ORGANIZATIONS IN THEIR LEGAL SETTING, 1016 pages, 1977. Teacher's Manual available. (Casebook) 1981 Supplement.

WESTON, FALK AND D'AMATO'S INTERNATIONAL LAW AND WORLD ORDER—A PROBLEM-ORIENTED COURSEBOOK, Second Edition, approximately 1305 pages, 1990. Teacher's Manual available. (Casebook) Documents Supplement.

Interviewing and Counseling

BINDER AND PRICE'S LEGAL INTERVIEWING AND COUNSELING, 232 pages, 1977. Teacher's Manual available. Softcover. (Coursebook)

BINDER, BERGMAN AND PRICE'S LAWYERS AS COUNSELORS: A CLIENT CENTERED APPROACH, Approximately 400 pages, October, 1990 Pub. Softcover. (Coursebook)

SHAFFER AND ELKINS' LEGAL INTERVIEWING AND COUNSELING IN A NUTSHELL, Second Edition, 487 pages, 1987. Softcover. (Text)

Introduction to Law—see Legal Method and Legal System

Introduction to Law Study

HEGLAND'S INTRODUCTION TO THE STUDY AND PRACTICE OF LAW IN A NUTSHELL, 418 pages, 1983. Softcover. (Text)

KINYON'S INTRODUCTION TO LAW STUDY AND LAW EXAMINATIONS IN A NUTSHELL, 389 pages, 1971. Softcover. (Text)

Judicial Process—see Legal Method and Legal System

Jurisprudence

CHRISTIE'S JURISPRUDENCE—TEXT AND READINGS ON THE PHILOSOPHY OF LAW, 1056 pages, 1973. (Casebook)

Juvenile Justice

FOX'S CASES AND MATERIALS ON MODERN JUVENILE JUSTICE, Second Edition, 960 pages, 1981. (Casebook)

FOX'S JUVENILE COURTS IN A NUTSHELL, Third Edition, 291 pages, 1984. Softcover. (Text)

Labor and Employment Law—see also Employment Discrimination, Social Legislation

FINKIN, GOLDMAN AND SUMMERS' LEGAL PROTECTION OF INDIVIDUAL EMPLOYEES, (The La-

Labor and Employment Law—Cont'd

bor Law Group). 1164 pages, 1989. (Casebook)

GORMAN'S BASIC TEXT ON LABOR LAW—UNIONIZATION AND COLLECTIVE BARGAINING, 914 pages, 1976. (Text)

LESLIE'S LABOR LAW IN A NUTSHELL, Second Edition, 397 pages, 1986. Softcover. (Text)

NOLAN'S LABOR ARBITRATION LAW AND PRACTICE IN A NUTSHELL, 358 pages, 1979. Softcover. (Text)

OBERER, HANSLOWE, ANDERSEN AND HEINSZ' CASES AND MATERIALS ON LABOR LAW—COLLECTIVE BARGAINING IN A FREE SOCIETY, Third Edition, 1163 pages, 1986. (Casebook) Statutory Supplement.

RABIN, SILVERSTEIN AND SCHATZKI'S LABOR AND EMPLOYMENT LAW: PROBLEMS, CASES AND MATERIALS IN THE LAW OF WORK, (The Labor Law Group). 1014 pages, 1988. Teacher's Manual available. (Casebook) 1988 Statutory Supplement.

Land Finance—Property Security—see Real Estate Transactions

Land Use

CALLIES AND FREILICH'S CASES AND MATERIALS ON LAND USE, 1233 pages, 1986. (Casebook) 1988 Supplement.

HAGMAN AND JUERGENSMEYER'S HORNBOOK ON URBAN PLANNING AND LAND DEVELOPMENT CONTROL LAW, Second Edition, Student Edition, 680 pages, 1986. (Text)

WRIGHT AND GITELMAN'S CASES AND MATERIALS ON LAND USE, Third Edition, 1300 pages, 1982. Teacher's Manual available. (Casebook) 1987 Supplement.

WRIGHT AND WRIGHT'S LAND USE IN A NUTSHELL, Second Edition, 356 pages, 1985. Softcover. (Text)

Legal History—see also Legal Method and Legal System

PRESSER AND ZAINALDIN'S CASES AND MATERIALS ON LAW AND JURISPRUDENCE IN AMERICAN HISTORY, Second Edition, 1092 pages, 1989. Teacher's Manual available. (Casebook)

Legal Method and Legal System—see also Legal Research, Legal Writing

ALDISERT'S READINGS, MATERIALS AND CASES IN THE JUDICIAL PROCESS, 948 pages, 1976. (Casebook)

BERCH AND BERCH'S INTRODUCTION TO LEGAL METHOD AND PROCESS, 550 pages, 1985. Teacher's Manual available. (Casebook)

BODENHEIMER, OAKLEY AND LOVE'S READINGS AND CASES ON AN INTRODUCTION TO THE ANGLO-AMERICAN LEGAL SYSTEM, Second Edition, 166 pages, 1988. Softcover. (Casebook)

DAVIES AND LAWRY'S INSTITUTIONS AND METHODS OF THE LAW—INTRODUCTORY TEACHING MATERIALS, 547 pages, 1982. Teacher's Manual available. (Casebook)

DVORKIN, HIMMELSTEIN AND LESNICK'S BECOMING A LAWYER: A HUMANISTIC PERSPECTIVE ON LEGAL EDUCATION AND PROFESSIONALISM, 211 pages, 1981. Softcover. (Text)

KEETON'S JUDGING, 842 pages, 1990. Softcover. (Coursebook)

KELSO AND KELSO'S STUDYING LAW: AN INTRODUCTION, 587 pages, 1984. (Coursebook)

KEMPIN'S HISTORICAL INTRODUCTION TO ANGLO-AMERICAN LAW IN A NUTSHELL, Third Edition, approximately 302 pages, 1990. Softcover. (Text)

REYNOLDS' JUDICIAL PROCESS IN A NUTSHELL, 292 pages, 1980. Softcover. (Text)

Legal Research

COHEN'S LEGAL RESEARCH IN A NUTSHELL, Fourth Edition, 452 pages, 1985. Softcover. (Text)

COHEN, BERRING AND OLSON'S HOW TO FIND THE LAW, Ninth Edition, 716 pages, 1989. (Text)

COHEN, BERRING AND OLSON'S FINDING THE LAW, 570 pages, 1989. Softcover reprint from Cohen, Berring and Olson's How to Find the Law, Ninth Edition. (Coursebook)

Legal Research Exercises, 3rd Ed., for use with Cohen, Berring and Olson, 229 pages, 1989. Teacher's Manual available.

ROMBAUER'S LEGAL PROBLEM SOLVING—

Legal Research—Cont'd

ANALYSIS, RESEARCH AND WRITING, Fourth Edition, 424 pages, 1983. Teacher's Manual with problems available. (Coursebook)

STATSKY'S LEGAL RESEARCH AND WRITING, Third Edition, 257 pages, 1986. Softcover. (Coursebook)

TEPLY'S LEGAL RESEARCH AND CITATION, Third Edition, 472 pages, 1989. Softcover. (Coursebook)

Student Library Exercises, 3rd ed., 391 pages, 1989. Answer Key available.

Legal Writing

CHILD'S DRAFTING LEGAL DOCUMENTS: MATERIALS AND PROBLEMS, 286 pages, 1988. Softcover. Teacher's Manual available. (Coursebook)

DICKERSON'S MATERIALS ON LEGAL DRAFTING, 425 pages, 1981. Teacher's Manual available. (Coursebook)

FELSENFELD AND SIEGEL'S WRITING CONTRACTS IN PLAIN ENGLISH, 290 pages, 1981. Softcover. (Text)

GOPEN'S WRITING FROM A LEGAL PERSPECTIVE, 225 pages, 1981. (Text)

MELLINKOFF'S LEGAL WRITING—SENSE AND NONSENSE, 242 pages, 1982. Softcover. Teacher's Manual available. (Text)

PRATT'S LEGAL WRITING: A SYSTEMATIC APPROACH, 422 pages, 1989. Teacher's Manual available. (Coursebook)

RAY AND RAMSFIELD'S LEGAL WRITING: GETTING IT RIGHT AND GETTING IT WRITTEN, 250 pages, 1987. Softcover. (Text)

SQUIRES AND ROMBAUER'S LEGAL WRITING IN A NUTSHELL, 294 pages, 1982. Softcover. (Text)

STATSKY AND WERNET'S CASE ANALYSIS AND FUNDAMENTALS OF LEGAL WRITING, Third Edition, 424 pages, 1989. Teacher's Manual available. (Text)

TEPLY'S LEGAL WRITING, ANALYSIS AND ORAL ARGUMENT, 576 pages, 1990. Softcover. Teacher's Manual available. (Coursebook)

WEIHOFEN'S LEGAL WRITING STYLE, Second Edition, 332 pages, 1980. (Text)

Legislation

DAVIES' LEGISLATIVE LAW AND PROCESS IN A NUTSHELL, Second Edition, 346 pages, 1986. Softcover. (Text)

ESKRIDGE AND FRICKEY'S CASES AND MATERIALS ON LEGISLATION: STATUTES AND THE CREATION OF PUBLIC POLICY, 937 pages, 1988. Teacher's Manual available. (Casebook) 1990 Supplement.

NUTTING AND DICKERSON'S CASES AND MATERIALS ON LEGISLATION, Fifth Edition, 744 pages, 1978. (Casebook)

STATSKY'S LEGISLATIVE ANALYSIS AND DRAFTING, Second Edition, 217 pages, 1984. Teacher's Manual available. (Text)

Local Government

FRUG'S CASES AND MATERIALS ON LOCAL GOVERNMENT LAW, 1005 pages, 1988. (Casebook)

MCCARTHY'S LOCAL GOVERNMENT LAW IN A NUTSHELL, Third Edition, approximately 400 pages, 1990. Softcover. (Text)

REYNOLDS' HORNBOOK ON LOCAL GOVERNMENT LAW, 860 pages, 1982, with 1990 pocket part. (Text)

VALENTE'S CASES AND MATERIALS ON LOCAL GOVERNMENT LAW, Third Edition, 1010 pages, 1987. Teacher's Manual available. (Casebook) 1989 Supplement.

Mass Communication Law

GILLMOR, BARRON, SIMON AND TERRY'S CASES AND COMMENT ON MASS COMMUNICATION LAW, Fifth Edition, 947 pages, 1990. (Casebook)

GINSBURG'S REGULATION OF BROADCASTING: LAW AND POLICY TOWARDS RADIO, TELEVISION AND CABLE COMMUNICATIONS, 741 pages, 1979 (Casebook) 1983 Supplement.

ZUCKMAN, GAYNES, CARTER AND DEE'S MASS COMMUNICATIONS LAW IN A NUTSHELL, Third Edition, 538 pages, 1988. Softcover. (Text)

Medicine, Law and

FURROW, JOHNSON, JOST AND SCHWARTZ' HEALTH LAW: CASES, MATERIALS AND PROBLEMS, 1005 pages, 1987. Teacher's Manual available. (Casebook) 1989 Supplement.

HALL AND ELLMAN'S HEALTH CARE LAW AND

Medicine, Law and—Cont'd

ETHICS IN A NUTSHELL, 401 pages, 1990. Softcover (Text)

KING'S THE LAW OF MEDICAL MALPRACTICE IN A NUTSHELL, Second Edition, 342 pages, 1986. Softcover. (Text)

SHAPIRO AND SPECE'S CASES, MATERIALS AND PROBLEMS ON BIOETHICS AND LAW, 892 pages, 1981. (Casebook)

SHARPE, BOUMIL, FISCINA AND HEAD'S CASES AND MATERIALS ON MEDICAL LIABILITY, Approximately 500 pages, September, 1990 Pub. (Casebook)

Military Law

SHANOR AND TERRELL'S MILITARY LAW IN A NUTSHELL, 378 pages, 1980. Softcover. (Text)

Mortgages—see Real Estate Transactions

Natural Resources Law—see Energy and Natural Resources Law, Environmental Law

Negotiation

GIFFORD'S LEGAL NEGOTIATION: THEORY AND APPLICATIONS, 225 pages, 1989. Softcover. (Text)

WILLIAMS' LEGAL NEGOTIATION AND SETTLEMENT, 207 pages, 1983. Softcover. Teacher's Manual available. (Coursebook)

Office Practice—see also Computers and Law, Interviewing and Counseling, Negotiation

HEGLAND'S TRIAL AND PRACTICE SKILLS IN A NUTSHELL, 346 pages, 1978. Softcover (Text)

STRONG AND CLARK'S LAW OFFICE MANAGEMENT, 424 pages, 1974. (Casebook)

Oil and Gas—see also Energy and Natural Resources Law

HEMINGWAY'S HORNBOOK ON OIL AND GAS, Second Edition, Student Edition, 543 pages, 1983, with 1989 pocket part. (Text)

KUNTZ, LOWE, ANDERSON AND SMITH'S CASES AND MATERIALS ON OIL AND GAS LAW, 857 pages, 1986. Teacher's Manual available. (Casebook) Forms Manual. Revised.

LOWE'S OIL AND GAS LAW IN A NUTSHELL, Second Edition, 465 pages, 1988. Softcover. (Text)

Partnership—see Agency—Partnership

Patent and Copyright Law

CHOATE, FRANCIS AND COLLINS' CASES AND MATERIALS ON PATENT LAW, INCLUDING TRADE SECRETS, COPYRIGHTS, TRADEMARKS, Third Edition, 1009 pages, 1987. (Casebook)

MILLER AND DAVIS' INTELLECTUAL PROPERTY—PATENTS, TRADEMARKS AND COPYRIGHT IN A NUTSHELL, Second Edition, approximately 440 pages, 1990. Softcover. (Text)

NIMMER'S CASES AND MATERIALS ON COPYRIGHT AND OTHER ASPECTS OF ENTERTAINMENT LITIGATION ILLUSTRATED—INCLUDING UNFAIR COMPETITION, DEFAMATION AND PRIVACY, Third Edition, 1025 pages, 1985. (Casebook) 1989 Supplement.

Products Liability

FISCHER AND POWERS' CASES AND MATERIALS ON PRODUCTS LIABILITY, 685 pages, 1988. Teacher's Manual available. (Casebook)

NOEL AND PHILLIPS' CASES ON PRODUCTS LIABILITY, Second Edition, 821 pages, 1982. (Casebook)

PHILLIPS' PRODUCTS LIABILITY IN A NUTSHELL, Third Edition, 307 pages, 1988. Softcover. (Text)

Professional Responsibility

ARONSON, DEVINE AND FISCH'S PROBLEMS, CASES AND MATERIALS IN PROFESSIONAL RESPONSIBILITY, 745 pages, 1985. Teacher's Manual available. (Casebook)

ARONSON AND WECKSTEIN'S PROFESSIONAL RESPONSIBILITY IN A NUTSHELL, 399 pages, 1980. Softcover. (Text)

MELLINKOFF'S THE CONSCIENCE OF A LAWYER, 304 pages, 1973. (Text)

PIRSIG AND KIRWIN'S CASES AND MATERIALS ON PROFESSIONAL RESPONSIBILITY, Fourth Edition, 603 pages, 1984. Teacher's Manual available. (Casebook)

ROTUNDA'S BLACK LETTER ON PROFESSIONAL RESPONSIBILITY, Second Edition, 414 pages, 1988. Softcover. (Review)

SCHWARTZ AND WYDICK'S PROBLEMS IN LE-

Professional Responsibility—Cont'd

GAL ETHICS, Second Edition, 341 pages, 1988. (Coursebook)

SELECTED STATUTES, RULES AND STANDARDS ON THE LEGAL PROFESSION. Softcover. Approximately 600 pages, 1990.

SMITH AND MALLEN'S PREVENTING LEGAL MALPRACTICE, 264 pages, 1989. Reprint from Mallen and Smith's Legal Malpractice, Third Edition. (Text)

SUTTON AND DZIENKOWSKI'S CASES AND MATERIALS ON THE PROFESSIONAL RESPONSIBILITY FOR LAWYERS, 839 pages, 1989. Teacher's Manual available. (Casebook)

WOLFRAM'S HORNBOOK ON MODERN LEGAL ETHICS, Student Edition, 1120 pages, 1986. (Text)

Property—see also Real Estate Transactions, Land Use, Trusts and Estates

BERNHARDT'S BLACK LETTER ON PROPERTY, 318 pages, 1983. Softcover. (Review)

BERNHARDT'S REAL PROPERTY IN A NUTSHELL, Second Edition, 448 pages, 1981. Softcover. (Text)

BOYER'S SURVEY OF THE LAW OF PROPERTY, Third Edition, 766 pages, 1981. (Text)

BROWDER, CUNNINGHAM, NELSON, STOEBUCK AND WHITMAN'S CASES ON BASIC PROPERTY LAW, Fifth Edition, 1386 pages, 1989. Teacher's Manual available. (Casebook)

BRUCE, ELY AND BOSTICK'S CASES AND MATERIALS ON MODERN PROPERTY LAW, Second Edition, 953 pages, 1989. Teacher's Manual available. (Casebook)

BURKE'S PERSONAL PROPERTY IN A NUTSHELL, 322 pages, 1983. Softcover. (Text)

CUNNINGHAM, STOEBUCK AND WHITMAN'S HORNBOOK ON THE LAW OF PROPERTY, Student Edition, 916 pages, 1984, with 1987 pocket part. (Text)

DONAHUE, KAUPER AND MARTIN'S CASES ON PROPERTY, Second Edition, 1362 pages, 1983. Teacher's Manual available. (Casebook)

HILL'S LANDLORD AND TENANT LAW IN A NUTSHELL, Second Edition, 311 pages, 1986. Softcover. (Text)

KURTZ AND HOVENKAMP'S CASES AND MATERIALS ON AMERICAN PROPERTY LAW, 1296 pages, 1987. Teacher's Manual available. (Casebook) 1988 Supplement.

MOYNIHAN'S INTRODUCTION TO REAL PROPERTY, Second Edition, 239 pages, 1988. (Text)

Psychiatry, Law and

REISNER AND SLOBOGIN'S LAW AND THE MENTAL HEALTH SYSTEM, CIVIL AND CRIMINAL ASPECTS, Second Edition, approximately 1127 pages, 1990. (Casebook)

Real Estate Transactions

BRUCE'S REAL ESTATE FINANCE IN A NUTSHELL, Second Edition, 262 pages, 1985. Softcover. (Text)

MAXWELL, RIESENFELD, HETLAND AND WARREN'S CASES ON CALIFORNIA SECURITY TRANSACTIONS IN LAND, Third Edition, 728 pages, 1984. (Casebook)

NELSON AND WHITMAN'S BLACK LETTER ON LAND TRANSACTIONS AND FINANCE, Second Edition, 466 pages, 1988. Softcover. (Review)

NELSON AND WHITMAN'S CASES ON REAL ESTATE TRANSFER, FINANCE AND DEVELOPMENT, Third Edition, 1184 pages, 1987. (Casebook)

NELSON AND WHITMAN'S HORNBOOK ON REAL ESTATE FINANCE LAW, Second Edition, 941 pages, 1985 with 1989 pocket part. (Text)

Regulated Industries—see also Mass Communication Law, Banking Law

GELLHORN AND PIERCE'S REGULATED INDUSTRIES IN A NUTSHELL, Second Edition, 389 pages, 1987. Softcover. (Text)

MORGAN, HARRISON AND VERKUIL'S CASES AND MATERIALS ON ECONOMIC REGULATION OF BUSINESS, Second Edition, 666 pages, 1985. (Casebook)

Remedies

DOBBS' HORNBOOK ON REMEDIES, 1067 pages, 1973. (Text)

DOBBS' PROBLEMS IN REMEDIES. 137 pages, 1974. Teacher's Manual available. Softcover. (Coursebook)

DOBBYN'S INJUNCTIONS IN A NUTSHELL, 264 pages, 1974. Softcover. (Text)

Remedies—Cont'd

FRIEDMAN'S CONTRACT REMEDIES IN A NUTSHELL, 323 pages, 1981. Softcover. (Text)

LEAVELL, LOVE AND NELSON'S CASES AND MATERIALS ON EQUITABLE REMEDIES, RESTITUTION AND DAMAGES, Fourth Edition, 1111 pages, 1986. Teacher's Manual available. (Casebook)

MCCORMICK'S HORNBOOK ON DAMAGES, 811 pages, 1935. (Text)

O'CONNELL'S REMEDIES IN A NUTSHELL, Second Edition, 320 pages, 1985. Softcover. (Text)

SCHOENBROD, MACBETH, LEVINE AND JUNG'S CASES AND MATERIALS ON REMEDIES: PUBLIC AND PRIVATE, Approximately 807 pages, 1990. Teacher's Manual available. (Casebook)

YORK, BAUMAN AND RENDLEMAN'S CASES AND MATERIALS ON REMEDIES, Fourth Edition, 1029 pages, 1985. Teacher's Manual available. (Casebook)

Sea, Law of

SOHN AND GUSTAFSON'S THE LAW OF THE SEA IN A NUTSHELL, 264 pages, 1984. Softcover. (Text)

Securities Regulation

HAZEN'S HORNBOOK ON THE LAW OF SECURITIES REGULATION, Second Edition, Student Edition, approximately 1000 pages, 1990. (Text)

RATNER'S MATERIALS ON SECURITIES REGULATION, Third Edition, 1000 pages, 1986. Teacher's Manual available. (Casebook) 1989 Supplement.

Statutory Supplement. *See Selected Securities Regulation*

RATNER'S SECURITIES REGULATION IN A NUTSHELL, Third Edition, 316 pages, 1988. Softcover. (Text)

SELECTED STATUTES, REGULATIONS, RULES, DOCUMENTS AND FORMS ON SECURITIES REGULATION. Softcover. 1272 pages, 1990.

Social Legislation

HOOD, HARDY AND LEWIS' WORKERS' COMPENSATION AND EMPLOYEE PROTECTION LAWS IN A NUTSHELL, Second Edition, 361 pages, 1990. Softcover. (Text)

LAFRANCE'S WELFARE LAW: STRUCTURE AND ENTITLEMENT IN A NUTSHELL, 455 pages, 1979. Softcover. (Text)

MALONE, PLANT AND LITTLE'S CASES ON WORKERS' COMPENSATION AND EMPLOYMENT RIGHTS, Second Edition, 951 pages, 1980. Teacher's Manual available. (Casebook)

Sports Law

SCHUBERT, SMITH AND TRENTADUE'S SPORTS LAW, 395 pages, 1986. (Text)

Tax Practice and Procedure

GARBIS, STRUNTZ AND RUBIN'S CASES AND MATERIALS ON TAX PROCEDURE AND TAX FRAUD, Second Edition, 687 pages, 1987. (Casebook)

MORGAN'S TAX PROCEDURE AND TAX FRAUD IN A NUTSHELL, Approximately 382 pages, 1990. Softcover. (Text)

Taxation—Corporate

KAHN AND GANN'S CORPORATE TAXATION, Third Edition, 980 pages, 1989. Teacher's Manual available. (Casebook)

WEIDENBRUCH AND BURKE'S FEDERAL INCOME TAXATION OF CORPORATIONS AND STOCKHOLDERS IN A NUTSHELL, Third Edition, 309 pages, 1989. Softcover. (Text)

Taxation—Estate & Gift—see also Estate Planning, Trusts and Estates

MCNULTY'S FEDERAL ESTATE AND GIFT TAXATION IN A NUTSHELL, Fourth Edition, 496 pages, 1989. Softcover. (Text)

PENNELL'S CASES AND MATERIALS ON INCOME TAXATION OF TRUSTS, ESTATES, GRANTORS AND BENEFICIARIES, 460 pages, 1987. Teacher's Manual available. (Casebook)

Taxation—Individual

DODGE'S THE LOGIC OF TAX, 343 pages, 1989. Softcover. (Text)

GUNN AND WARD'S CASES, TEXT AND PROBLEMS ON FEDERAL INCOME TAXATION, Second Edition, 835 pages, 1988. Teacher's Manual available. (Casebook) 1990 Supplement.

HUDSON AND LIND'S BLACK LETTER ON FEDERAL INCOME TAXATION, Third Edition, approximately 390 pages, 1990. Softcover. (Review)

Taxation—Individual—Cont'd

KRAGEN AND MCNULTY'S CASES AND MATERIALS ON FEDERAL INCOME TAXATION—INDIVIDUALS, CORPORATIONS, PARTNERSHIPS, Fourth Edition, 1287 pages, 1985. (Casebook)

MCNULTY'S FEDERAL INCOME TAXATION OF INDIVIDUALS IN A NUTSHELL, Fourth Edition, 503 pages, 1988. Softcover. (Text)

POSIN'S HORNBOOK ON FEDERAL INCOME TAXATION, Student Edition, 491 pages, 1983, with 1989 pocket part. (Text)

ROSE AND CHOMMIE'S HORNBOOK ON FEDERAL INCOME TAXATION, Third Edition, 923 pages, 1988, with 1989 pocket part. (Text)

SELECTED FEDERAL TAXATION STATUTES AND REGULATIONS. Softcover. Approximately 1650 pages, 1991.

SOLOMON AND HESCH'S PROBLEMS, CASES AND MATERIALS ON FEDERAL INCOME TAXATION OF INDIVIDUALS, 1068 pages, 1987. Teacher's Manual available. (Casebook)

Taxation—International

DOERNBERG'S INTERNATIONAL TAXATION IN A NUTSHELL, 325 pages, 1989. Softcover. (Text)

KAPLAN'S FEDERAL TAXATION OF INTERNATIONAL TRANSACTIONS: PRINCIPLES, PLANNING AND POLICY, 635 pages, 1988. (Casebook)

Taxation—Partnership

BERGER AND WIEDENBECK'S CASES AND MATERIALS ON PARTNERSHIP TAXATION, 788 pages, 1989. Teacher's Manual available. (Casebook)

Taxation—State & Local

GELFAND AND SALSICH'S STATE AND LOCAL TAXATION AND FINANCE IN A NUTSHELL, 309 pages, 1986. Softcover. (Text)

HELLERSTEIN AND HELLERSTEIN'S CASES AND MATERIALS ON STATE AND LOCAL TAXATION, Fifth Edition, 1071 pages, 1988. (Casebook)

Torts—see also Products Liability

CHRISTIE AND MEEKS' CASES AND MATERIALS ON THE LAW OF TORTS, Second Edition, 1264 pages, 1990. (Casebook)

DOBBS' TORTS AND COMPENSATION—PERSONAL ACCOUNTABILITY AND SOCIAL RESPONSIBILITY FOR INJURY, 955 pages, 1985. Teacher's Manual available. (Casebook) 1990 Supplement.

KEETON, KEETON, SARGENTICH AND STEINER'S CASES AND MATERIALS ON TORT AND ACCIDENT LAW, Second Edition, 1318 pages, 1989. (Casebook)

KIONKA'S BLACK LETTER ON TORTS, 339 pages, 1988. Softcover. (Review)

KIONKA'S TORTS IN A NUTSHELL: INJURIES TO PERSONS AND PROPERTY, 434 pages, 1977. Softcover. (Text)

MALONE'S TORTS IN A NUTSHELL: INJURIES TO FAMILY, SOCIAL AND TRADE RELATIONS, 358 pages, 1979. Softcover. (Text)

PROSSER AND KEETON'S HORNBOOK ON TORTS, Fifth Edition, Student Edition, 1286 pages, 1984 with 1988 pocket part. (Text)

ROBERTSON, POWERS AND ANDERSON'S CASES AND MATERIALS ON TORTS, 932 pages, 1989. Teacher's Manual available. (Casebook)

Trade Regulation—see also Antitrust, Regulated Industries

MCMANIS' UNFAIR TRADE PRACTICES IN A NUTSHELL, Second Edition, 464 pages, 1988. Softcover. (Text)

OPPENHEIM, WESTON, MAGGS AND SCHECHTER'S CASES AND MATERIALS ON UNFAIR TRADE PRACTICES AND CONSUMER PROTECTION, Fourth Edition, 1038 pages, 1983. Teacher's Manual available. (Casebook) 1986 Supplement.

SCHECHTER'S BLACK LETTER ON UNFAIR TRADE PRACTICES, 272 pages, 1986. Softcover. (Review)

Trial and Appellate Advocacy—see also Civil Procedure

APPELLATE ADVOCACY, HANDBOOK OF, Second Edition, 182 pages, 1986. Softcover. (Text)

BERGMAN'S TRIAL ADVOCACY IN A NUTSHELL, Second Edition, 354 pages, 1989. Softcover. (Text)

BINDER AND BERGMAN'S FACT INVESTIGATION: FROM HYPOTHESIS TO PROOF, 354 pages, 1984. Teacher's Manual available. (Coursebook)

Trial and Appellate Advocacy—Cont'd

CARLSON AND IMWINKELRIED'S DYNAMICS OF TRIAL PRACTICE: PROBLEMS AND MATERIALS, 414 pages, 1989. Teacher's Manual available. (Coursebook)

GOLDBERG'S THE FIRST TRIAL (WHERE DO I SIT? WHAT DO I SAY?) IN A NUTSHELL, 396 pages, 1982. Softcover. (Text)

HAYDOCK, HERR, AND STEMPEL'S FUNDAMENTALS OF PRE-TRIAL LITIGATION, 768 pages, 1985. Softcover. Teacher's Manual available. (Coursebook)

HEGLAND'S TRIAL AND PRACTICE SKILLS IN A NUTSHELL, 346 pages, 1978. Softcover. (Text)

HORNSTEIN'S APPELLATE ADVOCACY IN A NUTSHELL, 325 pages, 1984. Softcover. (Text)

JEANS' HANDBOOK ON TRIAL ADVOCACY, Student Edition, 473 pages, 1975. Softcover. (Text)

LISNEK AND KAUFMAN'S DEPOSITIONS: PROCEDURE, STRATEGY AND TECHNIQUE, Law School and CLE Edition. 250 pages, 1990. Softcover. (Text)

MARTINEAU'S CASES AND MATERIALS ON APPELLATE PRACTICE AND PROCEDURE, 565 pages, 1987. (Casebook)

NOLAN'S CASES AND MATERIALS ON TRIAL PRACTICE, 518 pages, 1981. (Casebook)

SONSTENG AND HAYDOCK'S TRIAL: THEORIES, TACTICS, TECHNIQUE, Approximately 650 pages, 1990. Softcover. (Text)

SONSTENG, HAYDOCK AND BOYD'S THE TRIALBOOK: A TOTAL SYSTEM FOR PREPARATION AND PRESENTATION OF A CASE, 404 pages, 1984. Softcover. (Coursebook)

WHARTON, HAYDOCK AND SONSTENG'S CALIFORNIA CIVIL TRIALBOOK, Law School and CLE Edition. Approximately 300 pages, 1990. Softcover. (Text)

Trusts and Estates

ATKINSON'S HORNBOOK ON WILLS, Second Edition, 975 pages, 1953. (Text)

AVERILL'S UNIFORM PROBATE CODE IN A NUTSHELL, Second Edition, 454 pages, 1987. Softcover. (Text)

BOGERT'S HORNBOOK ON TRUSTS, Sixth Edition, Student Edition, 794 pages, 1987. (Text)

CLARK, LUSKY AND MURPHY'S CASES AND MATERIALS ON GRATUITOUS TRANSFERS, Third Edition, 970 pages, 1985. (Casebook)

DODGE'S WILLS, TRUSTS AND ESTATE PLANNING–LAW AND TAXATION, CASES AND MATERIALS, 665 pages, 1988. (Casebook)

KURTZ' PROBLEMS, CASES AND OTHER MATERIALS ON FAMILY ESTATE PLANNING, 853 pages, 1983. Teacher's Manual available. (Casebook)

MCGOVERN'S CASES AND MATERIALS ON WILLS, TRUSTS AND FUTURE INTERESTS: AN INTRODUCTION TO ESTATE PLANNING, 750 pages, 1983. (Casebook)

MCGOVERN, KURTZ AND REIN'S HORNBOOK ON WILLS, TRUSTS AND ESTATES–INCLUDING TAXATION AND FUTURE INTERESTS, 996 pages, 1988. (Text)

MENNELL'S WILLS AND TRUSTS IN A NUTSHELL, 392 pages, 1979. Softcover. (Text)

SIMES' HORNBOOK ON FUTURE INTERESTS, Second Edition, 355 pages, 1966. (Text)

TURANO AND RADIGAN'S HORNBOOK ON NEW YORK ESTATE ADMINISTRATION, 676 pages, 1986. (Text)

UNIFORM PROBATE CODE, OFFICIAL TEXT WITH COMMENTS. 615 pages, 1989. Softcover.

WAGGONER'S FUTURE INTERESTS IN A NUTSHELL, 361 pages, 1981. Softcover. (Text)

WATERBURY'S MATERIALS ON TRUSTS AND ESTATES, 1039 pages, 1986. Teacher's Manual available. (Casebook)

Water Law—see also Energy and Natural Resources Law, Environmental Law

GETCHES' WATER LAW IN A NUTSHELL, Second Edition, approximately 441 pages, 1990. Softcover. (Text)

SAX AND ABRAMS' LEGAL CONTROL OF WATER RESOURCES: CASES AND MATERIALS, 941 pages, 1986. (Casebook)

TRELEASE AND GOULD'S CASES AND MATERIALS ON WATER LAW, Fourth Edition, 816 pages, 1986. (Casebook)

AN INTRODUCTION TO THE LAW OF EVIDENCE

Second Edition

By

Graham C. Lilly
Henry and Grace Doherty
Professor of Law
University of Virginia

WEST PUBLISHING CO.
ST. PAUL, MINN., 1987

50 West Kellogg Boulevard
P.O. Box 64526
St. Paul, Minnesota 55164–0526

Printed in the United States of America

Library of Congress Cataloging-in-Publication Data

Lilly, Graham C., 1938–
An introduction to the law of evidence.

Includes index.
1. Evidence (Law)—United States. I. Title.

KF8935.L54 1987 347.73'6 87–13965
347.3076

ISBN 0–314–59288–1

Lilly, Evidence, 2nd Ed.
2nd Reprint—1990

To Margaret Kemper Lilly

*

Preface and Acknowledgements Second Edition

It has now been nearly a decade since the "little green book," as my students call it, was published in its first edition. In this second edition, the little book approaches adolescence and, characteristic of that age, has grown noticeably in size and, I venture the hope, even in maturity. Despite its greater length, necessitated by recent developments and the increased adoption of evidence codes modeled after the Federal Rules, I have tried to keep the book within the bounds defined in the first preface: "a comparably concise treatment" of the law of evidence.

The reasons for an introductory text, set out in the preface to the first edition, seem to me as plausible in 1987 as they were in 1978. Much of the original volume remains intact, but the reader will notice a decided shift in emphasis toward the Federal Rules of Evidence. These Rules, now adopted wholly or substantially by more than thirty states,* have become the dominant influence in evidence law. But the common law, from which the Rules drew their essential character, is still given considerable attention. In some states, of course, appellate decisions continue to be the principal source of evidentiary rules. Furthermore, it is difficult to understand the Federal Rules without at least some appreciation of their common-law heritage. Of necessity, the Rules speak with a statutory terseness that cannot capture the richness of the judicial opinions that informed their content and, even today, enlighten their construction.

It is customary, at the beginning of a comparatively short work, to intone solemnly the usual cautions about the hazards of brevity and generalization. I shall simply trust that my readers will appreciate the limitations of treating the complex subject of evidence in fewer than 550 pages. Fortunately, it is not necessary to resolve the tension between the educational extremes of teaching "more and more about less and less" and "less and less about

* A list of states that have adopted the Federal Rules appears at page xiii.

more and more." The specialist and the generalist both have important roles, and progress in law and elsewhere depends on the contributions of each. Although this book aims principally at those who seek to learn (or relearn) the fundamentals of evidence law, I have tried to make the volume useful to a wider readership by documenting the text with primary and secondary authorities. I have also seized many opportunities to comment on the rules of evidence and, insofar as possible, to knit them together into a single fabric.

I should like to acknowledge my debts and gratitude to those whose help made this second edition possible. First, my deepest thanks to my student assistants over the last three academic years and to those who served in a similar capacity during the summer months: Molly Campbell, Greg Giammittorio, Christopher Mugel, Paula Scordato and, especially, to Albert Coons who served during both the summer and academic terms and dedicated many hours to the project. And I owe a special debt to three students, Roger Brooks, Yvonne Facchina, and Burton Spivak, who, during the last four weeks of manuscript preparation, simply appeared at my door and, despite burdensome law review responsibilities, offered their help. It was gratefully received. I pay special tribute to Madeline Branch, my secretary for this project, who can lay claim to having typed every word that appears in the first and second editions. Her professional skills are matched only by her patience, good humor, and serenity in the midst of disorder and impending deadlines. Finally, my warmest thanks go to my friend and Dean, Richard A. Merrill, and to the Law School Foundation; their joint support was essential to the inception and completion of this second edition.

GRAHAM C. LILLY

Charlottesville, Virginia
June, 1987

Preface and Acknowledgements First Edition

My reader deserves a brief explanation why, in a field abundant with fine texts and treatises, I add yet another volume devoted to the law of evidence. I have long felt that students of evidence—broadly including all of those who inquire into the rules and principles of judicial proof—need a comparatively concise treatment of the subject, one that presupposes little or no prior knowledge in the field. Even practicing professionals often seek recourse to an introductory text, either to refresh their memories or to learn for the first time a subject not formally studied in law school; for this reason, I have endeavored to include within these pages adequate citations to primary and secondary sources.

But how will this book serve the law student who enrolls in a basic evidence course? Presumably, he or she has a coursebook and ready access to the great works in the field of evidence. My hope that this text may have at least a supplementary role in the formal educational process is based in part upon conversations with my own students. They find the law of evidence relatively simple in its separate parts, but elusive and difficult to grasp as a whole. They also affirm the widespread recognition among educators that the demands imposed by important new areas of law curtail the time available for the traditional legal subjects. The old ground must be covered more efficiently and quickly than in the past. Finally, I sense among my colleagues who teach evidence a restive attitude, a growing conviction that new pedagogic techniques must be developed both to engage the students' interest and to free the teacher from the arid repetition of the evidential basics.* Perhaps a book of this kind will have utility for those seeking a fresh approach in the classroom.

My debts to those who have encouraged and assisted me in writing this book are too numerous fully to recount here. I

* A coursebook that breaks new ground by abandoning the traditional case method of study is Lempert & Saltzburg, A Modern Approach to Evidence, West Publishing Co. (1977).

particularly want to thank Dean Monrad G. Paulsen and his successor Dean Emerson G. Spies for their support, and to gratefully acknowledge that officials of the University of Virginia made available to me a grant under the Sesquicentennial Associateship Program of the Center for Advanced Studies, enabling me to devote a semester to writing and research. I am especially indebted, also, to my colleague, Professor Stephen A. Saltzburg who patiently read each page of the manuscript and made many valuable suggestions, and to the following of my student assistants who by laboring far beyond the limits imposed by their meager financial compensation contributed immeasurably to the final product: Robert Cave, David Hunt, Christopher Farley, Andrew Merdek, Ann Mische, Russell Pollack, Michael Ross, and Daniel Rowley. I could not close these acknowledgements without expressing special gratitude to Madeline Branch, my typist, whose stenographic skill and fortitude played a significant role in production of this book.

GRAHAM C. LILLY

Charlottesville, Virginia
August, 1978

Author's Note on Coverage, Style and Citations

The coverage of this text typifies that of a basic three- or four-hour course in Evidence. All of the major evidentiary rules and principles are discussed, except for those constitutionally based rules of exclusion—principally grounded on the Fourth Amendment—that usually are included in the course in Criminal Procedure. Ideally, this book should be read sequentially from beginning to end; at least it was so designed. But the format and an ample index permit selective reference. To accommodate the user who will not read the book in its entirety, the footnotes contain many cross-references. As a further convenience, there is occasional repetition in the textual discussion.

The use of the masculine gender throughout this book should not suggest that the author is indifferent either to the growing number of women in the legal profession or to the significance of their contribution. This usage, which accords with accepted grammatical practice, is simply to spare the reader the distraction of alternating pronouns.

The citations to certain references have been abbreviated in accordance with the illustrations below. These sources, especially the standard works of Weinstein & Berger, Louisell & Mueller, Wigmore, and McCormick, appear frequently throughout the text and footnotes. Professor McCormick's treatise, revised and updated in 1972 and 1984 under the general editorship of Professor Edward W. Cleary, remains the most comprehensive and scholarly single-volume treatment of the field of evidence.

*

Abbreviated Citations

1. Carlson, et al. at 281

   R. Carlson, E. Imwinkelried & E. Kionka, Materials for the Study of Evidence: Cases and Materials, 281 (1983).

2. Cleary & Strong at 281

   E. Clearly & J. Strong, Evidence: Cases, Materials & Problems, 281 (3d ed. 1981).

3. Graham, Handbook of Federal Evidence at 281

   M. Graham, Handbook of Federal Evidence, 281 (2d ed. 1986).

4. Kaplan & Waltz at 281

   J. Kaplan & J. Waltz, Cases and Materials on Evidence, 281 (5th ed. 1984).

5. Ladd & Carlson at 281

   M. Ladd & R. Carlson, Cases and Materials on Evidence, 281 (3d ed. 1972).

6. Lempert & Saltzburg at 281

   R. Lempert & S. Saltzburg, A Modern Approach to Evidence, 281 (2d ed. 1982).

7. 2 Louisell & Mueller at 281

   2 D. Louisell & C. Mueller, Federal Evidence, 281 (1977).

8. McCormick, § 99, at 213

   C. McCormick, McCormick on Evidence, § 99, at 213 (3d ed., Cleary, 1984).

9. Morgan & Weinstein at 281

   E. Morgan & J. Weinstein, Basic Problems of State and Federal Evidence, 281 (5th ed. 1976).

10. Saltzburg & Redden at 281

    S. Saltzburg & K. Redden, Federal Rules of Evidence Manual, 281 (4th ed. 1986).

11. 2 Weinstein & Berger, ¶ 601(04), at 28

    2 J. Weinstein & M. Berger, Weinstein's Evidence: Commentary on Rules of Evidence for the United States Courts and Magistrates, ¶ 601(04), at 601–28 (1982).

12. Weinstein & Mansfield, et al. at 281

    J. Weinstein, J. Mansfield, N. Abrams & M. Berger, Cases and Materials on Evidence, 281 (7th ed. 1983).

* 13. VII Wigmore, § 1946, at 76 (Chadbourn)

    VII J. Wigmore, Evidence in Trials at Common Law, § 1946, at 76 (Chadbourn rev. 1981).

* Other revised volumes are also noted with the reviser's name in parentheses.

States Adopting the Federal Rules of Evidence

The following states have evidence codes (or rules of court) based wholly or substantially upon the Federal Rules of Evidence: Alaska, Arizona, Arkansas, Colorado, Delaware, Florida, Hawaii, Idaho, Iowa, Maine, Michigan, Minnesota, Mississippi, Montana, Nebraska, Nevada, New Hampshire, New Mexico, North Carolina, North Dakota, Ohio, Oklahoma, Oregon, South Dakota, Texas, Utah, Vermont, Washington, West Virginia, Wisconsin, Wyoming.

*

Summary of Contents

	Page
PREFACE AND ACKNOWLEDGEMENTS, SECOND EDITION	xxiii
PREFACE AND ACKNOWLEDGEMENTS, FIRST EDITION	xxv
AUTHOR'S NOTE ON COVERAGE, STYLE AND CITATIONS	xxvii
ABBREVIATED CITATIONS	xxix
STATE ADOPTING THE FEDERAL RULES OF EVIDENCE	xxxi
TABLE OF CASES	xliii

Chapter		
I.	Evidence in Context	1
II.	Relevance: An Introduction	23
III.	Procedural Concepts and Consequences	47
IV.	Competency of Witnesses and the Process of Trial	84
V.	Relevance: Recurring Problems of Circumstantial Proof	122
VI.	The Hearsay Rule: Its Nature and Rationale	180
VII.	The Hearsay Rule: Selected Exceptions and Statutory Nonhearsay	218
VIII.	Impeachment	337
IX.	Privilege	381
X.	The Role of Judge and Jury: A Summary	452
XI.	Offer of Proof and Objections	469
XII.	Expert Testimony and Scientific Evidence	483
XIII.	Real Evidence and Writings	511

Appendix 536
Index 575

*

Table of Contents

Page

PREFACE AND ACKNOWLEDGEMENTS, SECOND EDITION xxiii
PREFACE AND ACKNOWLEDGEMENTS, FIRST EDITION xxv
AUTHOR'S NOTE ON COVERAGE, STYLE AND CITATIONS xxvii
ABBREVIATED CITATIONS xxix
STATE ADOPTING THE FEDERAL RULES OF EVIDENCE xxxi
TABLE OF CASES xliii

CHAPTER I. EVIDENCE IN CONTEXT

Section

1.1 The Role of Evidence in the Process of Adjudication 1
1.2 Evidence: Definition and Professional Evaluation 2
1.3 The Bases of Evidentiary Restriction: A Prefatory View 3
1.4 Building an Evidentiary Record: Allocation of Responsibility for Input and Exclusion 4
1.5 Use and Evaluation of the Admitted Evidence: Allocation of Responsibility 5
1.6 The Role of Judge and Jury: A General View 7
1.7 The Changing Shape of the Adversarial Model in Modern Litigation 9
1.8 Factfinding Outside the Record: Judicial Notice 13

CHAPTER II. RELEVANCE: AN INTRODUCTION

2.1 Basic Concepts 23
2.2 The Test of Probative Value 27
2.3 Assessing Probative Value 30
2.4 The Assumptive Admissibility of Relevant Evidence 33
2.5 Discretionary Exclusion Based on Considerations of Practical Policy 34
2.6 Conditional Relevancy 40
2.7 Circumstantial and Direct Evidence 43

CHAPTER III. PROCEDURAL CONCEPTS AND CONSEQUENCES

Section Page

3.1 Burdens of Persuasion and Production 47
3.2 Presumptions: General Nature and Effect 55
3.3 Some Sample Presumptions 57
3.4 Presumptions: Impact Upon Opponent and Effect of Rebuttal Evidence 59
3.5 Presumptions in Criminal Cases: Constitutional Problems 65
3.6 Presumptions: Instructing the Jury 78
3.7 Presumptions Under the Federal Rules of Evidence 80

CHAPTER IV. COMPETENCY OF WITNESSES AND THE PROCESS OF TRIAL

4.1 Introduction: Scope 84
4.2 Competency: In General 85
4.3 Competency: The Dead Man's Statutes 87
4.4 The Components of Trial: Opening Statement 90
4.5 The Components of Trial: Format and Order of Proof 90
4.6 Examining the Witness: Leading, Misleading, and Argumentative Questions 93
4.7 Examining the Witness: Refreshing Recollection 98
4.8 Examining the Witness: Past Recollection Recorded 104
4.9 Examining the Witness: The Opinion Rule 105
4.10 Examining the Witness: The Scope of Cross-Examination 110
4.11 Examining the Witness: The Interaction of the American Rule and Certain Rules of Privilege 114
4.12 The Components of Trial: Closing Argument and Judge's Charge 118

CHAPTER V. RELEVANCE: RECURRING PROBLEMS OF CIRCUMSTANTIAL PROOF

5.1 Scope 122
5.2 Character Evidence: In General 123
5.3 Character Evidence: Character An Essential Element of a Claim, Charge, or Defense 125
5.4 Character Evidence: Character Used Circumstantially 127

Section Page
5.5 Character Evidence: Circumstantial Use of Character in Civil Cases 127
5.6 Character Evidence: Circumstantial Use of Character in Criminal Cases 130
5.7 Character Evidence: Presenting and Cross-Examining the Reputation or Opinion Witness 134
5.8 Character Evidence Pertaining to a Victim or Other Non-Party 138
5.9 Rape Shield Provisions 142
5.10 Reputation, Incidents, and Threats as Bearing Upon the Defendant's State of Mind 144
5.11 Evidence of Habit 145
5.12 Other Criminal Acts: In General 148
5.13 Other Criminal Acts: Degree of Certainty With Which Collateral Crime Must be Shown 150
5.14 Other Criminal Acts: Application of the Governing Principle 153
5.15 Other Criminal Acts: Balancing the Competing Considerations that Govern Admissibility 161
5.16 Similar Incidents in Civil Cases 168
5.17 Public Policy Considerations in Circumstantial Proof: Subsequent Remedial Action and Offers to Compromise or Plead Guilty 172

CHAPTER VI. THE HEARSAY RULE: ITS NATURE AND RATIONALE

6.1 General Principle and Rationale 180
6.2 Application of the General Principle 183
6.3 Conduct as Hearsay 193
6.4 Prior Statements of a Witness 198
6.5 The Hearsay Rule and the Federal Rules of Evidence 208

CHAPTER VII. THE HEARSAY RULE: SELECTED EXCEPTIONS AND STATUTORY NONHEARSAY

PART A. PARTY ADMISSIONS

7.1 In General 218
7.2 Party Admission: An Illustration 220
7.3 Party Admission by Conduct and Implication 221

Section | Page
7.4 Vicarious or Representative Admissions ... 223
7.5 Statements of Coconspirators ... 232
7.6 Party Admissions Under the Federal Rules: A Summary ... 233

PART B. SPONTANEOUS DECLARATIONS

7.7 In General ... 236
7.8 Present Sense Impression ... 237
7.9 Excited Utterance ... 239

PART C. PHYSICAL OR MENTAL CONDITION

7.10 In General ... 244
7.11 Present Physical Condition ... 245
7.12 Present State of Mind: In General ... 247
7.13 State of Mind to Prove Conduct: Use and Limitations 249

PART D. RECORDED RECOLLECTION

7.14 In General ... 259
7.15 Recorded Recollection: Rationale and Application ... 260

PART E. RECORDS OF BUSINESS AND RELATED ENTERPRISES

7.16 In General ... 263
7.17 Records of Business and Related Enterprises: Illustrations and Refinements ... 265

PART F. PUBLIC RECORDS

7.18 In General ... 271
7.19 Public Records: Application of the Exception ... 272

PART G. JUDGMENT OF A CRIMINAL CONVICTION

7.20 Theory and application ... 278
7.21 Transitional Note: The Hearsay Exceptions and Declarant's Unavailability ... 283

PART H. FORMER TESTIMONY

Section		Page
7.22	In General	285
7.23	Former Testimony: Application of the Exception	286

PART I. DYING DECLARATIONS

Section		Page
7.24	In General	292
7.25	Dying Declarations: Application of the Exception	294

PART J. DECLARATIONS AGAINST INTEREST

Section		Page
7.26	In General	296
7.27	Declarations Against Interest: Application of the Exception	297

PART K. HEARSAY AND EXCEPTIONS: PAST AND FUTURE

Section		Page
7.28	Change Through Evolution and the Residual Exceptions	304

PART L. THE CONFRONTATION CLAUSE

Section		Page
7.29	The Confrontation Clause: Historical Context	311
7.30	Early Construction of the Confrontation Clause	319
7.31	Recent Interpretation of the Confrontation Clause	325

CHAPTER VIII. IMPEACHMENT

Section		Page
8.1	In General	337
8.2	Impeachment of One's Own Witness	338
8.3	Techniques of Impeachment: Character Traits Reflecting Mendacity	343
8.4	Techniques of Impeachment: Bias	357
8.5	Techniques of Impeachment: Prior Inconsistent Statements	361
8.6	Techniques of Impeachment: Extrinsic Evidence to Contradict and the Restriction Applicable to Collateral Matters	367
8.7	Accrediting the Witness (Rehabilitation)	373

CHAPTER IX. PRIVILEGE

Section Page
9.1 Rationale and Characteristics 381
9.2 Privilege Under the Federal Rules of Evidence 384
9.3 Spousal Privilege for Confidential Communications .. 386
9.4 Spousal Privilege to Prevent Adverse Testimony in a Criminal Trial 390
9.5 Attorney-Client Privilege: Introduction and Overview 394
9.6 Attorney-Client Privilege: Basic Requirements, Scope, and Duration 396
9.7 Attorney-Client Privilege: Special Problems of Sharing and Dissemination of Privileged Information... 405
9.8 Attorney-Client Privilege: Corporate Context 412
9.9 Attorney-Client Privilege: Nonapplicability and Waiver 417
9.10 Physician-Patient Privilege 419
9.11 The Privilege Against Self-Incrimination: Scope, Application, and Waiver 423
9.12 The Privilege Against Self-Incrimination: Special Application in Custodial Interrogation 436

CHAPTER X. THE ROLE OF JUDGE AND JURY: A SUMMARY

10.1 Factual Determinations Made by the Judge and Jury: In General 452
10.2 The Judge's Role in Evaluating the Evidence as a Whole 454
10.3 The Judge's Factual Determinations Regarding Individual Offers of Proof of Fact 454
10.4 The Judge's Role in Determining Competence and Applying Technical Exclusionary Rules 457
10.5 Factual Determinations Necessary for the Application of an Evidentiary Rule: Special Situations 460

CHAPTER XI. OFFER OF PROOF AND OBJECTIONS

11.1 The Offer, Objection, and Motion to Strike: In General 469
11.2 Offer of Proof: Proponent's Responsibilities 471
11.3 Objection: Waiver and Appellate Review 472

Section Page

11.4 Offers of Proof and Objections Under the Federal Rules of Evidence 476
11.5 Curative Admissibility ("Open Door" Theory) 477

CHAPTER XII. EXPERT TESTIMONY AND SCIENTIFIC EVIDENCE

12.1 Role and Qualification of the Expert Witness 483
12.2 The Expert Witness: Direct Examination 485
12.3 The Expert Witness: Cross-Examination and Impeachment 491
12.4 Scientific Proof: General Principles 493
12.5 Scientific Proof: Illustrations 496

CHAPTER XIII. REAL EVIDENCE AND WRITINGS

13.1 Real and Demonstrative Evidence: In General 511
13.2 Real and Demonstrative Evidence: Conditions of Admissibility and Required Foundation 513
13.3 Pictorial Evidence: Photographs, X-rays, and Motion Pictures 519
13.4 Experiments 520
13.5 Writings and Other Recordations: In General 522
13.6 Authentication: In General 523
13.7 Authentication by Evidence Extrinsic to the Writing 525
13.8 Self-Authentication 527
13.9 The Best Evidence Rule 529

Appendix 536

Index 575

*

Table of Cases

References are to Section and Footnote (n.) or Author's Note (Note)

Abbott, State v.—§ **11.3, n. 3.**
Abel, United States v.—§ **8.4;** § **8.4, n. 7, 12.**
Acosta, United States v.—§ **8.3, n. 48.**
Adams, People v.—§ **13.7, n. 7.**
Adcock, United States v.—§ **7.12, n. 2.**
Addison, United States v.—§ **12.5, n. 31.**
Adrian, State v.—§ **7.30, n. 10.**
Affleck, United States v.—§ **12.1, n. 11.**
Agosto, In re—§ **9.3, n. 11;** § **9.4, n. 13.**
Agrella v. Rivkind—§ **9.11, n. 36.**
Ahrens, United States v.—§ **3.7, n. 2.**
Alabama By-Products Corp. v. Killingsworth—§ **3.7, n. 8.**
Alamo, People v.—§ **8.3, n. 60.**
Albertson v. Subversive Activities Control Bd.—§ **9.11, n. 21.**
Albertson, People v.—§ **5.13, n. 4.**
Alcalde, People v.—§ **7.13;** § **7.13, n. 13, 15.**
Alford v. United States—§ **4.5, n. 6.**
Alker, United States v.—§ **7.3, n. 4.**
Allen v. County Court, Ulster County—§ **3.5;** § **3.5, n. 39, 40, 44, 46, 48.**
Allen v. Illinois—§ **9.11, n. 17.**
Allen v. McLain—§ **7.9, n. 3.**
Allen v. Matson Nav. Co.—§ **4.9, n. 9.**
Allen, United States v.—§ **5.14, n. 21.**
Aluminum Co. of America, United States v.—§ **1.8, n. 23.**
Aluminum Industries v. Egan—§ **4.5, n. 6.**
Amerada Hess Corp., United States v.—§ **9.6, n. 26.**
American Cyanamid Co., United States v.—§ **7.17, Note 2.**
American Tel. & Tel. Co., United States v.—§ **7.19, n. 21.**
Ammar, United States v.—§ **7.31, n. 26, 45.**
Anderson v. Florence—§ **12.5, Note 6.**
Ando v. Woodberry—§ **5.17, n. 18.**
Andresen v. Maryland—§ **9.11, n. 22, 27.**
Annunziato, United States v.—§ **7.13, n. 2, 24.**
Anstine v. McWilliams—§ **13.7, n. 8.**
Apfelbaum, United States v.—§ **9.11, n. 35.**
Apodaca, United States v.—§ **9.4, n. 11.**
Appeal of (see name of party)
Apple v. Commonwealth—§ **13.7, n. 2.**
Arcola v. Wilkinson—§ **11.3, n. 11.**
Arias, United States v.—§ **7.19, n. 11.**
Armour & Co. v. Industrial Commission of Colorado—§ **7.9, n. 7.**
Arpan v. United States—§ **7.3, n. 5.**
Arroyo, People v.—§ **7.31, n. 26.**
Ashcraft v. State of Tennessee—§ **9.12, n. 8, 15.**
Astling, United States v.—§ **5.13, n. 5.**
Atkins, United States v.—§ **7.27, n. 15.**
Atlantic Greyhound Corporation v. Eddins—§ **8.5, n. 21.**
Ault v. International Harvester Co.—§ **5.17, n. 3.**
"Automatic" Sprinkler Corp. of America v. Coley & Petersen, Inc.—§ **7.16, n. 2.**

Bailey v. Southern Pac. Transp. Co.—§ **7.23, n. 13.**
Baker v. Elcona Homes Corp.—§ **7.15, n. 6.**
Baker, United States v.—§ **7.17, n. 5.**
Baldwin, State v.—§ **7.12, n. 5.**
Baller, United States v.—§ **12.4, n. 3, 9;** § **12.5, n. 32.**
Ballou v. Henri Studios, Inc.—§ **2.7.**
Banks v. Schweiker—§ **1.8, n. 23.**
Banks, State v.—§ **13.2, n. 6.**
Barber v. Page—§ **7.30, n. 5, 13, 18;** § **7.31, n. 2, 14, 24, 57.**
Barker, United States v.—§ **4.12, n. 2.**
Barnard, United States v.—§ **8.1, n. 3.**
Barnes v. United States—§ **3.5;** § **3.5, n. 34.**
Barnhart, People v.—§ **6.3, n. 9.**
Baroda State Bank v. Peck—§ **13.9, n. 23.**
Barrera v. Gonzalez—§ **7.27, n. 3.**
Barrett v. State—§ **5.8, n. 6.**

Barrett, United States v.—§ **5.14, n. 25;** § **7.27, Note 2.**
Bay, United States v.—§ **8.3, n. 38.**
Beardsley v. Irving—§ **1.8, n. 3.**
Beechum, United States v.—§ **5.13, n. 5.**
Bell v. Harmon—§ **7.1, n. 8.**
Bell, United States v.—§ **7.5, n. 9.**
Bellis v. United States—§ **9.11, n. 4, 8.**
Bensinger Co., United States v.—§ **7.4, n. 10.**
Benson v. Commonwealth—§ **13.9, Note 3.**
Berger v. California—§ **7.30, n. 9.**
Berkemer v. McCarty—§ **9.12, n. 29.**
Bernhard v. Bank of America Nat. Trust & Savings Ass'n—§ **7.20, n. 3.**
Berry v. Chaplin—§ **12.5, n. 15.**
Betts v. Betts—§ **7.12, n. 4.**
Biener, United States v.—§ **6.4, n. 4.**
Big Mack Trucking Company, Inc. v. Dickerson—§ **7.4, n. 3.**
Big O Tire Dealers, Inc. v. Goodyear Tire & Rubber Co.—§ **5.17, n. 14.**
Billstrom, State v.—§ **5.13, n. 4.**
Blackburn v. Alabama—§ **9.12, n. 10.**
Blackshear, United States v.—§ **11.3, n. 1.**
Blau v. United States—§ **9.11, n. 15.**
Block v. Bourbon County Com'rs—§ **7.20, n. 2.**
Bloodgood v. Lynch—§ **11.3, n. 11.**
Blunt, United States v.—§ **1.8, n. 3.**
Bock, State v.—§ **5.14, n. 24.**
Boeing Airplane Company v. Brown—§ **5.17, n. 9.**
Bond, State v.—§ **13.7, n. 3.**
Booth, United States v.—§ **12.1, n. 4.**
Borgy v. Commonwealth—§ **7.29, n. 21.**
Bourjaily v. United States—§ **10.5, n. 11, 17, 18.**
Boulden, Commonwealth v.—§ **5.15, n. 2.**
Bouton, People v.—§ **5.6, n. 7.**
Boyd v. United States—§ **9.3, n. 2;** § **9.11, n. 26.**
Bracey v. Herringa—§ **7.17, n. 15.**
Bracey v. United States—§ **5.15, n. 22.**
Bradley, State v.—§ **7.15, n. 1.**
Bradshaw, State v.—§ **4.7, n. 6.**
Brady v. State of Maryland—§ **4.7, n. 19.**
Brady, Commonwealth v.—§ **4.9, n. 9.**
Bram v. United States—§ **9.12, n. 11.**
Branzburg v. Hayes—§ **9.12, Note 3.**
Brashier, United States v.—§ **8.3, n. 36.**
Brettholz, United States v.—§ **5.14, n. 14.**
Brewer v. United States—§ **13.2, n. 17.**
Brewer v. Williams—§ **9.12, n. 49.**
Bridges v. State—§ **6.5, Note 4.**
Briley, State v.—§ **9.4, n. 7.**
Brown v. Board of Education of Topeka, Shawnee County, Kan.—§ **1.8;** § **1.8, n. 12, 15.**
Brown v. Darcy—§ **12.5.**
Brown v. State—§ **13.4, n. 1.**
Brown v. State of Mississippi—§ **9.12;** § **9.12, n. 4, 16.**
Brown v. United States—§ **4.11, n. 11, 12;** § **9.11, n. 43, 48.**
Brown, Commonwealth v.—§ **7.24, n. 4, 7.**
Brown, People v.—§ **7.27, n. 11;** § **12.5, n. 12.**
Brown, United States v.—§ **5.2, n. 5;** § **8.3, n. 44;** § **8.4, n. 3;** § **12.4, n. 3.**
Bruton v. United States—§ **7.30, n. 3, 4, 11.**
Bryant v. State—§ **8.7, n. 1.**
Builders Steel Co. v. Commissioner of Internal Rev.—§ **1.2, n. 4.**
Bullard v. United States—§ **5.14, n. 21.**
Bunn v. Caterpillar Tractor Co.—§ **2.5, n. 17.**
Burch, United States v.—§ **8.3, n. 54.**
Burdis v. Texas & P. Ry. Co.—§ **7.20, n. 5.**
Burns Baking Co., Jay v.—§ **1.8, n. 13.**
Bush v. State—§ **5.6, n. 7.**
Butler, Commonwealth v.—§ **8.7, Note 3**
Byrd, United States v.—§ **5.15;** § **5.15, n. 10, 12, 15;** § **9.3, n. 5.**

Caldero v. Tribune Pub. Co.—§ **9.12, Note 3.**
California v. Byers—§ **9.11, n. 20, 21.**
California v. Green—§ **6.4, n. 11;** § **7.29, n. 6;** § **7.30, n. 6, 11, 12, 14;** § **7.31, n. 15, 16.**
Callahan, United States v.—§ **4.10, n. 11;** § **5.11, n. 9.**
Camp, State v.—§ **12.5, n. 15.**
Campion, United States v.—§ **2.6, n. 5.**
Cantrell, State v.—§ **8.3, n. 33.**
Canty v. State—§ **5.15, n. 3.**
Carbo v. United States—§ **5.10, n. 2;** § **7.5, n. 8;** § **10.5, n. 15.**
Cardillo v. Zyla—§ **7.6, Note 1.**
Carlson, United States v.—§ **7.21, n. 6.**
Carranco, United States v.—§ **7.17, n. 2.**

Carter v. United States—§ **5.14, n. 31; § 5.15, n. 3.**
Carter v. Yardley & Co.—§ **5.16, n. 7.**
Carver v. Howard—§ **7.24, n. 2.**
Castaneda v. Partida—§ **12.5, n. 5.**
Castro-Ayon, United States v.—§ **6.5, n. 12.**
Casualty Insurance Co. of California v. Salinas—§ **7.11, n. 1.**
Catanese, State v.—§ **12.4, n. 8.**
Cavallo, State v.—§ **12.4, n. 3.**
Cellamare v. Third Avenue Transit Corporation—§ **13.9, n. 11.**
Central Mut. Ins. Co. v. D. & B., Inc.—§ **12.1, n. 6.**
Cestero v. Ferrara—§ **7.17, n. 20.**
Chacko, Commonwealth v.—§ **13.2, n. 6.**
Chambers v. Mississippi—§ **7.27, Note 3; § 8.2, n. 4.**
Chambers v. Silver—§ **13.4, n. 6.**
Champion Intern. Corp., United States v.—§ **6.4, n. 19.**
Chapman v. State of Cal.—§ **7.30, n. 8.**
Chappell, United States v.—§ **7.31, n. 26, 32.**
Chart v. General Motors Corp.—§ **5.17, n. 2.**
Chatterton v. State—§ **7.29, n. 14.**
Cheek v. Avco Lycoming Division—§ **13.2, n. 10.**
Cheetham v. Union R.R. Co.—§ **13.4, n. 2.**
Chibbaro, United States v.—§ **9.11, n. 19.**
Chicago & N W Ry Co v. C C Whitnack Produce Co—§ **3.2, n. 2.**
Christy v. United States—§ **5.3, n. 2.**
Cicale, United States v.—§ **7.13, n. 16.**
City of (see name of city)
Clark v. South Central Bell Tel. Co.—§ **1.8, n. 3.**
Clark v. State—§ **9.6, n. 7.**
Clark, United States v.—§ **9.4, n. 10, 11, 16.**
Clay v. Johns-Manville Sales Corp.—§ **7.23, n. 9.**
Clere v. Commonwealth—§ **8.7, n. 18.**
Cleveland Bd. of Ed. v. LaFleur—§ **3.2, n. 5.**
Cleveland, City of v. Cleveland Elec. Illuminating Co.—§ **7.17, n. 5.**
Cluck, United States v.—§ **8.3, n. 58.**
Clutchette v. Rushen—§ **9.6, n. 17.**
Coades, United States v.—§ **5.15, n. 15.**
Coca, People v.—§ **4.2, n. 11.**
Coil v. United States—§ **8.3, n. 68; § 9.11, n. 58.**
Cole, State v.—§ **9.10, n. 4.**
Coleman v. State—§ **9.3, n. 7; § 9.4, n. 12.**
Coleman, People v.—§ **8.7, n. 19.**
Collins, People v.—§ **12.5; § 12.5, n. 1.**
Colorado v. Spring—§ **9.12, n. 31.**
Coltrane v. United States—§ **8.7, n. 18.**
Commercial Molasses Corp. v. New York Tank Barge Corp.—§ **3.4, n. 15.**
Commissioner of Welfare of City of New York ex rel. Tyler v. Costonie—§ **12.5, n. 15.**
Commodity Futures Trading Com'n v. Weintraub—§ **9.8, n. 17; § 9.9, n. 4.**
Commonwealth v. ______ (see opposing party)
Complaint of Am. Export Lines, Inc.—§ **7.17, Note 2.**
Conkling v. Conkling—§ **4.10, n. 1.**
Conley v. Mervis—§ **4.11, n. 2.**
Conley, United States v.—§ **5.15, n. 14.**
Connecticut v. Barrett—§ **9.12, n. 48.**
Conner v. Dart Transp. Service—§ **5.3, n. 1.**
Connor, People v.—§ **8.2, n. 7.**
Contemporary Mission, Inc. v. Famous Music Corp.—§ **12.5, n. 5.**
Cook, United States v.—§ **2.5, n. 16.**
Coolidge, State v.—§ **12.5, n. 26.**
Corke v. Corke and Cooke—§ **6.5, n. 1.**
Coughlin v. Capitol Cement Co.—§ **6.5, n. 11.**
County Court of Ulster County, New York v. Allen—§ **3.5; § 3.5, n. 37.**
Crane v. Kentucky—§ **7.30, n. 8.**
Crawford v. Commonwealth—§ **8.5, n. 21.**
Crawford, United States v.—§ **8.3, n. 30.**
Crider v. Com.—§ **5.14, n. 26.**
Crocker v. Lee—§ **13.2, n. 15.**
Cunningham, United States v.—§ **2.5, n. 8; § 8.2, n. 14.**
Curcio v. United States—§ **9.11, n. 7.**
Curtis v. Bradley—§ **7.15, n. 8.**
Curtis, United States v.—§ **5.7, n. 5, 12.**
Cyphers, United States v.—§ **5.14, n. 11.**
Czajka v. Hickman—§ **8.3, n. 51.**

D'Avella, Commonwealth v.—§ **12.5, n. 15.**
Daghita, People v.—§ **9.3, n. 9.**

Dallas County v. Commercial Union Assurance Co.—§ **7.28, n. 8.**
Damen, People v.—§ **6.4, n. 26;** § **7.9, n. 1.**
Daniell v. State—§ **4.9, n. 7.**
Dantonio, State v.—§ **12.5, n. 18.**
Darling v. Charleston Community Memorial Hospital—§ **13.2, n. 3.**
Darling, State v.—§ **5.14, n. 14;** § **5.15, n. 6.**
Davis Transport, Inc. v. Bolstad—§ **7.9, n. 3.**
Davis v. Alaska—§ **4.7, n. 26;** § **7.30, n. 7.**
Davis v. State—§ **13.4, n. 2.**
Davis v. State of North Carolina—§ **9.12, n. 13.**
Davis v. Williams Bros. Const. Co.—§ **13.9, n. 7.**
Davis, People v.—§ **10.4, n. 6.**
Davis, State v.—§ **5.13, n. 4;** § **9.12, n. 13.**
Davis, United States v.—§ **5.6, n. 2, 12;** § **5.15, n. 2;** § **7.21, n. 8;** § **7.23, Note 3;** § **9.4, n. 14;** § **9.11, n. 28.**
Day, United States v.—§ **5.13, n. 8.**
Deane Buick Co. v. Kendall—§ **7.13, n. 1.**
Deaton, Gassaway & Davison, Inc. v. Thomas—§ **4.3, n. 8.**
Del Toro Soto, United States v.—§ **8.3, n. 44.**
Delaware v. Van Arsdall—§ **7.30, n. 8.**
DeLawder, State v.—§ **5.9, n. 11.**
Dellums v. Powell—§ **9.12, Note 5.**
Demasi v. Whitney Trust & Savings Bank—§ **7.27, n. 5.**
Dement, People v.—§ **7.31, n. 27.**
Denaro v. Prudential Ins. Co. of America—§ **9.10, n. 7, 8.**
Dennis, United States v.—§ **8.5, n. 18.**
Di Carlo v. United States —§ **6.4, n. 10.**
Diamond v. Stratton—§ **9.9, n. 4.**
Dibona v. Philadelphia Transportation Co.—§ **4.6, n. 12.**
Dick v. New York Life Insurance Co.—§ **3.7, n. 4.**
Diez, United States v.—§ **7.5, n. 2.**
Diggs v. Lyons—§ **8.3, n. 51.**
Dillon v. United States—§ **5.14, n. 11.**
Dinapoli, United States v.—§ **8.4, n. 6.**
Dinner v. Thorp—§ **4.10, n. 1.**
Disbrow, People v.—§ **9.12, n. 39.**
Doe, United States v.—§ **9.6, n. 13;** § **9.11, n. 24, 27.**
Dollar v. Long Mfg., N.C., Inc.—§ **5.17, n. 11.**
Dolliole, United States v.—§ **5.13, n. 4.**
Douglas v. People of State of California—§ **9.12, n. 18.**
Douglas v. State of Ala.—§ **7.30, n. 3, 4;** § **7.31, n. 3.**
Dovico, United States v.—§ **7.27, Note 1.**
Downing, United States v.—§ **12.1, n. 12;** § **12.4, n. 6, 9.**
Drew v. United States—§ **5.14, n. 24.**
Dudley, United States v.—§ **5.14, n. 14.**
Duncan v. Smith—§ **7.27, n. 6.**
Durns v. United States—§ **5.14, n. 24.**
Durrant, State v.—§ **4.9, n. 8.**
Dutton v. Evans—§ **7.30, n. 11, 15, 17, 18;** § **7.31, n. 8, 31, 39, 45.**

Eastern Renovating Corp. v. Roman Catholic Bishop of Springfield—§ **7.6, n. 1.**
Edwards v. Arizona—§ **9.12;** § **9.12, n. 34.**
Edwards v. Jackson—§ **7.19, n. 1.**
Edwards, State v.—§ **7.31, n. 28.**
Edwards, United States v.—§ **7.14, n. 2.**
Eilers, State ex rel. State Highway Commission v.—§ **13.3, n. 1.**
Eisentrager v. State—§ **13.2, n. 18, 22.**
Elam v. State—§ **8.7, n. 3.**
Elemy, United States v.—§ **6.5, Note 3.**
Ellis v. United States—§ **9.11;** § **9.11, n. 61, 62.**
Ellison, United States v.—§ **4.10, n. 11.**
Emens v. Lehigh Val R Co—§ **7.8, n. 5.**
Erie R. Co. v. Tompkins—§ **3.7;** § **3.7, n. 4;** § **9.2, n. 1.**
Ernster v. State—§ **5.13, n. 4.**
Escobedo v. State of Ill.—§ **9.12;** § **9.12, n. 1, 20.**
Estate of (see name of party)
Estelle v. Smith—§ **9.11, n. 32.**
Eubanks v. Winn—§ **10.4, n. 7.**
Evans v. State—§ **7.29, n. 14.**

F.A. Potts and Co., Inc., In re—§ **9.8, n. 15.**
Fairchild, United States v.—§ **5.14, n. 26.**
Farber, State v.—§ **7.31, n. 26.**
Farner v. Paccar, Inc.,—§ **5.17, n. 7.**
Favors, People v.—§ **8.2, n. 7.**
Fearwell, United States v.—§ **8.3, n. 42, 46.**

Federal Trade Commission v. TRW, Inc.—§ **9.7, n. 8.**
Felice v. Long Island R. Co.—§ **7.17, n. 21.**
Ferguson v. Commonwealth—§ **13.3, n. 3.**
Ferguson v. Smazer—§ **7.27, n. 8.**
Ferguson v. State of Georgia—§ **8.3, n. 68.**
Fernandez v. Chios Shipping Co., Ltd.—§ **12.1, n. 8.**
Ferry v. Ramsey,—§ **3.5, n. 2.**
Fidelity Service Ins. Co. v. Jones—§ **7.11, n. 1.**
Fields v. Riley—§ **6.2, n. 14.**
Figueroa-Paz, United States v.—§ **9.3, n. 21.**
Figueroa, United States v.—§ **5.15, n. 9.**
Finch v. Weiner,—§ **4.11, n. 2.**
Finkley, State v.—§ **7.30, n. 20.**
Finley, State v.—§ **5.15, n. 23.**
Firlotte v. Jessee—§ **2.3, n. 2;** § **5.16, n. 10.**
First National Bank of Boston v. Bellotti—§ **9.11, n. 6.**
Fisher v. Commonwealth—§ **7.23, n. 5.**
Fisher v. United States—§ **9.6;** § **9.6, n. 11;** § **9.11, n. 23, 27.**
Flaherty, State v.—§ **5.9, n. 3.**
Fleegar v. Consumers' Power Co.—§ **8.2, n. 3.**
Flett, State v.—§ **2.5, n. 20.**
Flores, United States v.—§ **10.3, n. 1.**
Folkes, State v.—§ **7.15, n. 8.**
Fondren, State v.—§ **10.4, n. 9.**
Fontana, United States v.—§ **4.10, n. 8.**
Ford v. United States—§ **13.9, Note 1.**
Fortescue & Coake's Case—§ **7.29, n. 25.**
Foster, United States v.—§ **7.31, n. 45.**
Foundation Reserve Insurance Company v. Starnes—§ **4.9, n. 2.**
Fountain, United States v.—§ **8.3, n. 66.**
Fox, People v.—§ **5.15, n. 7.**
Francis v. Franklin—§ **3.5;** § **3.5, n. 14, 56.**
Frangos v. Edmunds—§ **7.11, n. 1, 2.**
Fratello v. United States—§ **9.11, n. 12.**
Freeman, State v.—§ **9.4, n. 12.**
Friedman, Commonwealth v.—§ **6.4, n. 25;** § **8.7, n. 9.**
Frye v. United States—§ **12.4;** § **12.4, n. 2.**
Fuller v. State—§ **5.14, n. 11.**
Funk v. United States—§ **9.4, n. 8.**
Furtado v. Bishop—§ **8.3, n. 51.**

Gaitan v. People—§ **8.2, n. 13.**
Gann, United States v.—§ **9.6, n. 6.**
Gardineer, People v.—§ **8.7, n. 19.**
Garfole, State v.—§ **5.17, Note 4.**
Garner v. Wolfinbarger—§ **9.8, n. 18.**
Garner, United States v.—§ **7.28, n. 12.**
Garrity v. State of N.J.—§ **9.11, n. 5.**
Garver, State v.—§ **4.9, n. 8.**
Gaskill v. Gahman—§ **8.3, n. 21.**
Gault, Application of—§ **9.11, n. 16.**
George, United States v.—§ **8.3, n. 36.**
Gideon v. Wainwright—§ **9.12, n. 18.**
Gilbert v. State of Cal.—§ **9.11, n. 19.**
Giles v. Valentic—§ **8.5, n. 2.**
Gill, People v.—§ **5.17, n. 12.**
Givens, United States v.—§ **8.3, n. 44.**
Glascock v. Anderson—§ **13.1, n. 8.**
Glatt v. Feist—§ **5.11, n. 6.**
Glenn, United States v.—§ **7.9, n. 3.**
Goins, United States v.—§ **7.27, n. 13.**
Gonzalez, United States v.—§ **7.27, n. 4.**
Good v. A.B. Chance Co.—§ **5.17, n. 3.**
Gorden, State v.—§ **7.27, n. 9.**
Gordon v. United States—§ **8.3, n. 30.**
Gortarez, State v.—§ **12.5, n. 31.**
Gould, United States v.—§ **12.4, n. 9.**
Grady, United States v.—§ **7.19, n. 17.**
Graham v. Danko—§ **6.4, n. 23.**
Grand Jury Proceedings, In re—§ **9.6, n. 22.**
Grand Jury Proceedings Involving Berkley and Co., Inc., In re—§ **9.6, n. 9.**
Grand Jury Proceedings on Feb. 4, 1982, In re—§ **9.6, n. 12.**
Grand Jury Subpoena Duces Tecum Issued on June 9, 1982, to Custodians of Records, Matter of—§ **9.6, n. 5.**
Grapp, United States v.—§ **11.2, n. 2.**
Gray, State ex rel. Steiger v.—§ **12.5, n. 15.**
Greenwald v. Wisconsin—§ **9.12, n. 14.**
Grenada Steel Industries, Inc. v. Alabama Oxygen Co., Inc.—§ **5.17, n. 4, 5.**
Griffin v. State—§ **5.14, n. 20.**
Griffin v. State of Cal.—§ **8.3, n. 68;** § **9.11, n. 13.**
Griffin, People v.—§ **5.15, n. 5.**
Grosso v. United States—§ **9.11, n. 21.**
Grunewald v. United States—§ **9.11, n. 13.**
Guedon v. Rooney—§ **5.3, n. 2, 6.**

Guffey, State v.—§ **7.3, n. 5.**
Guillette, United States v.—§ **7.27, n. 15.**
Gutridge v. State—§ **9.3, n. 12.**

Haggins v. Warden, Fort Pillow State Farm—§ **7.9, Note 4;** § **7.31, n. 26.**
Hale v. Firestone Tire & Rubber Co.—§ **11.5, Note 2.**
Hale v. Henkel—§ **9.11, n. 4.**
Hall, United States v.—§ **8.3, n. 36.**
Hamilton v. Alabama—§ **9.12, n. 19.**
Hamilton v. State—§ **5.6, n. 7.**
Hans, United States v.—§ **8.3, n. 38.**
Hansel v. Com.—§ **7.24, n. 2.**
Hansen, United States v.—§ **7.19, n. 16.**
Hanson v. Johnson—§ **6.2, n. 2.**
Hardin, United States v.—§ **7.19, n. 8.**
Harper v. Bolton—§ **13.2, n. 4.**
Harper & Row Publishers, Inc. v. Decker—§ **9.8;** § **9.8, n. 9.**
Harrington v. California—§ **7.30, n. 4.**
Harris v. Harris—§ **8.2, n. 4.**
Harris v. New York—§ **4.11, n. 8;** § **9.12, n. 39.**
Harris, United States v.—§ **6.5, n. 2.**
Harrison v. Blades—§ **7.29, n. 28.**
Harrison v. United States—§ **7.31, n. 26.**
Hartzog v. United States—§ **7.17, n. 14.**
Harvey v. Aubrey—§ **4.12, n. 2.**
Harvey, United States v.—§ **8.5, n. 1;** § **8.6, n. 16.**
Hashagen v. United States—§ **9.11, n. 15.**
Hatfield v. Levy Bros.—§ **1.5, n. 1.**
Hawkins v. United States—§ **1.8, n. 11;** § **4.11, n. 4;** § **9.4, n. 14.**
Hawkinson Tread Tire Co. v. Walker—§ **11.3, n. 3.**
Hayes v. Coleman—§ **4.12, n. 2.**
Haynes v. United States—§ **9.11, n. 21.**
Haynes v. Washington—§ **9.12, n. 8, 15, 16.**
Hayutin, United States v.—§ **8.4, n. 5.**
Hearst, United States v.—§ **4.11, n. 12;** § **5.15, n. 4.**
Helina, United States v.—§ **11.5, n. 10.**
Henderson v. Illinois Cent. Gulf R. Co.—§ **5.16, n. 1.**
Henderson v. Snider Bros., Inc.—§ **7.20, n. 2.**
Henderson, State v.—§ **7.30, n. 21;** § **8.3, n. 48.**
Henson v. State—§ **9.10, n. 4.**
Herman v. Eagle Star Ins. Co.—§ **8.7, Note 3.**
Herman, United States v.—§ **5.17, n. 18.**
Hernandez, United States v.—§ **4.11, n. 11, 12.**
Herrera, State v.—§ **8.7, n. 4.**
Hershberger v. Hershberger—§ **13.7, n. 2.**
Hess v. Marinari—§ **5.5, n. 7.**
Hewitt v. Grand Trunk Western R. Co.—§ **7.17, n. 4.**
Hickman v. Taylor—§ **9.12, Note 1.**
Higginbotham v. State—§ **13.1, n. 3.**
Hill, United States v.—§ **5.6, n. 11.**
Hilliker, People v.—§ **9.7, n. 14.**
Hillman v. Funderburk—§ **13.2, n. 7.**
Hinds v. John Hancock Mut. Life Ins. Co.—§ **3.4, n. 8, 17, 18.**
Hines v. Com.—§ **7.27, n. 10.**
Hiser, People v.—§ **8.7, Note 3.**
Hiss, United States v.—§ **8.1, n. 3;** § **8.7, Note 3.**
Hitsman, United States v.—§ **7.28, n. 9.**
Hodas v. Davis—§ **7.15, n. 1.**
Holland v. Holland—§ **7.1, n. 8.**
Holland v. State—§ **7.24, n. 5.**
Hollaris v. Jankowski—§ **4.2, n. 7.**
Holt v. United States—§ **9.11, n. 18.**
Home Ins. Co. v. Allied Tel. Co.—§ **7.27, n. 6.**
Hopkins v. Baker—§ **5.16, n. 7.**
Horowitz v. Sacks—§ **9.10, n. 8.**
Housholder, People v.—§ **4.12, n. 3.**
Housing Foundation of America, United States v.—§ **9.11, n. 12.**
Houston Oxygen Co. v. Davis—§ **7.8;** § **7.8, n. 1.**
Howard v. State—§ **4.9, n. 6;** § **5.14, n. 31.**
Howard, United States v.—§ **5.14, n. 29.**
Howard-Arias, United States v.—§ **13.2, n. 26.**
Huff v. White Motor Corp.—§ **7.28, n. 9.**
Hughes v. Meade—§ **9.6, n. 15.**
Humphreys, People v.—§ **11.3, n. 2.**
Hunydee v. United States—§ **9.7, n. 25.**
Hurt, State v.—§ **8.3, n. 11.**
Hutcher, United States v.—§ **11.1, n. 2.**
Hutchins v. Wainwright—§ **7.31, n. 26.**
Hutchison, State v.—§ **7.9, n. 7.**
Hyde, State v.—§ **5.13, n. 4.**

Iaconetti, United States v.—§ 6.4, n. 24; § 6.5, n. 14.
In re (see name of party)
Inadi, United States v.—§ 7.31; § 7.31, n. 47.
Ingram v. McCuiston—§ 12.2, n. 6.
International Security Life Ins. Co. v. Melancon—§ 5.3, n. 2.
Iron Shell, United States v.—§ 7.9, Note 4; § 7.11, Note.
Irwin v. Town of Ware—§ 7.17, n. 4.
Isaacs v. National Bank of Commerce of Seattle—§ 13.1, n. 3.
Ismail, United States v.—§ 5.14, n. 20.

Jackson v. Cherokee Drug Co.—§ 7.17, n. 18.
Jackson v. Denno—§ 10.5, n. 1.
Jackson v. State—§ 10.4, n. 9.
Jackson v. Virginia—§ 7.31, n. 16.
Jackson, United States v.—§ 2.5, n. 14; § 8.1, n. 3.
Jamerson, United States v.—§ 11.3, n. 1; § 11.4, n. 2.
James v. River Parishes Co., Inc.—§ 3.7, n. 10.
James, United States v.—§ 7.5, n. 9.
Janus v. Akstin—§ 7.6, Note 2.
Jaques, State v.—§ 9.4, n. 11.
Javins v. First Nat. Realty Corp.—§ 1.8; § 1.8, n. 14.
JD v. MD—§ 3.4, n. 13.
Jenness, State v.—§ 8.3, n. 6; § 8.7, Note 1.
Jett v. Com.—§ 6.4, n. 16.
John Doe Corp., In re—§ 9.7, n. 10; § 9.8, n. 14.
Johnson v. City of Tulsa—§ 1.8, n. 24.
Johnson v. Lutz—§ 7.17; § 7.17, n. 3.
Johnson v. State—§ 4.2, n. 3; § 8.7, n. 1.
Johnson v. United States—§ 4.11, n. 8; § 9.11, n. 46, 48.
Johnson, State v.—§ 5.14, n. 2.
Johnson, United States v.—§ 5.15, n. 12; § 11.5, n. 10.
Jordan v. Mace—§ 12.5, n. 15.
Jordan v. People—§ 7.15, n. 4.
Jordano, United States v.—§ 6.5, n. 12.
Jorgensen, State v.—§ 8.7, Note 3.
Juarez, United States v.—§ 5.15, n. 9.
Julian, Inc., James v. Raytheon Co.—§ 4.7, n. 15.

Kain, State v.—§ 5.9, n. 3.
Kansas City Southern R Co v. Jones—§ 11.3, n. 9.
Kaplan, United States v.—§ 5.14, n. 26.
Kastigar v. United States—§ 9.11, n. 33.
Kaufman v. Edelstein—§ 12.5, Note 6.
Kearney, United States v.—§ 12.5, n. 9.
Keefe v. State—§ 7.9, n. 1.
Keegan v. Green Giant Co.—§ 13.6, n. 4.
Kelley, People v.—§ 5.15, n. 15, 25.
Kelley, United States v.—§ 5.17, Note 4.
Kelly v. Sheehan—§ 7.17, n. 20.
Kelly v. Wasserman—§ 7.17, n. 6.
Kelly, United States v.—§ 7.15, n. 4; § 12.5, n. 28.
Kendrick v. State—§ 7.29, n. 21.
Kerlin v. State—§ 5.15, n. 24.
Kickham v. Carter—§ 7.11, n. 1.
Kidd v. People—§ 8.4, n. 3.
Kidd v. State—§ 7.24, n. 7.
King v. State—§ 5.14, n. 16.
King, People v.—§ 13.9, n. 11.
King, State v.—§ 5.14, n. 24.
King, United States v.—§ 7.19, n. 26; § 10.5, n. 15.
Kingsley v. Baker/Beech-Nut Corp.—§ 6.5, n. 8.
Kirby v. United States—§ 7.20, n. 10; § 7.30, n. 1.
Kline, Com. v.—§ 5.15, n. 2.
Korch for Use of Doody v. Indemnity Ins. Co. of North America—§ 13.9, Note 3.
Kordel, United States v.—§ 9.11, n. 54.
Korte v. New York, N.H. & H.R. Co.—§ 7.17, n. 14.
Kostan, Commonwealth v.—§ 8.3, n. 7.
Kovel, United States v.—§ 9.7, n. 14.
Krohn, United States v.—§ 5.14, n. 17.
Kronk, People v.—§ 5.6, n. 7.
Kuecker, United States v.—§ 8.3, n. 37.
Kuhn v. United States—§ 8.2, n. 12.
Kusior v. Silver—§ 12.5, n. 15.
Kutas, United States v.—§ 6.2, n. 5.

Lamar v. State—§ 5.15, n. 22.
Landfield v. Albiani Lunch Co.—§ 6.3, n. 4.
Lanford v. People—§ 13.2, n. 3.
Langley, State v.—§ 5.14, n. 27.
Lapin, People v.—§ 5.15, n. 25.
Larson v. Dougherty—§ 11.3, n. 11.
Latta, State v.—§ 5.14, n. 25.

Lawless, United States v.—§ **9.6, n. 5.**
Lawrence, State v.—§ **1.8, n. 8.**
Lawrence, Village of v. Greenwood—§ **5.16, n. 8.**
Le Beau, People v.—§ **8.2, n. 14.**
Lee v. Illinois—§ **7.30, n. 4;** § **7.31, n. 38.**
Lee v. United States—§ **8.2, n. 12;** § **8.3, n. 54.**
Lefkowitz v. Turley—§ **9.11, n. 5.**
Leggett, United States v.—§ **6.4, n. 23;** § **8.7, n. 1, 2.**
Lego v. Twomey—§ **10.5, n. 8.**
Lehner, People v.—§ **8.3, n. 73.**
Lehr v. Rogers—§ **8.3, n. 63.**
Leland v. State of Oregon—§ **3.5, n. 7.**
Lembeck v. United States Shipping Board Emergency Fleet Corporation—§ **13.8, n. 1.**
Lembke v. Unke—§ **9.10, n. 11.**
LeMere v. Goren—§ **12.3, n. 3.**
Leon, United States v.—§ **9.12, n. 17.**
Leonard v. United States—§ **5.14, n. 17.**
Leone, People v.—§ **8.7, Note 3.**
Leslie, United States v.—§ **8.4, n. 6.**
Lestico v. Kuehner—§ **13.2, n. 18.**
Letendre v. Hartford Acc. & Indem. Co.—§ **6.4, n. 1.**
Levitsky v. Prince George's County—§ **9.7, n. 15.**
Lewis, United States v.—§ **5.7, n. 8;** § **6.5, Note 3;** § **8.3, n. 46.**
Life & Casualty Ins. Co. of Tennessee v. Garrett—§ **4.6, n. 13.**
Lifschutz, In re—§ **9.10, n. 12.**
Lindsay v. Lipson—§ **9.7, n. 12;** § **9.10, n. 5.**
Lindstrom v. Yellow Taxi Company of Minneapolis—§ **7.17, n. 20.**
Lindstrom, United States v.—§ **9.10, n. 15.**
Lines, People v.—§ **9.7, n. 12.**
Linskey v. Hecker—§ **8.3, n. 44.**
Lipscomb, United States v.—§ **8.3, n. 30.**
Little, State v.—§ **5.13, n. 8;** § **5.14, n. 19.**
Little, United States v.—§ **5.14, n. 19.**
Lloyd v. American Export Lines, Inc.—§ **7.23, n. 9.**
Lloyd v. Professional Realty Services, Inc.—§ **7.17, n. 16.**
Loar, Commonwealth v.—§ **6.4, n. 15.**
Long Const. Co., Inc., James E., In re—§ **2.6, n. 4.**
Loper v. Andrews—§ **7.17, n. 17.**
Lora v. Board of Ed. of City of New York—§ **3.7, n. 2;** § **9.10, n. 12.**
Lord Morley's Case—§ **7.29, n. 29, 30.**
Luce v. United States—§ **8.3, n. 26, 27, 28.**
Luck v. United States—§ **8.3, n. 30.**
Lutwak v. United States—§ **9.4, n. 11.**
Lykus, Commonwealth v.—§ **12.5, n. 18**
Lyle, State v.—§ **5.14, n. 3.**
Lyles v. State—§ **5.13, n. 10.**
Lynumn v. State of Illinois—§ **9.12, n. 9, 14.**

McA, Inc. v. Wilson—§ **7.8, n. 4.**
McAndrews v. Leonard—§ **13.2, n. 1.**
McCarthy, People v.—§ **9.12, n. 39.**
McClard, State v.—§ **5.14, n. 17.**
McClintock, United States v.—§ **8.3, n. 37.**
McCormick, People v.—§ **8.3, n. 58.**
McDonald's Corp. v. Grissom—§ **5.16, n. 5.**
McFarland v. McFarland—§ **13.7, n. 6.**
McFarlin, State v.—§ **5.15, n. 26.**
McGautha v. California—§ **4.11, n. 12;** § **9.11, n. 46.**
McGee v. State—§ **8.3, n. 6.**
McGinty v. Brotherhood of Railway Trainmen—§ **9.10, n. 3.**
McGuire v. State—§ **13.9, n. 13.**
McI Communications Corp. v. American Tel. and Tel. Co.—§ **2.5, n. 19.**
McIntosh v. Pittsburgh Railways Co.—§ **8.3, n. 4.**
McKenna, State v.—**9.11, n. 19.**
McKinley, United States v.—§ **2.5, n. 8.**
McMillian, United States v.—§ **2.5, n. 8;** § **5.14, n. 25.**
McMonigle, People v.—§ **5.14, n. 25.**
McNabb v. United States—§ **9.12, n. 2.**
McPartlin, United States v.—§ **9.7, n. 25.**
McRae, United States v.—§ **13.2, n. 7.**
McSloy, State v.—§ **4.5, n. 9.**
McWhorter v. Commonwealth—§ **5.14, n. 17.**
Mackey, United States v.—§ **9.2, n. 3.**
Madda, United States v.—§ **13.9, n. 13.**
Madron v. Thomson—§ **7.4, n. 12, 14.**
Maestas, United States v.—§ **5.14, n. 24.**
Magri, People v.—§ **12.5, n. 17.**
Mahlandt v. Wild Canid Survival & Research Center, Inc.—§ **7.6, n. 4.**
Main, State v.—§ **1.8, n. 8.**
Maine v. Moulton—§ **9.12, n. 50.**

Mainline Inv. Corp. v. Gaines—§ **1.8, n. 3.**
Major v. Treen—§ **7.19, n. 9.**
Malfitano, Appeal of—§ **9.4, n. 5, 16.**
Mallory v. United States—§ **9.12, n. 2.**
Malloy v. Hogan—§ **9.11;** § **9.11, n. 2, 15, 47;** § **9.12, n. 3, 11.**
Mancari v. Frank P Smith, Inc—§ **13.6, n. 4.**
Mancusi v. Stubbs—§ **7.30, n. 18;** § **7.31, n. 8, 15, 24, 25, 38, 57.**
Mandel, United States v.—§ **7.13, n. 24.**
Manhattan Oil Co v. Mosby—§ **12.1, n. 7.**
Mapp v. Ohio—§ **9.12, n. 17.**
Marchand, United States v.—§ **6.5, Note 3.**
Marchetti v. United States—§ **9.11, n. 21.**
Marchildon, United States v.—§ **5.14, n. 14.**
Marchini, United States v.—§ **7.28, n. 12.**
Markwell v. Sykes—§ **9.1, n. 5.**
Marquez, State v.—§ **5.14, n. 18.**
Marshall v. Thomason—§ **7.9, n. 2.**
Marshall, United States v.—§ **7.15, n. 4.**
Martin v. State—§ **9.3, n. 22.**
Martino, United States v.—§ **8.3, n. 68.**
Mason v. Robinson—§ **12.5, Note 6.**
Mason, People v.—§ **6.4, n. 25.**
Massachusetts v. Sheppard—§ **9.12, n. 17.**
Master Key Antitrust Litigation, In re,—§ **7.23, n. 9.**
Masters v. Dewey—§ **13.2, n. 7.**
Mastropieri, United States v.—§ **10.5, n. 17.**
Mathis, United States v.—§ **7.28, n. 20;** § **9.4, n. 11.**
Matlock, People v.—§ **5.17, Note 4.**
Matlock, State v.—§ **8.2, n. 11.**
Matter of (see name of party)
Mattox v. State—§ **5.14, n. 29.**
Mattox v. United States—§ **7.29, n. 33;** § **7.30, n. 1.**
Mays, State v.—§ **8.5, n. 13.**
Mead v. Scott—§ **8.5, n. 3.**
Meagher, United States v.—§ **9.10, n. 15.**
Meany v. United States—§ **7.11, n. 6.**
Medico, United States v.—§ **7.8, n. 6.**
Mehrmanesh, United States v.—§ **8.3, n. 30.**
Mempa v. Rhay—§ **9.12, n. 20.**
Menefee v. Com.—§ **9.3, n. 9.**
Meredith, People v.—§ **9.6, n. 17.**
Merrill Trust Co. v. Bradford—§ **1.8, n. 26.**
Meyers v. United States—§ 11.5, n. 8; § 13.9, n. 3.
Michaels, People v.—§ **8.2, n. 15.**
Michelson v. United States—§ **5.6, n. 9;** § **5.7, n. 5, 6, 7.**
Michigan v. Tucker—§ **9.12, n. 38.**
Middleton v. Palmer—§ **5.17, Note 3.**
Miller Brewing Co. v. Jos. Schlitz Brewing Co.—§ **7.20, n. 3.**
Millings, United States v.—§ **8.3, n. 46.**
Mincey v. Arizona—§ **9.12, n. 42.**
Minnehaha County, S.D., v. Kelley—§ **7.19, n. 10.**
Minnesota v. Murphy—§ **9.11;** § **9.11, n. 30.**
Mintz v. Premier Cab Ass'n—§ **5.17, Note 3.**
Miranda v. Arizona—§ **7.3, n. 6, 7;** § **9.12;** § **9.12, n. 1, 22, 23;** § **10.5;** § **10.5, n. 2.**
Miranda-Uriarte, United States v.—§ **4.11, n. 11, 12.**
Mireles, People v.—§ **13.2, n. 6.**
Mobile, J & K C R Co v. Turnipseed—§ **3.5, n. 3.**
Monroe, State v.—§ **5.14, n. 14.**
Montalvo, United States v.—§ **5.14, n. 28.**
Montgomery, In re—§ **7.30, n. 10.**
Montgomery, People v.—§ **8.3, n. 30.**
Moore, Commonwealth v.—§ **4.9, n. 17.**
Moran v. Burbine—§ **9.12, n. 33.**
Morgan v. Washington Trust Co.—§ **8.5, n. 17.**
Morgan, United States v.—§ **5.6, n. 8;** § **5.7, n. 9.**
Moultrie v. Martin—§ **12.5, n. 5.**
Mountain, People v.—§ **12.5, n. 9.**
Mucci v. Lemonte—§ **11.2, n. 3.**
Mucci, State v.—§ **4.7, n. 6.**
Mullaney v. Wilbur—§ **3.1, n. 3;** § **3.5;** § **3.5, n. 10, 12.**
Murphy v. Waterfront Commission of New York Harbor—§ **9.11;** § **9.11, n. 37.**
Murphy Auto Parts Co v. Ball—§ **7.9;** § **7.9, n. 4.**
Murray v. New York Cent. R. Co.—§ **8.2, n. 3.**
Muscato, United States v.—§ **6.5, Note 4.**
Musgrave, United States v.—§ **11.3, n. 2.**

Mutual Life Ins Co of New York v. Hillmon—§ **7.13; § 7.13, n. 2, 4, 7, 14.**
Myers v. Genis—§ **7.17, n. 19.**
Myers, People v.—§ **8.7, Note 3.**
Myers, United States v.—§ **5.14, n. 24.**
Myre v. State—§ **7.8, n. 6.**

Narciso, United States v.—§ **7.11, Note.**
Navarro-Varelas, United States v.—§ **6.5, n. 14.**
Needham v. United States—§ **7.19, n. 7.**
Neely v. Kansas City Public Service Co.—§ **7.27, n. 6.**
Neff v. Neff—§ **4.7, n. 3.**
Neff, United States v.—§ **7.31, n. 37.**
Neil v. Biggers—§ **7.31, n. 16.**
Nelson v. Brunswick Corp.—§ **5.16, n. 2.**
Nelson v. O'Neil—§ **7.30, n. 4.**
New Jersey v. Portash—§ **9.11, n. 34.**
New York v. Quarles—§ **9.12; § 9.12, n. 45.**
Newton v. Higdon—§ **7.15, n. 1.**
Nichols v. Sefcik—§ **8.5, n. 3.**
Nick, United States v.—§ **7.30, n. 20.**
Nixon v. Administrator of General Services—§ **9.12, Note 5.**
Nixon, United States v.—§ **9.12, Note 5.**
Nobero Co. v. Ferro Trucking Inc.—§ **7.4, n. 6, 9.**
Noble, State v.—§ **4.2, n. 7.**
Noble, United States v.—§ **8.3, n. 40.**
Nobles, United States v.—§ **9.11, n. 10, 48.**
Nordstrom, State v.—§ **7.30, n. 10.**
North Carolina v. Butler—§ **9.12, n. 26.**
Northern Oil Co. v. Socony Mobil Oil Co.—§ **7.4, n. 14.**
Noumoff v. Rotkvich—§ **7.15, n. 6.**
Nowell By and Through Nowell v. Universal Elec. Co.—§ **7.28, n. 9, 21.**
Nunez v. United States—§ **5.15, n. 2.**
Nuttall v. Reading Company—§ **7.8, n. 7.**

O'Connor v. Venore Transp. Co.—§ **8.6, n. 15.**
O'Connor, United States v.—§ **10.4, n. 10.**
O'Dea v. Amodeo—§ **3.4, n. 16.**
O'Malley v. United States—§ **10.4, n. 7.**
O'Neal v. Morgan—§ **6.5, n. 4.**
Oates, United States v.—§ **7.19; § 7.19, n. 16, 22; § 7.31, n. 32, 37.**
Oates' Trial—§ **7.29, n. 30.**
Ocasio, People v.—§ **8.3, n. 59.**
Oertel, State v.—§ **12.1, n. 6.**
Ohio v. Roberts—§ **7.29, n. 5; § 7.31; § 7.31, n. 1, 3, 27, 32, 37, 48.**
Ojala, United States v.—§ **6.5, n. 8.**
Oliphant, People v.—§ **5.15, n. 7.**
Olson v. Hodges—§ **7.2, n. 1.**
Olson v. Tyner—§ **13.2, n. 3.**
Olwell, State ex rel. Sowers v.—§ **9.6, n. 15.**
Ondis v. Pion—§ **12.5, Note 6.**
Oneida Indian Nation of New York v. State of N.Y.—§ **1.8, n. 23.**
Oregon v. Elstad—§ **9.12, n. 38, 43.**
Oregon v. Hass—§ **9.12, n. 39.**
Orozco, United States v.—§ **7.17, Note 2.**
Osborne v. McEwan—§ **8.5, n. 3.**
Ostapenko v. American Bridge Div. of United States Steel Corp.—§ **1.5, n. 1.**
Osterhoudt, In re—§ **9.6, n. 23.**
Ostrowski v. Mockridge—§ **9.10, n. 6.**
Oswalt, State v.—§ **8.6, n. 7, 9, 11.**

Padgett v. Southern R. Co.—§ **7.11, n. 6.**
Padula, State v.—§ **5.8, n. 12.**
Page v. Barko Hydraulics—§ **7.28, n. 21.**
Page, United States v.—§ **7.17, n. 1.**
Palermo v. United States—§ **4.7, n. 19, 23.**
Palmer v. Hoffman—§ **7.17; § 7.17, n. 11.**
Palmer, United States v.—§ **4.11, n. 12.**
Palozie, State v.—§ **7.17, n. 6.**
Palumbo, United States v.—§ **8.3, n. 33.**
Parker v. Gunther—§ **12.1, n. 14.**
Parker v. Hoefer—§ **4.9, n. 6.**
Parker v. Randolph—§ **7.30, n. 4.**
Parker, United States v.—§ **5.6, n. 7.**
Parson v. State—§ **12.5, n. 9.**
Patterson v. New York—§ **3.1, n. 3; § 3.5, n. 9, 12, 59.**
Payne v. State of Arkansas—§ **9.12, n. 7.**
Payton, People v.—§ **8.4, n. 5.**
Pazsint, United States v.—§ **7.18, n. 2.**
Peacock, United States v.—§ **7.8, n. 7.**
Peete, People v.—§ **5.13, n. 10.**
Pekelis v. Transcontinental & Western Air—§ **7.17, n. 13.**
Pena, United States v.—§ **7.4, n. 5; § 7.6, n. 2.**
Pendleton v. Pendleton—§ **9.1, n. 5.**

People v. ______ (see opposing party)
Perez, People v.—§ **4.12, Note 7; § 9.11, n. 41.**
Perry v. People—§ **5.14, n. 20.**
Peters v. United States—§ **5.14, n. 21.**
Peterson v. Richards—§ **7.2, n. 2.**
Peterson v. Richfield Plaza—§ **7.11, n. 6.**
Petrozziello, United States v.—§ **7.5, n. 8.**
Pfeiffer, United States v.—§ **7.17, n. 4.**
Pheaster, United States v.—§ **7.13, n. 5, 6, 17; § 9.12, n. 27.**
Philadelphia, City of v. Westinghouse Elec. Corp.—§ **9.8, n. 7.**
Phillips v. Neil—§ **7.30, n. 21.**
Phillips, State v.—§ **8.3, n. 60.**
Pigford v. People—§ **5.15, n. 22.**
Pipkins, United States v.—§ **9.7, n. 16.**
Pittman v. Littlefield—§ **5.16, n. 4.**
Player v. Thompson—§ **6.2, n. 6, 13.**
Plough, Inc. v. Mason and Dixon Lines—§ **3.7, n. 10.**
Podor, State v.—§ **7.5, n. 5.**
Pointer v. State of Tex.—§ **7.30, n. 2, 10.**
Poland, People v.—§ **7.9, n. 2.**
Pollock, United States v.—§ **2.5, n. 18.**
Porter, United States v.—§ **6.5, n. 4, 8.**
Poston v. Clarkson Const. Co.—§ **2.3, n. 1; § 5.16, n. 7.**
Powers v. J.B. Michael & Co.—§ **5.17, n. 10.**
Primeaux v. Kinney—§ **7.15, Note.**
Proctor, State v.—§ **7.25, n. 1.**
Puco, United States v.—§ **7.30, n. 20.**
Puett, State v.—§ **7.25, n. 1.**
Purtell, People v.—§ **8.2, n. 15.**

Quezada, United States v.—§ **7.19, n. 17.**

Rabata v. Dohner—§ **12.2, n. 7.**
Radetsky v. Leonard—§ **13.2, n. 15.**
Radiant Burners, Inc. v. American Gas Ass'n—§ **9.8, n. 5.**
Ramseyer v. General Motors Corp.—§ **13.4, n. 4, 5.**
Rappy, United States v.—§ **4.7, n. 2.**
Rauser v. Toston Irr. Dist.—§ **7.19, n. 4.**
Ravich, United States v.—§ **2.5, n. 8.**
Reardon v. Boston Elevated R. Co.—§ **4.6, n. 13.**
Reed v. Allen—§ **4.9, n. 2.**
Reed v. State—§ **12.5, n. 31.**
Reina v. United States—§ **9.11, n. 38.**
Rendini, United States v.—§ **7.11, n. 8.**
Reynolds, United States v.—§ **6.3, n. 14; § 9.12, Note 4.**
Rhine v. State—§ **5.15, n. 23.**
Riccardi, United States v.—§ **4.7, n. 3.**
Rich v. Cooper—§ **5.5, n. 11.**
Richardson, United States v.—§ **13.3, n. 2.**
Ridling, United States v.—§ **8.7, Note 3.**
Rife, People v.—§ **5.14, n. 21.**
Rivers v. Black—§ **4.9, n. 8.**
Robbins v. Farmers Union Grain Terminal Ass'n—§ **5.17, n. 7.**
Robbins v. Whelan—§ **7.19, n. 20.**
Roberson v. State—§ **5.8, n. 14.**
Roberts v. Russell—§ **7.30, n. 9.**
Roberts v. State—§ **4.12, n. 2.**
Roberts, State v.—§ **7.31, n. 2.**
Roberts, United States v.—§ **5.14, n. 31.**
Robinson v. Commonwealth—§ **13.2, n. 24.**
Robinson v. Pennsylvania R Co—§ **4.12, n. 2.**
Robinson v. Shapiro—§ **7.28, n. 10, 14.**
Robinson v. State—§ **8.3, n. 25.**
Robinson, State v.—§ **5.8, n. 12.**
Robinson, United States v.—§ **2.2; § 2.2, n. 4, 5, 8; § 2.5; § 2.5, n. 4, 9; § 8.6, n. 16.**
Rocha, United States v.—§ **5.14, n. 14.**
Roder, People v.—§ **3.5, n. 48.**
Rogall v. Kischer—§ **8.5, n. 15; § 8.6, n. 15.**
Rogers v. Richmond—§ **9.12, n. 8.**
Rogers v. United States—§ **9.11; § 9.11, n. 55.**
Rolls, State v.—§ **12.5, n. 6, 7, 11.**
Rovetuso, United States v.—§ **8.6, n. 3.**
Roviaro v. United States—§ **9.12, Note 6.**
Roybal, State v.—§ **8.4, n. 4.**
Rubey v. City of Fairbanks—§ **7.30, n. 10.**
Rudzinski v. Warner Theatres, Inc.—§ **7.4, n. 5.**
Ruhala v. Roby—§ **6.4, n. 5, 7, 21.**
Ruhs v. Pacific Power & Light—§ **1.8, n. 24.**
Russ, State v.—§ **8.3, n. 4.**
Russell v. Coffman—§ **13.2, n. 4.**

Russo v. Russo—§ **1.8, n. 3.**
Ruth v. Fenchel—§ **12.3, n. 5.**

Sacasas, United States v.—§ **7.25, n. 8.**
Sachs v. Aluminum Co. of America—§ **9.7, n. 18.**
Safeway Stores, Inc. v. Combs—§ **6.2, n. 3, 8, 13.**
Sampol, United States v.—§ **8.7, n. 20.**
San Francisco, City & County of v. Superior Court In and For City and County of San Francisco—§ **9.7, n. 7;** § **9.10, n. 5, 22.**
Sanders, State v.—§ **7.27, Note 1.**
Sandoval, People v.—§ **8.3, n. 59.**
Sandstrom v. Montana—§ **3.5;** § **3.5, n. 14, 50, 54.**
Sandstrom, State v.—§ **3.5, n. 52.**
Santiago, State v.—§ **8.3, n. 33.**
Saporen, State v.—§ **6.1, n. 8.**
Sawyer, United States v.—§ **7.19, n. 26.**
Scalf, State v.—§ **5.6, n. 8.**
Schad, State v.—§ **7.31, n. 26.**
Schlak, State v.—§ **5.15, n. 24.**
Schmerber v. California—§ **9.11, n. 18.**
Scholle, United States v.—§ **6.4, n. 27;** § **6.5, n. 12;** § **7.17, Note.**
Schwartz, United States v.—§ **7.15, n. 3.**
Scott v. Spanjer Bros., Inc.—§ **12.3, n. 3.**
Seaboard Citizens Nat. Bank of Norfolk v. Revere—§ **4.3, n. 6.**
Sealed Case, In re—§ **9.6, n. 25.**
Seamons v. Andersen—§ **8.2, n. 13.**
Securities and Exchange Commission v. Capital Gains Research Bureau, Inc.—§ **1.8, n. 21.**
Semprini v. Boston & M.R.R.—§ **7.4, n. 5.**
Shanks v. State—§ **12.5, n. 6, 9.**
Shapiro v. United States—§ **9.11, n. 21.**
Sharpe, State v.—§ **7.17, n. 10.**
Shea, People v.—§ **5.14, n. 14.**
Shendal v. United States—§ **9.11, n. 56.**
Shepard v. United States—§ **7.13;** § **7.13 n. 19;** § **7.25, n. 1.**
Shingleton v. Armor Velvet Corp.—§ **8.3, n. 39.**
Shoupe, United States v.—§ **4.6, n. 7.**
Shows v. M/V Red Eagle—§ **8.3, n. 51.**
Shultz v. State—§ **9.10, n. 6.**
Silver v. New York Cent. R. Co.—§ **6.3, n. 4.**
Silvers, United States v.—§ **11.3, n. 4.**
Simmons v. United States—§ **4.11, n. 8;** § **7.31, n. 16.**
Singer, People v.—§ **8.7, n. 19.**
Sisk v. State—§ **13.3, n. 3.**
62.96247 Acres of Land, State v.—§ **9.7, n. 15.**
Skelton v. Sinclair Refining Co.—§ **12.1, n. 4.**
Skogen v. Dow Chemical Co.—§ **2.5, n. 17.**
Slattery v. Marra Bros.—§ **13.2, n. 3.**
Slocinski, State v.—§ **8.7, n. 9.**
Small v. Rose—§ **7.27, n. 3.**
Smith v. Illinois—§ **9.12, n. 32, 48.**
Smith v. Lohr—§ **8.2, n. 16.**
Smith v. Ohio Oil Co.—§ **13.1, n. 1.**
Smith v. Southern National Life Insurance Company—§ **7.6, Note 1.**
Smith v. State of Ill.—§ **7.30, n. 7.**
Smith v. Universal Services, Inc.—§ **7.19, n. 4.**
Smith, State v.—§ **12.5, n. 27.**
Smith, United States ex rel. Edney v.—§ **9.7, n. 5.**
Smith, United States v.—§ **4.9, n. 9, 16, 17;** § **7.17, n. 6;** § **7.19, n. 12;** § **8.3, n. 36;** § **9.3, n. 10;** § **12.1, n. 12.**
Snead v. State—§ **5.7, n. 4;** § **5.14, n. 13.**
Sneed, State v.—§ **12.5, n. 2.**
Soles v. State—§ **10.4, n. 6;** § **10.6.**
Sorge, People v.—§ **8.3, n. 59, 60, 63.**
Sowers, State ex rel. v. Olwell—§ **9.6, n. 15.**
Spence v. Farrier—§ **12.5, Note 4.**
Spencer, People v.—§ **13.4, n. 3.**
Spinosa, People v.—§ **8.2, n. 13.**
Spitaleri, People v.—§ **5.17, n. 19.**
Sporck v. Peil—§ **4.7, n. 8.**
Spreigl, State v.—§ **5.15, n. 13, 24.**
Sprynczynatyk v. General Motors Corp.—§ **11.5.**
Stadter, United States v.—§ **5.14, n. 20.**
Stafford, State v.—§ **7.9, n. 2, 3.**
Staiger v. Gaarder—§ **7.9, n. 2, 3.**
Stallone, Com. v.—§ **7.24, n. 5, 6.**
Stanchich, United States v.—§ **10.5, n. 17.**
Standafer v. First Nat. Bank of Minneapolis—§ **2.2, n. 2.**
Stanley v. Illinois—§ **3.2, n. 5.**
Stark v. Allis-Chalmers and Northwest Roads, Inc.—§ **5.16, n. 5.**
Starr v. Morsette—§ **7.8, n. 3.**
State v. ______ (see opposing party)

State ex rel. v. ______ (see opposing party and relator)
State Highway Commission, State ex rel. v. Eilers—§ **13.3, n. 1.**
State Highway Commission, State ex rel. v. Yackel—§ **1.5, n. 1.**
Stearns v. State—§ **5.8, n. 14.**
Steele v. Coxe—§ **4.7, n. 2.**
Steiger, State ex rel. v. Gray—§ **12.5, n. 15.**
Stephens v. Dichtenmueller—§ **3.4, n. 15.**
Stevens, State v.—§ **5.17, n. 13.**
Stifel, United States v.—§ **12.1, n. 2;** § **12.5, n. 26, 28.**
Stout, State v.—§ **12.5, n. 25, 26.**
Stover, United States v.—§ **5.14, n. 13.**
Stuard, State v.—§ **9.11, n. 18.**
Subpoenas Duces Tecum, In re—§ **9.8, n. 13.**
Subramaniam v. Public Prosecutor—§ **6.2, n. 4.**
Suburban Sew 'N Sweep, Inc. v. Swiss-Bernina, Inc.—§ **9.6, n. 9.**
Sullivan v. State—§ **8.3, n. 11.**
Sullivan, People v.—§ **9.3, n. 9, 22.**
Sunray Sanitation, Inc. v. Pet Inc.—§ **13.9, Note 3.**
Sutton, State v.—§ **7.15, n. 5.**
Sweazey v. Valley Transport—§ **6.4, n. 27.**

Taglione, United States v.—§ **7.12, n. 2.**
Tague v. Louisiana—§ **9.12, n. 25.**
Tait v. Western World Insurance Company—§ **7.9, n. 2.**
Taylor v. Baltimore & O.R. Co.—§ **8.2, n. 11.**
Taylor v. Commonwealth—§ **9.3, n. 21.**
Taylor v. State—§ **8.4, n. 5.**
Taylor, State v.—§ **4.9, n. 17.**
Tennessee v. Street—§ **7.31, n. 59.**
Texas Dept. of Community Affairs v. Burdine—§ **3.7, n. 9.**
Thevis, United States v.—§ **12.1, n. 11.**
Thomas v. Chicago Transit Authority—§ **13.4, n. 4.**
Thomas v. Fred Weber Contractor, Inc.—§ **7.17, n. 18.**
Thompson v. American Steel & Wire Co.—§ **2.5, n. 17.**
Thornton v. Vonallmon—§ **8.4, n. 4.**
Tigh v. College Park Realty Co.—§ **8.5, n. 21.**
Tillotson v. Boughner—§ **9.1, n. 5.**
Tims, State v.—§ **7.30, n. 10;** § **7.31, n. 32.**
Tomlin v. Beto—§ **7.30, n. 10.**
Tomlinson v. Croke—§ **7.29, n. 25.**
Toshishige Yoshino, State v.—§ **5.14, n. 18.**
Townsend, State v.—§ **7.3, n. 1.**
Trammel v. United States—§ **1.8, n. 11;** § **4.11, n. 4;** § **9.2, n. 4;** § **9.3, n. 7;** § **9.4, n. 2, 4, 13, 15.**
Transowski, People v.—§ **5.14, n. 13.**
Travelers Fire Ins. Co. v. Wright—§ **7.20, n. 9;** § **7.23, Note 1.**
Travellers' Ins. Co. of Chicago v. Mosley—§ **7.9, n. 7, 9.**
Truttmann v. Truttmann—§ **4.2, n. 8.**
Tucker v. State—§ **5.13, n. 10.**
Tucker v. Welsh—§ **8.5, n. 2.**
Tumblin, United States v.—§ **8.3, n. 22.**
Turbyfill v. International Harvester Co.—§ **7.28, n. 11.**
Turner v. Spaide—§ **7.17, n. 4.**
Turner v. United States—§ **3.5;** § **3.5, n. 17.**
Turner Const. Co. v. Houlihan—§ **1.5, n. 1.**
Tuthill v. Alden—§ **8.5, n. 13.**

United Services Auto. Ass'n v. Wharton—§ **7.25, n. 5.**
United States v. ______ (see opposing party)
United States v. Schlansky—§ **9.11, n. 28.**
United States ex rel v. ______ (see opposing party and relator)
United States for Use and Benefit of Carter Equipment Co., Inc v. H.R. Morgan, Inc.—§ **6.5, n. 3.**
University of Illinois v. Spalding—§ **13.7, n. 5.**
Unterseher, State v.—§ **12.5, n. 17.**
Upjohn Co. v. United States—§ **9.8;** § **9.8, n. 6, 15.**
Usery v. Turner Elkhorn Mining Co.—§ **3.5, n. 1;** § **3.7, n. 2.**

Vacca, United States v.—§ **7.17, n. 6.**
Valdes, United States v.—§ **13.3, n. 1.**
Valdez, State v.—§ **8.7, Note 3.**
Van Drunen, United States v.—§ **9.4, n. 10.**
Van Hook, United States v.—§ **7.19, n. 11.**
Van Meerbeke, United States v.—§ **4.2, n. 8.**
Varcoe v. Lee—§ **1.8, n. 3.**
Vassar v. Chicago, B. & Q.R. Co.—§ **8.4, n. 3.**

Vaughn v. Love—§ **8.3, n. 48.**
Vigil v. People—§ **9.11, n. 19.**
Village of (see name of village)
Villavicencio, State v.—§ **5.14, n. 31.**
Vinson, United States v.—§ **2.6, n. 6;** § **10.5, n. 11.**
Vinyard v. Vinyard Funeral Home, Inc.—§ **6.2, n. 10.**
Vlandis v. Kline—§ **3.2, n. 5.**

Wade v. Lane—§ **7.4, n. 1.**
Wade, United States v.—§ **9.11, n. 18.**
Wakefield, State v.—§ **5.13, n. 8.**
Walder v. United States—§ **9.12, n. 40.**
Walker v. Larson—§ **7.15, n. 1.**
Walker v. United States—§ **2.5, n. 8.**
Walker, State v.—§ **7.30, n. 20.**
Walker, United States v.—§ **8.3, n. 73.**
Wallulatum, United States v.—§ **7.31, n. 32.**
Walstad, State v.—§ **12.4, n. 8.**
Washington v. Commonwealth—§ **13.2, n. 6.**
Washington v. State of Tex.—§ **4.2, n. 3.**
Washington, State v.—§ **12.5, n. 12.**
Watkins v. Prudential Ins. Co. of America—§ **3.3, n. 2.**
Webb v. Van Noort—§ **5.11, n. 5.**
Weil, United States v.—§ **6.4, n. 27.**
Weinberger v. Salfi—§ **3.2, n. 5.**
Welborn, United States v.—§ **5.14, n. 14.**
Westberry v. State—§ **7.24, n. 6.**
Western & A.R.R. v. Henderson—§ **3.5, n. 3.**
Whalen v. Roe—§ **9.10, n. 2.**
Wheeler v. United States—§ **13.2, n. 19.**
Wheeler, State v.—§ **12.5, n. 32.**
Wheeling-Pittsburgh Steel Corp. v. Underwriters Laboratories, Inc.—§ **4.7, n. 14.**
White v. Holderby—§ **2.3, n. 3.**
White v. State of Maryland—§ **9.12, n. 19.**
White, United States v.—§ **9.11, n. 4, 8.**
Whiteman v. State—§ **5.14, n. 24.**
Williams v. Alexander—§ **7.17, n. 20.**
Williams v. Florida—§ **1.8, n. 11.**
Williams v. Graff—§ **4.10, n. 8.**
Williams v. State—§ **5.15, n. 3.**
Williams, United States v.—§ **7.15, Note;** § **8.3, n. 41;** § **12.4, n. 6;** § **12.5, n. 32.**
Wilson v. State—§ **7.25, n. 1;** § **13.2, n. 5.**
Wilson, People v.—§ **8.4, n. 4.**
Wilson, United States v.—§ **3.7, n. 3.**
Wimberly v. City of Paterson—§ **13.2, n. 5.**
Winchester v. Padgett—§ **5.3, n. 2.**
Winfrey v. State—§ **7.25, n. 2.**
Winship, In re—§ **3.1, n. 3;** § **3.5;** § **3.5, n. 5, 13, 53;** § **7.31, n. 16.**
Winston, United States v.—§ **11.5, n. 10.**
Witham, State v.—§ **11.5, n. 8.**
Witt, United States v.—§ **9.10, n. 17.**
Wofford Beach Hotel, Inc. v. Glass—§ **8.7, n. 18.**
Wolfe v. Madison Avenue Coach Co.—§ **8.5, n. 19.**
Wolfle v. United States—§ **9.3, n. 12.**
Wood, In re Estate of—§ **3.4, n. 22.**
Wood, State v.—§ **5.9, n. 4.**
Woods, United States v.—§ **5.13, n. 10;** § **5.14, n. 28.**
Woodward & Lothrop v. Heed—§ **13.1, n. 7.**
Wright v. Farmers Co-Op of Arkansas and Oklahoma—§ **7.17, n. 6.**
Wright v. State—§ **8.3, n. 59.**
Wright v. Swann—§ **7.9, n. 1;** § **10.4, n. 8.**
Wyatt v. United States—§ **9.4, n. 7.**
Wyman, State v.—§ **5.14, n. 14.**

Yackel, State ex rel. State Highway Commission v.—§ **1.5, n. 1.**
Yale's Estate, In re—§ **4.6, n. 13.**
Yates v. Bair Transport, Inc.—§ **7.17, n. 14.**
Yates, United States v.—§ **7.17, n. 5.**
York, Commonwealth v.—§ **3.5, n. 15.**
Young v. Group Health Cooperative of Puget Sound—§ **12.3, n. 3.**
Young Bros., Inc., United States v.—§ **7.17, n. 2.**

Zavala, People v.—§ **12.5, Note 4.**
Zdanis, State v.—§ **4.11, n. 14.**
Zenith Radio Corp. v. Matsushita Elec. Indus. Co. Ltd.—§ **7.17, n. 2.**
Zippo Mfg. Co. v. Rogers Imports, Inc.—§ **6.5, Note 6.**
Zuniga, In re—§ **9.10, n. 2, 12, 15.**

Chapter I

EVIDENCE IN CONTEXT *

§ 1.1 The Role of Evidence in the Process of Adjudication

The introduction and use of evidence is but one part of the complex process of litigation. This process formally begins with the filing of a complaint and terminates with the entry and satisfaction of a final judgment or decree. During the course of the various judicial proceedings, the parties' lawyers participate in a variety of matters: pleadings and motions, investigation and discovery, settlement negotiations, the presentation of evidence, closing argument, and (where appeal takes place) the preparation of the appellate brief and the delivery of oral argument.

Two concerns are central to all phases of litigation: first, a concern with establishing facts; and, second, a concern with the choice and application of legal rules. The formal study of law emphasizes the choice, construction, and impact of legal rules and principles. This academic preference has pedagogic advantages, but it obscures a basic reality: the outcome of most cases is determined by counsel's success in establishing *facts* favorable to his client. The governing rules of law are contested with much less frequency than is suggested by a study of the reported cases. Furthermore, the factual posture of a controversy often has a decisive effect upon extra-judicial disposition such as voluntary dismissal or settlement. Thus, facts, and consequently *evidence of facts,* can have a profound influence upon the resolution of disputes. Understandably, trial lawyers spend a substantial part of

* This chapter is designed to set out some of the fundamental characteristics of the adversarial system, especially those that bear upon the factual component of a case. At various points, some knowledge of civil procedure is assumed. The reader may wish to consult F. James & G. Hazard, Civil Procedure (3d ed. 1985), especially pp. 1–8, 333–371, 385–408; 2 F. Harper and F. James, The Law of Torts, §§ 15.1–15.5 (1956).

their professional lives developing and analyzing evidence in an effort to establish facts favorable to their clients.

§ 1.2 Evidence: Definition and Professional Evaluation

For present purposes, we may define evidence as any matter, verbal or physical, that can be used to support the existence of a factual proposition.[1] This definition is useful because it emphasizes the perspective of the legal profession, which associates evidence with the facts of a case.

Another aspect of "evidence," uniquely associated with the legal profession, is not directly related to the definition or inherent qualities of evidence but rather consists of the criteria by which lawyers assess the usefulness or probative worth of evidence. When attorneys contemplate litigation, their evaluation of prospective evidential materials departs sharply from that of other professionals or lay persons: [2] lawyers must anticipate the impact the rules of evidence will have upon the *admissibility* of these materials should a judicial trial be necessary.[3] At trial, the rules of evidence may operate to exclude all or part of the proffered testimony or tangible items; evidence so rejected will not be considered in the decisional process of the tribunal.[4] As a conse-

§ 1.2

1. For a different and more comprehensive definition of the term, see I Wigmore, § 1, at 3–6; see also Hart and McNaughton, Evidence and Inference in the Law, in Evidence & Inference 48 (Lerner, ed. 1958).

2. Cf. Hart and McNaughton, supra n. 1 at 52–53.

3. The rules of evidence that bar admissibility usually are not enforced in hearings before administrative agencies. McCormick, § 351, at 1005–06. Of course, evidence that would be rejected as untrustworthy in a judicial proceeding may not be given much weight by the hearing officer. For a complete discussion of the reasons underlying the admissibility and use of evidence in administrative proceedings, see K. Davis, Administrative Law Treatise, §§ 14.01–14.17 (1952 & Supp.1970); K. Davis, Administrative Law of the Seventies, §§ 14.00–14.17 (1976). As a practical matter, administrative tribunals may have to adhere to the evidentiary rules established by the courts that review administrative findings. See, e.g., cases cited in Saltzburg & Redden at 1086–1089.

4. In trials held before a judge sitting without a jury, there is a decided tendency to relax the exclusionary rules and admit evidence that might be rejected in a jury trial. See McCormick, § 60, at 153. If incompetent evidence is *admitted* in a nonjury case, a reviewing appellate court is likely to sustain the judgment below if, within the trial record, competent evidence can be found that is sufficient to support the judge's findings. Builders Steel Co. v. Commissioner, 179 F.2d 377, 379 (8th Cir.1950) (dictum). The trial judge is presumed to have ignored or discounted the evidence that was wrongly admitted. Conversely, erroneous *exclusion* by the judge will result in reversal in those cases where the rejected evidence is likely to have a significant impact on the outcome. See Builders Steel Co. v. Commissioner, 179 F.2d 377 (8th Cir.

quence, these materials are diminished in importance even before trial, despite their apparent relevance.

§ 1.3 The Bases of Evidentiary Restriction: A Prefatory View

There is no simple answer to the question of why the law should turn its face against evidentiary materials that investigators and factfinders generally would deem useful. The purpose of this book is to provide the reader with a framework that will facilitate analysis of this issue. For the moment, it suffices to note that judicial trials are different from other investigations. The evidence is presented by adversaries, each one offering evidence favorable to himself and each demanding a fair chance to challenge the reliability of the other's proof. As a consequence, evidence (such as hearsay) that may be plausible, but that cannot be tested adequately by the adversary's cross-examination, often is rejected. Trials are distinctive, also, in that the factfinders often are lay persons (the jury), not trained experts. This suggests a need to exclude evidentiary materials that pose a substantial risk of jury misuse. Finally, trials are public affairs; the evidence often reveals to the community and media confidential information. Instances arise in which the interests served by the preservation of confidentiality should take precedence over those interests advanced by the use of evidentiary material. In these circumstances, the evidence is said to be privileged and is deemed inadmissible.

There are other distinctive features of judicial trials,[1] but the foregoing characteristics—partisan presentation, the lay jury, and the public nature of the proceedings—provide an introduction to the reasons for rules that limit or exclude evidence. Note that at least one of the characteristics of judicial trials, the use of a jury, can sometimes be accommodated by a control device other than exclusion. In some instances, for example, the judge may provide guidance to the jury through cautionary instructions; this serves as an alternative to exclusion where the risk of the jury's misuse of evidentiary material is not great. Arguably, similar guidance

1950). Note the usual necessity for the judge to acquaint himself with the evidence *before* he intelligently can rule upon its formal admissibility. Thus, in non-jury trials the factfinder, by reason of practical necessity, usually is exposed to inadmissible evidence.

§ 1.3

1. See Hart and McNaughton, supra § 1.2 n. 1, at 56.

also could suffice where apparently reliable evidence cannot be tested fully by the adversary of the party offering the evidence. In any event, it is important to emphasize that the framework of trial and the nature of the adversary system yield rules that restrict the admissibility (input) of evidence or circumscribe its use in some way.

§ 1.4 Building an Evidentiary Record: Allocation of Responsibility for Input and Exclusion

We have seen that a lawyer's development of facts often critically affects the outcome of litigation, and that at trial, facts are established by an adversarial presentation of evidence. It is the responsibility of each party to gather and present his own evidence, either in the form of witnesses (testimonial evidence) or tangible things (real evidence) such as documents or chattels. This principle of party presentation is a fundamental tenet of Anglo-American adjudication.[1] The operative effect of this principle is to leave the development of a case largely in the hands of the adverse parties, whose interests usually are represented by counsel.[2] Only evidence that the parties proffer will be considered by the trier. The assumption is that each partisan will present the evidence that he deems most advantageous. This mode of presentation is thought to encourage a full evidentiary record. But the theory does not require a full record in fact. The proceedings satisfy the public interest if each party has been afforded a fair *opportunity* to proffer evidence and to test the evidence offered by his adversary, even in cases where the resulting evidentiary record is meager or incomplete.[3] Generally, the

§ 1.4

1. See Millar, The Formative Principles of Civil Procedure, 18 Ill.L.Rev. 1, 9 (1923); F. James & G. Hazard, Civil Procedure, § 1.2, at 4–5 (3d ed. 1985).

2. Professor Millar distinguishes party presentation, which makes it incumbent upon the parties to define the scope and content of a case, from party-prosecution, which makes the parties responsible for moving a case forward. See Millar, supra n. 1, at 9, 19. The adversary system embraces both of these characteristics.

Currently gaining support is a proposal to make lawyers advocates for full and candid disclosure, as well as for their clients. See, e.g., Frankel, The Search for Truth: An Umpireal View, 123 U.Pa.L.Rev. 1031 (1975); Uviller, The Advocate, The Truth and Judicial Hackles: A Reaction to Judge Frankel's Idea, 123 U.Pa.L.Rev. 1067 (1975). But see Freedman, Judge Frankel's Search for Truth, 123 U.Pa.L.Rev. 1060 (1975).

3. In simple adversary trials, only the parties are directly affected by the outcome of the trial; the public interest in this context lies only in ensuring that those parties have available a competent and neutral forum for resolving their dispute. Increasingly, however, certain kinds of litigation, such as those dealing with welfare, prison conditions,

Anglo-American adversarial trial has not embraced a policy that the judge[4] or some representative of the public supply evidence that the parties, through error or by design, withhold from the tribunal.

In addition to controlling the evidentiary presentation, a party can exert another influence upon the evidentiary record: by making a timely objection, he can sometimes block the admission of evidence offered by his adversary. The success of such an objection depends upon whether the judge determines that an exclusionary rule dictates rejection of the proffered evidence. A party, however, is not required to object, even though an exclusionary rule is available to prevent the admission of the evidence. If, by careless omission or deliberate inaction, a party makes no objection,[5] the evidence against him is admitted and becomes part of the material available to the trier of fact. Only in extreme cases, usually involving a criminal charge, will the judge intervene and exclude the evidence on his own motion. Again, the Anglo-American judicial system places primary reliance upon the partisan interests of the opposing parties, acting through counsel, to shape the factual basis of the dispute.

§ 1.5 Use and Evaluation of the Admitted Evidence: Allocation of Responsibility

The trier of fact (or factfinder) has the responsibility of evaluating the evidence and deciding what occurred; that is, the trier determines the adjudicative or historical facts. In cases where there is no right to a jury (generally, those formerly entertained in equity courts) the judge is the factfinder. In other

the environment, or racial and sexual discrimination are being perceived as quasi-public in nature. Participation (intervention) by interested parties has been frequent. Here, the interests of nonparties are bound up in the court's decision. According to some observers, protection of these nonparty interests calls for modifications of the adversarial process. See § 1.7. See also Fed.R.Civ.P. 24 (specifying conditions of intervention).

4. There is little doubt that the judge can call and (or) examine witnesses, although he is under no duty to do so. See Fed.R.Evid. 614, 706; McCormick, § 8. Judges sometimes exercise this power, especially in cases where each side has presented expert testimony and the experts' conclusions (opinions) are conflicting. The judge may appoint and call to the stand an impartial expert. Fed.R.Evid. 706. Nevertheless, primary responsibility for evidentiary presentation remains with the parties. IX Wigmore, § 2483 (Chadbourn). As to the wisdom of appointing experts to testify for the court, see Diamond, The Fallacy of the Impartial Expert, 3 Archives of Crim.Psychodynamics 221 (1959), reprinted in part in Lempert & Saltzburg at 979–83.

5. The rules governing objections are set out in Chapter XI.

cases the jury acts as the trier of fact, unless the parties have failed to assert, or agreed to waive, their right to trial by jury. Thus, a trial consists principally of the presentation of evidence to the factfinder.

After the presentation of all of the evidence in the case, each party has an opportunity to make a closing argument. In this forensic presentation, counsel for each litigant attempts to convince the trier to accept certain evidence as reliable and to draw inferences favorable to his client. Thus, the parties can influence the factfinder's conclusions by debate and persuasion. Closing argument is the principal phase of the trial that is directed to the meaning and weight of evidence, rather than to the presentation of evidence.

In a jury case, the parties also may attempt to affect the trier's evaluation of the evidence by persuading the judge to give certain instructions that guide the jury in its use of the evidence. These instructions are of three general kinds: a *cautionary* instruction, advising that certain evidence should be weighed with care because of a risk that it is untrustworthy; a *limiting* instruction, restricting the use of designated evidence to one or more stated purposes; and a *peremptory* (finding) instruction, directing that certain evidence must be believed, or that if certain evidence is believed, then specified consequences (such as a verdict for the plaintiff) must ensue.

When appropriate, the judge may give instructions even where none have been requested by the parties. It generally is regarded as the judge's responsibility to charge the jury correctly on the basic aspects of the case. However, if the judge charges the jury with regard to the applicable substantive law, he usually is not required to go further and give evidentiary instructions. To ensure that the judge's charge includes evidentiary instructions, the interested party must make a specific request that identifies the instruction(s) he desires. His failure to do so is dispositive in a subsequent appeal.[1] Once again party activity, or lack of it, can be a determinant in the factfinding process.[2]

§ 1.5

1. See Fed.R.Civ.P. 51; Fed.R.Evid. 105; Ostapenko v. American Bridge Div. of United States Steel Corp., 267 F.2d 204, 205–206 (2d Cir.1959); Turner Const. Co. v. Houlihan, 240 F.2d 435, 439 (1st Cir.1957); Hatfield v. Levy Bros., 18 Cal.2d 798, 810, 117 P.2d 841, 847 (1941); State ex rel. State Highway Comm'n v. Yackel, 445 S.W.2d 389, 393 (Mo.App.1969).

2. In a non-jury trial, the parties can request that the judge in his evaluation of the evidence apply the same

§ 1.6 The Role of Judge and Jury: A General View *

Lawyers sometimes use the expression that the jury decides questions of fact, and the judge resolves questions of law. This description of function loosely accords with prevailing practice. The rationale for such a division is obvious: the judge, through training and experience, is particularly qualified to resolve legal questions, while the jurors, who bring to the courtroom the common experience of the community, are better equipped to settle factual disputes. As we shall see, however, it is not as easy to make the division between judge-jury responsibility as this lawyers' colloquialism suggests.

The first qualification to this general statement of function is that the jury can discharge its factfinding role only in those cases where the state of the evidence reasonably justifies a finding in favor of either party. If from the evidence there is no *reasonable* dispute as to the historical (adjudicative) facts, the judge prevents the jury (by the use of an instruction, directed verdict, or other appropriate device) from making any finding that is contrary to the preponderating evidence. Thus, the function of adjudicating historical facts, a function that normally belongs to the jury, is assumed by the judge in cases where the evidence reasonably supports only one factual resolution.[1]

A second qualification to the general statement of judge-jury function arises where, by giving a general verdict, the jury applies the substantive law (as described in the judge's charge) to the particular facts of the case. In some instances, notably where community values and standards are thought to be particularly important, the standard contained in the applicable law is expressed by a very general phrase. A defendant is negligent, for example, if he fails to "act reasonably" or does not exercise "due

principles that would, in a jury trial, be expressed in instructions to the jury. However, there is no way of ascertaining the judge's mental evaluative processes unless he reveals his thoughts in his findings of fact and conclusions of law. See Fed.R.Civ.P. 52.

§ 1.6

* Chapter X discusses in detail the role of judge and jury. This section provides a general, prefatory statement of the division of functions between judge and jury in the adjudicatory process.

1. In criminal cases, by uniform tradition if not constitutional compulsion, the jury always applies the law to the facts unless the defendant waives his right to jury trial. Annot., 72 A.L.R. 899 (1931). See Fed.R.Crim.P. 29(a) (abolishing motions for directed verdicts in criminal cases). Of course, the judge can take the case from the jury and render a judgment in the *defendant's* favor by granting the defendant's motion for acquittal. See Fed.R.Crim.P. 29(a).

care." In these cases involving a broadly stated legal rule, the jury's application of law to fact involves a *characterization* of the adjudicative facts in the light of the jury's collective experience and in terms of the indeterminate language that constitutes the legal standard.[2] In a sense, the jury is giving the legal principles involved the necessary precision to resolve the case before them.[3]

The judge, too, assumes functions that vary from his more familiar task of deciding questions of law. He does, as we have seen, determine which rules of substantive law will apply in a particular case. But there are numerous occasions when the judge makes factual determinations. In the pre-trial process, he resolves factual questions pertaining to the jurisdiction of the court over the subject matter or over the parties. He settles factual disputes that may arise in connection with discovery proceedings. He also determines which issues are not reasonably in dispute in the course of a summary judgment proceeding or at a pre-trial conference. Even after a trial by jury is commenced, he monitors the evidence and, as already noted, removes from jury consideration any factual determinations that by reason of the state of the evidence could be resolved in only one way—that is, evidence that is not reasonably disputable. The judge also decides preliminary factual questions that accompany the application of the exclusionary rules of evidence.[4] The rules of evidence often are stated in terms that include a reference to the attending factual circumstances; the judge determines the existence or non-existence of these circumstances. For example, an evidence rule states that in proving the terms of a writing, the original document must be produced unless it is destroyed or otherwise unavail-

2. See 2 F. Harper and F. James, Law of Torts, § 15.3, at 880–83 (1956); Hart and McNaughton, supra § 1.2 n. 1, at 60–61.

3. There are control devices, including summary judgment, instructions, and directed verdict, that can be used to limit the jury's characterization. These devices ensure that the jury is not allowed to reach an irrational characterization of the conduct. See F. James & G. Hazard, Civil Procedure, § 7.11, at 345–49, §§ 7.12–7.22 (3d ed. 1985). For example, it would be irrational to characterize as negligent a hazardous, but correctly performed, surgical procedure if it were the only known means of saving the patient's life. But substantial latitude is inherent in such imprecise terms as "reasonable," and if the facts as well as the issue of reasonableness or due care are disputed, the jury's verdict normally is decisive. See F. Harper and F. James, Law of Torts, § 15.2, at 872–80 (1956); Weiner, The Civil Jury Trial and the Law-Fact Distinction, 54 Cal.L.Rev. 1867, 1872–74 (1966).

4. Chapter X explores his role in this regard. See, e.g., Fed.R.Evid. 104(a).

able.[5] Suppose the proponent claims that the original was destroyed or lost, but the opponent disputes this assertion.[6] In order to avoid prolonging the trial and overburdening or confusing the jury, the judge makes the preliminary factual determination necessary to apply the rule.

§ 1.7 The Changing Shape of the Adversarial Model in Modern Litigation

The Anglo-American adversary system has not been static. Rather, it has evolved over the years in response to pressures exerted by litigants and the public. Changes such as the introduction of discovery and the reduction of pleading technicalities, whatever one's view of the merits of these reforms, have had a significant impact on the system.[1] Yet generally speaking, the distinguishing features of the adversary system which we have seen—party control; bench passivity; issue identification through party exchange in the pleadings, during discovery, and at trial—have endured. But several features that limit party control should be noted.

The common law has long given judges considerable power over the process of trial. Within the limits of soundly exercised discretion, judges can control the mode and order of presentation at trial, ask questions of the witnesses called by the parties, call witnesses themselves, exclude inflammatory or prejudicial evidence, sum up the evidence, and even comment upon its weight.[2] Of course, some judges are more vigorous in the exercise of these powers than others. Probably, it is relatively rare to find a trial judge who fully exercises these various prerogatives in a single

5. This rule is discussed in § 13.9.

6. This example appears in McCormick, § 53, at 135.

§ 1.7

1. The most influential early reforms occurred in New York in 1848 with the adoption of the "Field Code," named after its principal architect, David Dudley Field. The adoption of the Federal Rules of Civil Procedure in 1938 and subsequent adoptions by many states represent the major procedural reform of the twentieth century. For a discussion of such reforms, see R. Field, B. Kaplan, and K. Clermont, Materials for a Basic Course in Civil Procedure, 391–98 (5th ed. 1984).

Of recent significance are the 1983 amendments to the Federal Rules of Civil Procedure, especially revised Rule 16 concerning the pretrial conference and amended Rule 26 on discovery. See Fed.R.Civ.P. 16 & 26 and Adv. Comm.Notes on the 1983 amendments.

2. McCormick, §§ 4, 5, 8. These common law powers have largely been codified in the Federal Rules. See, e.g., Fed.R.Evid. 104 (preliminary questions), 403 (exclusion of relevant evidence on grounds of prejudice, confusion, or waste of time), 611 (mode and order of interrogation), 614 (calling and interrogation of witnesses by the court), and 615 (exclusion of witnesses).

trial. Further, some states have constitutions or statutes that forbid the judge from exercising one or more of these powers, often by negating his power to comment on the evidence or even to summarize it.[3] In the federal system, however, and in many states, judges continue to hold the full range of common law powers. There is also a national movement, as yet of uncertain force and breadth, to increase the judge's authority over the litigation process. This trend has two characteristics: judges are encouraged to employ more fully their existing powers and to assert at least some managerial control over the entire adversarial process, especially in its pretrial phases.[4] In the federal system and some states, there have been formal amendments to procedural rules (or statutes) so that the judge's authority is insured.[5] For example, Rules 26(f) and 16 of the Federal Rules of Civil Procedure endow the judge with considerable authority over the scope and length of discovery and permit rather extensive management of both pre-trial and trial proceedings.

Before exploring further this trend toward a "managerial judge," it should be reiterated that the extent of the movement is not yet clear. Comprehensive statistical evidence is not available, so there is no documented record supporting a general shift by most judges toward systemic judicial control. There is, however, evidence that in complex, multi-party cases, such as securities and anti-trust litigation, judges are assuming a more dominant role in the adversarial process of litigation.[6] In some measure, the impetus for increased judicial control is found in the dramatic increase in cases filed in recent years.[7] Leaving the pace of litigation

3. See Vanderbilt, Minimum Standards of Judicial Administration, 224–29 (1949). Generally speaking, these restrictive provisions reflect the view that juries should have wide latitude in deciding cases and that if the judge directly or impliedly commented on the evidence, the jury might feel obliged to adhere to his view. For a discussion of the historical development and debate over judicial comment on the evidence, see 1 Weinstein & Berger, ¶ 107[01], at 7–20.

4. Fed.R.Civ.P. 16 and Adv.Comm. Note to the 1983 amendments; see generally Wright, Law of Federal Courts, § 91 (4th ed. 1983) (discussing the role of pretrial conferences in the pre-amendment context).

5. Fed.R.Civ.P. 16, 26 and Adv. Comm.Notes to the 1983 amendments; see generally Wright, supra n. 4, § 83.

6. The Federal Judicial Center has prepared special guidelines for such cases. See Federal Judicial Center, Manual for Complex Litigation, Second (1985).

7. For example, annual filings in federal district courts increased from 59,284 in 1960 to 87,321 in 1970, to 168,789 in 1980 and then to 241,842 in the twelve-month period ending June 30, 1983. Annual Report of the Administrative Office of U.S. Courts (1983). There have also been substantial increases in the caseloads of state courts. For instance, between 1976 and 1978

entirely to the parties ignores the pressing need to move an overload of cases efficiently through the system. Of course, in addition to the problem of overcrowded dockets, there are, among many observers, serious reservations about the adversarial system itself.[8] For example, critics point to inequities they perceive in its operation. Disparities between the professional skills of opposing attorneys may influence the outcome of litigation as much as the "merits" of the case. Disparate financial resources of the opposing parties may also be a principal determinant in the outcome of litigation. A party with superior resources may burden his opponent with protracted and expensive discovery, thus forcing a favorable settlement. Beyond these considerations, there is one kind of case in which some increased control by the judge appears both prudent and inevitable. This case is, for lack of a more specific label, the so-called institutional lawsuit.

Perhaps no category of complex litigation so dramatically challenges the traditionally passive role of judges than does the suit against public institutions—school systems, prisons, police departments, mental institutions, and the like. These unwieldy suits cannot be adequately shaped for trial or efficiently brought to judgment without significant management by a judicial officer, such as a judge or magistrate. Not only do the complexity and sheer size of these suits encourage increased judicial control, but the frequent divergence of interests among parties on the "same side" of the dispute induces the judge to assume an active posture. Further, many of these suits are filed as class actions—a form of lawsuit in which there traditionally has been active participation

filings of all types (including criminal, civil, juvenile, etc.) increased from 7.2 million to 7.8 million in California and from 1.7 million to 1.9 million in Virginia. See The National Center for State Courts, The Business of State Trial Courts (1983); Council on the Role of Courts, The Role of Courts in American Society (1984). For a thorough analysis suggesting that the growth in court filings represents neither a radical expansion of per capita litigation nor an increasing contentiousness among citizens, but instead reflects a broader growth in disputes and mediation that attends an increasingly interactive society and educated populace, see Galanter, Reading the Landscape of Disputes: What We Know and Don't Know (and Think We Know) About Our Allegedly Contentious and Litigious Society, 31 UCLA L.Rev. 1 (1983).

8. See, e.g., Frankel, The Search for Truth: An Umpireal View, 123 U.Pa.L. Rev. 1031 (1975); National Conference on the Causes of Popular Dissatisfaction with the Administration of Justice, April 7–9, 1976, 70 F.R.D. 79 (1976) (address delivered at forum sponsored by the Judicial Conference of the United States and the Conference of Chief Justices of the American Bar Association). For a review of cases illustrating the limitations of the adversary system, see Cleary & Strong, Ch. 2.

by the judge, who must protect the interest of the absent class members.[9]

These institutional lawsuits pose additional problems that strain the principle of party control. Typically, the plaintiffs seek major reforms in the target institution. The radiating effects of such fundamental changes may involve practically everyone within the defendant entity, those members of the public who have an immediate connection with the institution (such as the family of an inmate), and the general public who, through tax assessments or some other revenue measure, may ultimately have to finance the court-ordered reforms. Finally, when relief is granted, often in the form of a decree ordering the defendants to take far-reaching affirmative steps, its implementation usually requires long and detailed judicial supervision.[10]

Whether and to what extent it is appropriate for courts to be the instruments of far-reaching institutional reform is currently the subject of serious attention and debate.[11] Often the entity that the plaintiffs attack is a part of the executive branch, but established and funded by the legislature. Court-ordered reform raises the danger of hostility and resistance not only for the general public, but also from coordinate government branches. Additional tension arises when *federal* courts order expansive changes in *state* institutions. The counterbalance to these difficulties, it may be argued, is that when the political process fails to protect legal rights adequately, the only recourse is to the courts.

For our purposes, it suffices to sketch the difficulties of institutional litigation and to note the uneasy accommodation between the adversary model and the judiciary's role in this and related types of modern litigation. Many modern suits require a degree of management and control that probably cannot be provided by the parties. Beyond this, the interests of persons who are not named parties may be so significantly affected by the outcome of trial that special protective steps are required. Active involvement by a judge or other judicial officer is a predictable response to unwieldy litigation with far-reaching consequences. The chal-

9. See Fed.R.Civ.P. 23; Wright, supra n. 4, § 72, at 473–76, 486.

10. See, e.g., Chayes, The Role of the Judge in Public Law Litigation, 89 Harv.L.Rev. 1281 (1976); Diver, The Judge as Political Powerbroker: Superintending Structural Change in Public Institutions, 65 Va.L.Rev. 43 (1979); Fletcher, The Discretionary Constitution: Institutional Remedies & Judicial Legitimacy, 81 Yale L.J. 635 (1982); Mishkin, Federal Courts as State Reformers, 35 W & L L.Rev. 4 (1978).

11. See supra n. 10.

lenge lies in adapting the adversary system to modern conditions without sacrificing those features, such as judge neutrality, that are desirable. It is uncertain whether and how this challenge will be successfully met.

§ 1.8 Factfinding Outside the Record: Judicial Notice

An interesting accommodation of the roles of judge, counsel, and jury exists in the traditional doctrine of judicial notice. Judicial notice allows the court to introduce well-established propositions into the record as conclusive facts, the formal proof of which then becomes unnecessary.

Notice most commonly is taken of an historical or "adjudicative" fact, that is, one relating to the circumstances giving rise to the dispute. Such facts, were it not for judicial notice, ordinarily would be determined by a jury.[1] The modern standard of certainty required for a judicial notice of an adjudicative fact is that it "must be one not subject to reasonable dispute in that it is either (1) generally known within the territorial jurisdiction of the trial court or (2) capable of accurate and ready determination by resort to sources whose accuracy cannot reasonably be questioned."[2] The fact that Mission Street is a place of business activity is generally known to those in San Francisco; the time of sunrise or sunset can be ascertained from reliable sources, as can many historical, geographical, or scientific facts.[3] Such facts as these would be routinely noticed by the judge.

The judge may take judicial notice on his own motion. Under the preferred view, he must do so (assuming it is appropriate) if requested by counsel and provided with such information as may be necessary to facilitate the process.[4] At one time, there was a

§ 1.8

1. Adjudicative facts are those "concerning the immediate parties—who did what, where, when, how, and with what motive and intent. . . ." Fed.R.Evid. 201, Adv.Comm.Note.

2. Fed.R.Evid. 201(b).

3. Varcoe v. Lee, 180 Cal. 338, 347, 181 P. 223, 227 (1919) (character of Mission Street); Beardsley v. Irving, 81 Conn. 489, 491, 71 A. 580, 581 (1909) (whether June 3, 1906 fell on a Sunday). See McCormick, §§ 329–330. With the Varcoe case, compare Russo v. Russo, 21 Cal.App.3d 72, 90, 98 Cal.Rptr. 501, 541 (1971) (not common knowledge that Haight-Ashbury district unsafe for children). See also Mainline Investment Corp. v. Gaines, 407 F.Supp. 423, 426–27 (N.D.Tex.1976), where judicial notice was taken of a series of increases in oil prices; United States v. Blunt, 558 F.2d 1245 (6th Cir.1977) (federal prison on federal land); but see Clark v. South Central Bell Tel. Co., 419 F.Supp. 697, 704 (W.D.La.1976) (refusal to notice population of parish 30% black).

4. Fed.R.Evid. 201(c), (d). In some jurisdictions, it apparently is the rule that the judge *must* take judicial notice

vigorous debate over whether the noticed fact must be accepted by the jury as conclusively established or whether the opponent could attempt to persuade the jury to make a contrary finding.[5] If judicial notice of adjudicative facts is limited to those that are indisputable, it seems incongruous to permit a contrary finding by the jury.[6] Thus, most jurisdictions hold that, at least in civil cases, judicial notice is conclusive, and disproof by contrary evidence and argument is not allowed.[7] In criminal cases, however, there is a decided tendency to let the jury refuse to find any contested fact adverse to the accused, whether or not it is reasonably disputable.[8] The rationale is that the accused's right to jury trial, which prevents the judge from directing a verdict against him, makes it similarly inappropriate to bind him by judicial notice.[9] Thus judicial notice in criminal trials usually takes the form of an instruction to the jury that they *may* find certain facts even though not formally supported by evidence in the record.

The court may also judicially "notice" so-called "legislative facts"—those observations or conclusions about general conditions and behavior that form the factual basis of a policy or rule of law.[10] Legislative facts pertain to, yet transcend, the particular dispute before the court; often they are the sociological, economic,

of those facts that are commonly known and indisputable. See Morgan & Weinstein at 4–5, 9.

5. See, e.g., McNaughton, Judicial Notice—Excerpts Relating to the Morgan-Wigmore Controversy, 14 Vand.L. Rev. 779 (1961).

6. The Federal Rules of Evidence provide that in civil actions any fact judicially noticed must be accepted by the jury as conclusively established. Fed.R.Evid. 201(g).

7. Fed.R.Evid. 201(g); McCormick, Judicial Notice, 5 Vand.L.Rev. 296, 321–22 (1952). For a collection of representative cases, see Morgan & Weinstein at 9 n. 32.

8. See State v. Main, 94 R.I. 338, 180 A.2d 814 (1962); State v. Lawrence, 120 Utah 323, 234 P.2d 600 (1951). Fed.R. Evid. 201(g) provides that in criminal cases the judge "shall instruct the jury that it may, but is not required to, accept as conclusive any fact judicially noticed." But see Fla.Stat.Ann. § 90.206.

9. See House Judiciary Comm. Report on H.R.Res. 5463, H.R. No. 650, 93rd Cong., 2nd Sess. (1974), reprinted at 28 U.S.C.A. §§ 823, 828 (1975); Adv. Comm.Note to Fed.R.Evid. 201(g); Preliminary Draft of Proposed Rules of Evidence, 46 F.R.D. 161, 205. If judicial notice is limited to matters beyond reasonable dispute, it appears illogical in any case, civil or criminal, to sanction what purports to be countervailing evidence and to permit a finding at odds with certainty. Why should there be a right to trial by jury as to a fact that reasonably can not be disputed? The answer must lie in the jury's right to interdict an "unjust" application of law.

10. See the leading articles by Professor Kenneth Davis: An Approach to Problems of Evidence in the Administrative Process, 55 Harv.L.Rev. 365, 404–07 (1942), and Judicial Notice, 55 Colum.L.Rev. 945, 952–59 (1955). See also Graham, Judicial Notice of Adjudicative and Legislative Facts, 17 Crim. Law Bull. 241 (1981). Legislative facts may be pertinent "when deciding upon

political, or scientific assumptions that underpin the rule of law in question. Thus, a court may rely upon data indicating the probable effect of reducing the size of a jury from twelve persons to six, or cite the effects on the institution of marriage of allowing adverse testimony by one spouse against another.[11] Usually, it is an appellate—as opposed to a trial—court that uses legislative facts in its decisional process. It is, of course, appellate tribunals that bear significant responsibility for monitoring and, sometimes, modifying the substantive law. Since these courts enjoy greater authority than do trial courts to declare or change a substantive rule, they are naturally more attentive to discovering the reality of the environment in which the pronounced rule will operate.

Legislative facts by their nature are usually not indisputable. It would often be impractical to restrict a court to only those legislative facts beyond reasonable dispute. In creating or applying common law or in interpreting an ambiguous statute, the court must often settle for the conclusion that a fact or set of facts pertaining to a legal rule is probable.[12] Of course, when deciding the *constitutionality* of a statute, it is usually necessary only to conclude that data about existing conditions *were sufficient to cause a reasonable legislature* to enact the measure it did.[13] The court need not itself believe the factual assumption upon which the legislature acted. In other contexts, however, such as changing the common-law requirements governing the insanity defense in a criminal trial, the court generally decides which, among competing hypotheses or theories, is most probably correct. Thus, in Javins v. First National Realty Corp.,[14] the Court of Appeals for the District of Columbia, in ruling that an implied warranty of habitability runs with residential leaseholds, supported its holding

the constitutional validity of a statute, interpreting a statute, or [creating], extending, or restricting a common law rule." McCormick, § 331, at 928.

11. Williams v. Florida, 399 U.S. 78 (1970) (jury size); Hawkins v. United States, 358 U.S. 74, 77 (1958) (adverse spousal testimony would likely destroy marriage). See also Trammel v. United States, 445 U.S. 40 (1980), rejecting the assumptions of the *Hawkins* case.

12. Here the judge evaluates the validity in fact of the proposition. In Brown v. Board of Education, for example, the Court looked not to whether past decisions and statutes sanctioning segregation were grounded on then-reasonable perceptions, but instead upon contemporary data on the effects of segregated education. Brown v. Board of Education of Topeka, 347 U.S. 483 (1954), supplemented 349 U.S. 294 (1955); McCormick, § 331, at 929 n. 19.

13. McCormick, § 331, at 928–29; see, e.g., Jay Burns Baking Co. v. Bryan, 264 U.S. 504 (1924).

14. 428 F.2d 1071 (D.C.Cir.1970), cert. denied, 400 U.S. 925 (1970); see 1 Louisell & Mueller, § 56, at 396–98.

with certain factual assumptions about urban housing markets and the skills of low income tenants. Likewise, in the famous case of Brown v. Board of Education,[15] the United States Supreme Court relied upon sociological findings about the adverse effects of racially segregated schools.

If legislative facts can be judicially noticed even though their existence is less than certain, should not the parties have an opportunity to challenge the noticed facts?[16] The argument for such an opportunity is particularly compelling when judicially noticed extra-record facts are used without prior knowledge to the disputants to form the core of a court's holding. Although one may urge that parties to a suit should invariably have the right to challenge the accuracy of legislative facts, it seems inevitable that appellate courts almost always take account, expressedly or impliedly, of the world outside the courtroom doors. Discovering the realities of that world is not an easy task, and books, reports of investigations, scientific experiments, and the like are often the best available evidence. Perhaps the most that can be said about the notice of legislative facts is, first, that their source should be sufficiently reliable to support a conclusion that they exist and, second, that it is desirable, when practicable, to allow parties to present their views about the existence of pertinent legislative facts. When such facts are advanced at trial or in an appellate brief, the parties may exchange their views and arguments. When an appellate court makes its own investigation, especially after briefing and oral argument, party participation becomes more difficult.

The Federal Rules of Evidence expressly govern only judicial notice of adjudicatory fact;[17] they do not, however, foreclose notice of legislative facts.[18] Rule 201 authorizes notice of adjudica-

15. 347 U.S. 483, 494 n. 11 (1954), supplemented 349 U.S. 294 (1955).

16. See Saltzburg & Redden at 60: "We do not claim that Judges cannot rely on a broad range of facts to force the law forward. We suggest only that the parties should be permitted to participate in the march." For an early appeal for party participation as well as for the use of masters and court appointed experts in the observance of legislative facts in both trial and appellate courts, see Note, Social and Economic Facts—Appraisal of Suggested Techniques for Presenting Them to the Courts, 61 Harv.L.Rev. 692 (1948).

17. Fed.R.Evid. 201(a).

18. "[The view governing judicial access to legislative facts] renders inappropriate any limitation in the form of indisputability, any formal requirement of notice other than those already inherent in affording opportunity to hear and be heard and exchanging briefs, and any requirement of formal findings at any level" Fed.R.Evid. 201, Adv. Comm.Note.

tive fact when the factual proposition in question is indisputable. The Rule also guarantees to opposing parties an opportunity to be heard as to the correctness of taking notice.[19] Neither of the Rule's provisions applies to notice of legislative facts.[20] Such facts are not so easily governed by detailed provisions, and hence the drafters left the contours of judicial notice of legislative fact to case-by-case development.

Problems arise when a given fact can rationally be treated as either legislative or adjudicative.[21] In this event, the propriety of taking notice, as well as an opposing party's unqualified right to be heard, may turn on how a fact is characterized. In some instances, this characterization is not an easy task. Generally, the more closely the facts are identified with the particular activities of the parties—what happened, when, and to whom[22]—the stronger is the argument that the facts are adjudicative and cannot be judicially noticed unless the standard of indisputability is met. Judge Learned Hand was once faced with the question whether, five years after the trial of an antitrust case involving the Aluminum Company of America, he and his colleagues on the Second Circuit could judicially notice the report of the "Truman Committee." That report detailed the annual production of various producers of aluminum and set out the extent of certain reserves of ore. It was held that the document was not an appropriate source for assessing the correctness of the findings below, but it nonetheless was a legitimate informational tool for use in fashioning an appropriate remedy.[23] Thus the report

19. Fed.R.Evid. 201(b). The opportunity to be heard had not gained wide recognition until adoption of the Rule. Even today the right probably is not often asserted, either because the judge fails to indicate that he is taking notice or, more likely, because the noticed fact is not disputed by the parties. An opportunity to be heard nevertheless may be important even when the court takes notice of legislative facts, as the Javins case, discussed in the text, suggests.

20. See Fed.R.Evid. 201, Adv.Comm. Note.

21. See, e.g., Securities & Exchange Comm'n v. Capital Gains Research Bureau, Inc., 191 F.Supp. 897 (S.D.N.Y. 1961), aff'd, 300 F.2d 745 (2d Cir.1961), aff'd on rehearing en banc, 306 F.2d 606 (2d Cir.1962), rev'd, 375 U.S. 180 (1963) (propriety of judicially noticing whether purchase by an international advisory service of securities that the service was also recommending to clients was an artificial stimulant to market for those stocks); see generally 1 Louisell & Mueller, § 56, 405–416.

22. Davis, Judicial Notice, 55 Colum. L.Rev. 945, 952, 977 (1955).

23. United States v. Aluminum Co. of America, 148 F.2d 416, 445–46 (2d Cir.1945). See also Oneida Indian Nation v. New York, 691 F.2d 1070, 1086 (2d Cir.1982), on remand 649 F.Supp. 420 (N.D.N.Y.1986) (review of treaties and legislation affecting Indian relations); Banks v. Schweiker, 654 F.2d 637, 640–642 (9th Cir.1981) (judicial notice of practices of social security office used to reject testimony of benefit recip-

seemed to have been used as a source of legislative rather than judicial fact.

The term "judicial notice" also applies to the process by which a judge, usually with the assistance of counsel, determines or discovers the procedural or substantive law in his or some other jurisdiction. Usually the judge can consult and apply statutes, regulations, and prior case law (precedents) whether or not such materials have been introduced into evidence. If counsel wishes the judge to consult a particular source, he simply calls the judge's attention to it and supplies a citation. However, in instances where there is no widely available source (as there is with most American codes and case reports), it may be necessary for counsel formally to provide evidence of the pertinent rule of law.[24] For example, foreign law, the content of which may pose difficulties of discovery and interpretation, is not routinely judicially noticed. Unless a statute provides for judicial notice, the content of the foreign law must be proved by official documents and, when necessary, expert witnesses.[25] The treatment of municipal ordinances varies. Typically, these will not be noticed absent a statutory authorization; thus one relying upon such an ordinance may have to prove its content by an official or "true" copy.

The foregoing sketch provides a condensed description of at least the most important aspects of judicial notice.[26] It should be

ient, ruled improper on appeal as the fact was adjudicative and the party was entitled to an opportunity to be heard, even in an administrative hearing where Rule 201 did not apply).

24. See Ruhs v. Pacific Power & Light, 671 F.2d 1268, 1273 (10th Cir. 1982) (municipal ordinances may not be judicially noticed by courts of general jurisdiction, but must be proven as would any other fact); Johnson v. City of Tulsa, 97 Okl.Cr. 85, 258 P.2d 695, 700 (App.1953) (certified copy or some other means of proof must be used to enter into evidence the provisions of municipal ordinance).

25. See, e.g., Ore.R.Evid., 202(6) (1981); see generally McCormick, § 335, at 942–43. Where formal proof of foreign law is still required, there has been some relaxation in many jurisdictions as to what constitutes sufficient proof. See id. at 942.

26. Still other types of facts can be judicially noticed. First, courts routinely "notice" certain fundamental facts assumed in the course of presenting and challenging testimony. When a witness to an accident refers to a "car," all assume the vehicle to have been an automobile rather than a railroad car. All cases involve thousands of such "non-evidence" facts, the formal proof of which would result in enormous and unnecessary delay. Fed.R.Evid. 201, Adv.Comm.Note.

Second, judges sometimes judicially notice "evaluative" facts. For example, a judge concludes, usually on the basis of circumstantial evidence, that a particular condition must have existed and uses this "finding" in evaluating the evidence before him. A judge may notice, for instance, that precise navigation of a boat is inherently difficult in the adverse weather conditions in which the accident sued upon occurred.

reiterated that judicial notice of adjudicative fact is a substitute for formal proof; that is, it relieves counsel from the obligation formally to introduce evidence to support a noticed fact. His obligation does not extend beyond supplying the judge with such information as may be necessary to demonstrate that the proposition in question is beyond reasonable dispute. Note that judicial notice of adjudicative facts serves two functions: it expedites the trial of a case and, by imposition of an indisputability standard, serves as a method by which the judge can prevent highly improbable findings by the jury.

Judicial notice of legislative facts, by contrast, enables the judge more confidently to select or modify the substantive law he applies to the particular case before him. The facts "used" seldom are indisputable; they may be hotly contested in counsels' briefs or observed independently by the court. The judge exercises substantial discretion over when and how to notice legislative facts, and through effective use of the device, especially at the appellate level, can influence the development of broad areas of substantive law.

Notes

1. *Bases of Evidentiary Rules.* It has been said that the law of evidence is a "product of the jury system . . . where ordinary untrained citizens are acting as judges of fact." Thayer, A Preliminary Treatise on Evidence 509 (1898). However, not all of the evidentiary rules reflect a concern for the jury's lack of expertise. Certainly the protection of confidential information, which is conferred by the various rules prohibiting the evidential disclosure of "privileged" communications, is not grounded in concerns about the lay jury. In any event, subject to the qualifications set out in § 1.2 n. 4, the rules of evidence apply in trials without a jury. An article that traces the evolution of the jury's role, explores the nature of legal evidence, and proposes that the exclusionary rules be relaxed is Forkosch, The Nature of Legal Evidence, 59 Cal.L.Rev. 1356 (1971).

2. *Civil Law System.* Roughly ninety percent of the world's jurisdictions use the "inquisitorial" as opposed to the "adversarial" approach to trial procedure. The inquisitorial system is the hallmark of the civil law as it exists in Europe. The label "inquisitorial" often connotes reprehensible past practices on the Continent, documented

Merrill Trust Co. v. Bradford, 507 F.2d 467, 469 (1st Cir.1974). Evaluative facts resemble adjudicative facts. Both take account of the circumstances of the particular dispute. See generally 1 Louisell & Mueller, § 56, at 399–411.

in history, and featuring "secret, written proceedings, *ex parte* judicial investigations, the presumption of guilt, torture, and other sanctions to enforce the accused's duty to confess." Volkmann-Schluck, Continental European Criminal Procedures: True or Illusive Model?, 9 Am. J.Crim.L. 1 (1981). Procedure on the Continent today involves a more liberal accusatorial process, and thus may more aptly be described as "nonadversarial" than "inquisitorial." *Id.* at 3. Nonetheless, the Continental system still diverges from the Anglo-American procedures in important respects:

> In non-adversary procedure the attorneys play a significantly lesser role. The judge calls and questions witnesses, and chooses the order of procedure; his allegiance is, theoretically, to the truth. Typically he has a written dossier of prior testimony which also contains the report of an investigating official, but he is not bound by it. His questions range wider than those permitted in adversary trials. The investigating official (juge d'instruction or magistrate) theoretically conducts an independent preliminary investigation apart from police, court and attorneys, though they may be present when the accused is questioned.

Gross, Adversaries, Juries and Justice, 26 Loy.L.Rev. 525, 526 (1980).

It must be recognized that generalizations about the various systems of adjudication in Europe can be misleading in at least two respects. First, there are significant differences among the various civil law countries both in the theory underlying the adjudicative process and in the implementing provisions declared in statutes and other official sources. Second, the actual adjudicative practices may depart sharply from what one would expect from examining the official sources. See Goldstein and Marcus, The Myth of Judicial Supervision in Three "Inquisitorial" Systems: France, Italy, and Germany, 87 Yale L.J. 240 (1977). For example, a court may have extensive powers to take the initiative, ex officio, in controlling the scope of a judicial action or in developing the evidence, but in practice these powers may be used only partially or infrequently.

Subject to these cautions, it can be said that typically the judge in a Continental country is more active than his English-American counterpart in the following areas: controlling the progress of the litigation; shaping the alleged claims and defenses; dismissing and adding parties; and developing the proof. In the last regard, the judge may order additional documentary evidence or (in some countries) call for witnesses who were not presented by the parties. A notable feature of civil law adjudication is that the judge, not the lawyers, is primarily responsible for examining the witnesses. The examination typically permits the witness a wide latitude to give a narrative account, following which the judge will ask questions. Counsel may suggest topics for inquiry and, in some countries, ask questions or submit a list of questions to the judge. For an interesting comparison between the role of the judge in both the adversary and non-adversary systems, see Devlin, The Judge, 54–83 (1979).

The absence of a jury in many proceedings on the Continent (except in certain cases involving serious offenses) and the strict judicial control over the police in the preliminary stages of an investigation obviate some of the concerns about restricting the admission of evidence. In short, there is usually no basis for apprehension about jury misuse of evidence or abuse of police power in gathering evidence. While common law systems, like that used in the United States, have an explicit "exclusionary rule" to protect individual rights and deter police from illegally gathering evidence, most Continental systems have no such explicit rule. However, they do have certain proscriptions on the use of evidence—that is, some evidence may not be considered suitable legal proof. For example:

> . . . [t]he German Code of Criminal Procedure prohibits entirely the use of evidence extorted from the accused by means of physical abuse, drugs, torture, weariness, hypnosis, deceit, or unlawful threats or promises . . .. The High Federal Appellate Court . . . went a step further and developed the so-called sphere-of-individual rights doctrine. This doctrine allows evidence to be excluded from criminal prosecution when investigating officers intrude into the constitutionally protected sphere of fundamental civil rights.

Volkmann-Schluck, supra at 15. For interesting and concise descriptions of many of the existing nonadversarial systems, see M. Cappelletti & J. Jolowicz, Public Interest Parties and the Active Role of the Judge in Civil Litigation, 197–238 (1975), and Brouwer, Inquisitorial and Adversary Procedures—A Comparative Analysis, 55 Austl.L.J. 207, 208–221 (1981).

Criminal trials on the Continent are somewhat different from civil trials because the former may involve a jury (used in a few countries for serious crimes) or, if not, will probably involve lay assessors who sit with the judges. Further, Continental judges generally are more active in criminal than in civil trials. For an insightful comparison between adversarial and inquisitorial criminal trials, with special emphasis upon the admissibility and use of evidence, see Damaska, Evidentiary Barriers to Conviction and Two Models of Criminal Procedure: A Comparative Study, 121 U.Pa.L.Rev. 506 (1973).

Some American scholars suggest that the American adversarial system be modified by the adoption of certain nonadversarial features of European criminal procedure. The prohibition against plea-bargaining in civil law systems is an example sometimes cited as a practice that could be borrowed by the American system as a means of reducing the abuse of prosecutorial discretion. See Volkmann-Schluck, supra at 6–7. For an interesting discussion of how adoption of certain features of the inquisitorial system might improve the adversarial system, see Schlesinger, Comparative Criminal Procedure: A Plea for Utilizing Foreign Experience, 26 Buffalo L.Rev. 361 (1977).

Chapter II

RELEVANCE: AN INTRODUCTION

§ 2.1 Basic Concepts

Relevance is the basic, unifying principle of the evidentiary rules. The threshold test of admissibility is the test of relevance; if evidence is not relevant, it is not admissible.[1]

What is meant by the term "relevant evidence"? In its simplest form, relevant evidence helps persuade the trier of the existence (or nonexistence) of some fact that is germane to the dispute between the parties. Drawing upon an observation of Jeremy Bentham, we can say that the effect of relevant evidence "when presented to the mind, is to produce a persuasion concerning the existence of some . . . matter of fact—a persuasion either affirmative or disaffirmative of its existence."[2] Of course, all evidence tends to prove or disprove *some* fact, but in a judicial trial the substantive law, or perhaps the state of the pleadings, circumscribes those facts that have legal consequences. Thus, evidence that *V*, the victim of a robbery, consumed four alcoholic drinks one hour before he was robbed tends to show some degree of intoxication at the time of the crime. But this fact—intoxication during the robbery—may be of no consequence in a trial in which defendant, *D*, is prosecuted. Intoxication of the victim would not be a defense to the criminal charge of robbery.

It is understandable that the law restricts evidence to that which is relevant. This limitation is partly based on the goal of

§ 2.1

1. Fed.R.Evid. 402. Not all relevant evidence, however, is admissible. See §§ 2.4, 2.5.

2. Rationale of Judicial Evidence, Specially Applied to English Practice, Vol. 1 at 16 (1827).

efficiency: it is wasteful to receive irrelevant evidence since it has no appropriate bearing on the case. The relevance restriction also furthers the objective of rational factfinding within the framework of the substantive law: the admission of evidence that does not rationally assist in the resolution of pertinent factual issues raises unnecessarily the possibility of inappropriate use by the trier. The trier, for example, may disapprove of excessive drinking, but it should not express that disapproval by acquitting one who committed a crime against an intoxicated victim.

Although we loosely think of relevant evidence as that which "tends to persuade," it is important to note that the principle of relevance embodies two distinct relationships. First, relevance connotes the probative relationship between the testimonial or real evidence proffered and the factual proposition to which that evidence is addressed. Stated otherwise, one aspect of relevance is concerned with whether evidence is logically probative of the proposition toward which it is directed. The second aspect of relevance is concerned with whether the proposition to which the evidence is directed is "consequential" under the substantive law. Thus, evidence is relevant only if it (1) tends to prove or disprove a proposition of fact that (2) is of consequence under the substantive law as made applicable by the pleadings.[3] In a subsequent section we shall explore more fully the degree of probative force necessary to satisfy the requirement that evidence tend to "prove or disprove" a factual proposition. It is important, however, first to clarify and reiterate the requirement that evidence is relevant only if it supports a factual proposition that is "of consequence" to the outcome at trial.

Determining what facts are consequential involves a careful analysis of the controlling substantive law found in statutes, judicial opinions, and other primary sources. These substantive provisions, made applicable by the pleadings,[4] specify and limit the

3. The dual aspect of relevance is captured in Fed.R.Evid. 401: "Relevant evidence means evidence having any tendency to make the existence of any fact that is of consequence to the determination of the action more probable or less probable than it would be without the evidence." See text infra at n. 7.

4. Evidence can be inconsequential because the pleadings have precluded debate on the issue to which it is directed. In a contracts case in which the defense of forgery must be specially pleaded, evidence that the plaintiff had made plans to forge the defendant's name would be relevant (consequential) to show a false signature only if the defendant's pleading asserted (or was amended to assert) the affirmative defense of forgery. Similarly, other actions by opposing attorneys, such as stipulations or admissions during the discovery process, may render evidence "inconsequential."

legal effects that will attach to the establishment of certain propositions of fact. It is these propositions that are sometimes called the elements of a criminal charge, civil claim, or defense. Evidence is, therefore, consequential (or, under the older terminology, "material" [5]) whenever it tends to establish the existence or nonexistence of an element (of a charge, claim, or defense) that is derived from the controlling substantive law. Suppose in a suit for assault and battery, filed by *A* against *B*, the latter offers evidence that he mistakenly thought that *A* was another person, *C*. This evidence should be rejected if the proposition to which it is directed—mistaken identity—is of no legal consequence under the substantive law. That is, if the law of intentional torts imposes liability notwithstanding this kind of mistake, the evidence should be declared irrelevant.[6]

Although the requirement of consequentialness involves an analysis of the relationship between the substantive law and the factual proposition supported by the evidence, the effect of pleadings or other procedural devices such as stipulations should not be ignored. These may serve to narrow the dispute and, hence, confine the range of evidence that is consequential. Evidence pertaining to a defense that had not been pleaded would be inconsequential. Furthermore, if a party has stipulated or otherwise conclusively admitted a fact of consequence, there is no reason to receive evidence bearing upon the conceded proposition. Thus, generally speaking, evidence is consequential only if it relates to a properly *contested* element of a claim or defense.

To this general principle that evidence is consequential only if it bears upon a contested factual event, we must add a qualification: in order fully to convey the "story of a case" to the trier—that is, to permit the judge or jury comprehensively to understand the occurrences that gave rise to the lawsuit—it is usually necessary to present considerable background or contextual information. The trier needs to know some of the details about the

5. "Immaterial" historically meant that the proffered evidence bore no relationship to the legal issues raised by the substantive law made applicable by the pleadings, although the term often was used indiscriminately to refer merely to a lack of probative force between the evidence proffered and a consequential proposition. See Adv.Comm. Note to Fed.R.Evid. 401.

6. Of course, if mistaken identity were a factor that under the law of damages could be considered in determining the amount of the award, evidence of mistake would be of consequence, not to excuse liability, but to assess the appropriate damage award.

parties and their relationship to the events that are the subject of the litigation. This information usually is conveyed through testimony or, perhaps, a document. Often a witness's testimony is augmented by the use of maps, charts, or photographs that illustrate the physical setting in which the conduct under judicial investigation took place. This background evidence, needed in order to provide a contextual setting, is routinely admitted even though it may not, strictly speaking, be contested.

It should also be noted that the trier often needs to know information about a *particular witness* in order to evaluate his credibility and thus the accuracy of his testimony. Perhaps the witness, in the past, has been convicted of perjury or has engaged in other forms of deceptive conduct. These and other prior events may cast doubt on his credibility. Reconsider the example, given above, of the robbery of an intoxicated victim. Although the fact of the victim's intoxication is not directly relevant to the criminal guilt of the accused, it may nonetheless aid the jury in determining whether the victim correctly identified his assailant. Evidence of drunkenness supports the inference of impaired faculties and hence casts doubt on the victim's testimony directed to the consequential proposition that *D* was the offender. Thus, when we say that evidence must point to a fact "of consequence" we embrace within that phrase evidence that assists the trier in determining credibility. In short, evidence directed to the credibility of a witness is received because it ultimately bears on the contested facts to which the witness has testified.

Federal Rule of Evidence 401, which governs proceedings in United States courts[7] and has been adopted by many states, contains the following definition:

> "Relevant evidence" means evidence having any tendency to make the existence of any fact that is of consequence to the determination of the action more probable or less probable than it would be without the evidence.

In this concise provision, the rulemakers have captured the dual aspects of relevance. In sum, evidence is relevant if it (1) increases the probability [the first relationship] of (2) a consequential fact [the second relationship]. If the proposition to which the evidence is directed is consequential, only slight probative force is required to satisfy the other component of the test. The evidence

7. Fed.R.Evid. 101.

need only affect the probability that the proposition does (or does not) exist.

§ 2.2 The Test of Probative Value

We have seen that relevance involves a probative relationship between evidence and a consequential factual proposition. Suppose that in April a prison guard, V_1, is murdered and that in May another guard, V_2, is murdered. The investigation by authorities intensifies and, in late May, *D*, a prisoner, tries to escape from prison. In a subsequent trial for the murder of V_1 in which *D* is named the accused, is *D*'s attempted escape relevant? [1]

Persons responding to this question may disagree. Clearly the evidence does not establish the accused's guilt, but this is not the point. Only the total evidence introduced need be sufficient to justify a finding of guilt. A single item of evidence is relevant if it has any tendency to increase the probability of a consequential factual proposition. It is not even necessary to demonstrate that it is *more probable* that escape was motivated by the fear of detection in connection with V_1's murder than by other possible motives such as feared detection in connection with V_2's murder or simply the desire to gain freedom.[2] The question is whether the probability that the accused committed the murder for which he is on trial is to some degree increased by evidence that he attempted to escape. So put, it may be argued that the evidence is relevant and hence it should be considered along with other circumstantial evidence (such as fingerprints, blood stains, and so forth) in the determination of guilt beyond a reasonable doubt.

The examples discussed thus far in this chapter suggest that the test of probative value is derived from commonplace experience. That is, the test usually involves no more than a commonsense determination, made in the light of human observation and experience, that certain events or conditions either are causally connected or normally associated with other events or conditions. In the words of Professor Thayer, relevance is an "affair of experience and logic, and not at all of law." [3] Common observa-

§ 2.2

1. This problem, with some variation, is posed in McCormick, § 185, at 544.

2. McCormick, § 185, at 542–43. But see Standafer v. First Nat'l Bank, 236 Minn. 123, 52 N.W.2d 718 (1952) (circumstantial evidence must, to be admissible, make the desired proposition more likely than other propositions that are contrary to the proponent's position).

3. Thayer, A Preliminary Treatise on Evidence 269 (1898).

tion teaches that if one fled the scene of a robbery, his guilt thereby is made somewhat more probable than it would be in the absence of the flight. Similarly, human experience indicates that if one had a motive for murder, it is more probable that he murdered than it would be if no motive existed. The touchstone of relevance, at least in the first sense—probative value—is the presence of a logical relationship between the evidence and the ultimate proposition [4] that the evidence is offered to support.

United States v. Robinson [5] vividly illustrates both the kind of inquiry typically undertaken in resolving questions of relevance and the strength of the probative relationship that must exist between the evidence and the related proposition. The accused was prosecuted for a bank robbery committed by four persons. Only one person (who admittedly was involved in the robbery and who was cooperating with the government at the time of trial) could identify the accused as one of the participants. To strengthen the government's evidence bearing on identification, the prosecutor introduced evidence that when the accused was arrested ten weeks after the robbery, he had in his possession a .38 caliber revolver. There was evidence that at least one (and perhaps two) of the pistols used in the robbery were of this caliber. Aside from a similarity in caliber, however, there was no evidence that the gun in the accused's possession was used in committing the offense. The government argued, first, that from possession at the time of arrest it could be inferred that the accused possessed the gun at the time of the robbery, and, second, that the fact that the accused had a weapon of the same caliber as one that apparently was used in the commission of the offense increased the likelihood that he was a participant. The trial judge admitted evidence of the accused's possession of the gun and instructed the jury that they could consider this evidence for such probative value as it might have on the issue of identity.

On appeal, the defense did not contest the relevance of the evidence, but argued that its probative value was substantially outweighed by its prejudicial effect—an argument we shall examine later in this chapter. The Court of Appeals, on rehearing

4. See also Saltzburg & Redden at 111:

> There is no litmus paper test or simple formula for applying the general definition [of relevance]. Logic and experience together must supply the Judge with skills in determining whether a given piece of evidence tends to prove a disputed proposition.

5. 544 F.2d 611 (2d Cir.1976), rev'd en banc 560 F.2d 507 (2d Cir.1977).

en banc, reversed its initial panel decision, held the contested evidence admissible, and affirmed the conviction. It is significant, however, that with only a brief discussion both the panel and the full court concluded that the evidence was relevant because it tended to make the accused's participation in the offense more probable than it would be without the evidence.[6] For present purposes, it is enough to note that even though the probative force of the evidence was attenuated by the several inferential steps necessary and by the rather modest probabilities associated with each step, the court concluded that the basic test of relevance had been satisfied.

Professor Edmund Morgan has provided a revealing illustration of the process involved in drawing the inferences essential to the use of circumstantial proof.[7] Suppose that in the prosecution of *D* for the premeditated murder of *V*, the government offers in evidence a love letter written by *D* to *V*'s wife. The trier is asked to infer from the letter that *D* loved *V*'s wife, that his love caused him to desire her exclusive attention and affection, that this desire led to a concomitant desire to "get rid" of *V*, which in turn led to a plan[8] to accomplish the murder, which, finally, led to the execution of the plan. For each inferential step, one can construct an unarticulated premise: for example, "A man who writes a love letter to a woman is probably in love with her [premise one]; . . . A man who loves a woman probably desires her for himself alone [two]; . . . A man who loves a married woman and desires her for himself alone desires to get rid of her husband [three]; . . . A man who desires to get rid of the husband of the woman he loves probably plans to do so [four]; . . . and . . . A man who plans to get rid of the husband of the woman he loves is probably the man who killed him [five]."[9]

In assessing the probative force of the love letter to establish the ultimate proposition (that *D* killed *V*), it becomes apparent that two major determinants are involved: the first is the number of inferential steps and the second is the degree of probability that

6. Evidence of the possession of the gun may have been a decisive factor in the conviction. See the further discussion of this case in § 2.5.

7. See Morgan & Weinstein at 168–71.

8. In circumstances where the killing appeared to be the result of sudden passion, the premise concerning a plan would be inappropriate, as would several of the other premises and their associated inferences.

9. Morgan & Weinstein at 169.

exists between the inferential links.[10] The *more inferences* one must draw to reach the desired conclusion, the weaker the probative force. The *weaker each inferential link* (that is, the less likely each sequential inference derived from the basic fact), the less the probative force. Note that even if most links were strong, probative force would always be limited by the weakest link. In the foregoing example there were five inferential steps. Some of the inferential links are comparatively strong (e.g., from love letters to deep affection), yet others are comparatively weak (e.g., from the desire to possess to a plan to kill). Does the love letter still pass the test of relevance? It does because it increases somewhat the likelihood that *D* committed the murder.[11] Of course, whether the prosecution can establish beyond a reasonable doubt that the accused committed the offense charged is an entirely different matter which depends upon the combined probative effect of all of the inculpatory evidence introduced at trial.

Evidence of the love letter would not, standing alone, support belief beyond a reasonable doubt that *D* killed *V*. But suppose the prosecution also offered evidence that (1) *D* threatened to kill *V*; (2) *D* possessed a gun of the type and caliber used to kill *V*; (3) D purchased a duplicate key to *V*'s house; and (4) *D*'s fingerprints were found near the scene of the murder. These items of evidence are all relevant; each has a tendency to make more probable the consequential proposition that *D* murdered *V*. At the conclusion of the prosecutor's evidence, the judge must decide if a reasonable trier could conclude from all of the evidence that *D* was the murderer.

§ 2.3 Assessing Probative Value

Questions of relevance, which arise constantly in the course of litigation, ordinarily are not resolved by the explication of assumed premises, nor even by detailing all of the serial inferences. In the illustrative case of the love letter, the prosecutor might assert merely that the proffered love letter was relevant because it demonstrated *D*'s love of *V*'s wife, and that this affection was the

10. Id. at 169. For a more comprehensive analysis of the illustrative problem, see id. at 169–71.

11. See Saltzburg & Redden at 109:

> The important thing for the Judge and for counsel to remember is that the evidence does not by itself have to prove the ultimate proposition for which it is offered; nor does it have to make that ultimate proposition more probable than not. To be relevant it is sufficient that the evidence has a *tendency* to make a consequential fact even the least bit more probable or less probable than it would be without the evidence.

motive for the murder. However, careful consideration of the nexus between proffered evidence and the ultimate proposition to which it is directed is useful in planning trial strategy, in the formulation of evidential argument to the jury, and in advocacy before trial and appellate judges. Different items of circumstantial evidence that support a single proposition normally will vary in probative value. If the issue in an action for property damage is whether the defendant's blasting operation caused the damage to plaintiff's property or whether, as defendant asserts, the damage resulted from faulty construction, it would be relevant to show that neighboring structures also were damaged at the time of the explosions in question.[1] Evidence of damage simultaneously occurring to a house adjacent to that of the plaintiff and constructed of similar materials has considerable probative value indicating that the explosion caused the damage to plaintiff's house. Quite obviously, evidence of damage to a structure composed of less substantial materials and located nearer to the site of the explosion is less convincing.

A further example: suppose *A* makes an oral lease with *B* in which the latter grants to *A* grazing rights for *A*'s livestock during the summer. Subsequently, a dispute develops regarding whether *B* reserved the right to graze a certain number of his cattle on the leased land.[2] The following evidence might be available:

(a) The parties had a similar lease during the two preceding summers for the same land, and *B* had reserved grazing rights.

(b) The parties had a lease the preceding summer involving different acreage and different terms (e.g., rent, watering rights, fence repair, etc.), but *B* had reserved grazing rights.

(c) *B* had, several years before, leased the same acreage to *X* and, in a lease similar to the present one with *A*, reserved grazing rights.

(d) *B* had seven leases (covering various tracts of land) during the present summer with a number of persons, including *A*. These leases varied in their terms, but in five of the lease arrangements, *B* had reserved grazing rights.

It is apparent that some of these evidentiary offerings are more persuasive than others. In the circumstances given, the

§ 2.3

1. See Poston v. Clarkson Const. Co., 401 S.W.2d 522 (Mo.App.1966); Annot., 45 A.L.R.2d 112 (1956).

2. See Firlotte v. Jessee, 76 Cal.App. 2d 207, 172 P.2d 710 (1946).

degree of relevance increases roughly in proportion to the similarity of conditions between the lease in question and the other executed leases. Other factors being equal, it is arguable that prior arrangements between *A* and *B* are more probative than arrangements that *B* may have made with third parties. A past agreement between the immediate parties is probative, to some extent, to show *A*'s willingness (or lack thereof) to agree to joint use of the property. Thus, evidence that the principal parties had entered into similar oral leases for the same land over a period of several years and that each lease contained a reservation of grazing rights clearly is probative that there was a reservation during the summer in question. Conversely, evidence indicating dissimilar circumstances (different land, different parties, different terms) has little or no tendency to persuade the trier that grazing rights were reserved. The point to be stressed is that an important aspect of proving one's case involves careful selection of the most probative evidence that can be offered to support a desired factual proposition.

Thus far, we have assumed that probative force depends upon variations in the evidential material used to support inferentially a desired proposition. It should be apparent, however, that the probative value of the *same* evidence may be stronger or weaker depending upon the proposition to which it is directed. Consider, for example, the exhibition of an infant to the jury in a paternity case, where the plaintiff seeks to display the infant to the trier for the purpose of establishing, by comparison of facial features, that the defendant is the father. If the child is quite young, this evidence is of doubtful probative force, at least in the absence of some distinctive inherited trait possessed by both the putative father and the infant. Suppose, however, that an issue in the case were the race of the infant. Directed toward the question of race, the exhibition of the child would be more persuasive.[3]

A leading evidence casebook[4] recites the Biblical story[5] of two women, who each claimed the same infant as her son. The king directed that the child be severed and that each claimant be given a half. One claimant assented to this solution, but the other pleaded with the king to spare the child and give it to her rival. Is the evidence (the reaction of the claimants) directed at the proposition that the litigant willing to give up the baby was the

3. See White v. Holderby, 192 F.2d 722 (5th Cir.1951) (involving school segregation).

4. Kaplan & Waltz at 66.

5. I Kings 3:16–28.

biological mother? Or is it directed at the proposition that the forfeiting claimant would be the "better parent," regardless of whether she was the biological mother? Arguably it is more probative of the latter proposition than the former.

To summarize, probative value can be increased or decreased by changing the evidence offered to establish a particular proposition; similarly, as the last examples show, probative force can be altered by changing the proposition to which the evidence is directed. Because evidence frequently supports more than one proposition of consequence, the proponent may have the opportunity to select the proposition for which the evidence is offered. Thus, careful assessment of probative value involves scrutiny both of the available evidence and of the related consequential factual propositions.

§ 2.4 The Assumptive * Admissibility of Relevant Evidence

Because by definition relevant evidence helps to prove a fact of consequence to the case, it could (but need not necessarily) follow "that unless excluded by some rule or principle of law, all [evidence] that is logically probative is admissible."[1] There are, as we have seen,[2] rules of exclusion, such as hearsay and privilege, that operate to disallow evidence that has probative value. Additionally, statutory enactments[3] or constitutional provisions[4] may render relevant evidence inadmissible. These various exclusionary provisions rest upon diverse grounds. But each rule of exclusion is thought to be supported by a reason or policy that justifies withholding from the trier probative testimony or documents. However, unless there is some specific basis for excluding relevant evidence, a basic principle—that of assumptive admissibility—

§ 2.4

* The word "assumptive" is used in place of the commonly encountered term "presumptive" because the latter term, when carefully used, refers to a prescribed effect that is accorded to evidence already admitted. See § 3.2.

1. Thayer, Preliminary Treatise on Evidence, 265 (1898).

2. See § 1.3.

3. For example, in suits for personal injury or death, Virginia bars defendants from introducing evidence of reimbursement of income to the plaintiff (or his decedent) from any source, no matter how relevant such payments may be to the court's calculation of lost income or compensatory damages. Va. Code 1977, § 8.01–35. Virginia also excludes admission of any testimony or documentary evidence prepared by state highway safety investigators who surveyed an accident that is the subject of litigation before the Court, presumably to assure that parties to such mishaps will be candid with safety researchers. Va.Code 1977, § 8.01–402.

4. Consider, for example, exclusion under the Fifth Amendment of self-incriminating statements that might be highly probative. See §§ 9.11–9.12.

dictates that such evidence be received.[5] For example, the Federal Rules of Evidence state:

> All relevant evidence is admissible, except as otherwise provided by the Constitution . . . by act of Congress [or] by these rules. . . . Evidence which is not relevant is not admissible.[6]

This provision makes clear that as a general rule relevant evidence is admissible, subject to such exceptions as may be declared by particular, contrary provisions.

In the chapters ahead, many of the specific exclusionary provisions will be considered in detail. We then shall see that most exclusionary rules, such as hearsay and privilege, apply to certain limited classes or types of evidence. There is, however, an exclusionary principle of general application that is applied to every item of relevant evidence. It is examined in the following section.

§ 2.5 Discretionary Exclusion Based on Considerations of Practical Policy

Every item of relevant evidence must be measured against several practical bases of exclusion. Thus, relevant evidence which assumptively is admissible will be rejected by the trial judge if he determines that the probative value of the evidence is substantially outweighed by considerations of prejudice, confusion of the issues, misleading the jury, undue consumption of time, or, possibly, unfair surprise. These policy considerations [1], founded on practical concerns, are counterweights to relevance, justifying

5. See Thayer, Preliminary Treatise on Evidence, 264–66 (1898):

> There is a principle—not so much a rule of evidence as a presumption involved in the very conception of a rational system of evidence . . . which forbids receiving anything irrelevant, not logically probative. . . .
>
> There is another precept . . .; namely, that unless excluded by some rule or principle of law, all that is logically probative is admissible. . . .
>
> In stating our two large fundamental conceptions, we must not fall into the error of supposing that relevancy, real or supposed, is the only test of admissibility. . . . Some things are rejected as being of too slight a significance, or as having too conjectural and remote a connection; others in being dangerous, in their effect upon the jury, and likely to be misused or overestimated by that body; others, as being impolitic, or unsafe on public grounds; others, on the bare ground of precedent.

6. Fed.R.Evid. 402.

§ 2.5

1. The same considerations underlie some of the specific exclusionary rules. See, e.g., §§ 5.1, 5.2, 5.4, 5.5, 5.12.

exclusion in instances where the probative benefit of the evidence significantly fails to outweigh the practical burdens of its admission.

The decision whether the probative value of the evidence outweighs one or more of the counterweights is made by the trial judge, usually after objection by counsel.[2] Appellate courts wisely have reposed in the trial court considerable discretion in applying this balancing test. Unless there is a clear abuse of this discretion, no error is committed.[3]

Chapter V deals with some specific recurring situations in which appellate courts, after an assessment of relevance and the applicable counterweights, have directed the trial court either to admit or to exclude particular items or types of evidence. These appellate pronouncements, which have hardened, more or less, into absolute rules, govern the trial judge's action in resolving certain recurring evidentiary issues. Nonetheless, many issues of relevance are not governed by such rules. These issues often arise in circumstances peculiar to the case being tried. Hence, questions involving evidence claimed by the proponent to be relevant and admissible are often resolved by the trial judge on an ad hoc basis. He first determines if the proffered evidence is relevant, and he then measures the probative value of the evidence against the practical reasons for exclusion.

The *Robinson* [4] case, discussed earlier,[5] illustrates the process. The accused in a bank robbery prosecution argued that evidence that he possessed a .38 caliber revolver when arrested should have been excluded because of its unfair prejudicial effect—that is, its likely tendency to distort the rational fact-finding process by unjustifiably arousing the trier's hostility. In the first trial, the presiding judge excluded this evidence and the jury "hung," with eight of twelve jurors favoring conviction. In the second trial, the judge admitted evidence of the accused's possession of the gun and, after long deliberation, the jury convicted Robinson. The issue on appeal was whether the trial judge had abused his discretion in admitting this evidence; the focus of the appellate court was upon whether the probative value of the evidence was overcome by its prejudicial effect. Federal Rule of Evidence 403 states:

2. See § 1.4.

3. See McCormick, § 185, at 546–47.

4. United States v. Robinson, 544 F.2d 611 (2d Cir.1976), rev'd en banc 560 F.2d 507 (2d Cir.1977), cert. denied 435 U.S. 905 (1978).

5. See § 2.2 at nn. 5–6 and accompanying text.

> Although relevant, evidence may be excluded if its probative value is substantially outweighed by the danger of unfair prejudice, confusion of the issues, or misleading the jury, or by considerations of undue delay, waste of time, or needless presentation of cumulative evidence.

Acknowledging that the trial judge has wide discretion in the application of this balancing process,[6] a panel of the Court of Appeals nonetheless held that the admission of the contested evidence was reversible error. The panel, which later was reversed on rehearing en banc, characterized as weak the required inferences: (1) that possession of a .38 caliber weapon at the time of arrest suggests that there also was possession at the time of the offense, and (2) that possession of a pistol of the same caliber as the weapon used by the bank robber suggests that the possessor was the robber. In weighing the probative force of the evidence against its prejudicial effect, the panel noted a serious risk that the evidence might cause the jury to rest its decision on an improper basis. An armed arrestee, singled out by the authorities for apprehension and, subsequently, for prosecution, is likely to be viewed by the jury as a person who would use his weapon for an illegal purpose. Thus, said the panel, there was a substantial risk that the trier would "conclude that the possessor of the gun is a dangerous person who ought to be segregated from society."[7] Because, in the panel's view, the evidence had little probative force toward a legitimate proposition (the identification of the accused) and a high potential for prejudice, it held that the trial judge erred in admitting it.[8]

6. 544 F.2d at 616.

7. Id. at 618–19.

8. The *Robinson* case should be contrasted with an earlier case in the same Circuit, also involving a bank robbery. In United States v. Ravich, 421 F.2d 1196, 1203–05 (2d Cir.1970), cert. denied, 400 U.S. 834 (1970), the accused and his codefendants were found in possession of six .38 caliber pistols, a box of .38 ammunition, and more than $95,000. The court upheld the admission of the guns as a proper exercise of the trial judge's discretion, even though the only evidence that any of these weapons were used in the robbery was "attenuated" and served to connect only three of the six weapons. The basis for sustaining the trial judge's exercise of discretion was that possession of the guns was "relevant to establish opportunity or preparation to commit the crime charged, and thus . . . tended to prove the identity of the robbers, the only real issue in this trial." Id. at 1204. See also United States v. McMillian, 535 F.2d 1035 (8th Cir.1976), cert. denied, 434 U.S. 1074 (1978); Walker v. United States, 490 F.2d 683 (8th Cir. 1974); United States v. McKinley, 485 F.2d 1059 (D.C.Cir.1973); United States v. Cunningham, 423 F.2d 1269 (4th Cir. 1970).

The reader may wish to reconsider the hypothetical posed at the outset of the chapter with a view to weighing the

In a subsequent opinion (following an en banc rehearing), the full court, with two judges dissenting, took a different view.[9] Emphasizing the broad discretion reposed in the trial judge, the court declared that when the trial judge has measured probative value against prejudice and the other practical counterweights, his decision on admissibility will not be disturbed absent a showing that he acted arbitrarily or irrationally. The court found that the evidence of possession at the time of arrest increased the probability that Robinson possessed the weapon on the day of the bank robbery—a factual proposition supported by the co-felon who testified against the accused. Further, if Robinson possessed a .38 caliber revolver at the time of the offense, this possession added to the probability that he was a participant in the robbery: it made it more likely (than it would be without the evidence) that he was engaged in criminal activity involving the same type of weapon. The court reinforced its conclusion that the contested evidence was relevant on the issue of identity by declaring that the evidence both corroborated the government's principal witness and, independently of that use, "tended to show that [Robinson] had the 'opportunity' to commit the bank robbery, since he had access to an instrument similar to that used to commit it." [10]

Note, however, that the corroborative effect of the evidence is dependent upon its probative value to establish identity. Furthermore, citing opportunity as an independent reason for admitting the evidence adds little to the relevance argument, at least under the facts of this case. The showing that Robinson had the opportunity to commit the crime simply increases the likelihood that he (as opposed to someone who did not possess a .38 caliber revolver) participated in its commission—a proposition that admittedly bears upon identity but is not separable from it.[11] In any event, the en banc court, noting that the trial judge had carefully assessed the possible prejudicial effect of the disputed evidence and had cautioned the jury not to draw unwarranted or prejudicial inferences, held that the lower court did not abuse its discretion.

probative value of evidence of an attempted escape from prison against its prejudicial impact.

9. United States v. Robinson, 560 F.2d 507 (2d Cir.1977), cert. denied, 435 U.S. 905 (1978) (en banc).

10. Id. at 513.

11. Id. at 520–21 (Oakes, J., dissenting).

Although the full court's narrow holding probably is justified, its opinion offers little guidance for future cases. Doubt remains as to the degree of convincing force necessary to sustain the inference that Robinson possessed a .38 caliber revolver on the day of the robbery. Suppose that the arrest had been made one year after the offense. Should the court admit evidence that the arrestee-accused possessed a revolver of similar caliber? Note the ultimate inference that the trier is asked to draw: the accused's possession, on the day of the robbery, of a gun having the same caliber as a gun used in committing the offense *increases somewhat* the probability that the accused was the offender. The ultimate inference cannot be made, however, unless the trier first believes that the accused possessed such a gun at the time of the offense. Possession of a similar weapon immediately after the offense is much more likely to sustain such a belief than possession one year thereafter. Of course, evidence of possession at the later time (one year) might, in combination with other evidence (such as the accused's remark that he had long owned a .38 caliber pistol) sustain the conclusion that the accused possessed the gun at the time of the offense.

The *Robinson* opinion is also somewhat equivocal as to the effect, if any, that might come from other evidence (aside from the gun) of participation in the offense charged.[12] For example, if bank photographs taken during the robbery and eyewitnesses to the offense convincingly showed that Robinson was a participant, would evidence of the gun still be admitted? Here the degree to which evidence of possession would alter the jury's conclusion about the probability of Robinson's participation is slight; the potential for prejudicial influence, however, is not abated. Hence, the existence of other evidence probably strengthens the argument for rejecting evidence that the accused possessed a weapon similar to that used by one of the robbers.

Of course, it could be argued that when the prosecution's case is weak, special care should be taken to bar prejudicial evidence, since the jury's prejudice could be decisive in the outcome of the case. The courts have not always been consistent in assessing the effect of other evidence upon the admission of an item of evidence characterized by doubtful probative force and a potential for prejudice. The *Robinson* majority asserted that the presence or absence of other evidence is of no consequence to the ruling on the

12. Id.

contested evidence.[13] However, some courts tend to view the existence of other evidence as reducing the need (and, in a sense, the probative contribution) of the contested evidence, so that the general effect of other evidence is to influence the judge to exclude the controverted item.[14] In any event, it is clear that in the absence of a serious abuse of discretion by the trial judge, appellate courts are hesitant to disturb a trial court ruling that weighs probative value against prejudicial effect.[15]

Although the *Robinson* court was concerned with the prejudicial effect of relevant evidence, other reported cases contain many examples of the application of the additional practical reasons for the exclusion of relevant evidence.[16] In an action against a manufacturer for damages to plaintiff's farm resulting from fumes, considerations of time consumption and jury confusion justified the rejection of evidence concerning the condition of other agricultural lands twenty miles away; [17] in a prosecution for tax evasion, distraction and confusion of the jury were sufficient reasons to reject complicated exhibits from civil litigation relating to the funds in question; [18] in a complicated antitrust case, the probability of cumulative evidence, jury confusion, and wasted time caused the judge to limit the period during which each side could present its case in chief; [19] and finally, unfair prejudice was a valid reason to reject evidence of a wife's infidelity (offered to show her ill will toward the husband-victim in the murder prose-

13. Id. at 516 n. 11.

14. For a trial court decision that discusses thoroughly the process of balancing the need for certain evidence against its possible prejudicial effect, see United States v. Jackson, 405 F.Supp. 938, 942–45 (E.D.N.Y.1975). See also Adv.Comm.Note to Fed.R.Evid. 403; 2 Louisell & Mueller, § 126, at 26–27; Dolan, Rule 403: The Prejudice Rule in Evidence, 49 So.Cal.L.Rev. 220, 250–54.

15. 1 Weinstein & Berger, ¶ 403[03], at 29–57.

16. See generally McCormick, § 185, at 545–47; IA Wigmore, § 29a, at 979–980 (Tillers), and additional sections cited therein (note, however, that Wigmore also discusses situations in which a fixed rule dictates exclusion). For a federal case that applies the balancing test, see United States v. Cook, 538 F.2d 1000 (3d Cir.1976).

17. Thompson v. American Steel & Wire Co., 317 Pa. 7, 175 A. 541 (1934). See also Skogen v. Dow Chemical Co., 375 F.2d 692, 705–06 (8th Cir.1967) (products liability trial was long, and testimony of another expert witness in rebuttal would have been cumulative); Bunn v. Caterpillar Tractor Co., 415 F.Supp. 286 (W.D.Pa.1976), aff'd, 556 F.2d 564 (3d Cir.1977) (judge finds that to admit all of P's evidence would be too time consuming).

18. United States v. Pollock, 394 F.2d 922 (7th Cir.), cert. denied, 393 U.S. 924 (1968).

19. MCI Communications Corp. v. AT & T, 708 F.2d 1081, 1170–71 (7th Cir.1983), cert. denied, 464 U.S. 891 (1983).

cution of the wife) when the infidelities occurred months before the offense.[20]

Federal Rule of Evidence 403, set forth above, generally accords with the common-law rule as developed in most federal and state cases.[21] Two points, however, should be noted. If the balance is close between probative force and one or more counterweights, the federal rule favors admissibility.[22] That is, it provides for exclusion only if one or more practical reasons for rejection "substantially" outweigh probative value. Further, the federal rule, in contrast to some state provisions and common law cases,[23] does not include unfair surprise as a basis for rejecting relevant evidence. This omission represents a judgment that in cases where surprise occurs, a continuance, rather than exclusion of the evidence, is the preferred remedy.[24]

§ 2.6 Conditional Relevancy

It now should be apparent that the test of relevancy is infinitely less stringent than the tests to determine whether the totality of the evidence is *sufficient* to justify a finding for the party who must prove the affirmative—ordinarily the government in a criminal case and the plaintiff in a civil case. The measures of sufficiency are, in a criminal prosecution, proof beyond a reasonable doubt and, in a typical civil trial, proof by a preponderance[1] of the evidence. These standards mean that the total

20. State v. Flett, 234 Or. 124, 127–28, 380 P.2d 634, 636 (1963) (however, evidence of illicit sexual acts nearer in time to the alleged killing was held properly admitted).

21. Adv.Comm.Note to Fed.R.Evid. 403. Exclusion of relevant evidence under Federal Rule 403 on the ground of prejudice is considered extensively in Dolan, Rule 403: The Prejudice Rule in Evidence, 49 S.Cal.L.Rev. 220 (1976).

22. The common law cases do not usually make clear this choice, for they often speak in terms of probative force being only "outweighed" by the various counterweights. See generally Maguire, Evidence, Common Sense and Common Law, 201–03 (1947). Alaska's Rule 403 does not include the requirement that probative force be "substantially" outweighed, thus allowing exclusion of evidence with a prejudicial or other adverse effect only slightly greater than its probative value. Alaska R.Evid. 403 and Commentary.

23. McCormick, § 185, at 545 n. 27.

24. Adv.Comm.Note to Fed.R.Evid. 403.

§ 2.6

1. The word "preponderance" does not mean a greater quantity of evidence, but rather refers to the probative (convincing) force of the evidence. In general, the preponderance standard is met if the evidence would reasonably justify a finding that the existence of the facts necessary to sustain the party with the affirmative burden of persuasion is more likely than their nonexistence. F. James & G. Hazard, Civil Procedure, § 7.6, at 316–17 (3d ed. 1985). A more demanding standard of proof is required in certain civil cases.

evidence must be sufficiently probative to permit a rational trier to find that the party bringing the action (or, specifically, the party with the burden of persuasion) has established his facts to the required degree of probability. If he were required to show that every item of evidence makes the proposition to which it is directed more likely than not (or likely beyond a reasonable doubt), the introduction of evidence would be restricted severely. As McCormick notes, "a brick is not a wall";[2] the question at the conclusion of the case is whether all items of evidence *taken together* meet the applicable standard.

Sometimes, however, the preponderance test, which imposes a "more-probable-than-not" standard,[3] applies to a *single* item of evidence. This more demanding standard applies whenever the existence of one fact, *A*, conditions (is necessary for) the relevance of evidence of an allied fact, *B*. Put conversely, the relevance of allied fact *B* is dependent (conditioned) upon the existence of underlying fact *A*. In this circumstance, it is necessary to provide sufficient evidence of fact *A* to enable the trier to use the evidence of fact *B* for a consequential purpose.

Relevance is conditioned upon the existence of an underlying fact in the following illustrative situations: (1) On the issue whether *X* committed suicide, the proponent offers a page from a diary, alleged to be the diary of *X*, which reflects that the writer was mentally depressed (fact *B*). Mental depression is probative of suicide, but the trier cannot consider the diary as evidence of *X*'s depression (and hence, by further inference, of suicide) unless it finds that *X* made the diary entry (fact *A*);[4] (2) On the issue whether *X* drove negligently at the point of an automobile collision (a curve in the highway), the proponent offers evidence that a black sedan of American manufacture was traveling at a high rate of speed one half mile from the curve (fact *B*). This increases the likelihood that the car was speeding at the curve, but the trier can not consider the evidence unless it finds that *X* was the driver of the black sedan (fact *A*); (3) On the issue whether *X* assumed the risk of flying a private plane with a mechanical defect, the proponent offers evidence that an aircraft mechanic stated to several persons that the defect existed (fact *B*). The trier cannot

For example, some jurisdictions require that fraud must be established by clear and convincing evidence.

2. McCormick, § 185, at 543.

3. See supra n. 1; see § 3.1 at n. 3.

4. For a federal case applying the conditional relevance rule to a document, see In re James E. Long Const. Co., 557 F.2d 1039 (4th Cir.1977).

use this evidence to find that *X* assumed the risk unless it finds that *X* overheard or had knowledge of the mechanic's statement (fact *A*); (4) On the issue whether *X* killed *V* with a knife, the proponent offers evidence that gloves found in a garbage container near *X*'s apartment were stained with blood of the same type as *V*'s. The trier cannot use the evidence to increase the probability that *X* was the killer (fact *B*) unless it finds that *X* wore the gloves (fact *A1*) *and* that the blood on the gloves is in fact *V*'s (fact *A2*) and not that of some other person with the same blood type.

In all of the foregoing situations, the application of the basic test of relevance, which inquires whether the evidence has some probative force, is dependent or conditioned upon a conclusion that an underlying fact exists. The judge must ensure that there is sufficient evidence upon which the jury can find that the existence of the underlying fact is more probable than its nonexistence. Federal Rule 104 states in part:

> (b) Relevancy conditioned on fact. When the relevancy of evidence depends upon the fulfillment of a condition of fact, the court shall admit it upon, or subject to, the introduction of evidence sufficient to support a finding of the fulfillment of the condition.

The rule recognizes the practical accommodation that must accompany the receipt of evidence conditioned upon the existence of an underlying fact. In the strict sense, evidence of the underlying fact (e.g., that *X* inscribed the diary page) is not relevant without the associated conditioned evidence (that the writer was depressed) and vice-versa.[5] The judge determines whether the proponent's order of presentation is satisfactory and, under federal as well as common-law practice, he may permit the proponent first to introduce either evidence of the underlying (conditioning) fact or evidence of the conditioned fact. However, unless circumstances make it clear that the connecting evidence will be forthcoming, the judge should seek assurances from the proponent that he has the linking evidence and that it is in an admissible form. The proponent's subsequent failure to connect the admitted evidence with sufficient evidence of the underlying fact dictates that the

5. Morgan & Weinstein at 39. For a federal case presenting a problem of conditional relevance, see United States v. Campion, 560 F.2d 751 (6th Cir.1977) (papers reflecting payment to some person for relaying results of races cannot be used to implicate accused in illegal gambling because evidence is insufficient that accused was the person designated in the papers). The court in *Campion* cites only Fed.R.Evid. 402, but Rule 104(b) is also apposite.

judge strike evidence of the conditioned fact from the record and instruct the jury to disregard it. Because the possible relevance of the conditioned fact often is apparent to the jury, there is a risk of improper influence from exposure to the stricken evidence. For example, if the jury hears evidence that a black sedan was speeding, it may be influenced by this evidence even though the evidence subsequently is struck because the judge concludes that the evidence that *X* was driving is insufficient to support a finding that he was the operator. This risk of improper influence is most acute when there is *some* properly admitted evidence to suggest that *X* drove the speeding black sedan. Despite the proponent's failure satisfactorily to "connect up" his evidence by meeting the sufficiency test, the jury may conclude that *X* was driving the speeding vehicle. If the jury is erroneously exposed to evidence that might have a large impact on a central issue, an instruction from the judge to disregard the evidence may not suffice; he may have to declare a mistrial.[6]

§ 2.7 Circumstantial and Direct Evidence

Whether evidence is characterized as circumstantial or as direct turns upon whether or not the evidence requires the trier to reach the ultimate factual proposition to which the evidence is addressed by a process of inference. Testimony that the accused was seen in possession of the instrument used in a criminal assault is circumstantial evidence that he was the assailant; testimony that he was seen making the attack is direct evidence that he was the assailant. Observe that even though testimony relating to the defendant's possession of an instrument is *direct* evidence of the proposition that he possessed the object, it is *circumstantial* evidence of the ultimate proposition that he was the assailant. The relationship of the evidence to the *ultimate* factual proposition it supports determines its character; that is, if the evidence ultimately is directed toward an inferred fact, it is circumstantial, even though it is directly supportive of the initial proposition from which inferences are to be drawn.

When direct evidence of a consequential proposition is presented (as, for example, when a witness testifies that he saw *D* attack *V*), the trier is concerned solely with whether to believe the witness. But when circumstantial evidence is introduced (as, for

6. United States v. Vinson, 606 F.2d 149 (6th Cir.1979), cert. denied, 445 U.S. 904 (1980).

example, when a witness testifies that *D* fled the scene of the assault), the trier not only must be concerned with whether to believe the witness, but also with whether the evidence increases the probability of the proposition to which it is directed (that *D* was the assailant). It will also be observed that whether evidence is direct or circumstantial determines the degree of analysis necessary for the judge to resolve issues of relevance. Where direct evidence is offered, the judge need only inquire whether the factual proposition to which the evidence relates is consequential. When circumstantial evidence is offered, the judge must determine whether the ultimate proposition to which the evidence is directed is consequential *and* whether the evidence affects the probability of the existence of that proposition. This additional step should not, however, be taken as an indication that circumstantial evidence is intrinsically inferior (less probative) than direct evidence. Suppose, for example, *D* is accused of breaking into *V*'s apartment in the nighttime and stealing a diamond brooch. He denies the offense and claims that he was in another city on the night of the crime, but his fingerprints are found on *V*'s windowsill and jewelry box. This circumstantial evidence may be more convincing than testimony by *V*'s husband that he saw *D* take the brooch, particularly if the lighting were bad, the time for observation fleeting, or *D*'s physical or facial features partially obscured.[1] The probative force of both circumstantial and direct evidence is determined by the particular evidence presented and the surrounding circumstances, not by its formal classification.

Notes

1. *The Counterweight of Time Consumption.* Although undue time consumption may warrant the trial judge's rejection of relevant evidence, there is little point in making an appellate issue of his admission of time-consuming evidence. The time lost obviously cannot be recaptured, and appellate argument on the point represents an additional drain on judicial resources.

2. *Prejudice as a Basis of Exclusion.* All jurisdictions recognize that relevant evidence may be excluded if its probative force is overcome by its prejudicial effect. It is important to note, however, that "prejudice" does not refer simply to the fact that the evidence is very damaging to the party opposing it. Evidence is prejudicial only

§ 2.7

1. For a good discussion of possible distinctions between circumstantial and direct evidence, see Carlson, et al. at 140–42.

if it distorts the rational fact-finding process, as, for example, by misleading or inflaming the jury. See Adv.Comm.Notes to Fed.R. Evid. 403; Ballou v. Henri Studios, Inc., 656 F.2d 1147 (5th Cir.1981).

3. *Judge's Role: Evidentiary Issues.* Note that with regard to questions of relevance, the judge is acting as a monitor of the evidence. He ensures that a reasonable trier could find the evidence probative and, in the case of conditional relevance, that the trier could find the existence of the underlying fact. However, where the application of an exclusionary rule of evidence (including the competence of a witness) requires a factual resolution, the judge actually determines the facts. His role in this regard is treated in detail in Chapter X. Major disadvantages would attend the practice of having the jury decide the facts pertinent to the application of an exclusionary rule of evidence. Such a practice would unduly burden the jury with numerous "subsets" of fact-finding determinations that involve the admissibility of evidence. Further, many of the exclusionary rules are founded in whole or in part on policy considerations that would not be understood or appreciated by the jury. This unappreciated policy basis adds to the risk that the jury would be influenced improperly by exposure to evidence that, in accordance with the judge's instructions, it later determined was inadmissible. Federal Rule of Evidence 104 provides in part:

> (a) Questions of Admissibility Generally. Preliminary questions concerning the qualification of a person to be a witness, the existence of a privilege, or the admissibility of evidence shall be determined by the court. . . .

4. *Relevance; Materiality.* Examine the following passage, noting particularly the sense in which "relevant" is used:

> Unfortunately, . . . theoretical and practical difficulties surround the very concept of the "facts of the case" and these blur any distinctions that may be drawn between the material truth on the one hand, and the truth according to the allegations of the parties, on the other. It is common for lawyers and others to speak and write of "the facts of a case" as if this phrase conveyed a simple meaning, but as soon as it is qualified by the addition of the essential word "relevant," so as to make the phrase read "the relevant facts of the case," its apparent simplicity disappears. In the context of civil litigation, "relevant" must mean relevant for the resolution of the dispute in accordance with the law, and the test of relevancy is thus the law itself. It is, however, impossible to know what principles of law are applicable in a given case unless the relevant facts are known, and the argument thus proceeds in a circle.

M. Cappelletti & J. Jolowicz, Public Interest Parties and the Active Role of the Judge in Civil Litigation 254 (1975). How, as a practical matter, can one deal with the dilemma posed by the authors? Consider Rule 15 of the Federal Rules of Civil Procedure that provides for amendments to the pleadings. With leave of court, amendments may be made late in the trial, even after judgment has been entered.

The reader who is familiar with trials probably will agree that many disputes about relevance center upon the materiality or consequentialness of the proponent's proposition of fact. It is quite likely that he has correctly perceived the existence of a probative relationship between his evidence and the proposition of fact that it is offered to support. Often, the problem is how that proposition relates to the governing substantive law.

5. *Legal Relevance.* A few courts and commentators use the term "legal relevance" to characterize evidence that has sufficient probative force to overcome any counterweights to admission, such as prejudice, confusion, or delay. This term, then, simply describes evidence that passes the balancing test because probative value is not substantially outweighed by practical concerns. See Carlson, et al. at 237–38.

6. *The Distracting Charm of Irrelevance.* Trials, which are practical affairs, often do not strictly adhere to admissibility (or exclusion) as prescribed by the rules of evidence. For example, experienced practitioners often refrain from objecting to irrelevant evidence for fear of appearing obstructive to the jury. As a result, juries, while attempting to apply complicated instructions from the judge, may find themselves swayed by reactions to details wholly irrelevant to any legal issue. Consider Judge Bok's example:

> Irrelevance can be highly enlightening. The witness who starts with what she ate for breakfast and remembers it was Thursday because her husband's sister came down with the measles when she shouldn't if she had only gone to the doctor, the one with glasses—should be a delight to the judge's heart and make the jury feel at home. Behind this leisurely sweep of incident they can follow her as they please, and it will give them at least her barometric pressure at the time when she signed the note at the bank without reading it. After listening to enough of it, any idiot would know that she was an accommodation endorser who had done it to help her husband and had got nothing out of it herself. . . .

Bok, I Too, Nicodemus 322 (1946).

7. *Conditional Relevance.* Does United States v. Robinson, discussed in §§ 2.2 and 2.5, involve a problem of conditional relevance?

Chapter III

PROCEDURAL CONCEPTS AND CONSEQUENCES

§ 3.1 Burdens of Persuasion and Production

We have seen that a judicial trial employs the principles of party presentation and persuasion, but places the responsibility for dispute resolution in the hands of neutral participants—the judge and jury. In a jury trial, the judge instructs or "charges" the jury concerning the elements of a claim or defense and directs them, first, to ascertain the historical (adjudicative) facts from the evidence, and, then, by applying the law as described in the charge, to determine whether the claim or defense is established. For example, the judge may instruct the jury that slander consists of a defamatory statement [which would be further defined], that was communicated or "published" to one other than the person allegedly defamed, and that caused the defamed person to sustain pecuniary damage or harm to reputation. Depending upon what defenses are asserted, the judge also may instruct the jury that if they find that the statement is true or that it is privileged [which would be further explained], there is no liability. Of course, in a nonjury trial, the judge alone determines the historical facts and applies the governing legal principles—that is, he alone determines the existence or nonexistence of the elements.

In both judge and jury trials, there is a need to specify the consequences of the trier's determination that all (or alternatively only some) of the elements of a claim or defense are satisfactorily proved. This specification takes the form of allocating to the plaintiff and defendant their respective obligations with regard to proving the elements of a claim or defense. Thus, in a civil trial for slander the judge should make it clear to the jury that the plaintiff, if he is to recover, must convince them of the existence of all of the elements of slander: the defamatory statement, its publication, and the resulting damage or harm. The assertion of certain defenses (called "affirmative" defenses) requires additional instructions that make it clear that as to these defenses the defendant has the responsibility of proof. For example, if the defendant pleads the affirmative defense of truth, the judge will charge the jury that *if the defendant* convinces them that the defamatory statement is true, he is not liable.

This allocation of the responsibility for proof is not made on an ad hoc basis, but in accordance with precedent or statutory provisions. In most instances, especially in civil cases, a party is obligated to plead those elements for which he bears the responsibility of proof. A number of considerations influence the rules allocating the burden of proof, such as which party seeks to have the court alter the status quo, whether one party alleges an event that appears improbable, whether any social or public policy militates for or against recovery, and whether certain evidence is available more readily to one party than to the other.[1]

It is no simple matter to predict which of these factors may be dominant, but it is relatively easy to ascertain from statute or precedent the allocative rules of a particular jurisdiction. The rules loosely are spoken of as governing the "burden of proof"; the more precise phrase is "burden of persuasion" (or, alternatively, "the risk of nonpersuasion"), because it connotes that the party with the responsibility for particular elements has the burden of persuading (or bears the risk of not persuading) the trier that each of these particular elements exists.[2] The burdened party must persuade the trier of the existence of these elements according to a standard or degree of certainty mandated by the type of proceeding: in a criminal trial, the government must prove the elements of an offense beyond a reasonable doubt; in a typical civil case, a party must prove the elements of his claim by a preponderance of the evidence (sometimes expressed by the phrases "greater weight of the evidence" or "more probable than not").[3] There also are

§ 3.1

1. For a discussion of these and other factors, see F. James & G. Hazard, Civil Procedure, § 7.8 (3d ed. 1985).

2. The phrase "burden of proof" often has been used to refer to two separate and distinct responsibilities of the parties: the "burden of persuasion" and the "burden of production." Id., § 7.8. The distinction between these two responsibilities is discussed in this section.

3. McCormick, §§ 339, 341, at 957, 962. In criminal cases, an accused may

intermediate standards, such as "clear and convincing" proof,[4] that apply in particular kinds of civil cases or to particular elements within them. For example, where a party claims that his opponent engaged in fraudulent conduct, he may be required to prove the elements of fraud by clear and convincing evidence.[5]

These standards are intended to indicate the convincing force of the evidence required to meet the burden of persuasion, not quantitatively to measure the evidence.[6] A defendant who presents five witnesses will not always prevail over a plaintiff who presents one. What is important is the factfinder's belief in the existence or nonexistence of the disputed elements. Believability is not necessarily a function of the number of witnesses or quantity of evidence presented.[7]

The diagrammatic framework below illustrates an allocation of the burdens of persuasion to the respective parties for the various elements of the foregoing defamation case. To establish the framework for a particular case, one must know or assume the elements of the claims or defenses asserted. Here, assume the plaintiff must plead and prove three elements by a preponderance of the evidence: the existence of the defamatory statement [A], the communication or publication to a third party [B], and the resulting damage (or harm) [C]. Assume that the defendant denies that

be assigned the burden of persuading the trier of the existence of certain affirmative defenses by a preponderance of the evidence. See Patterson v. New York, 432 U.S. 197 (1977). However, there are some limits upon the state's power to allocate a burden of persuasion to the accused. In re Winship, 397 U.S. 358 (1970), held that the prosecutor was obliged to prove beyond a reasonable doubt each element or fact necessary to constitute the crime charged. *Winship,* as applied in Mullaney v. Wilbur, 421 U.S. 684 (1975), was construed to prohibit Maine from assigning to the accused the burden of proving provocation. The case turned, however, on the fine distinction that Maine viewed provocation as simply a means of disproving "malice aforethought"—an essential element of the offense charged. See Patterson, 432 U.S. at 215–16. Thus, it appears that a state retains considerable latitude to place upon the accused the burden of persuasion for specified defenses. However, care must be taken to define the defense (or perhaps the criminal offense itself) so that it does not negate or rebut an essential element of the crime charged. This distinction has been the subject of considerable debate. See generally McCormick, § 348, at 998 n. 4 (and articles cited therein). See also § 3.5.

4. The phrasing of an intermediate standard varies from state to state, but it generally includes the terms "clear" and "convincing." See McCormick, § 340, at 959–60.

5. The clear and convincing standard also applies to the impeachment (contradiction) of a notary's seal of acknowledgment. For other examples, see Id. at 960–61; IX Wigmore, § 2498, at 424–31 (Chadbourn).

6. James & Hazard, supra n. 1, § 7.6, at 316.

7. Id.

he made the statement and pleads, as a second defense [D], that the alleged defamatory statement is true. The latter defense traditionally is an affirmative one,[8] and the defendant normally bears the burden of persuading the factfinder that the statement is true.[9] Thus, each party has an affirmative responsibility of proof, although the defendant will prevail if either the plaintiff fails to persuade the trier of the existence of elements A, B, and C or the defendant does persuade the trier that the alleged statement is true (element D).

Because the jury resolves only those questions that reasonably can be disputed, the plaintiff, as a first step, must offer evidence sufficient to allow jury consideration of the existence of each element.[10] That evidence must be at least adequate to permit a reasonable jury, viewing it most favorably to the plaintiff, to find that the existence of the essential elements is more probable than their nonexistence. In the diagram below, the evidence at a minimum must justify the jury resolution signified by block II. If evidence pertaining to one or more elements is insufficient to raise a jury question (that is, insufficient to move all elements in the plaintiff's case to block II), the judge, on proper motion, will direct a verdict against the plaintiff on the ground that he failed to produce sufficient evidence to support his case. Put otherwise, if plaintiff's evidence has failed to create a *reasonable* dispute as to one or more elements, the case is resolved by the judge (block I).

Plaintiff's Elements	**Existence of Element Reasonably Disputable**	**Defendant's Element**
I	II	III
[Judge Resolution in Favor of D] A (defamatory statement) B (publication) C (damage or harm)	[Jury Resolution Based on the Evidence]	[Judge Resolution in Favor of P] D (truth)

8. A defendant generally must *plead* such a defense affirmatively. A mere denial of the plaintiff's allegations is not sufficient to raise an affirmative defense. Id., § 4.5, at 196.

9. W. Prosser & W. Keeton, The Law of Torts, § 116, at 839 (5th ed. 1984).

10. James & Hazard, supra n. 1, §§ 3.14, 7.11, at 162–63, 339.

Thus, ultimately to meet his burden of persuasion, the plaintiff must first satisfy the essential preliminary requirement of producing evidence sufficient to move all the elements necessary to his recovery from block I (resolution by the judge) to block II (resolution by the jury). Unless his opponent has conceded the existence of one or more elements,[11] the plaintiff begins this process of proof by producing evidence to support each element. This burden of coming forward with the evidence needed to avoid an adverse resolution by the judge is called the *burden of producing evidence* (or "burden of production"). It is a responsibility distinct from the burden of persuasion—the *ultimate* burden of *convincing* the factfinder of the existence of the essential elements of a claim or defense. However, by meeting the immediate responsibility imposed by the burden of production, the plaintiff avoids a directed verdict and moves the dispute at least as far as block II. In short, he paves the way toward meeting his second and greater burden, that of persuasion.

Of course, the plaintiff, if he can, will present evidence so convincing on one or more elements that no reasonable jury could find against him. Absent persuasive rebuttal evidence by the defendant on elements so established, there would be a judge resolution (block III) *in favor* of the plaintiff. The judge either would enter a directed verdict for the plaintiff (if all elements indisputably were present) or would take from jury consideration, through a peremptory instruction, those elements that indisputably were proven. If the plaintiff, during his case in chief, were able to produce evidence of such convincing force that the existence of all the necessary elements was indisputable, the state of the evidence would be reflected as follows:

11. The element might be conceded, for example, in the pleadings, by stipulation, or by an admission made during discovery. Furthermore, if the facts constituting a particular element were judicially noticed, no production of evidence would be necessary. See § 1.8.

Plaintiff's Elements	Existence of Element Reasonably Disputable	Defendant's Element(s)
I	II	III
[Judge Resolution]	[Jury Resolution]	[Judge Resolution]
A (defamatory statement) →	→	→ A
B (publication) →	→	→ B
C (damage or harm) →	→	→ C
		D (truth)

Before the judge resolves the presence of any or all elements in plaintiff's favor, however, he must give the defendant the opportunity to rebut plaintiff's evidence. The depicted state of the evidence, therefore, requires that the defendant take steps toward rebuttal or else face a directed verdict. The burden of *producing evidence now has shifted to the defendant,* although the burden of persuasion has remained fixed upon the plaintiff. Because the plaintiff must show the existence of all three elements in order to recover, the defendant can avoid a directed verdict (that is, he can meet the shifted burden of production) by rebutting at least one element so that he raises a jury question as to that element.[12]

Ideally, the defendant strives to present evidence of such convincing force that one or more elements would be resolved in his favor by the judge (block I of diagram), thus entitling him to a directed verdict. If the defendant were thus successful, the burden of production on the element(s) in block I would shift to the plaintiff, who would attempt to produce sufficient rebuttal evidence to move the issue of the existence of the element(s) back into block II. As a practical matter, however, multiple shifts in the burden of production are unusual because it is not often that the state of the evidence fluctuates back and forth between the extremes represented by blocks I and III; more frequently the determination of whether an element exists depends upon a jury assessment of credibility (block II).

12. As to those elements not rebutted (i.e., not moved out of block III by the defendant), the judge will give a peremptory instruction that these elements shall be taken as established.

The defendant, of course, is not limited to evidence that negates the plaintiff's evidence concerning elements A, B, and C. He also can avoid liability by establishing the affirmative defense of truth. To do so, he must first meet his burden of production by providing sufficient evidence of the truth of his statement to raise a jury question (that is, to move element D into block II). If the evidence of truth were highly convincing, thus moving the affirmative defense to block I, the defendant could shift the burden of production for this element to the plaintiff. Note, however, that the burden of *persuasion* on the element of truth would not shift to the plaintiff, but would remain fixed upon the defendant, where it was originally allocated.

Various assumptions about the state of the evidence, including the allocation of the burdens of production and persuasion, can be depicted in the diagram. Suppose, for example, that *at the conclusion* of the case, the following state of the evidence exists:

Plaintiff's Elements	**Existence of Element Reasonably Disputable**	**Defendant's Element(s)**
I	II	III
[Judge Resolution]	[Jury Resolution]	[Judge Resolution]
A (defamatory statement) ———	———————	———→ A
B (publication) ———	———————	———→ B
C (damage or harm) ———	———→ C	
	D ←———	——— D (truth)

The judge would instruct the jury that it shall take as an established fact that the defendant uttered (published) a slanderous statement to a third person (elements A and B). Jury questions exist, however, as to whether damage or harm was incurred (element C) and as to whether the statement was true (element D). Regarding these reasonably disputed elements, both plaintiff and defendant have discharged their respective *burdens of production* and must now meet their *burdens of persuasion.* Accordingly, it is necessary to instruct the jury that the plaintiff has the burden of persuasion on the element of damage or harm and the defendant has the burden of persuasion on the element of truth. If the jury does not believe that damage or harm occurred, it will render a defendant's verdict. If it finds (by a preponderance of the evidence) that there was damage or harm and if it is not persuaded by the defendant that the statement was true, it will return a verdict for the plaintiff. On the other hand, if the jury is persuaded that the statement was true, it will return a defendant's verdict regardless of whether the plaintiff sustained damage or harm.

Suppose, however, that the jury is in a state of indecision or equipoise regarding the issue of damage (harm) or truth.[13] When the jury agrees that the probabilities of the existence or nonexistence of an element are equal, the *allocation of the burden of persuasion becomes decisive in determining who prevails.* Because the party to whom that burden is allocated has failed to convince the jury affirmatively of the existence of the element(s) for which he is responsible, that party has not discharged his burden of persuasion and the jury, in obedience to proper instructions from the court, should find against him. Thus, if the jury concludes that it is equally likely that plaintiff did or did not suffer damage (or harm) from the alleged defamatory statement, the plaintiff loses. He has failed to meet his burden of persuading the jury that it is more likely than not that he sustained a loss. Correspondingly, if the jury believes that the probabilities of the truth or falsity of the defamatory statement are equal, the defendant has failed to carry his burden of persuasion on the affirmative defense.

As noted earlier, the substantive law dictates what elements constitute a civil or criminal offense and what element(s) comprise an affirmative defense. It is usually easy to determine which party bears the ultimate responsibility of proving by a preponderance of the evidence his claim or defense. Whether a party who has met his burden of producing sufficient evidence (by moving his case to block II) has also met his burden of persuasion depends simply upon whether the trier, at the conclusion of the case, is

13. The problem of a jury in a state of decisional balance can arise regarding the existence of any element of a claim or defense that, because of the state of the evidence, is the proper subject of jury resolution. As to any element in block II, the jury may conclude that the probability of the existence of the element is equal to the probability of its nonexistence. Of course, if the judge is the factfinder—that is, there is no jury—the judge also resolves disputed issues of fact in accordance with the allocation of the burden of persuasion. Note again that in the illustration in the text, the defendant prevails if either the plaintiff fails to carry his burden of persuasion on all essential elements or the defendant carries his burden of persuasion on the element of truth.

persuaded by the evidence favoring that party. In a jury trial, the verdict will signify the trier's determination of whether or not a party has carried his burden. Of course, a general verdict ("We find for the defendant") may not be completely informative about which party discharged his burden of persuasion. If the defendant has denied the plaintiff's allegations supporting a recovery and also has offered an affirmative defense (e.g., truth), a verdict for the defendant can mean either that the plaintiff failed to carry his burden or that the defendant successfully carried his burden. In a trial to the judge, there is usually a more explicit indication in the record (often contained in an opinion, memorandum, or statement of findings) disclosing the basis upon which a judgment is given.

The section that follows will explore the effects of a presumption upon the burden of persuasion and the burden of production. A true presumption always affects the burden of production, but in most jurisdictions a presumption does not, generally speaking, affect the burden of persuasion.

§ 3.2 Presumptions: General Nature and Effect

A trial involves many instances in which the trier of fact makes a factual determination by a process of inference. The factfinder first accepts the existence of a certain fact or set of facts and then infers the existence of a related fact or facts. Human experience yields countless situations in which a fact or group of facts, if believed to exist, can by the process of inferential reasoning lead to a related factual conclusion. For example, if there is evidence that a letter was addressed properly and thereafter posted, it may be inferred that the addressee received the letter. As further examples: if a vehicle is labeled with the name of a person or company, it may be inferred that the name is that of the owner; if a person cannot be found and neither family nor acquaintances have heard from him for many years, it may be inferred that he is dead.[1] In each of these situations certain *basic* facts (proper mailing, name on vehicle, absence without word) support a finding of the *inferred* facts (receipt, ownership, death).

Although the number and variety of basic facts that can lead to inferential conclusions are countless, certain patterns, such as those found in the foregoing illustrations, frequently recur. The courts and legislatures have singled out many sets of basic and

§ 3.2

1. For further examples, see § 3.3.

inferred facts such as mailing-receipt, absence-death, labeling-ownership, and have given to them the status of presumptions. In many of these recurring instances, there appears to be a strong likelihood of the existence of the inferred or, more accurately, *presumed* conclusion. In other instances, the probative force of the basic facts may not be so convincing, yet some policy rationale or procedural convenience may make the presumed conclusion desirable. Thus, when an article is found to be damaged after having been transported by more than one carrier, a presumption is raised that the last carrier caused the damage.[2] Here, as among several carriers, the probative value of the presumption that the damage occurred while the property was in the custody of the last carrier may appear weak. Absent any evidence that pinpoints the cause of damage, it could be argued that it is no more probable that damage occurred while the goods were on the terminal carrier than it is that the damage occurred on one of the prior carriers. On the other hand, if the goods already were damaged at the time the last carrier took custody, it perhaps is probable that the last carrier would have noted or recorded the damaged condition. More important, the presumption here serves as a procedural device that gives to the plaintiff (who in the setting just described is disadvantaged in ascertaining the facts) a fair chance to recover by tentatively placing the damage with the last carrier.

At this point, a presumption must be distinguished from an inference. Although the language used with reference to presumptions is exasperatingly indiscriminate, a genuine presumption is raised by a basic fact or facts that, when accepted as true by the trier,[3] give rise to a *mandatory* inference, properly called a presumed fact. *Once the basic facts are believed,* the resulting presumed fact must be accepted by the trier *unless* it is rebutted by contravening evidence. An inference never has such a compulsory effect. The trier always is at liberty either to accept or reject an inferred fact. Note further that because a presumption founded on established facts creates a compulsory finding that remains obligatory until the presumed fact is rebutted, the raising of a presumption has a mandatory procedural effect: generally, it shifts to the opposing party the *burden of producing evidence.*

2. Chicago & N.W. Ry. v. C.C. Whitnack Produce Co., 258 U.S. 369 (1922); 1 Louisell & Mueller, § 68, at 541.

3. The existence of the basic fact could be proved at the trial or established by pleadings, stipulation, or judicial notice.

This is not true of an inference, which results only in creating a jury question whether the inferred fact exists.

Although the terms "presumption" and "inference" as defined above have gained general usage, terminology in this area is not uniform. For example, judges and lawyers sometimes speak of "permissive presumptions" or "presumptions of facts," by which terms they usually mean inferences. The cases also contain the term "presumption of law," which usually means a rebuttable presumption [4] of the kind herein denominated simply a presumption. A "conclusive presumption," often encountered in statutes, is not really a presumption at all, but rather is a rule of substantive law. This "presumption" declares that certain basic facts, once established, give rise to an *irrebuttable* conclusion. For example, it may be presumed conclusively that a child under the age of seven years cannot commit a felony. This rule, although stated in presumptive language, is merely a substantive principle that serious criminal responsibility may not be imposed upon one under the age of seven.[5]

§ 3.3 Some Sample Presumptions

Although presumptions are found in all jurisdictions, what one jurisdiction considers a presumption, another may classify as an inference. Since there are dozens, if not hundreds, of presumptions, the illustrative list that follows is but a small sample.[1]

4. IX Wigmore, § 2491, at 305 (Chadbourn). The slippery language that permeates the area of presumptions should make the cautious reader or practitioner reserve judgment on what is meant by a particular term until a careful inquiry is made. For the varying meanings of the word "presumption," either standing alone or with various modifiers, see Morgan & Weinstein at 25–26; Ladd and Carlson at 1216–17; Laughlin, In Support of the Thayer Theory of Presumptions, 52 Mich.L.Rev. 195, 196–207 (1953); Louisell, Construing Rule 301: Instructing the Jury on Presumptions in Civil Actions and Proceedings, 63 Va.L.Rev. 281, 289–291 (1976).

5. Morgan & Weinstein at 25; Louisell, supra n. 4, at 289–90. As substantive rules, "conclusive presumptions" must comport with due process and equal protection tests. Weinberger v. Salfi, 422 U.S. 749 (1975) (upholding a conclusive statutory definition of "widow" for Social Security eligibility requirements); Cleveland Bd. of Educ. v. LaFleur, 414 U.S. 632 (1974) (invalidating a conclusive school board regulation on maternity leave); Vlandis v. Kline, 412 U.S. 441 (1973) (invalidating a conclusive statutory definition of "residents" for university tuition); Stanley v. Illinois, 405 U.S. 645 (1972) (invalidating a conclusive presumption against parental fitness of unwed father).

§ 3.3

1. For a more comprehensive list see McCormick, § 343, at 968–73; 1 Weinstein & Berger, ¶ 301[05], at 89–91; West's Ann.Cal.Evid.Code §§ 600 et seq.

There is a measure of probative force in each of the correlative groupings below. Other considerations, however, including superior knowledge or easier access to the evidence (numbers 1, 2, 6, 7, 8) and policies favoring the settlement of estates (4, 5), the protection of survivors (3, 4), or the recovery of damages in cases of accident (2, 6), appear to be operative.[2] The next section will examine whether the considerations behind a particular presumption support a departure from the traditional rule that a presumption shifts the burden of producing evidence, but does not disturb

Basic Fact(s)	Presumed Fact
1. Letter regularly addressed and mailed	Received by addressee
2. Vehicle lawfully stopped is struck from rear by second vehicle	Driver of second vehicle negligent
3. Violent death from external means	Death was an accident (not a suicide)
4. Absence for 7 years without explanation or any communication to family or friends; inquiries unavailing	Absentee deceased
5. Will cannot be found	Revoked by testator
6. Employee in accident while driving vehicle owned by employer	Employee was acting within scope of employment
7. Goods delivered to bailee in good condition, but damaged when returned	Bailee negligent
8. Goods damaged during transit provided by more than one carrier	Last carrier caused damage

2. See McCormick, supra n. 1; Louisell, supra § 3.2 n. 4, at 292–93. In Watkins v. Prudential Ins. Co., 315 Pa. 497, 504, 173 A. 644, 648 (1934), the court stated:

> Presumptions arise as follows: They are either (1) a procedural expedient, or (2) a rule of proof production based upon the comparative availability of material evidence to the respective parties, or (3) a conclusion firmly based upon the generally known results of wide human experience, or (4) a combination of (1) and (3).

The court fails to mention social policy, but this basis for creating presumptions is widely recognized. 1 Louisell & Mueller, § 68, at 540–45.

the burden of persuasion, which remains fixed upon the party to whom it originally was assigned.

§ 3.4 Presumptions: Impact Upon Opponent and Effect of Rebuttal Evidence

It will be recalled that the effect of a presumption always may be avoided by proving the nonexistence of the basic facts that support the presumed fact. However, rebuttal evidence showing the nonexistence of the basic facts often is not so compelling as to cause the judge, by instructions or otherwise, to remove from the case altogether any consideration of a presumption. If the evidence against the existence of the basic facts is not so persuasive as to cause the judge to resolve the question of their existence, he will instruct the jury that the presumed fact arises only if the jury first finds the existence of the basic facts. For example, where the evidence conflicts on whether a letter was regularly addressed and mailed, the judge will charge the jury that no presumption of receipt will arise unless the jury finds that the letter was properly posted.

The foregoing discussion does not consider what general effect is to be given to a presumption after the basic facts are found to exist, nor does it address the related issue of the measure of rebuttal evidence necessary to negate the presumed fact. The jurisdictions lack uniformity in their approach to these fundamental aspects of presumptions. There are two dominant views regarding the general effect of a presumption; each has substantial support. The (apparent) majority view, which was first associated with Professor James Bradley Thayer,[1] a 19th century evidence scholar, holds that when a presumption arises after the establishment of the basic facts, its only procedural effect is to shift the burden of producing evidence to the opponent.[2] The opponent must meet the shifted burden of producing evidence, but he does not bear the ultimate burden of convincing the trier of fact of the nonexistence of the presumed fact. The second view, embraced by a growing minority of jurisdictions, holds that the procedural effect of establishing the basic facts is usually to shift the burden

§ 3.4

1. Thayer, Preliminary Treatise on Evidence (1898). See especially pp. 314, 336–37. There is some doubt about precisely what Thayer's view was concerning the extent to which a presumption should persist in the face of rebuttal evidence. See McCormick, § 344, at 974 n. 7.

2. See McCormick, § 344, at 974. Thayer's position gained the support of Wigmore. See IX Wigmore, § 2491, at 305 (Chadbourn).

of persuasion.[3] This latter position, often called the Morgan view because of its advocacy by the late Professor Edmund Morgan,[4] places great weight both on the probative link between basic and presumed facts and on the supposed utility of presumptions in advancing desirable social policy.[5] The minority approach gives considerably greater effect to most presumptions: a shift in the burden of persuasion results in placing upon the opponent the burden of convincing the trier that the nonexistence of the presumed fact is more probable than its existence. This shift in the persuasion burden occurs if the existence of the basic facts is conceded; it also occurs, even where the basic facts are contested, if the proponent of the presumption shows that the basic facts cannot be reasonably disputed (i.e. no jury question exists). Of course, the existence of the basic facts could be an issue for the jury. If so, the proponent attempts to carry *his* burden of convincing the trier of the truth of the basic facts so that the burden of persuasion to show the nonexistence of the presumed fact will be cast upon the opponent of the presumption.[6]

It is important to recognize, however, that few if any jurisdictions invariably adhere either to the Thayer or Morgan view of the effect of presumptions. The marked tendency is to endorse generally one view or the other, but to make occasional exceptions for selected presumptions. Thus, a jurisdiction adopting Thayer's position may nonetheless determine that, in the case of a certain presumption, special considerations warrant the greater presumptive effect of shifting the burden of persuasion.[7]

The debate over which general approach to presumptions—Thayer or Morgan—is the more desirable one is not likely to be decisively concluded. The difficulty is that such a variety of reasons underlie presumptions that a single approach to all presumptions seems destined to failure. Thus, the majority (Thayer)

3. See, e.g., Me.R.Evid. § 301; Wis. Stat.Ann. 903.01; West's Ann.Cal.Evid. Code §§ 603–06.

4. Morgan, Some Problems of Proof, 74–81 (1956).

5. See id. at 81; see also McCormick, § 344, at 980–81.

6. For a strenuous criticism of the Morgan approach, pointing out the confusion that can attend its implementation, see Lansing, Enough is Enough: A Critique of the Morgan View of Rebuttable Presumptions in Civil Cases, 62 Ore.L.Rev. 485 (1983).

7. 1 Weinstein & Berger, ¶ 300[02], at 9. Most state statutes adopt either the Morgan or Thayer position but provide for special exceptions. For compilations of state statutes see 1 Louisell & Mueller, Ch. 3 appendix (Supp.); IX Wigmore § 2493k (Chadbourn). At least two state statutes purport to treat all presumptions alike. See Mont.R. Evid. 301; Or.R.Evid. 308.

approach can be criticized when it is applied to certain presumptions—for example, those that are supported by convincing probative force and strong policy grounds. Once the basic facts are established, the cogent considerations of policy and probability that were instrumental in the initial assignment of the burden of persuasion support a reallocation of this burden.[8] The argument for reassigning the burden of persuasion applies when *either* probative force *or* policy considerations appear particularly strong. On the other hand, the minority (Morgan) view can be criticized when it is applied to some presumptions, for its procedural effect on many routine presumptions may be greater than desirable.[9] Thus, the continuing problem faced by legislatures and courts is whether to adopt, with minor exceptions, the Thayer approach or the Morgan approach or, alternatively, to adopt an intermediate scheme that somewhat favors one view or the other but has a generous provision for the alternative approach.[10] One scheme, for example, is to shift the burden of persuasion when there is a substantial probative relationship between the basic facts and the presumed fact.[11] In the absence of such a nexus, a presumption shifts only the burden of production. Another approach, usually associated with the evidence rules of California, is to shift the burden of persuasion for those presumptions identified by the legislature or courts as based upon "public policy";[12] presumptions outside the public-policy category shift only the burden of producing evidence. Because many presumptions have at least some public policy underpinnings, the determination of which presumptions are within the persuasion-shifting category is not easy. Obviously, any dual approach to presumptions necessitates

8. See, e.g., Hinds v. John Hancock Mutual Life Insurance Co., 155 Me. 349, 365, 155 A.2d 721, 730 (1959) (on the presumption of accidental death, "[I]t seems pointless to create a presumption and endow it with coercive force, only to allow it to vanish in the face of evidence of dubious weight or credibility"); Morgan, Instructing the Jury Upon Presumptions & Burden of Proof, 47 Harv.L.Rev. 59, 80 (1933) (on presumptions designed to elicit disclosure of information, "Surely, the courts do not raise such a presumption merely for the purpose of making the opponent of the presumption cause words to be uttered. . . .").

9. See, e.g., Fed.R.Evid. 301, Comment from the Report No. 93–650 of the House Committee on the Judiciary.

10. McCormick, § 344, at 981–820. There is no consensus as to exactly what considerations (policy, probative force, or both) dictate which presumptions should have the effect of relocating the burden of persuasion.

11. E.g., Kan.Stat.Ann. 60.414 (1983); Okl.Stat.Tit. 12 § 2303 (1980).

12. West's Ann.Cal.Evid.Code §§ 603–606.

careful inquiry by student and practitioner as to the procedural effect that is assigned to a particular presumption.

Caution must be exercised even in a jurisdiction that purports to adhere to a single view of the effect of presumptions. As previously noted, several exceptions will usually be found; that is, some presumptions will be singled out by statute or judicial opinion for special treatment. The reasons for this departure from the normal scheme will vary, but factors (singly or in combination) such as policy concerns, fairness, or probative force may justify distinguishing certain presumptions. For example, the forceful policy favoring the legitimacy of children, coupled with strong probability, gives a special strength to the presumption that a child born in wedlock is the legitimate offspring of the husband.[13]

One must be alert for yet another variance. As noted below, even among those jurisdictions that generally restrict the effect of a presumption to shifting only the burden of production, some interjurisdictional differences are found in the measure of rebuttal evidence that is ordinarily considered sufficient to negate the presumed fact. Fortunately, most jurisdictions that adhere to the Thayer view concerning the effect of a presumption (namely, that of shifting only the production burden) also endorse Thayer's apparent view [14] concerning the measure of counterevidence necessary to rebut the presumption. That view is that a presumption disappears after the introduction of rebuttal evidence that is sufficiently probative to allow a reasonable trier to find the nonexistence of the presumed fact. In practical terms, this usually means that the opponent has produced evidence sufficient for the trier to find the opposite of the presumed fact—for example, to find the *nonreceipt* of a properly mailed letter.[15] Once adequate

13. Not only does this presumption uniformly shift the burden of persuasion, but in most jurisdictions the rebuttal evidence must meet some higher-than-usual standard such as clear and convincing. See McCormick, § 343, at 972. See also J.D. v. M.D., 453 S.W.2d 661, 663 (Mo.App.1970) (presumption of legitimacy must be rebutted by "clear, convincing and satisfactory proof that no copulation occurred or was possible between husband and wife"). Maine, which normally follows the Morgan approach shifting the burden of persuasion, Me.R.Evid. § 301, provides that the presumption of legitimacy can be rebutted only by proof beyond a reasonable doubt of illegitimacy. Me.R.Evid. § 302.

14. See supra n. 1.

15. Stephens v. Dichtenmueller, 207 So.2d 718, 725 (Fla.App.1968), rev'd on other grounds, 216 So.2d 448 (1968) ("A legal presumption will not disappear if no countervailing evidence is introduced or evidence is only a scintilla, or amounts to no more than speculation, surmise or conjecture."); Commercial Molasses Corp. v. New York Tank

rebuttal evidence is presented, the presumption disappears from the case. The trier ultimately decides the issue in question—that is, the existence or nonexistence of the fact that was the subject of the presumption—just as if no presumption were ever in the case. Under this pure Thayerian approach, the presumption is extinguished by the presentation of sufficient rebuttal evidence; it is of no consequence to the *disappearance of the presumption* that the trier *did not in fact believe* the counterevidence.[16] The judge simply determines whether the rebuttal evidence was sufficient to support a belief contrary to that expressed in the presumption.

A small number of variant jurisdictions, discontented with the comparative ease by which the opponent of a presumption can negate its effect, depart from Thayer in one important respect: while adhering to his view that a presumption shifts only the burden of production, they have taken steps to increase the opponent's burden of rebuttal. These jurisdictions have rules that, roughly, occupy a middle ground between the Thayer and Morgan positions. For example, a few jurisdictions allow a presumption to disappear only when the rebuttal evidence is substantial. In other of these "hybrid" jurisdictions, the presumption persists unless the rebuttal evidence makes the nonexistence of the presumed fact at least as probable as its existence.[17] Although these compromise positions appear to avoid some of the asserted shortcomings of both the majority and minority approaches, they often cause confusion and practical difficulties, especially in jury trials. For example, what constitutes substantial or equal evidence defies description and, often, recognition as well. Further, it is not always clear whether the judge or jury makes the determination of the sufficiency of the rebuttal evidence. When the determination is left to the jury and the rebuttal evidence reasonably could be considered substantial, but is not indisputably so, the jury may be instructed concerning the existence of a presumption, but should be told that the presumption is to be

Barge Corp., 314 U.S. 104, 111 (1941) (presumption does no more than impose upon the party against whom it is asserted the burden to "go forward with evidence sufficient to persuade that the nonexistence of the fact, which would otherwise be inferred, is as possible as its existence. It does not cause the burden of proof to shift . . .").

16. Morgan & Weinstein at 28; Louisell, supra § 3.2 n. 4, at 301; but see O'Dea v. Amodeo, 118 Conn. 58, 65–66, 170 A. 486, 488 (1934).

17. Various intermediate formulations are set out in Morgan & Weinstein at 28–30. For a case reviewing these formulations, their rationale, and the decisions implementing them, see Hinds v. John Hancock Mutual Life Ins. Co., 155 Me. 349, 155 A.2d 721 (1959).

disregarded if in their view the rebuttal evidence is substantial. Such an instruction is invariably difficult to follow. Finally, if the rebuttal evidence is of sufficient strength to create a jury question, yet falls below the persuasive effect necessary to cause the judge (or perhaps the jury) to find that the presumption has disappeared, it is the practice of some courts to give the case to the jury under an instruction that permits them to consider the presumption along with other evidence.[18] This confusing procedure appears to transform a presumption, which is a rule about how evidence is evaluated, into a part of the evidence itself.[19]

As previously suggested, it is difficult to support a single approach that applies to all presumptions. Thus, a flexible scheme that treats differently various presumptions within a jurisdiction might be preferable. Yet disparate approaches introduce further complexity and confusion to an area already cluttered with ambiguity and misunderstanding. Perhaps a practical compromise, admittedly imperfect, offers the best solution. As a starting point, there is much to be said for adopting a general approach that applies to all presumptions except those relatively few that for compelling reasons are singled out for different treatment. This concession to uniformity avoids the difficulty of classifying a large number of presumptions into different procedural categories. As a general approach, the Thayer view, which has been adopted by the Federal Rules of Evidence and by a slim majority of states, suffers no greater disadvantages than the competing theories. It is true, as the critics point out, that the Thayer approach does not always give a sufficient effect to presumptions.[20] The critics are, of course, also correct in their observation that it is comparatively easy to rebut a Thayer presumption. As noted, an opponent need only present enough rebuttal evidence to permit a reasonable trier to find the nonexistence of the presumed fact. On the other hand, the Thayer view is easy to understand and administer. It avoids the problem of confusing juries by dividing the burden of persuasion (basic fact to proponent; presumed fact to opponent) on what is essentially a

18. Hinds v. John Hancock Mutual Life Ins. Co., 155 Me. 349, 355, 155 A.2d 721, 726 (1959).

19. For a criticism of this metamorphosis, see S.Rep. No. 93–1277, 93d Cong., 2d Sess. (1974) reprinted in 1974 U.S. Code Cong. & Admin. News 7051, 7056.

20. These critics have given the Thayer approach such unappealing names as the "bursting bubble theory" and have analogized it to Maeterlinck's male bee, which "having functioned" disappears. McCormick, § 344, at 974 n. 6.

single factual issue—a division that is necessary under the Morgan view.[21] Further, the Thayer approach does not usually dissipate the force of the presumption altogether: because almost all presumptions are supported by a logical relationship between the basic and presumed fact,[22] the destruction of the presumption does not negate the probative force yielded by the basic facts. That is, the disappearance of a presumption only removes its compulsory effect; after a presumption vanishes, there still remains the inference that arises from the basic facts. In many jurisdictions, the judge may instruct the jury concerning the existence of this residual inference;[23] it seems especially desirable to give such an instruction in cases where either the probative relationship between the basic and presumed fact is very strong or the rebuttal evidence is barely sufficient to eliminate the presumption. Such a practice makes the Thayer view more acceptable, and may represent the best compromise in an area marked by severe disagreement and by the practical difficulties of trial administration.

§ 3.5 Presumptions in Criminal Cases: Constitutional Problems

Once the basic facts are established, a true or mandatory presumption compels a finding of the presumed fact in the absence of contrary evidence. This compulsion suggests a strong probative connection between the basic facts and the presumed fact. Indeed, it may be argued that in order to surmount a constitutional challenge there must be *some* probative association between them. Thus, even though many presumptions rest largely upon policy grounds, it is perhaps required by the due process clause that the presumed fact rests in part upon probative basic facts. In making this assertion, however, one must distinguish between criminal and civil cases. In the latter, where there are comparatively few constitutional restraints, probably no more is required by the Constitution than a showing of at least some rational connection

21. See supra n. 6 and accompanying text.

22. Even some presumptions commonly thought to originate only in procedural convenience or fairness (e.g., goods damaged during transit: damage caused by last carrier in the series) may be regarded as based upon logical inferences. See In re Woods Estate, 374 Mich. 278, 288–89 n. 3, 132 N.W.2d 35, 42 (1965). See § 3.2.

23. See Louisell, supra § 3.2 n. 4, at 303–04, quoting McCormick, § 345, at 821 (2d ed. 1972); H.Rep. No. 1597, 93d Cong., 2d Sess. 5–6 (1974) (Conference Report on H.R. 5463) reprinted in 1974 U.S. Code Cong. & Admin. News 7099. But see McCormick, § 345, at 979.

between the basic facts and the presumed fact.[1] This requirement, in practice, demands only minimal probabilistic ties. It is uncertain whether a civil presumption based *entirely* upon policy (or some other nonprobative ground) would meet constitutional standards. In fact, there is reason to predict that such a presumption would be sustained,[2] but the cases offer no definitive answer.[3] In any event, the constitutionality of presumptions in civil cases is usually a distant concern.[4]

In criminal cases, special considerations limit the scope of allowable presumptions. A directed verdict against the accused is never permitted; further, a conviction must rest upon the trier's belief beyond a reasonable doubt that each element of the charged offense exists.[5] Of course, these propositions should not necessarily forbid the use of a rebuttable presumption against the accused. The Constitution does not forbid placing upon the accused certain obligations to offer proof: it has long been an accepted practice to assign to him certain procedural burdens with respect to so-called "affirmative defenses."[6] These defenses, such as insanity, provocation, self-defense, and entrapment, can either exonerate the accused or, in some instances, reduce the degree of his culpability. If the accused wishes to offer one of these defenses, he is usually required not only to enter an appropriate plea, but also to offer supporting evidence. Depending upon the jurisdiction and the particular affirmative defense, the accused must either carry the

§ 3.5

1. Usery v. Turner Elkhorn Mining Co., 428 U.S. 1, 28 (1976). See McCormick, § 345, at 985.

2. If by a reformulation of the substantive law the state could eliminate altogether the presumed fact from the claim or defense of which it presently is a part, then the state should have the option of providing that such fact will be presumed until sufficiently rebutted. For example, suppose a legislature enacted a presumption that if a product were shown to be defective, the manufacturer would be presumed to have been negligent. Of course, in reality this presumption has at least some probative force. But suppose it were supported only by the policy of spreading the cost of product-related injury and of encouraging care in the design and manufacture of products. The legislative power to eliminate negligence (the presumed fact) and make the manufacturer strictly liable for its defective product suggests that the state can take the intermediate step of retaining negligence, but presuming its presence. In short, the greater power includes the lesser. See Ferry v. Ramsey, 277 U.S. 88, 94 (1928).

3. Compare Western & Atlantic R.R. v. Henderson, 279 U.S. 639 (1929), with Mobile, J. & K.C. R.R. v. Turnipseed, 219 U.S. 35 (1910). See McCormick, § 345, at 985.

4. McCormick, supra n. 3. For instances in which constitutional concerns may exist, see 1 Weinstein & Berger, ¶ 301[01], at 25–27.

5. In re Winship, 397 U.S. 358 (1970).

6. See supra § 3.1 n. 3.

burden of producing evidence or discharge the greater burden of persuading the trier (usually by a preponderance of the evidence[7]) of the existence of the defense.

The widespread recognition of affirmative defenses and the general approval of their constitutionality[8] suggest that presumptions, which like affirmative defenses place procedural burdens upon a criminal defendant, should be allowable even when invoked against the accused. The usual effect of a presumption is to shift to the opponent only the burden of producing evidence; the burden of persuasion is normally left undisturbed and, in the present context, would remain with the prosecution. Since even affirmative defenses that call upon the accused to carry the burden of persuasion seem to fall within constitutional bounds,[9] it would appear that presumptions having a similar or weaker procedural effect should not raise serious constitutional concerns. Whatever the logic of the foregoing suggestions, however, the United States Supreme Court has emphatically rejected them.

In the discussion that follows, the reader should carefully distinguish between two types of presumptions. As used by the Supreme Court a "mandatory presumption" is one which, once the basic facts are shown, *requires* the factfinder to find the presumed fact unless the defendant introduces at least some contrary evidence; a "permissive presumption" (also called an inference), is one which permits but *never* requires the factfinder to infer the presumed fact from the basic facts. Courts have not always been careful to state which form of presumption they are addressing, but proper classification is easy enough once one realizes that if a presumption shifts *any* evidentiary burden to the accused, it is mandatory. Obviously, a mandatory presumption has a greater impact on the accused than does a permissive presumption, since the former casts a burden on the accused to respond with rebuttal evidence. We shall see, however, that even permissive presumptions have been subjected to close constitutional scrutiny.

In Mullaney v. Wilbur,[10] the Court held unconstitutional Maine's mandatory presumption that shifted to the accused the

7. LaFave & Scott, Criminal Law 152 (1972). The Supreme Court, however, has held that the state may "impose upon the . . . [accused] the burden of proving his insanity beyond a reasonable doubt." Id. See Leland v. Oregon, 343 U.S. 790 (1952), reh. denied 344 U.S. 848 (1952).

8. See supra § 3.1 n. 3; 1 Weinstein & Berger, ¶ 303[05], at 29.

9. See Patterson v. New York, 432 U.S. 197 (1977); McCormick, § 347, at 990.

10. 421 U.S. 684 (1975).

burden of proving provocation. The judge had instructed the jury that if they found that the accused unlawfully and intentionally killed the victim, they should presume malice aforethought unless they were convinced by the accused that he acted from sudden provocation.[11] It was significant that under Maine law a showing of provocation was viewed as negating malice aforethought—an essential element of murder.[12] Thus, in the Court's view, the effect of the presumption was to relieve the prosecution of the burden, imposed by the leading case of In Re Winship,[13] of proving beyond a reasonable doubt every element of the crime charged.

Mullaney, decided in 1975, was not the first case in which the Supreme Court had invalidated a criminal presumption. However, the tenor of the Court's opinion and its emphasis upon the state's inescapable duty to prove all elements of the crime charged raised the question whether a mandatory presumption could *ever* be used against an accused. As interpreted in later cases, *Mullaney* meant *at least* that a presumption may not, consistent with the requirements of due process, shift to the accused the burden of proof with regard to an element of the crime.[14] Beyond that the decision was ambiguous. It was, of course, possible to read the *Mullaney* opinion narrowly: the presumption in that case operated to shift the burden of persuasion (not simply the burden of production); furthermore, there was not an especially strong probative nexus between the basic facts (illegal and intentional killing) and the presumed fact (malice aforethought).[15] But a broad application of *Mullaney* could render unconstitutional any presumption that shifted a procedural burden (production or persua-

11. Id. at 686. The defendant had to prove provocation by a preponderance of the evidence.

12. Id. at 686–87. Patterson v. New York, 432 U.S. 197, 215–16 (1977), upholding the constitutionality of an affirmative defense almost identical to the *Mullaney* presumption, distinguished *Mullaney* on this ground. See also supra § 3.1 n. 3.

13. 397 U.S. 358 (1970).

14. See Sandstrom v. Montana, 442 U.S. 510, 527 (1979), on remand 184 Mont. 391, 603 P.2d 244 (1979) (Rehnquist, J., concurring); Francis v. Franklin, 471 U.S. 307, 314 (1985).

15. The Court never explicitly assessed the probative strength of the contested presumption. It did quote a dissenter in an early Massachusetts case, characterizing the same presumption as "arbitrary and unfounded." Commonwealth v. York, 50 Mass. 93, 128 (1845) (Wilde, J., dissenting). The Court also stated that "the Due Process Clause demands more exacting standards before the state may require a defendant to bear this ultimate burden of persuasion." 421 U.S. at 703 n. 31. Thus it appears that an underlying factor in the Court's consideration of this presumption was its questionable probative force.

sion) to the accused. As noted later, the effect of *Mullaney* remains uncertain.

Mullaney is one of a series of perplexing cases [16] that have raised as many doubts as they have resolved. Whatever the precise meaning of these decisions, it is clear that the Court has imposed severe limits upon the use of presumptions against an accused. As will be seen, distinct standards seem to emerge from this line of decisions that govern presumptions in criminal cases. These standards vary, depending on the evidentiary effect of raising a particular presumption against the accused. The greater the burden of rebuttal, the more stringent the constitutional requirements. A review of some of the leading cases follows. It will be noted in the case descriptions that the Supreme Court has sometimes gauged the constitutional validity of a criminal presumption by assessing the probative nexus between the basic facts and the presumed facts, while on other occasions, the Court has focused upon whether or not the presumption under review operates to relieve the prosecution of its burden of proving each element of the offense charged. The usage in recent cases suggest that mandatory presumptions will be subjected to the much more demanding "burden of proof" analysis, while permissive presumptions will be evaluated under the "probative nexus" analysis.

In the 1970 case of Turner v. United States,[17] the accused, at the time of his arrest, possessed both heroin and cocaine. He was subsequently charged with several violations of the federal narcotics laws. One of the charged substantive offenses [18] consisted of "(1) knowingly receiving, concealing, and transporting heroin which (2) was illegally imported and which (3) [the accused] knew was illegally imported." [19] There was ample evidence that Turner knowingly possessed heroin (element (1) above). For proof of elements (2) and (3), the government relied upon a statutory inference (permissive presumption) that allowed—but did not require—the jury to infer from the defendant's unexplained possession that the heroin was illegally imported *and* that the defendant knew of the illegal importation.[20] The Court held that element (2) was amply supported by numerous, unchallenged studies and

16. The cases are carefully reviewed in 1 Weinstein & Berger, ¶¶ 303[04]–303[05].

17. 396 U.S. 398 (1970), reh. denied, 397 U.S. 958 (1970).

18. See id. at 401 n. 1 [quoting 21 U.S.C.A. § 174 (repealed 1970)].

19. Id. at 405.

20. Id. at 406–07.

reports[21] which concluded that virtually all heroin within the United States has been illegally imported.[22] The inferred fact of importation, said the Court, satisfies both a "more-likely-than-not standard . . . [and] the more exacting reasonable doubt standard normally applicable in criminal cases."[23] Furthermore, since little or no heroin is domestically produced and none is legally imported, the Court was "confident that . . . [the accused] was aware [element (3)] of the 'high probability' that the heroin in his possession had originated in a foreign country"[24] and had been smuggled into the United States.

Turner was also charged with the substantive offense of purchasing heroin in a form other than in (or from) the original stamped package.[25] The absence of appropriate tax-paid stamps on the container of heroin in the defendant's possession *permitted,* in the absence of an explanation, a statutory inference that his acquisition was from an unstamped package. This inference was also sustained by the Court. Again noting that nearly all heroin found in the United States was illegally imported and hence unstamped, the Court concluded that it was "extremely unlikely that a package containing heroin would ever be legally stamped."[26] Thus, possession of unstamped heroin left "no reasonable doubt"[27] that the source package was also unstamped.

Other counts in the indictment charged Turner with crimes in connection with his possession of cocaine. These offenses paralleled those alleged with regard to his possession of heroin. Furthermore, to prove the cocaine violations, the government relied upon the identical statutory inferences that supported its heroin charges: from the accused's unexplained possession of cocaine the trier could infer illegal importation and knowledge; from his unexplained possession of unstamped cocaine, the trier could infer an unstamped source. The Supreme Court ruled, however, that as applied to cocaine, these inferences were unconstitutional. The inference that the cocaine in Turner's possession was illegally brought into the United States was weakened by studies and

21. The Court's use of these materials is an example of judicial notice of legislative facts. See § 1.8.

22. 396 U.S. at 408–16. Even if some heroin were manufactured in the U.S., the amount that could be manufactured here would constitute less than 1% of the total present in the country. Id. at 414–15.

23. Id. at 416.

24. Id.

25. See id. at 402 n. 2 [quoting 26 U.S.C.A. § 4704(a) (repealed 1970)].

26. 396 U.S. at 421.

27. Id. at 422.

reports concluding that more cocaine is lawfully manufactured in this country than is smuggled into it from abroad. Thus, a significant portion of cocaine may have been stolen from a legally produced source.[28] The Court therefore invalidated the inference of illegal importation because it failed even to satisfy a more-likely-than-not standard. Using similar reasoning, the Court found constitutionally infirm the inference that Turner's cocaine came from an unstamped package. Since legally manufactured domestic cocaine is likely to be packaged in a stamped container, the origin of a significant portion of stolen cocaine (i.e. that purloined from legal channels) is traceable to a stamped source. This, said the Court, raises the "reasonable possibility" that Turner or his supplier obtained the cocaine from a stamped package.[29]

Although the *Turner* Court expressly refrained from holding that if a presumption or inference is to be used against a criminal defendant, the basic facts must imply the presumed fact "beyond a reasonable doubt," Justice White's majority opinion could be read as suggesting that such a standard was applicable.[30] He spoke with seeming approval of the "more exacting reasonable-doubt standard normally applicable in criminal cases." [31] However, the Court did not provide a precise definition of this reasonable-doubt standard, and the standard adopted by the Court is not obvious from the opinion. The facts the Court cites in support of the heroin presumption seem to lead *necessarily* to the conclusion that "[t]o possess heroin *is* to possess imported heroin" [32] (emphasis in original). Therefore it is possible to conclude from this opinion that the standard of near certainty requires not simply a probative connection *sufficient* for the trier to find the presumed fact beyond a reasonable doubt, but rather "a virtually inevitable connection" [33] between the basic fact and the presumed fact.

As a matter of fact, however, permissive presumptions have not been required to satisfy *either* variant of the reasonable-doubt test in cases following *Turner*. The first clarification came in Barnes v. United States,[34] where the Court expressly refrained from embracing a reasonable-doubt standard (however defined) to the exclusion of one requiring only a more-likely-than-not link. At issue was the common law presumption—or, more accurately,

28. Id. at 418–19.

29. Id. at 423–24.

30. McCormick, § 347, at 995.

31. 396 U.S. at 416.

32. Id.

33. McCormick, supra note 30.

34. 412 U.S. 837 (1973).

inference—that the unexplained possession of recently stolen goods (the basic fact) supported an inference that the possessor knew that the goods were stolen (inferred fact). After reviewing its prior decisions, the Court acknowledged that their "teaching . . . is not altogether clear." [35] However, wrote Justice Powell, the precedents at least establish:

> that if a statutory inference submitted to the jury as sufficient to support conviction satisfies the reasonable-doubt standard (that is, the evidence necessary to invoke the inference is sufficient for a rational juror to find the inferred fact beyond a reasonable doubt) as well as the more-likely-than-not standard, then it clearly accords with due process.[36]

The Court went on to hold that the defendant's possession of recently stolen treasury checks (initially payable to others) allowed the inference beyond a reasonable doubt that the defendant had knowledge of their prior illegal course. Thus the standard expressly approved as constitutionally permissible requires only that the basic facts be *sufficiently probative* of the presumed fact *to allow* a reasonable trier to find the latter beyond a reasonable doubt; the Court left open the constitutionality of a simple probability standard, but impliedly rejected the more stringent reasonable doubt or "inevitable connection" standard that could be inferred from *Turner.*

In 1979 the Court again considered the constitutionality of criminal permissive presumptions. County Court of Ulster County v. Allen [37] involved the prosecution by New York authorities of four persons (three male adults and a female minor) for various offenses, including the illegal possession of handguns. A car occupied by the defendants was stopped for speeding. The investigating officer noticed that the open handbag of the sixteen-year-old passenger was in the front seat area, and he observed within it two large-caliber handguns. At trial, the prosecutor relied upon a statutory "presumption" [38] that allowed an inference of illegal possession by all persons occupying a vehicle upon a showing of the basic fact that a firearm, not on the person of any particular occupant, was within the automobile. The trial judge instructed the jury that it was permissible to infer possession by all of the defendants from their presence in the vehicle containing the

35. Id. at 843.

36. Id.

37. 442 U.S. 140 (1979).

38. New York—McKinney's Penal Law § 265.15(3).

handguns, but that such an inference was not mandatory; it could be ignored even if the defendants produced no rebuttal evidence. It was thus clear that the presumption was permissive, not mandatory.

The defense attacked the statute as so broad on its face that it failed to satisfy due process. By its terms, it was argued, it would sweep within the presumption (1) occupants who may not know that the vehicle in which they are riding contains a gun, and (2) persons who, even though aware of the gun, were not permitted access to it.[39] Thus, the argument continued, the statutory presumption lacks the minimal probative force essential to its constitutionality.

The Court first responded by holding that the validity of a *permissive* presumption (inference) was to be judged in the context of the case in which it was invoked—that is, as applied to the particular circumstances of the defendant who opposes it. Although the validity of a *mandatory* presumption must be judged on its face, a facial assessment of a permissive presumption was deemed inappropriate. The critical difference is that the trier must abide by the mandatory presumption until it is dispelled. Absent rebuttal, the trier is not free to make its own independent evaluation of the presumed facts. However, when a presumption is permissive, the trier is always free of any obligation to draw the suggested inference; it may consider other evidence that tends to confirm or deny the "inferred" fact.

This predicate thus established, the Court held that as applied to the circumstances in *Allen*,[40] the inference of possession by all of the defendants was "entirely rational"[41]—that is, the inferred fact was "more likely than not to flow from the . . . [basic facts]."[42] It is not appropriate, held the Court, to require that a permissive presumption meet a reasonable-doubt standard: that more stringent measure of proof applies to the evidence as a whole and has no applicability to a permissive presumption that consti-

39. The Court of Appeals found these arguments persuasive. See Allen v. County Court, Ulster County, 568 F.2d 998, 1007 (2d Cir.1977), cert. granted, 439 U.S. 815 (1978).

40. The opinion emphasized that the defendants were not hitchhikers or casual passengers, that the guns were in plain view, that it was improbable that a sixteen-year-old was sole custodian of two large-caliber handguns, and that circumstances suggested an inept attempt to conceal the weapons when the defendants' vehicle was stopped for speeding. 442 U.S. at 163–64.

41. Id. at 163.

42. Id. at 165.

tutes only part of the proof.[43] Finally, the Court reiterated the important distinction between permissive and mandatory presumptions.[44] Because the latter must be accepted by the jury

> even if it is the sole evidence of an element of the offense . . . the prosecution [which] bears the burden of establishing guilt . . . may not rest its case entirely on a presumption unless the fact proved is sufficient to support an inference of guilty beyond a reasonable doubt.[45]

Ulster County thus teaches that permissive presumptions are allowable if either the basic facts or additional confirming evidence makes the inferred fact more likely than not. Mandatory presumptions, however, must meet a reasonable doubt standard on their face, at least where the presumed fact is an element of the offense charged.[46]

One feature of the *Ulster* Court's discussion of mandatory presumptions deserves special note. The Court's dictum suggests that a mandatory presumption is permissible whenever the basic facts supply a *sufficient* basis for finding the presumed fact beyond a reasonable doubt. Whether the Supreme Court would actually permit such a judge-imposed finding is open to question. To do so would relieve the prosecution of the burden of actually convincing the jury of the presumed fact. It may be that the Court would never uphold a truly mandatory presumption, even one that shifted to the accused only the burden of production. If this suggestion is accurate, the dictum in *Ulster County* that assumes the constitutionality of mandatory presumptions will not in fact be followed. On the other hand, if a mandatory presumption is allowable—if the trier may under some circumstances *be required*

43. It would be a different matter if the permissively presumed fact were the *sole* basis for a finding of guilt, since a reasonable-doubt standard would necessarily apply. Id. at 167.

44. Four Justices strongly dissented in *Ulster County,* essentially on the ground that jurors are influenced by permissive presumptions and, hence, it is important to insure that the basic facts *standing alone* make the presumed fact more likely than not. Id. at 175–77.

45. Id. at 166–67.

46. Most presumptions bear upon the elements of an offense and hence come within the constitutional limitations set out in *Ulster County* and other cases. In theory—but rarely in practice—a criminal presumption could relate to a matter sufficiently distant from the elements of an offense (and hence from the guilt of the accused) so that the constitutional restrictions generally applicable to criminal cases would not apply. See generally 1 Weinstein & Berger, ¶ 303[01], at 9, 16, and Adv.Comm.Note to S.Ct. Stand. 303, discussing differences in standards for inferences.

to find one fact after first finding another—then it seems likely that the Court will hold that the due process clause requires an "inevitable connection"[47] between the basic and the presumed facts.[48]

In any event, a consistent theme of the recent cases is the important difference between a permissive and mandatory presumption. And the Supreme Court has been concerned with the actual, not the formal or statutory effect of a presumption. Where the jury instructions might have led jurors to believe that they were *obliged* to find the presumed fact if the basic facts were established and no contrary evidence was introduced, then the presumption will be held to the standard required of mandatory presumptions.[49] The Court has also looked to jury instructions rather than statutory or case law to determine whether a mandatory presumption shifts to the accused the burden of persuasion, or merely the burden of production. In Sandstrom v. Montana,[50] decided two weeks after the *Ulster County* case, the accused was charged with purposely or knowingly causing the victim's death, an offense that Montana denominated "deliberate homicide." The accused admitted the killing, but claimed that he did not act with the requisite purpose or knowledge and, therefore, was guilty of a lesser offense. At the conclusion of the evidence, the trial judge instructed the jury that "[t]he law presumes that a person intends the ordinary consequences of his voluntary acts."[51] Under state law the intended effect of the *Sandstrom* presumption was to shift to the accused only the burden of producing some contrary evidence; the burden of persuasion remained with the prosecution.[52] However, the Supreme Court concluded that there was a significant risk that the instruction given to the jury had been misunderstood: they may have thought that they were peremptorily directed to find the requisite intent or, at least, that they were directed by a mandatory presumption shifting the burden of persuasion to find intent unless the defendant proved the contrary. Under either of these possible constructions, the presumption had unconstitutional consequences. First, since the

47. See supra note 33 and accompanying text.

48. In People v. Roder, 33 Cal.3d 491, 498 n. 7, 189 Cal.Rptr. 501, 505 n. 7, 658 P.2d 1302, 1308 n. 7 (1983), the California Supreme Court noted this apparent inconsistency in the *Ulster County* opinion.

49. See McCormick, § 348, at 997.

50. 442 U.S. 510 (1979), on remand, 184 Mont. 391, 603 P.2d 244 (1979).

51. Id. at 513.

52. State v. Sandstrom, 176 Mont. 492, 497, 580 P.2d 106, 109 (1978), cert. granted, 439 U.S. 1067 (1979).

state is obliged to prove beyond a reasonable doubt "*every fact* necessary to constitute the crime . . . charged" [53] and since there is no doubt that intent is an essential element of "deliberate homicide," a *conclusive* (peremptory) presumption would be unconstitutional. According to the Court, such a presumption would have the untoward effects of lifting from the prosecution its assigned burden of proving intent and of abridging the defendant's status of innocence until proven guilty of each element of the offense charged.[54] Second, constitutional infirmities would also result from a presumption that shifted to the accused the burden of the requisite state of mind.[55] When the state proved the basic fact of homicide—a fact that did not itself establish that the killing was knowing or purposeful—the jury might erroneously have presumed the element of intent unless persuaded otherwise by the accused.

In the 1985 case of Francis v. Franklin,[56] the Court again condemned a jury instruction about a presumption. The *Francis* instruction, unlike the instruction that was invalidated in *Sandstrom,* posed no risk that the jury might have construed the presumption in question as preemptive. Nonetheless, a closely divided Court ruled that there was a reasonable possibility that the jury had interpreted the trial court's instruction as shifting the burden of persuasion on the essential element of intent, in violation of *Mullaney* and *Sandstrom.*[57]

The *Francis* Court expressly refused to rule on the constitutionality of presumptions that shift only the burden of production.[58] But observe that if a defendant fails to meet the burden of production respecting an element, the prosecution is in fact relieved of its burden of proving the element, even though technically there has been no shift in the burden of persuasion. There is an additional difficulty in cases where the defendant himself is the only person who can provide the rebuttal evidence; as a practical matter, he must testify even though he might prefer to exercise his fifth amendment right not to take the stand. It may be, therefore, that the Court's decisions, taken as a whole, are leading toward the invalidation of *all* mandatory presumptions. Nonethe-

53. In re Winship, 397 U.S. 358, 364 (1970).

54. Sandstrom v. Montana, 442 U.S. 510, 521–23 (1979), on remand, 184 Mont. 391, 603 P.2d 244 (1979).

55. Id. at 524.

56. 471 U.S. 307 (1985).

57. See supra note 14 and accompanying text.

58. Id. at 314 n. 3.

less, there is an important difference between a mandatory presumption that shifts the burden of persuasion and a mandatory presumption that shifts only the burden of producing rebuttal evidence.

In any event, a legislature can probably achieve precisely the same effect that the Court has seemingly condemned. Suppose that a statutory reform converted a fact formerly the subject of a presumption into one that constituted an affirmative defense. For example, suppose that the Maine legislature, confronted with the *Mullaney* ruling, redefined murder as simply unlawful and intentional killing (excising the "malice aforethought" element), and made lack of malice aforethought an affirmative defense which, if proved, would reduce the grade of the crime to second degree murder.[59] Affirmative defenses, even those that call upon the accused to carry the burden of persuasion, are usually found constitutional.[60] It will thus be seen that despite the Supreme Court's rather stringent requirements surrounding presumptions, a sovereign is still permitted considerable latitude in allocating elements of an offense (or defense). First, it may take an element that could be used to define the crime (e.g., lack of provocation) and denominate it an affirmative defense (provocation). Furthermore, the state apparently has rather broad authority to eliminate altogether one or, perhaps, more elements of an offense.[61] For example, the state might define a crime as the illegal entry [element 1] into a dwelling [element 2] in the nighttime [element 3] with the intent to commit a felony therein [element 4] or it might state the offense more broadly, for example, by including only element 1 or some other combination of fewer than 4.

59. The Supreme Court upheld a murder statute essentially identical to that described in the hypothetical above in Patterson v. New York, 432 U.S. 197 (1977).

60. See supra note 8 and accompanying text.

61. For example, American legislatures have sometimes created strict liability offenses by eliminating the state's burden of establishing any *mens rea* on the part of the accused. See Jeffries & Stephan, *Defenses, Presumptions, and the Burden of Proof in Criminal Law,* 88 Yale L.J. 1325, 1373–76 (1979). The authors urge that legislatures should be free to employ any affirmative defenses, mandatory presumptions, or inferences free of restrictive analysis by the courts so long as the remaining elements of the offense are proven beyond a reasonable doubt and comprise a constitutionally adequate basis for the punishment contemplated. Id. at 1365. Thus, if a legislature could constitutionally (i.e., consistent with principles of substantive due process and proportionality) define a felony of illegal entry without including element (3) (see text), then courts should not concern themselves with whether element (3) is cast as a presumption or an affirmative defense.

In light of the ability of the state largely to avoid the impact of the Supreme Court's decisions restricting presumptions, it is not clear why the Court has insisted upon such strict constitutional requirements. Perhaps the answer lies in the Court's view of the jury's role, especially in criminal cases. That role is not, of course, one of simply finding facts by relying upon credible evidence and drawing rational inferences. The jury's historic protective role—its interposition between the power of the state and the individual accused—carries with it the unfettered right of acquittal. Presumptions, created by the state and administered by an authoritative state official, may have undue influence and effect. Thus, while the Court generally will allow the state legislature to redefine a crime or allocate to the defendant an affirmative defense, a majority of the Justices are uneasy with any procedure that seems to slant the trial court's fact-finding process against the accused. For this reason, mandatory presumptions are particularly suspect and may not survive constitutional challenge.[62]

§ 3.6 Presumptions: Instructing the Jury

In civil cases, under both the predominant Thayer view of presumptions and the minority Morgan view, it is not necessary to use the term "presumption" in instructing the jury. Avoiding this term is desirable because the jury may misunderstand its function and effect. Under the Thayer view, if there is no rebuttal evidence and the existence of the basic fact is undisputed, the judge either directs a verdict (if the presumed fact is dispositive) or instructs the jury that they shall consider the presumed fact as proven. In the latter instance, use of the term presumption is unnecessary.[1] The judge simply describes the presumed fact: "You shall find that the letter in question, written by *A* and addressed to *B*, was received." If the basic fact is contested, but there is no evidence rebutting the presumed fact,[2] it still is unnecessary to mention the term presumption: the judge simply instructs the jury that "If from the evidence you believe that the letter in question was regularly addressed and mailed, you shall

62. The difficulty of clearly instructing a lay jury about the nature and effect of a presumption may also help explain the Supreme Court's hostility toward presumptions in criminal cases.

§ 3.6

1. See Morgan & Weinstein at 33.

2. As a practical matter, this is unlikely to occur because the opponent will probably also offer evidence rebutting the presumed fact. But it could occur (as, for example, where the addressee is not available as a witness) that there is no evidence available to rebut the presumed fact.

find that it was received." Finally, if there is sufficient rebuttal evidence directed at the presumed fact so as to entitle a reasonable jury to find the nonexistence of that fact, the presumption disappears from the case in a Thayer jurisdiction. In recognition of any residual inference, however, the judge should, if permitted by local practice, instruct the jury that if they conclude that the letter was properly addressed and mailed, they *may* find that it was received.[3] Despite the simplicity and seeming appeal of the foregoing, the cases reveal inconsistent practices.[4]

In jurisdictions that hold that presumptions (or at least certain presumptions) shift the burden of persuasion, the jury also may receive the case without mention of the term presumption. If, for example, the basic facts are admitted or indisputably established and the opponent of the presumption attacks only the presumed fact, the judge should instruct the jury [to continue the example] that "you will find that the letter in question was received, unless from the evidence you believe its nonreceipt is more probable than its receipt." This instruction gives the maximum effect to the presumption by shifting the burden of persuasion on the issue of receipt to the party against whom the presumption operates. If the opponent attacks both the basic facts and the presumed fact, the judge should instruct "that if from the evidence you believe that the letter in question was addressed properly and thereafter mailed, then you also shall find that it was received, unless you believe that its nonreceipt is more probable than its receipt."

Other variations could be described, but it is sufficient to reemphasize that the minority approach, which shifts the burden of persuasion, shares with the majority approach, which shifts the burden of production, the advantage of avoiding instructions that inform the jury of a presumption and thus entwine them in determining the presumption's effect.[5] Conversely, the intermediate approaches that seek to invest presumptions with a somewhat greater effect than the Thayer view, but which do not go as far as to shift the burden of persuasion, often involve the jury in complex

3. See § 3.4, n. 23 and accompanying text. McCormick warns that some jurisdictions may consider this instruction an opinion on the facts. McCormick, § 344, at 979.

4. See McCormick, § 344, at 978–79; IX Wigmore, § 2491, at 306 and nn. 5–6 (Chadbourn).

5. However, courts often do not seize the opportunity to avoid a charge that contains language about presumptions. McCormick, § 345, at 978–80.

determinations. Frequently, the judge's instructions set out the meaning of presumptions and explain their allowable impact. For example, the jury may be directed to measure the probative strength of rebuttal evidence or to consider and weigh a presumption along with other evidence.[6]

In criminal cases, as previously indicated, the Supreme Court has not gone so far as to hold directly that so-called "mandatory presumptions" (that shift either the burden of production or persuasion) may never be raised against the accused. Yet, as elsewhere noted,[7] it is doubtful whether the Court would sustain a presumption that applied to an essential element of the crime and shifted to the accused either the burden of production or the greater burden of persuasion. If such a presumption were valid and if it were not rebutted, the judge would instruct the jury that if they find the basic facts,[8] they shall find the presumed fact. In short, mandatory presumptions in criminal cases would be treated essentially as ordinary presumptions are treated in civil cases.

As we have seen, "permissive presumptions" or inferences may usually be raised against the accused without violating the Constitution.[9] It is essential, however, that the judge make it absolutely clear to the jury that they are free to accept or reject the inference, that the prosecution must prove every element of the offense beyond a reasonable doubt, and that the permissive presumption casts no burden upon the accused. The Court is acutely sensitive to the jury's unfettered prerogative to acquit the accused and will carefully scrutinize any action by the judge that might suggest to the jury his support of the prosecution's case.[10]

§ 3.7 Presumptions Under the Federal Rules of Evidence

Rules 301 and 302 of the Federal Rules of Evidence deal with presumptions. No provision is made for presumptions in criminal cases, largely because at the time of the passage of the Federal Rules these presumptions were being considered in connection with a revision of the federal criminal code. This revision, however, was never enacted. In addressing civil cases, the Federal Rules neither define nor enumerate presumptions, but only state their

6. See § 3.4, nn. 17–19 and accompanying text.

7. See § 3.5, nn. 47–49.

8. The judge should instruct the jury that they must find the basic facts beyond a reasonable doubt. 1 Weinstein & Berger, ¶ 303[06], at 38.

9. See § 3.5.

10. See § 3.5, n. 61.

function and probative effect.[1] In proceedings where federal substantive law governs the claim or defense, Rule 301 adopts the Thayer view, specifying that "a presumption imposes on the party against whom it is directed the burden of going forward with the evidence to rebut or meet the presumption, but does not shift to such party the burden of proof in the sense of the risk of nonpersuasion . . . ."[2]

The Rules also contain an accommodation to the varying state approaches to presumptions. Rule 302 specifies that "the effect of a presumption respecting a fact which is an element of a claim or defense as to which State law supplies the rule of decision is determined in accordance with State law."[3] Students of civil procedure will recognize that this accommodation accords with the policy, if not the command, of Erie Railroad Co. v. Tompkins.[4] The Rule defers to state law only as to those presumed facts that constitute an element of a claim or defense; presumptions of lesser impact are governed by the Thayer approach of Federal Rule 301—even in diversity cases where state law is applicable.[5] Of course, the Thayer approach, embodied in Rule 301, governs with regard to facts underlying a federal claim or defense, even if these are joined with state claims or defenses. Thus, in a case involving both federal and state claims, as well as in cases involving state claims supported by a presumption and an incidental matter also supported by a presumption, the judge and jury may have to deal with several presumptions of differing force and effect. When this occurs, it may be difficult to instruct the jury in

§ 3.7

1. Fed.R.Evid. 301 & 302 and accompanying Report, Senate Committee on the Judiciary, supra § 3.4, n. 19.

2. Fed.R.Evid. 301. See Usery v. Turner Elkhorn Mining Co., 428 U.S. 1, 27–31 (1976); United States v. Ahrens, 530 F.2d 781 (8th Cir.1976); Lora v. Board of Educ., 74 F.R.D. 565 (E.D.N.Y. 1977). The phrase "risk of nonpersuasion" is synonymous with "burden of persuasion." As previously noted in the text, the party with the burden of persuasion bears the risk that he will lose his case if he is unable to persuade the trier. For a discussion of the measure of rebuttal evidence that will negate the presumption, see Saltzburg & Redden at 87–88. Professor Louisell argues that an intermediate approach may be taken in the implementation of Rule 301, rather than a pure Thayer approach. Louisell, supra § 3.2 n. 4 at 312–20.

3. Fed.R.Evid. 302 and accompanying Adv.Comm.Note. See, e.g., United States v. Wilson, 433 F.Supp. 57 (N.D. Iowa 1977).

4. 304 U.S. 64 (1938). See Dick v. New York Life Ins. Co., 359 U.S. 437 (1959). For an incisive analysis of the impact of the Federal Rules of Evidence on state law, with special attention to privileges, see C. Wright, Law of Federal Courts, 621–27 (4th ed. 1983).

5. 1 Weinstein & Berger, ¶ 302[01], at 4–5.

understandable terms as to the proper effect of the various presumptions.[6]

Rule 301 does not, of course, mean that all civil presumptions arising under federal law are treated in accordance with Thayer. Congress may enact a particular statutory presumption and specify its effect, for example, by stipulating that it shall persist until rebutted by clear and convincing evidence[7] or that it shall shift the burden of persuasion.[8] Sometimes courts must struggle to determine whether a statutory presumption supersedes Rule 301. For example, the courts have divided on the procedural effect of the presumption of illegal discrimination that arises under various antidiscrimination statutes. Generally, the statutes provide that a presumption of discrimination arises upon the showing of a possibly discriminatory practice, such as the rejection of a qualified minority applicant for employment. The Supreme Court has at least partially resolved the dispute. Under one major statutory scheme—Title VII—the Court has said that the defendant needs only to meet the burden of production by presenting evidence justifying his employment practices (showing a nondiscriminatory motive).[9] Finally, despite the passage of Rule 301, the federal courts have occasionally upheld the continuing validity of certain presumptions with early statutory or common-law origins that, usually for compelling policy or probative reasons, have been consistently construed as shifting the burden of persuasion.[10]

Notes

1. *Presumptions Against the Burdened Party.* There is usually little point in raising a presumption if the presumed fact countervails an element of a claim or defense upon which the opponent of the presumption already has the burden of persuasion. In discharging his burden, the opponent will negate the effect of a presumption

6. For a suggested approach to the problem of conflicting federal and state presumptions, see Saltzburg & Redden at 105–106.

7. See, e.g., 26 U.S.C.A. § 6653 (underpayment of tax treated as presumptively negligent unless taxpayer shows otherwise by clear and convincing evidence).

8. See Alabama By-Products Corp. v. Killingsworth, 733 F.2d 1511, 1514–15 (11th Cir.1984).

9. See Texas Department of Community Affairs v. Burdine, 450 U.S. 248 (1981), on remand 647 F.2d 513 (5th Cir. 1981).

10. James v. River Parishes Co., Inc., 686 F.2d 1129 (5th Cir.1982) (longstanding presumption of maritime common law that a vessel found adrift was operated negligently shifts the burden of persuasion; unaffected by Rule 301); Plough, Inc. v. Mason & Dixon Lines, 630 F.2d 468 (6th Cir.1980) (Rule 301 does not affect prior statutory presumption of the 1906 Carmack Amendment imposing on common carriers the burden of persuasion in rebutting the presumption of carrier liability).

under either the Thayer or the Morgan view. Of course, a presumption against the party already having the burden of persuasion would have an effect if it raised the level of persuasion required for rebuttal of the presumed fact. Thus, an opponent who already had the burden of proof would nonetheless be adversely affected by a presumption that could not be rebutted by the greater weight of the evidence, but rather could be rebutted only if the contrary evidence was at least clear and convincing.

2. *Conflicting Presumptions.* It is possible for evidence in a case to establish two sets of basic facts which then give rise to conflicting presumptions. For example, when there is evidence of a legal marriage between *H* and *W,* there often is a presumption that their marital status continues. Another presumption often arises when the basic fact of a ceremonial marriage between *H* and *W–2* is shown: any prior marriage is presumed to have been dissolved. In a case where evidence supporting both sets of basic facts is introduced, how is the court to handle the "conflicting presumptions"? It is obvious that both presumptions cannot operate with full force. One solution, favored by Thayer and adopted by some courts, see IX Wigmore, § 2493, at 308 (Chadbourn), is simply to ignore both presumptions. In essence, the presumptions negate each other. Thus it is possible, in the context of conflicting presumptions, to give some effect to the presumption raised against the party who normally has the burden of persuasion: the opposing presumption can at least have the effect of negating his presumption and of forcing him to produce evidence without the benefit of it. Permitting such an effect, that is, allowing the opposing presumption to dispel the presumption that favors the party with the burden of proof, reaches the result favored by Thayer. Both presumptions disappear from the case. Another probable resolution, suggested by the discussion in Note 1 above, would be to ignore only the presumption that was *raised against* the party with the burden of persuasion. The party with the burden would still have the benefit of his presumption.

Those jurisdictions that do not routinely negate both presumptions usually inquire whether one of the two presumptions is supported by the "weightier considerations of policy and logic," 1 Louisell & Mueller, § 68, at 543 n. 50. If one of the presumptions is so supported (and the other is not), it is given preference and the lesser presumption is ignored. Assuming the surviving presumption is in favor of the party with the burden of persuasion, the case goes forward with one operative presumption. In the example above, the presumption favoring the legality of the current marriage has strong support on both policy and probability grounds, and it would be preferred in many jurisdictions.

Chapter IV

COMPETENCY OF WITNESSES AND THE PROCESS OF TRIAL

---

§ 4.1 Introduction: Scope

In this chapter we examine the competency of witnesses, the format of a trial, and certain procedures applicable to eliciting testimonial evidence. Competency, once a major consideration in the law of evidence, has been reduced in importance by modern evidence codes and, even in common-law jurisdictions, by statutory reform. This subject is given only brief attention in the following materials, which are largely devoted to trial format and the procedures of interrogation. Understanding the trial format promotes a contextual understanding of the exclusionary rules that screen out some relevant evidence; knowledge of the constraints imposed upon interrogating counsel by the evidentiary rules provides a further indication of the impact of the adversarial system on the process of proof.[1] Offers of proof and objections to evidence, although fundamental aspects of evidentiary procedure, are reserved for a later chapter,[2] at which point we will have encountered most of the exclusionary rules which demonstrate the practical impact of these procedures.[3]

§ 4.1

1. The basic principles underlying the adversarial system are discussed in Ch. I.

2. See Ch. XI. The study of expert opinion is also postponed (Ch. XII); the materials contained in Ch. VI and VII will lay the groundwork for understanding the hearsay problems that arise in connection with expert testimony. Finally, the admission of tangible evidence, including writings, is covered late in the text (Ch. XIII). Documents often raise many of the evidentiary problems (such as those associated with hearsay and privilege) that are encountered in earlier chapters.

3. Two major themes have influenced the order of presentation in this text: the materials that generally are applicable to problems of proof, such as relevance, burdens of proof, and trial process, are collected in the early chapters of the book; materials that are

§ 4.2 Competency: In General

The word "competent" is often used to describe evidence that is admissible to prove a consequential proposition. So used, the term signifies that the evidence is not only relevant, but also is beyond the reach of the various exclusionary rules. As applied to a witness, "competent" denotes that a person called to testify has the necessary testimonial qualifications. This latter application of the term is the concern of this chapter.

At early common law, rigid and, often, illogical rules of incompetency precluded many potentially helpful witnesses from testifying. The rules of preclusion were based largely upon apprehensions about inaccurate or perjured testimony. A major basis of disqualification was interest in the outcome of the litigation, and this ground served to disqualify even the parties to an action from taking the witness stand. Other disabilities resulting in incompetence were the witness's infancy, insanity, disbelief in a supreme being, conviction of a crime, and marriage to a party.

Over the course of the last century, statutory and code reform has largely abolished these objections to competency.[1] Under some statutes and codes, a disability that formerly resulted in incompetency may still support the claim of a privilege not to testify. This transformation from incompetency to privilege occurred, for example, with regard to the disability arising from marriage to a party. In most jurisdictions a marital privilege can be claimed so as to prevent one spouse from testifying against an accused spouse in a criminal proceeding.[2]

Not all grounds of incompetency, however, have been transformed or removed by statute. Vestiges of the common-law proscriptions may still be found.[3] Furthermore, all jurisdictions have

either comparatively difficult or that require a substantial understanding of related parts of the law of evidence are deferred, insofar as possible, to the middle and latter portions of the text.

§ 4.2

1. Morgan & Weinstein at 86–88.

2. E.g., 22 Okl.Stat.Ann. § 2504; Va.Code 1950, § 19–2–271.2. In some jurisdictions the privilege is given to the accused, in others to the testifying spouse, and in still others to both spouses. Many jurisdictions recognize exceptions to the marital privilege, as, for instance, when the spouse is the victim of the crime with which the accused is charged. See § 9.4 for a discussion of the privilege.

3. E.g., Ala.Code § 12–21–162 (conviction of perjury disqualifies). But in Washington v. Texas, 388 U.S. 14 (1967), on remand, 417 S.W.2d 278 (1967), the Supreme Court declared unconstitutional a state statute which prohibited co-participants in the same crime from testifying for each other. Similar constitutional concerns prevent Alabama from applying its perjury dis-

rules designed to ensure the neutrality of the judicial tribunal. Typically, such rules govern (and usually forbid) testimony by judges and jurors in cases in which they are officially participating.[4] With regard to witnesses generally,[5] however, the modern approach is to disqualify a witness only when he is shown to be incapable of perceiving, remembering, or describing the event in question, or when he is deemed unable to appreciate his duty to testify truthfully.[6] The application by the trial judge of these general criteria can result in a ruling of incompetency in instances where the proffered witness is extremely young [7] or suffers from a certain kind (or degree) of mental illness.[8] Even where a statute or code provision prevents disqualification of a witness on grounds of incompetency, the disability formerly asserted as the basis of the claim of incompetence often bears upon credibility, and for this latter purpose evidence of the disability is admissible.[9] Thus, evidence that the witness has been convicted of a felony or has a financial interest in the outcome of the suit may be admitted to discredit or impeach his testimony.[10]

The trial judge decides whether a proffered witness is competent. In making his decision, he may find it necessary to hear and formally enter evidence bearing upon competency into the record.

qualification in criminal cases, at least as to witnesses for the defendant. Johnson v. State, 292 Ala. 208, 291 So. 2d 336 (1974), on remand, 52 Ala.App. 707, 291 So.2d 338 (1974), on rehearing, 53 Ala.App. 354, 300 So.2d 392 (1974), cert. denied, 293 Ala. 760, 300 So.2d 396 (1974).

4. E.g., Fed.R.Evid. 605, 606; West's Ann.Cal.Evid.Code §§ 703, 704.

5. The competency of expert witnesses is discussed in Ch. XII. Generally, the competence of these witnesses hinges upon whether they have special training, acquired by formal education or experience (or both).

6. See, e.g., West's Ann.Cal.Evid. Code §§ 700–702; Fed.R.Evid. 601–04 (generally limiting incompetency to lack of personal knowledge and failure to declare that he will testify truthfully). See § 4.3, n. 13.

7. State v. Noble, 90 N.M. 360, 563 P.2d 1153 (1977), limited 95 N.M. 205, 619 P.2d 1249 (1980); Hollaris v. Jankowski, 315 Ill.App. 154, 42 N.E.2d 859 (1942).

8. Truttmann v. Truttmann, 328 Ill. 338, 159 N.E. 775 (1927) (test for incompetency because of mental infirmity held to be whether derangement or feeblemindedness is such as to make the proffered witness untrustworthy). Few witnesses, however, are disqualified because of a lack of mental capacity. See Weihofen, Testimonial Competence and Credibility, 34 Geo.Wash.L.Rev. 53 (1965); Adv.Comm.Note to Fed.R.Evid. 601; see § 4.3, n. 13. See generally United States v. Van Meerbeke, 548 F.2d 415 (2d Cir.1976), cert. denied, 430 U.S. 974, 97 S.Ct. 663, 52 L.Ed.2d 368 (1977) (witness allowed to continue testifying even though under the influence of opium).

9. See, e.g., Conn.Gen.Stat.Ann. § 52–145.

10. See §§ 8.3–8.4. See also Adv. Comm.Note to Fed.R.Evid. 601.

If such a hearing is required, the judge must decide whether a risk of prejudice, embarrassment, or some other consideration dictates that he receive this evidence out of the jury's presence.[11]

§ 4.3 Competency: The Dead Man's Statutes

In some jurisdictions there is one aspect of contemporary litigation where the legacy of the common-law rules governing incompetency still has a disquietingly sharp effect. The common law rejected entirely the testimony of parties and other persons who had a direct pecuniary or proprietary interest in the outcome of the trial. This rule of exclusion assumed that testimony given by an interested party would be biased and, perhaps, perjured. It was of no consequence which side sought to call the disabled witness to the stand. Whatever the actual incidence of these supposed abuses, the cost of the prohibition became increasingly apparent. The rules of incompetency frequently barred from the witness stand the persons who had the most knowledge about the event in question. Thus, statutory reform was inevitable. Reform is seldom achieved, however, without compromise. Those with allegiance to the common-law rule barring parties and other interested persons from testifying urged its retention in a civil suit between two parties, one of whom is representing a deceased (or otherwise incapacitated) person. Their argument was appealing: if the surviving party is allowed to testify, an adversarial imbalance will result because the party representing the decedent will usually suffer a disadvantage in rebutting the survivor's testimony. Since death or some other disability (such as severe mental incapacity) precludes the testimony of one of the individuals most apt to have knowledge of the event in question, special rules of competence should apply to equalize the adversaries' opportunities to produce evidence.

This argument was sufficiently persuasive to produce a host of state statutes designed to equalize the adversarial posture of litigants in cases where one party represents the interests of someone deceased or otherwise incapacitated. In their most extreme form, these "dead man's statutes" simply prohibit the surviving party from testifying—a solution which one commenta-

11. See, e.g., People v. Coca, 39 Colo. App. 264, 564 P.2d 431 (1977). See Fed. R.Evid. 104(c). "Voir dire" is the name sometimes given to such a hearing held outside the jury's presence, although the term more frequently applies to the examination of prospective jurors.

tor described as "blind and brainless."[1] The injustice that results from this rule is apparent in cases where the survivor has a valid claim stemming from an oral agreement with the deceased or from a personal injury caused by the decedent. The living party is unable to substantiate his claim by his own testimony, which may be the best and, perhaps, only available evidence to support his recovery.

In recent years there has been general recognition of the injustices produced by the dead man's statutes, and statutory and code reforms negating or ameliorating their effect have gained widespread support. However, there is still no uniform approach. Differences among the statutes as originally passed have been compounded by variations resulting from the amending process. The only feature common to the present statutes is that each is still designed to equalize the opportunities of proof in litigation involving a decedent and survivor where the subject matter of the suit is a transaction or event that occurred when both were living.[2] Even today, some of the statutes bar the survivor from testifying to any conversation with the deceased,[3] while others broadly prohibit the survivor's testimony about any transaction with, or act done by, the deceased.[4] A liberalizing statutory provision that has gained favor in recent years permits the survivor to testify, but offsets this supposed advantage by admitting relevant hearsay statements of the decedent.[5] Some jurisdictions that have abandoned the absolute prohibition nonetheless require that the survivor's testimony will not sustain a judgment in his favor unless his interested testimony is corroborated by other evidence.[6] Other approaches include raising the standard of proof that the survivor

§ 4.3

1. McCormick, § 65, at 160, attributing this description to Jeremy Bentham.

2. Good introductory materials are collected in Weinstein & Mansfield, et al. at 242–54.

3. E.g., West's Fla.Stat.Ann. § 90.602. But an exception or waiver may operate in certain circumstances as, for example, where the interested survivor is called to the stand by the adversary. McCormick, § 65, at 159.

4. E.g., Ky.Rev.Stat. 421.–210(2).

5. E.g., Conn.Gen.Stat.Ann. § 52–172; Va.Code 1950, § 8.01–397. Illustrative statutes are collected in Weinstein & Mansfield, et al. at 254.

6. E.g., Va.Code 1950, § 8.01–397. Cases and statutes are collected in Annot., 21 A.L.R.2d 1013 (1952). This approach raises difficulties when the survivor is not a claimant, but rather a defendant. Weinstein & Mansfield, et al. at 254. One approach is to strike the defendant's uncorroborated testimony and to instruct the jury to disregard it. See Seaboard Citizens National Bank of Norfolk v. Revere, 209 Va. 684, 166 S.E.2d 258 (1969).

must meet [7] or vesting the trial judge with a discretionary power to admit the survivor's testimony where exclusion would cause hardship or injustice.[8]

Thus, an increasing number of states no longer prohibit a survivor from testifying,[9] although it is common for these jurisdictions to admit the deceased's hearsay statements or otherwise try to equalize opportunities of proof; this approach probably points the way of the future. The Federal Rules of Evidence accommodate the policy of those states that have dead man's statutes by providing that in "civil actions and proceedings, with respect to an element of a claim or defense as to which State law applies the rule of decision, the competency of a witness shall be determined in accordance with State law." [10] This deference to state rules of competence has the general effect of incorporating into the Federal Rules of Evidence a state dead man's statute in cases founded upon diversity of citizenship, although the language of the federal rule encompasses any other state rules that restrict competency.[11] However, in federal criminal proceedings and in federal civil proceedings not dependent upon a state claim or defense "[e]very person is competent to be a witness except as otherwise provided" [12] by the Federal Rules of Evidence. Aside from the general command of Rule 602 that a witness should have personal knowledge about the matter to which he testifies, the only specific rules that would disqualify a witness are 603 (requiring oath or affirmation), 605 (barring the presiding judge), and 606 (barring jurors). However, the trial judge still has authority to exclude the testimo-

7. E.g., N.J.Stat.Ann. 2A:81–2.

8. See Ariz.Rev.Stat. § 12–2251. For a state case confining the reach of a dead man's statute (which has since been repealed), see Deaton, Gassaway, & Davison, Inc. v. Thomas, 564 P.2d 236 (Okl.1977).

9. See West's Ann.Cal.Evid.Code §§ 700 et seq., 1261; N.J.Stat.Ann. 2A:81–2; N.Mex.Stat.Ann. 1978, § 601; R.I.Gen.Laws 1956, § 9–17–12.

10. Fed.R.Evid. 601. Presumably, where state law provides the claim or defense, the federal court will apply a state dead man's statute even if it provides that the survivor can testify, but contains protections or offsetting provisions such as corroboration or admissibility of the decedent's hearsay statements. It should not matter that the state may not characterize its statute as one of "competence." Saltzburg & Redden at 298.

11. 3 Weinstein & Berger ¶ 601[03] contains a survey of possible grounds of incompetency under state law. As noted in the text, however, most jurisdictions now have abolished the various grounds of incompetency that existed at common law. See § 4.2, nn. 1–9 and accompanying text. Congress recognized that the provision incorporating state rules of competency would apply primarily to dead man's statutes. H.Rep. No. 93–650, 93d Cong., 2d Sess. 9, (1973), reprinted in 1974 U.S.Code Cong. & Admin.News 7075, 7083.

12. Fed.R.Evid. 601.

ny of a witness if reasonable men could not believe that he observed, remembers, or is able to relate the event in question.[13]

§ 4.4 The Components of Trial: Opening Statement

At the commencement of trial, the plaintiff's counsel or, in a criminal case, the prosecutor customarily makes an opening statement. These opening remarks are simply to acquaint the trier with the case and to set out, usually in a general way,[1] what the claimant (or state) expects to prove. Although counsel tries to outline his case in an appealing, persuasive way, an opening statement (in contrast to a closing statement) is not, strictly speaking, an argument. Rather, it is an introduction to the case and to the contentions that the forthcoming evidence is intended to support.

In most cases, the plaintiff's or prosecutor's opening statement is followed immediately by the defendant's opening statement. However, in some jurisdictions the defendant may reserve his opening statement until later in the case. When he does so, the defense counsel delivers his opening statement after the plaintiff has completed his principal evidential presentation and just before the defendant presents his main evidence.[2]

§ 4.5 The Components of Trial: Format and Order of Proof

The party initiating a legal action—whether it is criminal or civil—presents his real and testimonial evidence first. Since, in order to secure a conviction or recovery, he must establish the existence of the factual elements that the substantive criminal or civil law prescribes, he has the burden of persuasion, meaning that he must ultimately persuade the trier.[1] This burdened party also

13. 3 Weinstein & Berger, ¶ 601[01], at 10. This exclusion could be based upon lack of relevancy. See id. ¶ 601[04].

§ 4.4

1. There is a tactical risk in detailing exactly what the forthcoming evidence will show. If some of the witnesses testify otherwise than expected, the opposing counsel can point to this discrepancy in his closing argument. The availability of modern discovery, however, has enabled counsel to make more detailed statements about the evidence that will follow.

2. See § 4.5 for a description of the order of proof.

§ 4.5

1. If after deliberation by a jury in a civil trial their minds are at a state of equipoise, the party with the burden of persuasion will lose because he has failed to carry his burden. See § 3.1. In a criminal trial, of course, the prosecutor has the burden of convincing the jury beyond a reasonable doubt.

has, initially at least, another burden: that of producing evidence.[2] He must produce sufficient evidence supporting his claims to avoid a directed verdict. This initial presentation of evidence is usually called the plaintiff's (or government's) case in chief. The plaintiff calls in turn each of his witnesses to the stand, and each witness takes the oath or, in lieu thereof, makes an affirmation.[3] Then the plaintiff's counsel conducts the direct examination. This interrogation consists of a series of question and answer exchanges: counsel simply asks questions of the witness that elicit from him an account of pertinent facts and occurrences.

How closely does counsel control and direct the testimony of his witness? At one end of the scale is the possibility of minimal guidance: occasional questions which direct the witness's attention to pertinent incidents, but which allow considerable freedom of narration. At the other extreme is the possibility of asking a number of narrow, highly directive questions that call upon the witness to respond in a sentence or two.[4] To some extent, whether counsel uses the technique of free narrative or that of specific question and answer depends on the circumstances of the case: he will be influenced by the capabilities of his witness and the nature of the testimony expected. If the witness is articulate and can be expected to make an orderly, favorable presentation, counsel might decide to exercise only minimal direction. The trial judge, however, has considerable discretionary authority over the form in which testimony is elicited.[5] Many judges, and even more opposing attorneys, prefer the question-and-answer technique. Frequently it is more efficient. It also facilitates anticipation by opposing counsel, making it easier to interpose an objection between the examining counsel's question and the expected inadmissible answer. Consequently, the court often responds favorably to a request by opposing counsel that testimony be elicited by specific questions.

After the direct examiner completes the first phase of questioning, the opposing counsel may, as a matter of right,[6] conduct his cross-examination. Of course, a lawyer is always entitled to

2. The burden of producing evidence sometimes shifts to the opposing party. Under the orthodox rule, the burden of persuasion remains with the party to whom the law initially assigned it. See § 3.1.

3. An affirmation simply is a solemn declaration that the declarant will tell the truth. See Adv.Comm.Note to Fed. R.Evid. 603.

4. McCormick, § 5, at 9–10.

5. McCormick, § 5, at 10.

6. Alford v. United States, 282 U.S. 687, 691 (1931). See Aluminum Industries Inc. v. Egan, 61 Ohio App. 111,

waive cross-examination and, for reasons of trial strategy, it is usually sound practice to do so unless the direct testimony of the witness has been harmful. Further interrogation always presents the risk that the witness's answers may damage the cross-examiner's case. This risk should be avoided when the direct testimony has been innocuous, unless counsel finds it necessary to the proof of his claim or defense to elicit additional testimony from the witness. Even in these circumstances it may be necessary for the cross-examiner to call the witness later in the case, for in most jurisdictions the scope of inquiry on cross-examination cannot exceed that of direct.[7]

Theoretically, a cross-examiner has the same leeway to elicit narrative testimony as has the direct examiner. In practice, however, the cross-examiner usually tries to control closely the witness by asking precise, narrowly-drawn questions which call for specific answers, often a "yes" or "no." This high degree of direction responds to the hostility normally existing between a witness and his cross-examiner. If counsel were to ask broad, general questions, calling for a lengthy narrative response, the witness could use the opportunity to repeat and emphasize his direct testimony or to give additional testimony which could be unfavorable. Of course, if the witness is not hostile, the examiner may relax the usual tightly structured exchange.

Following cross-examination, the counsel who called the witness may conduct redirect examination. Although the scope of redirect examination is subject to the discretionary control of the court, the judge must permit the examiner to ask questions regarding aspects of the witness's testimony that were first revealed during cross-examination.[8] Finally, there may be a fourth phase of interrogation: recross-examination. This last part of the examination process is likely to be at or near the point of diminishing returns. Accordingly, the trial judge may exercise his discretion to disallow recross questions, although he should permit recross as to new points developed during redirect questioning.[9]

116–17, 22 N.E.2d 459, 462–63 (1938); McCormick, § 19, at 47–48.

7. See § 4.10.

8. See McCormick, § 32, at 69–70. New, specific matters may arise on cross that are within the general scope of inquiry of the direct examination. In cases where the cross-examiner raises new matters that exceed the proper scope of inquiry, his examination is subject to several procedural consequences. These consequences are discussed in § 4.10. Note also that some jurisdictions do not limit the inquiry of cross-examination to that of direct.

9. For a further discussion of this rule, see State v. McSloy, 127 Mont. 265, 271–73, 261 P.2d 663, 665–67

Just as interrogation of a witness may have four distinct phases (direct, cross, redirect, and recross), so too the trial of a case may consist of a four-part sequence. After the plaintiff's (or prosecutor's) case in chief, in which he presents the witnesses and real evidence necessary to permit his recovery, the defense presents its case.[10] (Here, of course, the defense counsel calls witnesses for direct examination and plaintiff's counsel becomes the cross-examiner). The next phase of trial is the plaintiff's case in rebuttal, after which comes the final phase: the defendant's case in rejoinder.

Observe, however, that all of the evidence might be presented during the first two trial stages, or even during plaintiff's case in chief. The defendant may elect to present no case in defense, choosing instead to rely upon his cross-examination to negate the trier's belief in the plaintiff's evidence. Furthermore, at the conclusion of plaintiff's case in chief the defendant may move for a directed verdict (or, in a criminal case, an acquittal), arguing that he is entitled to a judgment as a matter of law because the plaintiff (or prosecutor) has failed to present sufficient evidence to establish his claim (or charge). To revert to an earlier discussion, the defendant is arguing that the plaintiff has not discharged his burden of production because he has failed to provide evidence sufficient to enable a reasonable trier to find the existence of an essential element of the plaintiff's case.

§ 4.6 Examining the Witness: Leading, Misleading, and Argumentative Questions

Much of the law of evidence, as we shall see, rests upon assumptions about human conduct. Subsequent chapters contain illustrations of evidentiary rules grounded upon suppositions about how a jury will evaluate certain types of evidence, and about the conditions under which a person is likely to speak truthfully.

The familiar rule that generally forbids the use of leading questions during direct examination rests upon two assumptions. The first, a factual assumption, is that a cooperative relationship exists between the direct examiner and his witness. Presumably, the witness will give testimony favorable to the examiner's client; further, it is likely that examining counsel and witness have met

(1953), modified 686 P.2d 193 (1984); McCormick, § 32, at 71 n. 18.

10. See § 3.1. In rare instances, court rules or decisions permit or require that one party interrupt the other's case to present evidence "out of order." See generally VI Wigmore § 1866 (Chadbourn).

prior to trial and discussed or even rehearsed the latter's testimony. The second assumption, a psychological one, is that if the direct examiner phrases his questions in language that impliedly suggests the desired answer, the witness will conform to the suggestion and tailor his answer accordingly. The second assumption is based on the first: the friendly witness will respond to suggestive questions.[1]

Accordingly, as a general rule, the direct examiner is prohibited from asking leading questions—that is, he is usually forbidden to ask questions that suggest the desired answer. The judgment whether a question is leading is a contextual one, which takes account of such factors as phrasing and voice intonation. In a suit for breach of contract for the sale of goods the following would constitute a leading question: after establishing that the defendant had spoken with the plaintiff, counsel for the plaintiff asks the witness:

> "During this conversation, didn't the defendant declare that he would not deliver the merchandise?"

On the other hand, counsel could rephrase his question:

> "Will you state what, if anything, the defendant said, during this conversation, relating to the delivery of the merchandise?"

and thereby avoid the suggestiveness that makes the first question improper.

The leading questions doctrine embodies the view that the trier should hear the witness's unadulterated testimony, not that implanted by partisan counsel. The objective of minimizing partisan influence is promoted by prohibiting leading questions during direct examination.[2] Three points, however, should be noted. First, practical considerations sometimes militate against objecting to a leading question. The damage caused by the leading question may not justify the interruption or jury impatience occasioned by an objection.[3] Second, the trial judge is rarely reversed solely on the ground that he ruled erroneously on objec-

§ 4.6

1. For an account of behavioral research that indicates that the wording of a question has a profound effect upon the respondent's answer, see Loftus & Zanni, Eyewitness Testimony: The Influence of the Wording of a Question, 5 Bull. of Psychonomic Society 86 (1975).

2. The theory that leading questions may cause bias is supported by behavioral research. Supra n. 1; McCormick, § 6, at 11 n. 1. But see Cleary, Evidence as a Problem in Communicating, 5 Vand.L.Rev. 277, 287 (1952).

3. Experienced counsel generally objects sparingly, reserving his objections

tions to leading questions. Third, there are situations outside the reach of the general prohibition, and in these, leading questions are deemed proper.[4] Leading questions are permitted, for example, in eliciting preliminary information that is not in contention. Counsel can use leading questions to establish his witness's identity, address, and other incidental or nondisputed facts. Leading questions are also proper, at least for a brief period, if the witness is forgetful. Counsel may attempt to prompt recollection[5] by directing the witness's attention to the specific event in question. There is some risk that if the leading questions do not revive memory, the witness may nonetheless give an answer based upon the suggestion implied by the examiner's question. Whatever the theoretical extent of this risk, it is minimized by the practical controls, first, of the opponent's right to object that recollection has not been refreshed and, second, of further testing, during the cross-examination, of the witness's memory. Leading questions are also usually permitted in the interrogation of a very young witness. Again, some risk is encountered, especially since a youthful witness is presumably quite susceptible to suggestion. As a practical matter, however, leading questions may present the only effective method of eliciting his testimony. Finally, as developed below in greater detail, leading questions may be used to interrogate a hostile witness. Where leading questions are allowed during direct examination, the trial judge has ample power to prevent abuse, and on objection, or occasionally on his own initiative, he can restrict or terminate a leading inquiry.

The prohibition against leading questions is generally inapplicable during cross-examination. Here the assumption is that the cross-examiner and the witness are antagonistic, and that there has been no preparatory conference between them. It is further assumed that an uncooperative witness is not amenable to implied suggestion. In short, leading questions are proper during cross-examination because the risks assumed to be present in direct examination are thought to be absent in the supposedly hostile atmosphere of cross-examination.[6] Note that the use of leading

for situations in which he wishes to exclude evidence capable of significantly harming his case. A constant objector does not draw favor from the jury. Unless leading questions constitute a pattern or pertain to a significant point, it usually is advisable not to object.

4. Morgan & Weinstein at 51–52.

5. See §§ 4.7–4.8 for a discussion of what additional techniques are available when a witness's memory fails.

6. For further discussion of the reasons for the different treatment of direct and cross-examination, see Lempert & Saltzburg at 17–19.

questions aids the cross-examiner in controlling an adverse witness. His inquiries can be narrow and specific, designed to limit the range of response, and consciously framed to induce the witness to give the desired answer. Thus, the cross-examiner can question a hostile witness on his—the cross-examiner's—own terms, thereby lessening the damage that might otherwise accrue.

It should be apparent that the factual assumptions of cooperativeness (during direct examination) and hostility (during cross) which underlie the rule governing leading questions may be inaccurate with regard to many witnesses. Some witnesses have no allegiance to either of the parties. Furthermore, tactics may force the direct examiner to call a hostile witness, or the cross-examiner may have the opportunity to interrogate a witness who is friendly. If, for a particular witness, the usual assumption is erroneous, the opposing counsel may request a change in the mode of examination. The trial judge has the power to permit or deny leading questions, depending upon the actual relationship between examiner and witness. Federal Rule of Evidence 611, which codifies the common-law practice, contains the following pertinent provisions:

> (a) Control by Court. The court shall exercise reasonable control over the mode and order of interrogating witnesses and presenting evidence so as to (1) make the interrogation and presentation effective for the ascertainment of the truth, (2) avoid needless consumption of time, and (3) protect the witnesses from harassment or undue embarrassment.
>
> . . .
>
> (c) Leading Questions. Leading questions should not be used on the direct examination of a witness except as may be necessary to develop his testimony. Ordinarily leading questions should be permitted on cross-examination. When a party calls a hostile witness, an adverse party, or a witness identified with an adverse party, interrogation may be by leading questions.[7]

Note that the rule makes special reference to calling an adverse party. In this situation, a hostile exchange can be predicted. Consequently, the general rule is that the sponsoring counsel can, from the outset, treat the adverse party as a hostile witness.

7. See United States v. Schoupe, 548 F.2d 636 (6th Cir.1977) for an illustration of excessive use of leading questions by a prosecutor interrogating an uncooperative witness whom he had called to the stand.

In many states this rule is contained in a statute or rule of court which declares that a party opponent may be questioned under the rules that normally apply to cross-examination. For example, Illinois law provides:

> [A]ny party . . . may be called and examined as if under cross-examination at the instance of any adverse party. . . .[8]

The general thrust of this and similar provisions is to allow leading questions of adverse parties. This practice is based on the recognition that the assumption of friendliness is usually inapplicable. In addition, many jurisdictions, either by judicial interpretation or by express statutory provision, also permit the party calling his adversary to the stand to impeach the latter,[9] that is, to present evidence that raises doubts about his credibility.[10]

Closely allied with leading questions are so-called argumentative questions, which are improper during either direct or cross-examination. As the term suggests, an argumentative question is one designed to induce the witness to affirm counsel's interpretation of the evidence.[11] The question "From your testimony that *X* pointed to the building that was on fire, we can assume, can't we, that the fire was visible?" would be argumentative[12] and, on objection, should be struck or rephrased. Although argumentative questions are always improper (since the jury, not counsel and the witness, is supposed to draw the inferences), judges sometimes permit cross-examiners to ask questions that, in the strict sense, fall into this category.

Misleading questions[13] are also inappropriate during either direct or cross-examination. The vice of a misleading question is that it assumes as true a fact that either is not in evidence or is in

8. Ill.Rev.Stat.1982, ch. 110, ¶ 2–1102.

9. Id.; Utah R.Civ.P. 43(b); McCormick, § 38, at 84 n. 12. The Federal Rules of Evidence go further and permit the impeachment of *any* witness, by either party. Fed.R.Evid. 607. For a discussion of the relationship between impeachment and leading questions, see Saltzburg & Redden at 564–65.

10. See § 8.2. As noted elsewhere, the common law generally forbids a party from impeaching witnesses he calls to the stand. Id.

11. McCormick § 7.

12. See Dibona v. Philadelphia Transp. Co., 356 Pa. 204, 207, 51 A.2d 768, 770 (1947). Judges and lawyers sometimes use the adjectives "misleading" and "argumentative" loosely, or even interchangeably.

13. For some illustrations, see Life & Cas. Ins. Co. v. Garrett, 250 Ala. 521, 523–24, 35 So.2d 109, 111 (1948); In re Yale's Estate, 164 Kan. 670, 675, 191 P.2d 906, 909 (1948); Reardon v. Boston Elev. R. Co., 311 Mass. 228, 231, 40 N.E.2d 865, 866–67 (1942).

dispute. For example, the question "At any time during this assault, did anyone attempt to leave?" assumes the existence of the assault, yet the fact of the assault may be contested. Of course, if the witness in the foregoing example had just testified that there was an assault, the question would be relatively harmless. Sometimes, however, counsel uses the misleading question in an attempt to get a second witness to affirm the testimony of an earlier witness. For example, suppose one witness testifies to the assault, and another witness gives testimony about persons leaving the scene of the alleged affray. The question to the second witness, "Did anyone leave during the course of the assault?", is misleading because an affirmative answer might mean (1) only that someone left the scene or (2) that there was an assault and someone left. The problem is whether the witness affirmed the premise of the question or simply its specific inquiry, and it is this ambiguity that makes the question misleading.[14]

§ 4.7 Examining the Witness: Refreshing Recollection

Leading questions, we have noted, are permitted in circumstances in which they serve as a catalyst to recollection. This form of interrogation is not, however, the only courtroom technique that can be used to stimulate memory. Sometimes it is possible to revive the memory of a forgetful witness by showing him some object, often a writing prepared by himself or another, or by allowing him to listen to a recording. The association of the "reminder" with the forgotten event may induce recollection.[1] Although the item used to aid the witness with a faltering memory is frequently a writing, anything, including "a song, a scent, or a photograph,"[2] may be used to revive the witness's present memory. Under the majority and preferred view, the witness can refer to this writing (or other recordation), even though it describes the event about which he is to testify.[3] It is important to recognize, however, the limited purpose for which the document or

14. McCormick § 7. A question is also misleading when it assumes a fact for which there is no supporting evidence. The question "Did you stop using narcotics before or after these headaches about which you complain?" would be misleading if there were no evidence of narcotics use.

§ 4.7

1. See Annot., 125 A.L.R. 19 (1940), supplemented by Annot., 82 A.L.R.2d 473 (1962), discussing the subject of refreshing recollection.

2. United States v. Rappy, 157 F.2d 964, 967 (2d Cir.1946), cert. denied, 329 U.S. 806 (1947); see also Steele v. Coxe, 225 N.C. 726, 36 S.E.2d 288 (1945).

3. United States v. Riccardi, 174 F.2d 883 (3d Cir.1949), cert. denied, 337 U.S. 941 (1949), is a leading case. See Neff v. Neff, 96 Conn. 273, 278–79, 114

other reminder is used: it serves *only to refresh* the witness's recollection and not as an independent source of evidence. If, for example, after examining the writing, the witness states that he now has a present recollection of the event, he may continue his testimony. Even though he may occasionally consult the writing, it is his *testimony,* given from his restored memory, that constitutes the evidence received. This is an important distinction and lies at the heart of the proposition that whenever memory is in fact restored by the use of a writing or recording (or any other means), the testimony of the witness, not the object used to refresh memory, is the actual evidence in the case.[4]

The procedure for refreshing present recollection often calls upon the trial judge to make a difficult judgment, particularly when the object used to refresh recollection is a writing that contains an account of the occurrence in question. He must determine if the witness's recollection has actually been refreshed or whether the witness is merely reciting the contents of the document. An affirmation by the witness that his memory is restored is a persuasive, but not controlling, factor, especially if he continues to falter. It is apparent, of course, that if the judge determines that recollection has not been revived, he can no longer assume that the witness's testimony constitutes primary evidence. The primary evidence is the writing itself. Whether this writing is admissible is a separate question addressed in the next section.

The theory that denies evidentiary status to the writing, recording, or other object used to refresh present recollection has a practical consequence: even though the examiner has the object marked as an exhibit for purposes of identification, he is not entitled to admit it into evidence. This means that he cannot, for example, submit the exhibited writing for jury examination; the trier must rely entirely upon the testimony of the witness.

At the end of his examination the questioner relinquishes the writing to his opponent who may then use the item in conducting his adverse examination. This affords the opponent an opportunity to test the extent to which the witness actually recalls the event in question: he can attempt to expose discrepancies between the witness's testimony and the writing or otherwise try to demonstrate that memory is not revived or is inaccurate. Most jurisdic-

A. 126, 127–28 (1921). But see Morgan & Weinstein at 55–56.

4. McCormick, § 9, at 18.

tions also allow the opponent to introduce the writing into evidence for purposes of impeachment. These jurisdictions permit the jury to examine the document and assess the witness's testimony in light of the writing, even though the writing can be used only for the limited purpose of determining credibility.[5]

In most cases, of course, a direct examiner has consulted his witness prior to calling him to the stand. Thus, the refreshing of the witness's memory, if any such prompting is necessary, normally takes place outside the courtroom. When this occurs, the cross-examiner may not know whether or not his opponent has used a writing to stimulate the witness's memory. Sometimes, however, through investigation, discovery, or cross-examination, the opponent learns that a document has been used to refresh recollection. The question then arises whether counsel has a right to use this item during his cross-examination. A convincing argument can be made that refreshing a witness's recollection before trial, when the process cannot be observed by the trier, should give the cross-examiner the same right of access to the underlying writing as he has when the process of refreshing memory takes place in the courtroom. Some authorities, particularly in criminal trials, so hold.[6] In general, however, courts have been apprehensive that an adversary's right to inspect documents used to refresh recollection prior to trial would be too invasive of the files of counsel and client. Thus, at least at common law, the marked tendency was to deny or severely restrict access to such writings.[7]

Rule 612 of the Federal Rules of Evidence provides in part:

> Except as otherwise provided [by the Jencks Act, 18 U.S.C.A. § 3500] . . ., if a witness uses a writing to refresh his memory for the purpose of testifying either—
>
> (1) while testifying, or
>
> (2) before testifying, if the court in its discretion determines it is necessary in the interests of justice,
>
> an adverse party is entitled to have the writing produced . . . to inspect it, to cross-examine the witness thereon, and

5. This is an example of limiting the use of evidence to a particular purpose. See §§ 1.5, 6.2, 6.4. The subject of impeachment is covered in Ch. VIII.

6. See, e.g., State v. Mucci, 25 N.J. 423, 436–40, 136 A.2d 761, 766–70 (1957); State v. Bradshaw, 101 R.I. 233, 240–41, 221 A.2d 815, 818–19 (1966). In civil matters, documents that have been or might be used "to refresh" often can be reached through the discovery process. See Fed.R.Civ.P. 34. But see Fed.R.Civ.P. 26(b)(3).

7. 3 Weinstein & Berger, ¶ 612[01], at 16.

to introduce in evidence those portions which relate to the testimony of the witness.

Under these provisions, there is no absolute right to compel production of a writing used to refresh a witness's memory prior to his courtroom appearance but neither is such a writing invariably protected from disclosure. Access to the writing previously used lies within the judge's discretion, influenced by such factors as the importance of the testimony and the nature of the document used to refresh. The rule reflects a judgment that in view of other means, notably discovery, available to parties [8] to gain access to pertinent materials in the adversary's hands, it suffices to leave to the judge's discretion the issue of whether the opponent is entitled to a writing used to aid memory before trial.

Two further points deserve comment and both of these are pertinent when—and only when—a writing is used to refresh a witness's memory prior to his testimony at trial. The question often arises whether a judge may order the production of a document, previously used to refresh recollection, if that document would ordinarily be protected by an evidentiary privilege, such as that bestowed upon communications between client and attorney or between spouses.[9] A similar question arises with respect to a writing protected by work product immunity—the immunity that, in the absence of special need, protects from disclosure documents prepared by a party or his representative in anticipation of litigation.[10] By refreshing a witness's memory *prior* to trial, the party entitled to the privilege or immunity has avoided directly introducing the protected writing into the courtroom proceedings. Thus, the opponent's claim that any protection is waived—a claim that is uniformly upheld when memory is refreshed *during* a witness's testimony [11]—is not necessarily compelling. The issue is a close one, and the response of the courts has not been uniform.[12] Certainly, the fact that a protected writing was used to refresh

8. See H.Rep. No. 93–650, 93d Cong., 2d Sess., reprinted in 1974 U.S.Code Cong. & Admin.News 7086. Neither the federal rule nor the accompanying Advisory Committee Report makes clear whether a claim of privilege overrides the court's power under this rule to order one side to show the other a document. Probably, the privilege will prevail. Saltzburg & Redden at 584–85. See also United States v. Schoupe, 548 F.2d 636 (6th Cir.1977); Sporck v. Piel, 759 F.2d 312 (3d Cir.1985), cert. denied, 106 S.Ct. 232, ___ U.S. ___ (1985). But see text at note 16.

9. See §§ 9.2–9.3, 9.5–9.10.

10. Fed.R.Civ.P. 26; Friedenthal, Kane, & Miller, Civil Procedure, § 7.5 (1985).

11. McCormick, § 94, at 226.

12. Id.

recollection is an important factor in the judge's decision whether to exercise his discretion and order production. But if he concludes that under Rule 612 "it is necessary in the interest of justice" [13] to have the writing produced, there is some case authority holding that neither privilege [14] nor work product immunity [15] will defeat an order to produce.[16]

The second point is a troublesome one and ought to be clarified by an amendment to Rule 612. The opening phrase of that Rule states that its provisions governing disclosure are subject to any contrary provisions in the so-called Jencks Act.[17] That Act, which predated the passage of Rule 612, both facilitates and restricts the access of a criminal defendant to certain prosecution documents. Access is granted to a prior statement of any prosecution witness if it deals with the subject matter of his testimony and if it is, roughly speaking, an authenticated verbatim statement of the witness.[18] It is immaterial under the Act whether or not the statement was used to refresh the witness's recollection prior to trial. Other statements, including those that are not substantially verbatim, those that are unauthenticated summaries prepared by a government agent, and those of nontestifying witnesses, are protected from disclosure.[19] Further, even when disclosure of a statement is commanded by the Act, the defendant's

13. Fed.R.Evid. 612.

14. Wheeling-Pittsburgh Steel v. Underwriters Laboratories, 81 F.R.D. 8 (N.D.Ill.1978).

15. James Julian, Inc. v. Raytheon Co., 93 F.R.D. 138 (D.Del.1982). The work product doctrine affords only a qualified protection; the trial judge has discretion not to protect materials for which the opponent demonstrates "substantial need." Fed.R.Civ.P. 26(b).

16. A judge can refuse to recognize a privilege in two ways: he can find waiver of the privilege in the use of the material to refresh a witness's memory or he can simply construe the language of Rule 612 to grant the trial judge the discretion to weigh "the interests of justice" against the policies served by the privilege. Courts and even commentators frequently fail to distinguish the two theories. See, e.g., McCormick, § 94, at 226.

17. 18 U.S.C.A. § 3500.

18. "The term 'statement' . . . means—

(1) a written statement made by said witness and signed or otherwise adopted or approved by him;

(2) a stenographic, mechanical, electrical, or other recording, or a transcription thereof, which is a substantially verbatim recital of an oral statement made by said witness and recorded contemporaneously with the making of such oral statement; or

(3) a statement, however taken or recorded or a transcription thereof, if any, made by said witness to a grand jury." 18 U.S.C.A. § 3500(E).

19. See Palermo v. United States, 360 U.S. 343, 352–53 (1959), rehearing denied, 361 U.S. 855 (1959); McCormick, § 97, at 240; but see Brady v. Maryland, 373 U.S. 83 (1963) (prosecution must provide defense with evidence in its possession "favorable to [the] ac-

right to inspect the document does not accrue until after the direct testimony of the prosecution witness.[20] This last point, however, loses significance in the practical implementation of the Jencks Act: in order to avoid the delay that would ensue if accused's counsel had to study the prior statement while the prosecution witness was on the stand, most prosecutors deliver the statement at some convenient earlier time.[21]

Thus far, then, the technical complications arising from the interplay of Rule 612 and the Jencks Act seem manageable. The Act may require disclosure even when the Rule would not, and the Act may deny production even when, under the Rule alone, there would be discretion in the judge to order it. Difficulties arise, however, because in December of 1980 the Jencks Act, in a somewhat amended form, was embodied in Rule 26.2 of the Federal Rules of Criminal Procedure.[22] Although in practical effect the Act was superseded by the Criminal Rule, the statute was not formally repealed and, as noted above, is still expressly referred to in Rule 612 of the Federal Rules of Evidence. That the current reference in Rule 612 is to a statute that has been superseded by Criminal Rule 26.2 would be of little consequence were it not for several significant differences between the statute and Criminal Rule 26.2 which supersedes it. Rule 26.2 governs access not only of the defendant to statements of prosecution witnesses, but also of the prosecutor to statements of defense witnesses; more importantly, the Rule contains language from the Jencks Act that *grants access* to substantially verbatim authenticated statements but omits language from the Jencks Act that had been generally interpreted as *blocking production* of other statements such as those noted in the discussion above.[23]

cused"), discussed in 3 Weinstein & Berger, ¶ 612[02], at 17–18.

20. "In any criminal prosecution brought by the United States, no statement or report in the possession of the United States which was made by a Government witness or prospective Government witness (other than the defendant) shall be the subject of subpoena, discovery, or inspection until said witness has testified on direct examination in the trial of the case." 18 U.S.C.A. § 3500(a).

21. 3 Weinstein & Berger, ¶ 612[02], at 19, 20.

22. Id. at 19.

23. See text at n. 19. Rule 26.2 does not contain a provision corresponding to subsection (a) of the Jencks Act, quoted supra n. 20. In *Palermo,* cited supra n. 19, the Supreme Court held that "statements . . . which cannot be produced under [the Jencks Act] cannot be produced at all." The Court relied primarily on the legislative history of the Act to reach this result. It is not clear whether the "exclusivity" of the Jencks Act survives in Rule 26.2; see McCormick, § 97, at 240–41 (concluding that it does not); 3 Weinstein & Berger, ¶ 612[02], at 24–25.

Let us thus suppose that a witness refreshes his memory prior to trial by consulting a statement of another witness or by examining a report or summary prepared by a government agent. May the trial judge, acting pursuant to Rule 612, order disclosure of the document that was used to refresh memory? Production would be barred by the Jencks Act, which has not been formally repealed, but which arguably has been rendered ineffectual by the Criminal Rule that replaced it. Put otherwise, the present problem is whether to construe Rule 612 as if it no longer refers to the Jencks Act but rather refers to the more recently enacted Criminal Rule 26.2. It might also be asked, assuming Rule 612 does incorporate Rule 26.2, whether Rule 26.2 permits the use of material that the Jencks Act was construed to prohibit. The solution is far from clear.[24] Most of the legal commentary favors a construction that avoids the restricted access of the Jencks Act,[25] a view that is consonant with the trend toward increased discovery in criminal cases and consistent with the broad principle that a witness's credibility always should be subject to inquiry and testing.[26] The final answer has yet to be worked out by the courts or, preferably, by a clarifying amendment to Rule 612.

§ 4.8 Examining the Witness: Past Recollection Recorded

This subject is explained in detail elsewhere,[1] where it is treated as an exception to the hearsay rule. A brief exposition appears here because past recollection recorded (variously called recorded recollection or recorded past recollection) is governed by a rule that bears close kinship to the rule pertaining to refreshing present recollection. Nonetheless, these two rules should be sharply distinguished, for they rest upon distinct theories and apply in different situations.

The rule pertaining to past recollection recorded is not applicable, at least under the orthodox approach, if the witness is able to testify from revived memory. However, if resort to the procedures described in the preceding section fails to restore memory, it may be possible to introduce into evidence a writing that describes

24. For a comprehensive article that addresses the problem and assesses possible solutions, see Foster, The Jencks Act—Rule 26.2—Rule 612 Interface—"Confusion Worse Confounded," 34 Okla.L.Rev. 679.

25. 3 Weinstein & Berger, ¶ 612[02], at 25; McCormick, § 97, at 241–42.

26. Cf. Fed.R.Evid. 607; Ch. VIII; Davis v. Alaska, 415 U.S. 308 (1974).

§ 4.8

1. See Ch. VII, Part D.

the unrecalled event. It is necessary, however, to establish carefully a foundation comprised of the several requirements of admissibility. First, the witness must testify that the writing was made soon after the event in question and at a time when memory was fresh. If the writing was made by someone other than the witness, it suffices that the witness testify that he verified its accuracy while his memory was fresh. That is, even though the witness has no present recollection of the event, he must recognize the writing and be able to state that he remembers making it or verifying it soon after the event. Second, the witness must state that he presently believes the writing is accurate. These requirements are necessary to ensure the accuracy and reliability of the writing, which are particularly important since the cross-examiner, faced with a witness who cannot remember the event, will probably find it impossible to disprove the event by cross questions.

Notice that past recollection recorded, unlike present recollection refreshed, involves the use of the writing itself as evidence. Typically the contents of the writing which represent the witness's past recollection are read to the jury. The establishment of a proper foundation and the proffer of the writing are steps that usually are taken by the counsel who called the witness. However, the cross-examiner, if he is able to elicit from the witness the required foundation, can use the technique of past recollection recorded.

§ 4.9 Examining the Witness: The Opinion Rule

In deciding the historical facts, the factfinder (often a jury) frequently must rely on circumstantial evidence. When direct proof is unavailable, the trier finds the historical facts by a process of inference: from the evidence supporting one fact, the trier infers the existence of a related fact. Since the jury has the principal responsibility of deciding the facts through the inference-drawing process, it is generally deemed inappropriate for a lay witness to incorporate in his testimony his own inferences in the form of an "opinion" or "conclusion." This prohibition against lay opinion applies generally to any testimonial statement or description in which the lay witness's opinion is *unnecessary.* Put otherwise, the rule forbidding opinions is applicable in circumstances where the witness could, if requested, describe his observations in "factual" terms. If the witness can adequately reveal the "facts," his opinion is superfluous, because the jury, when provided these facts, is able to draw the necessary inferences.[1]

It will thus be seen that one justification for the rule against opinion is the apprehension that testimonial opinion might unduly influence the jury. Perhaps there is some risk that the trier's factual determinations will be improperly influenced by a witness's gratuitous opinion. The fundamental and more persuasive rationale for excluding lay opinion, however, rests upon the assumption that if the jury is in a position to draw the appropriate inferences, opinion offered by a lay witness is superfluous. Many courts now accept this modern rationale, and recent cases display a tendency to permit a witness's opinion when it appears helpful to the trier.[2] This preferred view also explains the long-standing practice by courts to admit expert opinion (which is usually helpful) while prohibiting most, but not all, lay opinion.

The traditional formulation of the rule against opinion holds that a lay witness should recite the observed "facts," but should not offer his "opinion." The difficulty of administering this rule is that there is no precise method of classifying a testimonial statement as either fact or opinion. Almost every statement contains some degree of inference. As McCormick indicates, the difference between fact and opinion is one of degree.[3] When a witness describes a tree as "gnarled and decaying" he is, in the strict sense, giving an opinion, although, as we shall see, the courts would deem this statement one of fact. The same is true when a witness states that the voice he heard was that of *X*. Brief reflection about routine social and business conversation demonstrates that it is saturated with inferences. What, then, is the judicial dividing line between fact and opinion?

The more general and conclusory a statement, the more likely it will be classified an opinion. Conversely, the closer a statement comes to describing the separate components of an observation, the more likely it will be deemed a statement of fact.[4] The statement "*X* is drunk" is a statement of opinion[5] (although

§ 4.9

1. VII Wigmore, § 1917, at 10 (Chadbourn).

2. See, e.g., Reed v. Allen, 522 S.W.2d 339 (Tenn.App.1974); Foundation Reserve Ins. Co. v. Starnes, 479 S.W.2d 330 (Tex.Civ.App.1972).

3. McCormick, § 11, at 27.

4. Professor McCormick presents a particularly illuminating discussion of the fact-opinion distinction. Id.

5. This testimonial statement might significantly assist the trier and, hence, many modern courts would allow it. See infra n. 8.

admissible in most courts anyway); the statement "*X* had poor muscular control and the odor of alcohol on his breath" is a statement of fact, as that term is used by the courts. Obviously, these two statements are not diametrically opposed. The difference between them is the degree to which the separate bases of a conclusion are individually identified and described. The opinion rule poses no barrier to any testimony that is deemed factual. However, the rule bans most, but not all, lay testimony that is cast in the form of an opinion.

A guiding principal of general application is one founded on practicality: lay opinion is usually inadmissible if it is reasonably practical and efficient for the witness to express the separate factual components underlying it. If it is feasible to break an opinion into its rudimentary factual parts, then, presumably, the trier will be in as favorable a position as the witness to draw inferences. The opinion, thus unnecessary, is inadmissible. Conversely, when it is impractical to place the trier in a position of equal competence to draw inferences, the witness may give his opinion.[6] Suppose, for instance, the witness testifies that "*X became angry* when his appointment was cancelled" or that "*Y looked fatigued and worried* when he reported to work." These statements are, under the usual judicial classification, opinions. Nonetheless, they are admissible opinions because of the impracticality of reducing them into their component parts. It will thus be observed that all statements of fact and some statements of opinion are admissible.

Although most generalizations in this area can be challenged by some of the many disparate court rulings,[7] it is possible to characterize further that class of statements regarded as permissible lay opinion. Where the observer-witness forms an impression immediately upon perceiving an event—that is, where he would naturally gain an impression or opinion without time for reflection and deductive reasoning—he can usually convey his perception to the trier in a conclusory statement. This spontaneity is usually associated with a perception that is not sequential: the

6. Many illustrations are contained in Parker v. Hoefer, 118 Vt. 1, 100 A.2d 434 (1953). For a case allowing lay opinion concerning vehicle speed and intoxication, see Howard v. State, 346 So.2d 918 (Miss.1977).

7. See, e.g., Daniell v. State, 37 Ala. App. 559, 563–64, 73 So.2d 370, 373 (1954), cert. denied, 261 Ala. 145, 73 So. 2d 375 (1954), which collects a sample of the many conflicting authorities. See also Weinstein & Mansfield et al. at 327–33.

witness perceives a thing or an event at once, as a unified whole. Thus, when a witness testifies that a car "passed at high speed," or that "*Y* looked old," an objection based upon the opinion rule should fail. The same may be said of the statement "*X* was drunk", although one could argue (and a few courts have held) that it is feasible to dissect this statement into such components as impaired speech, telltale breath, poor physical coordination, and so forth. Often, however, observers do not isolate these separate manifestations; rather they perceive drunkenness as an integrated whole. Even where separate observations can be detailed, the witness's account may not adequately convey the total impression, and thus his opinion is still helpful. Accordingly, many decisions have approved lay opinion that the actor in question was intoxicated.[8]

A number of cases express the principle that lay opinion on the ultimate issue is improper. It appears, however, that this should be true only in certain circumstances. A witness's opinion should be rejected if it contains conclusions or expressions of opinion that are superfluous and unhelpful (e.g., testimony that a party was negligent).[9] The same is true where his opinion contains a legal component that has not been adequately explained, and consequently might be misunderstood by the witness or jurors.[10] An example of this latter circumstance is found in testimony that "*X* had the capacity to make a valid will." [11] Standing alone, this is objectionable opinion. Most jurisdictions explicitly define testamentary capacity in a rather technical manner as including a capacity to know the nature and extent of one's property, to identify the objects of one's bounty, and to understand the nature and effect of a will. During the evidence-taking stage

8. E.g., Rivers v. Black, 259 Ala. 528, 531, 68 So.2d 2, 4 (1953); State v. Durrant, 55 Del. 510, 515–516, 188 A.2d 526, 529 (1963) (witness detailed separate observations, then gave opinion); F. Busch, Trial Procedure Materials 319 (1961). Courts also have been lenient in receiving statements of general physical condition. See, e.g., State v. Garver, 190 Or. 291, 314–318, 225 P.2d 771, 782–783 (1950). As to lay opinion about the subject's sanity, see VII Wigmore §§ 1933–38 (Chadbourn), indicating a general receptivity. Note that such an opinion may or may not be formed spontaneously, again demonstrating that no statement describing the ambit of the opinion rule can provide more than broad guidance.

9. Allen v. Matson Navigation Co., 255 F.2d 273, 278 (9th Cir.1958); Commonwealth v. Brady, 370 Mass. 630, 351 N.E.2d 199 (1976); McCormick, § 12, at 30–31. For a federal case allowing opinion on the ultimate issue, see United States v. Smith, 550 F.2d 277 (5th Cir.), cert. denied, 434 U.S. 841 (1977).

10. See Fed.R.Evid. 701, 704 and Adv.Comm.Notes.

11. McCormick, § 12, at 32.

of trial, neither the witness nor the jury may be aware of these legal requirements; thus a witness's opinion concerning *X*'s capacity may be subject to ambiguity and misunderstanding. However, in situations where an opinion involving a legal criterion would be helpful to the trier, there is recent authority supporting admissibility if the legal concept is adequately explained to the witness and the jury.[12]

In the eighteenth century, a distinguished English jurist remarked that an opinion is not evidence.[13] This assertion, which may have referred only to situations where the witness had no personal knowledge of the event in question, cannot be given a literal reading in the light of modern developments. A lack of personal knowledge about the subject of one's testimony is one thing; rendering testimony in a general or conclusory mode is quite another. We have already seen that certain opinions are freely admitted for jury consideration and that the traditional justification of the opinion rule is that there is usually no need for lay opinion.[14] An opinion that is correctly permitted over objection or even one that comes in without objection may be considered as evidence by the factfinder. The only time an opinion does not constitute evidence is when a judge, on motion or objection, rules that the opinion is improper and orders it stricken from the record or instructs the jury to disregard it.

Federal Rule of Evidence 701 [15] provides:

> If the witness is not testifying as an expert, his testimony in the form of opinions or inferences is limited to those opinions or inferences which are (a) rationally based on the perception of the witness and (b) helpful to a clear understanding of his testimony or the determination of a fact in issue.

This provision eliminates most of the useless quibbling that has been associated with enforcement of the rule against opinion. The first condition of the Federal Rule simply ensures that the witness has perceived the subject or event about which he gives opinion testimony. This is a familiar requirement, which has been uni-

12. Fed.R.Evid. 704 and Adv.Comm. Note. See McCormick, § 12 at 32.

13. The statement is traced to Lord Mansfield in VII Wigmore, § 1917, at 6 (Chadbourn). For a full and illuminating history of the opinion rule, see id. § 1917.

14. McCormick, § 11, at 28.

15. For similar provisions, see West's Cal.Evid.Code § 800; N.J.Evid. Rule 56(1).

formly recognized.[16] The second condition is a modest, but useful innovation. It shifts the focus of admissibility from practical *necessity,* still the principal criterion of admissibility in many common-law jurisdictions, to *helpfulness.* Whether an opinion is, under the formulation of the Federal Rule, "helpful to a clear understanding of . . . [the witness's] testimony" does not necessarily depend upon such factors as the spontaneity of the opinion or the ease with which its component parts may be separately stated. These factors are relevant, but not determinative. Accordingly, an opinion such as one in which *A* testifies that *B* was present and "should have heard *C*'s warning" or that "B knew of and understood certain regulations" should be helpful, even though under the traditional approach it might be excluded.[17]

§ 4.10 Examining the Witness: The Scope of Cross-Examination

The majority of jurisdictions in this country have adopted what is commonly called the American Rule (or Federal Rule). It limits cross-examination to subjects or topics that were covered by the direct examiner and to matters relating to the witness's credibility.[1] This limitation is intended to achieve an orderly evidentiary presentation, supposedly resulting in a fuller understanding by the jury; the presentation of one party's case is not interrupted by proof of other facts that the opponent wishes to establish.

An incidental effect of the application of the American Rule is that it allows the party who makes the opening presentation of evidence (plaintiff or prosecutor) to present a more convincing case in chief since, by controlling the scope of his direct examination, he thereby limits the range of adverse testimony that can be elicited during cross-examination. Consequently, the opening party can sometimes postpone evidence bearing upon unfavorable

16. See Adv.Comm.Note to Fed.R.Evid. 701. See, e.g., United States v. Smith, 550 F.2d 277 (5th Cir.1977); United States v. Butcher, 557 F.2d 666 (9th Cir.1977).

17. See United States v. Smith, 550 F.2d 277 (5th Cir.1977), cert. denied, 434 U.S. 841 (1977). Compare Commonwealth v. Moore, 323 Mass. 70, 76, 80 N.E.2d 24, 27 (1948) with State v. Taylor, 57 S.C. 483, 485–86, 35 S.E. 729, 730 (1900). See Annot., 10 A.L.R.3d 258 (1966).

§ 4.10

1. See, e.g., Conkling v. Conkling, 185 N.W.2d 777, 783 (Iowa 1971); Dinner v. Thorp, 54 Wash.2d 90, 95, 338 P.2d 137, 140 (1959). The rule is variously stated as limiting the cross-examiner to the "same points" or "subjects" or "connected facts." McCormick, § 21, at 52.

aspects of his case until his adversary presents the case in defense. Even if the adversary then adduces this adverse evidence, the direct examiner may have gained a psychological advantage by initially establishing a strong case. More importantly, the opponent will sometimes decide to abandon the point that he could not pursue on cross: the tactical advantage that might be gained in an immediate examination may be lost when the witness has a period of time away from the stand to collect his thoughts and, perhaps, listen to other witnesses or confer with friendly counsel.[2] In short, the point that would have been explored on cross-examination, were it not for the American Rule, may not be worth the trouble and risk of recalling an adverse witness.

Obviously, situations arise in which it is debatable whether the cross-examiner is probing the topics covered on direct or whether he is inquiring into new matters.[3] To begin with, there are slight variations among the jurisdictions in the wording of the American Rule. Some formulations may connote more restrictiveness than others.[4] Furthermore, even when the rule is couched in traditional terms (same "topics" or "subjects" covered on direct), difficulties arise. The mosaic of human events does not always permit sharp lines between descriptive testimony. The amorphous division between testimonial subjects often leads to debate between counsel and, unfortunately, is the source of a number of appeals. The trial judge should be granted broad discretion to determine when the cross-examiner has exceeded permissible bounds. The rule limiting the scope of cross-examination is intended as a regulation governing the order in which evidence is presented and, as such, it should be administered with considerable latitude and practical adaptability.

A minority of jurisdictions follow the English (or Massachusetts) Rule, which does not limit cross-examination. The cross-examiner can thus inquire into any relevant matter.[5] He can, for

2. McCormick, § 23, at 55. There also is confusion as to whether a cross-examiner who recalls a witness may use leading questions. This issue should be resolved on the basis of the relationship between the witness and the examiner (i.e., whether the witness clearly is identified with one side or the other) and not by the automatic application of the general rule that the party calling a witness cannot lead him. See generally IIIA Wigmore §§ 909–18 (Chadbourn).

3. It seems clear that the direct examiner should not be entitled to elicit only a fragment of a transaction or statement, thereby presenting a misleading or distorted account, and to confine the cross-examiner strictly to the scope of the testimony on direct. See McCormick, § 23, at 52.

4. Id.

5. McCormick, § 21, at 51.

example, not only attempt (as under the American Rule) to get the witness to retract or qualify part of his direct testimony, but also to have the witness testify about matters bypassed by the direct examiner, including those that aid in establishing a counter-claim, cross-claim, or affirmative defense. Finally, the cross-examiner may, as under the American Rule, probe topics which go to the witness's credibility.[6] This English or "wide-open" rule is easy to administer and minimizes the need for recalling witnesses.

A few jurisdictions have chosen a middle course between the American Rule and the English Rule. Under their approach, the cross-examiner may elicit any testimony that directly contests his opponent's allegations. He may not elicit testimony that goes solely to establish his own affirmative defense, counter-claim, or cross-claim, or other aspect of his case that does not controvert the opponent's allegations. In general, this means that the cross-examiner may not elicit testimony designed to substantiate his claims or to avoid liability by disclosing additional facts. In short, he cannot use cross-examination to adduce evidence in support of propositions for which he bears the burden of persuasion.[7] Under this intermediate rule, as under the American Rule, it is necessary to make topical discriminations in order to forbid testimony that does not properly belong within the scope of cross-examination.

Note that in all jurisdictions the cross-examiner may ask questions directed to credibility or impeachment. This means that he may propound questions designed to impugn the witness's motive to be truthful or to demonstrate aspects of the witness's prior conduct that cast doubt upon his veracity.[8] For example, the examiner may inquire whether the witness holds a grudge against one of the parties, whether he has a financial stake in the outcome of the case, or whether he has been convicted of a crime that may raise doubts about his credibility. Even though inquiry about these facts carries the cross-examiner beyond the scope of direct examination, it is everywhere permissible to elicit testimony pertinent to impeachment. Two reasons justify this practice: first, credibility is always implicitly in issue and, second, a central

6. J. Maguire, Evidence, Common Sense and Common Law, 46 (1947); McCormick, § 22, at 54.

7. VI Wigmore, § 1889, at 712 (Chadbourn). The rule operates to prohibit the plaintiff from premature examination as to those new matters that he should reserve for his case in rebuttal. McCormick, § 21, at 53.

8. See, e.g., United States v. Fontana, 231 F.2d 807, 809–12 (3d Cir. 1956); Williams v. Graff, 194 Md. 516, 522, 71 A.2d 450, 452 (1950). Impeachment is discussed in Ch. VIII.

purpose of cross-examination is to weaken or negate the testimony given during direct examination. Although the cross-examiner is always free to probe a witness's credibility, it does not follow that the examiner can interrupt his opponent's evidentiary presentation by calling witnesses to impeach his opponent's witness. Normally, he must call these impeaching witnesses during a stage of the trial (such as the case in defense) allocated to his evidentiary presentation.

Except for questions pertaining to impeachment, the American Rule, as we have seen, obliges the cross-examiner to stay within the subject-matter bounds set by the direct examiner. On occasion, however, the cross-examiner will exceed the permissible scope. The question then arises as to what consequences attend this violation.[9] The opposing counsel can, of course, successfully object to the excessive questions, thereby containing the interrogation within the proper bounds; or he can permit the cross-examiner to pursue these inquiries. As to those matters beyond the scope of direct examination, the cross-examiner is said to have "made the witness his own." That is, as to these new subjects, the witness is treated as if he had been called by the cross-examiner. Thus, the direct examiner may successfully object to the cross-examiner's use of leading questions in regard to any new subject matter. In some jurisdictions, the cross-examiner is also forbidden to impeach the witness,[10] at least as to the testimony that is beyond the boundaries set by the direct examiner.

Federal Rule of Evidence 611 [11] provides:

> Scope of cross-examination. Cross-examination should be limited to the subject matter of the direct examination and matters affecting the credibility of the witness. The court may, in the exercise of discretion, permit inquiry into additional matters as if on direct examination.

Although these provisions ensure that federal courts will continue to apply the American (or Federal) Rule, they also reaffirm, and perhaps enlarge, the trial judge's discretion to permit the cross-examiner to inquire about subject matter beyond the scope of direct. If this discretion is exercised and new topics are explored,

9. See McCormick § 24.

10. The rule against impeaching one's own witness is considered (and criticized) in § 8.2. Fed.R.Evid. 607 freely allows impeachment.

11. Fed.R.Evid. 611(b). See United States v. Callahan, 551 F.2d 733 (6th Cir.1977), appeal after remand, 579 F.2d 398 (6th Cir.1978); United States v. Ellison, 557 F.2d 128 (7th Cir.), cert. denied, 434 U.S. 966 (1977).

the interrogation must proceed in the mode of direct examination which means, under normal circumstances, without the use of leading questions. However, if the witness is actually hostile or uncooperative and leading questions are therefore justified, the cross-examiner should be entitled to continue to lead the witness, even in connection with the new topics.[12] This is but another way of saying that whether leading questions are appropriate should not invariably depend upon who called the witness or upon the scope of an examination, but rather upon the responsiveness or hostility of the witness.[13] This guiding principle, generally recognized by modern authorities, should govern all phases of interrogations, whether direct or cross. Finally, exceeding the scope of direct examination under the quoted Federal Rule has no effect upon the cross-examiner's right to impeach, since another Federal Rule ensures that either party may attack the credibility of any witness.[14]

§ 4.11 Examining the Witness: The Interaction of the American Rule and Certain Rules of Privilege

A major difficulty with the American Rule is the practical application of the amorphous standard "same subject or topic." [1] As a measure of the permissible range of cross-examination, this standard necessarily generates disagreements at trial and on appeal concerning the boundaries of interrogation that must be observed by the cross-questioner. Indeed, a few appellate courts have made a dispositive point of the housekeeping rule governing scope of interrogation, and have reversed judgments because the trial judge permitted (or denied) cross-examination in accordance with the dictates of the American Rule.[2] The cases also suggest that courts have sometimes applied the American Rule, combined with a rule of privilege, in a manner that absolutely precludes the admission of evidence that, arguably, should have been admitted at some point in the trial.

12. Fed.R.Evid. 611(c); S.Rep. No. 93–1277, 93d Cong., 2d Sess., reprinted in 1974 U.S.Code Cong. & Admin.News 7072. See 3 Louisell & Mueller, § 336, at 434.

13. VI Wigmore, § 1887, at 704–05 (Chadbourn). In jurisdictions with wide-open cross-examination, the use of leading questions similarly should be regulated.

14. Fed.R.Evid. 607.

§ **4.11**

1. See § 4.10, nn. 1–3 and accompanying text.

2. Compare Conley v. Mervis, 324 Pa. 577, 188 A. 350 (1936) with Finch v. Weiner, 109 Conn. 616, 145 A. 31 (1929). It should be noted that it may be unfair for the cross-examiner to ask leading questions throughout a far-reaching examination, especially if the witness is not hostile. See § 4.10, nn. 2, 13.

As elsewhere noted,[3] rules of privilege grant to the privileged person (called the "holder") the right to withhold relevant, but privileged, testimony from the factfinder. For example, by either statute or judicial opinion, confidential communications between attorney and client and those between husband and wife have been given a privileged status. As privileged matter, these communications are protected from disclosure, absent a waiver. A few rules of privilege do not simply protect specified communications from compelled disclosure, but include the broader right to refuse to give any testimony or, as it is more often stated, to decline to take the witness stand. For example, one spouse may be privileged from being called by the prosecution to testify against his spouse in a criminal case.[4] If the spouse testifies for the defense, he is of course subject to cross-examination. However, if cross-examination is restricted to the topics covered on direct (as under the American Rule), most authorities hold that the prosecutor cannot subsequently call the witness and examine him with respect to other relevant topics.[5] Thus, in this setting, the scope-of-direct rule affects more than just the order of proof; it affects the range of admissible evidence.

The constitutional privilege against self-incrimination also interacts with the scope-of-direct rule to limit the evidence that may be disclosed. As applied to ordinary witnesses, in either criminal or civil proceedings, this privilege may be selectively invoked to avoid responding to any question that calls for an answer that may incriminate the witness.[6] The privilege is broader when applied to the accused in a criminal case. Any question put by the prosecution presumably aids the government in obtaining a conviction. Thus, the accused in a criminal trial is entitled to more than selective invocation of the privilege: he enjoys the broader right to avoid altogether the prosecutor's inquiries and he is entitled to exercise this right by refusing to take the witness stand.[7] Suppose, however, that the accused elects to take the stand in order to give testimony on his own behalf. The question raised is whether he has now waived completely his

3. See § 9.1.

4. E.g., Hawkins v. United States, 358 U.S. 74 (1958) (adopting common-law rule that wife may not testify against husband over his objection). See also Proposed Fed.R.Evid. 505. But see Trammel v. United States, 445 U.S. 40 (1980) (only testifying spouse may claim privilege). Neb.Rev.Stat. § 27–505(2).

5. See McCormick, § 23, at 55.

6. Id. at § 136.

7. Id., § 130, at 315; VIII Wigmore, § 2276, at 459, § 2260, at 369 (McNaughton).

constitutional protection, with the result that (at least *insofar as the Constitution* is concerned) he may now be cross-examined on any topic relevant to the offense charged.

There is one line of authority suggesting that if the accused elects to testify, he thereby completely waives any protection conferred by the constitutional privilege against self-incrimination as to the offense charged.[8] It is not clear whether the broad waiver extends so far to allow incriminating inquiries that bear *solely* upon the credibility of the witness-accused. Frequently, however, a nonconstitutional rule of evidence like Federal Rule 608(b) specifies that the "giving of testimony . . . does not operate as a waiver . . . with respect to matters which relate only to credibility."[9] In any event, the rule of broad waiver permits the prosecutor, free of constitutional restraint, to pursue all topics relevant to the offense charged. If this constitutional interpretation is correct, the only barrier to a complete cross-examination is the scope-of-direct rule. Since this rule is intended to govern only the order of proof,[10] it would seem that the judge should either waive the rule and allow a full cross-examination or, in the alternative, he should apply the rule during cross-examination, but permit the government subsequently to call the accused as its own witness and make additional inquiries about the offense charged. Each of these procedures recognizes that the rule of evidence limiting the scope of cross-examination is a rule only of trial administration, designed to regulate the order of proof. It does not embody a major policy or principle underlying the factfinding process.

8. Johnson v. United States, 318 U.S. 189, 195–96 (1943), rehearing denied, 318 U.S. 801 (1943); VIII Wigmore § 2276, at 465–66 (McNaughton). This complete waiver may reach all matters relevant in the case, or all relevant matters except those relating only to the credibility of the accused, or all relevant matters except those indicating guilt of some other crime. 3 Louisell & Mueller, § 337, at 441–42. The extent of the accused's waiver is discussed in § 9.11. An accused may testify in connection with a preliminary motion without effecting a waiver for trial purposes. Simmons v. United States, 390 U.S. 377, 389–390 (1968), on remand, 395 F.2d 769 (7th Cir.1968), appeal after remand, 424 F.2d 1235 (7th Cir.1970); Fed.R.Evid. 104(d). But see Harris v. New York, 401 U.S. 222 (1971). Generally, testifying in one proceeding does not preclude invoking the privilege in a separate and independent proceeding. McCormick, § 132, at 326.

9. Fed.R.Evid. 608(b). See 3 Weinstein & Berger ¶ 608[07], pointing out that incriminating evidence seldom affects *only* the defendant's credibility.

10. McCormick, § 23, at 54–55; 3 Louisell & Mueller, § 336, at 428.

In fact, however, most cases,[11] either expressly or by implication, make the rule prescribing scope the determinative factor governing the extent to which the accused is deemed to have waived his privilege against self-incrimination. Thus, by offering only selective testimony on direct examination, the accused testifying in a jurisdiction that follows the American Rule thereby limits his waiver and confines the prosecutor to the subject or topics covered during direct examination. Under the rationale of these cases, the prosecutor not only is prohibited from exceeding the scope of direct examination, but also is forbidden to later recall the witness, who has not waived his privilege against self-incrimination as to those matters outside his direct testimony. Thus, a lowly rule designed to produce trial efficiency takes on the far-reaching significance of prescribing the boundaries of a great constitutional principle.[12] Aside from this anomaly, the use of the

11. E.g., Brown v. United States, 356 U.S. 148, 154–56 (1958), rehearing denied, 356 U.S. 948 (1958); United States v. Miranda-Uriarte, 649 F.2d 1345, 1353–54 (9th Cir.1981); United States v. Hernandez, 646 F.2d 970, 978–79 (5th Cir.1981), cert. denied 454 U.S. 1082 (1981).

12. Brown v. United States, supra n. 11, used language suggesting that the extent of the accused's waiver of the privilege against self-incrimination was controlled by the scope of allowable cross-examination under the American (or Federal) Rule. Most federal trial and appellate courts have construed *Brown* to mean that a constitutional restraint operates to confine cross-examination within the scope of direct. However, a passage in McGautha v. California, 402 U.S. 183, 213 (1971), rehearing denied, 406 U.S. 978 (1972), decided thirteen years after *Brown*, states that cross-examination may extend to "matters reasonably related to the subject matter of . . . direct examination." Many courts have seized upon this language to broaden somewhat the scope of cross, while at the same time acknowledging that the scope-of-direct rule limits the extent of the constitutional waiver. See, e.g., United States v. Hernandez, 646 F.2d 970, 979 (5th Cir.1981), cert. denied 454 U.S. 1082 (1981). The "reasonably-related" test of the allowable scope of cross has an amorphous quality; thus it is not surprising that federal Courts of Appeals have often reposed in trial judges considerable discretion to determine if a topic was expressly or impliedly broached on direct and if a question on cross bears a reasonable relationship to a subject raised during direct. Some federal appellate decisions uphold trial court determinations that, in effect, come close to permitting any question that is relevant to the case as a whole. See, e.g., United States v. Miranda-Uriarte, 649 F.2d 1345 (9th Cir.1981); United States v. Palmer, 536 F.2d 1278 (9th Cir.1976); United States v. Hearst, 563 F.2d 1331 (9th Cir.1977), cert. denied, 435 U.S. 1000 (1978). Note that a liberal determination of what is allowable under the scope-of-direct rule is not the same as a judge's discretionary ruling pursuant to Federal Rule 611(c) to allow the range of cross-examination to exceed the scope of direct. The exercise of discretion under the rule is an acknowledgment that cross is broader than direct; such a 611(c) ruling could not be sustained if the fifth amendment waiver, occasioned by giving direct testimony, is not wide enough to remove the constitutional protection of the "new topics" that the judge, acting pursuant to the rule, allows the cross-examiner to explore.

rule regulating cross-examination to determine the extent to which the privilege against self-incrimination is waived produces the incongruity of a narrow waiver in a jurisdiction adhering to the American Rule, but a broad waiver in a jurisdiction following the English Rule. It is not easy to explain why a defendant taking the stand in Louisiana (which applies the English Rule)[13] triggers a broad waiver of his constitutional rights, whereas a defendant testifying in Connecticut (which applies the American Rule)[14] does not.[15]

§ 4.12 The Components of Trial: Closing Argument and Judge's Charge

After the close of the evidence, the lawyers have an opportunity to address the trier and to state their respective arguments concerning the evidence and what it proves. The plaintiff's counsel (or, in a criminal case, the prosecutor) makes his closing argument first. The defendant's lawyer then delivers his closing argument and following this, the plaintiff's counsel gives his argument in reply. Observe that the party who has the burden of persuading the jury of the existence of the facts necessary for a recovery (or conviction) has the opportunity to make the final forensic presentation.

Counsel have considerable latitude in setting the form and content of closing argument.[1] They may urge the factfinder to believe certain evidence and to draw reasonable inferences from it.[2] They may not, however, allude to evidence that was not offered or that was rejected, nor may they urge that evidence admitted only for a limited purpose be considered for another, improper purpose.[3]

13. La.Stat.Ann.–Rev.Stat. 15:462.

14. State v. Zdanis, 173 Conn. 189, 195, 377 A.2d 275, 279 (1977), appeal after remand, 182 Conn. 388, 438 A.2d 696 (1980), cert. denied, 450 U.S. 1003 (1981).

15. For commentators' views of what criteria should govern the extent of the waiver, see 3 Weinstein & Berger, ¶ 611[03], at 47–50; 3 Louisell & Mueller, § 337, at 445–46.

§ 4.12

1. For a helpful discussion of closing argument with an emphasis upon tactical considerations, see R. Keeton, Trial Tactics and Methods, § 7.12 (2d ed. 1973).

2. Roberts v. State, 346 So.2d 473 (Ala.Crim.App.1977), cert. denied, 346 So.2d 478 (1977). Compare Hayes v. Coleman, 338 Mich. 371, 382, 61 N.W.2d 634, 640 (1953) with Harvey v. Aubrey, 53 Ariz. 210, 214–15, 87 P.2d 482, 483–84 (1939). For cases in which counsel exceeded permissible bounds, see United States v. Barker, 553 F.2d 1013, 1024–25 (6th Cir.1977); Robinson v. Pennsylvania R.R., 214 F.2d 798, 800–03 (3d Cir.1954).

3. See People v. Housholder, 74 Mich.App. 399, 253 N.W.2d 780 (1977);

In the federal system and in most states, the judge instructs the jury after, rather than before, the closing arguments of counsel.[4] In his charge, the judge always sets out the applicable law; he may also include instructions to guide the jury in the proper use or evaluation of the evidence.[5] As elsewhere noted,[6] some jurisdictions permit the judge to comment on the evidence.

Notes

1. *Stages of a Jury Trial.* The selection of a jury is, in the broad sense, part of the trial. In a jury case, the phases of a typical trial may be summarized as follows:

(a) Jury Selection (Voir Dire)

(b) Counsels' Opening Statements

(c) The Presentation of Evidence
Plaintiff's Case in Chief
Defendant's Case in Defense
Plaintiff's Case in Rebuttal
Defendant's Case in Rejoinder

(d) Counsels' Closing Arguments

(e) Judge's Charge

(f) Jury Deliberation and Verdict

2. *Order of Counsels' Argument.* The plaintiff or prosecutor, it will be recalled, gives his opening argument first, makes the first evidentiary presentation, and is entitled to make the first and last closing argument. Are there psychological (forensic) advantages in having the first and last "word"? Consider the following closing argument to the jury by defense counsel:

VI Wigmore, § 1807, at 352 (Chadbourn). See also I Wigmore, § 13, at 694–97 (Tillers). Counsel can make reference to matters that are judicially noticed. VI Wigmore, § 1807, at 358–59 (Chadbourn). For examples of potential abuses in closing argument, see Lempert & Saltzburg at 1163–79.

4. Charging the jury before closing argument rather than afterwards makes it more convenient for counsel to argue about the jury's duties under the instructions as, for example, where counsel stresses the elements that must be found to constitute fraud or assumption of risk. However, the prevailing view, which reserves the judge's instruction until last, has the advantage of concluding the trial on an impartial note. Furthermore, counsel's preceding arguments are made with knowledge of what the instructions will be, since the lawyers and judge already have conferred in chambers over the latter's charge and he has made a final decision concerning what instructions he will give.

5. See § 1.5.

6. See § 1.7, n. 2.

The plaintiff's counsel, Mr. Agee, made the first opening statement, he presented his evidence first, he made the first closing argument and in a moment he will have yet another chance to address you. I was second in line to present my evidence, and this is my only opportunity to address you with a closing presentation. Perhaps it is fair that the plaintiff has the first and last word, because as His Honor will instruct you, the plaintiff has the burden of persuasion in this case. He must convince you that his alleged facts are the true facts and, if you don't believe that, you are sworn to return a verdict for my client, Mr. Woodson.

And I would like to make one other point before I review the evidence with you. If you will bear with me during this one chance I have to speak, if you will closely observe the weaknesses in the plaintiff's case and the ways in which the evidence fails to support it, then, if Mr. Agee should confront you with some new argument, please ask yourself, Ladies and Gentlemen, what I might say to answer that argument if I were able to address you again.

Turning now to the evidence, you will recall that the very first witness, Mrs. Kline, stated that she was uncertain whether the . . ..

3. *Order of Presentation: Effect on the Jury.* Research by social psychologists on the effect that the order of presentation of arguments and evidence has on jurors carries tactical implications for trial attorneys. Studies reveal, among other things, a "recency effect" (arguments heard most recently will have the most influence) and a "primacy effect" (when information about other *people* is received, as opposed to information about events or situations, the *first* information received has the strongest effect). Lind, The Psychology of Courtroom Procedure, in Kerr & Bray, The Psychology of the Courtroom, 25 (1982). This accords with research indicating that *in general* jurors remember the beginning and end of a trial better than the middle. For a discussion of the use of psychology to explain jury behavior, exploring the reactions of jurors to a variety of stimuli, see Vinson, Litigation: An Introduction to the Application of Behavioral Science, 15 Conn.L.Rev. 767 (1983).

4. *Past Recollection Recorded.* Under the orthodox approach, the rule allowing the introduction of a witness's prior writing as past recollection recorded is not applicable if the witness is able to testify from present (aided or unaided) recollection. Why should a witness's prior written account of an event not be admissible even if he can testify from memory, especially if the writing was not prepared for litigation?

5. *Opinion Rule.* A distinguished professor has commented on the opinion rule as follows:

> The rule of evidence that (normally) excludes from judicial proof laymen's opinions is designed to keep the witness' language at the neutral descriptive level and to exclude his erroneous or biased references; and the exceptions to the rule show recognition that the language of common nouns and adjectives is inadequate to communicate to a jury the data from which it can infer that, for instance, a voice heard by the witness was X's voice. Hence the witness is allowed to state directly that the voice he heard was X's voice.

E. Patterson, Jurisprudence, Men and Ideas of the Law, § 1.15, at 47 (1953).

6. *Scope of Cross-Examination.* Most jurisdictions applying the American Rule make it applicable to all witnesses, including parties who testify. In a few state jurisdictions, when a civil party calls himself as a witness, the opponent (cross-examiner) can exceed the scope of direct examination. McCormick, § 25, at 57. Is there any reason why the usual restriction should be lifted in this instance?

7. *Cross-Examination and Self-Incrimination: Waiver When Offenses are Joined for Trial.* Suppose that in one trial the accused is tried for multiple offenses—for example, for three robberies occurring at different times. If *D* takes the stand and testifies as to offenses one and two, may he be cross-examined on offense three? The answer probably turns upon whether the third offense is so closely related to the first two that its commission by *D* is relevant to show that he committed the other two or, perhaps, to show his state of mind in committing the other two. See People v. Perez, 65 Cal.2d 615, 55 Cal. Rptr. 909, 422 P.2d 597 (1967), cert. granted 390 U.S. 942 (1968), cert. dismissed 395 U.S. 208 (1969); see § 5.14. In short, the third offense may be reasonably related to offenses one and two which were the subject of *D*'s voluntary testimony.

The single trial for multiple offenses poses an additional dilemma for the accused. If he testifies only as to some of the offenses, his silence as to the others may increase the likelihood that the trier would find him guilty of the other charges. Further, if he is deemed to have waived his fifth amendment privilege as to the others, the prosecutor will be allowed to comment on the silence. The general prohibition against prosecutorial comment on the accused's exercise of a valid fifth amendment privilege would not apply. See *People v. Perez,* supra.

Chapter V

RELEVANCE: RECURRING PROBLEMS OF CIRCUMSTANTIAL PROOF

---

§ 5.1 Scope

The requirement of relevance, we have noted elsewhere,[1] is one of general application. Even when this fundamental requisite of admissibility is satisfied, however, a trial judge has general discretionary authority to exclude evidence if he determines that its probative value is substantially outweighed by such practical considerations as prejudice, confusion of the issues, time consumption, or misleading the jury.[2] The application of this balancing process takes full account of the particular facts and circumstances of the case being tried; differences among cases, coupled with the broad discretionary authority vested in the trial judge, limit the precedential value of these ad hoc rulings.

The materials in this chapter focus upon recurring patterns of circumstantial proof. Certain issues of evidence have repeatedly arisen, and courts and legislatures have responded by pronouncing rules of exclusion (or admissibility) that are intended to yield uniform results in similar situations. The bases underlying these rules are varied, but the dominant influences are probative force, the countervailing practical considerations noted above, and various public policies discussed later in this chapter. To the extent these rules are formulated as specific, absolute directives (as opposed to broad principles subject to the trial judge's exceptions) they restrict or eliminate ad hoc discretionary rulings by the trial judge.[3] Thus, these rules add an element of uniformity to evi-

§ 5.1

1. § 2.1.

2. § 2.5.

3. McCormick, § 185, at 547.

dence law; they also produce predictable tensions and some diverse judicial responses when, as is often the case, the "similar" situations purportedly governed by one of the rules have in fact significant differences among them. This chapter examines many of these rules, their underlying bases, and their effect upon the trial process.

§ 5.2 Character Evidence: In General

Character evidence is one area in which specific rules have been developed in an effort to strike the proper balance between the probative value of evidence and the opposing practical or policy considerations.[1] The potential probative force of character evidence is not difficult to see. We know that historical or adjudicative facts often are established at trial by circumstantial proof. In many instances, issues of fact involve questions about someone's conduct. Because character evidence is often circumstantially probative of one's actions, it is usually relevant. There are a variety of situations in which character evidence could be important, but several examples will illustrate typical contexts:

(1) In an automobile accident case, the only issue may be whether either or both of the two parties were negligent. The plaintiff wants to introduce evidence that the defendant often drives carelessly and has been responsible for several automobile accidents. The trier would be asked to infer that the defendant negligently caused the accident that injured the plaintiff.

(2) In a case for assault and battery, the defendant may claim that he acted in self-defense because the plaintiff was the first aggressor. To support this allegation, the defendant offers evidence that the plaintiff is a turbulent and violent person. The defendant seeks to have the trier infer that the plaintiff began the hostilities.

(3) In a prosecution for larceny, the prosecutor may offer to show that the accused has a record of past convictions for shoplifting, embezzlement, and robbery. The prosecutor argues that since the accused committed other crimes, it is more probable that he committed this one.

In all of these examples, one can reasonably argue that the evidence of the actor's character is probative of the specific conduct in question. The character trait of the party seems to have a

§ 5.2

1. McCormick, § 186, at 549–50.

"tendency to make the existence of [a] fact . . . of consequence . . . more probable . . . than it would be without the evidence."[2] The countervailing considerations, however, should also be apparent. Evidence of carelessness, turbulence, or past crimes may be given excessive weight by the jury or may cause it to judge the actor on his past rather than on his present conduct. Character evidence may also distract the jury from the central elements of the case, and its introduction may considerably lengthen the trial.

Recognition of these potential countervailing dangers has produced strict limits on the admissibility of character evidence. These limits respond to three determinants: the purpose for which character is to be used, the form of character evidence offered, and the type of proceeding, civil or criminal. The most important factor is the ultimate purpose for which evidence of character is offered, that is, whether the character that is supported by the evidence is to be used directly or circumstantially. Note that in the three foregoing hypothetical illustrations, the proponent seeks to use character circumstantially: from the evidence offered, the trier is, first, to infer the existence of the relevant aspects of character *and, then, to infer* that the subject acted consistently with that character. In contrast, the direct use of character occurs when character, or more specifically a character trait, is an essential element in the case. This direct use is freely allowed in all courts.[3] Circumstantial use of character, however, is disallowed in most jurisdictions in civil cases and, although everywhere allowed in criminal cases, its use in criminal trials is hedged with restrictive rules. The major restrictions limit the circumstances in which character evidence is admissible, specify the party who can introduce it, and prescribe what form or type of evidence is admissible to show character.

Possible forms of character evidence include (1) specific instances of past conduct that are probative of the relevant character trait; (2) testimony by a witness who is familiar with the person in question and who can state his opinion whether the subject has a certain character trait; and (3) evidence of the subject's community reputation for possessing the character trait in question. All of these types of character evidence carry dan-

2. Fed.R.Evid. 401.

3. Character is an essential element in only a few types of civil suits; it is very rarely an essential element in a criminal proceeding. See McCormick, § 187, at 551–52.

gers of prejudice, confusion, misleading the jury, and time-consumption; these practical counterweights must be balanced against the potential probative value of character evidence. Arguably, evidence of specific acts has the greatest potential to show character accurately, and evidence of community reputation has the least. However, courts historically have emphasized judicial expedition (probably at the expense of probative force) and have shown a distinct preference for reputation evidence because its presentation and rebuttal require comparatively little time. Only in recent years has opinion evidence gained favor, largely because the shift in residential patterns from small towns to urban centers has weakened the assumption that most people have a community reputation.[4] Because evidence of specific instances is likely to consume considerable time (as well as to arouse prejudice), its admission is limited to those cases in which character is a central element in the litigation, that is, cases in which character is "an essential element of a claim, charge, or defense."[5] In these instances its greater probative force is a prevailing consideration; further, since character is a central issue, evidence that reveals character cannot be said to distract the trier from the principal features of the case.

§ 5.3 Character Evidence: Character An Essential Element of a Claim, Charge, or Defense

The substantive law sometimes makes character a dispositive issue at trial: the existence or nonexistence of a character trait is itself an issue that directly determines the outcome of the case. In these instances, the trier does not use character as the basis for inferences about particular past conduct—that is, circumstantially. Such a case is a libel or slander suit where character is defamed and the defense is truth.[1] The defendant, for example, states that the plaintiff is "corrupt and dishonest"; in the resulting suit for defamation, the defendant bases his defense upon the truth of his statement. Plaintiff's character for dishonesty and

4. Courts also have begun to admit evidence of a person's reputation in his employment community as well as his residential community. See § 5.6, n. 6; § 8.3(c).

5. Fed.R.Evid. 405(b). See United States v. Brown, 547 F.2d 438, 445 n. 4 (8th Cir.1977), cert. denied, 430 U.S. 937 (1977).

§ 5.3

1. See McCormick, § 187, at 551 n. 1; Weinstein & Mansfield, et al. at 992–93 n. 4; Conner v. Dart Transp. Serv., 65 Cal.App.3d 320, 135 Cal.Rptr. 259 (1976).

corruption is directly in issue, and the inferential chain stops with the establishment of these traits. Further inferences about particular conduct are not required. Likewise, where an employer is sued for negligently engaging an employee of uncontrollable temper or intemperance, the character of the employee is placed directly in issue.[2] In criminal trials character is seldom directly in issue. An example of a charge that places character in issue is the seduction of a woman of chaste (i.e. high moral) character [3]; where the character of the victim is an element of the criminal charge.

The distinguishing characteristics of the cases above, or of any action in which character is said to be "directly in issue," is that character constitutes an essential "element of a charge, claim, or defense." [4] In these cases, of course, there exists no question as to the relevance of character evidence. Because character is itself a dispositive issue in the case, evidence intended to establish (or refute) the character trait in issue is always received.[5] Furthermore, many jurisdictions admit any *form* of character evidence that has probative value including testimony of (1) specific past acts; (2) opinions held by qualified observers; and (3) reputation in the community.[6] This generous receptivity stands in marked contrast to the begrudging approach that has traditionally prevailed when character is used circumstantially. In the latter instance, which is described in more detail below, not only are there strict limitations as to when character may be shown, but there are additional restrictions upon the type of evidence that may be used to establish character.

2. See, e.g., Christy v. United States, 68 F.R.D. 375 (N.D.Tex.1975); Winchester v. Padgett, 167 F.Supp. 444, 448 (N.D.Ga.1952); Guedon v. Rooney, 160 Or. 621, 87 P.2d 209 (1939). Cf. International Security Life Ins. Co. v. Melancon, 463 S.W.2d 762 (Tex.Civ.App. 1971).

3. See, e.g., Va.Code § 18.2–68.

4. Adv.Comm.Note to Fed.R.Evid. 404. Fed.R.Evid. 405(b) uses this phrase in declaring that specific instances of conduct are admissible to prove character only when it is an essential element in the action. For other cases, see McCormick § 187.

5. IA Wigmore, § 69.1, at 1457 (Tillers). See Adv.Comm.Note to Fed.R. Evid. 404.

6. See Fed.R.Evid. 405; West's Ann. Cal.Evid.Code § 1100, Law Rev.Comm. Comment; Morgan & Weinstein at 200. Contra, Guedon v. Rooney, 160 Or. 621, 87 P.2d 209 (1939). McCormick asserts that the particular kind of character trait in issue sometimes determines which of these various types of evidence will be received. McCormick, § 187, at 553.

§ 5.4 Character Evidence: Character Used Circumstantially

As we have seen, the circumstantial use of character involves not only the establishment of the relevant character trait, but also the inference that the particular conduct in question was consistent with the actor's character. If, for example, the issue in a prosecution for criminal assault is who attacked first, the defendant or the victim, the defense may wish to offer evidence that the victim has an aggressive and violent character; the desired inference is that his actions were commensurate with his character and, hence, that he attacked first. Specifically, the inferential chain is this: from the evidence presented, the factfinder infers a particular character trait, from which it further infers relevant actions that are manifestations of this trait. Used circumstantially, character serves only the subsidiary function of helping the trier reach an ultimate proposition about conduct (or, possibly, state of mind). The probative value of character evidence is thus attenuated and such convincing force as it does possess must be measured against the countervailing practical costs attending its introduction.[1]

It should be emphasized, however, that the probative value of character evidence can vary considerably from case to case. The degree of probative force associated with this evidence is affected by the strength and nature of the character trait (i.e., how dominant and specific it is), by the forcefulness of the evidence to establish that trait, and by the strength of the inference that the act in question is likely to result from the character trait. Some further examples, set out in subsequent sections, will illustrate these points.

§ 5.5 Character Evidence: Circumstantial Use of Character in Civil Cases

Arguably, one could have a character trait of carelessness or, more specifically, of carelessness in performing a certain activity such as driving.[1] Should the trier of fact be permitted to infer, in accident litigation, that an automobile driver who had such a trait was at fault on the occasion in question?[2] The risk in drawing

§ 5.4

1. Adv.Comm.Note to Fed.R.Evid. 404.

§ 5.5

1. Likewise, one could have a trait of exercising due care in the performance of certain activities.

2. For a thoughtful article that suggests a negative answer, at least where

this inference is that careless drivers often drive properly and, to state the obvious but inverse proposition, even generally careful drivers sometimes drive carelessly. Nonetheless, the evidence has a degree of probative force that seemingly satisfies the basic test of relevance: it increases somewhat the probability that the generally careless driver was at fault.[3]

Observe that the value of this evidence of a specific character trait (careless driving) appears to have more probative value than would evidence demonstrating a general carelessness in all activities. But even the inference from frequent lapses in driving care to a specific, contested act or omission (e.g., speeding or failure to stop or look at an intersection) carries with it several probative difficulties. First, the actor's careless driving may not be manifested in the particular negligent conduct at issue in the suit: one's careless disregard of speed limits, for example, is not very revealing on the issue of whether he failed to signal that his car was turning. Secondly, as noted above, due care may have been exercised on the occasion in question despite a pattern of careless driving. These considerations weaken the case for admitting character evidence because they present uncertainty and heighten the apprehension that the trier might give undue weight to evidence of "negligence character."

Arguably, in another context the probative force of character evidence is stronger. Suppose the plaintiff has a propensity toward truculence and physical violence. Injured in an affray with the defendant, he brings suit for assault and battery. The defendant pleads self-defense and offers evidence of the plaintiff's violent character to support the inference that the latter was the initial aggressor. The test of relevance is clearly satisfied: evidence of the character trait makes it more probable than it would be without the evidence that the plaintiff was the aggressor.[4] Of course, a violent or aggressive person will sometimes exercise restraint, thereby acting inconsistently with his character trait. However, the inference from aggressive character to violence may be stronger than the inference from traits of carelessness to a specific careless act. Physical aggression is purposeful activity; carelessness is often the result of inattention. Therefore, one could argue, a trait of turbulence and violence is likely to be

accident proneness is involved, see James and Dickinson, Accident Proneness and Accident Law, 63 Harv.L.Rev. 769 (1950).

3. See §§ 2.2–2.3.

4. See supra n. 3 and § 5.2, nn. 1–2.

manifested in a physical encounter, whereas carelessness, even in driving, can be evinced in a variety of ways. The validity of these tentative assertions remains an open question. The courts, however, have had to make both tentative assumptions and practical judgments in determining the admissibility of character evidence.

The civil cases dealing with character evidence reflect an inconsistent pattern. The dominant view, embodied in the Federal Rules, is that character evidence offered to support the circumstantial use of character in civil cases is generally not worth its cost in time, distraction, prejudice, etc., and is, accordingly, completely rejected.[5] A minority view admits certain character evidence in limited cases, such as those involving fraudulent misconduct or assault and battery. The distinguishing feature of these cases is that the alleged conduct usually involves moral turpitude or at least carries the stigma of strong societal disapprobation;[6] typically, punitive damages are available to the complaining party. The quasi-criminal nature of these civil suits has persuaded some courts to extend to the civil party against whom such misconduct is alleged a right that, as we shall see, is usually reserved for the accused in a criminal case. Perhaps the fact that activity with criminal overtones represents such a marked departure from the expected civil norm causes these minority courts to decide that the probative worth of character evidence has special force—that is, the greater one's deviation from the norm, the more one's character is implicated. In any event, in these jurisdictions the party charged with misconduct may introduce evidence that his character is good and thus inconsistent with the conduct alleged.[7] Of course, the favorable character trait he seeks to establish must be inconsistent with the alleged activity or else its probative value would be marginal or nonexistent. A character trait of honesty would be inconsistent with an allegation of deceitful misrepresentation and hence probative, but a character trait for nonviolence would not.

The minority of courts which do allow character evidence in specific kinds of civil cases have had their greatest precedential influence in one particular type of case: assault and battery where the defendant claims self-defense. Here, many courts that gener-

5. Fed.R.Evid. 404(a). Note, however, that character evidence can be used circumstantially to impeach a witness. See § 8.3(c).

6. McCormick § 192.

7. McCormick § 192. An early leading case supporting this minority view is Hess v. Marinari, 81 W.Va. 500, 94 S.E. 968 (1918).

ally disallow character evidence in civil cases when character is used circumstantially permit the defendant to introduce not only evidence of his peaceful character, but also to introduce evidence of the victim's propensity for violence or aggression.[8] The evidence is offered, of course, to support by inference the defendant's claim that the victim was the aggressor.[9] The victim-claimant may respond to the evidence by introducing evidence of the defendant's turbulent or aggressive character [10] (or, for that matter, by rebuttal evidence that the victim's character is nonviolent). The more general acceptance of character evidence in assault and battery,[11] but not in other civil contexts, is difficult to explain. Perhaps this receptivity is an implied acknowledgment that the probative relationship between a violent character and truculent conduct is stronger than the usual character-to-conduct nexus.[12]

§ 5.6 Character Evidence: Circumstantial Use of Character in Criminal Cases

Because most criminal acts involve deliberate conduct, it is plausible that the trier would be especially aided by knowledge of the accused's character. If the accused is generally disposed toward criminal acts, this disposition increases the likelihood that he committed the act with which he is charged. Further, the probative link between character and conduct is strengthened in cases where a *specific* character trait directly relates to particular alleged conduct. For example, the character trait of dishonesty relates directly to a criminal act involving fraud, cheating, or deception. Again, however, the probative value of character evi-

8. 91 A.L.R.3d 718 (1979).

9. A related, but distinct, situation exists when the civil defendant offers evidence of the victim's reputation for violence and couples this evidence with evidence that the defendant *was aware* of the victim's reputation. Here, admissibility is widespread. McCormick, § 192, at 571 n. 5. The theory is that the victim's reputation bears upon defendant's apprehension and, of course, the defendant's state of mind is a significant factor in determining whether he acted reasonably. The defendant could also show that he knew of specific acts of violence by the plaintiff (and hence was afraid).

10. Id. Contra, Fed.R.Evid. 404(a)(1)(2) which uses the terms "accused" and "prosecution," making it clear that the circumstantial use of character evidence is restricted to criminal cases.

11. In Rich v. Cooper, 234 Or. 300, 380 P.2d 613 (1963), the Oregon Supreme Court refused to extend the circumstantial use of character evidence to civil cases other than assault and battery where the defendant claims self-defense. A police officer, sued by the plaintiff-arrestee for assault and battery, sought to introduce evidence of the plaintiff's violent character for the inference that the plaintiff was likely to resist arrest. The court held this evidence inadmissible.

12. See supra, text at n. 4.

dence must be weighed against the policies of exclusion. At least two related risks of serious prejudice to the accused attend the use of character evidence. First, the trier might accord undue probative force to evidence of the accused's bad character, using it as the major determinant of guilt in the crime charged. Secondly, the trier might deemphasize the risk of an incorrect determination of the crime charged because evidence of the accused's unfavorable character provokes the belief that he should be confined or otherwise penalized. These dangers of prejudicial effect, when combined with the counterweights of time consumption, distraction, and confusion of the issues, have caused the courts to unite in a general principle: the prosecution may not initially show the defendant's bad character trait(s) for the inference that he is more likely to have committed the crime charged.[1]

The accused, on the other hand, is entitled to use character evidence in presenting his defense. The gravity of a criminal conviction, involving the possible loss of life or liberty, has influenced all courts to give special dispensation to an accused: he is permitted to show character traits (e.g., honesty, peacefulness) inconsistent with the crime charged.[2] The dangers of prejudice to the accused do not exist with respect to evidence of a relevant trait of "good" character offered by the accused, although the potential costs to the trial process of increased time consumption and distraction are present. The courts, however, consider paramount the accused's interest in protecting his freedom and hence they subordinate the countervailing practical considerations.

The principle that the accused may "place his character in issue,"[3] as the cases often express it, does not answer the question of what kind of evidence is admissible for this purpose. In addressing this issue, it first should be recalled that the basic requirement of all evidence is that of relevance. In the present context, the principle of relevance demands a showing that the character trait portrayed by the defendant is inconsistent with the

§ 5.6

1. McCormick, § 190, at 557–58; Fed.R.Evid. 404(a).

2. McCormick, § 191, at 566; Fed.R. Evid. 404(a)(1). But see United States v. Davis, 546 F.2d 583 (5th Cir.1977), cert. denied, 431 U.S. 906 (1977), excluding good behavior evidence offered to negate willfulness in trial for prison escape; a difficulty with admitting this evidence is that it supports good character by specific acts. See § 5.2.

3. McCormick notes that this phrase is misleading because character is still being used circumstantially. McCormick, § 191, at 568. Character is almost never an element of a charge or defense in a criminal case. 2 Louisell & Mueller, § 141, at 146.

crime charged. We have noted that this requirement would not be satisfied, for example, where an accused charged with criminal fraud offered evidence that he was a nonviolent person. Assuming relevance is satisfied, there are several types of character evidence that have probative value to establish the accused's favorable character traits. These are, as we have already observed: (1) previous acts relevant to the character trait in question; (2) opinion testimony given by one or more witnesses who know the accused and who testify as to his (relevant) good character; and (3) testimony of witnesses familiar with his (relevant) good reputation.

The traditional view, which emphasizes judicial expedition, still prevails in some jurisdictions and limits the accused to evidence of his community reputation.[4] His "character witnesses" are subjected to a comparatively brief period of interrogation during which they state their familiarity with his reputation.[5] Increasingly, however, courts have come to doubt the existence of a community reputation for many persons, especially those who reside in large metropolitan areas.[6] A partial escape from the restrictions of the orthodox rule is found in those jurisdictions that allow evidence of reputation within the employment community where the accused works.[7] A more direct approach, endorsed by the Federal Rules and probably by a majority of jurisdictions, is to

4. McCormick, § 191, at 567.

5. "In America the usual method of proof of character . . . is by general reputation after foundation testimony has been given to show that the character witness knows the reputation of the person in question. Following the foundation proper questions are: Does the person have a general reputation as to the trait involved (designating it) in the community of (naming it) or in larger centers in the area in which he is well known (stating it)? Do you know that reputation? Is it good or bad?" M. Ladd & R. Carlson, Cases and Materials on Evidence 223 (1972).

6. "Such a faith [in reputation evidence as a measure of character] is a survival of more simple times. It was justified in days when men lived in small communities. Perhaps it has some justification even now in rural districts. In the life of great cities, it has made evidence of character a farce." Cardozo, Nature of the Judicial Process, 157 (1921).

7. People v. Bouton, 50 N.Y.2d 130, 428 N.Y.S.2d 218, 405 N.E.2d 699 (1980); United States v. Parker, 447 F.2d 826, 830–31 (7th Cir.1971); People v. Kronk, 326 Mich. 744, 40 N.W.2d 788 (1950); Hamilton v. State, 129 Fla. 219, 176 So. 89 (1937). But see Bush v. State, 149 Ga.App. 448, 254 S.E.2d 453 (1979). See also Mass.Gen.Laws Ann. c. 233, § 21A (1959). McCormick states that evidence of reputation is increasingly permitted when the reputation has been developed within "other substantial groups of which the accused is a constantly interacting member." McCormick, § 191, at 568. Fed.R.Evid. 803(21) excepts from the hearsay rule "reputation of a person's character among his associates or in the community."

permit proof of character either by reputation or by receiving the opinion of persons who are sufficiently familiar with the accused to be able to testify concerning the trait in question.[8] The probative force of opinion evidence usually surpasses that of reputation evidence: the former is the product of direct observation and conclusion; the latter is merely the recital of an opinion or conclusion that is based on the more remote source of community hearsay.[9]

Proof by opinion evidence may, however, take more time than proof by reputation because the cross-examiner can (within reasonable limits set by the trial judge) probe the specific occurrences and observations that underlie the opinion.[10] Surely, however, this expenditure of time is a small price for the increased probative force of personal opinion. Additional reasons supporting the admissibility of opinion by a knowledgeable witness are, first, the practical difficulty of finding a qualified "reputation witness" willing to testify and, second, the superiority of opinion in providing the trier with a basis for making an intelligent evaluation of the subject's character. It should be noted that opinion witnesses need not be confined to lay persons. The Advisory Committee Notes and subsequent cases establish that a psychiatrist, for example, may testify to his opinion of the accused's character.[11]

Observe, however, that most courts do not permit the accused to establish his character by introducing evidence of specific instances of past conduct. Evidence of specific occurrences is potentially the most time consuming and distracting of the three possible means of showing character.[12] Admitting this evidence would put the principal focus of both direct and cross-examination

8. Fed.R.Evid. 405(a); United States v. Morgan, 554 F.2d 31 (2d Cir.1977), cert. denied, 434 U.S. 965 (1977). State v. Scalf, 254 Iowa 983, 119 N.W.2d 868 (1963); McCormick, § 191, at 567 n. 14. See VII Wigmore § 1986 (Chadbourn).

9. Michelson v. United States, 335 U.S. 469, 477 (1948) (characterizing reputation evidence as opinion-based-on-hearsay).

10. These include, but are not limited to, events that would affect the subject's reputation. As will be discussed in the next section, a prosecutor may probe a reputation witness's knowledge of rumors and certain occurrences which should be generally known to the community. This inquiry, however, usually is limited to a yes or no answer by the witness and hence ordinarily does not consume as much time as the cross-examination of an opinion witness.

11. Adv.Comm.Note to Fed.R.Evid. 405; United States v. Hill, 655 F.2d 512, 516–17 (3d Cir.1981), cert. denied, 464 U.S. 1039 (1984).

12. Fed.R.Evid. 405 and Adv.Comm. Note. See, e.g., United States v. Davis, 546 F.2d 583 (5th Cir.1977), cert. denied, 431 U.S. 906 (1977).

of the character witness upon selected past acts of the accused. These inquiries can raise collateral issues concerning the existence, number, or nature of past acts, thus exacting additional costs in time consumption, distraction, and, possibly, confusion and surprise.

§ 5.7 Character Evidence: Presenting and Cross-Examining the Reputation or Opinion Witness

The procedures that control the proof of character through the use of one or more reputation witnesses [1] promote trial expedition by sharply focusing the scope of the examination. A criminal trial provides a convenient illustration of proof by reputation, although the same principles apply in civil cases in which reputation evidence is admissible. Furthermore, there are significant similarities (but some differences) between the cross-examination of a reputation witness and the cross-examination of an "opinion" witness. These will be noted below. It suffices for the moment to reiterate that the reputation witness (who may or, perhaps, may not know the subject personally) testifies as to the subject's community reputation; the opinion witness (who always knows the subject) testifies that in his opinion the subject possesses certain character traits. Both types of witnesses are generically referred to as "character witnesses." Assume that the accused calls a character witness to give evidence of the accused's good reputation. The witness first states the association, such as residence in the accused's community, that enables him to be familiar with the accused's reputation for the relevant character trait.[2] The witness is then asked the nature of that reputation and, if he replies as expected, he will simply state, "It is good."

It should be apparent that this terse characterization not only lacks color and impact, but it also eludes a discriminating assessment because the trier is without any guidance as to the kind or number of occasions underlying the asserted reputation. Furthermore, the trier does not know if the witness personally observed any of these occasions, a fact that might have influenced his answer.[3] The process of cross-examination does, however, afford a

§ 5.7

1. See generally §§ 5.2–5.6.

2. Sample questions appropriate to establish the necessary foundation for a character witness are set out in Ladd, Techniques and Theory of Character Testimony, 24 Iowa L.Rev. 498, 519–527 (1939).

3. In theory the witness is testifying only to what he has heard; the observation of specific conduct is relevant to the formation of an opinion, but the

somewhat ritualistic test of the accuracy of the witness's assertion about the accused's reputation. As a first step, the prosecutor may further examine the witness's opportunity to know the accused's reputation. For example, he may inquire how long the witness has been a member of the accused's community. Second, he may ask the witness about damaging rumors of which one familiar with the accused's reputation should presumably be aware.[4] A major thrust of these questions, which usually must be asked in a "have-you-heard" form,[5] is to test the witness's familiarity with the accused's reputation. A further purpose of these inquiries is to ascertain the standard that the witness is applying in his assertion that the accused has a good reputation. Thus, the prosecutor might ask a question such as "Have you heard that the accused was convicted in 1984 for receiving stolen property?" In the leading case, Michelson v. United States,[6] the question "Have you heard that the accused *was arrested* for receiving stolen property?" was approved by the United States Supreme Court on the theory that an arrest (even when there is no subsequent conviction) affects one's reputation and, hence, inquiry into the witness's knowledge of the arrest was proper.

Note that if the character witness has not heard of an unfavorable event, his familiarity with the accused's character is brought into question; if he has heard of an unfavorable event, but nonetheless states that the accused enjoys a good reputation, his standard for determining that the reputation is favorable is brought into question. The event—or, more precisely, the rumor inquired about—must be one that would affect the reputation to

reputation the witness is portraying is the community's view of the accused.

4. See, e.g., Snead v. State, 243 Ala. 23, 8 So.2d 269 (1942) (character witness appearing in a prosecution for rape asked if he had heard of defendant's ravishing other women on specified occasions).

5. When character evidence is restricted to reputation only, the inquiries are addressed in the "have you heard" format rather than in the "did you know" mode because the former focuses on the witness's acquaintance with the general talk about the accused in the community, while the latter questions the witness's personal knowledge. Michelson v. United States, 335 U.S. 469, 482 (1948). The federal rules (which permit opinion evidence) avoid most problems over the form of cross-examination questions by stating "[o]n cross-examination, inquiry is allowable into relevant specific instances of conduct." Fed.R.Evid. 405 and Adv.Comm. Note. But see United States v. Curtis, 644 F.2d 263, 268–69 (3d Cir.1981), appeal after remand, 683 F.2d 769 (3d Cir. 1982), cert. denied, 459 U.S. 1018 (1982) (even though Federal Rules permit opinion as well as reputation evidence, a witness who has testified only as to reputation may be cross-examined only as to reputation).

6. 335 U.S. 469, 472–87 (1948).

which the witness has testified.[7] Thus, where the witness has testified that the accused has a good reputation for veracity, it would be improper to ask a have-you-heard question about an incident involving aggressive conduct.

The technique of cross-examination described above presents an overzealous prosecutor with opportunities for abuse. For example, the prosecutor might ask about a rumor for which there is not a reasonable basis. The courts therefore require that the cross-examiner ask only questions that he can propound in good faith—that is, questions based upon a reasonable belief of the actual existence of the rumor inquired about. Many authorities add the qualification that this belief is reasonable only if based upon reliable information that confirms the *actual existence* of the event giving rise to the rumor.[8] The trial judge has the responsibility of ensuring that the prosecutor's questions are not spurious. Misconduct should trigger the imposition of sanctions upon the offending attorney, and should also give rise to a mistrial where the transgression is too prejudicial to ameliorate by a curative instruction.[9]

During the prosecutor's case in rebuttal, he may present reputation witnesses to refute the accused's asserted good reputation for the particular character trait in question. This opportunity, of course, is conditioned upon the accused first placing his character in issue. Thus, if the accused has attempted to show that he has a good reputation for honesty and obedience to law, the prosecutor may try to show that he has a bad reputation for these traits. Just as the accused's reputation witnesses are subject to cross-examination, so too are the government's reputation witnesses. Their qualifications may be probed and they may be asked "have-you-heard" questions concerning an incident that is likely to be known in the community and which is consistent with the character portrayed by the defense.

Considerations of time consumption and distraction limit the inquiry that may be conducted by have-you-heard questions: the cross-examiner must settle for the answer of the witness. If the

7. In *Michelson,* the Court rejected the "Illinois rule" which would restrict inquiry about arrests only to "very closely similar if not identical charges." Id. at 483.

8. United States v. Lewis, 482 F.2d 632, 639 (D.C.Cir.1973).

9. McCormick, § 191, at 569. Such reversals, however, have been rare. Id. at n. 14. See generally Annot., 3 A.L.R.3d 965 (1965). For an example of appellate tolerance, see United States v. Morgan, 554 F.2d 31 (2d Cir.1977), cert. denied, 434 U.S. 965 (1977).

prosecutor's question is "Have you heard that the accused was arrested for receiving stolen property?" and the witness answers "No," the prosecutor's only recourse is to repeat the question—and even this tactic may be blocked if the judge, in his discretion, sustains the opponent's objection. The prosecutor may not present extrinsic evidence to demonstrate to the jury that the arrest occurred or, at least, that rumors to that effect exist. More importantly, neither the questioned witness nor the accused may attempt to erase the damaging inference of the question by proving the nonexistence of the arrest or any such rumors. Additional inquiry into this collateral subject is considered not worth the inpairment of judicial expedition and efficiency. This truncation of allowable proof underscores the importance of the cross-examiner's good faith.

Wigmore argues that the testing of an accused's reputation witness by "have-you-heard" questions is an unjustified practice.[10] In his view the jury is unable to limit its concern to the credibility of the reputation witness. Instead, it is likely to use the rumor communicated by the question to infer that the rumor exists and that it is true. The jury may then infer that the accused is likely to be guilty of the acts for which he is now on trial. Obviously, this technique of testing a witness's qualifications does involve risks of prejudice.[11] However, without such questions the trier has little or no basis for evaluating the character witness's assertion that the accused has a good reputation for the relevant character trait. It is true, of course, that the prosecutor can weaken the effect of the accused's reputation witness by presenting government witnesses who will state that the accused has a bad reputation for the trait in question. As a practical matter, however, such witnesses may be difficult to produce, since many persons might be reluctant to proffer this testimony. Furthermore, even if the prosecutor can produce one or more contradictory witnesses who will assert that the accused has a bad reputation, it is difficult for the trier to evaluate the conflicting lines of reputation evidence unless the witnesses' knowledge and standards are tested. A similar need exists for adequately testing—usually by questions in a "did-you-know" format—character witnesses who give opinion

10. IIIA Wigmore, § 988, at 920–21 (Chadbourn).

11. The prejudicial dangers are equally great with the "did you know" questions permissible in jurisdictions that allow opinion evidence to establish character.

testimony. Thus, the courts that allow opinion testimony permit the cross-examiner to test the basis of the witness's opinion.

There are additional reasons why probing the basis of the testimony of a character witness does not, on balance, treat the accused unfairly. The accused alone determines whether to make an issue of his character. If he decides to offer character evidence, he has a comparatively free choice in the selection of persons who will act as his reputation (or opinion) witnesses. These advantages, it seems, justify the current practice of allowing the cross-examiner to probe specific rumors or events that bear upon the direct testimony of a character witness.

As suggested above, there are obvious parallels between the use of reputation and opinion to establish character. The opinion witness, like the reputation witness, must also provide "foundation testimony." Here, however, the required foundation consists of testimony that reveals sufficient familiarity with the subject to form a reliable opinion about the character trait in question. The witness then states his opinion of the accused's character with regard to this trait. The cross-examiner may then probe the basis of this opinion and attempt to show that the witness's knowledge (familiarity) is incomplete or that the standard applied by the witness in concluding that the subject has a good character is questionable. Technically, in testing the basis of the witness's opinion, the cross-examiner should couch his inquiries in a "Do-you-know-that . . ." or "Are-you-aware-that . . ." format, but this distinction is often not observed. A have-you-heard question (usually reserved for testing the reputation witness) that is put to an opinion witness does little harm since, presumably, his opinion of the subject could be affected by what he hears as well as by what he sees.[12] Of course, a good-faith basis in asking about prior incidents inconsistent with the character claimed is essential.

§ 5.8 Character Evidence Pertaining to a Victim or Other Non-Party

In some circumstances, the character of one who is not a party is circumstantially relevant to an issue involving conduct. Because the circumstantial use of character usually is disallowed in

12. See Adv.Comm.Note to Fed.R. Evid. 405; but see United States v. Curtis, 644 F.2d 263, 268–69 (3d Cir.1981), appeal after remand, 683 F.2d 769 (3d Cir.1982), cert. denied, 459 U.S. 1018 (1982).

civil cases,[1] the issue of the admissibility of evidence of a non-party's character most frequently arises in a criminal setting. Usually the issue is whether either the accused or the prosecution can introduce evidence of the victim's character. A typical setting is a trial for murder in which an accused claims self-defense, alleging that the victim was the first aggressor. May the defendant introduce evidence that the victim was a violent and aggressive person? The accused's right to introduce character evidence as proof of conduct has been properly viewed as extending to the victim's character. A related context in which the issue formally arose with great frequency was in prosecutions for rape. When an accused claimed the defense of consent, he could usually support it with evidence of the victim's unchastity or sexual promiscuity.[2] In recent years, the passage of "rape shield" provisions has severely restricted the accused's opportunity to introduce evidence of the victim's prior sexual conduct or reputation.[3] Other instances in which a non-party's character is relevant to the guilt or innocence of an accused are theoretically possible,[4] but seldom arise.

In any event, the courts have generally permitted an *accused* to introduce evidence of a victim's character when the asserted defense makes it relevant.[5] In some jurisdictions the manner of proof is limited to evidence of reputation,[6] although there is a general trend toward allowing opinion testimony.[7]

Of course, when the accused presents testimony of the victim's character trait(s), the prosecutor may cross-examine the reputation or (where allowed) the opinion witness and may present reputation (or opinion) witnesses of his own.[8]

§ **5.8**

1. See § 5.5.

2. See Morgan & Weinstein at 181; Berger, "Man's Trial, Woman's Tribulation: Rape Cases in the Courtroom," 77 Colum.L.Rev. 1 (1977).

3. See § 5.9.

4. See Uviller, Evidence of Character to Prove Conduct: Delusion, Illogic, and Injustice in the Courtroom, 130 U.Pa.L.Rev. 845, 856 (1982), speculating that a defendant accused of bribery might assert a defense of extortion and offer to support it with proof of the bribed official's greed, or that one accused of "joyriding" might attempt to prove the victim's generosity to bolster his claim of permissive use of the vehicle.

5. Fed.R.Evid. 404(a)(2); IA Wigmore § 63 (Tillers); McCormick, § 193, at 571–72 (discussing homicide cases where self-defense is asserted).

6. See, e.g., Barrett v. State, 140 Ga. App. 309, 310–11, 231 S.E.2d 116, 117–18 (1976).

7. Fed.R.Evid. 404(a)(2) and 405(a) permit reputation and opinion evidence to show a victim's character. However, Rule 412, discussed in § 5.9, limits the use of such evidence in rape cases.

8. McCormick, § 193, at 572 (homicide cases).

A difficult question arises when the accused does not call any witnesses to testify about the victim's character, but through the pleadings and the evidence, makes an issue of the victim's conduct and, by inference, his character. This indirect attack on character occurs most frequently in a trial for violent homicide when the accused pleads self-defense and offers evidence that the victim was the first aggressor. A number of courts and the Federal Rules hold that in prosecutions for homicide, a plea of self-defense, coupled with evidence that the deceased was the first aggressor, is sufficient to trigger the prosecutor's right to offer rebuttal evidence that the victim was a person of peaceful character.[9] This position recognizes that in cases of physical violence, evidence of character has sufficient probative value to warrant admission. The special need for the evidence, occasioned by the unavailability of the victim, strengthens the case for admissibility. Furthermore, the risk of unfair prejudice to the accused is reduced in such instances because the evidence is directed to the victim's character, not to that of the defendant. In this circumstance, the trier is likely to use the evidence for its intended purpose: determining who was the first aggressor. Some risk does exist, however, that the prosecution's character evidence may arouse sympathy for a praiseworthy victim and provoke in the trier vengeful feelings against the accused. This possible prejudice may be largely avoided if the trial judge strictly limits character evidence to a showing of no more than the victim's nonviolent nature; testimony establishing other desirable character traits should be disallowed.

Some courts have rejected the arguments above, and have limited rebuttal evidence of a victim's peaceful nature to those cases in which the accused *directly attacks* the victim's character through the use of reputation or opinion witnesses.[10] This approach not only avoids the danger of the sympathetic trier and praiseworthy victim, but also adheres to the general principle that the criminal defendant has the exclusive privilege of initiating character evidence.[11] On the other hand, this restrictive approach denies the trier an opportunity to assess probative evidence that does not carry a significant risk of prejudice.

9. Fed.R.Evid. 404(a)(2); McCormick, § 193, at 572–73; Waltz, Criminal Evidence, 55 (1975).

10. IA Wigmore, § 63, at 1372 (Tillers); McCormick, § 193, at 572.

11. For discussion of the accused's privilege as to making his own character an issue in a criminal case, see § 5.6.

When the accused makes an issue of the victim's character through a direct attack, there is a diversity of opinion as to whether he has thereby placed his own character in issue. Some courts emphasize that it is difficult for the trier to evaluate evidence bearing upon initial aggression when the character evidence is limited to the victim—only one of the two participants in the occurrence.[12] While it is true that if the victim is a truculent person, he is more apt to have been the first aggressor than would a nonviolent person, it is also true that if the accused is likewise aggressive, the character trait of the victim may be entitled to little or no probative weight. Thus, the argument runs, in order to make a rational judgment based upon character, the trier needs to know the propensities of both defendant and victim: a direct attack by the accused upon the victim's character should permit counterbalancing evidence of the accused's character.[13] It should be stressed, however, that even if this argument is accepted, the accused does not open the door to a *general* attack upon his character; rather, he triggers the prosecutor's right to show that he has the same character trait as that which he imputes to the victim.

Another line of cases,[14] endorsed by the Federal Rules of Evidence and now representing the majority view,[15] holds that unless the accused first offers evidence of *his* character, the government is forbidden from doing so. These jurisdictions take a protective attitude toward the accused, emphasizing the fear of prejudice that, in part at least, underlies the accused's basic right to keep his character out of the proceeding.[16] It is argued that this right should not be forfeited simply because the accused bases his defense on the character of another person. Viewed from the standpoint of an accurate reconstruction of the facts, this latter position is difficult to defend; obviously, if the trier is made aware only of the victim's character, there is a greater chance that it

12. E.g., State v. Robinson, 344 Mo. 1094, 130 S.W.2d 530 (1939); State v. Padula, 106 Conn. 454, 459, 138 A. 456, 458 (1927). See also Comment, 99 U.Pa.L.Rev. 105 (1950).

13. Supra n. 12; IA Wigmore, § 63, at 1378–79 (Tillers).

14. E.g., Roberson v. State, 91 Okl. Cr. 217, 218 P.2d 414 (1950); Stearns v. State, 266 Ala. 295, 96 So.2d 306 (1957). See Comment, 99 U.Pa.L.Rev. 105 (1950).

15. Fed.R.Evid. 404(a)(1). See IA Wigmore, § 63, at 1379 n. 7 (Tillers), indicating "little authority" for the view that the accused opens the door to evidence of his character when he limits his evidence to the victim's character. Thus, it is likely that the view expressed in Fed.R.Evid. 4(a)(1) is favored in most jurisdictions.

16. See § 5.6.

may draw erroneous inferences. On the other hand, if there is a risk of undue prejudice against the accused resulting from evidence of his violent character, it seems unfair to attach the price of prejudice to his decision to reveal the victim's truculent character.

§ 5.9 Rape Shield Provisions

In recent years there has been a widespread movement to protect victims of rape from courtroom disclosures of their past sexual conduct.[1] Traditionally, the accused in a prosecution for rape could plead consent by the victim and then offer supporting evidence of the victim's unchaste character or promiscuous behavior.[2] The courts were not always in accord concerning what kind of evidence was admissible; reputation evidence disclosing an immoral or unchaste character was the preferred type,[3] although some courts admitted evidence of specific instances of consensual sexual relations with persons other than the accused.[4] In any event, such evidence, often of marginal probative value, was offered for the inference that if the victim voluntarily had intercourse with others, she was more likely to have consented to sexual relations with the accused.

The modern view, spurred by the realization that this line of proof could suppress the reporting of rapes and, in any event, often subjected rape victims to unfair attacks of dubious probative value, is expressed in so-called "rape shield" laws. In most jurisdictions the laws are embodied in statutes or evidence codes.[5] There are wide variations in these "shield" provisions, but all restrict admission of evidence of the victim's character trait(s) pertaining to sexual behavior. The federal rape shield provision is found in Federal Rule 412,[6] which illustrates in a general way the recent reforms. Its provisions are summarized below.

§ 5.9

1. IA Wigmore § 62 (Tillers); Berger, Man's Trial, Woman's Tribulation: Rape Cases in the Courtroom, 77 Colum.L.Rev. 1 (1977).

2. See McCormick, § 193, at 573; Morgan & Weinstein at 181; Annot., 140 A.L.R. 364, 380.

3. See, e.g., State v. Kain, 330 S.W.2d 842, 845 (Mo.1960); State v. Flaherty, 128 Me. 141, 146, 146 A. 7, 9 (1929).

4. See IA Wigmore, § 62, at 1264 n. 10 (Tillers); State v. Wood, 59 Ariz. 48, 122 P.2d 416 (1942).

5. As of 1983, forty-seven jurisdictions had such shield laws and several jurisdictions had provided similar protection through judicial decisions. See IA Wigmore, § 62, at 1264–95 (Tillers).

6. Federal prosecutions for rape are not numerous, but federal courts have jurisdiction, for example, over rape offenses that occur on Indian reservations and other federal lands. Rule 412 was

It will be recalled that in instances where character evidence is admitted for circumstantial use, the Federal Rules generally sanction both reputation and opinion evidence.[7] However, Rule 412, which applies to a prosecution for rape or assault to commit rape, makes an exception to the general rule and explicitly disallows "reputation or opinion evidence of past sexual behavior of an alleged [rape] victim." [8] Furthermore, the rule severely restricts any other evidence of "a victim's past sexual behavior," [9] that is, evidence of particular instances of prior sexual conduct. It does so by delineating only three circumstances in which such evidence can be received. They are:

(a) When the evidence "is constitutionally required to be admitted" [10] or, otherwise put, where rejection of the evidence would violate the due process clause, the accused's right of confrontation, or some other constitutional provision. The clear weight of modern cases rejects the proposition that the accused has a constitutional right to introduce evidence of a victim's prior sexual conduct with third persons.[11]

(b) When evidence of past sexual behavior with others is "offered by the accused upon the issue of whether . . . [he] was or was not, with respect to the alleged victim, the source of semen or injury." [12] Although the courts have not given a definitive interpretation of what is embraced in the term "injury" (e.g., is pregnancy included?), the gist of this second exception is clear. The provision allows evidence of past sexual acts with others that may account for the presence of semen—for example, in or on the victim's body—or may explain indications of physical abuse of the victim—such as bruises, cuts, or broken bones—that the victim claims was inflicted by the defendant.

(c) When the evidence of prior sexual behavior shows past sexual relationship(s) with the accused and is offered to support by inference the accused's claim that the victim con-

not a part of the Federal Rules of Evidence as originally passed in 1975; it was added by Congress in 1978. See Privacy Protection for Rape Victims Act of 1978, Pub.L. No. 95–540, 92 Stat. 2046.

7. Fed.R.Evid. 405(a); see § 5.6, at n. 8.

8. Fed.R.Evid. 412(a).

9. Fed.R.Evid. 412(b).

10. Fed.R.Evid. 412(b)(1).

11. 2 Louisell & Mueller, § 193, at 340 (1985 Supp.). But see State v. DeLawder, 28 Md.App. 212, 344 A.2d 446 (1975).

12. Fed.R.Evid. 412(b)(2)(A).

sented to the sexual intercourse that is the subject of the rape charge.[13] Here, of course, probative value is significantly higher than the probative value derived from evidence of the victim's sexual conduct with third persons.

In addition to the foregoing provisions, Rule 412 requires the accused to make a pre-trial offer of proof, setting forth the evidence that he contends falls within one or more of the limited categories of admissibility. The judge is directed to conduct a hearing in chambers and to determine whether the proffered evidence is admissible. Issues of conditional relevance are resolved by the judge and not, as is generally the practice,[14] by the jury. The Rule provides that only evidence the judge specifies as admissible shall be received at trial.

It is significant that Rule 412 contains its own test for striking the balance between probative value, on the one hand, and the risk of prejudice on the other. The judge may allow only relevant evidence possessing a probative value that "outweighs the danger of unfair prejudice." [15] This passage is not simply a restatement of Rule 403, elsewhere discussed,[16] which allows relevant evidence unless it is "substantially outweighed by the danger of unfair prejudice." [17] If the balance between probative force and prejudice is roughly equal, Rule 412 commands that the evidence in question be excluded. Thus, evidence that falls within the circumstances indicated in the last two categories above would nonetheless be rejected if its probative value did not pass the balancing test of Rule 412. The unfair prejudice contemplated by the Rule embraces not only the risk of arousing hostility or improper passions in the trier of fact, but also includes the damaging effects, such as embarrassment and humiliation, that disclosure may have upon the victim.[18]

§ 5.10 Reputation, Incidents, and Threats as Bearing Upon the Defendant's State of Mind

A criminal defendant who pleads self-defense raises the issue whether, in light of all of the circumstances, he acted reasonably in defending himself against the victim. Likewise, in a civil suit for assault and battery, a defendant who asserts self-defense poses

13. Fed.R.Evid. 412(b)(2)(B).

14. Fed.R.Evid. 104(b); see § 2.6.

15. Fed.R.Evid. 412(c)(3).

16. See § 2.5 at n. 21.

17. Fed.R.Evid. 403.

18. 2 Louisell & Mueller, § 193, at 344 (1985 Supp.).

the question of the reasonableness of his conduct. In either instance, the issue of whether the defendant's conduct was reasonable is normally one for jury resolution. The required determination involves an assessment of the defendant's actions in view of both the victim's conduct *and* the defendant's realistic apprehension of harm. This latter aspect of the determination requires an inquiry into the reasons why the defendant may have feared the victim. Hence, evidence of the victim's reputation, his threats against the defendant, or instances of violent conduct, *if known to the defendant,*[1] is admissible on the issue of the latter's state of mind. The purpose of the evidence is to demonstrate that the victim's reputation or activity made the defendant apprehensive or fearful, thus justifying his self-protective measures.[2] The evidentiary use just described requires, of course, a showing that the defendant had knowledge of the victim's threats, aggressive conduct, or reputation for violence. To this general requirement an exception should be noted: evidence of a *threat* directed at the defendant, but disclosed only to a third person, should also be admitted.[3] Admissibility in this latter instance, however, cannot rest upon relevancy derived from the probable effect of the threat upon the defendant's state of mind. The basis upon which the evidence is received is that the threat makes it more likely that the victim was the aggressor.[4]

§ 5.11 Evidence of Habit

The line between character and habit is not always easy to discern, but the division can mark the difference between exclusion and admissibility. Character evidence, as we have seen, is usually rejected in civil cases, except in those instances where character forms an essential element of the claim or defense.[1] Even in criminal cases the circumstantial use of character is not generally favored, and character evidence is admitted only in

§ 5.10

1. II Wigmore, §§ 246–248 (Chadbourn).

2. McCormick, § 295, at 850. Sometimes the *accused's* reputation if known to the victim is relevant. See Carbo v. United States, 314 F.2d 718, 740–41 (9th Cir.1963), cert. denied, 377 U.S. 953 (1964) (extortion accomplished by using underworld figure whose reputation for violence was known to victims).

3. I Wigmore, § 110, at 1685 (Tillers); McCormick, § 295, at 850.

4. A hearsay objection would usually not prevail. See Ch. VII, esp. §§ 7.12, 7.13. For discussion of the admissibility of evidence of the victim's *character,* even when unknown to the defendant at the time of the incident in question, see § 5.8.

§ 5.11

1. See §§ 5.2–5.3.

carefully prescribed circumstances.[2] On the other hand, evidence of habit, used circumstantially to prove particular conduct, generally is admissible.[3] The jurisdictions differ, however, in their degree of receptivity. In some courts, evidence of habit is admissible only if there is no eyewitness to the conduct in question.[4]

How is habit distinguished from character? Character may be thought of as a trait or disposition which can manifest itself in a variety of activities. So viewed, character is more general than habit; the latter is a particular activity, routine, or response that is frequently repeated over a protracted period of time. A person with a character trait for punctuality and orderliness may have a habit of picking up and sorting his mail each day at noon.

The probative value of habit is considered greater than that of character. When evidence of habit is introduced, the desired inference from habit to the conduct in question is grounded upon a series of specific, repetitious actions. The trier is asked to infer that on the occasion in question the actor conformed to habitual practice or procedure. When evidence of character is considered, the desired inference is grounded upon a trait, tendency, or disposition that may be displayed in somewhat varied circumstances. A general tendency to drive carefully could be displayed in a variety of driving behaviors. Thus, evidence that a person generally exercises care in driving is usually classified as evidence of character and rejected.[5] Conversely, evidence that each workday a person traversed a particular railroad track and always stopped before crossing is generally classified as habit.[6] The character-habit line becomes blurred when the evidence offered is

2. In most jurisdictions the accused alone determines if his character or that of the victim will be used circumstantially. See §§ 5.6–5.8.

3. Morgan & Weinstein at 185.

4. McCormick, § 195, at 576. This view is difficult to defend because its premise is the superior reliability of eyewitness testimony—a highly dubious proposition. A very good summary of the weaknesses of testimonial proof, which collects many authorities, appears in Weinstein & Mansfield, et al. at 216. Even if testimonial proof were considered reliable, should evidence of habit be rejected? It seems that this added evidence still should be presented for the trier's evaluation. The case for habit evidence is especially strong when the eyewitness is one of the parties (or identified with one of the parties) and evidence of habit is offered by the adversary.

5. E.g., Webb v. Van Noort, 239 Cal. App.2d 472, 48 Cal.Rptr. 823 (1966).

6. See, e.g., Missouri Pacific Ry. v. Moffatt, 60 Kan. 113, 55 P. 837 (1899). Cf. Glatt v. Feist, 156 N.W.2d 819 (N.D.1968). See McCormick, § 195, at 575.

that the actor always stopped at railroad crossings, but surely this is an area where the judge's discretion should be sustained.[7]

The business environment, which is characterized by standardized procedures and routines, offers many opportunities to develop evidence of habit. Frequently, courts refer to habit within a business organization as "custom," but this difference in label does not alter the requirement of a repeated response to a particular circumstance. Some courts have conditioned the admissibility of evidence of custom upon corroborating evidence that the custom was followed on the particular occasion in question.[8] This inadvisable limitation loses sight of the rationale of evidence showing a habit or custom: the theory is that a pattern of continuous activity increases the likelihood that the custom was followed on the particular occasion.

The modern approach to the admissibility of habit and custom evidence is expressed in the following provision of the Federal Rules of Evidence:

> Evidence of the habit of a person or of the routine practice of an organization, whether corroborated or not and regardless of the presence of eyewitnesses, is relevant to prove that the conduct of the person or organization on a particular occasion was in conformity with the habit or routine practice.[9]

Note that the Federal Rule expressly rejects the eyewitness requirement [10] and leaves open the question of what kind of evidence is admissible to prove habit or custom.[11] The usual method of proof is by the testimony of a witness who has observed the habit or custom over a sufficient period to state that it is a routine,

7. See generally IA Wigmore § 97 (Tillers); McCormick, § 195, at 574–76.

8. Slough, Relevancy Unraveled, 5 Kan.L.Rev. 404, 444–450 (1956).

9. Fed.R.Evid. 406. In a federal criminal case the trial judge was reversed for excluding evidence of business custom. United States v. Callahan, 551 F.2d 733 (6th Cir.1977), appeal after remand, 579 F.2d 398 (6th Cir. 1978).

10. See supra n. 4 and accompanying text.

11. The House Committee on the Judiciary deleted a provision that would have authorized the proof of habit by opinion evidence and evidence of specific instances of conduct. This deletion was made to allow the courts to deal with this issue on a case-by-case basis. The Committee noted that it did not intend to sanction a general authorization for the use of opinion evidence to show habit. H.Rep. 93–650, 93d Cong., 2d Sess. reprinted in 1974 U.S.Code Cong. & Admin.News 7075, 7079. In any event, it would appear that an opinion whether a habit was followed on the occasion in question would not be appropriate unless there was evidence of repetitious conduct. If there were such evidence, then a witness's opinion might be "helpful." See Fed.R.Evid. 701; § 4.9.

repeated practice. Sometimes, however, the proponent must resort to proof of a number of specific instances (usually through multiple witnesses) which, taken together, demonstrate the required regularity. This manner of proof is generally accepted, although dissimilarities between specific instances or the apparent lack of a sufficient number to establish a routine may result in the judge's discretionary rejection.[12] The Federal Rule also rejects the requirement, imposed by some courts, that business custom be corroborated as a condition precedent to its admission. Corroboration is viewed correctly as relating to the sufficiency of evidence rather than to its admissibility.[13]

§ 5.12 Other Criminal Acts: In General

Neither the prosecutor nor the civil plaintiff may initially use reputation or opinion evidence to show that the accused or defendant has a bad or criminal character consistent with the crime or conduct charged.[1] We already have observed in most jurisdictions that circumstantial evidence offered to establish a character trait is confined to criminal cases and its introduction is the exclusive right of the accused. The government may not elicit character evidence except in rebuttal.[2] From this, it follows that the government may not prove one or more past criminal acts in an effort to support the inference that the accused has a bad or criminal disposition.[3] Permitting this line of proof would be inconsistent with the general principle that disallows character evidence when offered for circumstantial use against the accused. Furthermore, the use of evidence of *specific acts* to establish bad character runs afoul of the accepted rule disallowing this *form* of evidence to establish a character trait, even in instances where circumstantial use of character is permitted. In short, the forbidden line of proof invokes with full force the considerations of distraction, confusion of the issues, time consumption and, especially, prejudice.

12. See McCormick, § 195, at 577.

13. Adv.Comm.Note to Fed.R.Evid. 406.

§ 5.12

1. In criminal trials, the accused has the exclusive privilege of initially using character evidence circumstantially. See supra § 5.6. In civil trials, a minority of courts permit a party charged with conduct of a quasi-criminal nature to introduce evidence supporting the circumstantial use of character. See § 5.5.

2. See § 5.6.

3. This section, and the one following, refer to past criminal and immoral acts of an accused, whether he was criminally convicted for the acts or not. The effect of an acquittal on the admissibility of the evidence is discussed in § 5.13, nn. 4–5 and accompanying text.

A different issue arises, however, when the prosecutor seeks to introduce evidence of other criminal acts not to show the accused's character or his criminal propensity, but rather to establish circumstantially an element of the crime charged.[4] When evidence of other crimes is so used, the factfinder is asked to engage in the following inferential reasoning: from a finding that the defendant has committed other criminal acts, the trier draws inferences about the accused's conduct or state of mind in connection with the offense for which he is now on trial. If, for example, the factfinder knows that a defendant now charged with embezzlement has committed criminal fraud on another occasion, it might disbelieve his defense of innocent mistake and conclude that he acted purposefully. To illustrate further: evidence showing that a defendant, who is being tried for the strangling of a drug addict, previously strangled another addict under the same distinctive circumstances may serve to identify him as the slayer. Here, evidence of another crime is circumstantially relevant to the accused's conduct.

In each of these hypotheticals, the evidence of other crimes reveals something more specific than simply the accused's defective character or general criminal disposition: it provides the basis for inferences concerning a particular element (either mental state or conduct) of the crime in question. In general, evidence of collateral crimes is admissible if its purpose is not simply to show criminal disposition (although the evidence may incidentally have this effect), but rather to prove immediately or ultimately one or more elements of the crime charged. The first task of the proponent is to convince the judge that the probative force of the proffered other-crimes evidence is directed toward a specific proposition that is either an element of the offense charged (such as intent) or else, if the proposition is more remote (as, for example, motive), its establishment provides a basis for inferring the existence of an element of the crime charged. Even when such a proposition is properly identified, the probative force of the other-crimes evidence must, as in the case of all evidence, be shown to overcome the practical reasons for exclusion: time consumption, confusion, distraction, and, particularly, prejudice.[5]

4. Although generally confined to criminal trials, evidence of other crimes may be relevant and admissible in certain civil cases, such as in a suit for a fraudulent act. See § 5.16.

5. Adv.Comm.Note to Fed.R.Evid. 404. Surprise is a practical reason for exclusion recognized in some states, but not included in Fed.R.Evid. 403 which specifies the counterweights to admissibility. See § 2.5.

§ 5.13 Other Criminal Acts: Degree of Certainty With Which Collateral Crime Must be Shown

A preliminary issue sometimes arising in connection with an offer of other-crimes evidence is the degree of certainty with which the commission of the collateral crime be shown. Arguably, before other-crimes evidence is admissible, the proponent should be required to show either that the accused was convicted of the collateral crime or that its existence is clear beyond a reasonable doubt. A rule imposing this standard of certainty ensures against the possibility of using evidence of a collateral crime of which the defendant was not in fact guilty. But a rule of such strictness is at odds with the basic principle that individual items of evidence need not meet a standard of proof intended to apply to the totality of evidence presented. Although the sum of all of the evidence presented in a criminal case must, in order to sustain a conviction, support belief beyond a reasonable doubt, the requirement that a reasonable-doubt standard be met for each item of evidence would make it virtually impossible to build an evidentiary record. Of course, no such general requirement exists; to the contrary, the basic test for the admission of evidence is satisfied if the evidence has a tendency to make the existence of a consequential fact more probable than not,[1] or, when relevance is conditioned on the existence of a fact [2] (such as the commission of another crime), the underlying fact normally must be supported by evidence sufficient to allow the trier to find its existence.[3] The telling impact of other-crimes evidence, however, coupled with its high potential for inducing prejudice, justifies some special safeguards. Accordingly, most authorities hold that the defendant's commission of the collateral crime must be shown by "substantial" evidence or, in some jurisdictions, by evidence that is "clear and convincing." [4] There is also authority, however, treating other-crimes evidence no differently from other evidence whose relevance is conditioned on an underlying fact and holding that evidence of other crimes

§ 5.13

1. § 2.2.

2. See § 2.6.

3. Fed.R.Evid. 104(b).

4. See, e.g., United States v. Dolliole, 597 F.2d 102, 106–07 (7th Cir.1979), cert. denied, 442 U.S. 946 (1979); State v. Davis, 449 So.2d 466 (La.1984); People v. Albertson, 23 Cal.2d 550, 145 P.2d 7 (1944); State v. Billstrom, 276 Minn. 174, 149 N.W.2d 281 (1967); State v. Hyde, 234 Mo. 200, 136 S.W. 316 (1911). Other cases are cited by McCormick, § 190, at 564 nn. 45–46. A few cases require that the collateral crime be established beyond a reasonable doubt. See, e.g., Ernster v. State, 165 Tex.Cr.R. 422, 308 S.W.2d 33 (1957).

need only meet the test of sufficiency.[5] This approach appears to minimize the protective role of the judge, but it is probably true that choosing the verbal formula said to prescribe the measure of proof is not nearly as important as how a particular formula (once selected) is applied by the trial judge.[6] The convincing force of evidence defies exact measurement. Furthermore, as will be noted shortly, whether evidence of a collateral crime is admissible should depend on a number of variables, one of which is the probability that the accused committed the other crime.

A special difficulty arises if the accused has been tried and acquitted for the commission of the collateral crime. In a technical sense, an acquittal means only that the jury (or, possibly, the judge) decided that the evidence was insufficient to convince it beyond a reasonable doubt of the existence of each essential element of the collateral offense. This finding does not preclude a subsequent determination of criminal conduct by a lesser standard, such as one calling for sufficient or clear and convincing evidence; nor does it preclude reconsideration of one particular aspect or element of a collateral offense. Observe the possibility that evidence in the collateral trial may have been very strong regarding conduct, but comparatively weak as to a mental element (such as intent) of the collateral offense. In the present trial for a different offense, the prosecutor may seek only to introduce evidence of the accused's conduct connected with the collateral offense. In short, the use of evidence of the other crime in the present trial should not be precluded by the *terms of the result* in the unsuccessful collateral prosecution, nor should use necessarily be foreclosed on grounds of untrustworthiness.[7]

Of course, there is a countervailing consideration: admission of evidence pertinent to a collateral crime for which the defendant has been acquitted does, in practical terms, cause him to defend against the same charge a second time. Even though different consequences may accompany the subsequent use of other-crimes evidence, the accused is required again to challenge and rebut evidence of an offense for which he has already won an acquittal. The force of this consideration, raising policy concerns that are related to those underlying collateral estoppel and the prohibition against double jeopardy, has caused a minority of courts to hold

5. United States v. Beechum, 582 F.2d 898 (5th Cir.1978), cert. denied, 440 U.S. 920 (1979); United States v. Astling, 733 F.2d 1446 (11th Cir.1984).

6. See 2 Weinstein & Berger, ¶ 404[10], at 56–58.

7. Id. at 58–59.

that other-crimes evidence cannot be used where the trial of the collateral crime resulted in an acquittal.[8]

Although this minority approach has immediate appeal, reflection suggests that it is unsound, at least when it operates as an absolute rule. Suppose, for example, an accused bookkeeper, prosecuted for the offense of embezzling funds from his employer, asserts the defense of innocent mistake, and, after a trial, is acquitted. Subsequently, he becomes employed by another firm, and thereafter similar bookkeeping discrepancies are discovered. If the accused is again prosecuted for embezzlement and again he asserts that the bookkeeping irregularities resulted from an innocent mistake, should the prosecutor be foreclosed from presenting evidence of the earlier incident? At the least, it appears unwise to reject out-of-hand the evidence of the other crime on the sole ground that the earlier prosecution resulted in an acquittal.[9] This is especially true where the losses sustained by the two employers reveal a similar pattern. The earlier trial put the accused on notice of the potential criminal nature of his activity, making it less likely that the subsequent discrepancies were innocent ones. A similar unsound result would occur in these circumstances: an accused is prosecuted for the arsenic poisoning of *A*, a child in her care. The evidence shows that the arsenic was administered in small doses over a period of time and that the accused was the beneficiary of a life insurance policy on *A*'s life. Nonetheless, the accused is acquitted. Subsequently, the accused is arrested and charged with poisoning, by similar means, *B*, another insured child in her custody; this trial too results in an acquittal. If, later, child *C* is found poisoned under similar circumstances, should evidence of the prior crimes be excluded in the resulting prosecution of the same accused? At some point in successive prosecutions, the *cumulative* prior circumstances become so highly probative [10] that evidence of the other instances should be admitted. Finally, it should be kept in mind that when evidence of a

8. See, e.g., United States v. Day, 591 F.2d 861 (D.C.Cir.1978); State v. Wakefield, 278 N.W.2d 307 (Minn.1979); State v. Little, 87 Ariz. 295, 350 P.2d 756 (1960); Annot., 86 A.L.R.2d 1132, 1146–47 (1962).

9. Some commentators note that cases such as those described in the text are rare, and they argue that other-crimes evidence should not be admissible after an acquittal unless later developments suggest the verdict was incorrect. Lempert & Saltzburg at 221.

10. For cases suggesting this kind of problem, see United States v. Woods, 484 F.2d 127 (4th Cir.1973), cert. denied, 415 U.S. 979 (1974); Tucker v. State, 82 Nev. 127, 412 P.2d 970 (1966); People v. Peete, 28 Cal.2d 306, 169 P.2d 924 (1946), cert. denied, 331 U.S. 783 (1947); Lyles v. State, 215 Ga. 229, 109 S.E.2d

collateral crime is relevant in the trial for the present offense, the prosecutor must present his own evidence of those relevant aspects of the other crime—he cannot simply rely upon a description of what witnesses in the collateral trial said.[11] This evidence may differ in probative quality from that presented in a prior prosecution for the other offense. Sometimes the evidence in the present proceeding will be stronger. In instances when the evidence concerning the collateral crime is significantly more convincing than that presented in the collateral trial, there is a reduced risk of using untrustworthy evidence (of a collateral crime) to convict the accused in the present trial.[12]

These various considerations suggest that it is undesirable to bar absolutely evidence concerning a collateral offense because of an earlier acquittal. What is desirable is a flexible policy that avoids an absolute rule, but recognizes the unfairness and general undesirability of causing an accused to respond twice to the same charge. In short, an acquittal of the collateral crime is one of several considerations, subsequently to be noted, that the trial judge should take into account when he rules upon admissibility.

§ 5.14 Other Criminal Acts: Application of the Governing Principle

The rule that forbids other-crimes evidence to establish criminal propensity, but admits this evidence to establish a specific consequential proposition, may be stated in either of two ways.[1] A positive or "inclusive" formulation of the rule is that relevant evidence of other criminal activity is admissible unless its *sole* probative effect is to show a criminal propensity or disposition. A negative or "exclusive" statement of the rule holds that evidence of other criminal activity is inadmissible unless the evidence has probative value to establish one or more *enumerated* propositions, such as knowledge, identity, absence of accident or mistake, intent, or motive.[2] A characteristic of the exclusive form of the rule is that it specifies these admissible purposes, not simply as an

785 (1959); McCormick, § 190, at 561 n. 26.

11. It may be, however, that the prosecutor can, in certain instances, introduce portions of the transcript from the collateral trial. See §§ 7.20–7.21.

12. Of course, this does not lessen the policy objection of having the accused respond twice to the government's assertions concerning the collateral offense.

§ 5.14

1. See Stone, The Rule of Exclusion of Similar Fact Evidence: America, 51 Harv.L.Rev. 988, 989 (1938).

2. See State v. Johnson, 183 N.W.2d 194 (Iowa 1971). For additional pos-

illustration, but rather as a complete list of the approved propositions to which other-crimes evidence may be directed. Under this formulation, evidence not fitting within an established category is rejected.[3]

A possible difficulty with the limited or exclusive formulation is that it lacks the breadth and flexibility to take account of the varied factual patterns in which evidence of other crimes may have probative force for a purpose other than simply showing criminal disposition. That is, the proffered evidence of other crimes may have a legitimate probative use, yet the proposition to which it is directed may not be listed among the enumerated permissible categories.[4] A system confined to limited, specified exceptions also has been criticized on the ground that judges sometimes routinely admit evidence that is relevant to one of the enumerated exceptions without a careful assessment of its probative value.[5] As will be emphasized shortly, the critical inquiry in considering evidence under either statement of the rule governing other-crimes evidence is a careful assessment of the purpose, probative worth, and possible prejudice of the evidence. Thus, the inclusive statement of the rule, which may encourage more careful analysis and does permit flexibility, is to be preferred. In most cases, however, either formulation of the rule will produce the same evidentiary result.[6]

Whenever a proponent offers evidence of a collateral crime, it is important that both counsel and judge identify clearly the consequential fact to which the evidence is directed. A criminal offense consists of proscribed conduct usually accompanied by a specified state of mind. It would appear, therefore, that the outer boundaries of the relevance of other-crimes evidence is established by inquiring if evidence of another crime provides a basis from which the trier can draw inferences about either the accused's conduct or state of mind in connection with the crime charged. Although the consequential facts to which the evidence might be addressed can vary widely, certain factual categories, such as

sibilities, see McCormick, § 190, at 558–64.

3. See State v. Lyle, 125 S.C. 406, 118 S.E. 803 (1923), discussed in Stone, 1006, supra n. 1.

4. Note, Other Crimes Evidence At Trial: Of Balancing and Other Matters, 70 Yale L.J. 763, 767–69 (1961).

5. See Stone, 1005–07, supra n. 1, where this and other criticisms of the exclusive formulation of the rule are forcefully detailed.

6. Weinstein and Berger state that the actual "decisions are not appreciably affected by the form of the rule." 2 Weinstein & Berger, ¶ 404[08], at 47.

those described below, are repeatedly cited by the courts; the frequency with which these arise justifies their careful consideration.

Federal Rule of Evidence 404(b), which forbids the use of evidence of other crimes to "to prove . . . character . . . in order to show that [the accused] acted in conformity therewith," nonetheless provides that this evidence "may . . . be admissible for other purposes . . . ." [7] By way of illustration, the Rule lists purposes such as "proof of motive, opportunity, intent, preparation, plan, knowledge, identity, or absence of mistake or accident." [8] From the language of the Rule and its legislative history, it is clear that the federal drafters created an open system in which a trial judge neither mechanically excludes, nor routinely accepts, other-crimes evidence: rather, he determines admissibility on the basis of such factors as probative value, potential prejudice, and the availability of alternative forms of evidence.[9] The elaborative material below contains a sampling of the circumstances in which consequential propositions normally can be established by the introduction of other-crimes evidence.[10]

> (1) In the prosecution of *D* for the murder of *V*, evidence that *V* had threatened to expose *D*'s participation in a land fraud scheme would be relevant to show *motive*, i.e., the inducement or reason why *D* might have committed the criminal offense charged.[11] Existence of a motive usually supports an inference about conduct, but motive might also have probative value in establishing a mental state such as intent (purpose).[12]

7. Fed.R.Evid. 404(b).

8. Id.

9. Id.; Adv.Comm.Note to Fed.R. Evid. 404(b); 2 Weinstein & Berger, ¶ 404[08], at 49, and ¶ 404[18].

10. For further examples, see Annot., 93 A.L.R.2d 1097 (1964) (other-crimes evidence in drug prosecutions); Annot., 78 A.L.R.2d 1359 (1961) (fraud prosecutions); Annot., 34 A.L.R.2d 777 (1954) (forgery prosecutions); Annot., 20 A.L.R.2d 1012 (1951) (bribery prosecutions).

11. United States v. Cyphers, 553 F.2d 1064 (7th Cir.1977), cert. denied, 434 U.S. 843 (1977) (defendant's purchase of $1000 worth of heroin after robbery relevant to show motive for the crime); Dillon v. United States, 391 F.2d 433, 435–36 (10th Cir.1968), cert. denied, 393 U.S. 825, 889 (1968) (accused's participation in abortion scheme supplied motive for present crime of bribery); Fuller v. State, 269 Ala. 312, 334–37, 113 So.2d 153, 172–76 (1959), cert. denied, 361 U.S. 936 (1960) (accused's receipt of illegal gambling payoffs supplied motive to murder nominee for public office who pledged to eradicate gambling and other illegalities in that county); McCormick, § 190, at 562–63.

12. See McCormick, § 190, at 562.

(2) In the trial of *D* for a criminal assault upon *V*, *D* asserts that he was in another city on the day in question. Evidence that on the same day *D* attempted to rob a liquor store in the city where the offense against *V* occurred would be relevant to show that *D* had the *opportunity* to commit the assault.[13]

(3) In the prosecution of *D* for the theft of a rented automobile, he asserts that he intended to return the car. Evidence of the theft of other rented cars would be relevant to establish *D*'s *intent*.[14] The term "intent" is, generally speaking, synonymous with "purpose"; it denotes "the desire to achieve a particular end" [15] and an awareness that the action undertaken is likely to produce it. Thus, since the crime of theft is usually defined so as to require a taking of goods with the purpose of depriving the owner (either permanently or for a substantial period of time), evidence of other thefts bears upon the mental element of intent.

13. See United States v. Stover, 565 F.2d 1010 (8th Cir.1977); People v. Tranowski, 20 Ill.2d 11, 169 N.E.2d 347 (1960), cert. denied, 364 U.S. 923 (1960). A similar result should obtain in a case in which D is prosecuted for the theft of jewelry from a retail shop, and evidence is introduced to show that he broke into and entered the building in which various retail shops, including the shop in question, were located. In Snead v. State, 243 Ala. 23, 8 So.2d 269 (1942) evidence of prior assaults was introduced to rebut defendant's claim that his physical incapacity prevented him from committing the assault in question.

14. See United States v. Dudley, 562 F.2d 965 (5th Cir.1977); United States v. Welborn, 322 F.2d 910 (4th Cir.1963). See also United States v. Rocha, 553 F.2d 615 (9th Cir.1977) (previous arrest for possession of marijuana admitted to show intent to distribute); United States v. Marchildon, 519 F.2d 337, 346–47 (8th Cir.1975) (other drugs in defendant's possession relevant to show intent to distribute drug in question); United States v. Brettholz, 485 F.2d 483, 488 (2d Cir.1973), cert. denied, 415 U.S. 976 (1974) (prior transactions with cocaine make it more likely that defendants intended to sell cocaine rather than purchase marijuana); State v. Monroe, 364 So.2d 570 (La.1978) (similar killing by defendant admitted to rebut claim of self-defense in murder prosecution); State v. Wyman, 270 A.2d 460 (Me.1970) (evidence that accused almost drove automobile into *B* and *C* while shouting "Do you want to be Number 2?" is relevant to show that accused intentionally ran into the first victim, *A*); State v. Darling, 197 Kan. 471, 475–81, 419 P.2d 836, 840–42 (1966) (that defendant intended to cause an abortion by use of certain therapy is shown by evidence that on other occasions he used the same medical procedures to produce abortion); People v. Shea, 147 N.Y. 78, 98–101, 41 N.E. 505, 511–12 (1894) (evidence of election fraud in connection with which accused armed himself and went to polls is relevant to show purposeful killing as opposed to a homicide that resulted from sudden passion). Federal cases are collected in 2 Weinstein & Berger ¶ 404[12].

15. 2 Louisell & Mueller, § 140, at 225.

(4) In the trial of *D* for exploding a bomb in a public building, evidence that a week before the bombing *D* stole explosive materials would be relevant to show his *preparation* for the crime charged.[16] Preparatory activity increases the likelihood that the act charged was performed. Note the overlap between preparation and activity. Observe also that preparation may reveal the state of mind of the actor, e.g., by showing deliberation or purposefulness.

(5) In the prosecution of *D* for arson of building *A*, evidence that *D* had wrongfully burned building *B* covered by similar insurance would be relevant, if coupled with other evidence, to show that *D* had a *plan* (scheme or design) to destroy these buildings in order to collect insurance proceeds.[17] If the crime charged is shown to be part of a plan, inferences can be drawn concerning conduct or, perhaps, state of mind. In its pristine form, this exception entails the evidentiary use of acts separate from the crime charged in order to infer the existence of a plan or scheme.[18] An inference is then drawn that the act charged is part of the larger scheme.[19] From this conclusion, further inferences can be made about the actor's conduct or intent (or other mental state) in connection with the offense charged. However, courts have occasionally admitted evidence of similar criminal acts under the rubric of plan, scheme, or design in circumstances that render it doubtful whether a general or comprehensive plan existed.[20]

16. King v. State, 230 Ga. 581, 582, 198 S.E.2d 305, 306 (1973); II Wigmore, § 238, at 38–39 n. 1 (Chadbourn).

17. State v. McClard, 81 Or. 510, 160 P. 130 (1916) (evidence of similar fire that destroyed other insured property). See United States v. Krohn, 560 F.2d 293 (7th Cir.1977), cert. denied, 434 U.S. 895 (1977) (scheme to use forged checks); Leonard v. United States, 324 F.2d 911 (9th Cir.1963) (scheme to forge and pass treasury checks); McWhorter v. Commonwealth, 191 Va. 857, 870–71, 63 S.E.2d 20, 26–27 (1951) (plan to persuade workers to quit their jobs; evidence of insults to worker admitted); II Wigmore, § 304, at 249 (Chadbourn).

18. See State v. Marquez, 222 Kan. 441, 447–448, 565 P.2d 245, 251 (1977); II Wigmore, § 304, at 249 (Chadbourn). But the plan may be conceived during or shortly after the commission of the collateral crime, as where *D* robs *A* and in so doing learns the location of *B* who possesses certain funds. *D* then seeks out and robs *B*. State v. Toshishige Yoshimo, 45 Hawaii 206, 364 P.2d 638 (1961).

19. See, e.g., United States v. Little, 562 F.2d 578 (8th Cir.1977). For a case in which the prosecution failed to provide sufficient evidence of a comprehensive scheme, see State v. Little, 87 Ariz. 295, 303–04, 350 P.2d 756, 761 (1960) (effect of prior acquittal also considered by court).

20. See, e.g., Perry v. People, 116 Colo. 440, 181 P.2d 439 (1947); Griffin v. State, 124 So.2d 38 (Fla.App.1960); Payne, Jr., The Law Whose Life is Not

(6) In the trial of *D* for receiving stolen property from *A*, evidence that on other occasions and under similar circumstances *A* had supplied *D* with goods known by *D* to have been stolen is relevant to show that *D* had *knowledge* that the goods in question were stolen.[21] The element of knowledge is closely related to and frequently overlaps that of intent (or purpose) since both require awareness. From an evidentiary standpoint, the difference between intent and knowledge is not critical because evidence offered to show knowledge also has probative value to show intent (or purpose). Similarly, because intent includes knowledge, evidence offered to establish intent would also have probative force on the element of knowledge. The substantive criminal law, however, sometimes distinguishes between intent and knowledge.[22] For some crimes, knowledge, unaccompanied by any intent or purpose concerning the actor's conduct, satisfies the culpability requirement for mental state. Other crimes are defined so that intent is a prerequisite to culpability as, for example, in the case of retaining possession of lost property with the intention of depriving the owner.[23]

(7) In the prosecution of *D* for passing a forged check for $75, purportedly made payable to *D* by *A* Company, evidence that *D* passed similar false checks from *A* Company under like circumstances (e.g., buying a small item and receiving a substantial sum in change) is relevant to *identify* *D* as the actor in the offense charged.[24] Evidence of other crimes is

Logic: Evidence of Other Crimes in Criminal Cases, 3 U.Rich.L.Rev. 62, 79–80 (1968). However, even though collateral acts may not be sufficiently integrated with the act charged to constitute an overall plan, the collateral acts nonetheless may be admissible for another purpose, such as motive, intent, etc. See United States v. Ismail, 756 F.2d 1253 (6th Cir.1985); United States v. Stadter, 336 F.2d 326 (2d Cir.1964), cert. denied, 380 U.S. 945 (1965).

21. Peters v. United States, 376 F.2d 839 (5th Cir.1967) (other transactions with counterfeit bills relevant to show accused knew that bills in question were counterfeit); United States v. Allen, 303 F.2d 915 (6th Cir.1962) (other stolen vehicles received); People v. Rife, 382 Ill. 588, 598–99, 48 N.E.2d 367, 373 (1943) (possession and concealment of similar items that were stolen); II Wigmore §§ 324, 326 at 227–32 (Chadbourn). But see Bullard v. United States, 395 F.2d 658 (5th Cir.1968) (willingness to defraud insurance company through car theft not probative of knowledge that another car was stolen).

22. See Model Penal Code § 2.02, Comment. See also II Wigmore § 300 (Chadbourn).

23. See Model Penal Code § 223.5.

24. State v. Bock, 229 Minn. 449, 39 N.W.2d 887 (1949); see Durns v. United States, 562 F.2d 542 (8th Cir.), cert. denied, 434 U.S. 959 (1977) (prior attempted kidnapping using same modus operandi); United States v. Maestas, 546 F.2d 1177 (5th Cir.1977) (similar use

admissible to prove identity when conduct is in question (that is, when the accused denies that he participated in a crime) and when the modus operandi of the collateral crime(s) and the crime charged are sufficiently distinctive and similar to be substantially probative of identity. In contrast, a mere showing that *D* has committed other crimes in the same class as the offense charged is insufficiently probative of identity to justify admission. However, even when the principal and collateral crimes are somewhat dissimilar, it may be possible to introduce evidence that a distinctive feature or instrumentality linking the defendant to the collateral crime(s) is also involved in the crime charged. For example, it may be possible to show that a certain unusual weapon was used in committing both crimes or that an instrumentality acquired during the collateral crime (e.g., a check-writing machine) was used in the commission of the crime charged (passing forged checks).[25] Note the possibility that a collateral crime may bear upon preparation and identity, or for that matter, other propositions.

(8) In the trial of *D*, a bookkeeper, for embezzling the funds of Company *A*, evidence that *D* embezzled the funds of Company *B* by making false entries is relevant to negate a defense that the erroneous entries in *A*'s records were the result of innocent *mistake*.[26] A similar theory of admissibility

of forged checks); State v. King, 111 Kan. 140, 206 P. 883 (1922) (other buried bodies, along with accused's possession of decedent's personal effects, relevant to identify *D* as murderer of *A*, whose buried body was also discovered on *D*'s premises and whose personal effects were in *D*'s possession); Whiteman v. State, 119 Ohio St. 285, 164 N.E. 51 (1928) (similar offenses characterized by using uniforms to impersonate officers). But see United States v. Myers, 550 F.2d 1036 (5th Cir.1977), cert. denied, 439 U.S. 847 (1978) (insufficient similarity between bank robbery charged and subsequent bank robbery); Drew v. United States, 331 F.2d 85, 92–94 (D.C. Cir.1964) (two ice cream stores held up by black with sunglasses; insufficient similarity especially since one of the offenses did not involve threat with gun).

25. United States v. Barrett, 539 F.2d 244 (1st Cir.1976) (extraordinary expertise in avoiding burglar alarm activation); United States v. McMillian, 535 F.2d 1035 (8th Cir.1976), cert. denied, 434 U.S. 1074 (1978) (same gun used in principal and collateral crime); State v. Latta, 246 Or. 218, 425 P.2d 186 (1967) (burglary trial; evidence admitted to show tool in defendant's possession was burglary tool); People v. McMonigle, 29 Cal.2d 730, 177 P.2d 745 (1947) (stolen naval T-shirt worn during commission of subsequent crime).

26. Crider v. Commonwealth, 206 Va. 574, 145 S.E.2d 222 (1965). See also United States v. Fairchild, 526 F.2d 185 (7th Cir.1975), cert. denied, 425 U.S. 942 (1976) (possession of counterfeit bills probative of intent and ability); United States v. Kaplan, 416 F.2d 103 (2d Cir. 1969) (possession of check issued with-

would permit evidence that *D*, who defends a murder charge on the ground of *accidental* shooting, fired at the decedent on another occasion.[27] Observe that showing the absence of mistake or accident can be equivalent to showing intent.

Each of the foregoing examples is directed either to the defendant's conduct or to his mental state. It is true that sometimes the evidence is ostensibly directed to a more remote proposition, such as plan, opportunity, or motive, that is not an element of the crime charged; however, from such an intermediate proposition, further inferences about conduct or mental state can be drawn. Of course, there are other consequential propositions, not included in the illustrations above, that ultimately bear upon conduct or state of mind and that usually can be shown by evidence of collateral crimes.[28] For example, the destruction of evidence or attempted flight, when apparently undertaken to avoid conviction or apprehension, can give rise to an inference of guilt.[29] Further, if the accused defends a charge by claiming entrapment, evidence of a collateral crime similar to the charged offense tends to weaken the accused's contention that government officials originated the idea of the crime charged and induced him to engage in it.[30] Finally, courts also admit evidence of a crime not charged when its commission is so closely related in time or circumstance to the principal crime that revelation of the collateral crime is necessary to a complete understanding of the principal offense.[31] It will again be observed that the various illustrative

out consideration relevant to present charge against bank teller of falsifying entry); II Wigmore, § 329, at 294 (Chadbourn) (where the author treats the basis of admissibility, at least in most cases, as intent).

27. State v. Langley, 354 N.W.2d 389 (Minn.1984); II Wigmore, § 302, at 241 (Chadbourn) (where author treats the basis of admissibility as intent).

28. See, e.g., United States v. Woods, 484 F.2d 127 (4th Cir.1973), cert. denied, 415 U.S. 979 (1974) (prior episodes of cyanosis of children in defendant's care probative that criminal activity was cause of the asphyxiation of child victim); United States v. Montalvo, 271 F.2d 922, 927 (2d Cir.1959), cert. denied, 361 U.S. 961 (1960) (possession of penknife caked with heroin shows accused about to join illegal enterprise); McCormick, § 190, at 558–64.

29. McCormick, § 190, at 562–63; United States v. Howard, 228 F.Supp. 939, 942–43 (D.Neb.1964) (in narcotics prosecution, evidence admitted that accused had murdered principal witness against him); Mattox v. State, 243 Miss. 402, 413–16, 137 So.2d 920, 922–24 (1962) (attempt to arrange murder of witness). Weinstein & Mansfield, et al. cites these and other cases at 894–96.

30. 2 Louisell & Mueller, § 140, at 129–33.

31. Carter v. United States, 549 F.2d 77 (8th Cir.1977); United States v. Roberts, 548 F.2d 665 (6th Cir.1977), cert. denied, 431 U.S. 920 (1977); Howard v. State, 346 So.2d 918 (Miss.1977); State v. Villavicencio, 95 Ariz. 199, 388 P.2d

purposes justifying other-crimes evidence often overlap, so that evidence of collateral crimes frequently falls within more than one category.

§ 5.15 Other Criminal Acts: Balancing the Competing Considerations that Govern Admissibility

Commentators have often been critical of the judicial treatment of other-crimes evidence.[1] Much of this critical comment has been directed toward decisions that admit this evidence under the various labels without a careful analysis. Certainly there are examples of evidential admission that cannot be reasonably justified under any theory.[2] Often, however, the courts simply have seized upon a wrong label to justify an otherwise proper ruling of admissibility.[3] This latter mistake, although regrettable because it muddles judicial analysis and adds to a body of divergent and confusing precedents, is harmless error in the case at hand.

Neither the commentators nor the courts have been completely successful in articulating an ideal formula for determining when evidence of collateral crimes should be admitted. All authorities agree that any rule governing the admission of other-crimes evidence must require a probative value greater than simply a showing of bad disposition or criminal proclivity. There is also general agreement that the judge should exclude any evidence whose probative value is substantially outweighed by the danger of prejudice (or some other adverse practical consequence).[4]

245 (1964); 2 Weinstein & Berger, ¶ 404[10], at 60–62.

§ 5.15

1. E.g., Payne, Jr., The Law Whose Life is Not Logic: Evidence of Other Crimes in Criminal Cases, 3 U.Rich.L. Rev. 62, 68–69, 85–87 (1968); Slough & Knightly, Other Vices, Other Crimes, 41 Iowa L.Rev. 325, 349–50 (1956).

2. E.g., Nunez v. United States, 370 F.2d 538 (5th Cir.1967) (per curiam) (discussed in 2 Weinstein & Berger, ¶ 404[16], at 88); Commonwealth v. Kline, 361 Pa. 434, 65 A.2d 348 (1949). But see Commonwealth v. Boulden, 179 Pa.Super. 328, 345–47, 116 A.2d 867, 875–76 (1955) (refusal to extend *Kline* decision). For a case in which the basis of admissibility is left in doubt, see United States v. Davis, 551 F.2d 233 (8th Cir.), cert. denied, 431 U.S. 923 (1977).

3. See, e.g., Carter v. United States, 549 F.2d 77 (8th Cir.1977) ("res gestae"); Canty v. State, 244 Ala. 108, 11 So.2d 844 (1943), cert. denied, 319 U.S. 746 (1943) ("res gestae"). In Williams v. State, 110 So.2d 654 (Fla.1959), cert. denied, 361 U.S. 847 (1959), a rape case, the court cited plan and identity as justifying evidence of a similar occurrence, yet the accused's defense was consent. Nevertheless, the collateral crime did have probative force to negate the likelihood of consensual conduct.

4. Fed.R.Evid. 403; Adv.Comm.Note to Fed.R.Evid. 404(b); 2 Weinstein & Berger, ¶ 404[08], at 49; McCormick, § 190, at 565: "[M]ost recent authority recognizes that the problem is not

But these are general propositions, abstractly stated. Disagreement attends their application to specific facts. Because of the great potential for prejudicial consequences inherent in other-crimes evidence, a judge often encounters difficult problems of analysis and balancing. His determination can involve a number of variables, and it is important that he identify these and assess each with care.

If there has been a trial of the collateral crime and an acquittal resulted, this fact should be considered an important, though not necessarily dispositive, element in the balancing process.[5] As noted earlier, if evidence of the other offense is used to show that the accused was on notice of the potential criminal nature of his conduct (and hence an innocent state of mind with regard to the present crime is unlikely), the fact of acquittal should not usually dictate exclusion.[6] Also, prior acquittals involving offenses with characteristics similar to those of the present crime may be admissible if the cumulative probative impact of the several offenses, considered together, justifies the costs of prejudice, distraction, or time consumption that may be involved in receiving evidence of the collateral offenses.[7] Other situations will arise in which admissibility is justified, despite an earlier acquittal. The strength of the evidence by which the collateral crime is shown is, of course, an important consideration.

Other-crimes evidence must, of course, meet the basic requirements of relevance. In making the relevance determination, it is always important to identify precisely the proposition to which such evidence is directed and to evaluate carefully its probative force. Other important factors include: (1) whether the accused contests the proposition for which the evidence is offered; and (2) whether other evidence, with less potential for prejudice, appears sufficient to establish the proposition.[8] It is sometimes easier to assess these variables after much of the evidence is in, the

merely one of pigeonholing, but of classifying and then balancing." See United States v. Hearst, 563 F.2d 1331 (9th Cir.1977), cert. denied, 435 U.S. 1000 (1978).

5. See People v. Griffin, 66 Cal.2d 459, 58 Cal.Rptr. 107, 426 P.2d 507 (1967); Annot., 86 A.L.R.2d 1132 (1962).

6. State v. Darling, 197 Kan. 471, 478–81, 419 P.2d 836, 842–44 (1966). See § 5.13.

7. See § 5.13; People v. Oliphant, 399 Mich. 474, 250 N.W.2d 443 (1976). Cf. People v. Fox, 126 Cal.App.2d 560, 569, 272 P.2d 832, 838 (1954) (evidence that accused gave same explanation for a previously dismissed charge that he gave in connection with present crime is admissible).

8. McCormick, § 190, at 565.

strength of the government's case against the accused is known, and the issues have been clarified. The judge should not hesitate to exercise his full control over the order of proof and, in appropriate cases, to postpone his decision regarding other-crimes evidence until near the end of the government's case in chief, or even until after the accused has presented his evidence in defense.[9] Often, it is advisable to receive the government's offer of proof of other-crimes evidence in chambers or elsewhere out of the jury's presence.

Judge Friendly's opinion in United States v. Byrd [10] is illustrative of the kind of assessment and careful balancing that is necessary when considering the admissibility of collateral-crimes evidence. This case involved the prosecution and conviction of an IRS employee for receipt of illegal fees in connection with his auditing of returns. The trial judge gave an erroneous instruction which, on appeal, resulted in a reversal. However, in the course of the appellate disposition, the court considered certain evidentiary points that were expected to arise again on retrial:

> One of these points concerns the admission by the trial court of evidence of Byrd's activities [receipt of payment] in connection with the auditing of the Sandberg tax return. The Government offered it as a part of its main case for the purpose of showing criminal intent. A vigorous objection was made by the defense but the court admitted it. The admissibility of this kind of evidence is "a matter in which the trial judge should be allowed a wide range of discretion." United States v. Feldman, 136 F.2d 394, 399 (2d Cir. [1943]). The exercise of discretion must be addressed to a balancing of the probative value of the proffered evidence, on the one hand, against its prejudicial character on the other. The probative value is measured by the extent to which the evidence of prior criminal activities, . . . closely related in time, and subject matter, tends to establish that the accused committed the criminal act charged in the indictment knowingly or with criminal intent or tends to negative the claim that the acts

9. 2 Weinstein & Berger, ¶ 404[09], at 49–50; McCormick, § 190, at 565 n. 58; United States v. Figueroa, 618 F.2d 934, 939 (2d Cir.1980). In United States v. Juarez, 561 F.2d 65 (7th Cir.1977), the court refused to find error in the trial judge's admission, during the government's case in chief, of evidence of a prior sale of heroin. Finding the evidence relevant to intent, the Court of Appeals ruled that since the accused could have contested intent, the prosecutor was not obligated to postpone the other-crimes evidence.

10. 352 F.2d 570 (2d Cir.1965).

were committed innocently or through mistake or misunderstanding.

It is generally recognized that there can be no complete assurance that the jury even under the best of instructions will strictly confine the use of this kind of evidence to the issue of knowledge and intent and wholly put out of their minds the implication that the accused, having committed the prior similar criminal act, probably committed the one with which he is actually charged. The court in its colloquy with defense counsel conceded that prejudice of this sort would result to Byrd in letting in the evidence.

From the quality of proof standpoint for proving knowledge and intent, its probative value was largely cumulative. The evidence came from the mouth of the same witness, Kaufman, who testified to the occurrences in the first two counts. If the jury believed his testimony as to those counts, the relating of the Sandberg incident added little, if anything, to a revelation of Byrd's state of mind. If they had disbelieved Kaufman's testimony about the first two counts, it is not very likely they would have believed his story about the Sandberg tax audit.

Another factor to be considered is whether the Government was faced with a real necessity which required it to offer the evidence in its main case. The defense had not, either in its claims or the statement of facts which it would seek to prove, "sharpened" the issue of intent by asserting that the act charged was done innocently or by accident or mistake. McCormick, Evidence, § 157 at 331 (1954). . . . Nor did the Government suffer from a lack of evidence of intent. Kaufman's testimony relating to the first two counts furnished ample evidence of knowledge and intent, of the same kind and quality as that shown by his testimony concerning the Sandberg tax return. There was therefore no pressing necessity that evidence of that prior occasion be offered on the Government's main case. . . . It is, of course, conceivable that in some cases proof of the offenses charged would contain little or nothing from which an inference of guilty intent could be drawn. In such a case a trial judge would, in the exercise of his discretion, be justified in admitting as part of the Government's case, proof of a prior similar offense to show knowledge or intent. For the present purpose of this discussion it is enough to point out that the scope of discretion does not include every offer of a prior similar offense which may contribute something to a showing of intent in the Government's main case. Where the prejudice is substantial and the probative value, through the nature of the evidence or the lack of any real necessity for it, is slight, its admission at that stage may be held to be an abuse of discretion. Under such circumstances the better practice would be to sustain the objection to the offer on the Government's main case without prejudice to its re-offer in rebuttal, if then warranted.[11]

A discriminating analysis of this kind fosters a sound result by clarifying the significant considerations in a given case. Of course, one should not expect the precedents to provide precise guidance. Inevitable differences from case to case in such factors as the degree of certainty that the other offense was committed and the probable costs of admissibility in terms of prejudice and efficient trial administration may have a decisive influence upon admissibility.[12] For example, the introduction of other-crimes evidence might surprise the accused, putting his defense counsel at a disadvantage in presenting rebuttal evidence. This consideration should either lead to a continuance or count heavily against admission.[13] Furthermore, various judges view the admission of other-crimes evidence differently because of their differing assessments of its probative force in a particular case or their varying appraisals of the policy considerations underlying its general exclusion. Judicial disagreement is illustrated by those cases in which evidence of a collateral crime is relevant to a necessary element of the crime charged—for example, the element of intent—but that element is not directly contested by the accused, who asserts only that he did not engage in the conduct charged. In this situation, some courts have permitted the use of other-crimes evidence to show intent,[14] while others have held that this evidence should be excluded because conduct and not intent is the

11. Id. at 574–75.

12. See, e.g., United States v. Johnson, 382 F.2d 280 (2d Cir.1967) (per curiam), where the court distinguished United States v. Byrd, 352 F.2d 570 (2d Cir.1965).

13. The Federal Rules prefer a continuance to avoid unfair surprise. Adv. Comm.Note to Fed.R.Evid. 403. In a few jurisdictions there is a rule that notice, in certain circumstances, is a prerequisite to admissibility. See, e.g., State v. Spreigl, 272 Minn. 488, 139 N.W.2d 167 (1965) (charge of indecent liberties with a minor). Usually, however, a lack of notice is but a factor to be considered.

14. See, e.g., United States v. Conley, 523 F.2d 650 (8th Cir.1975), cert. denied, 424 U.S. 920 (1976).

element specifically contested by the defense.[15] Although the latter resolution generally is preferable, an invariable rule dictating exclusion probably is unwise. Certain proscribed conduct (such as robbery) may be highly suggestive of the requisite mental state, but other criminal activity (such as passing a counterfeit bill) is not so cogently probative of the actor's state of mind. Thus, even if the principal controversy at trial is the accused's conduct, the prosecutor sometimes may need to present evidence bearing upon intent to establish this element beyond a reasonable doubt. Furthermore, the collateral criminal activity may have some probative value for a specific purpose other than intent, yet if used solely for this other purpose, the propriety of admission may be questionable. If the evidence also bears upon intent, this additional value may strike the balance in favor of admission. If the accused wishes to protect himself against the proffered evidence, he can enter a stipulation on the issue of intent. The judge will then instruct a jury that intent is not an issue and that they are to return a verdict of guilty, if the other element(s) of the offense are found beyond a reasonable doubt.[16]

The courts have been especially receptive to other-crimes evidence in the prosecution of sex crimes.[17] The usual justification for a liberal policy of admission is the assumed propensity of sex offenders to repeat their illegal sexual activity, although this general assumption is open to dispute.[18] Courts usually admit evidence of collateral (prior and subsequent) sexual activity between the accused and the victim on the ground that it shows a propensity to engage in an illegal sex act with a certain person.[19] This rule of admissibility is a special exception to the general prohibition against the use of other-crimes evidence to show criminal propensity. The distinction said to justify the exception is that between using other-crimes evidence to show a propensity for

15. See, e.g., United States v. Byrd, 352 F.2d 570 (2d Cir.1965); People v. Kelley, 66 Cal.2d 232, 57 Cal.Rptr. 363, 424 P.2d 947 (1967). In United States v. Coades, 549 F.2d 1303 (9th Cir.1977), the court disapproved of evidence of another crime introduced to show intent when the defense was clearly based upon a denial that the accused committed the act in question.

16. See § 1.5.

17. Annot., 77 A.L.R.2d 841, 846–49 (1961).

18. See Gregg, Other Acts of Sexual Misbehavior and Perversion as Evidence in Prosecutions for Sexual Offenses, 6 Ariz.L.Rev. 212, 231–35 (1965). A difficulty with the judicial assumption about the recidivism of sex offenders is that all such offenders are viewed as repeaters; there is evidence suggesting that the rate of recidivism as to most classes of sex offenses is low. Id. at 233.

19. See McCormick, § 190, at 560 n. 23.

a certain crime with different victims and using it to show a propensity for particular criminal activity with a *specific person.*[20] The underlying assumption is that there is considerable likelihood that illegal sexual acts with the same person will be repeated. The assumption is probably valid, at least when applied to consensual sex crimes; its application to sex crimes of force, however, is questionable.[21]

Some courts have failed to apply the limitations of this special exception and, citing such reasons as intent, design, or propensity, have admitted evidence of sexual acts with third persons.[22] Usually, but not always,[23] this extended exception is applied in prosecutions for behavior considered uncommon or perverted, such as sexual offenses against children.[24] Thus, in some prosecutions, evidence of other instances of generally similar conduct is admissible as bearing upon the accused's propensity to commit a certain kind of sexual offense. This broadened receptivity also departs from the rule prohibiting evidence of other similar offenses to show only a proclivity to commit the crime charged.[25] The principle of extended admissibility in prosecutions for sex offenses has met resistance from some commentators who assert that, at least in cases allowing acts with third persons to be shown, the general prohibition against other-crimes evidence has been abandoned without adequate justification.[26]

20. Lempert & Saltzburg at 229.

21. Id.

22. People v. Pigford, 197 Colo. 358, 593 P.2d 354 (1979); Bracey v. United States, 142 F.2d 85, 88 (D.C.Cir.1944), cert. denied, 322 U.S. 762 (1944) (dictum); Lamar v. State, 245 Ind. 104, 195 N.E.2d 98 (1964).

23. State v. Finley, 85 Ariz. 327, 338 P.2d 790 (1959) (rape of another woman under somewhat similar circumstances, five days before). Rhine v. State, 336 P.2d 913, 920–23 (Okl.Crim.App.1958) (evidence that accused doctor drugged other patients and then had intercourse). In each of these cases, the court justified admission on the basis of a plan or scheme. Query whether there was a broad plan embracing all of the sexual acts?

24. See, e.g., Kerlin v. State, 255 Ind. 420, 265 N.E.2d 22 (1970) (sodomy with boy; evidence of previous sodomy with adults admitted); State v. Spreigl, 272 Minn. 488, 139 N.W.2d 167 (1965) (sexual offense against young stepdaughter); State v. Schlak, 253 Iowa 113, 111 N.W.2d 289 (1961) (lewd act upon child); McCormick, § 190, at 560–61.

25. The general prohibition normally excludes evidence of other crimes to show propensity even in instances where the collateral crimes involve the same offense as the crime charged. See People v. Lapin, 138 Cal.App.2d 251, 291 P.2d 575 (1956); People v. Kelley, 66 Cal.2d 232, 57 Cal.Rptr. 363, 243–44, 424 P.2d 947, 957 (1967) (dictum); Morgan & Weinstein at 191–92.

26. For a thoughtful article on the subject of other-crimes evidence in sex cases, see Gregg, Other Acts of Sexual Misbehavior and Perversion as Evidence in Prosecutions for Sexual Offenses, 6 Ariz.L.Rev. 212 (1965). See

§ 5.16 Similar Incidents in Civil Cases

Many jurisdictions reject altogether the circumstantial use of character evidence in civil cases, even when the conduct alleged in the complaint or counterclaim has criminal overtones. When the civil case does not involve "quasi-criminal" conduct, there is overwhelming authority rejecting character evidence. Thus, evidence that a party acted negligently on prior occasions will not be received to show circumstantially that he was negligent at the time of the principal event. Reception of this evidence would not only violate the general rule forbidding the circumstantial use of character, but it would also contravene the rule that even when character can be shown for circumstantial use, it may not be shown by evidence of specific instances. Of course, evidence indicating a habit—a long-term, consistent response to a particular situation—will be received for the inference that the consistent practice was followed on the occasion in question. Finally, as we saw in the preceding sections, in criminal trials the law raises a general prohibition against evidence of other crimes, but marks out exceptions when the evidence shows more than a criminal disposition. We now turn to some selected problems in the civil area that bear a close kinship to those discussed above.

Suppose that *A* sues *B*, a service station owner, alleging that *B*'s attendant was negligent in placing a metal pipe over a walkway leading to a display rack. The plaintiff offers evidence that another person, *X*, tripped over the same pipe. *B*, on the other hand, offers evidence that in recent months many people have used the same walkway without an incident. The receipt of evidence of these collateral events may assist the trier in determining whether the walkway was hazardous and thus in resolving the issue of *B*'s negligence (or *A*'s contributory negligence). The probative force of these proffered items depends largely upon the coincidence of conditions that surround the earlier events and the event in question. Variables such as lighting, the condition of the walkway, and the attentiveness of *X* and the other pedestrians affect the strength of the inferences about the condition of the walkway at the time of *A*'s fall. These factors may be difficult to prove, and the introduction of the evidence pertaining to the variables may be time-consuming. Similarity is particularly hard to demonstrate when one wishes to compare the conditions sur-

also State v. McFarlin, 110 Ariz. 225, 517 P.2d 87 (1973) (limiting evidence of sexual acts with third persons, offered to show propensity or disposition, to those cases involving abnormal sexual behavior).

rounding an event (*A*'s fall) and one or more "non-events" (safe passage by the pedestrians who did not fall). These combined considerations—the cost in terms of time, distraction, and possibly prejudice, weighed against questionable probative value—have led most courts to condition the admissibility of such evidence on its meeting certain requirements.[1] These requirements, which are discussed below, are designed to ensure that other-accidents evidence will be admitted only when its probative value outweighs its cost. The standards, however, are broad; most appellate courts repose in the trial judge considerable discretion to determine the admissibility of this type of evidence.[2]

It is important to observe that evidence of other accidents alone does not establish that the defendant was negligent. Rather, it is offered to help establish that the surrounding conditions were dangerous or, if the other accidents were known to the defendant, that the defendant had notice that a possibly dangerous condition existed. When the evidence is offered to establish a hazardous condition, the desired inferences are (1) that the dangerous condition caused the other accident(s); (2) that the dangerous condition then existing also existed at the time of the plaintiff's injury; and (3) that this condition caused the plaintiff's injury. The ultimate question in a negligence suit, however, is whether the defendant acted unreasonably; proof of a dangerous condition alone is not usually dispositive of this question. Of course, this proof can be an important link in the process of establishing negligence, and its utility is seldom overlooked by claimants.

A careful proponent seeking to persuade a trial or appellate court that "other-accident" evidence is admissible should be prepared to state exactly why the evidence is relevant and why its probative force is sufficient to justify an exception to the usual prohibition. Note that not only is similarity of condition between the other accidents and the litigated event a critical point, but the number of other accidents can also be highly significant. It may be unreasonable to infer from a single prior accident that the condition alleged was in fact the cause. But two or more prior accidents at the same location, under substantially similar condi-

§ 5.16

1. See Henderson v. Illinois Central Gulf R.R., 114 Ill.App.3d 754, 70 Ill.Dec. 595, 449 N.E.2d 942 (1983); Carlson, et al. at 363–64.

2. See Nelson v. Brunswick Corp., 503 F.2d 376, 380 (9th Cir.1974); McCormick, § 200, at 587.

tions, buttress the inference that the faulty condition existed and was a causal factor.

The importance of repetition and similarity varies depending on the proposition to which the evidence of collateral events is directed. When prior accidents are used to show that the defendant was on notice that a possibly dangerous condition existed, even one accident known to the defendant has considerable probative force. Furthermore, when notice is the object of the proof, it is unnecessary to show that the other accident occurred under precisely the same condition as that involving the plaintiff;[3] it suffices that a dangerous condition, allegedly the cause of the present injury, was known or should have been known to the defendant because it was associated with a prior accident. This analysis again underscores the importance of carefully assessing and clearly stating probative value of the proffered evidence.

A defendant may encounter considerable difficulty when he wishes to show a lack of previous accidents for the inference that a dangerous condition did not exist. Although situations obviously vary, it generally holds true that evidence of an absence of other accidents is not so persuasive in demonstrating a safe condition as is evidence of prior accidents in demonstrating an unsafe condition. At least this is true in the common situation where the condition in question is subject to change. Someone, after all, must be the first to be harmed by an evolving hazardous condition.[4] There are circumstances, however, notably those involving fixed or stable conditions and safe use or passage by a considerable number of persons, where probative force justifies admission.[5] McCormick, with some judicial support, argues that the trial judge should be vested with discretion to admit evidence of a lack of prior accidents.[6] Furthermore, such evidence (a "good" safety record) should be admissible to rebut the inference of a hazardous condition in cases in which the judge has admitted evidence of a prior accident.

Other situations exist in which the probative value of a similar incident is high. In one case, for example, a plaintiff alleged that her skin was damaged by the defendant-manufactur-

3. McCormick, § 200, at 590.

4. See Pittman v. Littlefield, 438 F.2d 659 (1st Cir.1971).

5. See McDonald's Corp. v. Grissom, 402 So.2d 953 (Ala.1981); Stark v. Allis-Chalmers & Northwest Roads, 2 Wash. App. 399, 467 P.2d 854 (1970).

6. McCormick, § 200, at 590–91.

er's cosmetic. One of the defenses was that any skin damage resulted from a source or cause other than the defendant's product. The plaintiff offered to show that *X* and *Y*, both users of defendant's preparation, sustained skin damage similar to hers. The court correctly admitted the evidence for the purpose of showing what had caused the skin condition.[7] A like result is usually appropriate when the sale price of property similar to the property in question is offered as relevant to value.[8] In contractual disputes, reference to a course of dealing between the parties may shed light upon the terms or meaning of the disputed contract.[9] Of course, dissimilarities between the contested transaction and other contractual arrangements may render evidence of the other events inadmissible. Evidence of similar contractual transactions between one of the parties to the disputed agreement and a *third* party sometimes has only attenuated probative value. The early cases were reluctant to receive this evidence; modern authority generally recognizes that in some contexts similarities may be sufficiently strong to warrant admission.[10]

Although more commonly encountered in criminal trials, other-crimes evidence—which discloses a similar event—has a parallel role in the context of certain civil trials,[11] notably those involving a claim based upon deceitful conduct. For example, when a plaintiff seeks redress for an act of fraud or misrepresentation, he may introduce other, substantially identical acts to show a plan or scheme of which the present act is a part; such evidence then can be used to prove conduct or identity on the occasion in question.[12] Other fraudulent acts (bearing at least some similarity to the act in question) may also have substantial probative force to prove mental state, such as knowledge or intent.[13]

7. Carter v. Yardley & Co., 319 Mass. 92, 64 N.E.2d 693 (1946); Annot., 42 A.L.R.3d 780 (1972). Cf. Hopkins v. Baker, 553 F.2d 1339 (D.C.Cir.1977) (other persons' use of railroad yard relevant on issue whether plaintiff's presence was foreseeable). Cf. Poston v. Clarkson Const. Co., 401 S.W.2d 522 (Mo.App.1966) (blast damage to houses near plaintiff's relevant to whether blast caused damage to plaintiff's house).

8. Lawrence v. Greenwood, 300 N.Y. 231, 90 N.E.2d 53 (1949). See McCormick § 199, where a good discussion is accompanied by ample citations to authorities.

9. McCormick, § 198, at 583.

10. Id. at 583–84; Firlotte v. Jessee, 76 Cal.App.2d 207, 172 P.2d 710 (1946) (terms of lease in dispute; terms of *A*'s earlier offer of same land to *C* relevant to terms of disputed contract with *B*).

11. For a broader discussion of other-crimes evidence, see §§ 5.12–5.15.

12. McCormick § 197.

13. Id.

§ 5.17 Public Policy Considerations in Circumstantial Proof: Subsequent Remedial Action and Offers to Compromise or Plead Guilty

Public or social policy considerations frequently mold rules of evidentiary exclusion as, for example, in instances where evidence of a privileged communication is rejected. One rule of evidence thought to promote socially desirable ends is that which excludes evidence of subsequent (post-accident) repairs or remedial measures in negligence cases. For example, in a suit for liability arising out of a defective walkway, evidence that the defendant repaired the condition after the accident is not admissible to show a prior defective condition. The same exclusionary principle applies when the defendant makes design changes or institutes new safety regulations or practices following an accident. In both of these instances the proponent of the evidence is attempting to raise the inference that remedial steps were taken because the actor thought the prior condition was hazardous or harmful; therefore (the further inference goes), a dangerous or harmful condition in fact existed.

An issue of relevance is, of course, raised by this inferential chain. An after-the-incident precautionary measure may reflect merely the exercise of extraordinary caution to avoid any possibility of future injuries, and may not indicate the actor's belief that the condition in question was really hazardous. This hypothesis is sometimes cited as a reason for excluding post-injury measures.[1] It appears, however, that in many instances evidence of post-injury remedial steps increases the likelihood that the actor thought the prior condition or practice was unsafe. Thus, the traditional justification for refusing to admit evidence of repairs or other precautionary measures is that if this evidence could be used to establish the prior existence of a dangerous condition or practice, the person potentially liable would be reluctant to take corrective action. Since the law should foster the desirable policy objective of encouraging remedial action, it should reject evidence of post-injury protective measures offered for adverse use against the party charged with fault. Whether this rule of exclusion actually affects one's willingness to undertake remedial steps is

§ 5.17

1. As the Advisory Committee to the Federal Rules noted, "[A remedial measure] is not in fact an admission, since the conduct is equally consistent with injury by mere accident or through contributory negligence." Adv.Comm.Note to Fed.R.Evid. 407. The Committee notes, nonetheless, that it still is possible to infer fault. Id.

problematic and the assumption that it does has been seriously questioned.[2] Arguably, even if the evidence of remedial measures were admissible, the actor would still make the necessary repairs or take other corrective action. Failure to do so poses for him the risk that another person would injure himself; furthermore, the second claimant's case would be strengthened by the fact that the defendant had notice of a possibly dangerous condition by reason of the first accident. Doubts about the efficacy of the exclusionary rule have caused several courts to abandon it in strict liability cases.[3] However, the weight of modern authority adheres to the traditional exclusionary rule even in suits based upon a theory of strict liability.[4] Various arguments support the majority approach. The exclusion of evidence of subsequent precautionary measures may have an effect, at least in some cases, upon the willingness of the potential defendant to take corrective steps. Further, the probative force of this evidence is often meager or nonexistent; a rule that admits evidence of remedial action permits this evidence even in cases where the defendant was simply improving a product that was already safe. Finally, allowing proof of subsequent measures diverts the jury's attention from the critical inquiry, namely the circumstances at the time the product was manufactured.[5] It will be seen that these reasons combine a deference to social policy with concerns about relevance and its counterweights.[6]

Note that excluding evidence of remedial measures seems especially appropriate in cases based on negligence. Here, liabili-

2. See Schwartz, The Exclusionary Rule on Subsequent Repairs—A Rule in Need of Repair, 7 The Forum 1 (1971). Professor Schwartz provides a careful analysis and notes, among other things, that in many cases the evidentiary rule is unknown to the potential defendant and thus could not influence his conduct. Id. at 6. He also observes that the motive to repair and avoid future accidents is strong and would prevail even if evidence of subsequent repairs were admissible. For a case that can be read as supporting this thesis, see Chart v. General Motors Corp., 80 Wis.2d 91, 258 N.W.2d 680 (1977).

3. Ault v. International Harvester Co., 13 Cal.3d 113, 117 Cal.Rptr. 812, 528 P.2d 1148 (1974); Good v. A.B. Chance Co., 39 Colo.App. 70, 78–80, 565 P.2d 217, 224 (1977). See also Alaska R.Evid. 407.

4. Grenada Steel Industries, Inc. v. Alabama Oxygen Co., Inc., 695 F.2d 883, 887 (5th Cir.1983), reh. denied 699 F.2d 1163 (5th Cir.1983).

5. Id.

6. Maine departs from the usual practice and allows evidence of remedial or precautionary steps even in negligence actions. Field, The Maine Rules of Evidence: What They Are and How They Got That Way, 27 Maine L.Rev. 203, 217–19 (1975); Note, The Repair Rule: Maine Rule of Evidence 407(a) and the Admissibility of Subsequent Remedial Measures in Proving Negligence, 27 Maine L.Rev. 225 (1975).

ty attaches if the defendant acted unreasonably in view of the facts known (or which should have been known) to him before the incident in question. An after-incident remedial measure is usually taken on the basis of the additional facts revealed by the accident or injury. There is a risk that the trier, particularly a jury, might not keep this important distinction clearly in mind and might too easily infer prior knowledge from subsequent remedial acts that were generated by knowledge gained from the incident itself.

Federal Rule 407 is in accord with most common-law decisions. It provides:

> When, after an event, measures are taken which if taken previously, would have made the event less likely to occur, evidence of the subsequent measures is not admissible to prove negligence or culpable conduct in connection with the event. This rule does not require the exclusion of evidence of subsequent measures when offered for another purpose, such as proving ownership, control, or feasibility of precautionary measures, if controverted, or impeachment.

It is possible, of course, to interpret this rule as inapplicable to cases based on strict liability. One can argue, as a minority of federal (and state) courts have, that strict liability does not depend upon the defendant's culpable conduct and therefore Rule 407 is inapplicable by its terms;[7] the only issue is whether the product in question was in fact defective when made.

The second sentence in Rule 407 qualifies further the general rule of exclusion by adopting certain exceptions that were developed by the common law.[8] If a dispute arises over the ownership or control of property involved in an accident,[9] or if a defendant claims at trial that the condition in question cannot feasibly be corrected or made safer,[10] then remedial measures from which the trier can infer ownership, control, or feasibility may be entered in rebuttal. Occasionally, it may be necessary to reveal the fact of a repair or remedial step to impeach a witness by showing that he

7. Robbins v. Farmers Union Grain Terminal Ass'n, 552 F.2d 788 (8th Cir. 1977). See also Farnar v. Paccar, Inc., 562 F.2d 518 (8th Cir.1977). Contra, Grenada Steel Industries, Inc. v. Alabama Oxygen Co., Inc., supra n. 4.

8. Adv.Comm.Note to Fed.R.Evid. 407; II Wigmore § 283 (Chadbourn); Annot., 64 A.L.R.2d 1296 (1959).

9. See, e.g., Boeing Airplane Co. v. Brown, 291 F.2d 310 (9th Cir.1961).

10. See, e.g., Powers v. J.B. Michael & Co., 329 F.2d 674 (6th Cir.1964), cert. denied, 377 U.S. 980 (1964).

has acted or spoken inconsistently with his testimony at trial.[11] These various exceptions are applicable in both negligence and strict liability cases. In these instances the evidence is not offered for the purpose of showing an unsafe condition, and its probative force may be considerably greater when directed to one of these propositions not governed by the rule of exclusion. Observe that the Federal Rule does not purport to exhaust the propositions to which evidence of subsequent measures might be relevant. It is important, however, that the judge determine that an actual dispute exists concerning ownership, feasibility, etc. before he admits evidence of a remedial measure; otherwise there would be nothing left of the rule of exclusion.

Another example of an evidentiary rule designed to encourage socially useful conduct is that which excludes offers of compromise. Under this exclusionary principle, if there is an actual dispute between parties, evidence that one of the parties offered to settle or compromise the claim against him is inadmissible for the inference that he thought himself liable or that he had a weak claim.[12] Sometimes such an offer has very little probative value: it may not be an implied admission of probable liability, but simply an attempt to avoid the expense and trouble of litigation. However, in some instances, as where a defendant offers a large settlement sum constituting a high percentage of the amount claimed by the plaintiff, an inference is justified that the offering party believes himself liable. Nonetheless, all jurisdictions exclude evidence of the offer, usually on the grounds that compromise should be encouraged. The decisions vary, however, as to the admissibility of statements made during the course of compromise negotiations. A statement made by either party in hypothetical terms—usually prefaced by such phrases as "without prejudice" or "assuming, but not admitting"—is protected. But factual statements not so couched or conditioned are often admissible even if made during discussions about settlement possibilities.[13] Federal Rule 408, now of course adopted in many states, reflects a more protective attitude and broadens inadmissibility to include evidence of "conduct or statements made in compromise negotia-

11. See, e.g., Dollar v. Long Mfg., 561 F.2d 613 (5th Cir.1977), reh. denied, 565 F.2d 163 (5th Cir.1977) (defendant's design engineer who testified product in question was safe impeached by letter he wrote to dealers warning of hazards).

12. See, e.g., Fed.R.Evid. 408 and Adv.Comm.Note; People v. Gill, 247 Mich. 479, 226 N.W. 214 (1929).

13. State v. Stevens, 248 Minn. 309, 80 N.W.2d 22 (1956).

tions. . . ." [14] This formulation avoids the difficult distinction between hypothetical and factual statements. However, under the federal rule, as under the common-law decisions, evidence of compromise or statements made in connection therewith are admissible if relevant for other purposes such as showing bias or rebutting a contention of undue delay.[15] Further, if there is no actual dispute over liability or damages, the federal rule is inapplicable because its terms address only "a claim which . . . [is] disputed as to either validity or amount." [16]

Most jurisdictions also exclude evidence that one of the parties furnished or offered to furnish money in payment of medical or hospital expenses.[17] This "good Samaritan" rule is intended to encourage aid and assistance by preventing a disadvantage from accruing to a benefactor who provides economic benefits to an individual whose illness or incapacity might have been caused by the former's conduct. Similarly, in order to foster guilty pleas, evidence that an accused made an offer to plead guilty to the crime now charged or to a lesser charge is inadmissible.[18] Evidence that the accused pleaded guilty but later withdrew the plea is also usually excluded.[19] Generally, such a plea, once made, cannot be withdrawn unless the judge finds that it was improvidently entered.[20] Thus, the withdrawn plea should not carry adverse collateral consequences. Similarly, a nolo contendere plea, which does not admit culpability, should not be used adversely in a subsequent civil or criminal proceeding.[21]

Notes

1. *Evidence of Reputation.* As the text indicates in § 5.2, reputation evidence historically has been the preferred manner of proof in

14. Fed.R.Evid. 408 and Adv.Comm. Note. See, e.g., Big O Tire Dealers, Inc. v. Goodyear Tire & Rubber Co., 561 F.2d 1365 (10th Cir.1977), cert. denied, 434 U.S. 1052 (1978).

15. Fed.R.Evid. 408.

16. Id. The term "claim" should be given a contextual interpretation and not be construed to require that a lawsuit actually be filed.

17. The common-law rule is embodied in Fed.R.Evid. 409.

18. McCormick, § 274, at 814; Fed. R.Evid. 410, applying in civil and criminal proceedings. See United States v. Herman, 544 F.2d 791 (5th Cir.1977), reh. denied 549 F.2d 204 (5th Cir.1977). But see Ando v. Woodberry, 8 N.Y.2d 165, 203 N.Y.S.2d 74, 168 N.E.2d 520 (1960) (guilty plea in traffic court admissible in civil suit arising from accident).

19. Fed.R.Evid. 410; People v. Spitaleri, 9 N.Y.2d 168, 212 N.Y.S.2d 53, 173 N.E.2d 35 (1961).

20. See Saltzburg, American Criminal Procedure, 779–80 (2d ed. 1984).

21. Fed.R.Evid. 410.

those instances when character may be shown for circumstantial use. An increasing number of courts, including the federal courts, now also allow opinion evidence of character. When character is an essential part of a charge, claim, or defense, many courts admit any of the kinds of evidence that have a bearing on character: reputation, opinion, or specific acts. Other courts prefer the more probative evidence of specific acts.

Note, however, that sometimes evidence of reputation is admissible on the issue of the appropriate amount of damages in a suit based upon defamation. Normally, the measure of damage in such a suit is the harm done to the plaintiff's reputation. If that reputation was bad even before the defendant's remark, the additional harm caused by the defamatory statement may be very small. Thus, the defendant may show that prior to his statement the plaintiff already had a bad reputation for the unfavorable character suggested by the defamatory remark. Morgan & Weinstein at 183.

2. *Evidence of an Accused's Prior Bad Conduct.* Note the possibilities, already explored, of introducing evidence disclosing that an accused has engaged in other criminal conduct: (1) "Have-you-heard" questions during cross-examination of the reputation witness who, on direct, has asserted that the defendant has a good reputation (inconsistent with the crime charged), and, likewise, do-you-know questions put to the witness who on direct offers an opinion of the accused's good character; (2) Other-crimes evidence relevant to some proposition other than criminal propensity. In addition to these possibilities, a third avenue opens if the accused testifies. He is then subject to impeachment by evidence of criminal activity that bears on credibility. § 8.3.

3. *Other Claims by the Civil Plaintiff.* When a plaintiff has a history of bringing similar claims, the present defendant may wish to introduce this history into evidence, hoping the trier will conclude that the plaintiff makes a practice of bringing groundless claims. However, this contention by the defendant, especially in the absence of any clear indication that the previous claims *were* baseless or frivolous, is clearly prejudicial, and most courts will not allow evidence of other claims in such circumstances. Alternatively, the defendant may offer the evidence for the inference that the plaintiff is accident-prone or clumsy, arguing that the plaintiff's accident-proneness increases the likelihood that he was contributorily negligent in the accident in question. But the danger that the trier will improperly conclude that the plaintiff is a "litigious crank" is still present. Compare Middleton v. Palmer, 601 S.W.2d 759, 762 (Tex.Civ.App.1980) (previous claim(s) inadmissible to show "claim-mindedness," although

admissible to disprove claim that injuries were caused by accident sued on) with Mintz v. Premier Cab Ass'n, 127 F.2d 744, 745 (D.C.Cir. 1942) (admitting evidence of prior claims, the court held, "[i]t was for the jury to decide . . . whether [plaintiff] was merely unlucky or was 'claim-minded' "). See McCormick § 196; 1 Louisell & Mueller § 99.

4. *Other-Crimes Evidence Offered by the Accused.* Other-crimes evidence occasionally is offered by the accused to negate guilt as, for example, where criminal acts of the victim or of the accused himself support a factual hypothesis that negates or lessens the defendant's guilt. In People v. Matlock, 51 Cal.2d 682, 336 P.2d 505 (1959), the accused testified that he did not intend to strangle the victim but rather was participating with the victim in a scheme to defraud an insurance company by choking him until unconsciousness set in. It was held error to exclude evidence that victim had been convicted of fraud. See also United States v. Kelley, 545 F.2d 619 (8th Cir.1976), cert. denied, 430 U.S. 933 (1977) (construing Fed.R.Evid. 404(b) as applicable only to "other crimes" of the *accused*; those of victim not admissible.

The accused may also offer evidence of crimes similar to the crime charged but not, he claims, committed by him. For instance, he may argue that a series of rapes were so similar that they were probably committed by the same person, and although he cannot prove his innocence concerning the rape with which he is charged, he wants to try to prove (for example, by alibi) that he could not have committed the other, similar rapes. State v. Garfole, 76 N.J. 445, 388 A.2d 587 (1978), appeal after remand 80 N.J. 350, 403 A.2d 888 (1979). See also State v. Saavedra, 705 P.2d 1133 (NM, 1985) (Similar robberies for which another person convicted).

5. *Guilty Pleas.* Although an offer to plead guilty, like an offer to compromise, is excluded when offered to show a sense of guilt, a guilty plea that is made and received by the court is conclusive in the criminal case in which it is made and in some jurisdictions may be admitted in a civil case based upon the same conduct. Suppose, for example, *D* pleads guilty to the offense of reckless driving. This plea is a substitute for trial and has a conclusive effect. In a later civil suit grounded on the same allegedly reckless driving, some courts admit evidence of the guilty plea against *D* on the theory that it constitutes a party admission. See § 7.1.

6. *The Federal Rape Shield Rule.* Suppose, in a prosecution for rape, the victim states during direct examination that she had "a sexually innocent past" prior to the rape. See 2 Louisell & Mueller, § 193, at 342 (1985 Supp.). Is the accused now entitled to introduce evidence of the victim's past sexual activities that cannot be reconciled with her claimed innocence? The victim's assertion of high moral behavior is not, strictly speaking, relevant, yet such testimony

might increase the trier's sympathy for her. A counterattack by the accused, either during cross-examination or by extrinsic evidence, does not fit comfortably with the circumstances (detailed in Federal Rule 412) in which evidence of prior sexual activity is permissible. Professor Mueller suggests that the counter-evidence ought to be allowed, since impeachment by contradiction is widely approved and is generally allowed even when the impeaching evidence contravenes a specific rule of exclusion. 2 Louisell & Mueller, § 193, at 342 (1985 Supp.).

Chapter VI

THE HEARSAY RULE: ITS NATURE AND RATIONALE

§ 6.1 General Principle and Rationale

The general understanding among lay persons that hearsay evidence involves someone's courtroom repetition of what he has heard elsewhere is partially accurate. Hearsay does involve a serial repetition: one person, the witness, repeats what an individual, whom we shall call the declarant, previously has said outside the courtroom.[1] But not all statements by an out-of-court declarant are considered hearsay. To constitute hearsay, the repeated statement must be offered for the purpose of proving that what the declarant said is true—just as if the declarant were on the witness stand, giving testimony that the proponent wants the trier to believe. Assume, for example, the declarant stated to a witness that the heating system in a particular warehouse was inoperative during the winter; evidence of this statement is offered by the witness who overheard it to prove the system was not operating during this period. The proffered statement is hearsay. Unless an exception to the hearsay rule applies,[2] the opposing party can enter an objection and the judge will exclude the witness's testimony disclosing what the declarant said.

The basis for the rule against hearsay—and hence for sustaining the opponent's objection—is that the opponent is unable to

§ 6.1

1. Under the prevailing view, a prior out-of-court statement by a witness now on the stand is also treated as hearsay. See § 6.4. In these circumstances, of course, the witness and the out-of-court declarant are the same person. In initially understanding the hearsay rule, the reader may be helped by assuming that the witness and the declarant are different persons.

2. The exceptions are considered in Ch. VII.

confront and cross-examine the "real" witness (the declarant) and to expose weaknesses in his statement. It bears repeating, however, that a statement is classified as hearsay only if the proponent of the evidence seeks to have the trier believe that the declarant's out-of-court statement is true, that is, only if the proponent seeks to have the factfinder rely on the declarant's credibility.[3] It will be seen, momentarily, that it is only in instances in which a declarant's statement is "offered for its truth," as the cases say, that cross-examination of the declarant is necessary to protect the opponent. This proposition may be understood by recalling that the general purpose of cross-examination is to expose mistake or deception and thereby weaken or destroy the trier's belief in the truth of assertions made during direct examination. Thus, an adverse interrogation of the declarant is unnecessary when his declaration is not offered for the truth of its assertion. In such a case, the opponent's right to test the proponent's evidence is preserved, for he may cross-examine the witness-auditor to probe the accuracy of *his* testimony that the declarant actually made the out-of-court statement in question. If the statement or declaration is not offered for its truth, the only issue is whether the statement was made at all, and on this question there is an opportunity for effective cross-examination. As will be seen, an extra-judicial assertion can often be relevant and useful to the trier of fact for a purpose not entailing proof of the truth of the assertion.

The following example illustrates further the nature of hearsay and the need for cross-examination: in a prosecution for the sale of illegal weapons, witness *W* testifies that declarant *B* stated that he (*B*) observed the accused selling a machine gun. If the proponent offers *W*'s testimony to show that the accused made the sale, the trier is asked to believe *B*'s account of the facts—to rely upon his credibility. The cross-examiner, unable to confront and interrogate the absent *B*, will find it difficult to expose weaknesses in *B*'s statement. Cross-examination of the declarant, were he present, might reveal that he was deliberately lying or that, even though he was not consciously making a false assertion, his statement was inaccurate because of poor observation, faulty memory, or what might be called a "mistranscription" resulting from the declarant's unintended omission of a word or his ambigu-

3. The term "credibility" as here used includes both wilful and innocent (unknowing) misstatements. It may be thought of as synonymous with "accuracy."

ous use of language. In sum, if *B* were on the stand the cross-examiner could test not only whether *B* was willing to tell the truth, but also whether he had the ability to perceive the event clearly and to remember it adequately; the examiner could also ascertain whether *B* is using language he intended—language that renders an unambiguous account of what occurred. The cross-examiner's interrogation of the witness, *W*, however, can only test whether *W* is accurately *repeating* what was said by the declarant *B*. It cannot test the accuracy of *B*'s statement.

Since we often shall refer to the potential defects in a declarant's statement—the so-called hearsay "dangers" or "risks"—they are explained below:

(a) *Defects in perception*: the statement may be unreliable because the declarant did not observe or hear accurately.

(b) *Defects in memory*: the declarant's recollection may have been inaccurate or incomplete.

(c) *Defects in sincerity or veracity*: the declarant may simply not have told the complete truth.

(d) *Defects in narration or transmission*: mistransmissions may arise because the declarant's statement is ambiguous (as, for example, when he has used a word or phrase that has a special or unusual meaning within a particular group) or the declarant's statement is incomplete (as when he inadvertently omits the word "not" from a sentence). This potential defect is usually not considered by the courts to pose a significant risk.[4]

The assumption underlying the hearsay rule is that cross-examination reveals these infirmities; accordingly, the lack of opportunity for cross-examination is the fundamental reason for excluding hearsay evidence. Although other reasons for rejecting hearsay have been advanced (for example, that the declarant did

4. Although it is true that defects in transcription can be exposed by cross-examination of the declarant, this particular hearsay danger has received only limited attention in the reported cases. Possibly, this comparative indifference indicates the hazard is not frequently encountered or, perhaps, not frequently recognized. It should be noted, however, that when the declarant communicates with words, but uses a special or "slang" meaning, other witnesses can sometimes help establish the particular denotation or connotation. Mistranscription by ambiguity can also be a difficulty where the hearsay declarant communicates not by words, but rather by conduct. See § 6.3. However, mistranscription in this latter context is principally a problem of probative value, that is, the question is whether the actor's conduct is probative of the proposition for which it is offered.

not speak under oath and his demeanor could not be observed by the factfinder), the dominant view holds that it is the untested nature of hearsay evidence that justifies its exclusion. This rationale, of course, is consistent with a major tenet of the adversary system: cross-examination is essential for ensuring accuracy and discovering truth.[5] Despite this consistency, however, the mechanical application of the hearsay rule without exception would stultify judicial trials and impede accurate factfinding. Hence, as the next chapter demonstrates, there are numerous exceptions to the hearsay rule. Thus, in reading the present chapter, bear in mind that classification of a particular statement as hearsay does not necessarily mean that the statement will be excluded. Often the declaration is admissible under one of the various exceptions.

§ 6.2 Application of the General Principle

We have seen that the hearsay stigma attaches when, and only when, the proponent offers the declarant's assertion for a purpose that requires the trier to accept as true the facts it embodies. If the proponent's probative purpose can be achieved without the factfinder's reliance upon the truth of the declarant's statement, the hearsay rule is inapplicable. It thus becomes important to take close account of the purpose for which a statement is offered. Sometimes it is readily apparent that a particular statement is not being offered for its truth, as in the contracts example immediately below. On other occasions the statement may appear to have its greatest probative force if used as proof of the assertion it contains, yet it is offered for a relevant nonhearsay purpose and, so offered, is not blocked by the hearsay rule.

There are various patterns in which a serial repetition serves a recognized evidentiary purpose without requiring that the factfinder rely upon the declarant's credibility—in other words, situations in which the consequential fact is the making of the statement, not the truth or falsity of any facts that may be contained in the statement. One such pattern arises when the declarant's statement *is instrumental in creating a legal relationship* or, otherwise stated, the statement has a *legal significance independent* of the declarant's desire or capacity to be accurate and truthful. For example, when the issue is whether *B* accepted *A*'s offer for certain painting services, a witness *W* may testify that he

5. V Wigmore, § 1367, at 32 (Tillers).

overheard *B* say to *A*: "I accept your offer to paint my porch." Under the objective view of contract formation, the statement by *B* resulted in the formation of the agreement—assuming a reasonable offeror would have construed *B*'s statement as an acceptance. The proponent only need establish that the operative words forming the contract were spoken, not that these words were, in any sense, true. It is of no consequence that the cross-examiner is deprived of an opportunity to test the defects in *B*'s perception, memory, sincerity, or narration. What matters is that *B* spoke the words of acceptance, not (for example) that he may have been insincere because he secretly intended to reject *A*'s offer. Note that there is no proper hearsay objection as to whether *B* spoke the words of acceptance, because *W*, who asserts he overheard *B*, is in court and available for cross-examination. The cross-examiner can interrogate *W* concerning what *B* said—that is, he can probe fully the issue of what (if any) words were spoken. Hence, *W*, who was the *auditor of B*'s statement, can be fully cross-examined regarding what *B* said. *B*, the declarant, need not be examined because his statement is not offered for its truth.

The foregoing discussion reveals that there are two inquiries regarding the admissibility of a declarant's out-of-court statement. The first question is whether there is admissible evidence that the declaration was made. If the statement was oral, it usually is necessary to call as a witness the auditor, who can give testimony concerning what the declarant said. If the statement is in writing, it usually is required that the writing be produced and identified as having been authored by the declarant. The proponent of the evidence must be able to prove the statement was made without violating any rule of evidence, *including the hearsay rule.* Assuming there is admissible evidence that the statement was made, the second inquiry is whether the declarant's statement is being offered for its truth. In the illustration involving the formation of an oral contract, there was proper (admissible) evidence that the declarant-offeree spoke the words of acceptance. And since his declaration was not offered for its truth, it falls outside the exclusionary reach of the hearsay rule.

Consider Justice Holmes's classic example of the man who falsely shouts "fire" in a crowded theater.[1] Suppose that in the

§ 6.2

1. See Saltzburg & Redden at 719–20.

accused's prosecution for the resulting offense of disturbing the peace, a witness offers to testify that he heard the defendant shout "fire," and the defense objects on the grounds of hearsay. Because the statement is offered only to show that the declarant spoke the warning (and not to show that there was a fire in the theater), the objection fails. Note that the witness called to testify was an auditor-witness—that is, he claims to have actually heard the defendant shout the warning. What if the witness testified that another person, *B*, told him that the defendant called out "fire," but the witness himself had not heard the shout? The proffered testimony would be hearsay. The prosecution would be introducing the witness's testimony for a purpose (viz., to show that the defendant gave the false warning) requiring the trier to accept the *truth of B's statement.* The defect in this latter instance is that the proponent offers hearsay evidence that the statement ("fire") was uttered: instead of calling an auditor, he calls a witness who did not hear the defendant's shout, and hence who can testify only that the auditor *B* stated that the defendant shouted "fire." The cross-examiner is denied the opportunity to test the *auditor's* assertion that the defendant shouted the warning.

To summarize: in the last two illustrations, evidence of the statements of contractual acceptance and warning *do not themselves* constitute hearsay. If there is admissible, nonhearsay evidence that the declarant spoke the words, the statements may be received without violating the hearsay rule. These statements are not offered for their truth because the law prescribes a legal effect to their mere utterance. In other words, the statements are consequential in the legal actions in which they are offered, quite apart from whether they are true. This legal effect (the *formation* of a contract or the *utterance* of a prohibited warning) becomes operative without regard to the credibility of the declarant. This rationale of independent legal significance (or consequence) also applies to the utterance of a libel or slander, and to words that make a transfer a gift—assuming the substantive law provides that the gift is effected if delivery is accompanied *by words* of donation. Both defamatory words (e.g., "You are a thief") and the donative declaration (e.g., "Take this watch as a gift") are offered for their independent legal effect, without regard to the credibility of the declarant.

To extend our illustrations, suppose an issue at trial was whether *A* had impersonated a United States ambassador. *W* testifies that he leases limousines and that when *A* came to *W's* office, *A* said, "I am Ambassador Bruce." This evidence is not offered to prove that *A* is Ambassador Bruce, but that he spoke the words of impersonation which, we are assuming, had relevance (that is, were consequential) under the substantive law simply by the fact that they were uttered.

In a well-known case [2] involving a suit for conversion of plaintiff's corn by the defendant bank, it was necessary for the plaintiff to show that the corn in question belonged to him rather than to his tenant. The litigants agreed that one portion of the harvested corn belonged to plaintiff and the other portion belonged to the tenant; the issue was what corn belonged to whom. The plaintiff testified that prior to the alleged conversion by the bank, the tenant had pointed to certain cribs and stated for the first time that the corn in these belonged to the plaintiff. Was this hearsay? Under the controlling substantive law, the court correctly ruled that it was not. This holding was sound, despite the fact that the plaintiff was offering the statement to show that he owned the corn in question. Until the tenant's statement was made, the fungible crop had not been divided. Under the substantive law, the tenant's statement resulted in endowing the plaintiff with sole ownership of the designated portion of the corn. The mere utterance of the statement had the independent legal effect of vesting ownership. It was unnecessary to rely upon the credibility of the tenant-declarant, since ownership was conferred regardless of his subjective intent. The result would have been contrary had the corn earlier been divided. In that event, a *subsequent* statement by the tenant that identified certain *previously designated* corn as belonging to the plaintiff would have been hearsay because the trier then would be asked to accept as true the declarant's factual assertion that the portion of the corn to which he pointed already belonged to the plaintiff. Thus, whenever the mere utterance of certain words, independent of their truth and regardless of the declarant's subjective intent, is consequential under the substantive law, the hearsay rule is not violated. Such declarations are sometimes called "verbal acts."

Another pattern in which a statement is not offered for its truth is when the purpose of offering the statement is to *show its probable effect upon the state of mind of another person* who heard (or read) the statement. Suppose, for example, a patron sues a

2. Hanson v. Johnson, 161 Minn. 229, 201 N.W. 322 (1924).

grocery store for injuries sustained from slipping on the contents of a broken ketchup bottle.[3] The defendant store calls to the stand a checkout clerk (the auditor) who will testify that he heard the manager cry out to the patron: "Lady, please don't step on the bottle of ketchup." The evidence is consequential because the patron's conduct, which may involve contributory negligence, should be evaluated in light of the warning. Furthermore, the warning supports the contention that agents of the grocery store acted prudently. The purpose for which the evidence is offered is satisfied if the trier decides the words of warning were spoken. The trier is not being asked to use the declarant's statement as proof that there was a bottle of ketchup on the floor. Without reliance upon the truth of the declarant's statement, the trier can evaluate the plaintiff's conduct (and that of the store's management) in light of whether she was warned of the hazardous condition. On the issue of contributory negligence, the question is what effect the warning had or should have had upon her, a question that can be addressed without accepting the clerk's declaration for its truth. Indeed if the plaintiff maintains that she thought the manager was joking, she may so testify. Since the question of contributory negligence turns upon the reasonableness of the *plaintiff*'s conduct, and that is the issue on which the evidence is offered, it is immaterial whether or not the *declarant* actually thought there was a broken bottle of ketchup on the floor.

A similar rationale explains a British case involving a prosecution for the forbidden possession of ammunition in a battle zone.[4] In support of his defense of duress—grounded on the claim that he had been captured by enemy terrorists and forced to arm himself—the accused offered evidence of his captors' orders and threats. The statements of the captors were not hearsay because they were not offered for their truth. They were not offered, for example, to prove that the terrorists actually would have killed the accused had he not taken up arms. Rather, the statements were offered because their mere utterance was significant in proving duress. Evidence that the threats were made enables the trier to assess the probable effect of the statements upon the

3. The example is based on Safeway Stores, Inc. v. Combs, 273 F.2d 295 (5th Cir.1960); see Kaplan & Waltz at 95; Weinstein & Mansfield, et al. at 556.

4. Subramaniam v. Public Prosecutor, 100 Solicitor's Journal 566 (Judicial Comm., Privy Council 1956) reprinted in pertinent part in Kaplan & Waltz at 94–95.

accused's state of mind, permitting them to judge his conduct accordingly.[5]

In such cases as the foregoing, the fact that the statement was made is itself consequential because the utterance gives notice of a hazard or threatening circumstance that reasonably might affect the hearer's conduct. If the trier believes that the statement was made and that the actor heard it, it will weigh this evidence in deciding whether his actions were reasonable or justified. Thus, on the issue of whether *D* was negligent when he drove a car that had defective tires, a statement to *D* by *B*, the service station attendant, "These tires are bad," is not hearsay if offered to show *D*'s notice or knowledge.[6] Of course, the declaration would be hearsay if offered as proof that the tires were bad. To prove the defective condition of the tires, other evidence would be necessary. A final example: on the issue of *A*'s anxiety as an element of his injuries, his physician's statement giving an unfavorable diagnosis and discouraging prognosis would not be hearsay.[7]

Let us now compare the related but distinct case in which the substantive law makes it consequential that a declarant had an awareness or knowledge of a certain event or circumstance, and *he makes a statement disclosing that knowledge*. Here again the hearsay rule is usually held inapplicable. If, for example, it is consequential that the declarant knew that his brakes were defective, testimony that he stated that his brakes were bad would be admitted if the evidence were limited to showing that he had knowledge. A similar rationale would admit evidence that a declarant stated that his company's manufacturing process was poisoning nearby aquatic life. These statements would be hearsay if offered to show defective brakes or that the declarant's firm was contaminating the water. However, if the evidence is *limited to the issue of the declarant's knowledge*, which under the substantive law (we have assumed) is a determinant of liability, there is no hearsay violation. Again, the proponent would have to supply

5. In United States v. Kutas, 542 F.2d 527 (9th Cir.1976), cert. denied, 429 U.S. 1073 (1977), the Court of Appeals approved the admission of declarant's statement made in accused's presence on the nonhearsay ground that the statement reasonably could apprise the accused that the person he was harboring was an escaped prisoner. The fact that the person was an escapee was shown by other evidence; thus the declarant's statement could be used for the limited probative purpose of increasing the likelihood that the accused knew the person he was harboring was a fugitive.

6. Player v. Thompson, 259 S.C. 600, 193 S.E.2d 531 (1972).

7. Weinstein & Mansfield, et al. at 555.

other evidence showing that the brakes in fact were defective or that discharged pollutants in fact were killing fish. But the words spoken demonstrate a knowledge or awareness and for this limited purpose they may be admitted without violating the hearsay rule. Even though the statement of knowledge is couched in terms of the fact to be established, "[p]roof that one talks about a matter demonstrates on its face that he was conscious or aware of it, and veracity does not enter into the situation." [8]

In an earlier chapter, we observed that evidence may have probative force pointing toward two or more consequential propositions.[9] It should now be apparent that there are instances when evidence offered for one probative purpose runs afoul of the hearsay rule, but the same evidence offered for another purpose avoids a hearsay violation. Suppose, for example, golfer *A* sues country club *B* for injuries that resulted when *B* negligently provided *A* with a defective cart. It would be consequential that prior to *A*'s accident, *B* had knowledge that the cart was defective. Evidence is offered that golfer *C* (the declarant) had said to *B*'s agent in charge of the golf course, "Don't lease the red cart today; the brakes are bad." If this evidence is offered through an auditor-witness for the purpose of proving that the cart had defective brakes, a hearsay objection would be proper: the declarant made the statement out of court and the proponent offers it for the truth of the assertion that the brakes were defective. This use of the evidence requires that the trier rely upon the credibility of the declarant-golfer, yet his out-of-court assertion cannot be tested by cross-examination. It is possible, however, to introduce this evidence to prove that the defendant's agent had notice or knowledge of the defect [10] and thus acted carelessly in leasing the cart. Directed to the proposition of notice or awareness, evidence of the declarant's statement is not hearsay because its use does not require the trier to rely upon the truth of the statement, but instead upon the *making* of the statement.

The point to be emphasized is that a proponent, by carefully identifying the limited purpose for which evidence is offered, often can avoid application of the hearsay rule. When evidence is admitted for a limited, nonhearsay purpose, the opponent, upon request, is entitled to an instruction that the evidence is to be considered only for its admissible purpose. In the present illustra-

8. McCormick, § 250, at 741.

9. § 2.3.

10. See text supra at n. 4–5. Cf. Vinyard v. Vinyard Funeral Home, Inc., 435 S.W.2d 392, 396 (Mo.App.1968).

tion, the judge would instruct the jury to consider the golfer's statement only with respect to the question of notice, not for the purpose of deciding whether the brakes were defective.[11]

We now have encountered three general patterns or classes of statements that fall outside the hearsay rule. In the first, the act of speaking certain words has an *independent legal significance* (or consequence) quite aside from the truth or falsity of the assertion. The acceptance of a contract is a classic example; the same rationale classifies as nonhearsay a statement made by a depositor to his bank, directing that his deposit be held in trust for his daughter—assuming that under the substantive law the very utterance of the words creates a trust.[12] In the second class of cases, the words spoken are offered for their probable *effect upon the mind of the listener,* for example, the statement made by the declarant to *A* that *A* should be careful of the broken bottle in the aisle.[13] A similar rationale supports the admission of a threat to kill, made by declarant against the accused, if the purpose of the evidence is to show that the accused was reasonable in taking steps to defend himself when he encountered the declarant. A third class of nonhearsay statements consists of those assertions by a declarant that exhibit his *knowledge of a fact or condition* in a case where this knowledge is consequential. For example, a declarant states that his vehicle has defective brakes, and this statement is offered to show his knowledge or awareness. A similar rationale might admit a statement by the declarant that he was forbidden by court order from visiting his child: this statement exhibits an awareness of that provision of the order, and would not be hearsay if offered in a contempt proceeding for the limited purpose of showing that the declarant knew of the restriction.

Observe that in both the second and third classes, statements are offered, essentially, as circumstantial evidence of knowledge—by hearers or speakers—of the assertions the statements contain.

11. It is doubtful, however, that even a conscientious jury can be entirely obedient to such an instruction. Tactical considerations thus might dictate that the opponent forgo this request. It is difficult for the jury to abide by the instruction, and the instruction serves to remind the trier of evidence that is unfavorable to the opponent.

12. Lempert & Saltzburg at 360.

13. Safeway Stores, Inc. v. Combs, 273 F.2d 295 (5th Cir.1960). See also Player v. Thompson, 259 S.C. 600, 193 S.E.2d 531 (1972); Lempert & Saltzburg at 361.

A fourth class of cases, involving a declarant's statement disclosing his *state of mind,* falls on the borderline between hearsay and nonhearsay. Let us begin, however, with illustrations that rather clearly fall within the nonhearsay class. Suppose the issue is whether student *A* enrolled in Professor *X*'s class or whether, as the student contends, he (*A*) appeared on the class roll because of administrative error. Evidence is introduced that prior to registration, *A* had told another student (the auditor) that *X* graded unfairly, that the year before *X* had given a low grade to *A*, and that *X*'s lectures were confusing and that the student (auditor) should select another course. Could evidence disclosing these declarations be received as probative of the proposition that *A* was not likely to select Professor *X*'s course? The evidence satisfies the test of relevance, but the question remains whether the hearsay rule is a barrier to admission. The hearsay ban can be avoided by the straightforward analysis that these declarations are not offered to prove the faults of *X*, but rather to show circumstantially that *A* disliked *X*, and hence was unlikely to have registered for his course. A second example illustrates the same point. Suppose the issue at trial is whether Testator (*T*) intended to omit from his will Nephew (*N*). A witness testifies that several months before his death, *T* remarked: "*N* is an incorrigible spendthrift, too lazy even to hold a job, and shouldn't be allowed to spend our family into bankruptcy." This declaration is offered not as proof that *N* had these traits, but rather as circumstantial evidence that *T* disliked and distrusted *N*. The evidence increases the probability that *T* intended to omit *N* from his will; for this purpose, *T*'s statement is not hearsay. A like analysis would admit as nonhearsay the declarations of a wife, accusing her husband of neglect, infidelity, and inadequate financial support, when offered for the limited purpose of showing the wife's disaffection. This lack of affection would, of course, have to be consequential under the substantive law or at least point toward some consequential proposition. For example, suppose the husband were negligently killed by *D*. In many jurisdictions, damages in a resulting wrongful death action by the wife would be measured in part by the survivor's emotional loss.[14]

Now take the identical illustrations set out above, but imagine the declarants' statements to have been, respectively: (1) "I will never take another course from Professor *X*"; (2) "I will never

14. See, e.g., Fields v. Riley, 1 Cal. App.3d 308, 81 Cal.Rptr. 671 (1969).

leave any part of my estate to *N*"; and (3) "I hate my husband." These declarations appear to fall clearly within the hearsay rule, and, under the better view, they should be so classed. It could be argued, however, that these statements, even if untrue, have some circumstantial probative force to indicate a disaffected state of mind: the very fact that an uncomplimentary remark about the subject was made has some value to show the speaker's dislike of the subject. So viewed, the declarations would escape the hearsay rule because they are not offered for their truth, but to show circumstantially the state of mind in question. Under this rationale the mere utterance of a statement of praise, affection, distrust, or dislike, for example, has a probative value quite aside from the literal truth of the statement: the use of the words gives rise to an inference of an underlying state of mind consistent with the statement, even though the statement may not be literally true.

The difficulty with this nonhearsay analysis is that it ignores the commonsense proposition that the factfinder is probably incapable of the mental discriminations required to avoid the hearsay risks. It is highly likely that when the declarant has directly asserted his state of mind, the trier will judge that statement on its face as either true or false. Thus, declarations that *assert directly* the out-of-court speaker's state of mind should be classed as hearsay, even though neither the cases nor the commentators invariably take this view. Fortunately, the disagreements are largely conceptual because statements disclosing motive, intent, feeling, or other mental states, even if characterized as hearsay, usually are admissible under the firmly rooted hearsay exception for statements of mental or emotional condition.[15] Thus, with at least significant support in the cases and commentaries,[16] we shall consider as hearsay any off-the-stand declaration that directly asserts the declarant's state of mind if the declaration is offered for a purpose that will, as a practical matter, require that the trier consider the declaration for the truth of its assertion. Notice the application of this approach to the following case. Suppose the issue is whether the declarant is domiciled in New York. The out-of-court statement proffered at trial is "I like New York and want to live here permanently." This would be hearsay under the view suggested above, and thus would be admitted because it fell within

15. See Fed.R.Evid. 803(3).

16. See, e.g., 4 Louisell & Mueller, § 417, at 120–21.

the exception for mental state, not because it was used for a nonhearsay circumstantial purpose. Would the analysis be different if the declaration were simply, "New York is my favorite state"? The statement would still be hearsay. The factfinder is asked, first, to *believe* the statement and, second, to infer that the declarant intended to make New York his permanent home. The first step, of course, involves accepting the truth of the statement, and since this initial step (belief that New York *is* the declarant's favorite state) is essential to the second, the hearsay rule should apply. Again, however, the exception for mental state or emotion is applicable. Finally, suppose the declarant had said, "New York is the most exciting place in the country." This statement would be nonhearsay; it serves as circumstantial evidence of the declarant's selection of New York as his home.

None of the examples thus far discussed involves a written declaration, but it should be clear that assertive documentary evidence can be hearsay. If a declarant's writing is offered for the truth of the assertion it contains, the hearsay rule is applicable: the cross-examiner cannot test the reliability of the written assertion—unless, of course, the author testifies, in which case the writing may be superfluous.[17] As with verbal declarations, however, a writing may serve a nonhearsay purpose and, if properly offered, it escapes objection. Suppose, for example, *A* sues *B* for the fraudulent sale of a rare book. The complaint alleges that *B*, in connection with the sale, fraudulently stated that the volume bore the genuine signature of Thomas Jefferson. Could *B* introduce into evidence a written warranty from his supplier (the declarant), authenticating Jefferson's signature as genuine? If *B* offers the warranty to support the proposition that the signature is *genuine*, the written evidence (an out-of-court assertion by the supplier) is hearsay. But if *B* offers the evidence only to show that he had no intent to deceive *A* (thus attempting to negate the element of deceit), there is no violation of the hearsay rule. Offering the statement contained in the warranty for the limited purpose of showing its probable effect upon *B*'s mind enables the trier to consider the book supplier's assertion without relying upon his credibility.

§ 6.3 Conduct as Hearsay

Physical gestures, such as those used in sign language, in pointing out a person or object, or in nodding affirmatively in

17. But see § 7.14; § 13.9.

response to a question, often are used as a substitute for words. When the declarant intends to make an assertion by physical manifestations, and the proponent enters evidence of the declarant's actions for the truth of the assertion manifested, the hearsay rule applies. Thus, when *A*, asked by the police to identify his assailant, points to *B*, his assertion by gesture is the equivalent of the statement "*B* is the assailant."

A conceptually related but distinct situation arises when the declarant does not intend to make an assertion, but his actions imply or suggest circumstantially his belief in a relevant fact. A traveler who purchases a bus ticket and thereafter waits at a certain street corner may not intend to assert that a bus passes the corner, but his conduct implies this belief. If the traveler's conduct (standing at the corner with a bus ticket) is viewed simply as a substitute for words, equivalent in all respects to the statement "The bus passes this corner," then, like pointing or nodding, his conduct is hearsay if offered to show the passage of the bus. The argument, of course, is that since the declarant's out-of-court statement of the fact to be proved (the bus route) would be hearsay, so too should be his implied assertion of the same fact. This contention can be raised in many factual contexts. A sea captain inspects a vessel and then sets sail with his family aboard it. May a witness, offered by a party who seeks to show that the vessel was seaworthy, testify to the captain's actions? Again, the argument against admission rests on the ground that the captain's conduct belongs to the same prohibited hearsay class as his statement, "This ship is seaworthy." A similar question is posed by evidence that a doctor performed an operation of a kind that usually is administered for a certain spinal disability. May a proponent seeking to establish this disability introduce evidence of the operation? [1] Finally, on the issue of whether *A* or *B* won a footrace, may the court receive evidence that *C*, who placed his bet on *A*, was paid off by another gambler? Clearly an out-of-court statement by the gambler that "*A* won the race" would be subject to a hearsay objection.

It will be observed that in the illustrations above, only "pure conduct" is involved. The "declarant" has said nothing. But it is quite possible for verbal or written statements to contain implied

§ 6.3

1. See Weinstein & Mansfield, et al. at 572.

assertions. Suppose, for example, the issue is whether *A* had the authority to sell *B*'s property during the latter's absence.[2] Evidence is offered that immediately upon his return, *B* called the buyer and demanded that the property be surrendered.

A famous English case[3] considers in detail the issue of implied assertions. There, the proponents of a will sought to introduce letters to the testator from *X, Y,* and *Z* because the tone and content of the letters impliedly manifested the writers' belief that the recipient was sane and competent. So far as the letters ostensibly disclosed, the writers (declarants) intended only to communicate various business and social matters, but the letters were *not offered to prove anything expressly said therein*: they were offered for the *implied assertion* that the writers believed their addressee to be competent. In other words, the writers' use of normal, unguarded language, coupled with the fact that they entrusted to the testator the discharge of certain business and social affairs, implied that they thought he was sane—just as the sea captain's behavior implied that he thought his vessel was seaworthy.

Before attempting to resolve the hearsay status of what usually is called nonassertive conduct, it should be observed that in certain circumstances, silence or inaction also can be interpreted as an implied assertion of the existence or nonexistence of a certain fact. Suppose, for example, persons other than the plaintiff are exposed to an alleged condition that the plaintiff claims caused his injury, yet no one else complained or spoke about this condition. Can the trier draw an inference that the condition did not exist? This issue is sometimes posed when a plaintiff sues a restauranteur on the ground that the latter served unwholesome food. The hearsay question is whether the defendant can introduce evidence that no other customers complained.[4] In addition to the hearsay difficulty posed by this case, there is a problem of relevance. The probative force of evidence of "noncomplaints" depends, first, upon whether the other patrons ate the same food as the plaintiff and, second, whether they would have complained to the restauranteur had they become ill.

2. 4 Louisell & Mueller, § 414, at 83.

3. Wright v. Doe d. Tatham, 7 Adloph. & E. 313, 386, 112 Eng.Rep. 488 (Exch.Ch.1837) and 5 Cl. & F. 670, 739, 47 Rev.Rep. 136 (H.L.1838), reprinted in part in Lempert & Saltzburg at 533–39.

4. See Landfield v. Albiani Lunch Co., 268 Mass. 528, 168 N.E. 160 (1929); Silver v. New York Cent. R.R., 329 Mass. 14, 105 N.E.2d 923 (1952) (issue: whether railroad passenger car became cold; evidence offered: other passengers did not complain).

All of the foregoing are examples of conduct that apparently proceeds from the actor's implied belief that a certain condition exists—hence the phrase "implied assertion." For evidentiary purposes, however, a more important characteristic that these examples share is the fact that the declarant *did not intend to make the assertion* that his conduct (possibly including speech) implied. It is apparent that these nonassertive actions are different from those, such as gestures, in which conduct *intended as an assertion* is offered to prove the assertion. When nonassertive conduct is involved, the hearsay danger of insincerity is reduced or eliminated because the actor does not intend to make the assertion implied by his actions. The following illustration underscores this distinction: A question arises as to whether a particular day was warm or chilly. A witness, who on the day in question was in a building, testifies that he observed from his window that persons standing at a bus stop turned up their collars and placed their hands in their pockets.[5] One can distinguish these persons from the usual hearsay declarant because, in all likelihood, they did not intend to be making an assertion. They did not say to the witness, "The day is cold," nor did they affirmatively nod their heads when asked if it was chilly. Consequently, it is unlikely that they were being deceptive or insincere.[6]

The absence of the hearsay risk of insincerity in situations involving nonassertive actions has caused most commentators to place nonassertive conduct outside the hearsay ban. So viewed, this conduct is simply circumstantial evidence of the proposition it supports. Only recently, however, has this nonhearsay rationale expressly been adopted by courts and rulemakers. In the main, the older cases support a hearsay classification for nonassertive conduct.[7] But as Professor Falknor notes:

> In any of these situations [of nonassertive conduct] the hearsay objection is likely to be overlooked. This is especially

5. See Falknor, The "Hear-Say" Rule as a "See-Do" Rule: Evidence of Conduct, 33 Rocky Mountain L.Rev. 133 (1961).

6. In this particular instance there are no dangers from defects in the declarant's perception and memory because the actors were responding immediately to perceived climatic conditions. As to the danger of mistranscription, see § 6.1, n. 4.

Some conduct, of course, would raise dangers of defects in memory and perception as, for example, where letter-writers *X*, *Y*, and *Z* treat their addressee as if he were competent, yet their contact with him may have been limited (perception) and in the remote past (memory). See text at § 6.1, n. 4. Note that limited and remote contact also affects probative force.

7. McCormick, § 250, at 738.

> so when the evidence concerns "non-verbal" conduct because the hearsay rule is almost always, in the abstract, phrased in terms of "statements" or "utterances" and the possible application of the rule to "conduct" may not be immediately apparent. And the same is true, although perhaps to a lesser degree, when the evidence is of "verbal" conduct [of the sort involved in the English case of the letters] relevant only circumstantially. Cases are legion consequently where the hearsay objection, with strong supporting authority, might have been raised but was not.[8]

Thus, in a prosecution of the defendant for keeping a house for the purpose of taking bets, an appellate court approved, with little discussion, the admission of evidence that while police officers were apprehending the defendant they answered his telephone and discovered that the callers were placing bets.[9] A concurring justice, however, argued that evidence of the calls, when offered to establish that the defendant used his house for taking bets, violated the hearsay rule. Under his view, the act of placing a bet was the equivalent of the assertion "This house is used for betting."

The modern trend [10] toward removing nonassertive conduct from the hearsay prohibition is endorsed in the Federal Rules of Evidence.[11] The hearsay rule applies to an out-of-court "*statement* . . . offered in evidence to prove the truth of the matter asserted," [12] but, as defined in the Rules, a "statement" includes only an express assertion and "nonverbal conduct . . . *intended* . . . as an assertion." [13] [Emphasis added.] The rulemakers rejected a characterization of nonassertive conduct as hearsay on the ground that if the actor does not intend to make an assertion, there is little or no risk of insincerity.

Of course, cases will arise in which it is not clear whether the declarant intended to make the "implied assertion." [14] If he consciously "implied" the assertion—if he was aware of the com-

8. Falknor, The "Hear-Say" Rule as a "See-Do" Rule: Evidence of Conduct, 33 Rocky Mountain Law Review 133, 135 (1961).

9. People v. Barnhart, 66 Cal.App.2d 714, 153 P.2d 214 (1944).

10. McCormick, § 250, at 738–39.

11. Fed.R.Evid. 801(a)(2) and Adv. Comm.Note.

12. Fed.R.Evid. 801(c).

13. Fed.R.Evid. 801(a)(2).

14. See United States v. Reynolds, 715 F.2d 99 (3d Cir.1983); see also Finman, Implied Assertions as Hearsay, 14 Stan.L.Rev. 682, 687 n. 16 (1962), pointing out that commentators have sometimes come to opposite conclusions as to whether a particular declarant intended to make an assertion.

munication underlying his conduct (including words)—then the risk of insincerity is present. For instance, the letter writers in the English case may have believed their addressee was subject to periods of insanity, but not wishing to offend him, consciously expressed themselves in a manner that falsely implied confidence in his abilities. Other hearsay dangers may occasionally arise: the ticketed passenger awaiting the bus at the corner may have forgotten the bus route (memory); the sea captain may not have had time to make a complete inspection (perception), or may not have been inspecting the vessel at all, but rather was engaged in a search for a missing object ("mistranscription").[15] In most of these instances, however, the possible infirmities should reduce the weight accorded the evidence, rather than dictate exclusion.[16] The minimal risk of insincerity associated with ostensibly nonassertive conduct supports a general rule of admissibility, subject to the judge's exclusion in cases where one or more dangers pose a substantial risk of jury misuse.[17] The modern trend toward adopting the approach of the Federal Rules is slowly reposing an issue that has fascinated academics, but been of little practical consequence.

§ 6.4 Prior Statements of a Witness

At common law, the hearsay rule usually encompasses any statement entered for its truth *other than one made from the witness stand in the present proceeding*. This broad definition places within the hearsay ban even a prior out-of-court statement made by a witness who testifies at trial. The reason for including a witness's own prior statement within the rule is not immediately apparent; if the declarant testifies at trial, each party can examine him regarding both his present testimony and his earlier out-of-court statement. Since the basis of the hearsay rule is the opponent's lack of opportunity to cross-examine the declarant, it would seem that the rule is inapplicable when the declarant is a present witness. Why, then, should a witness's prior, extrajudicial statement be classified as hearsay?

Several preliminary points should be made. Although a majority of courts still take the view (subject to limited exceptions) that a witness's prior statement is hearsay, evidence of the prior

15. See Lempert & Saltzburg at 368.

16. McCormick, § 250, at 739.

17. Under the modern approach, the judge must determine as an initial matter that the conduct is nonassertive—that is, that the actor did not intend to communicate the proposition for which his conduct is offered. See § 10.4.

statement—even in these courts—often is admissible. Frequently, the earlier statement of a witness is inconsistent with his present testimony. In this circumstance, evidence of the prior statement is admissible for the limited purpose of impeachment. The immediate effect of revealing to the trier a prior contradictory statement is to discredit or impeach the witness's present testimony: one who gives inconsistent accounts of the same events should not readily be believed. All courts recognize the propriety of admitting evidence of prior inconsistent statements for this sole purpose of discrediting the witness. Difficulty arises, however, if the proponent, in order to prove his case, requires that the trier use the prior statement as substantive evidence—that is, as evidence of the truth of the facts asserted in the out-of-court statement.

The following cases illustrate this difficulty: *A* sues *B* on a fidelity bond written to indemnify *A*, an employer, for losses occasioned by the defalcation of his employees.[1] At trial, the employee who allegedly misappropriated the goods takes the stand and denies any wrongdoing. The plaintiff then impeaches him by introducing a prior inconsistent statement in which the witness admitted the defalcations. All courts allow evidence of this prior inconsistency for purposes of impeachment. But can the trier also use the employee's statement as evidence that he misappropriated the goods? Stated in hearsay terms, the question is whether the earlier statement can be offered for the truth of the assertion that the employee-declarant converted the plaintiff's goods. Under the orthodox approach, the prior statement is hearsay if used to prove the misappropriation, since for this purpose it is an out-of-court statement offered for its truth.[2] If the statement is used to prove the misappropriation, it must fit within a hearsay exception.

This traditional limitation upon the use of a prior statement becomes more than an academic formality in a case in which the proponent requires the substantive use of the impeaching evidence to prove an essential element in his case (that is, to satisfy his burden of production with regard to an element of his charge, claim, or defense upon which he has the burden of persuasion [3]).

§ 6.4

1. See Letendre v. Hartford Accident & Indemnity Co., 21 N.Y.2d 518, 289 N.Y.S.2d 183, 236 N.E.2d 467 (1968).

2. Of course, if the statement constitutes an exception to the hearsay rule, see Ch. VII, it is admissible for its truth. However, this does not alter its characterization as hearsay.

3. See § 3.1.

Assume, for example, in a prosecution for the illegal interstate transportation of a female for the purpose of prostitution, the government must prove as one element of the offense that the transported victim engaged in prostitution.[4] When called to the stand, the victim denies that she was a prostitute. As we have seen, she may be impeached by prior written or oral declarations to the contrary. These prior inconsistencies are allowed for the limited purpose of casting doubt on her present testimony; since they are not received for the truth of the assertions they contain, the hearsay rule is not violated. It is always possible, of course, that prior declarations of a witness will fall within an exception to the hearsay rule, and hence could be used for their truth. Assume, however, that they do not fit within an exception. In the case just put, unless the prosecutor has other evidence that the witness engaged in prostitution, he will be unable to obtain a conviction. The witness-declarant's prior statements cannot be used for the truth of their assertion that she engaged in prostitution, which is an essential element of the charge. Without additional evidence, the prosecutor would fail to meet his burden of production on the element of prostitution, and the judge would direct an acquittal. Similarly, in a wrongful death action against *B*, the plaintiff must prove that *B* and not *C* was the operator of a negligently driven vehicle.[5] Suppose plaintiff calls the only witness to the accident, who adversely testifies that *C*, not *B*, was the driver. The plaintiff then introduces evidence that the witness made an earlier written statement that *B* was the operator. If this prior statement cannot be used substantively, the plaintiff loses the case because there is no evidence to support the trier's finding that *B* was the driver.

Where there is other, sufficient evidence of the essential fact asserted in the prior inconsistent statement, the proponent suffers little or no practical disadvantage from the restriction that limits the earlier statement to the single purpose of impeachment. Although it is true that the opponent is entitled to an instruction directing the jury that the prior inconsistency is to be used solely to cast doubt on the witness's trial testimony, this restriction probably has little impact upon the jury's deliberations. Furthermore, it is impossible to ascertain whether the jury was obedient to the instruction. If the jury finds for the proponent and there is

4. See United States v. Biener, 52 F.Supp. 54 (E.D.Pa.1943).

5. See Ruhala v. Roby, 379 Mich. 102, 150 N.W.2d 146 (1967).

evidence aside from the earlier inconsistent statement to support the verdict, the resulting judgment will stand.

It is important to again emphasize that a prior inconsistent statement *can be used as substantive evidence (that is, entered for its truth) if it falls within one of the exceptions* to the hearsay rule.[6] This escape from the usual limitation that confines the trier's use of a prior inconsistent statement to the issue of credibility, however, does not alter the orthodox analysis that the statement is hearsay when used for substantive purposes: despite its hearsay character, it may be used for its truth because it fits within a hearsay exception.

What are the justifications for the traditional rule that prior inconsistent statements are hearsay? Various reasons have been advanced in support of the orthodox view. The principal ones are, first, that it is undesirable, especially in a criminal prosecution, to permit one to prove an element of his case by extra-judicial statements; and, second, that the examiner seeking to negate the effect of a prior inconsistent statement suffers a practical disadvantage that would not attend his attempts to nullify or weaken present testimony.[7] This claimed practical disadvantage rests in part on the notion that while cross-examination is usually effective to test the accuracy of testimony just rendered, it loses much of its efficacy when used to test the accuracy of a statement made in the past.[8] During the time between the prior extra-judicial statement and the cross-examination, the witness has had an opportunity to prepare himself to meet his interrogator's questions. The counterpoint to this observation is that, in many instances at least, the prior statement was made before the distorting influences of litigation—those associated with victory over the adversary—have had an effect. This increases the chances that the earlier statement is reliable. Beyond the claim that a "stale cross-examination" is less effective than one directed at statements just made, it is asserted that other disadvantages arise in particular contexts. We shall subsequently explore these, but let us first address the justification that, as a matter of sound

6. Selected exceptions are discussed in Ch. VII.

7. See Rept., New Jersey Supreme Court Committee on Evidence, 132–135 (1963), for arguments against liberalizing the traditional approach. For a judicial defense of the traditional view, see Ruhala v. Roby, 379 Mich. 102, 150 N.W.2d 146 (1967).

8. State v. Saporen, 205 Minn. 358, 362, 285 N.W. 898, 901 (1939).

policy, judicial proof should rest upon statements made in the courtroom—not those made prior to trial.

The objection to permitting proof of one's case by extra-judicial statements is rooted in the belief that the most reliable statements are those made from the witness stand. Courtroom testimony is attended by all of the conditioning devices of a judicial inquiry, including the oath, the opportunity for the factfinder to observe demeanor, and the officialism of the proceedings. Of course, if this rationale were extended to its logical end, the result would be to deny admission to all hearsay statements, even in the many instances where a statement falls within a hearsay exception. A related basis for the objection is the apprehension that permitting the substantive use of prior inconsistencies would encourage fabricated testimony. False evidence of prior inconsistent statements, it is feared, would be introduced in order to prove the essential elements of the proponent's case. It is doubtful, however, that the risk of fabricated testimony is greater in this instance than it is in many others, especially since the speaker is present in the courtroom to deny (or affirm) the inconsistency. The modification of a technical rule in order to permit the substantive use of prior inconsistent statements (which already are admissible to impeach) hardly seems the kind of reform that would increase significantly the incidence of perjury.

A more convincing defense of the traditional rule is the practical argument that effective interrogation relating to earlier inconsistent statements is difficult or impossible. To appreciate fully the basis of this contention, it is important to remember that the counsel who introduces evidence of the witness's prior inconsistent statement is trying to *neutralize* the witness's present assertions from the stand. Usually, it is the cross-examiner who introduces the prior contradictory statement, although occasionally the direct examiner, displeased or surprised by the testimony of his witness, offers evidence of a prior inconsistent and more favorable statement.[9] The next examination is conducted by the opponent, who wants the trier to believe the witness's present testimony and disbelieve the prior inconsistent statement. That is, assuming that when confronted with the prior inconsistent statement the witness denies making it or else denies that the prior statement represents the truth, the counsel next examining

9. As to impeaching one's own witness, see § 8.2; McCormick § 38.

the witness strives to support the witness's present testimony, while negating the impact of the evidence of the earlier inconsistency.

The obstacles faced by this subsequent examiner depend largely upon the witness's explanation of the evidence that he has made a prior contradictory statement. If he denies making the prior statement or at least asserts that he has no memory of it, the subsequent examiner is hampered somewhat in eliciting an explanation of why the *unacknowledged* prior statement is inaccurate; the interrogator usually will have to settle for having the witness reassert that his immediately preceding testimony, based upon present recollection of the event, is accurate. But the subsequent examiner faces a situation of even greater practical difficulty in the comparatively rare instance when the witness neither acknowledges the prior inconsistency, nor remembers the event allegedly described in his prior statement (which event, if it existed, would be at odds with his present testimony). Here the interrogator neither can elicit testimony about the event, nor can he show why the prior inconsistency is inaccurate. In this circumstance, it is very difficult, if not impossible, for the subsequent examiner to interrogate the witness so as to demonstrate why the prior account should be rejected by the factfinder.

Contrast the situation in which the witness acknowledges that he made the prior inconsistent statement, but denies its accuracy because he now purports to recall correctly the incident described in the statement. Here the subsequent examiner is not substantially handicapped. He can attempt to demonstrate why the facts he seeks to establish are shown reliably by the present testimony and why they should not be negated by the prior contradiction. As one source puts it:

> The declarant is in court and may be examined and cross-examined in regard to his statements and their subject matters. . . . The trier of fact has the declarant before it and can observe his demeanor and the nature of his testimony as he denies or tries to explain away the inconsistency. Hence, it is in as good a position to determine the truth or falsity of the prior statement as it is to determine the truth or falsity of the inconsistent testimony given in court.[10]

10. Calif.Law Rev.Comm.Comment on § 1235, West's Ann.Calif.Evid.Code. Compare Judge Learned Hand's observation in DiCarlo v. United States, 6 F.2d 364, 368 (2d Cir.1925), that if the jury "conclude[s] that what [the witness] says now is not the truth, but what he said before, they are nonethe-

Of course, the subsequent examiner of a witness who has been challenged with a prior inconsistency does have a role different from that of the usual hostile cross-examiner. The object of the subsequent interrogation is not to discredit the witness generally (since the interrogator seeks to support the witness's in-court testimony). But this difference does not weaken the point made above that the witness can be interrogated in the presence of the trier as to present and past statements. The fact that the witness may be interrogated by both attorneys concerning the subject matter of his testimony, the conditions surrounding his prior inconsistent statement, and the reasons for the apparent contradiction surely avoids or minimizes the hearsay dangers.[11]

The question remains whether the practical disadvantage sometimes suffered by the subsequent examiner, when coupled with a preference for evidence given from the witness stand, provides a convincing basis for the traditional rule denying the substantive use of prior inconsistent statements.[12] This question is not easily resolved; any arguments for the orthodox approach must be weighed against several factors that support the substantive use of prior inconsistencies.[13] As noted, apprehensions about the frailty of extra-judicial statements and the possibility of their abuse have not prevented the courts and legislators from fashioning more than twenty-five exceptions to the hearsay rule. These permit substantive use of out-of-court statements in many instances in which the declarant does not even appear as a witness. It is also significant that compared with testimony from the stand, the prior statement was made closer in time to the event in question when, presumably, memory was fresher. And as noted previously, in many cases the prior statement was made before the possibly distorting influences of litigation, which include the witness's identification with one party, the psychological urge to make one's testimony consistent with other evidence and believa-

less deciding from what they see and hear of that person and in court."

11. Cf. California v. Green, 399 U.S. 149, 160 (1970), on remand, 3 Cal.3d 981, 92 Cal.Rptr. 494, 479 P.2d 998 (1971) indicating that in such circumstances it also is clear that the confrontation clause is satisfied. See § 7.29.

12. For a defense of the orthodox view, see Beaver & Biggs, Attending Witness's Prior Declarations as Evidence, 3 Ind.L.Forum 309 (1970).

13. Note that the arguments supporting the orthodox view against admitting prior inconsistent statements for their substantive worth apply equally against letting in party admissions for their substantive value. The recent trend is to remove party admissions from the category of hearsay instead of treating them, as had been the practice, as an exception to the hearsay rule. See §§ 7.1, 7.6; Fed.R.Evid. 801(d).

ble, and the bias that may arise when an attorney prepares or "coaches" the witness.[14] These considerations have convinced a minority of jurisdictions to permit the substantive use of a witness's prior inconsistent statement, even in instances when the prior statement does not fit within a recognized hearsay exception.[15] A few jurisdictions have an even more liberal rule: Any prior statement of a witness, whether or not inconsistent, is admissible as substantive evidence.[16]

When a prior inconsistent statement qualifies as an exception to the hearsay rule, it may be used, even under the orthodox rule, both as impeaching evidence and as substantive proof.[17] For example, when a party-witness has made an earlier contradictory statement,[18] that statement is a party admission which may be received as substantive evidence.[19] At common law, party admissions constitute a well established exception to the hearsay rule. Of course, other exceptions, such as that for excited utterances, may also be applicable to the prior statement.[20] Another escape from the hearsay rule is provided when the witness not only admits the prior inconsistency, but also recants part or all of his present testimony by stating that the assertion in the earlier statement is accurate. Here the cases hold the witness has adopted or merged his prior statement into his present testimony and hence his assertions, in effect, are contemporaneous statements from the stand.[21]

It remains to be considered whether a prior *consistent* statement should be classified as hearsay. The orthodox definition of hearsay, embracing as it does any statement offered for its truth which is made other than from the witness stand in the present proceeding, includes prior consistent statements. However, there is a significant difference between prior consistent and prior

14. For careful and comprehensive analyses of the rule denying substantive effect to prior statements, see Lempert & Saltzburg at 507–16; McCormick § 251.

15. See Blakey, Substantive Use of Prior Inconsistent Statements Under the Federal Rules of Evidence, 64 Ky. L.J. 3, 35 n. 112 (1975). See also West's Ann.Calif.Evid.Code § 1235; Commonwealth v. Loar, 246 Pa.Super. 398, 399 A.2d 1110 (1979) (prior inconsistent statement of a present witness is admissible for truth and impeachment).

16. See, e.g., Jett v. Commonwealth, 436 S.W.2d 788, 792 (Ky.1969).

17. Exceptions to the hearsay rule are discussed in Ch. VII.

18. Ch. VII, Part A.

19. McCormick, § 262, at 774–75. See United States v. Champion Int'l Corp., 557 F.2d 1270 (9th Cir.1977), cert. denied, 434 U.S. 938 (1977).

20. See Ch. VII.

21. This analysis is discussed in Ruhala v. Roby, 379 Mich. 102, 150 N.W.2d 146 (1967).

inconsistent statements. When a prior statement is consistent with the trial testimony, the subsequent examiner has every opportunity for a full, forceful, and antagonistic interrogation. He may seek to impugn the general credibility of the witness, for the subsequent examiner is not trying to preserve one of the witness's accounts of an event while negating the other (as he must when a prior inconsistency exists). Thus, despite older precedents to the contrary, there is little logic to support the application of the hearsay rule to prior consistent statements.[22]

This does not mean, however, that prior consistent statements should be admitted freely. Evidence of these statements may constitute cumulative, superfluous proof; unlimited admission would encourage litigants and witnesses to strengthen their trial testimony by laying a groundwork of duplicative stories. Such a self-serving practice wisely is condemned by a generally recognized rule that prohibits bolstering a witness's testimony.[23] There are, however, occasions when a "fresh complaint" or prompt disclosure to a third party has special probative worth to show an event has occurred.[24] Indeed, silence by the victim of a crime might be viewed as inconsistent with the happening of the alleged occurrence. In many cases, especially those in which a criminal offense is alleged, there is often a special need for evidence of prompt disclosure because there are no eyewitnesses other than the perpetrator and the victim. Crimes such as rape or bribery, for example, are apt to be known only to the wrongdoer and the victim. Disclosure to a third person soon after an unusual occurrence is a natural and predictable response and, recognizing this, the courts have usually admitted evidence of a prior complaint or disclosure. Observe that by limiting the evidence to complaints occurring reasonably soon after the alleged event, the courts restrict the

22. See McCormick, § 251, at 747. It also would seem that the prior statement has been adopted by the witness and thus merges with his present testimony. See text supra at n. 21.

23. See, e.g., United States v. Leggett, 312 F.2d 566, 572 (4th Cir.1962); Graham v. Danko, 204 Va. 135, 129 S.E.2d 825 (1963).

24. United States v. Iaconetti, 540 F.2d 574 (2d Cir.1976), cert. denied, 429 U.S. 1041 (1977), rehearing denied, 430 U.S. 911 (1977). In theory, and under the practice in most jurisdictions, the evidence offered to strengthen the factual proposition that misconduct has occurred need only consist of testimony that the complaint was made; there is no need to recite to the trier the details of the disclosure or even the identity of the alleged wrongdoer. See IV Wigmore §§ 1135–36 (Chadbourn). But when prior consistent statements come in to rehabilitate a witness, details may be given. Id. §§ 1137–38.

possibility of abuse.[25] Since the evidence is entered to confirm the happening of the event, many courts permit only evidence that there was a complaint about the act in question, but do not permit evidence of any details that were disclosed by the complaint.[26]

Prior consistent statements also have a special value in cases in which a cross-examiner charges or implies that a witness's testimony is a recent fabrication developed for trial or that a witness has been corrupted or improperly influenced to distort or falsify his courtroom testimony. A prior consistent statement predating the corrupting motive, event, or influence helps to rebut the express or implied accusation that the witness's testimony is tainted.[27] In these situations of "rehabilitating" the witness after an accusation of contrived testimony, the older cases admit the evidence of prior consistent statements only for the purpose of bolstering credibility. Wisely, recent authority favors the use of this rebuttal or rehabilitative evidence for any purpose for which it is probative, including the truth of the assertion.[28] This accords with both sound theory and the practicalities of jury trial. Surely it is too much to ask a jury to accept a statement from the stand for its truth while using a prior consistent statement only as evidence of credibility.

Obedience to the traditional hearsay formula also precludes admission of prior out-of-court identifications of an individual. A pre-trial assertion, for example, that identifies the accused as the person who committed the act charged normally is offered for its truth and thus is hearsay. Yet often an identification made closer in time to the event in question may be more reliable than a subsequent courtroom identification. This is particularly true where the earlier identification took place in circumstances that

25. Although most cases impose the requirement that the complaint be made promptly, this condition is relaxed when there is a satisfactory explanation for the period of delay. People v. Mason, 301 Ill. 370, 379, 133 N.E. 767, 770–71 (1921). For a case admitting a "fresh complaint" in a bribery prosecution, see Commonwealth v. Friedman, 193 Pa.Super. 640, 165 A.2d 678 (1960).

26. See People v. Damen, 28 Ill.2d 464, 193 N.E.2d 25 (1963); IV Wigmore § 1136 (Chadbourn). But see Ch. VII, Part B.

27. See United States v. Scholle, 553 F.2d 1109 (8th Cir.1977), cert. denied, 434 U.S. 940 (1977); Sweazey v. Valley Transp., 6 Wash.2d 324, 107 P.2d 567 (1940); IV Wigmore, § 1128, at 268 (Chadbourn). See also § 8.7. But see United States v. Weil, 561 F.2d 1109 (4th Cir.1977) (no proof bolstering statement made *prior* to promise of leniency).

28. See Fed.R.Evid. 801(d)(1)(B); McCormick, § 251, at 747.

were not unfairly suggestive and the later courtroom identification occurred after a significant lapse of time. Other circumstances may cast doubt on the accuracy of a courtroom identification. The person to be identified may have changed his appearance, making identification more difficult. On the other hand, the courtroom setting, because of the arrangement of counsels' tables and other indications of identity, may make it comparatively easy to single out the person to be identified. The potentially greater reliability of earlier identification has prompted a growing number of courts to admit prior identifications as substantive evidence.[29] Most of these courts require that the identifying party be present and available for cross-examination.[30] Admission of a prior identification by one not present for cross-examination raises all the hearsay dangers, while not affording any opportunity for the cross-examiner to offset them.[31] Furthermore, such an admission may implicate the Confrontation Clause of the United States Constitution.[32]

§ 6.5 The Hearsay Rule and the Federal Rules of Evidence

Under Federal Rule 801, hearsay is an oral or written "statement, other than one made by the declarant while testifying at the [present] trial or hearing, offered in evidence to prove the truth of the matter asserted." [1] A hearsay "statement" includes nonverbal conduct, *but only if the declarant intends* to make an assertion by his physical action, as, for example, when he points a finger to make an identification or nods his head in answer to a question.[2] Nonassertive conduct which, as we have seen, is conduct not intended by the actor as an assertion, is not within the federal definition of hearsay.[3]

29. See Fed.R.Evid. 801(d)(1)(c); Saltzburg & Redden at 725–26; McCormick, § 251, at 747–48.

30. See Annot., 71 A.L.R.2d 449, 456 (1960).

31. If a witness who testifies is unable to identify the accused in the courtroom, yet did make an earlier identification, the cross-examiner still can explore the circumstances of the prior identification and inquire as to the degree of certainty the witness had at the time of the earlier identification.

32. See generally Ch. VII, Part L.

§ 6.5

1. Fed.R.Evid. 801(c).

2. Fed.R.Evid. 801(a)(2). In United States v. Harris, 546 F.2d 234 (8th Cir. 1976), a declarant's laughter, when asked if he was really hurt, was treated as a "statement" subject to hearsay analysis.

3. Fed.R.Evid. 801(a), (c); Adv. Comm.Note to Fed.R.Evid. 801(a). In United States ex rel. Carter Equip. Co. v. H.P. Morgan, Inc., 544 F.2d 1271, rev'd on other grounds, 554 F.2d 164 (5th Cir.1977) (en banc), the initialing of invoices was viewed as non-verbal asser-

Subsection (d) of Rule 801 contains further refinements to the basic hearsay definition. The first of these concerns party admissions. Statements made by a party or by his representative (or those adopted by a party) are not classified as hearsay when offered against that party.[4] Traditionally, such statements, attributed to a party either by reason of his own utterance or on principles of adoption or agency, have been admitted under the party admissions *exception* to the hearsay rule. Some commentators, while favoring the admission into evidence of party admissions, have nonetheless objected to the inclusion of party admissions among the various exceptions to the hearsay rule. They observed that exceptions to the hearsay rule generally are limited to those out-of-court statements attended by circumstances that increase their trustworthiness. Guarantees of trustworthiness are not always associated with party admissions, since the test of their admissibility generally is only that a party or his representative (as defined in the cases or rules) made or adopted the extrajudicial statement that his opponent offers against the party at trial. For example, there is no requirement that the party's statement be against his interest at the time it was made, although in most instances the statement will have been disserving when made. Thus a disserving quality—which underlies an important exception to the hearsay rule and is associated with several others—may bolster the trustworthiness of most, but not necessarily all, party admissions.[5] The possible absence from party admissions of an element of trustworthiness persuaded the federal drafters to define such admissions as nonhearsay, rather than include them, as common-law courts have done, among the exceptions to the hearsay rule.[6]

Of course, a party's previous statement is allowed for its truth regardless of whether it is viewed as an exception to the hearsay rule or as a specially defined instance of nonhearsay. Conceivably, however, the underlying rationale may be significant in defining the outer limits of admissibility.[7] Note that both the tradi-

tive conduct within the Rule 801 definition of statement.

4. Fed.R.Evid. 801(d)(2). See, e.g., O'Neal v. Morgan, 637 F.2d 846 (2d Cir. 1980), cert. denied, 451 U.S. 972 (1981); United States v. Porter, 544 F.2d 936 (8th Cir.1976).

5. One exception to the hearsay rule, declarations against interest, is grounded on the assumption that a declarant is not likely to make a disserving statement unless it is true. See Ch. VII, Part J.

6. Adv.Comm.Note to Fed.R.Evid. 801(d)(2).

7. "[T]he degree to which the [party] admissions doctrine should be extended to statements other than those of a par-

tional and federal approaches cause a party to confront and explain his prior statements or those made by his representative.[8] And whatever the theoretical justification for party admissions, their admissibility is consistent with the Anglo-American adversarial system, which long has allowed a party considerable freedom in prescribing the course of litigation while enforcing the consequences of an adversary's mistakes. The federal rulemakers and many commentators assert that it is this consistency with the adversarial trial itself which justifies admissibility.[9] Other commentators propose that the principle of party responsibility [10] underlies the long-standing practice of admitting evidence of a party admission. Observe that whether evidence of a party admission is presented is entirely in the hands of the adversary; a party cannot introduce his own admission.[11]

Finally, Rule 801 excludes certain prior statements of a declarant-witness from the definition of hearsay. Unwilling to remove the hearsay ban entirely in circumstances where the out-of-court declarant also is a trial witness, the drafters compromised by passing a provision that classifies a witness's prior statements as nonhearsay in limited, specific situations. If a prior *inconsistent* statement "was given under oath subject to the penalty of perjury at a trial, hearing, or other proceeding, or in a deposition," [12] the statement can be used as substantive evidence. This provision limits the substantive use of a prior inconsistent statement to

ty himself rests on an assessment of the proper basis for admissibility." 4 Weinstein & Berger, ¶ 801(d)(2)[01], at 185. The treatment of party admissions as nonhearsay has also led to drafting imperfections and ambiguities. For example, in the first sentence of Federal Rule 806, the drafters refer to hearsay statements and to nonhearsay party admissions, but in the second sentence they refer only to hearsay statements. The resulting difficulty is discussed in Saltzburg & Redden at 994–995.

8. See Kingsley v. Baker/Beech-Nut Corp., 546 F.2d 1136 (5th Cir.1977); United States v. Porter, 544 F.2d 936 (8th Cir.1976); United States v. Ojala, 544 F.2d 940 (8th Cir.1976) (party's failure to protest a damaging remark made by his counsel in his presence made the remark an "adoptive admission" and therefore it was held to be nonhearsay).

9. Adv.Comm.Note to Fed.R.Evid. 801; Morgan & Weinstein at 241; Strahorn, A Reconsideration of the Hearsay Rule and Admissions, 85 U.Pa.L.Rev. 484, 564 (1937).

10. Lempert & Saltzburg at 384. These commentators assert that the probable basis for the rule is the accepted notions of morality that consider an individual to be responsible for his own actions.

11. See Coughlan v. Capitol Cement Co., 571 F.2d 290, 306 (5th Cir.1978).

12. Fed.R.Evid. 801(d)(1)(A). United States v. Scholle, 553 F.2d 1109 (8th Cir.), cert. denied, 434 U.S. 940 (1977); United States v. Jordano, 521 F.2d 695 (2d Cir.1975). For a discussion of "other proceedings," see United States v. Castro-Ayon, 537 F.2d 1055 (9th Cir. 1976), cert. denied, 429 U.S. 983 (1976).

those situations where, as a practical matter, there usually will be convincing proof (often by a transcript or sworn deposition) that the statement was made. Typical examples are previous statements made in a deposition, at a preliminary hearing, before a grand jury, before an administrative tribunal, or during another trial. In these settings, there is almost always a written or tape-recorded record of the prior statement; hence, it is unlikely that an examiner wishing to negate the impact of the previous inconsistency will face a witness who denies the existence of the prior statement.[13] The Federal Rule also recognizes, as it should, that the prior inconsistent statement made under oath and under conditions from which a perjury charge could result increases the likelihood that the statement is reliable. The federal approach also encourages litigants who anticipate the need to offer a witness's prior statement for substantive purposes to take his deposition or, when possible, to call him to testify in a grand jury proceeding or preliminary hearing.

The treatment of prior *consistent* statements under Rule 801 largely is congruent with the common-law development. The Rule follows the common-law practice of admitting prior consistent statements of a witness when "offered to rebut an express or implied charge against him of recent fabrication or improper influence or motive . . . ." [14] Unlike the common law, however, the Rule, by calling the statement nonhearsay, allows the proponent to use such consistent statements not only to rehabilitate (accredit) the witness, but also as substantive evidence. As elsewhere noted,[15] permitting the substantive use of prior consistent statements accords with sound theory and practice. The Federal Rule also endorses a recent common-law trend by admitting prior identifications for their substantive use, provided the identifying witness is on the stand and subject to cross-examination.[16] No express provision is made for the admission of a "fresh complaint"—at least not under Federal Rule 801. But in some circumstances, such a complaint will fit within an exception.[17]

13. See § 6.4; § 8.5.

14. Fed.R.Evid. 801(d)(1)(B). See United States v. Navarro-Varelas, 541 F.2d 1331 (9th Cir.1976), cert. denied, 429 U.S. 1045 (1977); United States v. Iaconetti, 406 F.Supp. 554 (E.D.N.Y. 1976), affirmed, 540 F.2d 574 (2d Cir. 1976), cert. denied, 429 U.S. 1041 (1977), rehearing denied, 430 U.S. 911 (1977).

15. See § 6.4, n. 28.

16. Fed.R.Evid. 801(d)(1)(C); see § 6.4, n. 29.

17. In particular, note the possibility that the complaint may constitute an excited utterance. § 7.9.

Care must be taken to observe that Federal Rule 801(d)(1) prescribes specially defined categories of nonhearsay that constitute departures or exemptions from the general definition of hearsay—out-of-court statements offered for the truth of the matter asserted. Obviously, many statements are not offered for their truth, including prior inconsistent statements not previously made under oath, which are offered only for the purpose of discrediting the witness. Note also that Rule 801(d)(1), which covers various kinds of prior statements by a witness (inconsistent statements, consistent statements, and prior identifications), contains quite different criteria controlling when these statements fall outside the hearsay rule. The characterization of a prior inconsistent statement as nonhearsay depends upon whether the earlier statement was under oath and subject to the penalty of perjury, whereas the characterization of a prior consistent statement as nonhearsay is conditional upon whether it is used to rebut a charge of improper influence or recent fabrication. A prior identification is considered outside the hearsay rule if no more is shown than that the testifying witness, now subject to cross-examination, made an earlier identification of the person in question "after perceiving him." [18]

Notes

1. *Nonassertive Conduct.* Consider a divorce suit brought by husband against wife on grounds of wife's adultery with *X*. The wife denies having sexual relations with *X*, and wants to testify that after she and *X* were discovered together in wife's bedroom, the wife immediately insisted that a physician be called to examine her and to verify that she had not recently had intercourse. Assuming the physician could not be contacted, is the testimony of the wife's request hearsay? See Corke v. Corke and Cooke, 1 All E.R. 224 (1958), which holds that the wife's statements are inadmissible hearsay. Even if the wife intended to imply that she had not had relations, isn't the jury in a position to decide how much, if any, probative value should be accorded the wife's demand for an examination?

2. *Prior Statements.* How do you explain the fact that Fed.R. Evid. 801(d) classifies as nonhearsay only those prior inconsistent statements made under oath, while the same rule prescribes a nonhearsay classification for prior consistent statements offered to rebut a charge of recent fabrication even though the prior consistent statement was *not* attended by an oath?

18. Fed.R.Evid. 801(d)(1)(C).

3. *Prior Identifications.* As noted in the text, a prior "identification of a person made after perceiving him" is removed from the hearsay classification by subsection (C) of Rule 801(d)(1). Thus, if witness *W* has made a prior identification of *X*, then evidence that he, for example, pointed to *X* or said "*X* was the assailant" is admissible, assuming of course that no constitutional ban (such as the prohibition against improper police line-ups) is applicable. Likewise, one who was present at the earlier identification may testify that *W* made a prior identification of *X*. United States v. Elemy, 656 F.2d 507, 508 (9th Cir.1981). But if the prior identification is to gain a nonhearsay status, it is necessary that *W* be available for a courtroom examination about the prior identification. It is the chance to cross-examine the identifier that underlies the nonhearsay classification and thus the rule requires that the identifier testify at trial and be "subject to cross-examination concerning the [prior] statement" of identification. This requirement probably would not be satisfied if *W* disavowed any recollection of the earlier identification or simply refused to answer questions. 4 Louisell & Mueller, § 421, at 212–13.

Usually, the previous identification confirms (is consistent with) the in-court identification, but a prior identification that is at odds with the courtroom identification is also admissible. See United States v. Lewis, 565 F.2d 1248 (2d Cir.1977), cert. denied, 435 U.S. 973 (1978) (rejecting the contention that a prior inconsistent identification is subject to the conditions of Rule 801(d)(1)(A), which limits the admissibility of prior inconsistent statements).

Does Rule 801(d)(1)'s phrase "identification of a person" require a corporeal identification, or will identification of a photograph suffice? Suppose the previous identification was of a photograph of the subject, the photographic identification having been made after the identifier actually perceived the subject at an earlier time. There is considerable authority that this identification is nonhearsay under the Rule. United States v. Marchand, 564 F.2d 983, 996 (2d Cir.1977), cert. denied, 434 U.S. 1015 (1978); 4 Louisell & Mueller, § 421, at 206 n. 51.

4. *Hearsay: The Bridges Case.* Suppose that a child is taken to the defendant's house and molested. The victim subsequently describes to her mother what the house looked like and includes additional details about the appearance of the interior. At trial, the prosecutor introduces evidence describing the exterior and interior of the defendant's home. May the mother now testify as to her daughter's prior statements in which the child accurately recited what her captor's house looked like? If the prosecutor also supplied evidence that it was highly unlikely that the victim could have gained knowledge of these surroundings except by having been transported there

on the occasion in question, the little girl's prior statements ought to be admissible to show her knowledge. Her statements would not be offered to prove the appearance of the defendant's house—this having been established by other evidence. Nor are they offered to prove the appearance of the house in which she was molested, although of course she could repeat her description of the surroundings from the witness stand. Her out-of-court description, congruent with the *actual physical* appearance of the defendant's home, constitutes convincing circumstantial evidence that she once saw it, at least if there is sufficient detail in her account to distinguish the house in question from other houses. See Bridges v. State, 247 Wis. 350, 19 N.W.2d 529 (1945), rehearing denied, 247 Wis. 372, 19 N.W.2d 862 (1945).

For a modern application of the *Bridges* principle, see United States v. Muscato, 534 F.Supp. 969 (E.D.N.Y.1982). There *W* gave an accurate extra-judicial description of a gun having unique features. The opportunities for gaining this knowledge, other than by actually seeing the weapon in the circumstances claimed by *W,* were limited. The fact that *W* also identified the gun in the courtroom and was subject to cross-examination concerning other ways in which he might have gained knowledge of its appearance buttressed the prosecution's case for admissibility.

The trial judge in *Muscato* (Judge Jack Weinstein), after discussing *Bridges* and similar cases, allowed the previous description into evidence. He characterized the evidence, used not to prove the fact asserted but to prove the declarant's knowledge of the fact, as nonhearsay. Judge Weinstein acknowledged, however, that this kind of evidence might be highly influential to the jury, an influence that would be unwarranted if the witness might have gained his knowledge by more than one means. Nonetheless, in the case before him, not only was it unlikely that the witness gained the knowledge other than by seeing the gun (as claimed), but the witness also testified, identified the weapon again, and was subject to a full cross-examination about the source of his knowledge. Thus, applying Rule 403, the court ruled that the probative value of the nonhearsay, out-of-court declaration was not outweighed by the risk of jury misuse.

5. *Recognizing Hearsay.* Professor Laurence Tribe has made a significant contribution to an understanding of the hearsay rule and the exceptions that attend it. Tribe, Triangulating Hearsay, 87 Harv. L.Rev. 957 (1974). The following diagram draws upon his work, as does a portion of the accompanying discussion.

Suppose it is necessary for a party to show that the door of a storage building was left unlocked prior to a theft occurring on the evening of January 15. A witness testifies that a worker (declarant) at the building told the witness that the door in question "was not secured at the end of the workday on January 15." If this evidence is offered for the proposition that the door was not locked, all four hearsay dangers are present:

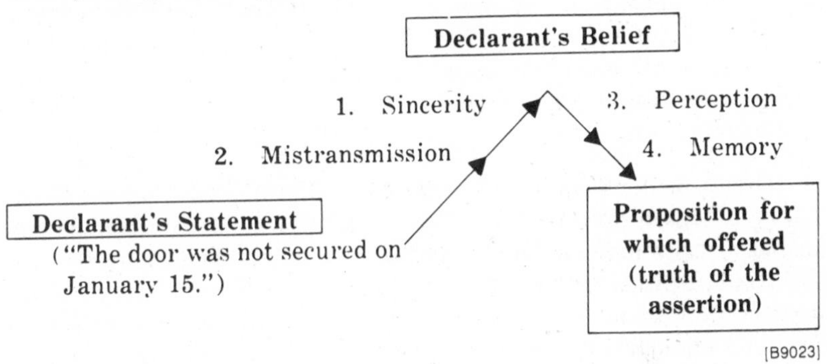

The trier must first conclude that the declarant actually *believed* (sincerity) that the door was *unlocked* (note also the possible mistransmission resulting from use of the word "secured"). Next the trier must conclude that the declarant's belief was correct—that he had a chance to *observe* the door (perception) and that he correctly *recalls* that it was unlocked on January 15 (memory). This line of reasoning, which proceeds from the declarant's statement to his belief and then to the accuracy of that belief, involves reliance upon the declarant's credibility. The hearsay prohibition clearly is applicable. The first two hearsay risks are encountered in step 1: deciding whether the declarant really believed what the auditor claims he (declarant) asserted. The last two hearsay dangers are encountered in step 2: deciding whether the declarant's belief, assuming he sincerely and accurately communicated it, faithfully portrays the past condition or event.

Suppose, however, the question is not simply whether the door was unlocked, but also whether the owner of the storage building took reasonable steps to keep its contents secure. A witness testifies that at the end of the workday on January 15th he overheard the declarant report to the owner that the door in question was not secured. Offered for the purpose of showing that the owner was made aware of a condition of insecurity, the evidence is not hearsay:

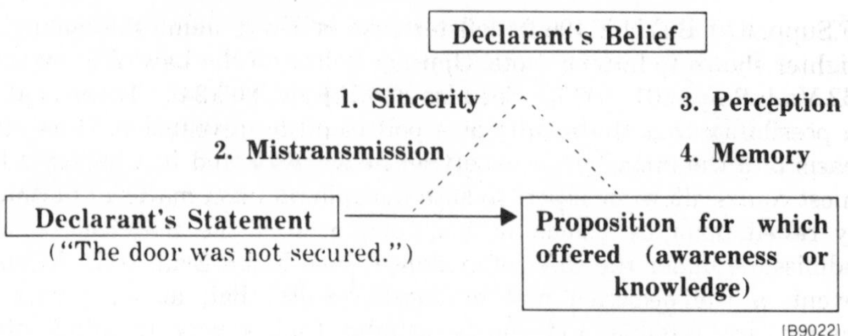

In using the evidence of declarant's statement, it is unnecessary for the trier to rely upon the declarant's credibility, and therefore the hearsay dangers are avoided. Other evidence must be introduced as the basis for a finding that the door was unlocked. Of course, the owner can explain why it was reasonable to take no action following the declarant's statement to him. He may say, for example, that he thought the declarant was mistaken in his assertion. However, it is still unnecessary for the trier to rely upon the declarant's credibility: the question is what the owner thought, or should have thought, in light of all surrounding circumstances, including the declarant's statement. The statement is admissible for the purpose of showing its effect on the mind of the listener.

6. *Polls or Opinion Surveys and the Hearsay Rule.* The applicability of the hearsay rule to opinion polls varies with the particular survey. Some surveys do not involve a hearsay response from the person polled. For example, a poll to determine how many people *express* an opinion on the subject of world disarmament does not involve a hearsay response: it is sufficient for purposes of the survey that the respondent does or does not express an opinion. If the survey seeks to determine how many people favor disarmament, it is necessary to believe the respondent's statement that he does or does not favor disarmament, thus raising the hearsay danger of insincerity. A poll not directed at opinion, but rather at determining what the respondent may have done in the past (e.g., whether he voted in a particular election) raises the additional hearsay danger of a defect in memory.

Nonetheless, even when the hearsay rule is applicable, courts increasingly admit the evidence under one of the traditional exceptions—for example, by finding that respondents' statements to pollsters were present sense impressions, declarations of mental state (see §§ 7.8, 7.12)—or under an exception of recent origin that is specifically addressed to polls. See Zippo Mfg. Co. v. Rogers Imports, Inc., 216

F.Supp. 670 (S.D.N.Y.1963) (pollster asks pollee to name the maker of lighter shown to latter); Note, Opinion Polls and the Law of Evidence, 62 Va.L.Rev. 1101 (1976). See also Fed.R.Evid. 803(24). There is also a possibility that the results of a poll could be revealed to show the basis of an opinion by an expert witness. As noted in Chapter XII, most courts allow an expert to base his opinion upon material normally relied upon by people in his field, even if the material is not admissible under the rules of evidence. See Fed.R.Evid. 703. In any event, a well-designed poll produces results that, at least within limits, are reliable and courts usually find a way to admit the findings. However, it is important to afford the cross-examiner an adequate opportunity to test the design and execution of the poll. Such factors as the selection of a sampling area, the determination of a random selection within it, the design of the questions, the experience of the poll-takers, and the execution of the interviews can be important.

Chapter VII

THE HEARSAY RULE: SELECTED EXCEPTIONS AND STATUTORY NONHEARSAY

PART A. PARTY ADMISSIONS

§ 7.1 In General

Although the Federal Rules and many similar evidence codes treat admissions by a party as nonhearsay,[1] the common law considers such statements hearsay but admits them under the party admissions exception to the hearsay rule. The federal departure in classification, now copied in many states, traces the rationale for admitting party admissions more to the spirit of the adversary system than to the considerations of trustworthiness which more commonly characterize the various hearsay exceptions.[2] Under the admissions exception (or nonhearsay classification), a party may introduce against his party opponent the latter's prior out-of-court declarations. Admission of this evidence is consistent with the adversary system since the opponent (or his agent) created this adverse evidence. Furthermore, the opponent is present at the trial to meet the adverse evidence by giving an explanation, offering counter-evidence, or otherwise providing a rebuttal.[3]

As elsewhere suggested,[4] however, neither the federal innovation nor the common-law view supplies a unifying theme that completely explains the admissibility of all party admissions.

§ 7.1

1. Fed.R.Evid. 801(d)(2).

2. Adv.Comm.Note to Fed.R.Evid. 801(d)(2). See § 6.5 at n. 4.

3. 4 Louisell & Mueller at 251.

4. § 6.5.

In any event, many modern codes of evidence, whether adopted through rules of court or directly by statute, treat party admissions as nonhearsay. It will be seen, however, that when a party's out-of-court declaration is offered to prove the truth of the matter asserted, the statement falls within the generally accepted definition of hearsay. Initially, then, we shall consider such a declaration hearsay and inquire whether it nonetheless is admissible under the party admissions exception. In due course, we will examine the nonhearsay classification of the Federal Rules of Evidence. Ultimately, it will be seen that the range of admissibility under federal and common law approaches is substantially similar—at least as between the federal scheme and the common law of those jurisdictions that have followed the modern trend of broadening the party admissions exception.

A party admission is a hearsay "statement" comprised of words or conduct, made or adopted by a party (or made or adopted by his representative, agent or "privy"), which is offered against the admitting party by his opponent. As a tactical matter, an adversary will present evidence of a party admission when the admission is inconsistent with the "admitting" party's contentions at trial.

Usually the out-of-court admission will have been against the interest of the admitting party when made, but this "against-interest" characteristic is not essential to admissibility. The only question is whether the party offering the admission believes it inconsistent (and hence damaging) with the admitting party's *posture at trial.* It is thus misleading to label a party admission as an "admission against interest." This loose and deceptive term, sometimes used by the courts, invites confusion between party admissions and another hearsay exception: declarations against interest. The latter exception is discussed separately.[5]

It is important to recognize that an extra-judicial party admission is not conclusive. After evidence of a party admission has been introduced, the admitting party may try to negate the evidence, either by denying the statement (if appropriate) or by rebutting the inferences which the proponent seeks to draw from it.[6] Suppose, for example, *A* offers against opposing party *B* the

5. §§ 7.26–7.27.

6. As discussed in § 6.1, the basis for the hearsay rule is the inability of the opposing party to cross-examine the declarant. Notice that when a party, as opposed to his representative, has made an admission, a hearsay objection lodged against evidence of the admission is really an assertion that the objector-party does not have an opportuni-

latter's extra-judicial admission that he was drinking beer at the time of an automobile accident. *B* may deny that he made the statement, admit making it but explain he was only joking, or seek to lessen the impact by testifying that his modest drinking was not the cause of the collision. A party admission, in other words, has only such evidential value as the trier accords it, and the adversaries are free to argue about its probative weight. This inconclusive feature distinguishes *evidentiary* party admissions from the parties' formal or *judicial* admissions which usually are made in the pleadings, through a discovery rule that permits one party to request another to deny in writing the truth of some relevant matter,[7] or by a stipulation. These formal admissions remove the fact conceded from further contest,[8] and are conclusive unless the matter is again placed in dispute by amendment or some other appropriate procedure.

Two themes recur in the many judicial opinions that address party admissions. First, the reported cases, taken together, illustrate the various ways in which a party, by his words or conduct, can make a party admission. Second, these cases often consider the extent to which a party should be held responsible for statements or actions of affiliated persons such as agents or privies. The first theme raises familiar issues of relevance, although problems associated with the technical requirements of the party admissions exception are sometimes involved. The second theme involves a policy issue concerning the ambit of party responsibility. We shall consider these major questions at appropriate places in the sections that follow.

§ 7.2 Party Admission: An Illustration

The most common party admission is an oral or written statement by a party that, in the context of litigation, is determined by his adversary to be disadvantageous to the admitting

ty to examine himself in order to test sincerity, etc. While the awkward posture of the objector serves as a rationale to justify admissibility when the objecting party is also the declarant, this rationale arguably does not extend to admissions made by representatives or by those in privity. See § 7.4.

7. See, e.g., Fed.R.Civ.P. 36.

8. Some courts hold that testimony by a party from the witness stand, as distinguished from extra-judicial statements, has a conclusive effect. This rule applies when he testifies concerning a matter within his personal knowledge and his testimonial statement contradicts his asserted claim or defense. See, e.g., Holland v. Holland, 217 Va. 874, 234 S.E.2d 65 (1977); Bell v. Harmon, 284 S.W.2d 812 (Ky.1955).

party and hence is offered in evidence against him. In an Iowa automobile accident case,[1] the defendant introduced as a party admission the plaintiff's signed statement that the defendant (in whose car plaintiff was a passenger) was not intoxicated and had driven carefully. The inconclusive nature of party admissions is demonstrated by the fact that the plaintiff testified in rebuttal that he had signed the statement (which had been drafted by defendant's insurance agent) without reading it and while in the hospital under the influence of pain-killing drugs.

The foregoing case illustrates another point about party admissions: frequently, admissions by an adverse party are inconsistent not only with the admitting party's contentions as advanced, for example, through his pleadings, but also with his trial testimony.[2] In this situation, the introduction of the earlier, extrajudicial statement serves both a substantive purpose and an impeaching or discrediting function. Hence, even though a party admission can be introduced against a party before he takes the stand (or even if he does not testify), it has enhanced probative value if it is inconsistent with the party's trial testimony. This additional value may induce the proponent of a party admission to postpone its presentation, anticipating that his opponent will take the stand and give testimony that conflicts with the prior admission.

§ 7.3 Party Admission by Conduct and Implication

Nonverbal action, such as flight from the scene of the crime[1] or changing one's appearance or name,[2] also can constitute a party admission, provided, of course, these actions have probative value. Such conduct usually is offered to demonstrate a sense of guilt or wrongful conduct. If a party conducts himself inconsistently with his trial contentions, his contradictory conduct may be introduced against him under the exception for party admissions. An alternative analysis finding increased acceptance characterizes conduct not intended as a substitute for words as nonassertive and thus outside the definition of hearsay.[3] Obviously, where this latter analysis prevails, it is unnecessary to invoke the present exception or to resort to the special nonhearsay classification that the

§ 7.2

1. Olson v. Hodges, 236 Iowa 612, 19 N.W.2d 676 (1945).

2. See, e.g., Peterson v. Richards, 73 Utah 59, 272 P. 229 (1928).

§ 7.3

1. State v. Townsend, 201 Kan. 122, 439 P.2d 70 (1968).

2. McCormick, § 271, at 803.

3. See § 6.3.

Federal Rules accord to party admissions. Thus, evidence of the accused's flight from the scene of the charged offense might be received as nonhearsay, circumstantial evidence, since it is unlikely that the person fleeing intended thereby to assert his guilt.

A failure to take action or to speak out sometimes may have probative value to confirm the existence of a certain fact or condition. This probative silence is most frequently found when a party, confronted with a statement or accusation, fails to deny or protest its accuracy. A failure to correct or deny such a statement constitutes an implied, or, as some courts say, adopted admission, assuming it reasonably can be expected that a person in the party's position would protest the statement were it untrue. An implied admission occurred, for example, in an early (pre-Rules) federal case [4] in which the evidence showed that the defendant in a tax evasion prosecution had removed bundles of money from a safe and stated to interested beneficiaries that each bundle contained $500. One of those present said to him "No; $5000," and the defendant remained silent. The court held that the defendant's failure to deny the accuracy of the onlooker's statement was an implied admission of the higher amount. Of course, this admission was not conclusive; the trier was still entitled to find that the bundles contained only $500.

A trial judge should exercise a high degree of care in admitting evidence of admissions implied because of silence. It first is essential that he determine that the statement was heard and understood by the admitting party, that the latter had an opportunity to reply, and that in the circumstances a protest, correction, or statement of disagreement would be probable if the statement were untrue. Of course, some statements or accusations, especially those which are exaggerated or inflammatory, may not warrant a reply. Consequently, the judge should exclude these statements because in the particular circumstances it is not probable that the nonanswering party acquiesced in the truth of the statement addressed to him.[5] In short, a reasonable person would not have made a statement of protest or correction.

4. United States v. Alker, 255 F.2d 851 (3d Cir.1958), cert. denied 358 U.S. 817 (1958).

5. State v. Guffey, 261 N.C. 322, 134 S.E.2d 619 (1964); see Arpan v. United States, 260 F.2d 649, 655 (8th Cir.1958); Heller, Admissions by Acquiescence, 15 U.Miami L.Rev. 161, 163–64 (1960). Suppose the subject matter of the unanswered statement is not within the knowledge of a party against whom the evidence is offered. Lack of knowledge would, in most circumstances at least, make it reasonable not to reply. McCormick, § 270, at 652–53.

The judge should also be alert to constitutional difficulties. It would violate one's constitutional right against self-incrimination to admit evidence that he failed to respond to a statement or allegation if he were properly exercising his fifth amendment right to remain silent.[6] An accused in a criminal proceeding must be warned of his constitutional right to remain silent when governmental officials deprive him of his "freedom of action in any significant way."[7] This right would be substantially undermined if the accused's silence could be used against him. Of course, even if the accused's freedom was not in fact restricted and he was not in any way coerced, he may have believed that he was properly exercising his right to remain silent; thus the better view is that where it is plausible for one to believe he is entitled to silence, his failure to speak should not be used against him.[8]

§ 7.4 Vicarious or Representative Admissions

A principal issue associated with party admissions is the range of party responsibility—the extent to which a party may be held responsible (in the evidentiary sense) for statements made by someone else. The strongest case for a representative or vicarious admission is found where the principal-party expressly has authorized an agent to speak for him on a particular subject or expressly has adopted another's prior statement. If, for example, an injured person commissioned his doctor or lawyer to speak for him at a hearing before an insurance claims adjuster, his representative's statements would constitute authorized party admissions and, as such, would be admissible against the authorizing party. Similarly, if a representative whose prior "speaking" authority was in doubt spoke at the hearing, and subsequently a party expressly assented to the former's statements, these would be admissible as adoptive party admissions.

A change in the facts requires a somewhat different analysis, grounded upon the principles of an implied admission discussed in the preceding section. Suppose a physician writes a letter to his patient setting out the former's diagnosis. If, for instance, the patient freely chooses to append the letter to his claim for disabili-

6. Adv.Comm.Note to Fed.R.Evid. 801. See Miranda v. Arizona, 384 U.S. 436, 468 n. 37 (1966), reh. denied, 385 U.S. 890 (1966), discussed in § 9.12.

7. Miranda v. Arizona, 384 U.S. 436, 444 (1966), reh. denied, 385 U.S. 890 (1966); see McCormick, § 161, at 353–58.

8. 4 Louisell & Mueller at 279.

ty compensation, and forwards it to an administrative tribunal, it might properly be inferred that he acquiesced in the physician's findings. In these circumstances, a court probably would find that the patient impliedly had adopted the physician's statement; hence the doctor's letter would be admissible against the patient as a party admission.[1] Of course, if in forwarding the claim the patient protested the doctor's appended findings, or if the administrative body required a statement from this particular doctor and other portions of the patient's proofs contradicted the doctor's statements, there would be no basis for an implied adoption. This absence of implied adoption does not, of course, preclude the proponent from attempting to show that the patient had previously *authorized* the physician to speak for him. Such a showing, if successfully made, would provide an alternative basis for admitting the physician's statements. Thus, if the patient requests that his physician examine him and that the doctor thereafter forward one copy of his report directly to the insurance company, it is likely that the doctor would be an authorized spokesman.

An adoptive admission, then, may be any statement expressly or impliedly accepted by the admitting party, even though authority to speak may not have existed prior to the statement in question.

As to other statements by third persons, admissibility traditionally has been restricted to previously authorized statements.[2] Until recently, the courts have drawn a sharp distinction between an agent's conduct, for which his principal may be vicariously liable under the substantive law, and an agent's statements, which for evidentiary purposes cannot be imputed to the principal absent a conferral of authority to speak. The fact that an agent speaks in connection with an *activity* that is clearly within the scope of his delegated duties does not mean that he *speaks for* his principal, even if he speaks about such activity. Authority to speak is a matter for separate determination.[3] Consequently, difficulty is encountered with statements made by agents not employed *to*

§ 7.4

1. See Wade v. Lane, 189 F.Supp. 661 (D.D.C.1960), aff'd, 290 F.2d 387 (D.C.Cir.1961). In the circumstances, the action by the party implies adoption; in the analogous situation discussed at § 7.3, n. 4, inaction in the form of silence resulted in adoption.

2. But see the discussion in § 7.5 pertaining to declarations by coconspirators.

3. See Restatement of Agency, Second, § 298; Big Mack Trucking Co., Inc. v. Dickerson, 497 S.W.2d 283 (Tex.1973).

speak for the principal,[4] but rather engaged primarily to perform physical acts such as making repairs, ushering, driving trucks, and so forth.[5] In these cases, many courts, especially in their early decisions, take the narrow view that the authority to speak is either nonexistent or does not extend to statements of fault or misdeeds that could result in the principal's liability.[6] A truck driver, the reasoning goes, is engaged to drive the principal's truck, not to speak for him; hence a post-accident statement by the driver that he was speeding is not a party admission of his employer-principal,[7] and cannot be admitted against the employer under a party admissions theory.

A second, related, restrictive doctrine may be found in many, but not all, common-law jurisdictions. Even if the agent is authorized to speak, there will be no party admission by the principal if that authorization covers only speech to designated persons within the business entity, such as a supervisor or fellow worker. For there to be a party admission by the principal, broader authority enabling the agent to speak to the "outside world" must be conferred. Only this broad conferral of speaking authority results in a party admission by the principal. For example, suppose a defendant's employee admits his failure to inspect certain machinery that may have injured the plaintiff, but the admission is made to a company supervisor who is investigating the accident. The agent's statement is not a party admission of the principal-employer who, it is assumed, may authorize statements to supervisors (or fellow servants) without creating adverse evidence against himself through the party admissions doctrine.[8] Note that even if the employee's statement had been made to someone outside the business, there would still be no admission of the principal since the agent would have *exceeded* his limited speaking authority. Of course, if the employee has himself made a party admission (either

4. As the drafters of the Federal Rules noted, "[s]ince few principals employ agents for the purpose of making damaging statements, the usual result was the exclusion of the statement." Adv.Comm.Note to Fed.R.Evid. 801(d)(2).

5. See, e.g., Semprini v. Boston & M.R.R., 87 N.H. 279, 179 A. 349 (1935); Rudzinski v. Warner Theatres, Inc., 16 Wis.2d 241, 114 N.W.2d 466 (1962). Are paid informants "agents" of the police with authority to speak? See United States v. Pena, 527 F.2d 1356 (5th Cir. 1976), cert. denied, 426 U.S. 949 (1976), where the issue is raised but not resolved.

6. IV Wigmore, § 1078, at 166 (Chadbourn). A review of cases applying the traditional view may be found in Nobero Co. v. Ferro Trucking, Inc., 107 N.J.Super. 394, 258 A.2d 713 (1969).

7. McCormick, § 267, at 788 n. 6.

8. Id. at 789–80.

to someone within or outside the business) pointing toward his own liability, his declaration may be entered in evidence against him—assuming he is named as a party to the suit in which the plaintiff seeks redress.

Fortunately, these restrictive views, which often result in excluding reliable, probative evidence, are losing favor. There is a clear trend toward admitting the agent's statement as the employer's party admission if the statement concerns a "matter within the scope of . . . [the] agency or employment, made during the existence of the [agency or employment] relationship." [9] It is immaterial whether the statement was made to a fellow employee, a member of the business management, or someone outside the business. The requirement that the employment or agency relationship exist at the time of the representative's statement protects the principal against disserving statements of former, perhaps disgruntled, employees.

Thus, in a majority of modern courts, an agent's declaration is admissible against the principal if there was adequate "speaking authority" (the traditional rule) or, even in the absence of such authority, if the agent spoke about a matter within the scope of his work. The proponent, of course, must provide the proper foundation for this evidence. Under the traditional approach, which requires authority to speak (and, in some jurisdictions, authority to speak to persons outside the business organization) there must be evidence, persuasive to the judge, that there was express or implied authority to speak. Similarly, in those modern jurisdictions that broaden admissibility to include statements about the subject matter of the agent's work, there must be proof that convinces the judge that the agent was in fact addressing a matter within the scope of his employment.

Even in those jurisdictions that abide by the orthodox approach and take a narrow view of the employee's authority to speak, careful evidentiary planning often results in the admission of his statement. To begin with, various exceptions to the hearsay rule, such as those for spontaneous declarations and declarations against interest, may apply with the result that an employee's statement is freely admissible against any party, including the principal. The rationale of admissibility is the satisfaction of the conditions of reliability prescribed by the applicable hearsay exception and not the rationale of adversarial responsibility which

9. Fed.R.Evid. 801(d)(2); see Nobero v. Ferro Trucking, Inc., 107 N.J.Super. 394, 258 A.2d 713 (1969); McCormick, § 267, at 641.

underlies party admissions. Furthermore, if the employee or agent is made a party, his prior statement usually will constitute *his own party admission,* even if it is not that of his principal. As always, the test of relevance must be satisfied, which in this context means that the prior statement must have probative value to establish the agent's liability. If the relevance test is satisfied and the agent is joined as a party defendant in the suit against the principal, the agent's statement is admissible against the agent himself, although, as we shall see, there are restrictions upon how this use affects the employer's liability.

Note that a possibly admissible statement by an agent might support one or more of the following propositions: (1) the agency relationship or scope of employment ("I was making a delivery."); (2) the agent's fault ("I forgot to give a signal."); (3) the principal's fault ("My employer told me to ignore the overloaded cargo and make the delivery by noon."). As to the first of these uses, the traditional requirement is that the fact and scope of the agency (including speaking authority) must be proved by evidence independent of the statement offered as a party admission [10]—to hold otherwise amounts to using the statement of agency as part of the proof of the foundation upon which its admissibility rests. However, since the question of agency with respect to the party admissions rule is properly a question for the judge, who is not, as to such preliminary questions, bound by the usual rules of evidence, modern authority often permits the judge to consider the agents' statement as part of the preliminary proof.[11]

If the proponent produces evidence of an agency relationship that includes "speaking authority," the agent's declaration then becomes admissible against the principal. Under the modern

10. IV Wigmore, § 1078, at 176 (Chadbourn); see, e.g., United States v. Bensinger Co., 430 F.2d 584, 593 (8th Cir.1970) ("It is a universally accepted rule of evidence that the fact of agency may not be proved by the alleged agent's extrajudicial statements."). See infra n. 1 at the end of Part A. Even the approach of the Federal Rules appears to require independent evidence that the employment or agency relationship existed at the time of the agent's statement. Further, if an issue arises under Federal Rule 801(d)(2) whether the agent's statement concerns "a matter within the scope of his agency or employment," the proponent should be required to produce independent evidence of the scope of the agency. Note, however, that the *judge* makes the necessary findings with regard to the existence of the employment relationship and what matters fall within it. See § 10.3. In making these determinations, he is "not bound by the rules of evidence except those with respect to privileges." Fed.R.Evid. 104(a).

11. Adv.Comm.Note to Fed.R.Evid. 104(a). See 1 Louisell & Mueller, § 29, at 208 (arguing, however, that the judge must consider the statement along with *some* independent evidence of agency).

view, it is only necessary to show that the agent spoke about a matter within the scope of his agency or employment. With respect to the second use, regarding the agent's fault, the evidence—as we just observed—constitutes the agent's party admission and is clearly admissible to establish his liability, assuming he is joined as a party. Note, however, that under principles of vicarious liability and respondeat superior, the superior is liable if the employee's conduct is actionable, regardless of any wrongful conduct on the part of the superior. Hence, the trier's use of the employee's declaration, *ostensibly only to find the employee's* wrongful conduct, nonetheless may affect the employer's liability. This indirect or derivative use of the evidence to impose liability on the employer [12] results from the substantive law; the evidentiary use is against only the employee. Some courts have not made this distinction and have resisted this derivative use by requiring "that the agent's liability be established by evidence also admissible against the principal" [13] before the principal can be held vicariously liable. These courts reason that in instances where a major portion of the evidence showing the agents' fault consists of his (but not his principal's) party admission, a suit by the plaintiff solely against the principal would probably be unsuccessful. The plaintiff's ability to join both defendants in one suit should not, these courts assert, produce a different result than that which would probably obtain in separate suits. Other courts, while technically adhering to the restriction that the agents' declaration is not admissible against the principal as a party admission, nonetheless countenance an indirect effect upon the principal: once the agent is found liable on the basis of evidence admissible against him, the principal is properly held vicariously liable under the substantive law. Finally, when the agent's statement speaks to the principal's fault, courts traditionally have required that the statement be made within the scope of the employee's employment *and* that there be preliminary evidence that the employee had the requisite authority to speak.[14]

12. A good analysis is found in Madron v. Thomson, 245 Or. 513, 419 P.2d 611 (1966), clarified, 245 Or. 513, 423 P.2d 496 (1976).

13. E. Cleary & J. Strong, Evidence, Cases, Materials, Problems, 616 (3d ed. 1981). See Annot., 27 A.L.R.3d 966 (1969); Note, 11 Hous.L.Rev. 481, 484 (1974).

14. See, e.g., Madron v. Thomson, 245 Or. 513, 518–20, 419 P.2d 611, 614–15 (1966). For a federal case decided prior to the effective date of the Federal Rules of Evidence, see Northern Oil Co. v. Socony Mobil Oil Co., 347 F.2d 81 (2d Cir.1965), appeal after remand, 368 F.2d 384 (2d Cir.1966).

Note again the modern trend toward admitting an agent's or employee's statement if it concerns a matter within the scope of his duties. Such a statement may inculpate either the agent or the superior or, for that matter, both of them. Under this modern trend, it is only necessary that the agent speak about a matter within the scope of his agency or employment and that the statement be made during the employment or agency relationship. If the conditions are shown, the agent's statements are freely admissible against the employer.

An interesting aspect of the early judicial development of vicarious or representative party admissions is the growth of coexisting doctrines illustrative of contrasting extremes between exclusion, on the one hand, and admissibility, on the other. As we noted above, a hinderance to the full exposure of relevant evidence is the doctrine—still viable in some jurisdictions—that renders inadmissible statements which the principal has authorized to be made *only* between agents or from an agent to himself. Under this restrictive doctrine, such statements are not party admissions of the principal for the reason that he conferred no authority to speak to third persons, but rather he gave only limited authority to speak to one or more designated persons (i.e., the principal or another agent). This restrictive view takes no account of the fact that an agent's statement about his work is likely to be trustworthy. The employee probably is in a position to know the truth and, further, is not apt to make a statement potentially harmful to both himself and his employer unless he believes his declaration is accurate. Nonetheless, where the old view prevails, the employer, by carefully curtailing his employees' speaking authority, can escape the unfavorable impact of adverse evidence that under general evidentiary standards of need, reliability, probative force, and the absence of unfair prejudice, ought to come in against him.

During the same period in which the older restrictive view was flourishing, the courts took a surprisingly receptive attitude t[illegible] another kind of party admission: those made by a party's [illegible] To understand this aspect of party admissions, it first is [illegible] to consider what is meant by the relationship of "privi-[illegible]ugh imprecise, the term (in the present context, at [illegible] a relationship between a party and another, derived [illegible] consensual undertaking (usually a transfer) that [illegible] something of value. A relationship of privity is [illegible]e one transfers to a party a right, title, or [illegible]ngible or intangible asset; in many jurisdictions, a relationship of privity also exists where a party and another jointly hold certain proprietary interests. Buyers and sellers stand in a relationship of privity, as do deceased persons and those who take their property through will or intestacy.[15] Many courts also apply the privity label to joint owners, joint tenants, and joint obligees.[16]

In its most important application, the doctrine of party admissions by a privy holds that statements by a predecessor in interest [17] which concern the property (or right) transferred *and* which are made while the predecessor-declarant purportedly owned the property [18] are admissible against the successor in interest. Thus, if *A* sold a painting to *B*, an earlier statement by *A* that the painting had a flaw that had been retouched would be admissible in litigation between *B* and *C* concerning the condition of the painting. That is, *C* could introduce *A*'s statement as *B*'s party admission, assuming *A* made the statement while he still owned the painting.

This result is supported by the dubious rationale that one taking property (or at least colorable title to it) [19] assumes the burdens of the evidentiary admissions that are traceable to his predecessor. This is not a satisfying ground for the admissibility of hearsay evidence. The major concern here ought to be trustworthiness. It is true that *A*'s prior position to know about the condition of the painting favors admissibility. But the application

15. McCormick, § 268, at 795–96.

16. Id. at 647; IV Wigmore § 1077 (Chadbourn). "Privity" is perhaps a confusing label to use in connection with the party admission of a joint holder, since it is not immediately apparent why a joint holder should be treated like a predecessor in interest—which aptly describes the other privity situations. But note that the party admissions doctrine is applicable only to joint ownership as distinguished from ownership in common. Morgan & Weinstein at 251–52. Apparently the theory is that "identity of substantive interests should determine the scope of admissible evidence." Id. at 252. In a joint tenancy, the interest of the deceased tenant passes to the surviving tenant; in a tenancy in common, the interest of the deceased tenant passes to his heirs or devisees. Thus each *joint* tenant is a potential transferee or a transferor.

17. In the case of joint owners the privy is not, technically, a predecessor, but one who holds the property contemporaneously. See supra nn. 15–16.

18. Colorable title would suffice. In Morgan, Basic Problems of Evidence, 180 (1963), the author notes the requirement that the predecessor make the statement " 'while owning the interest' [later transferred to a party] does not denote or connote actual or legal ownership of any interest. It means simply, while the declarant had whatever interest, if any, the party in the action is claiming to have derived from him, so that the party has the same legal position with reference to the property that the declarant had at the time of the declaration."

19. See supra n. 18.

of the present exception denies to *B* the chance to cross-examine *A* concerning the latter's assertion.[20] The major hearsay dangers of insincerity, inaccurate perception, and faulty memory all are present. Further, *A*'s relationship to *B* is an arm's length transaction; it carries no authority, express or implied, entitling *A* to speak for *B*. Thus, it is not clear why *B* should bear evidentiary responsibility for *A*'s statements. A weak analogy supporting admission is found in the increasingly accepted rule admitting an agent's statement concerning a matter within the scope of his employment if made during the employment relationship. The privity rule, by analogy, requires that the statement be made during the period of ownership and it admits only statements about the right, title, or interest transferred. However, the single arm's length transaction giving rise to privity is a tenuous link compared with the more substantial relationships that characterize other representative or vicarious party admissions. Further, the likelihood that the declaration concerns a subject about which he is knowledgeable does not lessen the danger of insincerity. One might urge that the exception for a predecessor's statement is supported by the fact that such a statement usually is against the financial or proprietary interest of the predecessor-declarant,[21] but this argument assumes too much: any statement, whether self-serving or disserving, made by the predecessor concerning his interest or title in the thing later transferred comes within the exception.[22] Furthermore, there is another exception to the hearsay rule that specifies when declarations against interest are admissible.[23] It is thus difficult to justify the admission of a predecessor's statements, at least on the grounds that normally support the introduction of party admissions. Beneath the surface of many of the cases, however, practical considerations such as the unavailability of the declarant, his known familiarity with the property in question, and, often, the fact that his statement was disserving when made, operate to subordinate sound theory to pragmatic considerations and account for the considerable common-law recognition of the rule extending party admissions to statements of a privy.

20. For a careful criticism of the privity rationale of party admissions, see Morgan, Admissions, 12 Wash.L. Rev. 181, 203 (1937).

21. See McCormick § 268 for a summary of the arguments for and against the privity exception.

22. Morgan, Basic Problems of Evidence, 279–280 (1963).

23. See Part J.

§ 7.5 Statements of Coconspirators

A discussion of party admissions would be incomplete without mention of the admissibility of the statements made by a coconspirator. A conspiracy is analogous to a business partnership in the sense that its participants act in concert to achieve a desired end.[1] Thus, the courts have viewed a party as having authorized all acts and declarations of a coconspirator made during and in the furtherance of the conspiracy.[2]

The exception for coconspirators' statements applies in both civil and criminal cases. It is unnecessary that the pleadings or indictment charge a conspiracy, and the declarant-coconspirator need not be a party to the proceeding in which his statement is introduced against a conspiring party. It suffices that the proponent of the evidence demonstrate that there was a conspiracy in which both declarant and party were participants, that the coconspirator made his statement during the course of it, and that the statement was "in furtherance" of the conspiracy.[3]

The line between declarations which further the conspiracy and those that do not is shadowy. Generally, the courts take a broad view of what declarations further the conspiratorial enterprise. As Professor McCormick notes, the criterion often applied in practice is whether the statement was made during the continuance of the conspiracy,[4] although cases can be found which reject statements on the ground that the declarations did not further the conspiracy.[5] A more common basis for exclusion is that the conspiracy had terminated before the statements were made. Yet here, too, there is room for a difference of opinion, and acts of concealment sometimes are considered within the conspiracy.[6]

There has also been a lively debate over the appropriate role of the judge in determining the admissibility of a coconspirator's statement. Under the emerging view, recently endorsed by the Supreme Court, the judge must decide, on a preponderance-of-the-evidence standard:[7] (1) that the conspiracy existed, (2) that the

§ 7.5

1. McCormick, § 267, at 782.

2. Morgan & Weinstein at 249; United States v. Diez, 515 F.2d 892 (5th Cir.1975), cert. denied, 423 U.S. 1052 (1976).

3. Fed.R.Evid. 801(d)(2)(E); McCormick, § 267, at 792 ("[G]enerally, [courts] have imposed the same test, namely that the declaration must have been made while the conspiracy was continuing, and must have constituted a step in furtherance of the venture.").

4. McCormick, § 267, at 792–94.

5. E.g., State v. Podor, 154 Iowa 686, 135 N.W. 421 (1912).

6. McCormick, § 267, at 793–94.

7. 1 Louisell & Mueller, § 29, at 100 (1985 Supp.). See infra n. 10.

declarant and the party were members of it and, (3) that the declarant made the statement in question in its furtherance.[8] Traditionally, the evidence used to establish the first two parts of this foundation had to be in addition to and independent of the declaration which the proponent offered as being within the coconspirator's admissions rule. However, the Federal Rules have now been construed to allow the judge, who (except for rules respecting privileged communications) is not bound by the rules of evidence in ruling on preliminary questions,[9] to consider the proffered declaration as part of the foundation proof.[10] This, in a sense, is a concession to reality, since the judge is obviously aware of the contested statement. Finally, some problems involving the proper roles of the judge and jury arise in criminal cases involving admissions by a coconspirator when a conspiracy is charged as a substantive offense. These difficulties are addressed elsewhere.[11]

§ 7.6 Party Admissions Under the Federal Rules: A Summary

As noted previously, the Federal Rules of Evidence remove party admissions from the classification of hearsay. In their nonhearsay form, admissions against a party opponent are gov-

8. There is disagreement among the courts concerning the proper role of the judge in assessing the evidence of a conspiracy. Under one view, the judge need only determine that the evidence supporting the proponent's claim that a conspiracy existed is sufficient to constitute a "prima facie" showing—that is, the evidence is sufficient for a reasonable jury to find that there was a conspiracy, that the declarant and the party against whom the declaration is offered were coconspirators, and that the statement in question was made in furtherance of the conspiracy. Carbo v. United States, 314 F.2d 718 (9th Cir. 1963), cert. denied, 377 U.S. 953 (1964). Under a second view, the judge himself must determine that there was a conspiracy and so forth; in making this determination, he assesses the credibility of the evidence offered. United States v. Petrozziello, 548 F.2d 20 (1st Cir.1977), cert. denied, 436 U.S. 947 (1978). A very good discussion of these and other approaches is contained in Saltzburg & Redden at 795–799. The role of the judge in connection with a coconspirator's admission is discussed further in § 10.5.

9. Fed.R.Evid. 104(a). See also United States v. James, 590 F.2d 575 (5th Cir.1979), cert. denied, 442 U.S. 917 (1979); United States v. Bell, 573 F.2d 1040 (8th Cir.1978) (both establishing that the trial judge decides whether the out-of-court statement of a coconspirator may be admitted).

10. Bourjaily v. United States, 55 U.S.L.W. 4962 (U.S. June 23, 1987). Prior federal decisions, however, disagreed as to whether the judge could consider the coconspirator's statement along with independent evidence of the conspiracy. See Saltzburg & Redden at 788–794 (and cases discussed therein); 1 Louisell & Mueller, § 29, at 209–212 (1977), 99–100 (1985 Supp.).

11. See § 10.5.

erned by Rule 801(d)(2).[1] A party's own statement may be offered against him whether he made it in his individual or representative capacity. Authorized statements made by a party's agent and offered against the party also are admissible; it is immaterial that the authorized statement was made to another agent or to the principal.[2] The restrictive common-law rule, recognized in some courts, that required authority to speak to persons outside the business entity is thus abandoned. Significantly, the rule also includes as a party admission a statement by an "agent or servant concerning a matter within the scope of his agency or employment," if the statement is made while the employment or agency relationship still exists. As noted, this provision is part of a modern trend toward eliminating the restrictive traditional approach that rejects evidence on the ground that the employee or agent was not authorized to speak for his principal. Arguably, the broader test adopted in the Rules is consistent with a party's adversarial responsibility: since he has engaged the agent to act on his behalf and he has some control over the agent's duties, it is fair that the statements of the agent related to his employment be admissible against the party-principal. Also, there is reason to think that an agent's statement made under the conditions prescribed by the Rule is reliable: the agent usually is well informed about matters related to his employment, and those of his statements which are introduced against his employer normally are against the interest of the agent, the employer, or both. It is not likely that the employee would make false inculpatory declarations or statements jeopardizing his continued employment.[3]

Rule 801(d) makes no provision for admitting the declarations of one in a relationship of privity to a party, a step which may trigger the demise of this aspect of party admissions. It is possible, however, that some declarations by a privy could be received

§ 7.6

1. The pertinent provisions exclude from the definition of hearsay:

> (2) *Admission by party-opponent.* The statement is offered against a party and is (A) his own statement, in either his individual or a representative capacity or (B) a statement of which he has manifested his adoption or belief in its truth, or (C) a statement by a person authorized by him to make a statement concerning the subject, or (D) a statement by his agent or servant concerning a matter within the scope of his agency or employment, made during the existence of the relationship, or (E) a statement by a coconspirator of a party during the course and in furtherance of the conspiracy.

2. Adv.Comm.Note to Fed.R.Evid. 801(d)(2). See United States v. Pena, 527 F.2d 1356 (5th Cir.1976), cert. denied, 426 U.S. 949 (1976).

3. See McCormick, § 267, at 788; Lempert & Saltzburg at 373.

under the "catchall" exceptions, 803(24) and 804(5),[4] designed to admit evidence deemed trustworthy, but which does not fit any of the specific exceptions. Furthermore, a privy's statement, if disserving when made, will qualify as a declaration against interest under Federal Rule 804(b)(3) if the declarant is unavailable as a witness.[5]

Finally, the Rule 801(d)(2)(E) expressly recognizes the admissibility of coconspirators' admissions. Although one can debate the wisdom of this exception,[6] conspiracies are by nature secret and elusive, making probative evidence difficult to secure. Statements that are highly suspect as to their reliability may be excluded in appropriate instances because their probative value is substantially outweighed by the risk of unfair prejudice.[7]

Notes

1. Sometimes a single transaction or event which involves an infraction of the criminal law also gives rise to one or more suits for civil damages. A traffic accident, for example, may involve both a misdemeanor (or felony) and a tortious activity. If the public offense is prosecuted first and a guilty plea is entered, many jurisdictions allow evidence of the plea to be introduced in the civil action based upon the same event. See Smith v. Southern Nat. Ins. Co., 134 So.2d 337 (La.App.1961). This evidence does not, however, have a conclusive effect in the civil action. Some jurisdictions deny admission to evidence of pleas of guilty in traffic offenses when later offered in a civil suit, but admit evidence of other guilty pleas. This position recognizes that a variety of reasons unrelated to guilt (such as expense or the inconvenience of contest) frequently account for guilty pleas in traffic cases. Although the status of a plea of nolo contendere has been debated, Federal Rule of Evidence 410 states that neither a plea of nolo contendere nor a withdrawn guilty plea is admissible in any other civil or criminal action. See § 5.17.

A different situation exists if an accused pleads not guilty but nonetheless is convicted. May his conviction be introduced in a civil trial based upon the same transaction? It is clear that there has been no party admission. There is growing authority, however, that the doctrine of collateral estoppel makes the first judgment conclusive as to those facts actually and necessarily decided. See Cardillo v. Zyla,

4. See § 7.28 and Fed.R.Evid. 803(24) and 804(5).

5. See § 7.28 and Fed.R.Evid. 804(b)(3).

6. Saltzburg & Redden at 728–729.

7. Fed.R.Evid. 403, discussed in § 2.5.

486 F.2d 473 (1st Cir.1973). Compare Eastern Renovating Corp. v. Roman Catholic Bishop of Springfield, 554 F.2d 4 (1st Cir.1977).

Another view, adopted in some jurisdictions that refuse a collateral estoppel effect, admits evidence of the criminal conviction in the civil trial, but permits the jury to accord to the evidence such weight as they desire. Finally, some courts, perhaps now a minority, exclude evidence of the criminal conviction. A factor which may be determinative is whether the party is in a defensive posture in the second proceeding or whether he is, as the courts say, "seeking to profit from his criminal acts." An example of the latter is where an individual is convicted of arson, but nonetheless brings suit against the insurer of the burned structure. Courts tend to admit evidence of the earlier conviction.

2. A basic principle of evidence is that personal knowledge of the witness or declarant is essential to admissibility. The speaker must have seen, heard, or otherwise perceived the event about which he speaks. But if the admissibility of a party admission is grounded on the adversary system, it is unnecessary that the party have personal knowledge of the event or condition about which he speaks. As noted in the main text, the cases so hold. Janus v. Akstin, 91 N.H. 373, 20 A.2d 552 (1941); see also Adv.Comm.Note to Fed.R.Evid. 801. Should this exemption from the usual requirement of personal knowledge apply when a party's agent, employee or privy makes the declaration in question? Since one basis of admitting another's declaration as an admission of a party is that the declarant probably knows the subject about which he speaks, it probably should be required that the representative have personal knowledge. See 4 Weinstein & Berger, ¶ 801(d)(2)(C)[01], at 215–218. However, the trend in the cases is to take the routine approach to party admissions and dispense with any requirement of personal knowledge. See Mahlandt v. Wild Canid Survival & Research Center, Inc., 588 F.2d 626 (1978).

PART B. SPONTANEOUS DECLARATIONS

(PRESENT SENSE IMPRESSIONS AND EXCITED UTTERANCES)

§ 7.7 In General

The term "spontaneous declaration" as used here includes two related but distinct hearsay exceptions for statements made under circumstances minimizing the dangers of insincerity and inaccurate memory.[1] The first of these exceptions is made for a statement of "present sense impression." Such a statement is considered trustworthy because it is made contemporaneously with, or immediately after, the event that it describes. The requirement of substantial contemporaneity minimizes the dangers of deliberate misrepresentation (since there is little time during which to conceive a false assertion) and of a faded memory. The second exception is made for a spontaneous declaration that usually is called an "excited utterance." This statement is made under a sense of excitement, shock, or stress and at a point in time fairly close to the event it describes. Here, it is the state of nervous excitement or shock that is thought to still the speaker's ability to practice deception. Requiring the statement to be made soon after the event in question helps ensure against defects in memory.

Both the statement of present sense impression and the excited utterance must pertain to the event that caused the immediate or excited response. A statement about an unrelated matter indicates that the speaker's attention was not confined to the contemporaneous or immediately preceding event, thus increasing the possibility of conscious deception. An unrelated event also may be farther in time from the declaration, and the greater the time lapse, the greater the possibility of a memory flaw. The admissibility of both types of spontaneous statements is conditioned upon a preliminary determination by the judge that the various requirements of the applicable exception have been met.

§ 7.8 Present Sense Impression

This exception is of comparatively recent origin. The leading case supporting it is Houston Oxygen Co. v. Davis,[1] decided by the Texas Supreme Court in 1942. Some courts have not recognized the exception as such, but nonetheless have admitted statements bearing the characteristics of a present sense impression.[2] Significantly, Federal Rule 803(1) expressly provides for this exception:

§ 7.7

1. The dangers of faulty perception and mistranscription, however, are still present. But note that excitement—which might impair the accuracy of perception—is not a requirement of the exception for a recent sense perception.

§ 7.8

1. 139 Tex. 1, 161 S.W.2d 474 (1942). See also Morgan & Weinstein at 298–300.

2. McCormick, § 298, at 860–61. The exception usually applied to justify admission is that for res gestae, the most amorphous of the exceptions. See n. 3 following Part B.

Present sense impression. A statement describing or explaining an event or condition made while the declarant was perceiving the event or condition or immediately thereafter.

Although judicial disagreement may develop concerning how soon after the event (or condition) the statement must be made, the central idea is that the statement follows the perception of the event so closely that deliberate falsification and memory defects are unlikely. Thus, the declarant's statement immediately following the overturning of her truck, that a passenger's seizing the wheel had caused the accident, falls within the exception.[3] It is not necessary that a declaration of present sense impression be attended by excitement, but the time lapse between the event and the descriptive statement must be very brief.

In most instances, the person who heard the declarant's statement about the event also will have been in a position to observe the circumstances described. This opportunity for confirmation further reduces the chance of a purposeful misstatement. The rule, however, does not require that the hearer be in a position to observe the event or condition. Nonetheless, the courts are likely to take this factor into account, especially when there is an issue concerning the lapse of time between the event or condition and the statement describing it.

Note that the Federal Rule requires that the declarant detail, or at least characterize, the perceived "event or condition" by "describing or explaining" it. The "event or condition" can take a variety of forms such as the playing of recorded music,[4] the failure of a train to sound its whistle at a crossing,[5] or even someone's [6]

3. Starr v. Morsette, 236 N.W.2d 183 (N.D.1975) (a witness who believed she arrived "a minute or two after" a pick-up truck overturned, was permitted to testify that the defendant driver said that defendant passenger had grabbed the wheel, causing the accident).

4. See MCA Inc. v. Wilson, 425 F.Supp. 443 (S.D.N.Y.1976), judg. aff'd and mod. 677 F.2d 180 (2d Cir.1981) (after hearing a song, declarant remarked that it sounded like "Bugle Boy"—a song to which *P* held the copyright).

5. See Emens v. Leigh Valley R. Co., 223 Fed. 810 (N.D.N.Y.1915) (to prove that the attention of the witness to a grade crossing accident was called to the train, his testimony that immediately prior to the accident his wife had said, "Do you suppose the people in that automobile see the train?" and "Why don't the train whistle?" was admitted). It seems clear that today the declarations in the *Emens* case would be admitted as present sense impressions.

6. There is no requirement that the declarant be identified for admissibility under the exception. See United States v. Medico, 557 F.2d 309 (2d Cir.1977), cert. denied, 434 U.S. 986 (1977) (unidentified bystander recites license plate number of getaway car in robbery). Cf. Myre v. State, 545 S.W.2d 820 (Tex.Crim.App.1977).

statement overheard (and described) by the declarant.[7]

A statement which may have been evoked by the event but which does not describe or explain what happened does not come within the exception.[8] Such a declaration is more likely to be attended by the hearsay risks of insincerity and faulty memory.

Several features of the exception should be reiterated in order to facilitate comparison with the next exception: excited utterances. The necessity for contemporaneity and the requirement that the statement must be strictly confined to the event or condition perceived are both rigorously enforced in connection with the exception for present sense impressions. However, as noted above, this exception does not require that the declarant be excited or under stress.

§ 7.9 Excited Utterance

The exception for an excited utterance requires that the declarant speak while under the stressful influence of a startling event or condition. The necessary state of excitement may embrace the consequent shock or emotional distress that may persist even after "excitement," in the narrow sense, has subsided.[1] The rationale supporting admission is that emotional stress suspends the process of reflective thought necessary for conscious fabrication, and that the recentness of the exciting event minimizes the danger of faulty memory. Federal Rule 803(2) adopts the exception as it has been developed by the common law in most jurisdictions:

> *Excited Utterance.* A statement relating to a startling event or condition made while the declarant was under the stress of excitement caused by the event or condition.

There are several distinctions and refinements to be made with regard both to the Rule and the common-law tradition which underlies it. The time lapse between the event and the declaration is obviously an important factor. A state of excitement or

7. The "event" perceived by the declarant can be a verbal statement. For example, in Nuttal v. Reading Co., 235 F.2d 546 (3d Cir.1956), statements made by a decedent husband in immediate response to a telephone call from his supervisor were admitted. See also United States v. Peacock, 654 F.2d 339 (5th Cir.1981), cert. denied, 464 U.S. 965 (1983).

8. 4 Weinstein & Berger, ¶ 803(1)[01], at 79–80.

§ 7.9

1. Wright v. Swann, 261 Or. 440, 493 P.2d 148 (1972); People v. Damen, 28 Ill.2d 464, 193 N.E.2d 25 (1963); Keefe v. State, 50 Ariz. 293, 297–98, 72 P.2d 425, 427 (1937); McCormick, § 297, at 855–57.

shock, of course, can linger for a period of time after the causal event has occurred, but the longer the interval between event and declaration, the greater the chance of exclusion.[2] Observe, however, that the required immediacy for present sense impressions does not necessarily accompany an excited utterance: if a declarant makes the statement as he regains his faculties after a period of unconsciousness or extreme shock, the passage of several or more hours between the exciting event and the statement usually is not fatal to admissibility.[3]

Related factors bearing upon the judge's preliminary decision of whether the requirements of the exception are satisfied are the condition of the declarant and the likelihood that the particular statement, judged by its contents, was prompted by the exciting event. There is no requirement that the declarant be a participant in the exciting event; he may be a bystander. Of course, the duration of the required emotional state of excitement might not be as long with a bystander as with a participant.

An important feature to consider is the directness with which the utterance must relate to the startling event. A present sense impression must describe or explain an event or condition, but the excited utterance need only relate to the startling event. This difference in scope is illustrated by Murphy Auto Parts Co. v. Ball,[4] a suit against a defendant-employer in which the action of an allegedly negligent employee had accidentally injured the plaintiff. An issue in the case was whether the employee was engaged in his employer's business at the time of the event. In a post-accident remark, the employee stated that he had been on an errand for his employer. The trial judge admitted this statement, and the Court of Appeals for the District of Columbia approved the admission, holding that the statement qualified as an excited utterance. The test, said the court, is whether there is an exciting event which prompts the declaration and if it is so prompted, it need not be confined only to a description of the event.

2. Staiger v. Gaarder, 258 N.W.2d 641 (N.D.1977); Tait v. Western World Ins. Co., 220 So.2d 226 (La.App.1969); Marshall v. Thomason, 241 S.C. 84, 127 S.E.2d 177 (1962). But see State v. Stafford, 237 Iowa 780, 23 N.W.2d 832 (1946).

3. United States v. Glenn, 473 F.2d 191, 194 (D.C.Cir.1972) ("Nor is it decisive that an appreciable time elapsed."). See Allen v. McLain, 75 S.D. 520, 530, 69 N.W.2d 390, 396 (1955); State v. Stafford, 237 Iowa 780, 23 N.W.2d 832 (1946); Davis Transport, Inc. v. Bolstad, 295 S.W.2d 941 (Tex.Civ.App.1956). See also 4 Weinstein & Berger, ¶ 803(2)[01], at 92, n. 26. But see Staiger v. Gaarder, 258 N.W.2d 641 (N.D.1977).

4. 249 F.2d 508 (D.C.Cir.1957), cert. denied, 355 U.S. 932 (1958).

This rationale suggests there should be no requirement that the declarant have first-hand (personal) knowledge of the *exciting* event, if he spoke with the requisite degree of excitement and *does* have first-hand knowledge of the *related* event described in his statement.

The *Murphy* case is interesting for still a second point. Under the traditional common-law view, the declaration in question would have qualified as a party admission if an agency relationship were shown to exist by evidence outside the employee's declaration *and,* under the older restrictive view, *if* the agent had authority to speak. The proponent of the evidence in *Murphy* had failed to prove these elements, so that the statement in question could not come in as a vicarious party admission. Yet it did qualify for admission as an excited utterance. Note that when a statement is admitted as an excited utterance, it can be used against *any* party to whom it is relevant. This stands in contrast to a party admission which, generally speaking, is admissible only against the party making or authorizing the statement. Thus, if the excited statement in *Murphy* had been the employee's declaration "I didn't see the other car" or "I was in a hurry to make a delivery," it would have been freely received against both employer and employee (assuming the latter is joined as a party defendant) without limitation. On the other hand, in some common-law jurisdictions, a party admission by the agent is received only against him and not against the employer unless the employer had conferred "speaking authority." [5] Thus, by offering the employee's statement as an excited utterance—and not as a party admission—the restrictions surrounding the latter exception are avoided. The point, made earlier in this text [6] but illustrated in *Murphy* is that imaginative thinking about possible alternate avenues of admission may yield positive results.

The proponent of an excited utterance may be faced with the question whether he must provide independent evidence (aside from the excited declaration itself) of the startling occurrence. Although there is some disagreement, the weight of authority appears to accept the declaration as proof that the exciting event has occurred.[7] The existence of an excited statement is, after all,

5. See § 7.4.

6. See §§ 2.3, 6.1.

7. E.g., Travelers Insurance Co. v. Mosley, 75 U.S. 397 (1869) (8 Wall); State v. Hutchison, 222 Or. 533, 353 P.2d 1047 (1960); Armour v. Industrial Comm., 78 Colo. 569, 243 P. 546 (1926). See Slough, Res Gestae, 2 Kan.L.Rev. 41 (1953).

probative of the existence of an exciting event.[8] The Federal Rule, which is silent on this point, probably will be interpreted so as to permit the declaration to serve as evidence that the event took place.[9] As a practical matter, however, there is usually other evidence confirming the existence of the event.

Notes

1. Arguments about the reliability of an excited utterance usually center upon the proposition that while one who is startled may not falsify, the chances of impaired perception are increased when he is excited. See Hutchins & Slesinger, Some Observations on the Law of Evidence—Spontaneous Exclamations, 28 Colum.L.Rev. 432 (1928). In short, as the risk of one hearsay danger goes down, the risk of another is increased. However, this infirmity need not result in exclusion, but rather could be considered in weighing the evidence. Apparently, no jurisdiction has rejected the excited utterance exception.

2. As suggested in the main text it is the responsibility of the trial judge to determine if the exception for excited utterances is applicable. In People v. Poland, 22 Ill.2d 175, 181, 174 N.E.2d 804, 807 (1961), the court stated that the necessary factors consisted of "(1) an occurrence sufficiently startling to produce a spontaneous and unreflecting statement; (2) absence of time to fabricate; and (3) the statement must relate to the circumstances of the occurrence." The fact that the declaration was in the form of an opinion or conclusion or that it was made in answer to a question should not preclude admissibility. The rule against opinion is designed to apply to testimony from the stand, where there is an opportunity to rephrase a question or answer. That an excited utterance was given in response to a question should not itself defeat admissibility; this fact, however, may be relevant in the judge's determination whether the declaration was made under the influence of excitement or stress. See McCormick, § 297, at 857–58.

8. See 4 Louisell & Mueller, § 439, at 495 for elaboration of this point.

9. See Traveler's Ins. Co. v. Mosley, supra n. 7; 4 Weinstein & Berger, ¶ 803(2)[01], at 87–88 discussing the *Mosley* case and Rule 803(2). The authors point out that Fed.R.Evid. 104(a) lends support to the assumption that the declaration may be received as evidence of the happening of the event. That Rule frees the judge from the rules of evidence (except with regard to privileges) in making preliminary determinations about the admissibility of evidence. This indicates that the hearsay declaration could be used to establish the event, at least at the critical juncture of the judge's preliminary determination. After the excited utterance is received in evidence, arguments that there was no exciting event or stress should affect only the weight that the trier accords the evidence.

3. The phrase "res gestae" still appears in judicial opinions despite widespread condemnation. A declaration is said to be admissible despite the hearsay rule if it constitutes a part of "the thing done." Often, the term is used to justify the admission of a statement having independent legal significance (a "verbal act"), that is, a statement that is consequential simply because it was uttered and regardless of its truth. See § 6.2. As we saw in the preceding chapter, such a statement is not hearsay and thus need not be entered under an exception. Unfortunately, the res gestae label is sometimes indiscriminately applied to hearsay declarations that fit within the exceptions for statements of excited utterance, present sense impression, physical condition, or state of mind. See Part C. The imprecision of the term, coupled with careless usage by the courts, has been a source of perplexity for students and lawyers. See generally VI Wigmore §§ 1757, 1766–70 (Chadbourn). Fortunately, the res gestae label continues to lose favor; the term is not included in the Federal Rules of Evidence. Some lawyers may lament its omission. "If you wish to tender inadmissible evidence," Lord Blackburn reminds us, "say it is a part of the res gestae." Tregarthen, The Law of Hearsay Evidence 21 (1915).

4. The exception for excited utterances has figured prominently in cases of sex offenses in recent years. The significance of the exception for such cases, particularly rape cases, lies in the possibility of admitting statements of the victim-declarant without that person having to testify or in addition to her testimony. Thus, if the declarant's statements meet the requirements of the exception, her hearsay declarations may be introduced to establish the facts recited in them. When children are alleged to have been sexually assaulted, the child-declarant's statements are subject to somewhat less strict requirements on the time lapse and spontaneity factors. See, e.g., United States v. Iron Shell, 633 F.2d 77 (8th Cir.1980), cert. denied, 450 U.S. 1001 (1980) (alleged assault of nine-year-old girl; court held that statements made by the child to officers between 45 minutes and one hour and fifteen minutes following event were properly received under excited utterance exception). See also Haggins v. Warden, Ft. Pillow State Farm, 715 F.2d 1050 (6th Cir.1983), cert. denied, 464 U.S. 1071 (1984) (statements of four-year-old victim of alleged assault to nurses and police officers identifying assailant held admissible under the exception). The introduction of excited utterances against the accused in criminal cases may pose questions under the confrontation clause. See §§ 7.29–7.31.

PART C. PHYSICAL OR MENTAL CONDITION

§ 7.10 In General

The hearsay exceptions for statements about the declarant's physical or mental condition are well established. Their recognition in part is based upon the realization that one's primary means of learning about another's bodily condition or state of mind often is through his statements. These exceptions also are defined so as to promote trustworthiness. Reliability is sought by the general requirement (subject to several qualifications) that the excepted statement must describe a currently existing physical or mental condition—that is, the declaration must refer to a condition that exists at the time of the statement and not to some past condition. This requirement of contemporaneity reduces somewhat the chance of reflective fabrication; [1] it also eliminates the risk of faulty memory. Note that faulty perception is usually not a problem—presumably, the declarant can reliably perceive his own physical or mental state. Arguably, out-of-court statements of presently existing physical or mental condition are as reliable as subsequent courtroom testimony.

Federal Rule 803(3), which is based upon the common law, provides a hearsay exception for:

> *Then existing mental, emotional, or physical condition.* A statement of the declarant's then existing state of mind, emotion, sensation, or physical condition (such as intent, plan, motive, design, mental feeling, pain, and bodily health), but not including a statement of memory or belief to prove the fact remembered or believed unless it relates to the execution, revocation, identification, or terms of declarant's will.

The following sections explore these provisions. Note, however, that the Federal Rule adopts the general requirement limiting the excepted declaration to a "then existing" condition, but suspends this requirement in cases involving a will. As we shall see, the courts have considered a declarant's statement relating to his will as falling within a special category and have been willing to

§ 7.10

1. On the other hand, such a statement is usually not capable of verification by the hearers; this might make it more likely that the declarant would lie or exaggerate.

broaden the exception to include a statement about past events or conditions.

§ 7.11 Present Physical Condition

Physical condition is a familiar courtroom issue. The existence of an injury to a party (or in some cases to a non-party) may be an element of a cause of action. And the extent of injury usually affects the damage award. Although many physical ailments and conditions can be ascertained by the trier's visual inspection or by a physician's testimony giving the results of a medical examination, it generally is helpful and sometimes essential to consider an individual's own statement of his physical condition. This is especially true with regard to such subjective internal symptoms as pain, headaches, nausea, and so forth.

The exception for present physical condition admits relevant hearsay declarations in which the declarant, either by exclamation or narration, indicates his then existing bodily condition.[1] Thus, a declarant's out-of-court statements that he was having difficulty hearing and that he was experiencing headaches would be admissible under the exception.[2] There is no danger of a defect in memory and only a minimal danger of erroneous perception. Although insincerity is a risk, the jury readily can appreciate the possibility of a self-serving motive. Furthermore, the judge has the authority to reject evidence of a statement of physical condition in instances where there appears to be a high risk of fabrication.[3]

The extra-judicial statement of bodily condition may be recounted by any witness who overheard it. There is no requirement (at least in the majority of jurisdictions) that the person overhearing the statement be a medical specialist.[4] However, in a growing number of jurisdictions it is significant whether the statement was made to a physician who is being consulted for purposes of treatment. In this setting, many jurisdictions, including the federal judiciary,[5] now expand the exception for physical

§ 7.11

1. Fidelity Service Ins. Co. v. Jones, 280 Ala. 195, 191 So.2d 20 (1966); Casualty Ins. Co. v. Salinas, 160 Tex. 445, 333 S.W.2d 109 (1960); Frangos v. Edmunds, 179 Or. 577, 173 P.2d 596 (1946); Kickham v. Carter, 335 S.W.2d 83 (Mo. 1960).

2. Frangos v. Edmunds, 179 Or. 577, 173 P.2d 596 (1946).

3. McCormick, § 291, at 839.

4. VI Wigmore, § 1719, at 109 n. 9 (Chadbourn); McCormick, § 291, at 838.

5. See Fed.R.Evid. 803(4), set out in the text infra at n. 8.

condition to include statements of *past* physical condition.[6] This relaxation of the usual requirement that the declaration describe a condition existing at the time of the statement rests on the rationale that effective treatment normally depends upon an accurate statement of condition; thus the patient has an incentive to be truthful. Statements of past physical condition, of course, raise the possibility of a defect in memory.

The common-law cases reflect a marked reluctance to admit declarations of condition made to a physician consulted not for treatment, but rather solely for the doctor's preparation of his expert testimony. In this setting, the rationale justifying the expanded exception for statements of past condition does not apply. Furthermore, many cases reject even statements of *present* condition when made to the medical expert not engaged in treatment or in diagnosis undertaken for purposes of treatment.[7]

Federal Rule 803(4) creates the following hearsay exception:

> *Statements for purposes of medical diagnosis or treatment.* Statements made for purposes of medical diagnosis or treatment and describing medical history, or past or present symptoms, pain, or sensations, or the inception or general character of the cause or external source thereof insofar as reasonably pertinent to diagnosis or treatment.

The Federal Rule is explicit in its provision that statements of past symptoms are admissible when made "for purposes of medical diagnosis or treatment. . . ." By not specifying that the statement be made directly to a physician, the Rule allows admission of remarks made to other medical attendants.[8] Note that the wording of the Rule is broad enough to admit statements made to a physician consulted for the purpose of enabling him to testify even if no treatment is contemplated. The Advisory Committee's Note explains that many common-law decisions allowed the nontreating physician to relate to the trier the patient's account of his past

6. Meaney v. United States, 112 F.2d 538 (2d Cir.1940); Peterson v. Richfield Plaza, Inc., 252 Minn. 215, 89 N.W.2d 712 (1958); Annot., 37 A.L.R.3d 778 (1971).

7. E.g., Padgett v. Southern Railway Co., 396 F.2d 303 (6th Cir.1968) (pre-Rules case). See McCormick § 293.

8. The drafters noted that under Rule 803(4) "[s]tatements to hospital attendants, ambulance drivers or *even members of the family* might be included." Adv.Comm.Note to Fed.R.Evid. 803(4) (emphasis added). See United States v. Rendini, 738 F.2d 530, 534 (1st Cir.1984) (notes by chairman of disability panel admissible as statements reasonably pertinent to diagnosis).

symptomatology when this testimony helped to explain the basis of the expert's diagnosis and prognosis. In theory, these statements were to be not considered for their truth, but rather for their bearing upon the physician-expert's opinions. The Committee thought the jury could not be obedient to this distinction and that, on balance, the declarations should come in and be accepted for their truth if the trier so wished to treat them.[9]

Note

Sometimes statements to a doctor include references to the cause of the accident, e.g., "I was struck on the right hip by a bicyclist." If the statement of the immediate cause of the accident is pertinent to treatment and if one safely can presume that the patient knew this, the patient's statement to a treating physician (or to other medical personnel associated with treatment) arguably encompasses even that portion of the statement which details the external cause of the injury. Thus viewed, the entire statement including reference to the external cause is admissible. Some courts have so held, but the greater number have refused, at least until quite recently, to receive statements of external cause. See McCormick, § 292, at 839–40. Federal Rule 803(4) quoted in the text above and now adopted in many jurisdictions does provide for the admission into evidence of a statement describing "the inception or general character of the cause or external source thereof . . .." Even this provision, which adopts the position of the most liberal cases, would not justify the admission of statements of fault, e.g., "I was injured by *X*, who drove his bicycle through a stop sign." Adv.Comm.Note to Fed.R.Evid. 803(4). See United States v. Iron Shell, 633 F.2d 77 (8th Cir.1980), cert. denied, 450 U.S. 1001 (1981). Cf. United States v. Narciso, 446 F.Supp. 252, 289 (E.D.Mich.1977) ("The rule [exception] is limited to facts related which are 'reasonably pertinent to diagnosis or treatment. It has never been held to apply to accusations of personal fault. . . .' ").

§ 7.12 Present State of Mind: In General

Professor McCormick reminds us of the frequency with which the "substantive law . . . makes legal rights and liabilities hinge upon the existence of a particular state of mind or feeling in a person involved in the transaction at issue."[1] The law inquires into one's mental state in both criminal and civil litigation. A crime normally is defined so as to require a particular mens rea or

9. Adv.Comm.Note to Fed.R.Evid. 803(4).

§ 7.12

1. McCormick, § 294, at 843.

state of mind; the measure of civil damages sometimes depends upon the mental suffering of the victim or the malicious intent of the defendant. The cases are replete with other instances in which mental state is an issue: the question of where one is domiciled is answered in part by ascertaining his intention; the issue of whether a will was validly executed (or whether it was revoked) may turn upon intent; the question whether one fraudulently conveyed assets is in part answered by intentions; a business tort may be defined so as to include the intention of the alleged wrongdoer. In these and other situations, the substantive law is drawn so that the existence or nonexistence of a particular state of mind itself is a pivotal element in the case.[2] In other words, mental state is often the ultimate proposition to which the evidence (whether direct or circumstantial) is addressed.

Observe, however, that state of mind, once established, also can serve as circumstantial evidence of behavior. In this situation, state of mind is not the ultimate proposition to be proven, but serves as an intermediate basis for further inferences about conduct. Suppose, for example, there is an issue in a case of whether an individual has left the United States. If it can be established (by direct or circumstantial evidence) that he intended to leave, this intention (state of mind) can be used as a basis for the further inference that he departed.[3]

The central problem of the following section is the scope and application of the exception to the hearsay rule that allows into evidence a declarant's statements of his mental condition when these statements are offered for the truth of their assertion. It should be observed, however, that some statements bearing upon mental attitudes, condition, or intent that appear to involve the present exception may be seen upon closer inspection not to require it. Close examination may show that the statement in question is not hearsay and thus needs no exception. If, for example, a declarant-testator refers to his son-in-law, *X*, as a "crooked politician" and evidence of this statement is offered in a case where the issue is whether the testator intended to include *X*

2. Extortion cases provide frequent examples. See United States v. Adcock, 558 F.2d 397 (8th Cir.1977), cert. denied, 434 U.S. 921 (1977); United States v. Taglione, 546 F.2d 194 (5th Cir.1977). For a collection of federal cases in which state of mind is an issue, see 4 Weinstein & Berger, ¶ 803(3)[03], at 112 n. 2–114 n. 12.

3. Note that even direct evidence of the actor's state of mind (e.g., his declaration "I intend to leave") is circumstantial evidence that he left. See § 2.7.

as a beneficiary under his will, the present exception need not be invoked. The proffered utterance is not offered for its truth (that is, to show that *X* is a dishonest politician), but only as circumstantial evidence of the declarant's dislike of his son-in-law. In contrast, if the testator's statement had been "I hate *X* and intend to exclude him from any share in my estate," evidence of this declaration should fall within the present exception. The trier is asked to believe that the declarant entertained the hatred and intention to foreclose *X*. In cases involving statements of mental condition, the first question to be asked is whether the intended use of the evidence requires that the trier accept as true the declaration of mental state.[4]

What elements of trustworthiness qualify a statement of mental condition as an exception to the hearsay rule? Because the declarant expresses an existing (as distinguished from a past) state of mind, there is no danger of faulty memory. Perception shoud not be a problem. The contemporaneous nature of the statement also reduces somewhat the possibility of insincerity, at least where the statement is made with apparent spontaneity.[5] Hence, in many instances, a declarant's hearsay statement describing an existing emotional or mental state carries as high a degree of reliability as does his subsequent testimonial statement describing retrospectively his mental condition.

§ 7.13 State of Mind to Prove Conduct: Use and Limitations

Selected illustrations from cases in which the substantive law makes mental state an ultimate (as opposed to an intermediate) issue have been set out in the preceding section. We have also

4. Consider in the setting of a child-custody case a statement by the child that her stepfather "killed my brother and he'll kill my mommie too." This declaration is not hearsay if offered only to show circumstantially that the declarant regarded the stepfather with fear and anxiety. Betts v. Betts, 3 Wash.App. 53, 473 P.2d 403 (1970). On the other hand, the statement, "I hate my stepfather and don't want to live with him," if offered to show the child's wishes concerning her custodian probably would be viewed as hearsay, but within the present exception. Some authorities, however, would hold that the statement had a circumstantial use to show the child's lack of affection and preferences for another guardian. The reasoning is that the use of the words, even if not accepted as true, show a lack of affinity and a probable preference for someone else as a guardian. See § 6.2, text accompanying n. 14 and thereafter.

5. If the statement appears to be a contrivance, the judge should exercise his discretion and exclude it. See Fed. R.Evid. 403. For an interesting case that calls for an analysis of the hearsay/nonhearsay distinction as well as careful consideration of the risk of insincerity, see State v. Baldwin, 47 N.J. 379, 221 A.2d 199 (1966), cert. denied, 385 U.S. 980 (1966).

seen that state of mind can be used as part of an inferential chain which, ultimately, is directed toward conduct.[1] For example, a declarant's intention to undertake a certain act increases somewhat the probability that he pursued his intention and accomplished the contemplated act. But when the evidence of an actor's state of mind consists of his own declarations, the factfinder's use of this evidence necessitates a reliance upon the truth of the declarant's statement, and the present hearsay exception must be invoked.

In the leading case of Mutual Life Ins. Co. v. Hillmon,[2] the central issue was whether a body discovered at Crooked Creek, Colorado, was that of Hillmon, the insured, or that of Walters, a companion. Part of the evidence offered by the defendant insurance company consisted of letters written by Walters to his family and fiancee in which he declared his intention to leave Wichita and journey with Hillmon to the vicinity of Crooked Creek. The United States Supreme Court held Walters's written statements admissible under the state of mind exception, since they showed his present intention to travel with Hillmon to Crooked Creek.[3] This intention was relevant because it increased somewhat the probability that Walters embarked upon his intended journey and reached his destination, thereby increasing the likelihood that the body was his.

Despite this straightforward analysis there is a latent question of relevance (and, as we shall see, an additional hearsay difficulty) in the *Hillmon* case that was not satisfactorily addressed by the court. Walters's communications indicated that he was going to accompany Hillmon to their common destination. Walters's journey to Crooked Creek appeared to have depended upon the cooperation of another (Hillmon); this contingency operates to reduce the probative force of the evidence, for if Hillmon decided not to undertake the journey, Walters probably would not have embarked for Crooked Creek.[4] However, so long as Walters's

§ 7.13

1. § 6.2 at n. 3. See Deane Buick Co. v. Kendall, 160 Colo. 265, 417 P.2d 11 (1966) (declarant's statement that he intended to return to work admitted on the issue of whether he was going to work when he sustained a fatal accident).

2. 145 U.S. 285 (1892).

3. For a detailed account of this case and its ramifications, see Maguire, The Hillmon Case—Thirty-three Years After, 38 Harv.L.Rev. 709 (1925).

4. Under the circumstances of *Hillmon*, the probability that Walters would not have gone to Crooked Creek alone or with a person other than Hillmon is increased by the fact that Walters was to be employed by Hillmon

declarations were offered to show his probable future conduct and not that of Hillmon, this contingency should affect only the weight to be given to the evidence, not its admissibility.[5] Likewise, a statement by Walters, "If the weather clears, I will go to Crooked Creek," should be admissible; the state of the weather is merely a contingency affecting probative force.

A more difficult question arises from the inferences that can be derived from the contingency that Walters was travelling with Hillmon. Suppose the question in the case were whether Hillmon had journeyed to Crooked Creek and suppose further that Walters's declarations were offered not to show his conduct, but to show that of Hillmon. To admit the portion of the declaration that Walters intended to accompany Hillmon allows the inference that Hillmon intended to accompany Walters and that, in fact, he did so.[6] This chain of proof permits a statement, admitted because of the exception for Walters's present state of mind, to show Hillmon's state of mind from which Hillmon's conduct is inferred.[7]

The rationale behind the state-of-mind exception does not support such an extension: the declarant's express or implied statement of the intent and conduct *of another person* possesses all the dangers of hearsay and none of the assurances associated with the present hearsay exception.[8] Despite this "theoretical awkwardness," [9] the language of the Supreme Court in the *Hillmon* case is broad enough to admit that portion of Walters's declaration alluding to Hillmon which carries the associated inference that Walters went with Hillmon.[10] It is to be stressed, however, that

when the latter found a satisfactory site for a sheep ranch. See Mutual Life Ins. Co. v. Hillmon, 145 U.S. 285, 288 (1892).

5. See United States v. Pheaster, 544 F.2d 353, 376 & n. 14 (9th Cir.1976), cert. denied, 429 U.S. 1099 (1977) (noting that contingencies always are present that could frustrate a person's asserted intentions).

6. See discussion id. at 377.

7. Note that the state of mind exception would allow Walters or any other competent witness to testify that *Hillmon stated his present intention* to make a certain trip. This would enlarge the probabilities that Hillmon undertook the journey.

8. Lempert & Saltzburg at 429.

9. United States v. Pheaster, n. 5 at 377.

10. Mutual Life Ins. Co. of New York v. Hillmon, 145 U.S. at 294–296: "Evidence that . . . [Walters] had the intention of leaving Wichita with Hillmon would tend . . . to show that he went from Wichita to Crooked Creek with Hillmon." Id. at 295. The court states: "The letters in question were competent . . . as evidence that, shortly before the time when other evidence tended to show that he went away, he had the intention of going, and of going with Hillmon, which made it more probable both that he did go and that he went with Hillmon. . . ." Id. at 295–96.

the issue in the *Hillmon* case was Walters's whereabouts; it was not argued that Hillmon was elsewhere than in the Crooked Creek area. Nonetheless, most courts have followed the apparent lead of the Supreme Court on this question of how much of a declaration is admissible and have permitted a declarant's statement of his present intention to undertake a course of action requiring the cooperation of another to serve as evidence that the declarant's *contemplated act was accomplished.*[11] The opponent of the evidence is entitled to a limiting instruction that directs the jury to consider the declarant's statement as evidence only of his conduct and not as evidence of the conduct of the other possible participant.[12]

This practice of limiting the use of the state-of-mind declaration may be of little efficacy where the real interest of the trier is not in the declarant's conduct, but in that of the coparticipant. In People v. Alcalde,[13] the exception for present state of mind was applied by the Supreme Court of California (over the strong dissent of Justice Traynor) in a most interesting set of circumstances. The prosecution was for murder, the accused was one Frank, and the victim was his girlfriend Bernice. In an effort to show that Bernice was with Frank on the evening of her murder, the state offered her statements to a witness that she was "going out [to dinner] with Frank tonight." A limiting instruction that the hearsay declaration could be used only as evidence of Bernice's intention was given, but it is arguable that the evidence should have been rejected. Neither Bernice's whereabouts at the time of her death, nor her identity as the victim was a point of dispute at trial. What was in dispute was whether Frank was with Bernice. Hence, the evidence was of little probative worth for its limited purpose of showing that the declarant went out to dinner, but was highly probative (or so the trier may have thought) to show that Frank was the declarant's companion. Note also that in the *Hillmon* case, although Walters declared his intention to travel to Crooked Creek with Hillmon, Walters's intention to go to Crooked Creek might have been fulfilled even if Hillmon had decided not to

11. Lempert & Saltzburg at 429:

"Most courts follow the Supreme Court . . . and allow a statement of an intention to engage in some action with another to support the inference that that action was done with the other and, since the two are not separable, to support the inference that the other did the action with the declarant."

12. McCormick, § 295, at 849. But see supra note 11.

13. 24 Cal.2d 177, 148 P.2d 627 (1944).

make the journey.[14] But in *Alcalde,* Bernice could not "go out *with Frank*" unless the latter consented to participate in this social engagement. The primary value of the evidence was not to show that she went out, but that Frank was her escort.

Despite the foregoing analysis, the result in *Alcalde* may be defensible. There was evidence in the record that Bernice dressed for dinner and that she left her apartment. One witness testified that she thought she saw Bernice leave in a car with a male. Would she have gone out with an escort other than Frank or, assuming the witness was mistaken, would she have gone out alone? Of course, these possibilities exist. It is significant, however, that she asserted an intention to pursue a course of conduct (go out to dinner) with a particular person (Frank) and there was some confirming evidence that the conduct was undertaken. In these circumstances, where there is evidence of a declarant's intention and additional evidence that she undertook the predicted course of conduct, the probability that the other individual participated is increased. The declarant's intention to go out with Frank is fulfilled only if he is her escort, and evidence showing that she went out (or further evidence showing that she went out with a male) serves to confirm the realization of her intention.[15] Likewise, were there independent evidence that the other alleged participant took steps to implement the contemplated joint activity (such as dressing to go out and thereafter driving in the direction of his purported companion's apartment), the dangers associated with the declarant's statement of intention would be lessened.

Under this suggested approach, the admissibility of a declarant's statement that he will undertake a course of conduct with *X*, when offered as evidence tending to show that the conduct was accomplished, depends upon (1) independent evidence that the declarant or *X* undertook the activity and (2) the likelihood that the declarant would not have undertaken it unless *X* participated (i.e., the degree of cooperation required of *X*). Hearsay dangers still exist: for example the declarant may have had a defective memory concerning the prior arrangement with *X*, or the declar-

14. In Walters's letters, he expressed a keen interest in seeing the part of the country to which he intended to travel. See Mutual Life Ins. Co. v. Hillmon, 145 U.S. 285, 288–89 (1892). But see supra n. 4.

15. A careful analysis of *Alcalde* appears in Lempert & Saltzburg at 429–30.

ant may have lied. But in the circumstances of a particular case, corroborating evidence may lessen the dangers enough to justify the admission of a declaration of the kind encountered in *Alcalde,* even in the face of a very real danger that the trier will use the declaration as evidence of *X*'s conduct.[16]

In a federal prosecution for a kidnapping conspiracy, the United States Court of Appeals for the 9th Circuit approved the trial judge's admission of the victim's statement that he intended to meet Angelo, the accused, in a nearby parking lot, obtain some marijuana, and then return.[17] Although there was no independent evidence that Angelo had travelled to the purported meeting place, there was undisputed evidence that the victim had left his companions with the avowed purpose of going to the parking lot to rendezvous with the accused. The victim was not heard from thereafter.

The admission into evidence of the victim's declaration of intention, including the name of the accused, makes it highly probable that the jury used the statement as evidence that Angelo was the individual whom the victim encountered after leaving his companions. The act of meeting Angelo required his cooperation, since the meeting place was a parking lot to which Angelo presumably would have to travel. All hearsay dangers are present. Against these persuasive reasons for rejection, it is necessary to weigh the corroborating evidence that the victim took the initial steps to accomplish the joint action. Undoubtedly, there was a pressing need for the evidence, but that need was to connect Angelo with the offense and not to show that the victim was to meet some unidentified person in the parking lot. Thus, the real utility of the evidence falls outside of its permissible limited use (to show only the victim's action). If admissibility is to be justified on the basis of the need to connect Angelo with the kidnapping,

16. See United States v. Cicale, 691 F.2d 95 (2d Cir.1982), cert. denied, 460 U.S. 1082 (1983) (use of declarant's statements of his own intentions admissible to prove act of third person when there exists independent, non-hearsay evidence of acts of third person).

17. United States v. Pheaster, 544 F.2d 353, 374–80 (9th Cir.1976), cert. denied, 429 U.S. 1099 (1977). The trial preceded the effective date of the Federal Rules of Evidence and both the trial and appellate courts applied Rule 26 of the Federal Rules of Criminal Procedure (The "admissibility of evidence" shall be governed by "the principles of common law as they may be interpreted by the courts of the United States in the light of reason and experience."). However, the Court of Appeals noted that under one interpretation of Federal Rule of Evidence 803(3), its decision would be the same even if the case had been tried after the effective date of the Rules. Id. at 379–80. See infra n. 18 and accompanying text.

the limiting charge instructing the jury to consider the victim's declaration only with regard to the victim's conduct not only belies the real purpose of the evidence, but also asks of the jury a discrimination at odds with common sense.

We see, then, that one line that may mark the boundaries of the present exception lies between a declarant's statements of present intention regarding his future conduct and his statements asserting the future conduct of another. This distinction is consistent with the language of Federal Rule 803(3). It is noteworthy that the House Judiciary Committee, which reviewed this rule, commented that it "intended that the Rule be construed to limit the doctrine of . . . Hillmon . . ., so as to render statements of intent by a declarant admissible only to prove his future conduct, not the future conduct of another person." [18] It remains to be seen whether the courts will take seriously the Committee's intention by denying admissibility or whether they will give it only the perfunctory attention of a limiting instruction.

Another major restriction on the use of the state-of-mind exception is illustrated by the leading case Shepard v. United States.[19] In *Shepard*, the United States Supreme Court again turned[20] its attention to declarations of mental state offered as circumstantial proof of conduct. Dr. Shepard was prosecuted for the murder of his wife. The indictment charged that death had been effected by means of poison. There was evidence that shortly before dying, Mrs. Shepard summoned her nurse and asked to examine the contents of a whiskey bottle. Stating that this was the liquor she drank just before collapsing, she inquired whether there was enough remaining in the bottle to permit a test for the presence of poison. She then remarked that the taste and smell were unusual and stated, "Dr. Shepard has poisoned me."

At the trial level, Mrs. Shepard's statements were admitted under the hearsay exception for dying declarations;[21] on appeal it was held that the prosecutor had failed to show all the necessary

18. H.R.Rep. No. 93–650, 93d Cong., 2d Sess. 13–14, reprinted in 1974 U.S. Code Cong. & Admin.News 7075, 7087. In United States v. Pheaster, the court notes that this quoted sentence reflects a cutback in the prevailing common law. It also notes that this restrictive interpretation apparently is contrary to the Advisory Committee's intent to incorporate the *Hillmon* doctrine in full. 544 F.2d at 379–80 (1976).

19. 290 U.S. 96 (1933).

20. Mutual Life Ins. Co. v. Hillmon, discussed supra at n. 2, was decided in 1892. The *Shepard* case was decided four decades later.

21. See Part I.

elements of the exception.[22] There remained, however, an additional appellate question: could the trial court's admission of the statements be sustained on other grounds? The government made two principal arguments that they could be: first, since they had probative value to rebut a defense contention that Mrs. Shepard may have committed suicide, they were not hearsay, and second, even if they were hearsay, they came within the state-of-mind exception to the hearsay rule.

There was testimony in the record that Mrs. Shepard had remarked at various times that she had no further will to live and that she might take her own life. Since these statements showed a depressed state of mind (a mental condition consistent with the defense theory of suicide), the government argued that Mrs. Shepard's statements, reflecting apprehension that she might have been poisoned, could be received for the limited purpose of rebutting the suicide defense. So used, no hearsay problem was involved because the declarations were entered, not for their truth, but as circumstantial evidence bearing on Mrs. Shepard's will to live. Alternatively, the government argued that even if the statements were hearsay their admissibility was sustainable under the state-of-mind exception because they reflected Mrs. Shepard's mental state.

The Court, in an opinion by Justice Cardozo, addressed and rejected each of the government's arguments. He also made a general point, applicable to the case before him because the government was trying to uphold the trial judge's admission of the contested statements on theories of limited admissibility that were not advanced at trial. Since the declarations in question were clearly treated by the trial judge as coming within the hearsay exception for dying declarations, it would be prejudicial to the defendant if, subsequently on appeal, admissibility were placed upon a different, restricted ground. If the different ground had been identified at trial, the accused could have objected to it. Further, even if the evidence had been admitted over his objection, he could have obtained a limiting instruction cautioning the jury that the declarations could only be considered for the narrow purpose for which they were offered.

Nonetheless, the Court went on to consider each of the government's alternative grounds of admission. It found unconvincing

22. There was not sufficient evidence demonstrating that the declarant had a sense of impending death. 290 U.S. at 99–100 (1933); see Part I, § 7.25.

the argument that Mrs. Shepard's statements could have been properly received by the trial judge for the limited, nonhearsay purpose of showing her will to live. In fact, said Cardozo, the declarations showed little about the victim's will to live, but were forceful, accusatory statements against the defendant. The jury would not have been capable of restricting its consideration to whatever light they cast upon the absence of a suicidal state of mind. Further, even if one were to concede that Mrs. Shepard's declarations might be offered for the nonhearsay purpose of showing circumstantially that she had the will to live, their modest probative value for this purpose was overcome by their potential for prejudice.

The next question was whether Mrs. Shepard's statements might properly be received under the state-of-mind exception to the hearsay rule. Observing that the principal probative force of the statements was directed toward past acts allegedly committed by another person, Cardozo emphasized the limits of the *Hillmon* doctrine:

> Declarations of intention, casting light upon the future, have been sharply distinguished from declarations of memory, pointing backwards to the past. There would be an end, or nearly that, to the rule against hearsay if the distinction were ignored.
>
> The testimony now questioned faced backward and not forward. This it did in at least its most obvious implications. What is even more important, it spoke to a past act, and more than that, to an act by some one not the speaker.[23]

This passage summarizes the major restrictions upon the use of the state-of-mind exception. Generally, the exception does not include statements of memory or belief about past actions or events,[24] nor does it usually include declarations offered to prove the actions of a person other than the declarant. Note also Justice Cardozo's concern that the hearsay rule would be weakened severely should "backward looking" declarations be viewed as within the exception for state of mind. A declarant's statement of past conduct ("I was in Chicago last January 15th"), involves

23. 290 U.S. at 105–06.

24. Occasionally a declaration looking toward future conduct is coupled with a related past event of recent origin ("*X* just called and demanded money and I intend to deliver it this afternoon."). There is authority for admitting the statement in its entirety. United States v. Annunziato, 293 F.2d 373 (2d Cir.1961), cert. denied, 368 U.S. 919 (1961). But see United States v. Mandel, 437 F.Supp. 262 (D.Md.1977).

the hearsay risk of a defective memory, a danger not involved with a declaration of intended conduct ("I intend to go to Chicago in January"). It also is possible—although no data exist—that the problem of doubtful veracity (sincerity) might be more severe where past conduct is concerned. Arguably, statements about past conduct, uttered in the light of subsequent events, might, on the whole, carry a greater risk of insincerity than statements of mere intention concerning future conduct.

Suppose the state-of-mind exception were broadened generally to include statements not only of the declarant's past conduct but also of "external" events, including the observed actions of others. *Every* relevant declaration about a past event then would be admissible under the theory that the declaration evinced a belief or memory about the event, and that this belief or memory constituted, in the broadest sense, a state of mind. It is apparent that statements of such "remembered" past events usually would present all the hearsay risks: faulty perception, defects in memory, insincerity, and mistransmission.[25] Thus, by the circuitous approach of enlarging the state-of-mind exception, the hearsay rule would be largely negated.

There is one area where the exception for mental state has been broadened so as to include at least statements of the *declarant's own past* conduct. Moved, perhaps, by a recognition of special need, the courts increasingly have been receptive to declarations by a deceased person concerning his estate or will.[26] The Federal Rules of Evidence acknowledge this trend and Rule 803(3) permits the admission of "a statement of memory or belief to prove the fact remembered or believed [if the statement] relates to the execution, revocation, identification, or terms of declarant's will."[27] It is likely, of course, that the declarant-testator knew the most about his will (that is, whether it had been executed, modified, or revoked). Often this knowledge, coupled with the unavailability of the declarant, creates a special need for evidence of his declarations. These considerations combine to persuade a majority of courts to admit even "backward looking" declarations in these limited circumstances. Nonetheless, the hearsay risks all are present. Perhaps the innovation for wills points toward a broader

25. See § 6.1.

26. McCormick, § 296, at 853.

27. The drafters observed that this exception rested "on practical grounds of necessity and expediency rather than logic." Adv.Comm.Note to Fed.R.Evid. 803(3).

recognition that in circumstances characterized by need and substantial probative value, the hearsay rule should yield. It should not be overlooked that the hearsay risks relating to perception, memory, sincerity and mistransmission are pertinent in deciding questions of evidentiary weight. Hence, the presence of dangers that account for the hearsay rule need not always result in exclusion, but can be considered in the trier's evaluative process.

Notes

1. The general limitation restricting the exception for mental condition to statements of existing state of mind does not, of course, prohibit the trier from reasonably inferring that the declared state of mind existed on another occasion. Suppose that on August 15 the declarant states that he is depressed. If the issue were whether the declarant committed suicide on August 20th, the proponent of the declaration would urge the trier to infer that the state of mind persisted (or that it returned) on August 20th. The only issue to be resolved by the trial judge in making his evidentiary ruling would be one of relevance.

2. There is some case support for the application of the mental state exception to statements of recently perceived events when these statements are coupled with a declaration that looks toward the future. A case in point is United States v. Annunziato, 293 F.2d 373 (2d Cir.1961), cert. denied, 368 U.S. 919 (1961), where the admitted declaration, backward looking at least in part, alluded to a recent phone call from *X* and an intention to respond to it by sending *X* some money. See McCormick, § 295, at 847; supra n. 24.

3. Suppose in the course of litigation the sanity of the declarant develops as an issue. Evidence is offered that the declarant frequently states that he is Fidel Castro. Under one view, this declaration is not hearsay because the proponent is not offering it for its truth; under another analysis, the statement is hearsay because it is the equivalent of the declaration "I think that I am Fidel Castro." Even under the latter approach, the statement is admissible because it constitutes a declaration of presently existing mental state. Of course, the trier may assess the danger of insincerity in deciding what weight to accord this evidence.

PART D. RECORDED RECOLLECTION

§ 7.14 In General

The exception now before us, past recorded recollection, should be considered in conjunction with the principles that govern refreshing a witness's present recollection. These principles, which are treated in more detail elsewhere,[1] may be summarized as follows: when a witness is unable to remember, interrogating counsel may attempt to revive the witness's memory by producing a writing (or some other item) intended to induce recollection. If the interrogator succeeds in restoring the witness's memory so that the latter can testify from present recollection, the only evidence received by the court is the witness's testimony, not the writing. The writing serves the limited purpose of aiding memory; consequently, the counsel who used the writing for this narrow purpose has no right to introduce it into evidence. Under these circumstances, which are usually designated "present recollection refreshed," there is no hearsay difficulty because no "off-the-stand" assertion is offered for its truth. The witness testifies from present (revived) recollection just as if he had not suffered a temporary memory lapse.

A different situation is encountered when the witness's memory cannot be revived satisfactorily and an earlier writing, authored or previously verified by the witness, if offered *in lieu of* his present testimony. If the proponent introduces the writing for a purpose which requires the trier to accept the truth of the assertions it contains, the writing is hearsay: the cross-examiner neither can cross-examine the writing, nor can he interrogate the witness about the details of the events described in it, since the witness is unable to recall these. Under these circumstances, admissibility must rest upon the use of some exception to the hearsay rule.[2] If the witness can provide a foundation which attests to the accuracy of the writing by reason of its timely and accurate preparation, the present exception for recorded recollection will suffice.

§ 7.15 Recorded Recollection: Rationale and Application

Although a forgetful witness may be unable to recall the event or condition described in an earlier writing, he may be able to testify that he prepared the writing (or at least verified its accuracy) when the event was fresh in his memory. If he also can affirm that the writing is accurate—either because he recalls making an accurate recordation or because it was his habitual

§ 7.14

1. See § 4.7.

2. United States v. Edwards, 539 F.2d 689 (9th Cir.1976), cert. denied, 429 U.S. 984 (1976); see Maguire and Quick, Testimony: Memory and Memoranda, 3 How.L.J. 1, 9 (1957).

practice to make correct notes—then the present exception applies.[1] The requirements for recorded recollection (timely preparation and an affirmation of accuracy) reduce the hearsay risks of insincerity and faulty memory.[2] Since the witness must testify in the presence of the trier (and subject to cross-examination) that the writing is accurate, there is some assurance of sincerity.[3] The further requirement that he testify that the writing was made at a time when he had a strong recollection of the event or condition in question minimizes the danger of a defective memory.

Federal Rule 803(5) describes the exception for recorded past recollection:

> *Recorded Recollection.* A memorandum or record concerning a matter about which a witness once had knowledge but now has insufficient recollection to enable him to testify fully and accurately, shown to have been made or adopted by the witness when the matter was fresh in his memory and to reflect that knowledge correctly. If admitted, the memorandum or record may be read into evidence but may not itself be received as an exhibit unless offered by an adverse party.

This statement of the exception generally is in accord with the case law.[4] Usually, the witness will have himself written the

§ 7.15

1. Walker v. Larson, 284 Minn. 99, 169 N.W.2d 737 (1969); State v. Bradley, 361 Mo. 267, 275, 234 S.W.2d 556, 560 (1950) (dictum); Annot. 82 A.L.R.2d 473, 525–31. Often, a notary, stenographer, or bookkeeper can testify to a habit of making correct entries. For a case which considers at length the requirements of a proper foundation, see Hodas v. Davis, 203 App.Div. 297, 196 N.Y.S. 801 (1922). The *Hodas* decision is criticized in Walker v. Larson, supra, 169 N.W.2d at 742–43. For an illustrative case, see Newton v. Higdon, 226 Ga. 649, 177 S.E.2d 57 (1970) (lawyer testifies to his practice respecting the witnessing of wills).

2. The risk of mistranscription also is reduced, since the witness probably can correctly interpret his earlier language.

3. Some cases require exclusion where a witness makes only an indirect assertion of the accuracy of the writing in question, at least if other circumstances call the accuracy into question. For example, the witness says, "I would not sign an untrue statement." See, e.g., United States v. Schwartz, 390 F.2d 1 (3d Cir.1968) (any guarantees of trustworthiness greatly outweighed by circumstances that statement made almost seven years after events and under threat of imminent sentencing for a prior conviction). The danger of insincerity is further reduced when the writing was made prior to the existence of any motive to falsify.

4. See United States v. Kelly, 349 F.2d 720 (2d Cir.1965), cert. denied, 384 U.S. 947 (1966); Jordan v. People, 151 Colo. 133, 376 P.2d 699 (1962), cert. denied, 373 U.S. 944 (1963); Annot., 82 A.L.R.2d 473 (1962). For a case construing Fed.R.Evid. 803(5) and upholding its validity against a Sixth Amendment claim of a denial of the right to confront an adverse witness, see United

memorandum or record that is offered as recorded recollection, but 803(5) expressly takes account of the case in which the witness was not the author. It is enough that the witness adopted the writing which, in this context, means that he examined the writing and affirmed its correctness at a time when memory was fresh.

There is no particular time after the event during which the recording must be made (or if made by another, its accuracy affirmed), but there should be proof that recollection was clear when the writing was made or verified.

Note that under the Federal Rule, applicability of the exception hinges upon a finding that the witness "now has insufficient recollection to enable him to testify fully and accurately . . . ." There still is disagreement among some state jurisdictions as to whether impaired memory is essential to the applicability of the present exception and, if so, whether there must be a complete inability to remember the pertinent event before the prior writing may be introduced. A minority of courts take the view that because the memorandum was prepared soon after the event which it describes, it is more reliable than subsequent courtroom testimony. Hence, it is admissible (if the other requisites of the exception are met) without regard to the present ability of the witness to remember the event.[5] Most courts, however, require a substantial or total loss of memory before the exception for recorded recollection is available.[6] In these courts there is concern that dispensing with the requirement of impaired memory would lead to the increased use of statements prepared for litigation and often drafted or influenced by interested parties, claims adjusters, or attorneys.[7] The requirement embodied in the Federal Rule (inability to "testify fully and accurately") strikes a sensible balance and is emerging as the dominant formulation.

The last sentence of the Federal Rule prohibits the proponent from treating the recorded recollection as an exhibit. The practi-

States v. Marshall, 532 F.2d 1279 (9th Cir.1976).

5. E.g., State v. Sutton, 253 Or. 24, 450 P.2d 748 (1969).

6. E.g., Baker v. Elcona Homes Corp., 588 F.2d 551 (6th Cir.1978), cert. denied, 441 U.S. 933 (1979) (police officer's memory sufficient, so accident report inadmissible under Rule 803(5); however report admissible as public record under 803(3)); Noumoff v. Rotkvich, 88 Ill.App.2d 116, 232 N.E.2d 107 (1967) (proponent of admission of a document under past recollection recorded exception must show (1) witness has no independent recollection of facts, and (2) witness is unable to refresh his recollection by reviewing the document).

7. McCormick, § 302, at 867.

cal effect of this prohibition is to prevent the jury from examining the writing and from carrying it to the jury room, unless, of course, the adverse party enters the writing as an exhibit. The position expressed in the rules has some case support, although the authorities are divided.[8] The rationale for prohibiting jury inspection, and thus treating the memorandum differently from other items of documentary evidence, apparently lies in the notion that the memorandum is a substitute for present testimony; consequently, the reasoning goes, the jury should have no greater exposure to the evidence than it has to other testimonial proof. This approach avoids the risk, if indeed there is one, that extensive jury use and inspection of the writing will lead the jury to exaggerate its probative force.

Note

An interesting problem of proof by means of recorded recollection arises when an observer reports facts to another, who records them. It then becomes important that the proponent produce both participants—the first to affirm that his oral transmission, rendered when his memory was fresh, correctly portrayed the facts observed, and the second to affirm that he faithfully recorded the verbal statements. See United States v. Williams, 571 F.2d 344 (6th Cir.1978), cert. denied, 439 U.S. 841 (1978) (witness's statement admitted where recorded by government agent and subscribed by witness.) Primeaux v. Kinney, 256 So.2d 140 (La.App.1971).

PART E. RECORDS OF BUSINESS AND RELATED ENTERPRISES

§ 7.16 In General

Every jurisdiction has created a hearsay exception permitting admission of the records of business concerns and related enterprises such as hospitals, educational institutions, and governmental departments.[1] The principal characteristic of a "business" is its engagement in regular, systematic activity. The overwhelming majority of jurisdictions provide for the so-called "business entry" exception by either statute or rule of court; a few states have

8. Compare State v. Folkes, 174 Or. 568, 150 P.2d 17 (1944), cert. denied, 323 U.S. 779 (1944) with Curtis v. Bradley, 65 Conn. 99, 31 A. 591 (1894).

§ 7.16

1. As to departments and agencies of the federal government, see Part F.

fashioned this exception through the common-law decisional process.[2]

Underlying the exception for business records is the recognition that business entities rely heavily upon regularly kept records and, consequently, that there is an organizational motivation to be thorough and accurate. While it may be true, as we shall see shortly, that some business entries are cast in self-serving terms, most entries are attended by circumstances that encourage accuracy. The general practice of reliable and prompt record-keeping reduces the hearsay dangers and justifies the admission of business records for the truth of their assertions. The exception for business records also is a practical necessity in the modern business environment because a "business transaction" often involves a number of participants, each of whom has personal knowledge of only a portion of the transaction. Thus, the central records of a department store chain may show that certain goods were shipped from warehouse inventory, received by a branch store, stocked, and then sold. Yet the shipping clerk can testify only that he placed the goods on a delivery truck, the driver only that he delivered certain packages to the branch store, the stock clerk only that the goods were shelved, and the sales clerk only that all of the goods were sold. Likewise, different individuals may participate in installing a telephone, repairing it, assigning the number, billing the user, and so forth. It would be highly burdensome to call as witnesses all participants in these segmented transactions. An attractive alternative is to present the composite business record, supported or sponsored by a custodian or other qualified person who can state (1) that the proffered record systematically was made in the course of regularly conducted business activity, and (2) that the information entered came from an individual with personal knowledge.

2. For example, Virginia judicially recognized the exception. See "Automatic" Sprinkler Corp. v. Coley & Petersen, Inc., 219 Va. 781, 250 S.E.2d 765 (1979).

The rule first developed at common law was called the "shopbook rule." It may be traced to the English practice of allowing a merchant to prove an account receivable upon which he brought suit. The shopbook rule was necessitated, both in England and America, by the rule of incompetence that disqualified parties from testifying. § 4.2. Admission of the merchant's books of account supplied the proof necessary to establish the debt claimed. Even though the merchant did not, technically at least, testify, he had to comply with elaborate procedures, such as taking a special ("suppletory") oath and opening his books to judicial inspection, designed to ensure the validity of his claim. For a concise, careful description of the common law and statutory development of the business entry exception, see Lempert & Saltzburg at 439–42.

§ 7.17 Records of Business and Related Enterprises: Illustrations and Refinements

Federal Rule 803(6) is illustrative of the statutory (or rule-of-court) provisions that govern the admissibility of business entries and related records. Under the Rule, an exception is made for:

> *Records of regularly conducted activity.* A memorandum, report, record, or data compilation, in any form, of acts, events, conditions, opinions, or diagnoses, made at or near the time by, or from information transmitted by, a person with knowledge, if kept in the course of a regularly conducted business activity, and if it was the regular practice of that business activity to make the memorandum, report, record, or data compilation, all as shown by the testimony of the custodian or other qualified witness, unless the source of information or the method or circumstances of preparation indicate lack of trustworthiness. The term "business" as used in this paragraph includes business, institution, association, profession, occupation, and calling of every kind, whether or not conducted for profit.

The Rule and its various counterparts in state jurisdictions contemplate that the person(s) who provides the basic information for the entry will have personal knowledge of the act or event that is recorded. There is no requirement, however, that this person be called to testify;[1] it suffices that the custodian or other qualified witness states that it is the business practice to base the entry upon data supplied by one with personal knowledge.[2] It is essential under the Federal Rule and its state counterparts that the report was made in the regular course of business, that it was the regular practice to make the kind of entry in question (thus ensuring that entries were not made simply for litigation purposes), and that the entry was made "at or near the time" of the condition or event described in the entry. The exception contem-

§ 7.17

1. United States v. Page, 544 F.2d 982 (8th Cir.1976).

2. 4 Weinstein & Berger, ¶ 803(6)[02], at 177–78. See United States v. Young Bros., Inc., 728 F.2d 682 (5th Cir.1984), cert. denied, 469 U.S. 881 (1984) (custodian of computer-generated records testifies to their authenticity, although he did not prepare them himself); United States v. Carranco, 551 F.2d 1197 (10th Cir.1977) (business manager provides necessary foundation and establishes that it is regular practice of company to make changes and additions on freight bill). Compare Zenith Radio Corp. v. Matsushita Elec. Industrial Co., 505 F.Supp. 1190, 1236 (E.D. Pa.1980) (testimony of custodian not necessary but proponent must make strong showing of regularity of records by other means).

plates that both the informer, who supplies the information from personal knowledge, and the entrant-recorder, who makes the written entry, act in the course of regular business duty.

On some occasions, of course, the informer and entrant will be the same person, as where an office manager routinely observes which of his employees are on duty and records their presence. Frequently, however, the informer will be different from the entrant, as where the doctor states that the patient has a broken wrist and the nurse records this information in the appropriate medical file.

A problem arises when either the informer or the entrant is not acting under a business duty. In the leading case of Johnson v. Lutz [3] several bystanders reported to a policeman certain observations about a traffic accident. The policeman recorded these statements in his police report, which later was offered into evidence for the purpose of proving the truth of the recorded facts. The Court of Appeals of New York ruled against admitting the report. Its holding was based principally on the view that the state statute governing business entries never was intended to support the admissibility of statements volunteered by observers not acting in the course of business. This construction of the statute is consistent with the rationale of the business entries exception, for it draws upon the reliability which presumably attends the dutiful conduct of those engaged in business. It can be argued that the entrant's business-motivated *recording* of information gratuitously supplied by an informer should satisfy the statute in cases where persons within the business organization would rely on the information. The courts, however, generally have adhered to the *Johnson* requirement and insisted upon the additional reliability present when all participants in the making of the record are acting under a business duty.[4] Although the language of the Federal Rule is somewhat ambiguous, it has

3. 253 N.Y. 124, 170 N.E. 517 (1930). For a criticism of this decision, see V Wigmore, § 1561b, at 507.

4. See, e.g., Turner v. Spaide, 108 A.D.2d 1025, 485 N.Y.S.2d 593 (1985), app. denied, 66 N.Y.2d 601, 496 N.Y.S.2d 1025 (1985), rearg. denied, 66 N.Y.2d 1036, 489 N.E.2d 1304 (1985); Irwin v. Town of Ware, 392 Mass. 745, 467 N.E.2d 1292 (1984); Hewitt v. Grand Trunk Western R. Co., 123 Mich. App. 309, 333 N.W.2d 264 (1983); Annot., 69 A.L.R.2d 1148 (1972); McCormick, § 310, at 879. The essential element is that the participants in the making of the business record act under a business duty. The involvement of separate business entries in the creation, use, or storage of a particular record does not defeat admissibility. See United States v. Pfeiffer, 539 F.2d 668 (8th Cir.1976).

likewise been construed to require that both the informer and the entrant-recorder act in the regular course of business.[5] This judicial requirement confirms that the court—not the business community—remains the primary arbiter of admissibility.

It should be noted that in those instances in which only one participant in the recordation is acting under a business duty, admissibility still can be gained if the statement of the non-business participant is not hearsay or qualifies under another hearsay exception.[6] For example, where the communication of the non-business declarant qualifies as a recent sense perception, excited utterance, or a party admission, the applicable exception *can be linked* with the business entry exception to render the entry admissible. Suppose, for example, a bystander excitedly reported to a policeman certain facts about a startling event and the latter (acting under a business duty) recorded the bystander's statement. The linking principle would be operative: the business-entry exception is used (in lieu of the entrant-policeman's testimony) to prove the statement was made; the excited-utterance exception is invoked to permit the trier to accept the bystander's statement for its truth. Of course, when one policeman—the informer—reports to another policeman—the entrant—there is no need to rely upon the principle of linking, since the exception for business entries is applicable both to the declaration and its recordation.[7]

Finally, note that when an entry fails to qualify under the business entry exception or any other, it may still be used to refresh a witness's recollection.[8] Of course, if the witness's recollection cannot be revived and no exception (such as past recollec-

5. See United States v. Baker, 693 F.2d 183 (D.C.Cir.1982); City of Cleveland v. Cleveland Electric Illuminating Co., 538 F.Supp. 1257 (N.D.Ohio 1980); United States v. Yates, 553 F.2d 518 (6th Cir.1977); 4 Weinstein & Berger, ¶ 803(6)[04], at 185–86; Saltzburg & Redden at 831–32.

6. Wright v. Farmers Co-op of Arkansas and Oklahoma, 681 F.2d 549 (8th Cir.1982) (business entry coupled with party admission); State v. Palozie, 165 Conn. 288, 334 A.2d 468 (1975); Kelly v. Wasserman, 5 N.Y.2d 425, 185 N.Y.S.2d 538, 158 N.E.2d 241 (1959). See United States v. Smith, 521 F.2d 957 (D.C.Cir.1975) (business entry may be used to show statement was made by one not under business duty; since statement not offered for its truth, but only to show inconsistency, no linking hearsay exception necessary). In United States v. Vacca, 431 F.Supp. 807 (E.D.Pa.1977), aff'd, 571 F.2d 573 (3d Cir.1978), the court overlooked the double hearsay problem arising when the informer is not acting under a business duty.

7. For a discussion of the admissibility of police reports under Fed.R.Evid. 803 and its statutory predecessor, see Annot., 31 A.L.R.Fed. 457 (1976).

8. See § 4.7.

tion recorded [9]) can be successfully invoked, the entry is blocked by the hearsay rule.[10]

Several restrictive interpretations of business-entry provisions call for cautious evidentiary planning. In Palmer v. Hoffman [11] the United States Supreme Court held inadmissible an accident report prepared and offered at trial by a defendant railroad because the entries were made primarily for purposes of litigation and not for the systematic conduct of the railroad's business. In the deceptively simple analysis of Justice Douglas, the record was not made " 'in the regular course' of business [railroading] within the meaning of the [then controlling federal] Act." [12] This approach would render inadmissible a variety of documents prepared in the regular course of activity, but in light of possible litigation.

The *Palmer* holding has not been construed broadly,[13] perhaps because of a realization that accident reports and other documents that may pertain to a potentially litigated event are prepared for a variety of reasons, including assessing present and projected financial losses, determining cause, undertaking the least costly remedial measures, and so forth. However, in circumstances suggesting a strong self-serving motivation, the *Palmer* result will obtain and the proffered business record will be rejected.[14] Nevertheless, in most of the modern cases, the *Palmer* rationale—that an entry made in anticipation of litigation is not in the course of business—has not applied, at least when there were both business and litigious motives to make the entry.[15] The tendency in recent decisions has been to recognize that many accident-related entries are in fact made in the course of business, yet self-serving motives

9. See Part D.

10. But see State v. Sharpe, 195 Conn. 651, 491 A.2d 345 (1985) (statement volunteered to police officer admissible when evidence is necessary and statement accompanied by guarantees of trustworthiness). See also Fed. R.Evid. 803(24), 804(5).

11. 318 U.S. 109 (1943), reh. denied, 318 U.S. 800 (1943).

12. Id. at 111.

13. See Pekelis v. Transcontinental & W. Air Inc., 187 F.2d 122 (2d Cir. 1951), cert. denied, 341 U.S. 951 (1951) and cases therein cited.

14. In Yates v. Bair Transport, Inc., 249 F.Supp. 681 (S.D.N.Y.1965) the court rejected medical reports prepared for purposes of litigation by doctors of the plaintiff's choice, but admitted physician's reports prepared at the request of the defendant. All of the reports were proffered by the plaintiff. See also Korte v. New York, N.H. & H.R. Co., 191 F.2d 86 (2d Cir.1951), cert. denied, 342 U.S. 868 (1951). See Hartzog v. United States, 217 F.2d 706 (4th Cir. 1954) (prosecution for tax evasion; error to admit deputy collector's worksheets prepared for case).

15. E.g., Bracey v. Herringa, 446 F.2d 702 (7th Cir.1972).

for the entries might nonetheless render them sufficiently suspect to justify their exclusion. Federal Rule 803(6) expressly provides for this result by directing that the exception for business entries will not be used to admit entries when "the source of information or the method or circumstances of preparation indicate lack of trustworthiness." [16] Generally, however, this provision should be invoked sparingly because the trier usually can identify the temptation to be self-serving and discount the weight of the evidence accordingly.

Two other problems attend the business entry exception. Some courts still engage in the restrictive practice of rejecting entries of medical diagnoses found by the judge, presumably aided by medical testimony, to be conjectural.[17] Other courts, expressing a similar concern about trustworthiness, purport to exclude from the present exception diagnostic "opinions," [18] thus confining the admissible evidence to medical findings that can be confirmed objectively either by sight or by standard testing procedures. These rather arbitrary rejections of medical evidence are, generally speaking, cast aside in Federal Rule 803(6), which expressly provides for the admission into evidence of "opinions, or diagnoses." [19] Of course, as noted above, the Rule also provides for the exclusion of any business record which, because of the source of its contents or the circumstances of its preparation, is deemed untrustworthy.

Some entries, especially those which give a prognosis in cases in which the medical condition is unusual, ought to be closely scrutinized by the trial judge. He often will be aided in his decision about admissibility by the testimony of a properly trained expert. Sometimes, of course, the materials of discovery will apprise the judge that considerable uncertainty surrounds the medical condition in question.

A second difficulty with the present exception is encountered when a medical record contains assertions as to the immediate

16. This provision was invoked, for example, in Lloyd v. Professional Realty Services, Inc., 734 F.2d 1428 (11th Cir.1984), cert. denied, 469 U.S. 1159 (1985), to reject corporate board minutes that, although prepared in the regular course of business, were submitted in a heavily marked draft version.

17. Loper v. Andrews, 404 S.W.2d 300 (Tex.Civ.App.1966).

18. See, e.g., Thomas v. Fred Weber Contractor, Inc., 498 S.W.2d 811 (Mo. App.1973); Jackson v. Cherokee Drug Co., 434 S.W.2d 257 (Mo.App.1968).

19. See Myers v. Genis, 235 Pa. Super. 531, 344 A.2d 691 (1975) (citing Fed.R.Evid. 803(6)).

cause of the patient's injury or assertions about fault. Although the cause of the injury (that is, whether it came from a fall, a collision, etc.) usually is pertinent to a medical determination regarding proper treatment, statements about fault ("*D* was speeding and hit patient") generally are viewed as outside the entrant's business duty to record.[20] Even when the recorded statement concerns only the immediate cause (as distinguished from fault) of the patient's condition, it usually is necessary to link the business entry with another hearsay exception in order to gain admissibility. Typically, the statement explaining the cause comes from the patient or some other person not under a business duty to speak. Consequently, even though the entrant may be under a business duty to record matters pertaining to immediate cause (and hence germane to treatment) it still is required that another exception be invoked to cover the patient's or other non-business speaker's statement.[21] Special consideration should be given to the possibility of linking the business entry exception with that for party admissions, excited utterances, or statements of physical condition made to medical personnel. When the linking principle applies, the medical record shows that the statement in question was made; the other applicable exception permits the statement to be used for its truth.

Notes

1. If a regularly-kept entry is admissible to show certain facts or events, the absence of an entry (that normally would be made if an event occurred) may have probative force to show that the event did not occur. To illustrate, if P company routinely records shipments of goods that are prepaid, the absence of an entry pertaining to certain goods indicates that there was no prepayment. Federal Rule 803(7) which permits showing the absence of an entry, is aligned with the weight of authority. Is the absence of an entry hearsay? See Adv. Comm.Note to Fed.R.Evid. 803.

2. Federal Rule 803(8) provides for the admission of records compiled by public offices or agencies. Most of the agencies are also business entities, since the term "business" is broadly defined in the typical business entry statute or rule to include "business, institution,

20. Williams v. Alexander, 309 N.Y. 283, 129 N.E.2d 417 (1955); Lindstrom v. Yellow Taxi Co., 298 Minn. 224, 214 N.W.2d 672 (1974); Kelly v. Sheehan, 158 Conn. 281, 259 A.2d 605 (1969). See Weinstein & Mansfield, et al. at 820–823. But see, Cestero v. Ferrara, 57 N.J. 497, 273 A.2d 761 (1971).

21. Felice v. Long Island Railroad Co., 426 F.2d 192 (2d Cir.1970), cert. denied, 400 U.S. 820 (1970).

association, profession, occupation and calling of every kind, whether or not conducted for profit." Fed.R.Evid. 803(6). There is authority that government records and reports are governed exclusively by Rule 803(8) and are not within 803(6). See, e.g., United States v. Orozco, 590 F.2d 789, 793 (9th Cir.1979); cert. denied 439 U.S. 1049 (1978); Complaint of American Export Lines, Inc., 73 F.R.D. 454, 459 (S.D. N.Y.1977); United States v. American Cyanamid Co., 427 F.Supp. 859, 867 (S.D.N.Y.1977). The relationship between Rule 803(8) and 803(6) is explored further in Part F.

3. The introduction of computer business records generally requires a more comprehensive foundation than that necessary for conventional records, since it usually is necessary to provide evidence of the methods used to gather, store, and retrieve information. See United States v. Scholle, 553 F.2d 1109 (8th Cir.1977); Roberts, A Practitioner's Primer on Computer-generated Evidence, 41 U.Chi.L. Rev. 254 (1974).

PART F. PUBLIC RECORDS

§ 7.18 In General

Most frequently created by statute or rule of court, the hearsay exception for public records rests upon the assumption that persons discharging the public's business will accurately maintain public records because of substantial reliance by users.[1] The force of public duty and the presence of routine, systematic practices combine to make the analogy to the exception for business records compelling. The shared characteristics of these exceptions account for the relatively abbreviated treatment given to certain features of the public records exception. Note, for example, the common problem of whether the informer and entrant were responding to an obligation that, either expressly or impliedly, arose from official duties. As a general rule, if only the entrant (or only the informer) has such a public duty, another hearsay exception, applicable to the statement of the declarant who is not under a duty, must be linked to that for public records to admit the record for the truth of its assertion.[2]

§ 7.18

1. Another practical reason asserted for the exception is "the unlikelihood that [a public official] will remember details independently of the record." Adv.Comm.Note to Fed.R.Evid. 803(8).

2. United States v. Pazsint, 703 F.2d 420, 424 (9th Cir.1983), appeal after remand, 728 F.2d 411 (9th Cir.1984) ("statements made by third persons under no duty to report may not be admitted under 803(8)"). See, however,

The use of the public records exception, however, often involves a hearsay problem not found with the business records exception because the former usually does not require that the public custodian (or other appropriate official) appear as a witness to provide foundation testimony. Typically, the public records exception is applicable if the entry or statement in question is a public record or part of a public record (as defined by statute, rule of court, or, perhaps, judicial opinion) *in the custody* of a public official. The frequency with which public records are used as evidence makes it impractical to require that the public custodian or his surrogate appear in court to verify that the record is genuine (that is, public) and is held in proper custody. Practical difficulties are also posed if the original record is removed from the public repository each time it is presented in court. Thus, most statutes provide that when the appropriate public custodian attests by official written certification or by seal that the original is a public record in his custody and that the proffered duplicate is a "true copy," the duplicate will be accepted for its truth on the basis of the custodian's hearsay statement that it is within the present exception.[3] There thus is no need for him to appear in court.

§ 7.19 Public Records: Application of the Exception

Because the judicial and statutory treatment of this exception varies among the jurisdictions, generalizations must be viewed with particular caution. The usual prerequisite for admissibility is a showing that the proffered document or written assertion was made by a public official or employee acting within his official duties. Some statutes specifically designate as admissible certain certificates or documents;[1] others, more general in application, are framed in terms of records, statements, or reports of public employees or agencies.[2] Typically, the public records exception, either by general provision or by a multiplicity of specific ones, includes rather generous provisions for the receipt in evidence of assertions or data from first-hand knowledge of persons acting under a public duty. It also usually is recognized that data and

§ 7.19 and especially the comment on investigative reports.

3. This statement of genuineness serves to authenticate the document. See § 13.8.

§ 7.19

1. See, e.g., Va.Code 1983, § 19.2–188 (reports by state medical examiners).

2. See, e.g., West's Ann.Cal.Code Evid., § 1280 (1966).

facts sent to a public agency by a "semi-public" agent such as a physician or clergyman come within the exception—at least where there is a statutory or professional duty to report.[3]

There is growing recognition that factual findings of official investigations should fall within the exception, despite the awareness that much of the factual information may come from persons with no public or business duty.[4] Admission here is justified, if at all, by the probability that the officials conducting the investigation (who themselves are under a public duty) will be careful and discriminating in selecting the factual data upon which to rely in reaching their findings and conclusions. Note the analogy to in-court expert testimony which, as we shall see in a subsequent chapter,[5] may be based upon inadmissible data or materials if these are ordinarily relied upon by professionals in the expert's field.

The Federal Rules of Evidence contain a number of provisions governing the admissibility of public documents.[6] Principal among these is Rule 803(8), which provides a hearsay exception for:

> *Public records and reports.* Records, reports, statements, or data compilations, in any form, of public offices or agencies, setting forth (A) the activities of the office or agency, or (B) matters observed pursuant to duty imposed by law as to which matters there was a duty to report, excluding, however, in criminal cases matters observed by police officers and other law enforcement personnel, or (C) in civil actions and proceedings and against the Government in criminal cases, factual findings resulting from an investigation made pursuant to authority granted by law, unless the sources of information or other circumstances indicate lack of trustworthiness.

Subsection (A) is typical of the widely recognized exception for records that disclose the activities of a public entity. The analogy to business records is clear; indeed there is often an overlap between the exception for public records and that for business entries. Included within subsection (A) are records such as those

3. McCormick, § 317, at 892–93.

4. See, e.g., Rauser v. Toston Irrigation District, 565 P.2d 632, 172 Mont. 530 (1977); Smith v. Universal Services, Inc., 454 F.2d 154 (5th Cir.1972), on remand, 360 F.Supp. 441 (E.D.La.1972); McCormick, § 316, at 890–91.

5. Ch. XII.

6. Fed.R.Evid. 803(8), (9), (10), (11), (12), (14).

of the Internal Revenue Service,[7] the Drug Enforcement Administration,[8] and legislative committees.[9]

Subsection (B) embraces recordations of "matters observed" pursuant to a public duty to observe and report as, for example, the Weather Bureau's observations of weather conditions [10] or an induction officer's observation that an individual refused to take a required oath.[11] Note, however, that records of matters observed by law enforcement personnel are inadmissible in criminal cases, at least when offered by the government *against* the accused.[12] Thus, for example, recorded observations made by the police at the scene of an arrest would not come within the public records exception.[13] The basis for this special restriction is the assumption, surely accurate in most circumstances, that the adversarial relationship between law enforcement officials and criminal defendants casts doubt on the objectivity of these officials' public entries detailing observations pertinent to the accused's guilt. Further, the admission of these entries would raise difficulties under the confrontation clause of the Constitution if the officer making them were not available for cross-examination by the accused.[14] In any event, entries by law enforcement personnel falling within the special restriction to sub-part (B) are inadmissible; generally speaking, if the police observations recorded in the public record are to be introduced, they must be presented by the observing officer, not by offering the public records as a substitute for the officer's testimony.[15]

7. Needham v. United States, 564 F.Supp. 419, 421–22 (W.D.Okl.1983) (IRS computer record showing that deficiency notice had been mailed).

8. United States v. Hardin, 710 F.2d 1231, 1237 (7th Cir.1983), cert. denied, 464 U.S. 918 (1983) (preparing statistical report of drug sales is an activity of the DEA).

9. Major v. Treen, 574 F.Supp. 325, 330 (E.D.La.1983) (transcripts of public hearings before state legislative committees).

10. See Minnehaha County, S.D. v. Kelley, 150 F.2d 356, 361 (8th Cir.1945); Adv.Comm.Note to Fed.R.Evid. 803(8).

11. See United States v. Van Hook, 284 F.2d 489 (7th Cir.1960), judg. rev'd on other grounds, 365 U.S. 609 (1961). See also United States v. Arias, 575 F.2d 253 (9th Cir.1978), cert. denied, 439 U.S. 868 (1978) (court reporter's transcript of trial).

12. Fed.R.Evid. 803(8)(B). The Rule has been interpreted not to exclude recorded observations offered by the accused. United States v. Smith, 521 F.2d 957, 968–69 (D.C.Cir.1975).

13. Graham, Handbook of Federal Evidence, § 803.8, at 840–42.

14. See § 7.25.

15. Of course the records could be used to refresh the officer's recollection, see § 4.7. Further as noted below, if the observing officer testifies, some courts then allow the public entries into evidence.

Although the general thrust of sub-part (B) is apparent, there remain significant problems of construction. It is unclear, for example, exactly who falls within the category "law enforcement personnel."[16] Beyond this, it is apparent that police and other law enforcement officials often make routine entries that, even though ultimately relevant to the accused's guilt, are made in a nonadversarial context. There is some judicial authority that admits these routine entries on the ground that they fall outside the purpose underlying the special restriction to the 803(B) hearsay exception.[17]

Subpart (C) is the most controversial section of Rule 803(8). It confers general admissibility upon investigative findings, but, again, not when offered against the accused in a criminal case. This protective provision is probably required by the accused's constitutional right to confront witnesses against him.[18] However, as set out in Rule 803(8), "in civil actions and against the Government in criminal cases, factual findings resulting from an investigation made pursuant to . . . law" are prima facie admissible. Thus, for example, an investigative report of the Bureau of Mines detailing the probable cause of an explosion or an investigative report by the Army setting out the extent and causes of lost military supplies should fall within sub-part (C).[19]

The Rule states that "factual findings" are admissible, raising the clear inference that opinions, conclusions, and evaluations are not within the present exception. Nonetheless, the line between factual assertions, on the one hand, and evaluations, conclusions, and opinions, on the other, is often hard to discern. Some courts correctly take a tolerant view on the question of what is sufficiently "factual" to come within the exception.[20] This receptive ap-

16. See United States v. Oates, 560 F.2d 45, 67–68 (2d Cir.1977) (Customs Service chemist who analyzed drug is within category of "other law enforcement personnel"); cf. United States v. Hansen, 583 F.2d 325, 333 (7th Cir. 1978), cert. denied, 439 U.S. 912 (1978) (city building inspector is not).

17. E.g., United States v. Grady, 544 F.2d 598 (2d Cir.1976) (recording of serial numbers of weapons); United States v. Quezada, 754 F.2d 1190, 1193–95 (5th Cir.1985), reh. denied, 758 F.2d 651 (5th Cir.1985) (INS warrant of deportation); see McCormick, § 316, at 892 n. 14.

18. U.S. Const.Amend. VI. See §§ 7.29–31. In the present context, some of those persons who have supplied information to the investigator may not even be known, or, assuming their identity is disclosed, may not have been speaking from first-hand knowledge.

19. See the cases collected in 4 Louisell & Mueller, § 455, at 734, some of which predate the Rules.

20. Robbins v. Whelan, 653 F.2d 47 (1st Cir.1981), cert. denied, 454 U.S. 1123 (1981).

proach recognizes that the value of investigative reports often lies in their conclusions which are not, strictly speaking, purely factual. Furthermore, there is within the Rule itself protection against speculation or unsubstantiated hearsay assertions. If the "sources of information or other circumstances" cast doubt on the reliability of assertions within the report, these may be excluded. In ruling upon admissibility, the judge may consider such factors as the expertise of the investigator, his possible bias or motive to distort, and whether the investigation included hearings so that opposing views could be expressed and weaknesses in the underlying information revealed.[21]

The kinship between Rule 803(6), governing business entries, and Rule 803(8), controlling public records, has already been noted. The term "business" is broadly defined in 803(6) so that it surely embraces most public entities such as agencies, commissions, departments, and the like. Therefore, many recorded hearsay declarations will meet the conditions of both 803(6) and 803(8) and may be received into evidence under either. It will be noted, however, that Rule 803(8) contains special protections for the accused in a criminal case. For example, as noted above, a recorded observation by a law enforcement official falls within the exclusionary restriction of 803(8)(B). Suppose a written statement meets the requirements of a business entry under Rule 803(6), but because of a special restriction in Rule 803(8) (such as that in 803(8)(B)) fails to qualify for admission under the latter. May the proponent nonetheless gain admission by offering his recordation pursuant to the terms of 803(6)? After all, a general governing principle of evidence holds that if evidence is admissible as offered, it is not to be rejected simply because it would be inadmissible if offered under another theory or for a different purpose. Yet in the particular setting under consideration, this general proposition should not apply. To receive freely under Rule 803(6) entries that would not be admissible against an accused under Rule 803(8) would emasculate the protective provisions of the latter. In the leading case of United States v. Oates,[22] the Court of Appeals for the Second Circuit found "clear legislative intent not only to exclude [reports by law enforcement personnel] from the scope of FRE 803(8) but from the scope of FRE 803(6) as well."[23] In *Oates,* the prosecution introduced a report by a Customs Service chemist

21. See United States v. American Tel. & Tel. Co., 498 F.Supp. 353, 359–60 (D.D.C.1980).

22. 560 F.2d 45 (2d Cir.1977).

23. Id. at 68.

concluding that the substance seized from the defendant was heroin. Although another chemist testified as to the procedures followed in chemical analysis, thus laying the foundation required by Rule 803(6), the chemist who performed the analysis did not testify. The court concluded that the report was a "factual finding" in connection with an "investigation" and hence barred by sub-part (C) of Rule 803(8). An alternative ground of exclusion, in which the court had less confidence, was to characterize the report as one which recorded "matters observed" by "law enforcement personnel" and thus within the prohibition of sub-part (B). In any event, the court buttressed its holding by noting Congress' apprehension that the accused's right to confront witnesses against him [24]—the reason for the restrictions on Rule 803(8) [25]—might be violated if these restrictions could be circumvented by reliance on another hearsay exception. Later courts, relying on legislative intent, have reasoned that Rule 803(8) forbids the use of law enforcement reports as a *substitute* for an officer's testimony; thus they have held that if the officer testifies, the public entries concerning the subject of his testimony become admissible.[26]

Note

Much litigation and judicial discussion have surrounded the question of the scope of the duty and authority of one who, in an official or professional capacity, reports vital statistics and related information to a public agency. Most jurisdictions have special statutes governing such matters as reports or certifications of births, marriages, deaths, and so forth. The scope and interpretation of these statutes varies considerably from jurisdiction to jurisdiction. Frequently litigated is the question of which of the various entries on a death certificate are admissible. See McCormick, § 317, at 892. When the statute provides that a death certificate can be received as proof of the facts therein stated, see, e.g., Va.Code Ann. § 32.1–272 (1985), most courts have held either that the official duty does not extend to entries about the cause of death (e.g., "suicide," "food poisoning") or that the "facts" referred to in the statute are only those facts of which the entrant

24. See n. 18.

25. Adv.Comm.Note to Fed.R.Evid. 803(8). See also the discussion of Rule 803(8) on the floor of the House of Representatives, Congressional Record, January 6, 1974, pp. 563–565, reprinted in 4 Weinstein & Berger, ¶ 803, at 15–22.

26. E.g., United States v. King, 613 F.2d 670 (7th Cir.1980). Cf. United States v. Sawyer, 607 F.2d 1190 (7th Cir.1979), cert. denied, 445 U.S. 943 (1980) (report admitted as recorded recollection of testifying officer).

had a first-hand knowledge, not those derived from third persons not under a public duty. See Edwards v. Jackson, 210 Va. 450, 171 S.E.2d 854 (1970). Thus, a death certificate may be admissible only to prove the fact of death (perhaps including date or time of death), not to show causation. Query whether such an interpretation would preclude admission where a medically observable cause of death (such as a crushed larynx) which may raise a strong inference (in the example, strangulation) is listed on the certificate by an entrant with a duty to report, but no first-hand knowledge.

Federal Rule 803(9) provides that "[r]ecords or data compilations, in any form, of births, fetal deaths, deaths, or marriages, if the report thereof was made to a public office pursuant to requirements of law" are not excluded by the hearsay rule. The federal courts are divided on whether conclusions that largely rest upon the inferences of the reporting official are properly within the Rule. The solution should turn upon whether, under the circumstances, the conclusion appears speculative or otherwise seems to lack a sufficient guaranty of trustworthiness. Note also the possibility that Rule 803(8)(C) would dictate exclusion. See generally 4 Louisell & Mueller at 777–85.

PART G. JUDGMENT OF A CRIMINAL CONVICTION

§ 7.20 Theory and Application

We have seen that a guilty plea to a criminal charge may constitute a party admission in subsequent litigation involving the occurrence that was the subject of the criminal proceeding.[1] For example, if *A* pleads guilty to a charge of willfully burning his warehouse (an act of arson), this plea—which is a conclusive judicial admission in the criminal trial—may constitute a party admission in a later civil suit in which *A* claims he is entitled to the proceeds of his fire insurance policy. The trier would be entitled to consider the plea as inconsistent with *A*'s claim in the civil suit that the destruction was accidental.

May the insurance company invoke principles of res judicata—more particularly, collateral estoppel, or issue preclusion—to establish conclusively that the fire was deliberately set? It probably may not, for the dominant judicial position applies collateral estoppel only to those facts that were *actually* and *necessarily*

§ 7.20

1. Note 1 following § 7.6.

litigated in the first proceeding—that is, only to those consequential facts that were contested by the parties and resolved by the trier.[2] Suppose, however, that there had been a trial of the criminal charge, culminating in *A*'s conviction of arson. The jury's finding that *A* purposefully burned his property might be conclusive (issue preclusive) in the subsequent civil case. Indeed many jurisdictions would make it so, and thus *A*'s suit for the recovery of fire insurance proceeds would be resolved against him by summary judgment—assuming, of course, that the substantive laws (or the insurance policy) disallowed coverage for the insured's willful destruction of his property.

Note also the possibility that the resolution of contested facts in the criminal proceeding would have no effect in subsequent litigation, which, after all, involves a different cause of action and at least one different party—the insurance company. However, the fact that *A was a party* to the first trial, that he had a full opportunity to contest the charge of purposeful destruction, and that the trier found him guilty beyond a reasonable doubt suggest convincingly that the earlier proceeding should not be completely ignored. The compelling force of this argument will be appreciated by recalling that a majority of jurisdictions would routinely apply collateral estoppel to a factual finding made in a prior *civil* suit where the standard of proof required only that facts be established by a more-probable-than-not measure. Thus, most jurisdictions give some effect to an earlier contested conviction and, as we have seen, are likely to construe a guilty plea as a party admission.

Our immediate problem is one of determining what effect shall be given in a present judicial proceeding to an earlier judicial result, traceable to either a plea or a factual finding. In part, this problem is addressed by the law of res judicata, not by the law of evidence. That is, when there was an actual trial in the first suit, the effect of that suit on a subsequent suit is determined in the first instance by the law of res judicata and, more particularly, collateral estoppel (issue preclusion) which, in most jurisdictions, makes the prior determination conclusive. A discussion of the law of collateral estoppel is beyond the scope of the present text. Generally speaking, however, a trier's determination of contested facts, including mixed questions of fact and law such as negli-

2. Restatement (Second) of Judgments, § 27 (1982); see Henderson v. Snider Bros, Inc., 409 A.2d 1083 (D.C. App.1979), on reh., 439 A.2d 481 (1981); see also Block v. Commissioners, 99 U.S. 686, 693 (1878).

gence, becomes conclusive in subsequent civil litigation (based on the same occurrence but a different cause of action) when introduced against one who was a party to the first trial.[3] This is true whether the first trial is civil or criminal, assuming the facts were contested in the earlier trial and were actually and necessarily resolved by the trier of fact.[4] Whether a prior determination was "actual" and "necessary" is, of course, a question allocated to the trial judge, who is free to examine the judicial record (transcript, instructions to the jury, findings, etc.) of the first trial.

However, some jurisdictions do not prescribe this conclusive collateral estoppel or "issue preclusive" effect even to matters properly litigated in the first trial. For example, some courts may refuse to apply collateral estoppel unless the second suit is between the same parties that contested the first suit; it is not sufficient that one of the parties (against whom issue preclusion is urged) is a litigant in the subsequent suit. Furthermore, as just noted, collateral estoppel operates when there was an actual contest and thus, under the prevailing view, has no application to stipulations, admissions in the pleadings, consent judgments, guilty pleas, or other concessions by the parties. In a broad sense, these consensual arrangements represent negotiations, concessions, or admissions that are not intended to have a *conclusive* effect beyond the first trial. By limiting the effect of these decisions not to offer a contest, the law encourages accommodations and settlements in the first trial. On the other hand, for reasons already noted, it may be inappropriate to deny *any effect* to previous actions by a party when they appear to weaken or negate his allegation in a subsequent suit. Hence, a guilty plea, statements in the pleading of the first trial, and similar concessions are often deemed party admissions in the subsequent trial. The trier in the later suit may consider the declarations in the

3. Restatement (Second) of Judgments, §§ 27, 29 (1982); Miller Brewing Co. v. Jos. Schlitz Brewing Co., 605 F.2d 990 (7th Cir.1979), cert. denied, 444 U.S. 1102 (1980); Bernhard v. Bank of America Nat. Trust & Savings Ass'n, 19 Cal.2d 807, 122 P.2d 892 (1942).

4. A different result is reached when findings from an earlier *civil* trial are offered in a later *criminal* proceeding. Since the state must prove each element of a criminal charge beyond a reasonable doubt, determinations made in the civil suit—which were made under a preponderance-of-the-evidence standard—are not conclusive in the criminal proceeding. Similar reasoning precludes the evidentiary use of those prior findings which are, in essence, hearsay declarations by the trier of fact in the preceding civil suit. Friedenthal, Kane & Miller, Civil Procedure 664–65 (1985).

earlier trial, attaching to them such weight as seems appropriate.[5] Similarly, if there has been a contest and an actual, necessary determination in the first trial, it may be appropriate at least to consider the prior finding *as evidence* should the court in the subsequent suit align itself with a minority view that such prior findings are not conclusive as a matter of collateral estoppel.

Observe, however, that a determination by the trier in the first trial, when introduced into evidence in a subsequent suit, will usually be hearsay. The earlier finding is, in essence, a declaration by the trier in the first proceeding that a certain fact exists—such as, for example, that *A* willfully burned the building in question. Thus, when a declaration from a prior proceeding is offered as evidence of its truth in the present trial, it is necessary to consider the rule against hearsay. Note that whereas a guilty plea or statements in a pleading may appropriately be considered a party admission and thus within a traditional exception to the hearsay rule, a declaration by the trier of fact in the first suit is not a party admission and, if received in evidence, must rest on other grounds. Federal Rule 803(22) provides:

> *Judgment of previous conviction.* Evidence of a final judgment, entered after a trial or upon a plea of guilty (but not upon a plea of *nolo contendere*), adjudging a person guilty of a crime punishable by death or imprisonment in excess of one year, to prove any fact essential to sustain the judgment, but not including, when offered by the government in a criminal prosecution for purposes other than impeachment, judgments against persons other than the accused. The pendency of an appeal may be shown but does not affect admissibility.

This exception does not address the scope of collateral estoppel. To determine the reach of this doctrine of preclusion, the judge in the subsequent proceeding should be guided by the res judicata law of the jurisdiction in which the first trial was held. Generally speaking, he should give the identical force and effect—that is, the "same full faith and credit" [6]—to the judgment that it would be given in the rendering jurisdiction. However, should collateral estoppel not make the earlier determination conclusive, Rule 803(22) permits evidentiary use of a final criminal conviction in

5. IV Wigmore, §§ 1065–66; see Burdis v. Texas & Pacific Ry. Co., 569 F.2d 320 (5th Cir.1978); supra note 1.

6. 28 U.S.C.A. § 1738 (1966).

the first trial. It is immaterial whether the judgment rests on a guilty plea or upon a conviction after trial, but the judgment must have resulted in the conviction of a felony-grade offense. An acquittal is not within the present exception since it implies only that some element necessary to the conviction was not found to exist beyond a reasonable doubt. The essence, then, of Rule 803(22) is that it permits, as an exception to the hearsay rule, the introduction of a prior felony conviction "to prove any fact essential to sustain the judgment." [7] The prior judgment may have been against a party to the present suit or, if the present suit is a civil proceeding, against one who is not a present party. Thus, in a civil suit in which *A*'s executor claims that *B* (and not *C*) negligently shot and killed *A*, *B* could introduce a judgment showing that *C* was convicted of the involuntary manslaughter of *A*.[8] Similarly, in the earlier illustration involving arson, the defendant insurance company could introduce against the claimants, business partners *A* and *B*, evidence that *A* had been convicted of deliberately burning the building in question.[9] A final example illustrates a restriction appearing on the face of Rule 803(22). Suppose that the present trial is a criminal proceeding in which *D* is charged with the receipt of stolen stamps. To prove that the stamps were in fact stolen, the government introduces a judgment, obtained in an earlier criminal trial, showing that *X* had been convicted of stealing the stamps in question. The prior judgment is offered for the hearsay assertion by the trier in the first trial that the stamps were stolen. Rule 803(22) would disallow the evidence.[10] The previous conviction was against a person "other than the accused" in the present trial; the evidence is not offered for the purpose of impeaching the credibility of a witness,[11] and, more importantly, the present accused is entitled to

7. Fed.R.Evid. 803(22).

8. See McCormick, § 318, at 896.

9. Under the substantive law, the "innocent" partner is usually not permitted to recover fire insurance proceeds when the "guilty" partner has deliberately burned the insured premises. Cf. Travelers Fire Insurance Co. v. Wright, 322 P.2d 417 (Okl.1958).

10. Cf. Kirby v. United States, 174 U.S. 47 (1899). A different situation is presented when the offense charged in the second trial contains as an essential element the existence of a prior conviction. If, for example, the charge is selling a firearm to a convicted felon, the status of the buyer as a felon could be shown by the judgment of his conviction. The judgment is a public record, and the admission of this record would not be barred by the restrictive provision of Rule 803(22). Id. at 54; Adv. Comm.Note to Fed.R.Evid. 803(22).

11. If the person convicted of stealing the stamps were to take the stand and testify, there is a possibility that the court would allow his conviction for theft of the stamps to be introduced for

confront the witness against him. The confrontation clause of the Constitution[12] accounts largely for the restriction on the hearsay use against the accused of the conviction of another person.[13]

§ 7.21 Transitional Note: The Hearsay Exceptions and Declarant's Unavailability

The applicability of the hearsay exceptions discussed so far is not conditioned upon whether or not the declarant is unavailable as a witness.[1] These foregoing exceptions (along with others omitted from the preceding discussions) are grouped under Federal Rule of Evidence 803. In most respects these exceptions are similar to those developed by the states through judicial decisions or statutory enactment. But the incorporation of these exceptions under a single federal rule emphasizes their salient common feature: the availability (or unavailability) of the declarant is immaterial to their application. This shared feature rests upon the assumption that the admissible declarations described in Federal Rule 803 have guarantees of trustworthiness that make them the substantial equivalent of testimony from the stand; this conclusion renders unimportant the question whether the hearsay declarant could be called to testify in person about the subject matter of his out-of-court statement. Since the hearsay statement is on an equivalent footing with live testimony, it comes into evidence either in addition to, or in lieu of, the testimony of the declarant. It should be added, however, that in criminal prosecutions the confrontation clause of the Constitution might compel the prosecution to produce, for cross-examination by the accused, available declarants whose hearsay statements would, under the usual rules of evidence, be admissible without regard to whether or not the declarant was available. This problem is discussed elsewhere.[2]

We now encounter additional exceptions, grouped under Federal Rule 804,[3] in which the evidentiary rules specify that the

the limited purpose of impeachment. However, the judge would have to conclude that the probative value of this restricted use outweighs the "prejudicial effect to the defendant." See Fed. R.Evid. 609(a); § 8.3.

12. See § 7.29.

13. See Adv.Comm.Note to Fed.R. Evid. 803(22).

§ 7.21

1. But note that the exception for past recorded recollection requires that the declarant be available to provide the necessary foundation. See § 7.15.

2. See § 7.31.

3. There are four specific exceptions and one "catch all" or residual exception contained in Rule 804(b). Three of the specific exceptions are discussed in

declarant's unavailability to testify is a condition of admissibility. Before these exceptions apply, the proponent must demonstrate to the judge that he cannot reasonably secure the declarant's testimony. Rule 804 exceptions, which generally are consistent with the common law, may be thought of as "second class" exceptions. The hearsay within these exceptions is not equal in quality to the "class one" exceptions of Rule 803 [4] (or, of course, to live testimony), but the statements are thought sufficiently reliable to be considered by the trier if the declarant is unavailable as a witness. In short, we introduce here the notion of preference: live testimony is preferred, but if the declarant is unavailable, his hearsay declaration will be received.

It is not always easy to predict the circumstances under which a declarant will be considered unavailable. This especially is true under the common law, where the requirement of unavailability usually was defined separately for each of the exceptions conditioned upon it.[5] The clear cases are those in which absence from the jurisdiction (with current address unknown), death, or some other incapacity (such as serious illness) renders it impossible to present the declarant as a witness. Federal Rule 804(a), which draws upon substantial common-law support, announces other conditions, such as the successful claim of a privilege or a persistent refusal to testify,[6] that satisfy the requirement of unavailability.[7] Under the Federal Rule, an inability to remember the event

the materials immediately following. One of the specific exceptions is briefly considered in § 7.28, n. 2. The residual exception is considered in the text at § 7.28.

4. This generalization, perhaps, is inaccurate when applied to former testimony. See § 7.23.

5. Adv.Comm.Note to Fed.R.Evid. 804. A good discussion of the unavailability requirement is found in McCormick § 253.

6. See United States v. Carlson, 547 F.2d 1346 (8th Cir.1976), cert. denied, 431 U.S. 914 (1977) (coconspirator who was granted use immunity refused to testify for fear of reprisals and was thereafter incarcerated for contempt; held unavailable).

7. *(a) Definition of unavailability.* "Unavailability as a witness" includes situations in which the declarant—

"(1) is exempted by ruling of the court on the ground of privilege from testifying concerning the subject matter of his statement; or

"(2) persists in refusing to testify concerning the subject matter of his statement despite an order of the court to do so; or

"(3) testifies to a lack of memory of the subject matter of his statement; or

"(4) is unable to be present or to testify at the hearing because of death or then existing physical or mental illness or infirmity; or

"(5) is absent from the hearing and the proponent of his statement has been unable to procure his attendance (or in the case of a hearsay exception under subdivision (b)(2), (3), or (4), his attendance or testimony) by process or other reasonable means.

to which the witness is asked to testify also renders the witness unavailable.[8] Common-law decisions, in contrast, are not uniform on the question whether a lack of memory suffices.[9]

PART H. FORMER TESTIMONY

§ 7.22 In General

This exception, invoked in various contexts, is applicable where the proponent in the present trial offers testimony given in an earlier hearing or proceeding. The hearsay dangers are minimized by the prior opportunity to test or develop the testimony. In one familiar setting, a witness is called by one side—for example, by the plaintiff—and, after direct examination, is made available for cross-questions. Subsequently, the case is appealed and, for reasons unrelated to the testimony of the witness, a new trial is ordered. If the witness cannot be produced to testify at the new trial, the original proponent (the plaintiff) now may offer to prove, usually by means of a transcript, the witness's testimony from the first trial. In theory, and occasionally also in practice, the *opponent* of the witness in the first trial (the defendant, in the present example) may introduce the prior testimony against the earlier proponent. Although this earlier proponent was not a cross examiner, his attorney presumably had ample opportunity to develop the witness's testimony.

In the foregoing illustration, the parties to both proceedings (the original and the new trial) are the same. Each had the opportunity to interrogate the witness at the earlier trial. Suppose, however, that the first suit was brought by one plaintiff and the second was initiated by another. This difference in plaintiffs would occur, for example, where the first suit resulted from a claim by an infant for injuries occasioned by the negligence of a defendant railroad, and the second suit resulted from a claim by a

"A declarant is not unavailable as a witness if his exemption, refusal, claim of lack of memory, inability, or absence is due to the procurement or wrongdoing of the proponent of his statement for the purpose of preventing the witness from attending or testifying."

Note that the proponent seeking to use the exceptions for (1) statements under belief of impending death ("dying declaration") or (2) statement against interest or (3) statement of family history ("pedigree") must show not only his inability to produce the witness by "process or other reasonable means" but also his reasonable inability to obtain the declarant's deposition. Fed.R.Evid. 804(a)(5).

8. See United States v. Davis, 551 F.2d 233 (8th Cir.1977), cert. denied, 431 U.S. 923 (1977).

9. McCormick, § 253, at 755.

parent for loss of the child's services. If the witness who testified against the railroad in the first trial is unavailable at the second trial, may his testimony be used by either party? Using the testimony against the railroad, which was a party to both suits and had an opportunity at the first trial to interrogate the witness, appears to fit comfortably within the exception. However, if the defendant railroad seeks to use all or part of the former testimony against the second plaintiff, a difficulty arises: the second plaintiff was not a party to the first suit and had no opportunity to interrogate the witness and to develop his testimony. This lack of opportunity has caused most courts to exclude the former testimony when offered against one not a party or not in privity with a party to the first suit.

As noted, however, there remains the possibility that the second plaintiff could introduce the former testimony against the defendant railroad which was a party to the earlier suit. Despite the apparently strong argument for allowing this evidence against the identical party, the early cases denied admissibility. The reasoning was this: since the railroad cannot use the former testimony against the second plaintiff, fairness dictates that the plaintiff not be permitted to use the prior testimony against the railroad. This logic underlies the so-called doctrine of mutuality which requires that there must be at least the possibility of mutual use of the former testimony before either party can introduce it. Modern scholarship and recent cases [1] reject the doctrine, taking the view that in a factfinding proceeding the concern only should be whether it is fair to offer the testimony against a party who also was a party to the prior trial.[2] Under this recent approach, fairness is not assessed on the basis of whether either party could offer the prior testimony. Instead, the question of fairness turns upon whether the party against whom the evidence of prior testimony is offered had an earlier opportunity to develop or test the former testimony.

§ 7.23 Former Testimony: Application of the Exception

When evidence of prior testimony is offered against an opponent who was a party to the earlier proceeding, it may not be

§ 7.22

1. McCormick, § 256, at 763–767.

2. See § 7.23 and Note 1 at the end of Part H, suggesting that the pertinent inquiry is whether a party to the prior suit conducted an interrogation with the same motive and interest as that of the present party. Under such a view, it is not essential that there be any identity of parties; the test is identity of interest.

apparent why the hearsay rule should apply at all. Since the rule barring hearsay rests upon the opponent's lack of opportunity to cross-examine, it seemingly is inapplicable where a full opportunity has been afforded. Arguably, then, there often is no reason to classify prior testimony as an *exception* to the hearsay rule; it seems appropriate to view the prior testimony as nonhearsay—at least in instances where the opponent already has had adequate opportunity to conduct an adverse examination of a witness testifying in court.

The traditional approach, however, which now has the endorsement of the Federal Rules of Evidence,[1] is to treat previous testimony as hearsay and then, under appropriate circumstances, to invoke the present exception. This treatment is consistent with the orthodox definition of hearsay, which brings within the rule *any statement* offered for its truth which was made at a time and place other than from the stand in the *present proceeding.* A plausible justification for treating prior testimony as hearsay is that its evidentiary use denies to the trier in the second trial the opportunity to assess the witness's demeanor. It should be noted, however, that the trustworthiness of prior testimony arguably is higher than the other "class two" exceptions, which (as we have seen) give a preference to live testimony by conditioning admissibility upon the unavailability of the hearsay declarant. Indeed, trustworthiness may be equal to, or even greater than, most of the exceptions contained in class one, thus casting doubt on the generalization made earlier in this text that class two exceptions are less trustworthy than their class one counterparts.[2]

Although many states have passed statutes governing the admission of former testimony, this exception took root and grew to maturity in the common-law tradition.[3] There are variations from state to state in statutory language (or rules of court) and in case-developed law, but the formulation contained in Federal Rule of Evidence 804(b)(1) has substantial support. If the declarant is unavailable, the court may receive in evidence:

> *Former testimony.* Testimony given [by one who was] . . . a witness at another hearing of the same or a different proceeding, or in a deposition taken in compliance with law in the course of the same or another proceeding, if the party against whom the testimony is now offered, or, in a civil action or proceeding, a predecessor in interest, had an oppor-

§ 7.23

1. See Fed.R.Evid. 804(b)(1).

2. See § 7.21 at n. 4.

3. McCormick, § 254, at 760.

tunity and similar motive to develop the testimony by direct, cross, or redirect examination.

The exception requires proof of unavailability, coupled with a showing that the party against whom the evidence now is offered had a fair opportunity and a probable motive to test or develop the testimony at the earlier proceeding.[4] The requirement is satisfied if there was an *opportunity* to examine the witness at the prior proceeding. It is not essential that there was an actual interrogation, so an earlier waiver of cross-examination does not render the exception inapplicable.[5] Although the Federal Rule does not expressly state that the prior testimony must have been given under oath or affirmation, such a setting no doubt is contemplated.[6]

In civil cases, it is sufficient that the *predecessor in interest* to the present party had an opportunity and a similar motive to examine the now-unavailable witness. Although the phrase "predecessor in interest" (which the courts frequently use interchangeably with the phrase "persons in privity")[7] has an exasperating inexactness about it, the expression generally refers to the predecessor from whom the present party received the right, title, interest or obligation that is at issue in the current litigation. For example, a decedent is a predecessor in interest to ("in privity with") both his personal representative and those, such as heirs and legatees, who take from him; so, too, is a grantor of property a predecessor to his grantee, as is a principal to his surety. Joint owners, joint obligors and joint obligees often have been considered within a relationship of privity.[8] It is not entirely clear, however, that a joint interest satisfies the Federal Rule, since, strictly speaking, a joint holder is not a *predecessor*. The funda-

4. Note that the Rule does not limit the use of former testimony only to the party *against* whom (or against whose predecessor) the earlier testimony was offered. The drafters reasoned that, for the purpose of the application of the present exception, direct and redirect examination of one's own witness is the equivalent of cross-examination of the opponent's witness. Adv.Comm.Note to Fed.R.Evid. 804(b). See Falknor, Former Testimony and the Uniform Rules: A Comment, 38 N.Y.U.L.Rev. 651 (1963).

5. McCormick, § 255, at 761. Some common-law decisions suggest, however, actual prior cross-examination is a condition of the present exception. See Fisher v. Commonwealth, 217 Va. 808, 232 S.E.2d 798 (1977).

6. See 4 Weinstein & Berger, ¶ 804(b)(1)[02], at 74–75.

7. For a discussion of the term privity as it is used in connection with the exception for party admissions, see § 7.4, nn. 15–23 and accompanying text. For an additional discussion in connection with the present exception, see 4 Louisell & Mueller at 1103–08.

8. Morgan & Weinstein at 251–52.

mental requirement of Rule 804(b)(1) is that the proponent of prior testimony show that the successor against whom the evidence is offered is attempting to protect or advance substantially the same interest as his privy-predecessor. If this requirement is satisfied, the term "predecessor" should be construed accordingly.[9] A functional approach is more desirable than one which emphasizes the arcane aspects of privity, most of which derive from property concepts.

The link of property or interest succession ("privity") infrequently applies in a criminal context. In cases where it arguably applies—as, for example, where two business partners are tried separately for the receipt and sale of stolen property—the confrontation clause of the Constitution casts doubt upon using prior testimony against the last party tried.[10] The constitutional doubt is avoided under the Federal Rule by limiting the privy-predecessor concept to civil actions.

It should be observed that the Federal Rule, in common with most states, limits the exception for prior testimony to circumstances in which the present opponent shares with the earlier examiner (whether himself or a predecessor) a "similar motive to develop the [prior] testimony by direct, cross, or redirect examination." [11] Similarity of motive is determined by ascertaining the interests and objectives of the party in the first proceeding and, where interrogation actually has taken place, by examining the prior interrogation. If the motive of the previous examiner is substantially different from that of the present party against whom the prior testimony now is offered, the earlier interrogation should not be an adequate substitute for present questioning.

It sometimes is said that a condition of the former-testimony exception is that the issues in the first and second trials be identical, but this overstates the requirement. When the judge in the second proceeding is trying to determine similarity of motive, he should determine only whether the issues to which the now unavailable declarant *directed his proffered testimony* are the

9. See Clay v. Johns-Mansville Sales Corp., 722 F.2d 1289 (6th Cir.1983), cert. denied, 467 U.S. 1253 (1984); Lloyd v. American Export Lines, 580 F.2d 1179 (3d Cir.), cert. denied, 439 U.S. 969 (1978); In re Master Key Antitrust Litigation, 72 F.R.D. 108 (D.Conn.1976) (federal government is predecessor in interest to private antitrust plaintiffs).

10. See 4 Weinstein & Berger, ¶ 804(b)(1)[05]. For further discussion of the confrontation clause, see Part L.

11. Fed.R.Evid. 804(b)(1); McCormick, § 256, at 765. See supra n. 9.

same, or substantially so, in both trials.[12] These are the issues that are determinative; congruence of other issues in the two cases is unnecessary. Circumstances, however, might dictate that the judge weigh the relative importance of the witness-declarant's testimony in both trials, at least where the role of the testimony in the first trial was so minor as to raise questions about the motive of the earlier party to develop or test it.

An illustration of the considerations that attend the application of the former testimony exception can be found by recourse to an earlier example. Suppose an injured child sues a railroad for installing a mechanically defective signal; subsequently the child's parent sues for loss of the child's services, alleging negligent maintenance of the signal. Testimony by a witness in the first trial (in which the infant was the plaintiff) that the signal was not working at the time of the accident would be material to both cases. In the second proceeding, where—we shall assume—the witness is unavailable, the testimony would be offered against the same party (the railroad) which defended the first suit, thus satisfying the condition of party similarity. If the judge concluded that the motive of the railroad in the first trial was similar to its motive in the second trial, the exception for former testimony would apply. Application of the exception should not be denied on the ground of a difference in the ultimate issue between the two trials; rather, the inquiry should be whether as to those issues to which the witness's testimony was responsive the railroad had a common motive.[13]

Notes

1. A minority of jurisdictions expressly do not require that the party to the first proceeding be either the same party who later opposes the former testimony or a predecessor in interest. Rather, these jurisdictions require only that the prior testimony was first developed or tested by a party who had the opportunity to examine the witness-declarant and who had an interest and motive *similar* to the opponent-party in the second trial. Thus, in some circumstances, former testimony is receivable against one who was neither a party to the first trial, nor a successor in interest. See Calif.Evid.Code, § 1292; Travelers Fire Ins. Co. v. Wright, 322 P.2d 417 (Okl.1958). Nonetheless, the broader rule is intended to ensure that the prior

12. McCormick, § 257, at 767.

13. For a recent application of the exception under the federal rules of evidence see Bailey v. Southern Pacific Transp. Co., 613 F.2d 1385 (5th Cir. 1980), cert. denied, 449 U.S. 836 (1980).

examination adequately protects the present party. Isn't this a more desirable approach than that of making admissibility dependent upon an analysis of whether the party to the first proceeding was a predecessor in interest?

2. Use of an official transcript is the most convenient and reliable method of proving that the testimonial statements from the first trial or proceeding were made by the witness-declarant. The official (public) records exception to the hearsay rule usually enables the proponent to introduce the transcript as proof that the testimonial statements in question were made. The proponent may, however, use other methods to prove the witness's prior statements. For example, one who heard the former testimony can take the stand in the present trial and state what the testimony was, i.e., recite what he heard the declarant say. If the witness had made notes, these might come into evidence as recorded recollection, or might be used to refresh recollection. See 4 Weinstein & Berger, ¶ 804(b)(1)[01], at 72–73. Observe that proving that the prior testimonial statements were made involves a hearsay problem when the evidence proffered is not live testimony but rather is an official transcript or a writing which is a recordation of past recollection. An exception (for public records or recorded recollection) allows the transcript or writing to serve as evidence that the prior statements were made. Of course, the second hearsay problem—that involving the use of the statements for their truth—normally is resolved by reference to the present exception for former testimony.

3. Suppose the prior testimony consists in part of statements by the (now unavailable) witness reciting what someone else (a declarant) said. To use the declarant's words for their truth, the proponent must invoke an appropriate exception if one can be found. Cf. United States v. Davis, 551 F.2d 233 (8th Cir.), cert. denied, 431 U.S. 923 (1977) (prior testimony recites statement of D; D's statement constitutes a party admission). In short, portions of the prior testimony offered under the present exception may still be objectionable because these portions violate some evidentiary rule of exclusion.

4. Assume that the testimony at the first trial would have been excluded had appropriate objection been made. At the second proceeding an opponent for the first time raises the proper objection. Is the objection waived? Most courts would answer that if the witness were present and testifying in the second trial, a proper objection would be entertained and sustained; therefore, the opponent can object when the witness's statements from the first proceeding are offered as former testimony. Note, however, that when the objection that could have been made attacks only the form of the testimony

(e.g., incomplete foundation, violation of the opinion rule, etc.) and not its relevance or competence (e.g., violation of the hearsay rule), it will not defeat admissibility in the second trial. McCormick, § 259, at 770.

PART I. DYING DECLARATIONS

§ 7.24 In General

The exception for dying declarations has had a curious history, revealing judicially imposed restrictions that range from debatable to senseless.[1] For our purposes, it suffices to say that during the Nineteenth Century, courts increasingly admitted *in criminal homicide prosecutions* the victim's dying statement identifying his slayer or revealing the cause of his impending death. Only in cases of homicide, it was reasoned, was there a special need because the alleged murderer has silenced the witness-victim.

Application of this arbitrary rule results in excluding dying declarations in all civil cases and in all criminal prosecutions except those for homicide.[2] This limitation gives little weight to the supposed reliability of any "deathbed statements" [3]—a reliability derived from the belief that one thinking himself about to die will be motivated to speak truthfully.[4] If this belief is suspect, it

§ 7.24

1. A cogent account appears in McCormick §§ 281–85.

2. See Carver v. Howard, 280 S.W.2d 708 (Ky.1955) (dying declaration not admissible in civil action for wrongful death and personal injury); Hansel v. Commonwealth, 260 Ky. 148, 84 S.W.2d 68 (1935) (dying declaration not admissible in prosecution for rape, even though victim died in resulting childbirth).

3. Adv.Comm.Note to Fed.R.Evid. 804(b)(2) (recognizing the "powerful psychological pressures" present at death). Consider also the following passage from William Shakespeare's King John, Act V, Sc. iv:

Melun. Have I not hideous death within my view,
Retaining but a quantity of life,
Which bleeds away, even as a form of wax
Resolveth from his figure 'gainst the fire?
What in the world should make me now deceive,
Since I must lose the use of all deceit?
Why should I then be false, since it is true
That I must die here and live hence by truth?

4. "Dying declarations in homicide cases have from ancient times been admitted in evidence either (1) because of solemnity—the solemnity of the occasion and the fear of punishment in the hereafter if one tells a lie just before death, or (2) because of necessity—since the victim of the homicide cannot testify its admission is necessary to protect the public against homicidal criminals and prevent a miscarriage of justice. . . . In our judgment, both grounds justify the admissibility of dying declarations . . .." Commonwealth v. Brown, 388 Pa. 613, 616–17, 131 A.2d 367, 369 (1957) (footnotes omitted).

should not support the admission of dying declarations in homicide cases, where the consequences of a conviction are quite serious. Indeed, one can argue that these declarations should be excluded in criminal cases, but admitted in civil cases where the results of erroneous factfinding are less severe. Of course, if the psychological assumption is valid, admissibility in a wide variety of cases should be sanctioned. As we shall see, the modern trend is to broaden the classes of cases in which dying declarations are admitted.

In homicide cases, courts generally sanction the exception for dying declarations, but have been unwilling to accept statements that do not pertain to the injury or death of the victim-declarant; they have restricted admissibility to those statements which describe the circumstances (including identity) surrounding the slaying. The basis for this restriction is the lack of immediacy of any other subject matter. Statements about other topics carry a greater risk of insincerity or faulty memory. Curiously, there also is older authority that the dying declaration must have been uttered by the victim whose murder is the subject of the trial where the declaration is offered.[5] Strictly applied in a case where the defendant contemporaneously kills two persons, the limitation results in excluding a statement of the declarant-victim in the trial for the murder of the other victim.[6] Such a limitation cannot be justified on the ground that a special need is lacking. It also is difficult to see how the assumed element of trustworthiness is weakened in these circumstances.

Thus, while the rhetoric of courts affirms that statements made in anticipation of death are likely to be accurate,[7] admissibility (especially in the older cases) often has been restricted in ways that cannot be reconciled with the premise of trustworthiness. Furthermore, as Professor Morgan has noted, the judicial rulings on admissibility cannot be reconciled with a rationale of special need, for even where there are eyewitnesses to the homicide, a

5. Holland v. State, 126 Ark. 332, 190 S.W. 104 (1916); Commonwealth v. Stallone, 281 Pa. 41, 126 A. 56 (1924). See McCormick, § 283, at 831.

6. A few courts have so held. See Westberry v. State, 175 Ga. 115, 164 S.E. 905 (1932) (soundly criticized in V Wigmore, § 1433, at 281 n.1 [Chadbourn]); Commonwealth v. Stallone, 281 Pa. 41, 126 A. 56 (1924).

7. E.g., Commonwealth v. Brown, 388 Pa. 613, 616–17, 131 A.2d 367, 369 (1957). But see Kidd v. State, 258 So.2d 423, 429–30 (Miss.1972) (concurring opinion).

dying declaration is admissible if the conditions of the exception are satisfied.[8]

§ 7.25 Dying Declarations: Application of the Exception

Despite the apparent inconsistencies noted in the preceding section, the central feature of dying declarations—and the condition that is essential to admissibility—is that the statement be made at a time when the declarant has a settled expectation of death. All hope of recovery must have been abandoned; equivocal statements ("I may die") are insufficient to satisfy the exception. The judge must find from all of the attending circumstances, including (when available) statements by the declarant, that the declarant felt a sense of impending death.[1] Of course, in jurisdictions still adhering to the traditional approach, admissibility is conditioned further: death must actually have ensued and the prosecution must be for the resulting homicide. If the prosecution is for some lesser offense—such as abortion or rape—the declaration is inadmissible even though death in fact ensued.[2]

An increasing number of jurisdictions have taken steps to expand the exception, sometimes by sanctioning admissibility in criminal prosecutions other than homicide or, more frequently, by allowing dying declarations in civil actions (such as wrongful death) where there necessarily is an inquiry as to cause of death.[3] The Federal Rules of Evidence contain the following provision: [4]

> *Statement under belief of impending death.* In a prosecution for homicide or in a civil action or proceeding, a statement made by a declarant while believing that his death was imminent, concerning the cause or circumstances of what he believed to be his impending death.

Note that this formulation extends to any civil case, subject, of course, to the requirements of relevance. For example, a dying declaration by a wife that her husband intentionally caused the automobile accident in which she sustained fatal injuries was admitted in a suit to determine insurance coverage.[5] However, on

8. Morgan & Weinstein at 268.

§ 7.25

1. Shepard v. United States, 290 U.S. 96 (1933); Wilson v. State, 86 Nev. 320, 468 P.2d 346 (1970).

2. Winfrey v. State, 174 Ark. 729, 296 S.W. 82 (1927); § 7.24 n. 2; Morgan & Weinstein at 268.

3. McCormick, § 287, at 834; Morgan & Weinstein at 268.

4. Fed.R.Evid. 804(b)(2).

5. In a pre-rules decision, United Services Automotive Association v. Wharton, 237 F.Supp. 255 (W.D.N.C. 1965), the district judge broke the common-law tradition and admitted the

the criminal side of the docket the exception is limited to prosecutions for homicide. This restriction apparently rests upon the old "necessity" theme.[6] In both criminal and civil cases, the exception is applicable only if there is a belief that death is imminent. However, in civil cases there is no requirement that the declarant actually die; it suffices that he is unavailable. Any of the reasons set out in Federal Rule 804(a) meet the unavailability requirement. (Of course, death will have occurred in homicide cases.) Finally, the Federal Rule incorporates the general limitation that the statement must refer to the cause or circumstances attending the supposed impending death.[7] Thus, a "deathbed" statement by one indicted for a bank robbery, that his co-indictee was innocent of the crime charged, fell outside the present exception because it did not describe the cause or circumstances of the declarant's impending death.[8]

Notes

1. Dying declarations most frequently are offered by the prosecution in an effort to convict the accused of the murder of the declarant. But the exception is equally available to the defense. See State v. Proctor, 269 S.W.2d 624 (Mo.1954); State v. Puett, 210 N.C. 633, 188 S.E. 75 (1936).

2. The argument has been made, usually without success, that a lack of religious conviction or belief should defeat admissibility because there is no fear of divine punishment. Courts generally have been satisfied that there is a psychological stimulus to be truthful when facing the uncertainties of death, even though the declarant has no fear of divine or supernatural sanction. Under this view, irreverence may be shown for the purpose of affecting the weight to be accorded the declaration, but not to defeat its admissibility. Weinstein & Mansfield, et al. at 840.

3. As with other evidence (except party admissions, Note 2 following Part A, and statements of family history, § 7.28, n. 2) there is a requirement that the proponent of a dying declaration show that circumstances support the conclusion that the declarant had first-

wife's declaration. Admissibility is now assured by the express provisions of Rule 804(b)(2).

6. Adv.Comm.Note to Fed.R.Evid. 804(b)(2).

7. The drafters of the Rule believed the influence of the impending death was not sufficient to ensure the trustworthiness of statements dealing with other matters. Id.

8. United States v. Sacasas, 381 F.2d 451, 454 (2d Cir.1967).

hand knowledge. However, if this requirement is met, the better-reasoned cases do not reject the declaration simply because it is phrased in terms that appear to violate the opinion rule. This position is sound, for it recognizes that the opinion rule should be confined in application to courtroom testimony that can be rephrased so as to eliminate unnecessary inferences or conclusions. Morgan & Weinstein at 267. See also § 4.9.

4. Note the overlap between dying declarations and excited utterances. To a significant degree the importance of the former is eclipsed by the latter. Thus, even though a proffered statement may not satisfy the conditions of a dying declaration, it may nonetheless qualify as an excited utterance. See 4 Weinstein & Berger, ¶ 804(b)(2)[01], at 113.

5. Does the exception for dying declarations implicate the confrontation clause of the Sixth Amendment, particularly where the victim is the only accusing "witness"? See § 7.31.

PART J. DECLARATIONS AGAINST INTEREST

§ 7.26 In General

Generally speaking, the present exception admits a hearsay statement of a nonparty when the statement was adverse to the declarant's interest. Statements or declarations against interest should be distinguished from party admissions: declarations against interest must be adverse to the interest of the declarant *at the time* of the utterance and the declarant must be unavailable. Unlike party admissions, which may be offered only against the admitting party, declarations against interest may be offered against *any* party. Party admissions, as we have seen,[1] do not have to be against interest when made and are not conditioned upon a showing of unavailability.

Because the use of a declaration against interest is conditioned upon a showing of unavailability, the exception has its most frequent application where the declarant is not a party. When the declarant is a party he is usually available to testify, and the hearsay exception more often applicable is that for party admissions. Although a party cannot introduce his own statement as a party admission, he can in theory (and does occasionally in prac-

§ 7.26

1. See § 7.1.

tice) put into evidence his declaration against interest. This seldom happens, of course, because of the dual requirements that the proffered statement be disserving when made and that the declarant be unavailable. From a tactical standpoint there usually is no incentive for the party-declarant to offer his disserving statement because it is apt to be inconsistent with his posture at trial. And, of course, the party-declarant usually is available, with the result that an essential condition of the exception for declarations against interest is not met. Hence, it may be generalized that declarations against interest are disserving statements, made by unavailable, nonparty declarants.[2]

The assumption that underlies the present hearsay exception is that a declarant is unlikely to make a disserving statement unless it is true. Common observation probably supports this proposition, putting aside special psychological conditions characterized by self-denigration. In this regard, it is interesting that until recent years statements coming within the declarations-against-interest exception were limited to those that were directly against the declarant's pecuniary or proprietary interest.[3] Thus, assertions coming within the exception have tended to have a business or financial flavor since they deal with matters of ownership or money. In this business context, the courts could, perhaps, more readily assume rational behavior. Statements against penal interest usually were rejected, although the law here has recently changed in many jurisdictions. Statements against one's social interest, often discussed by the commentators and considered in scattered cases, has gained only very limited support.[4]

§ 7.27 Declarations Against Interest: Application of the Exception

If the unavailable declarant has made a statement admitting that he owes money or acknowledging that he does not own property (or that his ownership is limited, impaired, or encumbered), he usually has satisfied the condition that his statement be against pecuniary or proprietary interest. Conversely, if the de-

2. For a comprehensive and incisive treatment of this exception, see Morgan, Declarations Against Interest, 5 Vand.L.Rev. 451 (1952); see also the influential article, Jefferson, Declarations Against Interest: An Exception to the Hearsay Rule, 58 Harv.L.Rev. 1 (1944).

3. McCormick, § 277, at 821.

4. See Adv.Comm.Note to Rule 804(b)(4) [now 804(b)(3)]; West's Ann. Cal.Evid.Code § 1230; Note 1 following Part J.

clarant has made a statement or a written entry indicating that he is owed $2,000 by *X*, the assertion normally is self-serving and outside the present exception. But a subsequent statement or entry showing that $2,000 has been received from *X* is an acknowledgment that the debt is no longer owing; thus, this last entry (the statement of receipt) has a disserving quality.[1] Although it is arguable that the trustworthiness of a statement of receipt of monies owed is suspect because the declarant may not realize that his assertion is against his interest, such a general contention probably should not defeat admissibility. Analytically, the courts correctly conclude that the statement of money received impairs or defeats a claim that a collectable debt still is outstanding.[2]

The question whether a statement is against interest must be answered in context, taking into account the circumstances attending the declaration. As we have seen, a statement that a debt is owed normally is against the declarant's interest. But it would not be so in circumstances where it is to the declarant's advantage to establish the debt. For example, it might be advantageous to the declarant to establish a debt in order to show that a transfer of his real property was not absolute, but was made only to secure an outstanding obligation.[3] To further illustrate, a statement by *X* that he is a member of a business partnership might be disserving if the partnership were in financial difficulty, but self-serving if the firm were solvent and the declarant wished to share in its proceeds.[4] In the usual case, the court will assess the nature of

§ 7.27

1. Knapp v. St. Louis Trust Co., 199 Mo. 640, 98 S.W. 70 (1906) (admitting not only that portion of a physician's entry regarding payment, but also that portion showing date of treatment and condition treated; see note 2 at the end of Part J).

2. A different problem is presented when an agent acknowledges receipt of money on behalf of his principal. Here the against-interest requirement arguably is satisfied because the agent indirectly is acknowledging his obligation to remit the sum received to his principal. A false entry might result in his liability to the principal for the amount recorded. See Jefferson, Declarations Against Interest: An Exception to the Hearsay Rule, 58 Harv.L.Rev. 1, 12 (1944).

3. Barrera v. Gonzalez, 341 S.W.2d 703 (Tex.Civ.App.1960), appeal after remand, 358 S.W.2d 233 (1962). Similarly, an entry of partial payment received, which arguably is against interest (because it is a recognition that part of the debt is no longer owed), made after the running of the statute of limitations may favor the declarant's interest if the effect of the payment is to revive the obligation. See Small v. Rose, 97 Me. 286, 54 A. 726 (1903).

4. V Wigmore, § 1463, at 337 (Chadbourn). For a federal case analyzing the "against requirement," see United States v. Gonzalez, 559 F.2d 1271 (5th Cir.1977).

the statement (as disserving or not) by inquiring whether, under all of the known circumstances, a reasonable man would consider the statement against his interest. The reasonable-man standard is relatively easy to apply and in most cases is the only practical measure of the nature of the declarant's statement, since discovering the subjective motivations of the absent declarant is not usually possible. The trial judge, however, will consider any evidence disclosing the motive or mental attitude of the particular declarant, and he will exclude the proffered hearsay declaration if he finds that this particular declarant did not consider the statement adverse to his interest.[5] This result is consistent with the rationale underlying the exception; that is, it would be inconsistent with the psychological basis of the exception for the judge to admit a declaration even though he was unable to satisfy himself that the *particular* declarant thought the statement disserving.

Courts have been faced with continuing pressure to expand the kinds of interests that will qualify under the exception. One argument finding increasing acceptance is that a statement sufficiently disserving should be admissible even though it may not *directly* or *immediately* address a proprietary or pecuniary interest: in other words, a contingent adverse economic interest should suffice. The major step in accepting this argument came when American courts began to hold that a statement indicating fault or other actionable conduct qualified as a declaration against pecuniary interest. A majority of courts now endorse the view that a statement which, if true, would render a declarant liable for damages in a tort action is sufficiently adverse to pecuniary interest to justify admission.[6] Similar reasoning should uphold the admissibility of any declaration that, if true, would result in civil liability, such as a statement indicating a breach of contract[7] or a declarant's assertion that he was the father of an illegitimate

5. The cases do not make this point clearly; however, most courts appear willing to consider evidence about the mental state of the particular declarant in question. See, e.g., Demasi v. Whitney Trust & Sav. Bank, 176 So. 703 (La.App.1937), where the court refers to the declarant as ignorant and not realizing the consequences of her statement. See also 4 Weinstein & Berger, ¶ 804(b)(3)[02], at 134–35. Rule 403 could be invoked to reject a declaration which, although disserving on its face, was apparently not construed by the particular declarant as against his interest. Id.

6. Home Ins. Co. v. Allied Telephone Co., 246 Ark. 1095, 442 S.W.2d 211 (1969); Neely v. Kansas City Pub. Serv. Co., 241 Mo.App. 1244, 252 S.W.2d 88 (1952); Duncan v. Smith, 393 S.W.2d 798 (Tex.1965). But see Morgan & Weinstein at 259, citing early cases that illustrate a "sharp conflict in the decisions."

7. See McCormick, § 277, at 822.

child.[8] Of course, a declarant's statement that his claim is weak or invalid is admissible as "against interest" if the other conditions of the exception are satisfied. A further extension, recognized in a growing number of jurisdictions, permits declarations against *penal* interest to come within the present exception. Thus, if the declarant makes a statement acknowledging conduct that would subject him to a criminal penalty, the statement is admissible. Some of the jurisdictions that admit this kind of disserving statement limit admissibility to *civil* trials where the criminal conduct described also constitutes a tort.[9] Thus, some courts bring declarations contingently against penal interest within the more familiar rule that recognizes the admissibility of statements acknowledging conduct that could lead to civil liability. Many jurisdictions, however, have taken a direct approach. They frankly recognize that statements against penal interest, which implicate both monetary loss and more severe penalties such as incarceration, potentially are the most disserving of all adverse statements.[10] These courts hold that declarations that could lead to criminal liability fall within the present exception, and admit these statements in both civil and criminal trials.[11]

A growing number of jurisdictions that generally extend the exception to penal interests nonetheless show apprehension about fabricated evidence, especially in criminal trials. This judicial skepticism most often occurs when an accused, attempting to raise a reasonable doubt, offers a hearsay declaration inculpating an unavailable declarant. The declaration is offered to show that the declarant, not the accused, committed the crime. When a defendant tries thus to implicate an absent third person, a court may suspect fabricated evidence. Consequently, it is a common requirement that the admissibility of the declaration against penal interest, offered in exculpation by the accused in a criminal trial, is conditioned on the existence of corroborative evidence that increases the likelihood that the absent declarant committed the

8. The latter statement, of course, raises the possibility of judicially imposed support payments. In Ferguson v. Smazer, 151 Conn. 226, 196 A.2d 432 (1963), the court acknowledged that such a declaration was against pecuniary interest, but then rejected the statement on several grounds that should have affected weight, not admissibility.

9. McCormick, § 278, at 823. Cf. State v. Gorden, 356 Mo. 1010, 204 S.W.2d 713 (1947) (statement held inadmissible).

10. See, e.g., Hines v. Commonwealth, 136 Va. 728, 117 S.E. 843 (1923).

11. See People v. Brown, 26 N.Y.2d 88, 308 N.Y.S.2d 825, 257 N.E.2d 16 (1970). See also N.J.Evid., Rule 63(10).

crime in question.[12] Such corroborative evidence, for example, might indicate the declarant's motive, establish his presence at the scene of the crime, or show other circumstances tending to confirm the trustworthiness of the declaration.

Federal Rule of Evidence 804(b)(3) adopts the holdings of recent decisions:

> *Statement against interest.* A statement which was at the time of its making so far contrary to the declarant's pecuniary or proprietary interest, or so far tended to subject him to civil or criminal liability, or to render invalid a claim by him against another, that a reasonable man in his position would not have made the statement unless he believed it to be true. A statement tending to expose the declarant to criminal liability and offered to exculpate the accused is not admissible unless corroborating circumstances clearly indicate the trustworthiness of the statement.

The Federal Rule uses a reasonableness standard for determining whether a statement is disserving, but this standard should not prohibit an inquiry by the judge as to whether the *particular* declarant in question viewed the statement as against his interest. In the great majority of cases, no issue arises whether circumstances peculiar to a particular declarant should render self-serving or neutral a statement that a reasonable man would find adverse. But where the opponent produces evidence to show that the declarant in question did not view the proffered statement as one against interest, the judge should exercise the power conferred by Federal Rule 403 to exclude the statement on the ground that its probative value is outweighed by the risk that it will mislead the jury.

One further circumstance requires clarification. Suppose the declaration is one that, on its face at least, is plainly against interest. It could be argued that despite its disserving character the statement is not within the present exception because the declarant believed that the listener would not reveal the statement to a third person. In short, the declarant did not believe that *making* the statement was against his interest, even though the *content* of the statement was disserving. It appears that the disserving content should bring the declaration within the exception, especially in circumstances where the declarant is likely to

12. See, e.g., N.M.R.Evid. 11–804(B)(4); Maine R.Evid. 804(b)(3).

be candid.[13] That is, the present exception should ordinarily embrace any declaration that by reason either of its content ("Just between us, I stole the car.") or context ("I'm a partner in [insolvent] ABC Firm.") is against the declarant's interest.[14]

Rule 804(b)(3) also takes a cautious approach to the introduction of a statement against penal interest offered to exculpate the accused in a criminal case. Admissibility of the against-penal-interest declaration is made dependent upon a showing of "corroborating circumstances [that] clearly indicate the trustworthiness of the statement." [15] Thus, in a criminal case, the accused seeking to show that another person committed the crime in question must couple his offer of the other person's inculpatory hearsay statement with a showing of corroborating evidence. As noted above, this corroboration can take various forms, such as a showing that the declarant had a motive to commit the crime, that he was at the scene of the offense, or that his subsequent conduct indicates guilt.[16]

Notes

1. Should a statement that exposes the declarant to hatred, ridicule, or disgrace come within the against-interest exception to the hearsay rule? Such statements against one's social interest have received more attention from the commentators than acceptance by the courts. Earlier drafts of the Federal Rules of Evidence contained a provision that included disserving social statements among those that qualified as "against interest." But Congress found such declarations "lacking sufficient guarantees of reliability" and deleted the provision. H.R.Rep. No. 650, 93rd Cong. 2d Sess. 16 (1973). For cases discussing declarations against social interests see United States v. Dovico, 261 F.Supp. 862 (S.D.N.Y.1966), aff'd, 380 F.2d 325 (2d Cir.), cert. denied, 389 U.S. 944 (1967); State v. Sanders, 27 Utah 2d 354, 357–59, 496 P.2d 270, 272–73 (1972). For statutes providing that such declarations are admissible, see West's Ann.Cal.Evid.Code § 1230, Nev.Rev.Stat. 51.345; Kan.R. Civ.Pro. § 60–460(j).

13. See United States v. Goins, 593 F.2d 88, 90–91 (8th Cir.), cert. denied, 444 U.S. 827 (1979).

14. See 4 Louisell & Mueller, § 489, at 1134–1147.

15. Compare United States v. Atkins, 558 F.2d 133 (3d Cir.), cert. denied, 434 U.S. 929 (1977) (corroboration sufficient) with United States v. Guillette, 547 F.2d 743 (2d Cir.1976), cert. denied, 434 U.S. 839 (1977) (insufficient).

16. 4 Louisell & Mueller, § 489, at 1159–1165.

2. Courts still struggle with the admissibility of statements that in part are disserving and in part are self-serving or neutral. Severance of the declaration by admitting *only* the disserving portions is one possibility, although in some contexts such a procedure may distort impact and meaning. (Also, it may be that only the self-serving or neutral portion of the statement is relevant to an issue.) Another possibility is for the trial judge to evaluate the statement as a whole to try to determine whether the disserving aspects preponderate. The cases are not harmonious. See McCormick, § 279, at 825; 4 Weinstein & Berger, ¶ 804(b)(3)[02], at 136–38. Where portions of the statement(s) that are not adverse are more or less neutral, the case for admission of the entire statement is strong. Where the balance is close and severance is not a practical alternative, much deference should be given to the trial judge's discretion. The most difficult case is a third person's assertion that he and another person (*X*) committed an illegal act. Assume that the act was committed either by the declarant and *X* or by the declarant and *D*, the accused in the present case. *D* offers the statement of the unavailable declarant to support the proposition that *X*, not *D*, was the accomplice. Assuming that there are corroborating circumstances required of statements against interest used for exculpatory purposes, the problem remains whether the relevant part of the declarant's statement (*X* was the accomplice) is sufficiently linked to the disserving portion of the statement to be admitted. See United States v. Barrett, 539 F.2d 244 (1st Cir.1976), in which the declarant's statement about *X* was admissible under the present exception. Two noted commentators make the suggestion that the judge should explain to the jury the rationale of the hearsay exception for against-interest statements so as to enable them to evaluate more accurately combined statements that are not entirely disserving. See 4 Weinstein & Berger, ¶ 804(b)(3)[02], at 138.

3. In certain circumstances, rejection of a declaration against penal interest, when coupled with other restrictive rulings, is a violation of due process. The leading case is Chambers v. Mississippi, 410 U.S. 284 (1973), the peculiar facts of which arguably confine the holding to comparatively few situations. Chambers, the accused, moved to call as an adverse witness *X*, an *available* declarant who had confessed to the crime of murder with which Chambers was charged. The trial judge denied this motion, but did allow Chambers to elicit from *X* during direct examination testimony that the latter had given a written confession admitting guilt for the crime in question; on cross, the prosecutor showed that *X* had repudiated the confession and, further, secured testimony from *X* that he was not at the scene of the crime when the fatal shot was fired. Because the court refused to permit Chambers' lawyer to treat *X* as an adverse

witness, counsel was denied the opportunity to conduct a hostile examination designed to weaken or destroy *X*'s claim of alibi and to attack the credibility of *X*'s repudiation of his written confession. Blocked from this line of proof, Chambers sought to present certain witnesses to whom *X* orally had admitted his (*X*'s) perpetration of the killing in question. The trial judge ruled the evidence inadmissible on hearsay grounds.

In reversing the conviction on the basis that the sum of the judge's rulings denied Chambers due process of law, the United States Supreme Court discussed declarations against penal interest. It found that the corroborating circumstances made *X*'s verbal declarations against penal interest trustworthy. These circumstances included testimony that *X* was at the scene, that he had a gun of the type used in the killing, that he had admitted his guilt soon after the murder and on more than one occasion, and that his declarations unequivocally were against his interest. The court also found it significant that *X* was in the courtroom and subject to examination under oath. Note, however, the usual requirement, applied in both federal and state cases and adopted in Fed.R.Evid. 804(b)(3), that the declarant be unavailable before the exception for declarations against interest is applicable.

PART K. HEARSAY AND EXCEPTIONS: PAST AND FUTURE

§ 7.28 Change Through Evolution and the Residual Exceptions

No aspect of Anglo-American evidentiary law has drawn more attention and commentary than the hearsay rule and its various exceptions. As with other controversial subjects, the hearsay rule has its ardent defenders and critics.[1] The basic rule and its exceptions—some of which are omitted[2] from this text—can be criticized as resting upon untested premises and assumptions.

§ 7.28

1. See, e.g., Taylor, The Case for Secondary Evidence, 81 Cas. & Com. 46 (Jan.-Feb. 1976); 2 Jones on Evidence, §§ 8:1–8:3 (6th ed. 1972) (collecting authorities pro and con); Maguire, The Hearsay System: Around and Through the Thicket, 14 Vand.L.Rev. 741 (1961).

2. The Federal Rules of Evidence contain twenty-nine exceptions to the hearsay rule, not including party admissions which the Federal Rules treat as nonhearsay. The exception for learned treatises appearing as 803(18) is briefly considered in connection with expert testimony. § 12.3. Note especially another Rule 803 provision, the exception for ancient documents. Rule 803(16) excepts from the hearsay exclusionary rule:

> Statements in ancient documents. Statements in a document in exis-

tence twenty years or more the authenticity of which is established.

Necessity plays a dominant role in this exception because the declarant who makes assertions in a document aged twenty or more years likely is unavailable or without sufficient memory to testify. Note, however, that the unavailability of the declarant is immaterial to the application of the exception. To the extent this exception rests on trustworthiness, such reliability probably is found in the fact that the statement far antedates the present controversy; if there was a motive to misrepresent, it is unlikely that the source of the motive is the controversy in which the aged document is offered. Furthermore, additional reliability is gained if the accuracy of the document—assuming its existence was continuously known—has not been challenged for twenty or more years. Presumably, if the case were otherwise and the document were suspect, the judge could exclude it. See Fed.R.Evid. 403.

Many, but not all, common-law jurisdictions recognize the exception for statements contained in ancient documents. At common law the document must be thirty or more years old. Some jurisdictions limit the exception to dispositive statements or recitals in documents that are likely to be drafted carefully. The hearsay exception for ancient documents should be distinguished from the ancient document rule pertaining to the authentication of writings. See § 13.7.

One use of the ancient documents exception is to prove family relationships where an issue of kinship arises. But all jurisdictions recognize in some form the "pedigree exception," which can be used in establishing family relationships such as births, marriages, divorces, degree of kinship, etc. This common-law doctrine is hedged with restrictions: where the issue concerns *X* (for example, his birth, death, etc.) or the relationship of *X* to *Y*, the proponent must show that the declarant was related by blood to *X* (in the first example) or to *X* or *Y* (in the second example). It also sufficed that the declarant was married to *X* (first example) or to *X* or *Y* (second example); affinity more distant than that of the spouse of the subject of the declaration would not suffice under the orthodox common-law view. Morgan & Weinstein at 301–02. Some courts even required that when the statement concerns *X* and *Y*, the proponent must show the declarant's relationship *to both*. Id. at 304. Thus although *Z*, a declarant married to *Y*, in *most* jurisdictions could make a statement about *Y* and *X* that would fall within the exception, members of *Z*'s family (unrelated to *X* or *Y* by blood) could not give admissible declarations about the relationship of *X* and *Y*. Recent decisions, however, extend the exception to include persons, such as a physician or minister, so situated as to know the facts even though the kinship is missing. Id. at 302.

The common law insisted that the declaration be made prior to the present controversy or, at least, before the controversy was known to the declarant. As developed under the common law, the reliability of this exception depends upon (1) the knowledge (even though not firsthand) that family members usually have about their own family and (2) absence of a motive to falsify. The assumption is that a family-member declarant is likely to speak truthfully about relationships within his own family; for one thing, his statements often are subject to verification by other family members. The common law also required that the declarant be unavailable, thus heightening the need for the hearsay evidence falling within the exception.

The Federal Rules expand the pedigree exception under the title "statement of personal and family history." Rule 804(b)(4) provides that when the declarant is unavailable, there shall be an exception for:

(A) A statement concerning the declarant's own birth, adoption, marriage, divorce, legitimacy, relation-

Arguably, the hearsay rule impairs the process of litigation because the basic rule operates to block valuable evidence, whereas many of the exceptions admit evidence that is suspect.[3] The validity of this hypothesis is doubtful and in any event cannot be tested here, but the rule and its exceptions deserve some further exploration.

The basic exclusionary rule, rejecting all extrajudicial statements offered for their truth and not within a recognized exception, accepts the proposition that cross-examination can expose evidentiary infirmities such as inaccurate perception, poor memory, insincerity, and mistransmission. Although it is difficult to imagine an adversarial system that accords no value to the efficacy of cross-examination, no one yet has empirically demonstrated that adversarial cross-questioning usually lays bare these infirmities. What repeatedly is shown by common experience, however, is that cross-examination often causes a witness to express uncertainty, give additional information, or, sometimes, modify or repudiate his direct testimony. Thus, even without a convincing demonstration that cross-examination is beyond any doubt "the greatest legal engine ever invented for the discovery of truth,"[4] a showing that it often causes a witness to change his testimony, either in emphasis or context, is enough to justify cross-questioning as a central feature of the adversary system. This suggests that attempts to abandon or nullify the rule against hearsay evidence are unlikely to be successful so long as the basic tenets of the adversary proceeding are retained. Because the adversarial posture demands the opportunity for cross-examination, the hearsay rule—which protects that right by rejecting "untested" evidence not within an exception—is not easily forsaken.

ship by blood, adoption, or marriage, ancestry, or other similar fact of personal or family history, even though the declarant had no means of acquiring personal knowledge of the matter stated; or (B) a statement concerning the foregoing matters, and death also, of another person, if the declarant was related to the other by blood, adoption, or marriage or was so intimately associated with the other's family as to be likely to have accurate information concerning the matter declared.

This provision discards by omission the common-law requirement that the declaration predate the controversy, extends the exceptions to include declarants closely associated with the family in question, and requires only a relationship between the declarant and one of the persons spoken of in the declaration.

3. Cf. Note, Erosion of the Hearsay Rule, 3 U. of Richmond L.Rev. 89, 103 (1968).

4. V Wigmore, § 1367, at 32 (Chadbourn).

As to the exceptions, these are the product of an evolutionary process that began two centuries ago.[5] The result of pragmatic accommodation, they lack the symmetry and consistency of a comprehensive design or preconceived plan. The behavioral assumptions underlying the exceptions more readily are traced to the judges' view of human nature than to the controlled inquiry of behavioral scientists. Research has confirmed the validity of some of these assumptions, while casting doubt upon others.[6]

The recognition or retention of an exception, however, should not depend entirely upon the law's accuracy in predicting conditions in which a declarant is likely to be truthful. The most important question is whether accurate factfinding is advanced or hindered by acceptance of the hearsay evidence in question. A reasoned answer to this depends not only upon the probable degree of reliability of the evidence, but also upon the tribunal's need for the evidence and the extent to which the trier can be alerted to its possible infirmities. Testimonial infirmities, such as defects in memory or sincerity, that underlie the hearsay rule also may be valuable in assessing the probative force of hearsay evidence. The justification for an exception need not rest upon a showing of high reliability; it is sufficient that the exception generally operates to admit evidence that has a sufficient degree of truthworthiness to promote accuracy in the factfinding process. Tested by this standard, the present exceptions are more defensible.

A suggestion that there is a degree of permanence to the present hearsay system, consisting of a basic exclusionary rule and multiple exceptions, should not imply that the system is static. Neither history nor logic suggests this. Both legislative and judicial movement have broadened existing exceptions and, with perhaps less frequency, created new ones. Illustrative of this trend are the decisions or legislative provisions (including court

5. V Wigmore, § 1426, at 257 (Chadbourn).

6. See, e.g., Stewart, Perception, Memory, and Hearsay: A Criticism of Present Law and the Proposed Federal Rules of Evidence, 1970 Utah L.Rev. 1; Hutchins & Slesinger, Some Observations on the Law of Evidence: Spontaneous Exclamations, 25 Colum.L.Rev. 432 (1928). Lempert & Saltzburg at 414–15 cite and comment upon the findings of Elizabeth Loftus and her associates, with special attention to the implications for the hearsay rule. See also Comment, Do the Eyes Have it? Psychological Testimony Regarding Eyewitness Accuracy, 38 Baylor L.Rev. 169 (1986); Lempert, Statistics in the Courtroom: Building on Rubinfield, 85 Colum.L.Rev. 1098 (1985).

rules) that have enlarged the exceptions for business entries, statements of physical condition, and dying declarations. The same processes of cautious, incremental movement also have given shape to exceptions of more recent origin, such as those for present sense impressions, opinion surveys, and prior identifications.[7] Additionally, both legislatures and courts have demonstrated inventiveness in providing for the admissibility of needed hearsay evidence found sufficiently reliable to justify consideration by the factfinder, but which does not come within an established exception.[8]

Federal Rule 803(24), a carefully drawn "residual" or "catch-all" exception to the hearsay rule, admits into evidence a probative statement, needed by the trier, when the "circumstantial guarantees of trustworthiness" are equivalent to those underlying the recognized exceptions. This Rule, which appears at the end of the exceptions grouped under Rule 803 (availability of declarant immaterial) and again at the end of the exceptions listed under Rule 804(b) (unavailability of declarant a condition of admissibility) provides:

> Other exceptions. A statement not specifically covered by any of the foregoing exceptions but having equivalent circumstantial guarantees of trustworthiness [is admissible], if the court determines that (A) the statement is offered as evidence of a material fact; (B) the statement is more probative on the point for which it is offered than any other evidence which the proponent can procure through reasonable efforts; and (C) the general purposes of these rules and the interests of justice will best be served by admission of the

7. The exception for learned treatises, also comparatively recent, is mentioned in § 12.3. See also Fed.R.Evid. 803(18). It should be noted that at least two jurisdictions have adopted an exception for statements of recent perception. See N.M.R.Evid. 11–4–804(B)(2). Wis.Stat.Ann. 908.045(2) provides that if the declarant is unavailable there shall be a hearsay exception for a:

> Statement of recent perception. A statement, not in response to the instigation of a person engaged in investigating, litigating, or settling a claim, which narrates, describes, or explains an event or condition recently perceived by the declarant, made in good faith, not in contemplation of pending or anticipated litigation in which he was interested, and while his recollection was clear.

8. See Mass.Gen.Laws Ann. c. 233, § 65 (admitting statements of a deceased person in civil actions if court finds declarations made in good faith upon personal knowledge); S.D.Codif. Laws 19–16–34 (admitting statements of decedent in suits by or against personal representatives); Dallas County v. Commercial Union Assur. Co., 286 F.2d 388 (5th Cir.1961) (newspaper account of fire in courthouse admitted to show fact of fire where cause of structural damage was in dispute).

> statement into evidence. However, a statement may not be admitted under this exception unless the proponent of it makes known to the adverse party sufficiently in advance of trial or hearing to provide the adverse party with a fair opportunity to prepare to meet it, his intention to offer the statement and the particulars of it, including the name and address of the declarant.

Generally speaking, this Rule has received a fairly sympathetic reading from most courts.[9] For example, the catch-all exception has been invoked to admit the statement of an unavailable superintendent concerning how the decedent-repairman was instructed to gain access to the roof of a garage; [10] to allow the unsworn statement of a since-deceased mechanic describing how a car ignited when the plaintiff attempted to start it; [11] and to receive statements made to a grand jury by a declarant who now refuses to testify.[12] The principal issue upon which admissibility turns is whether the proffered statement has "circumstantial guarantees of trustworthiness" [13] that are the "equivalent" of those that generally attend the recognized exceptions. Thus, factors such as a lack of motive to fabricate, strong indication that there was ample opportunity to perceive, a relatively brief period between the event and the hearsay statement describing it, and the consistency of the statement with other corroborating circumstances attending the event [14] are all features that point toward admissibility. The other requirements of the catch-all exception are relatively easy to satisfy. Even the notice requirement is often excused if the need for the hearsay does not arise until late in the

9. See, e.g., Nowell v. Universal Electric Co., 792 F.2d 1310 (5th Cir. 1986), cert. denied, ___ U.S. ___ (1986); United States v. Hitsman, 604 F.2d 443 (5th Cir.1979); Huff v. White Motor Corp., 609 F.2d 286 (7th Cir.1979). But the cases nonetheless show marked disparities. For a discussion of recent judicial treatment of the rule, see 4 Louisell & Mueller, § 472, and cases collected in the 1986 supplement at 233. See also Grant, The Equivalent Guarantees of Trustworthiness Standard for Federal Rule of Evidence 803(24), 90 Dick.L.Rev. 75 (1985). See n. 22 infra.

10. Robinson v. Shapiro, 646 F.2d 734 (2d Cir.1981).

11. Turbyfill v. International Harvester Co., 486 F.Supp. 232 (E.D.Mich. 1980).

12. United States v. Garner, 574 F.2d 1141 (4th Cir.1978), cert. denied, McKethan v. United States, 439 U.S. 936 (1978); United States v. Marchini, 797 F.2d 759 (9th Cir.1986).

13. See Fed.Rules 803(24) and 804(b)(5).

14. Robinson v. Shapiro, 646 F.2d 734 (2d Cir.1981); McCormick, § 324.1, at 908; Emerging Problems Under the Federal Rules of Evidence 279–94 (ABA Section of Litigation 1983). But see Grant, supra n. 9, criticizing the use of this last factor in assessing trustworthiness.

litigation and the trial judge grants a continuance that allows the opponent to prepare his rebuttal.[15]

Note, however, that the residual exception appears at the conclusion of the Rule 803 exceptions[16] (which are applicable whether or not the declarant is available) and in identical language at the end of the Rule 804 exceptions[17] (which apply *only* if the declarant is unavailable). Thus, in instances where the declarant is available or where there are doubts whether any of the "unavailability criteria" of Rule 804[18] have been satisfied, the proponent presumably will rely on the residual exception as set out in Rule 803, arguing that the availability of the declarant is immaterial. But the possible availability of the declarant is germane even to the residual exception contained in Rule 803: the exception applies only if the proffered hearsay statement "is more probative on the point for which it is offered than any other evidence which the proponent can procure through reasonable efforts."[19] This requirement will block the hearsay declaration if the trial judge determines the testimony or deposition of the declarant can be reasonably secured and is more probative than his hearsay statement.[20]

Although cases decided under the residual exceptions continuously increase, their precedential value is limited. The circumstances vary from case to case, and a measure of discretion is accorded the trial judge.[21] The salient feature of Rule 803(24) and its counterpart in Rule 804(b) is the frank recognition that no list of exceptions can account for the nuances or the endlessly varied contexts from which hearsay evidence may spring. Within the guidelines set forth in the Rule, a trial judge now can make a realistic appraisal of the variables that should determine admissibility.[22] Thus, the Rule not only accommodates previously unencountered or unforeseen situations, but also helps courts

15. Weinstein & Mansfield, et al. at 865.

16. See Fed.R.Evid. (803)(24).

17. See Fed.R.Evid. (804)(b)(5).

18. See Fed.R.Evid. (804)(a).

19. See Fed.R.Evid. (803)(24).

20. United States v. Mathis, 559 F.2d 294 (5th Cir.1977).

21. Again see Nowell v. Universal Electric Company, 792 F.2d 1310, 1315 (5th Cir.1986), cert. denied, ___ U.S. ___ (1986), and Page v. Barko Hydraulics, 673 F.2d 134, 140 (5th Cir.1982).

22. For an excellent discussion of the rule see 4 Louisell & Mueller, § 472, at 921–940, emphasizing the tension between the desire to admit evidence that appears trustworthy and the competing desire to invoke the residual exceptions sparingly so as to avoid substantially undermining the hearsay rule.

identify circumstances in which the creation of a new exception might be justified. This latter usage provides a convenient bridge between past and future.

PART L. THE CONFRONTATION CLAUSE

§ 7.29 The Confrontation Clause: Historical Context [1]

An intractable problem in criminal trials is to reconcile the accused's constitutional right "to be confronted with the witnesses against him" with the government's invocation of various exceptions to the rule against hearsay.[2] When applicable, these exceptions permit evidence detailing a hearsay declarant's out-of-court statement, enabling the trier of fact to consider this declaration for the truth of its content. In theory, hearsay that falls within an exception is attended by surrounding circumstances that make it more reliable than ordinary extra-judicial statements. This enhanced trustworthiness supposedly justifies admission of the excepted statements even though the declarant is not subjected to the usual requirement of cross-examination.[3]

Under one construction of the confrontation clause, the state's introduction of hearsay evidence sanctioned by an exception would be unconstitutional. The "witness against" the accused would be the hearsay declarant, and to ensure confrontation, the declarant's presence at trial would be constitutionally compelled. Without this confrontation, the hearsay declaration would be inadmissible. Under another construction the Constitution would be satisfied if evidence against the accused were presented through a witness subject to confrontation, as for example, a witness who testifies to the statement of the hearsay declarant. It would be of no constitutional concern that the accused could not test the basis and

§ 7.29

1. Portions of sections 7.29–7.31 are excerpted from Lilly, Notes on The Confrontation Clause and Ohio v. Roberts, 36 Univ. of Fla.L.Rev. 207 (1984).

2. The constitutional provision is found in U. S. Const. amend VI. A list of hearsay exceptions appears in Fed.R. Evid. 803–04; West's Ann.Cal.Evid.Code §§ 1220–1340. As of this writing, about 31 states have adopted evidence codes which are either identical or substantially similar to the Federal Rules of Evidence. Of course, the common law developed a catalogue of exceptions which served as the basis of the modern codes. For a general description and analysis of the various hearsay exceptions, see McCormick at 759–774 (1984).

3. Cross-examination is useful for testing defects in perception, memory, sincerity, and narration (mistranscription)—the latter denoting mistakes that occur because of ambiguities or unintended omissions in the declarant's statements. See § 6.1.

accuracy of the declarant's statement.[4] Under this construction, the Constitution would require only that the accused be permitted to confront and examine those persons who actually testify against him at trial. Between these extremes lie variant possibilities,[5] some of which will be sketched below. Preliminarily, however, a brief recourse to history will suggest the ambiguities that cloud the Framers' intentions.

"[T]he Confrontation Clause," remarked Justice Harlan, "comes to us on faded parchment."[6] Harlan's own search for historical explication of the clause yielded no convincing evidence of its intended meaning.[7] Commentators have associated the passage of the clause with the notorious abuses at the trial of Sir Walter Raleigh in 1603.[8] There the Crown's principal evidence to support its charge of conspiracy of treason consisted of highly suspect hearsay declarations. Raleigh repeatedly was denied the right to confront and examine his principal accuser. The trial concluded in a conviction, and Raleigh was eventually executed.[9]

No doubt this trial and perhaps others of similar notoriety largely account for the rule forbidding hearsay evidence.[10] Wigmore declared that the hearsay rule secured the right of cross-

4. Id. Presumably, the accused adequately could examine the in-court witness with respect to whether the declarant had made a statement and, if so, precisely what words were spoken. The accused, however, would be unable to test whether the declaration in question was credible because he could not test the accuracy of the declarant's perception, probe the strength of his recollection, or attempt to reveal his desire to be truthful. § 6.1.

5. The literature, replete with proposed constructions, is extensive. Ample bibliographies may be found in Ohio v. Roberts, 448 U.S. 56, 66 n. 9 (1980) and 4 Weinstein & Berger, ¶ 800[04], at 19–35.

6. California v. Green, 399 U.S. 149, 173–74 (1970) (Harlan, J., concurring).

7. Id. at 176 n. 8.

8. The connection seems first to have been made in Hadley, The Reform of Criminal Procedure, 10 Proceedings of the Academy of Political Science 396, 400–01 (1924). See also F. Heller, The Sixth Amendment 104 (1951) (stating simply that confrontation was a common law right which "had gained recognition as a result of the abuses in the trial of Sir Walter Raleigh."); Lempert & Saltzburg at 551 (noting that most scholars believe the "framers drafted the confrontation clause to curb abuses associated with such celebrated English trials as the trial of Sir Walter Raleigh.").

9. A description of the trial is given in Graham, The Right of Confrontation and the Hearsay Rule: Sir Walter Raleigh Loses Another One, 8 Crim.L.Bull. 99, 100–01 (1972). This account relies upon 2 T. Howell, State Trials 1 (1816). Other descriptions: 1 D. Jardine, Historical Criminal Trials 389–511 (1832); H. Stephen, "The Trial of Sir Walter Raleigh," Trans. Royal Hist. Soc'y 172 (4th series 1919); see also Pollitt, The Right of Confrontation: Its History and Modern Dress, 8 J.Pub.L. 381, 388–89 (1959).

10. V Wigmore, § 1364, at 22–28 (Chadbourn).

examination, which in his view was essentially the same as the common-law right of confrontation.[11] He noted, however, that these two common-law protections were sometimes referred to as if they were distinct.[12] In any event, the hearsay rule, perhaps the single most important evidentiary rule in American common law, originated in seventeenth century English practice.[13] The recognition and maturation of that rule, even if accurately attributable to the 1603 trial of Raleigh, nonetheless fails to explain why the Americans adopted a constitutional right of confrontation in 1791. One would at least expect a more immediate cause or, perhaps, some indication that over the long term the hearsay rule had failed to provide the accused adequate protection.

Even if Raleigh's trial was the major influence in the adoption of the confrontation clause, the meaning and reach of that clause is still doubtful. The assumption that the confrontation clause was designed to forbid the kind of flagrant abuses practiced in Raleigh's trial does not eliminate doubts about its intended reach. The evidence used against Raleigh apparently fits no hearsay exception, early or modern.[14] One could thus conclude that the

11. Id. §§ 1365 at 28, 1397 at 155–62.

12. Id. § 1365.

13. Id. § 1364.

14. The principal hearsay statements were those of Lord Cobham declaring, for example, that Raleigh had conspired with Cobham to commit treason and dethrone the Queen of England. Pollitt, supra n. 9, at 388. Cobham's statements implicating Raleigh would not be against Cobham's penal interest; therefore, under a strict construction of the exception for declarations against interest his statement would not be admissible. See McCormick, § 279, at 825. Furthermore, the exception for such declarations requires that the declarant be unavailable. See id. at 819, 827; Morgan, Declarations Against Interest, 5 Vand.L.Rev. 451, 475 (1952) (noting that "the English courts have been especially strict and have refused to recognize any cause [for admissibility of a declaration against interest] except death of the declarant. The early American cases put insanity in the same category as death but are generally hesitant about going further."). See also Jefferson, Declarations Against Interest: An Exception to the Hearsay Rule, 58 Harv.L.Rev. 1, 2–3 (1944) (noting that authorities established death as the test of unavailability). For a modern view of what constitutes unavailability, see Fed.R.Evid. 804(a).

Possibly, Cobham's statement would be admissible under the coconspirator exception. It does not appear, however, that Cobham's statements were made during and in furtherance of the conspiracy as required by most authorities. See McCormick, § 267, at 792–794 (the requirement that the statement must be made in furtherance of the conspiracy calls for the exclusion of admissions and confessions made "after the termination of the conspiracy."); Fed.R.Evid. 801(d)(2)(E). At least one state has broadened admissibility so as to embrace a co-conspirator's statement made during the period when the conspirators are trying to conceal their crime. See Official Code Ga.Ann. § 24–3–52 (1982); Chatterton v. State, 221 Ga. 424, 144 S.E.2d 726 (1965), cert. denied, 384 U.S. 1015 (1966). See McCormick at

confrontation clause was intended only to forbid hearsay evidence that falls outside a recognized exception;[15] so construed the clause would protect the accused from the type of gross transgression which led to Raleigh's conviction. This construction would not bar evidence that came within an established hearsay exception. Wigmore, because he equated the rights of confrontation and cross-examination, would apparently agree with this interpretation.[16] The obvious difficulty with this construction is that it permits the law of evidence to dictate the reach of a parallel constitutional provision. The resulting anomaly is that the scope of constitutional protection is placed in the hands of judges and legislators who fashion the hearsay exceptions.

Other historical interpretations, however, are also plausible. For example, the clause might have been the Framers' response to the much resented vice-admiralty courts. Established by the British, these tribunals gained jurisdiction to punish violators of acts that restricted the colonists' rights of international trade.[17] Initially, the colonial common law courts had jurisdiction over

793 ("attempts to expand the so-called 'concealment phase' to include all efforts to avoid detection have generally failed."). A few cases, criticized by McCormick, take a broad view of the "concealment phase" of the conspiracy. See, e.g., Evans v. State, 222 Ga. 392, 150 S.E.2d 240 (1966), aff'd, Dutton v. Evans, 400 U.S. 74 (1970). It remains difficult, however, to fit Cobham's assertions within even an expansive version of the conspiracy exception.

There is also evidence that Cobham was tortured in an effort to gain incriminatory statements about Raleigh. See Pollitt, supra n. 9, at 388–89. Of course, this would make the statements inadmissible quite aside from the hearsay rule.

15. This is essentially Wigmore's position. See V Wigmore §§ 1365, 1397 (Chadbourn). Often debated is his principal assertion that the mission of the confrontation clause is to assure that trials are conducted in the adversarial mode, notably including cross-examination of the in-court witness. If this proposition is accepted, and evidence of an out-of-court declaration is admitted under a hearsay exception sanctioned by the adversary system, the Constitution would not be offended. Id., § 1397, at 158. Note that Wigmore did not go so far as to urge that examination of the live witness always satisfied the constitutional requirement. For constitutional compliance, the in-court witness must be giving evidence that falls within a recognized hearsay exception. Id.

16. Id.

17. Regarding the vice-admiralty courts, one commentator noted, "[c]rown officials come later to regard these courts as suitable for enforcement of all Parliamental acts which regulated trade in the colonies." Lovejoy, Rights Imply Equality: The Case Against Admiralty Jurisdiction in America, 1764–1776, 16 Wm. & Mary Q. 459, 461–62 (1959). The final significant legislative development in admiralty jurisdiction was the Sugar Act in 1764, 4 Geo. III, ch. 15, § 41, in 26 Stat. (Pickering) 32, 49 (London 1761); a similar provision of such jurisdiction is found in the Stamp Act, 5 Geo. III, ch. 12, §§ 57–58, 49 Stat. (Pickering) 179, 202–03 (London 1761).

these offenders. The earlier prosecutions were conducted in the traditional adversarial mode, which included examination of witnesses in open court and trial by jury. The significance of the latter, coupled with British apprehension that colonial juries were unwilling to convict fellow colonists, led Parliament to enlarge the jurisdiction of the vice-admiralty courts.[18] These courts sat without a jury and their procedure was based upon civil law.[19] The colonists strenuously objected to this mode of trial which in England was carefully restricted. Indeed, the Virginia Declaration of Rights, upon which the confrontation clause appears to have been based, might have been an early attempt to curb the perceived abuses of the civil law procedure of the vice-admiralty courts.[20] By the constitutional adoption of the accused's right to confront adverse witnesses, the Framers provided formidable security against the inquisitional practice of examining witnesses in closed chambers. It is thus possible that the confrontation clause was intended to address only the general mode of trial by securing the common-law procedures enjoyed by Englishmen but denied to Americans in the courts of vice-admiralty. The drafters of the Sixth Amendment may not have had any intention of negating recognized exceptions to the hearsay rule. They simply wanted to insure adherence to the common-law adversarial system.

Even if this thesis is accurate, it does not inevitably follow that the confrontation clause is entirely neutral with regard to

18. Pollitt, supra n. 9, at 396.

19. Id. at 397. See also D. Towle, Records of the Vice-Admiralty Court of Rhode Island, 1716–1752, 91–93 (1936) ("The English Government set up in the American colonies a civil law court . . . a court the practices of which were very different from those of the common law."). Id. at 91.

20. The Virginia provision stated "[t]hat in all capital or criminal prosecutions a man hath a right . . . to be confronted with the accusers and witnesses." 6 American Archives, 1561 (P. Force, ed. 4th series 1846).

James Madison prepared and introduced into the First Congress proposed amendments designed to satisfy political disagreements so that the Constitution would be ratified. While campaigning for Congress, Madison had pledged himself to support a Bill of Rights to be added to the Constitution. Using the language of the Virginia Declaration of Rights, Madison drafted language for a national Bill of Rights and proposed this to the "committee of eleven" for consideration. See F. Heller, supra n. 8, at 28–30. The Virginia Bill of Rights seems clearly to have been the chosen framework for the sixth amendment. As one researcher concludes: "[I]n its basic structure, compactness of arrangement, and enumeration of rights the [sixth] Amendment follows the recommendation of the ratifying Convention of Virginia, which in turn was but an amplification of the corresponding section of the Bill of Rights drawn up by George Mason." Id. at 34. For an examination of the historical evidence suggesting that the confrontation clause was adopted because of American reaction to the vice-admiralty courts, see Lilly, supra n. 1, at 210–14.

hearsay exceptions. After all, the Americans rejected the civil law procedure in favor of the common-law system as it was known to them in the latter part of the Eighteenth Century. Perhaps, then, the clause was intended to render immutable one or more essential features of the recognized exceptions by constitutionalizing one or more of their characteristics. When the Sixth Amendment was submitted for ratification in 1789, exceptions to the hearsay rule were narrowly restricted.[21] Basically, the American common-law rule against hearsay was that extant in England during the same period.[22] At that time, English courts admitted hearsay evidence only in very limited circumstances: namely, when the declarant was unavailable.[23] If the declarant could be produced, the proffered hearsay was rejected. This same pattern appears in American law. Almost all of the Eighteenth Century American and English cases collected by Wigmore imposed on the government (and even civil litigants) a stringent obligation to produce the declarant.[24] Although these Anglo-American decisions are not totally harmonious, a prevailing principle threads throughout them: if the declarant was living and could be produced, he must appear at trial.[25] Hearsay exceptions generally

21. See, V Wigmore, § 1364, at 25 n. 49. See, e.g., Borgy v. Commonwealth, 51 Va. (10 Gratt.) 722 (1853) (the witnesses who had testified at the former trial were out of state, not dead, and the testimony was held inadmissible by the Court of Appeals of Virginia).

22. The Crown of England intended that the English common law would be followed in the colonies. F. Heller, supra n. 8, at 13–14. At first the colonists attempted their own "period of rude, untechnical popular law." Id. at 15 (quoting Reinsch, The English Common Law in the Early American Colonies, 2 Bulletin of the Univ. of Wis. (1899)). Later, they sought to apply the law of England to improve colonial conditions and secure fundamental rights, such as the right of confrontation. See Pollitt, supra n. 9, at 390–91. Pollitt asserts that the commissioners of the courts were "charged to do equal right to poor and to rich . . . as near as may be after the laws of the realm of England." Id. (quoting Reinsch, The English Common Law in the Early American Colonies, 1 Select Essays in Anglo-American History 367, 404–05 (1970)). Specifically, concerning common law rights at trial, including the accused's right to confront witnesses against him, trial proceedings had to be consistent with the "heretofore . . . constant practice;" in short, the practices and privileges enjoyed in England. Pollitt, supra n. 9, at 391. In support of his thesis, Pollitt cites Lightfoot, The Maladministration of Governor Nicholson of Virginia, 9 English Historical Documents 253, 257 (1955).

23. See infra nn. 24–31 and accompanying text.

24. V Wigmore, § 1364, at 23–25 n. 47 (Chadbourn).

25. See, e.g., Tomlinson v. Croke, 2 Rolle's Abv. 687, pl. 3 (1612) (deposition receivable if the deponent is dead, not if he is living); Fortescue & Coake's Case, 78 Eng.Rep. 117 (Godb. 193) (1613) (depositions of witnesses read at law only if "affidavit be made that the witnesses who deposed were dead.").

were limited to declarations made by deceased persons.[26] Besides death, courts found few acceptable excuses for nonproduction. It was no excuse that the declarant was overseas,[27] ill,[28] or, under some authorities, could not be found,[29] even after a diligent search.[30] As Thayer remarked in his Preliminary Treatise on Evidence, hearsay in England was generally admitted only upon "the original speaker's death, or, in some cases, his other disability." [31]

This restrictive attitude toward hearsay exceptions suggests a variant historical explanation of the purpose of the confrontation clause. Although adoption of the clause was largely a reaction to the vice-admiralty courts, the clause was perhaps designed to do more than simply insure an adversarial trial. The Framers may have also intended to give constitutional status to the common-law right of confrontation recognized in England and America. At its core, at least in the criminal context, this was the right of the accused to confront any witness against him whom the prosecutor could reasonably produce.[32] Arguably, this confrontation right was not, contrary to Wigmore's thesis, simply an embodiment of the hearsay rule, so that a permissible exception to the ban against hearsay was also an exception to the right of confrontation. Rather, the common law right of confrontation might have diverged from the hearsay rule in this particular: the declarant's presence was always preferred even though his statement may be sufficiently trustworthy to fall within a hearsay exception and

26. See C. McCormick, Handbook of the Law of Evidence 678 and n. 61 (2d ed. 1972).

27. Stephen v. Gwenap, 1 M. & Rob. 120, 174 Eng.Rep. 41 (Ex.1831) (although witness is "abroad . . . and altogether out of the power of a party to produce him as a witness," if still living he must be produced at trial).

28. Harrison v. Blades, 3 Camp. 457, 170 Eng.Rep. 1444 (N.P.1813) (illness insufficient, witness who is "still alive and within the jurisdiction of the Court" must appear at trial for testimony to be admitted). Id.

29. See, e.g., Lord Morley's Case, Kel. 55, 6 How.St.Tr. (Eng.) 770 (1666) (deposition may not be read simply because deponent cannot be found).

30. Oates' Trial, 10 How.St.Tr. (Eng.) 1227, 1285 (1685) (excluded deposition of a witness not found after a search); Lord Morley's Case, Kel. 55, 6 How.St.Tr. (Eng.) 770 (1666) (although party makes all endeavors to find witness and yet cannot, that is not sufficient to authorize admittance of testimony).

31. J. Thayer, A Preliminary Treatise on Evidence at the Common Law 501 (1898).

32. It was widely acknowledged that such a common-law right existed. See V Wigmore §§ 1365, 1397 (Chadbourn). But the precise nature of the right and its relation to the hearsay rule is unclear.

thus be admissible in his absence. Further support for this position is found in Thayer's conclusion that the best evidence rule, which favors the original of a document over a copy or verbal account of its contents, was applied during the eighteenth century to hearsay declarations. In short, the early history of hearsay is entwined with notions of a preference for the live witness. It is thus possible that the confrontation clause is silent regarding a hearsay exception when the declarant is unavailable and, at least in the modern context, has no impact upon a hearsay exception invoked in a civil trial. Perhaps the confrontation clause speaks with a single voice, commanding production of available witnesses against the accused in a criminal trial.[33]

If this interpretation were correct, the drafters of the Sixth Amendment would not have intended to arrest the development of exceptions to the hearsay rule. Rather, they would have sought to secure the common-law practice of requiring that witnesses against the accused should, if possible, give their testimony personally in open court, there to be confronted. Hearsay exceptions could be developed free from constraints of the confrontation clause, except that in criminal cases the state must secure the presence of available adverse witnesses.[34] This thesis is at times suggested in some of the Supreme Court cases construing the confrontation clause, but as will be seen below, no unified theory of the meaning of that clause has drawn the consistent support of the Court. The cases reflect a pragmatic approach with varying emphases upon the government's duty to produce an available witness, as well as upon the reliability of evidence traceable to an "unconfronted" declarant. It is unlikely that either history or the

33. This thesis is consistent with the early leading case of Mattox v. United States, 156 U.S. 237 (1895). There the Court approved the use of prior testimony when the former witnesses were dead. Justice Brown explained:

> [T]he primary object of the constitutional provision was to prevent depositions or ex parte affidavits, such as were sometimes admitted in civil cases, being used against the prisoner in lieu of a personal examination and cross examination of a witness in which the accused has the opportunity . . . of compelling [the witness] to stand face to face with the jury in order that they may look at him, and judge by his demeanor upon the stand and the manner in which he gives his testimony and whether he is worthy of belief. Id. at 242–43.

The Court observed that the constitutional right guaranteed to each citizen is that which "he already possessed as a British subject. . . ." The right of confrontation, though expressed in absolute terms, is "subject to exceptions, recognized long before the adoption of the Constitution. . . ." Id. at 244.

34. Of course, this reading of history is not definitive, but it offers a construction that is at least plausible.

Supreme Court will give a fixed and invariable meaning to the confrontation clause, but the puzzle of its purpose and meaning remains engaging.

§ 7.30 Early Construction of the Confrontation Clause

Since 1965,[1] when the Supreme Court held the confrontation clause applicable to the states,[2] the Court has applied the clause in a variety of contexts. The resulting interpretations are not easily reconciled. The initial series of opinions, rendered prior to 1970, indicated that the right of confrontation was a significant barrier to the use of hearsay in criminal trials. Two of these cases[3] involved trials in which the extra-judicial confession of one co-felon also implicated the other. Because the confessing felon could not be cross-examined by the implicated accused,[4] the Court held that the latter's right to confront an adverse witness was

§ 7.30

1. Mattox v. United States, 156 U.S. 237, 243–44 (1895) is an early leading case. There the Supreme Court upheld the use of prior reported testimony against the accused and, in dictum, approved the use of dying declarations. See also Kirby v. United States, 174 U.S. 47 (1899) which involved a prosecution for receipt of stolen goods. The Court held that the judgment against those convicted of stealing the property could not be used to establish that the goods received by the accused had in fact been stolen. Id. at 63–64.

2. Pointer v. Texas, 380 U.S. 400 (1965), mandate conformed, 391 S.W.2d 62 (1965) (use by state of transcript of witness' testimony given during preliminary hearing at which the accused was not represented by counsel violated the confrontation clause).

3. Bruton v. United States, 391 U.S. 123 (1968), appeal after remand, 416 F.2d 310 (8th Cir.1969), cert. denied 397 U.S. 1014 (1970); Douglas v. Alabama, 380 U.S. 415 (1965).

4. In Douglas v. Alabama, 380 U.S. 415 (1965), the previously convicted co-felon was called as a witness for the state. He refused to give testimony. Under the guise of refreshing recollection, the prosecutor read aloud the witness' earlier confession which implicated the accused. This procedure was condemned on confrontation grounds.

Bruton v. United States, 391 U.S. 123 (1968), appeal after remand, 416 F.2d 310 (8th Cir.1969), cert. denied, 397 U.S. 1014 (1970), was a joint trial in which a confession of one codefendant was introduced and it implicated the other codefendant. The confessing defendant did not take the stand. Despite the trial court's instruction that the confession could be used only with respect to the guilt of the confessor, the Supreme Court held that the implicated defendant was denied the right to confront a witness against him. Id. at 137.

Subsequent decisions have emasculated the *Bruton* holding. See Nelson v. O'Neil, 402 U.S. 622 (1971) (*Bruton* is not controlling when codefendant takes stand, denies inculpatory admission, and testifies favorably to accused); Harrington v. California, 395 U.S. 250 (1969) (*Bruton* violation can be harmless error; further, *Bruton* may be inapplicable when codefendant takes the stand and admits making the earlier statements). In Parker v. Randolph, 442 U.S. 62 (1979), a plurality of the Court took the position that where codefendants each confess, and the confession of a non-testifying defendant "interlocks" with and implicates the other accused, a *Bruton* violation will nearly always be reduced to harmless error if

denied. A third case[5] addressed the state's constitutional obligation to produce at trial a declarant, incarcerated in a federal prison, whose statements were used against the accused. The evidence in question was the transcript of the declarant's testimony given at the accused's preliminary hearing. The Supreme Court found that the state's use of the transcript denied the accused's right of confrontation: "[a] witness is not 'unavailable' for purpose of the [prior testimony] exception to the confrontation requirement unless the prosecutorial authorities have made a good faith effort to obtain his presence at trial."[6] These cases indicated that the confrontation clause placed strict but uncertain limits upon the state's ability to introduce "uncross-examined" testimony; further, the clause also obligated the state, at least in

the trial court gave a proper limiting instruction. Id. at 64. Recently, however, in Lee v. Illinois, 476 U.S. ___, 106 S.Ct. 2056 (1986), the Supreme Court reaffirmed the *Bruton* standard that admission of a non-testifying co-defendant's statement inculpating the accused can violate the latter's confrontation rights. Justice Brennan, writing for the Court, held that the presumptive unreliability of an accomplice's confession which incriminates the accused is not overcome simply because it interlocks in its factual recitations with the accused's statement. When the discrepancies between the confessional statements touch important disputed issues, such as premeditation, and affect the culpability of the accused, the statements are not sufficiently interlocking to avoid the prohibition of the confrontation clause. Since the unavailable co-defendant could not be cross-examined by the accused and his confession lacked independently sufficient indicia of reliability, its admission violated the Sixth Amendment. The majority rejected the state of Illinois' "categorization of the hearsay involved in this case as a simple 'declaration against penal interest.' That concept defines too large a class for meaningful confrontation clause analysis. We decide this case as involving a confession by an accomplice which incriminates a criminal defendant." Id. at ___ n. 5, 106 S.Ct. at 2064 n. 5. Justice Blackmun wrote a vigorous dissent.

5. Barber v. Page, 390 U.S. 719 (1968).

6. Id. at 724–25. The Court also held that the accused's failure to cross-examine the witness at the preliminary hearing did not result in a waiver of the right to cross-examine the witness at trial. The Court observed that even when the right to cross-examine at a preliminary hearing is exercised, this examination is not the equivalent of a cross-examination at trial:

> The right to confrontation is basically a trial right. It includes both the opportunity to cross-examine and the occasion for the jury to weigh the demeanor of the witness. A preliminary hearing is ordinarily a much less searching exploration into the merits of a case than a trial, simply because its function is the more limited one of determining whether probable cause exists to hold the accused for trial.

Id. at 725. In California v. Green, 399 U.S. 149 (1970), on remand, 3 Cal.3d 981, 92 Cal.Rptr. 494, 479 P.2d 998 (1971), petition for review dism'd, 404 U.S. 801 (1971) the Court discounted this observation and held that, at least in the circumstances of *Green*, cross-examination at the preliminary hearing satisfied the confrontation clause. See infra nn. 12–14 and accompanying text.

some circumstances, to rely upon live testimony instead of hearsay declarations.

Finally, in an opinion that applied the confrontation clause to the scope of cross-examination, the Supreme Court reversed a conviction because the accused was prohibited from asking the state's witness (an informer) his name and address.[7] It thus seemed clear that the confrontation clause also protected the accused against evidentiary rules that significantly undermine the effectiveness of cross-examination even though the witness against him had been questioned in open court. This view was recently affirmed in a case in which the Supreme Court held that the confrontation clause entitled the accused to a full opportunity to examine an adverse witness about the latter's possible bias.[8]

Although these early opinions did not condemn the use of all hearsay, they seemed destined to circumscribe closely the allowable use of hearsay declarations.[9] Those hearsay exceptions that traditionally applied without reference to the declarant's availability might be constitutionally inoperative unless the state could demonstrate its inability to produce the speaker. Those that applied only upon a showing of unavailability might sometimes be suspended: the state's constitutional obligation to produce the declarant could be more demanding than that required by a common-law or statutory hearsay exception. Finally, even if unavailability were substantiated, the proffered evidence nonetheless might be inadmissible because it lacked sufficient reliability to meet the constitutional standard.[10]

7. Smith v. Illinois, 390 U.S. 129 (1968). *See also* Davis v. Alaska, 415 U.S. 308 (1974) (right of confrontation dictates that accused is entitled to show that prosecution witness was on probation for juvenile offense).

8. Delaware v. Van Arsdall, 475 U.S. ___, 106 S.Ct. 1431 (1986). The Court recognized, however, that the harmless error rule announced in Chapman v. California, 386 U.S. 18 (1967), reh. denied, 386 U.S. 987 (1967), would preserve the conviction from reversal if the trial court's exclusion of the evidence concerning bias was harmless beyond a reasonable doubt. Delaware v. Van Arsdall, 475 U.S. at ___, 106 S.Ct. at 1436. See also Crane v. Kentucky, 476 U.S. ___, 106 S.Ct. 2142 (1986) (error to disallow evidence of circumstances surrounding defendant's voluntary confession).

9. As to the retroactive application of confrontation requirements, see Berger v. California, 393 U.S. 314 (1969), on remand, 77 Cal.Rptr. 617, 272 Cal.App. 2d 584 (1969) (*Barber* applied retroactively); Roberts v. Russell, 392 U.S. 293 (1968) reh. denied, 393 U.S. 899 (1968) (*Bruton* applied retroactively). Most of the major confrontation cases are collected and closely scrutinized in Lempert & Saltzburg, at 550–601.

10. Despite these specific apprehensions, the precise reach of the confrontation clause was in doubt and its analytical framework remained opaque. The uncertain landscape caused some lower courts to limit the scope of the

The 1970s brought on an apparent shift in the high Court's approach. During this period, its reading of the confrontation clause emphasized moderation. In particular, the resolution of two leading cases [11] marked a break in the vigorous application of constitutional standards, and a retreat from the strident language which characterized some of the earlier opinions. In the first decision,[12] the Court found no constitutional objection to a state rule of evidence that permitted a prosecution witness's prior out-of-court statement to be used for its truth. The fact that the witness was on the stand and testifying would, under most circumstances, allow adequate confrontation of his earlier declarations. In the same case, contrary to strong disapproving language in an earlier decision,[13] the Court allowed the use of a witness's prior testimony taken at a preliminary hearing. It rejected the accused's claim that because a preliminary hearing was for the limited purpose of inquiring into probable cause, there was diminished incentive to cross-examine fully and hence inadequate confrontation.[14]

recent decisions. See, e.g., Tomlin v. Beto, 377 F.2d 276, 277 (5th Cir.1967) (citing Pointer v. Texas, 380 U.S. 400 (1965), mandate conformed, 391 S.W.2d 62 (1965) where the court states that the right of confrontation is inapplicable to an exception to the hearsay rule); State v. Nordstrom, 104 R.I. 471, 244 A.2d 837 (1968) (*Pointer* found not to exclude admissible evidence under any well-established hearsay exception). Other courts, however, saw sweeping implications in the revitalized confrontation clause and responded accordingly. See, e.g., State v. Tims, 9 Ohio St.2d 136, 224 N.E.2d 348 (1967), overruled State v. Spikes, 67 Oh.St.2d 405, 423 N.E.2d 1122 (1981) (hospital records not admissible unless examining and recording physician was present and subject to cross examination); Rubey v. Fairbanks, 456 P.2d 470 (Alaska 1969) (admission of non-hearsay statement violates confrontation clause); In re Montgomery, 2 Cal.3d 863, 87 Cal.Rptr. 695, 471 P.2d 15 (1970) (only upon showing of unavailability may right of confrontation be dismissed); State v. Adrian, 51 Hawaii 125, 453 P.2d 221 (1969) (confrontation of witnesses must mean confrontation of hearsay declarant; otherwise the clause would be emasculated).

11. California v. Green, 399 U.S. 149 (1970), on remand, 3 Cal.3d 981, 92 Cal. Rptr. 494, 479 P.2d 998 (1971), petition for review dism'd, 404 U.S. 801 (1971); Dutton v. Evans, 400 U.S. 74 (1970), on remand, 441 F.2d 657 (5th Cir.1971). In addition to taking a more tolerant approach in the two cases, the Court also emasculated its holding in Bruton v. United States, 391 U.S. 123 (1968), appeal after remand, 416 F.2d 310 (8th Cir. 1969), cert. denied, 397 U.S. 1014 (1970). See supra n. 4.

12. California v. Green, 399 U.S. 149 (1970), on remand, 3 Cal.3d 981, 92 Cal. Rptr. 494, 479 P.2d 998 (1971), petition for review dism'd, 404 U.S. 801 (1971). For an analysis of this case and the unanswered questions that survive it, see IV Weinstein & Berger, ¶ 800[04], at 21–23; ¶ 801(d)(1)(A)[02]–[08], at 90–111.

13. Barber v. Page, 390 U.S. 719, 725 (1968).

14. However, the Court refrained from broadly approving all testimony given at a preliminary hearing that fell within a hearsay exception such as former testimony. It concluded simply that on the facts before it, testimony at the preliminary hearing was given "under circumstances closely approximating those that surround the typical

In the second case,[15] a bare majority [16] permitted the state to introduce a coconspirator's declarations under an exception to the hearsay rule even though they were not made "in furtherance" of the conspiracy.[17] Although the decision did not discuss whether there was normally an obligation to produce the declarant,[18] the excepted testimony in the case was not constitutionally objectionable even though the state failed to produce him. In approving the use of the coconspirator's statement against the accused, the plurality emphasized that the confrontation clause allowed the states considerable latitude to fashion and enlarge hearsay exceptions. Those Justices voting to affirm the conviction were influenced by the relatively inconsequential nature of the admitted declarations and the abundant evidence supporting the accused's guilt. One might conclude that a majority of the Justices were now prepared to give a flexible interpretation to the confrontation

trial" and that defense counsel had been afforded "every opportunity to cross-examine" the adverse witness. California v. Green, 399 U.S. 149, 165 (1970), on remand, 3 Cal.3d 981, 92 Cal. Rptr. 494, 479 P.2d 998 (1971), petition for review dism'd, 404 U.S. 801 (1971).

15. Dutton v. Evans, 400 U.S. 74 (1970), on remand, 441 F.2d 657 (5th Cir.1971).

16. A plurality of four Justices was joined by Justice Harlan in affirming the rejection of the accused's confrontation arguments.

17. The state rule in issue extended the co-conspirators exception to include statements made during the period when the conspirators were concealing the crime or their involvement in it. Dutton v. Evans, 400 U.S. 74, 78 (1970), on remand, 441 F.2d 657 (5th Cir.1971). Most jurisdictions confine the exception to statements made in furtherance of the conspiracy. See McCormick, § 267, at 792. Federal law, then and now, is in accord with the majority view. Dutton v. Evans, 400 U.S. 74, 81, on remand, 441 F.2d 657 (5th Cir.1971); Fed. R.Evid. 801(d)(2)(E).

18. A subsequent case, Mancusi v. Stubbs, 408 U.S. 204 (1972), casts further light upon the state's obligation to produce the declarant. In *Mancusi,* the requirement established in Barber v. Page, 390 U.S. 719 (1968), see supra nn. 5–6 and accompanying text, that the state make a good faith effort to secure the presence of a witness, was satisfied even though the prosecutor did not make an exhaustive attempt to produce a live declarant. The declarant, who had testified at the accused's earlier trial, had since moved to Sweden. The state's only effort to secure his presence was to send a subpoena to his last known address in the United States. The majority may have concluded that no bona fide attempt was required if it appeared that there would be little chance of such efforts succeeding. However, the Court expressly relied upon the inability of the state to compel a foreign resident to appear. There was, in short, no procedural mechanism for securing the witness' presence. Beyond this, the Court examined the prior testimony and concluded that the accused's opportunity to confront the adverse witness and his actual cross-examination of that witness was adequate to satisfy the Constitution. The earlier testimony "bore sufficient 'indicia of reliability' and afforded the 'trier of fact a satisfactory basis for evaluating the truth of the prior statement[s].'" 408 U.S. at 216 (quoting Dutton v. Evans, 400 U.S. 74, 89 (1970), on remand, 441 F.2d 657 (5th Cir.1971)).

clause, taking full account of the context of each case.[19] Perhaps, in the broadest sense, the confrontation clause imposed minimum standards of trustworthiness and adversarial fairness. Application of these standards would require an inquiry into the likely trustworthiness of the challenged hearsay evidence, its importance, and the ease with which the declarant could be produced. Arguably, these criteria were interlocking and the existence of one affected the others. For example, if reliability of the evidence were high, as might be the case where a well-established hearsay exception applied, the ease of producing the witness and centrality of the evidence might be given little or no consideration.

For more than a decade after these two decisions, the Court did not attempt to clarify further the meaning and scope of the confrontation clause. The Court's later, more tolerant decisions, however, set the tone for the lower courts as they assessed the constitutional restraints on the use of hearsay.[20] The hearsay exceptions were generally sanctioned, although the confrontation clause precluded the use of hearsay where there was a serious risk that uncross-examined statements would mislead the trier or where the hearsay was critical evidence.[21]

19. See V Wigmore, § 1397, at 184–85 (Chadbourn).

20. See, e.g., United States v. Nick, 604 F.2d 1199, 1203 (9th Cir.1979) (admission of youth's out-of-court statement identifying the man who sodomized him did not deny the defendant his right to confrontation even though boy was available but did not take stand; test for admissibility under *Dutton* is whether under all of the circumstances the evidence has a very high degree of reliability and trustworthiness and there is a demonstrated need for the evidence); United States v. Puco, 476 F.2d 1099, 1103 (2d Cir.1973), cert. denied, 414 U.S. 844 (1973) (co-conspirator's out-of-court identification of defendant allowed even though co-conspirator did not testify; hearsay evidence does not violate confrontation provided it is "clearly trustworthy and is not 'crucial' to the prosecution or 'devastating' to the defendant"); State v. Walker, 53 Ohio St.2d 192, 195, 374 N.E.2d 132, 136 (1978) (introduction of log books to establish proper working condition of breathalyzer is not violative of confrontation clause even though neither custodian nor maker of record testified; admissibility determined in light of purpose of confrontation clause to assure that the trier has a sufficient basis for evaluating the truth of statement); State v. Finkley, 6 Wash.App. 278, 492 P.2d 222 (1972) (medical record disclosing sperm in victim admitted over confrontation objection because record fell within business entry exception to hearsay rule).

21. See, e.g., Phillips v. Neil, 452 F.2d 337, 348 (6th Cir.1971), cert. denied, 409 U.S. 884 (1972) (opinion evidence in a psychiatric record violates confrontation clause because such use jeopardizes the "truth-determining process"); State v. Henderson, 554 S.W.2d 117, 122 (Tenn.1977), appeal after remand, 576 S.W.2d 10 (1978) (laboratory reports establishing substances purchased from defendant as marijuana are inadmissible; lack of cross-examination regarding a critical element of crime violates confrontation).

§ 7.31 Recent Interpretation of the Confrontation Clause

Two cases decided in the 1980's illustrate the Supreme Court's continued vacillation in construing the confrontation clause. In the first of these, Ohio v. Roberts,[1] the accused was charged with forging a check in the name of Bernard Isaacs and stealing the latter's credit cards. At the preliminary hearing, defense counsel called the victim's daughter, Anita. She testified during a lengthy direct examination that she knew the accused, Roberts, and that, with her permission, he had temporarily used her apartment while she was away. She denied, however, that she gave him her father's checks and credit cards. Despite this unfavorable testimony, defense counsel did not seek the court's permission to declare Anita a hostile witness and formally cross-examine her; the prosecutor asked no questions of Anita.

At trial, Roberts took the stand and testified that Anita gave him the credit cards and checks bearing her father's name with the understanding that he could use them. Pursuant to the state's hearsay exception for prior testimony, the prosecutor in rebuttal offered Anita's testimony from the preliminary hearing. He established the "unavailability" predicate of the hearsay exception by showing that five unanswered subpoenas had been issued for Anita at her parents' residence; he also elicited testimony from Anita's mother that Anita had left home more than a year prior to trial, that she had not contacted her parents for about seven months, and that they did not know where she was presently living. The trial judge admitted the transcript, and Roberts was convicted. The question before the United States Supreme Court[2] was whether the use of the transcript violated the accused's right of confrontation.

§ 7.31

1. 448 U.S. 56 (1980).

2. Ohio's intermediate appellate court reversed Roberts' conviction on the ground that the state had not exercised sufficient diligence in its attempts to produce Anita. In essence, the prosecutor's failure to pursue possible leads, and in particular to contact a social worker who previously had been in touch with Anita, fell short of the constitutional "good-faith standard" imposed by Barber v. Page, 390 U.S. 719 (1968). The Ohio Supreme Court affirmed, but on a different ground. The supreme court found that the prosecution had made sufficiently diligent efforts to present Anita's live testimony, but use of the transcript nonetheless violated the confrontation clause: because a preliminary hearing is only to determine the existence of probable cause, the mere opportunity to cross-examine a witness during such a hearing does not afford the accused his right of confrontation. State v. Roberts, 55 Ohio St.2d 191, 378 N.E.2d 492 (1978), judgment rev'd, 448 U.S. 56 (1980).

Justice Blackmun's majority opinion began by declaring "that the confrontation clause reflects a preference for face-to-face confrontation at trial, and that 'a primary interest secured by [the provision] is the right of cross-examination.'"[3] Even though countervailing considerations such as a state's "interest in effective law enforcement and in the . . . precise formulation of . . . rules of evidence" could suspend this right in some circumstances, the clause nonetheless restricts the scope of admissible hearsay in two ways.[4] The provision is, first, a statement of "preference for face-to-face accusation;"[5] therefore, the prosecution must either produce, or demonstrate the unavailability of, the declarant whose statement it wishes to use against the defendant.[6] Once unavailability is shown,[7] the clause has a second effect: it allows only hearsay that is accompanied by "indicia of reliability"[8] sufficient in the circumstances to justify dispensing with confrontation. The Court then noted that firmly rooted hearsay exceptions would presumptively bear such indicia, thus making it unnecessary to conduct a particularized search for their presence.[9]

Applying these criteria, the Court found that the prosecution's effort to produce Anita satisfied the good-faith standard imposed by the confrontation clause.[10] This requirement was met because the state took reasonable steps to locate the witness and there was a "great improbability"[11] that additional efforts would be fruitful. The state's satisfaction of the "unavailability" predicate did not, of course, end the constitutional inquiry. The Court also examined whether there was compliance with the reliability standard, and concluded that the contested hearsay bore sufficient indicia of reliability. Defense counsel's thorough interrogation of Anita, replete with leading questions, was in substance the equivalent of

3. Ohio v. Roberts, 448 U.S. 56, 63 (1980) (quoting Douglas v. Alabama, 380 U.S. 415, 418 (1965)).

4. 448 U.S. at 64–65.

5. Id. at 65.

6. Id.

7. Id.

8. Id. (quoting Mancusi v. Stubbs, 408 U.S. 204, 213 (1972)). There may also be a closely related but distinct requirement that the admitted hearsay afford "the trier of fact a satisfactory basis for evaluating the truth of the prior statement." Mancusi v. Stubbs, 408 U.S. 204, 216 (1972) (quoting Dutton v. Evans, 400 U.S. 74, 89 (1970), on remand, 441 F.2d 657 (5th Cir.1971) quoted in Ohio v. Roberts, 448 U.S. at 73. However, it is difficult to conceive of a case in which the admitted hearsay had the accouterments of reliability and yet was without a sufficient basis for evaluation by the trier.

9. 448 U.S. at 66.

10. From this conclusion, Justices Brennan, Marshall, and Stevens dissented. Id. at 77.

11. Id. at 76.

cross-examination. It served to test adequately the witness' credibility, including such components as accurate perception, sufficient memory, and sincerity.[12] Thus, the prior examination fit comfortably within the exception for former testimony and a further "particularized search for 'indicia of reliability' "[13] was unnecessary.

At first blush, *Roberts* appears to be an unexceptional application of principles established in prior cases. On another occasion the Court had required a constitutional "good-faith effort" to produce the declarant before resorting to his hearsay declaration.[14] In prior decisions the Court also had established a constitutionally imposed standard of reliability and had indicated that well-founded hearsay exceptions conformed to the standard.[15] Reinforcing the apparently routine disposition of Roberts' appeal is the opinion's pragmatic tone, suggesting the Court's willingness to accommodate constitutional requirements to the practical realities of criminal prosecutions.

It is possible, however, to give the *Roberts* opinion a construction of far-reaching significance. A solid majority of the Court agreed that the confrontation clause was, first, a rule of preference, and second, a constitutional bulwark against unreliable hearsay evidence. The justices appeared to endorse a constitutionally imposed duty, resting on the prosecution, to make a good-faith effort to produce in court any hearsay declarant whose extrajudicial declaration was offered against the accused. The fact that the declaration fell within a hearsay exception did not appear to excuse the government's duty to produce an available hearsay declarant. Further, the *Roberts* court reaffirmed the theme, found in earlier cases, that the confrontation clause imposed a reliability standard. Even if the prosecution was unable (after a good faith effort) to produce the declarant, the proffered hearsay declaration could still be rejected. Admissibility was dependent upon a showing that the statement bore sufficient indicia of reliability to meet the constitutional standard. Although the standard is not precisely defined, it appears to be approximately

12. See §§ 7.29 n. 3; 6.1 at nn. 3–4.

13. 448 U.S. at 72.

14. Barber v. Page, 390 U.S. 719 (1968).

15. Mancusi v. Stubbs, 408 U.S. 204, 213 (1972) ("even though the witness be unavailable his prior testimony must bear some indicia of reliability"); California v. Green, 399 U.S. 149, 161 (1970), on remand, 3 Cal.3d 981, 92 Cal. Rptr. 494, 479 P.2d 998 (1971), petition for review dism'd, 404 U.S. 801 (1971) (traditional exceptions usually possess indicia of reliability).

the same as that which is imposed by the due process clause.[16] Generally speaking, if the declaration lacks indicia of reliability there is a high probability that it might be false and, hence, it fails to satisfy the constitutional requirement. So viewed, the "reliability" requirement of *Roberts* makes little or no demand beyond existing law.

The same cannot be said of the apparently sweeping ambit of the preferential role of the confrontation clause. Here the *Roberts* opinion speaks broadly, apparently addressing all hearsay: the declarant must be produced unless the proponent meets the constitutional test of unavailability; only if unavailability is established is there a need to assess reliability. Yet, as we have seen, the vast majority of hearsay exceptions are not based upon the declarant's unavailability.[17] The Federal Rules of Evidence, illustrative of the common law and other evidence "codes," divide hearsay exceptions into two principal categories. The first (class 1) consists of exceptions (such as business and public records, learned treatises, excited statements, and statements of physical and mental condition)[18] which require that the excepted statement be made in circumstances that strongly suggest trustworthiness. Because attending circumstances indicate a similar degree of reliability as that of testimony given in court, it is not essential to cross-

16. California v. Green, 399 U.S. 149, 189 (1970), on remand, 3 Cal.3d 981, 92 Cal.Rptr. 494, 479 P.2d 998 (1971), petition for review dism'd, 404 U.S. 801 (1971). In a line of cases decided under the due process clause, the Court has determined that a defendant may not be found guilty unless there is "sufficient evidence to justify a rational trier of fact to find guilt beyond a reasonable doubt." Jackson v. Virginia, 443 U.S. 307 (1979), reh. denied, 444 U.S. 890 (1979). See also In re Winship, 397 U.S. 358 (1970), mandate conformed, 27 N.Y.2d 728, 314 N.Y.S.2d 536, 262 N.E.2d 675 (1970); Neil v. Biggers, 409 U.S. 188, 198 (1972) (quoting, Simmons v. United States, 390 U.S. 377, 384 (1968), on remand, 395 F.2d 769 (7th Cir.1968), appeal after remand, 424 F.2d 1235 (7th Cir.1970)). The due process standard is explicated in Westen, The Future of Confrontation, 77 Mich.L.Rev. 1185, 1190–91 (1979); Westen, Confrontation and Compulsory Process: A Unified Theory of Evidence for Criminal Cases, 91 Harv.L.Rev. 567, 575 n. 21 (1978). See also supra n. 8. Thus the confrontation clause's standard of reliability closely approximates that which is independently operative through the due process clause.

17. See McCormick, § 253, at 608. ("[T]he group of hearsay exceptions where unavailability is required are in a sense second class in comparison with the far larger number of exceptions where availability or unavailability is simply not a factor."). The Federal Rule of Evidence lists 24 exceptions which are not dependent on the absence of the declarant. Fed.R.Evid. 803; only five exceptions hinge upon unavailability. Fed.R.Evid. 804.

18. Fed.R.Evid. 803(6), (8), (18), (2), (3).

examine the declarant.[19] Conversely, the second category of exceptions (class 2) is generally thought to embrace less reliable declarations. These exceptions, partly the product of necessity, apply only if the declarant is unavailable.[20]

The *Roberts* Court did not in the course of its constitutional analysis differentiate between these classes of hearsay exceptions. The resulting inclusive application of the confrontation clause presumptively conditioned all hearsay exceptions upon a predicate of unavailability. Further, *Roberts* left uncertain the scope of the government's duty to produce the declarant. There are, of course, explications of what constitutes unavailability set forth in various decisional and codified evidence rules.[21] For example, a witness may be unavailable when he lacks memory, refuses to testify, cannot attend trial because of illness or infirmity, or is absent from trial and cannot be produced by reasonable means.[22] Definitions of "unavailability" traditionally are associated with those comparatively few hearsay exceptions (class 2) which are predicated on the inability to secure the declarant's live testimony.[23] Yet *Roberts* appeared to impose an unavailability requirement for all hearsay that is within the compass of the confrontation clause. Further, because the requirement is of constitutional origin,[24] the meaning of unavailability was a matter of constitutional dimension. Thus the courts were apparently left to define the precise boundaries of a prosecutor's "good faith" obligation to produce a witness against the accused. When the unavailability predicate for hearsay exceptions delineated in cases and statutes was not sufficient in criminal trials governed by the confrontation clause, the prosecutor was to be guided by the constitutional standard.

Obvious questions raised by *Roberts* were the extent of the government's duty when no procedural mechanism existed for requiring the declarant's presence,[25] the range of acceptable "ex-

19. See § 7.21. Adv.Comm.Note to Fed.R.Evid. 803.

20. See Fed.R.Evid. 804(b) and Adv. Comm.Note.

21. See, e.g., Fed.R.Evid. 804(a); West's Ann.Cal.Evid.Code § 240; V Wigmore, §§ 1403–1413, at 205–37 (Chadbourn) (lists common law bases of unavailability)

22. Fed.R.Evid. 804(a).

23. See, e.g., Fed.R.Evid. 804.

24. Prior cases support a constitutional standard. See Barber v. Page, 390 U.S. 719 (1968). Cf. Mancusi v. Stubbs, 408 U.S. 204 (1972).

25. In Mancusi v. Stubbs, 408 U.S. 204 (1972), the Court held that the state court was proper in finding the declarant unavailable when he was beyond the reach of the state's power, even though no attempt had been made to secure the declarant's voluntary appearance. Id. at 211–16.

cuses" for non-production,[26] and the extent to which the obligation to produce is affected by the significance of the evidence in question and/or its probable reliability.[27] These issues, arising in cases that frequently are distinguishable on their facts, are not yet resolved.[28]

Perhaps the most significant question associated with the *Roberts* preference rule was simply whether the obligation to produce encompasses all class 1 exceptions, as *Roberts* seemed to indicate.[29] A footnote in *Roberts* makes the laconic observation that "[a] demonstration of unavailability . . . is not always required" [30] and would not be where "the utility of trial confronta-

26. Post-*Roberts* cases addressing the issue are: Haggins v. Warden, Ft. Pillow State Farm, 715 F.2d 1050, 1055 (6th Cir.1983), cert. denied, 464 U.S. 1071 (1984) (youthful declarant unavailable because incompetent to testify); United States v. Ammar, 714 F.2d 238, 255 (3d Cir.1983) (declarants had eluded apprehension and thus were unavailable), cert. denied, 464 U.S. 936 (1983); United States v. Chappell, 698 F.2d 308, 312 (7th Cir.1983) (declarant dead, thus unavailability requirement satisfied), cert. denied, 461 U.S. 931 (1983); State v. Schad, 129 Ariz. 557, 569, 633 P.2d 366, 378 (1981), cert. denied, 455 U.S. 983 (1982) (declarant in serious accident, thus unavailable); Harrison v. United States, 435 A.2d 734, 736 (D.C. App.1981) (unavailability satisfied because declarant was 83 years old, sick, and would have to travel from Louisiana to D.C.); People v. Arroyo, 54 N.Y.2d 567, 573, 446 N.Y.S.2d 910, 914, 431 N.E.2d 271, 275 (1982), cert. denied, 456 U.S. 979 (1982) (declarant unavailable because disappeared day of trial after giving no indication to prosecutor of an unwillingness to testify); State v. Farber, 295 Or. 199, 666 P.2d 821, 826–27 (1983), appeal dism'd, 464 U.S. 987 (1983) (declarant unavailable because if called to stand would have claimed fifth amendment privilege). But see Hutchins v. Wainwright, 715 F.2d 512, 516 (11th Cir.1983), cert. denied, 465 U.S. 1071 (1984) (that police would not reveal informant's name did not make him unavailable).

27. In *Roberts,* the Court noted that a showing of unavailability was not always required if, for example, the utility of trial confrontation was remote. 448 U.S. at 65 n. 7. See People v. Dement, 661 P.2d 675, 682 (Colo.1983) (unavailability requirement not satisfied because utility of confrontation was high).

28. In the lower courts, judges have had to address the measure of the prosecutor's duty to produce the declarant. Under one view, for example, the state's effort to produce the declarant is to be measured by the supposed effort that the prosecutor would mount if he were without the hearsay evidence he proffers. State v. Edwards, 136 Ariz. 177, 182, 665 P.2d 59, 64 (1983). In a sense, this test is stringent, for it clearly contemplates prosecutorial efforts to secure a witness even though no compulsory mechanism is available. The test could be interpreted, but thus far has not, to contain a leavening feature: by taking account of centrality, the prosecutor's duty diminishes in proportion to the insignificance of the hearsay evidence.

29. For a discussion of the significant difficulties such an approach would bring to many of the most frequently invoked hearsay exceptions, see Kirkpatrick, Confrontation and Hearsay: Exemptions from the Constitutional Unavailability Requirement, 70 Minn.L.Rev. 665, 689–709 (1986).

30. 448 U.S. at 65 n. 7.

tion" [31] is sufficiently remote. Whether the escape from the usual duty to produce was available for such hearsay exceptions as business entries,[32] public records,[33] ancient documents,[34] commercial publications,[35] or learned treatises [36] remained problematic.

Under a broad reading of *Roberts* no out-of-court declaration could be entered for its truth unless the government first showed that it could not produce the declarant or, alternatively, the government produced the declarant, thus allowing the accused to confront the witness against him.

Roberts also left unresolved questions with respect to the "reliability" prong of the constitutional test. Even if production of the declarant were excused, the state's proffered hearsay may still run afoul of the confrontation clause. Admission would hinge upon whether the tendered evidence possesses sufficient "indicia of reliability." [37] These indicia include such factors or circumstances as an adequate chance to observe, spontaneity of speaking, likelihood of sufficient recollection, and absence of motive to falsify.[38] The *Roberts* Court reiterated a point made in earlier decisions that "[r]eliability can be inferred without more in a case where the evidence falls within a firmly rooted hearsay exception." [39] Whether "firm-rooting" is a function of the longevity of an exception, the number of jurisdictions recognizing it, or both remains uncertain. Are exceptions recognized by the Federal Rules of Evidence [40] firmly rooted? If so, acceptance at the federal level may suggest adequate constitutional reliability even though

31. Id. As an illustration the Court cites Dutton v. Evans, 400 U.S. 74 (1970), on remand, 441 F.2d 657 (5th Cir.1971). See also supra n. 27 and accompanying text.

32. See, e.g., Fed.R.Evid. 803(6), 803(7). The reach of rule 803(6) is already curtailed by 803(8). United States v. Oates, 560 F.2d 45, 71 (2d Cir. 1977), on remand, 445 F.Supp. 351 (E.D. N.Y.1978), aff'd, 591 F.2d 1332 (2d Cir. 1978). But see United States v. Picciandra, 788 F.2d 39, 44 (1st Cir.1986); United States v. Grady, 544 F.2d 598 (2d Cir.1976).

33. See, e.g., Fed.R.Evid. 803(8), 803(9), 803(10).

34. See, e.g., id. 803(16).

35. See, e.g., id. 803(17).

36. See, e.g., id. 803(18).

37. Ohio v. Roberts, 448 U.S. 56, 65–66 (1980). There must also exist a satisfactory basis for assessing the truth or falsity of the proffered hearsay declarations. Id. (quoting Mancusi v. Stubbs, 408 U.S. 204, 213 (1972)). However, the ability of the trier to evaluate the credibility of the hearsay evidence should turn in large part, if not exclusively, upon the presence or absence of indicia of reliability. See supra n. 8. See also Lee v. Illinois, 476 U.S. ___, 106 S.Ct. 2056 (1986).

38. See Dutton v. Evans, 400 U.S. 74, 88–89 (1970), on remand, 441 F.2d 657 (5th Cir.1971).

39. 448 U.S. at 66 (1980).

40. Of course, the "residual" exceptions, set out in Fed.R.Evid. 803(24) and 804(b)(5) only prescribe general criteria. See Comment, The Confrontation

some states either do not acknowledge the federal exception or narrowly restrict its scope.[41] Certainly, recognition by the federal rulemakers bolsters the argument that indicia of reliability are contained within the exception itself and need not be further explored. But there is still much room for case-by-case development and thus the significant possibility of a solution by decisional accretion.

One point, however, emerges clearly, not so much from the language of *Roberts* as from its underlying logic. Generally, hearsay declarations are divided into two categories: inadmissible hearsay (out-of-court statements offered for their truth) and admissible excepted hearsay (out-of-court statements that may be received for their truth because they fall within a hearsay exception). The Federal Rules of Evidence, however, reclassify certain common law exceptions, notably party admissions, as nonhearsay by exempting them from the usual definition of hearsay.[42] These nonhearsay declarations are admissible if relevant, provided they fit the special definition set out in the Rules. Nonetheless, these statements are out-of-court assertions offered for their truth "and thus resting for . . . [their] value upon the credibility of the out-of-court asserter."[43] Vicarious admissions, including those of a coconspirator, may constitute nonhearsay under the Federal Rules, but they surely come within the inner core of constitutional concern.[44] In short, *Roberts* applies full force. That leaves the close question whether these common law exceptions, now transformed by the Rules into nonhearsay, are sufficiently reliable to be received in evidence without the case-by-case scrutiny necessary for exceptions that are not firmly rooted. A major reason for the reclassification of party admissions was the Advisory Commit-

Clause and the Catch-all Exception to the Hearsay Doctrine: Hopkinson v. State, 17 Land & Water L.Rev. 703–26 (1982).

41. Generally speaking, the common law's recognition of hearsay exceptions is more restrictive than that of the federal rules. See, e.g., Adv.Comm.Notes to Fed.R.Evid. 803(4), 803(18), 804(b)(2), 804(b)(3). Many states, although generally adopting the Federal Rules, have refused to adopt certain hearsay exceptions. See, e.g., Fed.R.Evid. (Callaghan) [Finding Aids; State Correlation Table] Alaska p. 1, Fla. p. 1, Maine p. 1, Mich. p. 1. Massachusetts considered but rejected adoption of the Federal Rules. Id. at Mass. p. 1.

42. See Adv.Comm.Note to Fed.R. Evid. 801(d)(2).

43. McCormick, § 246, at 584.

44. See Dutton v. Evans, 400 U.S. 74, 80–83 (1970), on remand, 441 F.2d 657 (5th Cir.1971); United States v. Ammar, 714 F.2d 238 (3d Cir.), cert. denied, 464 U.S. 936 (1983); United States v. Foster, 711 F.2d 871 (9th Cir. 1983), cert. denied, 465 U.S. 1103 (1984). In *Ammar* and *Foster,* the court conducted a contextual review of the reliability of coconspirator's statements.

tee's view that admission of these declarations is more accurately traceable to the adversary system than to the trustworthiness criteria for hearsay exceptions.[45] This conclusion suggests that party admissions made by another (such as a coconspirator or employee) but imputed to the accused will be subjected to a particularized examination for indicia of reliability.[46]

Whatever apprehensions the *Roberts* case may have produced in prosecutors' ranks, the reach of the opinion was severely restricted in United States v. Inadi,[47] decided in 1986. Some of the questions raised by *Roberts* were addressed and resolved—at least for the present.

Inadi was a prosecution for conspiracy to manufacture and distribute narcotics. At trial, the government offered tape recordings of statements made by one Lazaro, an unindicted coconspirator, in telephone conversations with other conspirators. After listening to the statements in question, the trial judge concluded that they satisfied Federal Rule of Evidence 801(d)(2)(E) which, as we have noted, exempts such statements from the hearsay rule by defining them as nonhearsay. The defense then argued that the statements could not be received unless the prosecution first produced the declarant, Lazaro. Although the prosecution did subpoena the declarant, he failed to appear at trial, citing car trouble as the reason for his absence. The judge nonetheless ruled that the statements were properly received in evidence. The ruling was reversed by the Court of Appeals for the Third Circuit; it held that the confrontation clause, as construed in Ohio v. Roberts,[48] required the government to meet a constitutional standard of unavailability. This, the prosecution had failed to do. It was of no moment that the Federal Rules did not condition the admission of Lazaro's statement on unavailability.

The Supreme Court granted certiorari to "resolve the question whether the confrontation clause requires a showing of unavailability as a condition to admission of the out-of-court statements of a nontestifying coconspirator, when those statements otherwise satisfy the requirements of . . . Rule . . . 801(d)(2)(E)." [49] By a

45. Adv.Comm.Note to Fed.R.Evid. 801(d)(2); IV Wigmore, § 1048, at 4 (Chadbourn).

46. See supra n. 44.

47. 475 U.S. ___, 106 S.Ct. 1121 (1986), on remand, 790 F.2d 383 (3d Cir. 1986).

48. 448 U.S. 56 (1980).

49. 475 U.S. at ___, 106 S.Ct. at 1124.

vote of seven justices to two, the Court held that no such requirement existed.

Justice Powell wrote the majority opinion. He began by stating that Ohio v. Roberts should be confined to the question actually before the Court in that case and should not be read as "a wholesale revision of the law of evidence. . . ." [50] *Roberts,* he said, addressed only the question whether the prior reported testimony exception to the hearsay rule requires a showing of unavailability. He then pointed out that both the rules of evidence and constitutional precedents have consistently imposed such a requirement. But the case now before the Court, he asserted, was different. Here, neither the rules of evidence nor any decision under the confrontation clause demanded the application of an unavailability requirement.

The balance of the Court's opinion was devoted largely to a justification for not applying a constitutionally imposed unavailability standard to coconspirator's declarations. In contrast to statements contained in prior recorded testimony, conspiratorial statements often derive their significance from the context in which they are made. Declarations made by coconspirators in furtherance of their conspiracy will usually contrast sharply with statements made from the witness stand. These contextual statements, made while the conspiracy is still in operation, shed light on the criminal enterprise that is seldom equalled by subsequent testimony of the coconspirators. This inability to replicate conspiratorial statements is made more severe by the fact that at trial the former conspirators no longer have an alliance of interests: "[t]he declarant and the defendant will have changed from partners in an illegal conspiracy to suspects or defendants in a criminal trial, each with information potentially damaging to the other." [51] The ambivalence of the former coconspirators, often torn between aiding the prosecution in return for leniency and assisting a former partner, deepens the contrast between statements made during the conspiracy and those offered at trial. Thus, Justice Powell asserted for the majority, "[t]he admission of coconspirators' declarations . . . actually furthers the 'Confrontation Clause's very mission . . . to advance the accuracy of the truth-determining process. . . .' " [52]

On a more practical level, Justice Powell concluded that the application, in *Inadi,* of a constitutional unavailability require-

50. Id. at ___, 106 S.Ct. at 1125.

51. Id. at ___, 106 S.Ct. at 1126.

52. Id. at ___, 106 S.Ct. at 1127 (quoting from Tennessee v. Street, 471 U.S. 409, 415, 105 S.Ct. 2078, 2082 (1985).

ment would place a significant burden on the prosecution: the government would have to constantly monitor the whereabouts of declarants in order to produce them at trial. This appeared especially unwarranted since the declarant's out-of-court declaration would be admitted if he was produced for cross-examination and, of course, would also be admitted if he were shown to be unavailable.

One other feature of the majority opinion is noteworthy. Justice Powell stressed the fact that the accused was not rendered helpless by the decision not to condition admission of Lazaro's declarations on a showing of unavailability. The accused was free to exercise his right under the compulsory process clause [53] to subpoena the witness and to implement his right under Federal Rule of Evidence 806 to examine Lazaro "as if" the latter were "under cross-examination." [54] This allusion to self-help by the accused at least implies the following possibility: perhaps as to those hearsay exemptions and exceptions that the rules of evidence do not condition on unavailability, there will usually be no constitutional requirement to produce the declarant. Instead, the accused who wishes to cross-examine the declarant must have him subpoenaed.[55]

It is no easy task to reconcile *Inadi* with the sweeping approach of *Roberts*. Indeed, the two dissenters in *Inadi* complained that the majority's "effort to confine *Roberts* misconstrues both the meaning of that decision and the essential command of the Confrontation Clause." [56] It seems clear that the *Inadi* court has rejected the logical implications of the *Roberts* opinion. It is

53. U.S.Const. amend. VI.

54. Fed.R.Evid. 806 states:

"When a hearsay statement, or a statement defined in Rule 801(d)(2), (C), (D), or (E), has been admitted in evidence, the credibility of the declarant may be attacked, and if attacked, may be supported, by any evidence which would be admissible for those purposes if declarant had testified as a witness. . . . If the party against whom a hearsay statement has been admitted calls the declarant as a witness, the party is entitled to examine him on the statement as if under cross-examination."

55. United States v. Inadi, 475 U.S. 387, ___, n. 10, 106 S.Ct. 1121, 1128 n. 10:

"It is not clear from the Court of Appeals' opinion whether in order to meet its burden of showing unavailability, the prosecution, would be required to call the declarant as a witness, or only to ensure that the declarant is available for testimony if needed. The unavailability rule suffers from many of the same flaws under either interpretation, and in fact may be even less defensible under an interpretation requiring the prosecution to call each declarant as a witness."

For a discussion of this problem see Lilly, Notes on the Confrontation Clause and Ohio v. Roberts, 36 Univ. of Fla.L.Rev. 207, 229–32 (1984).

56. 475 U.S. at ___, 106 S.Ct. at 1130.

equally plain that the Court has not—and probably will not—embrace a uniform, systematic approach to the confrontation clause. The framework, such as it is, will be awkwardly erected in response to pragmatic factors. At least as to those hearsay exceptions conditioned upon the unavailability of the declarant, there is probably an independent constitutional standard that the prosecution must satisfy. Whether this constitutional standard is appreciably more demanding than the unavailability requirement imposed by the rules of evidence is uncertain. It is likely, however, that the good-faith effort required by the confrontation clause will not always be satisfied by a showing that the evidentiary criteria governing unavailability have been met.[57]

There is also a reliability requirement imposed by the confrontation clause. Indeed the *Inadi* Court was careful to note that the issue of whether Lazaro's statements bore sufficient indicia of reliability to satisfy the confrontation clause was not before it.[58] The Court of Appeals had held that whether or not Lazaro's statements were reliable, they were inadmissible because the *Roberts* standard of unavailability had not been satisfied by *Inadi*. This constitutional standard will usually be satisfied when the hearsay declaration in question fits within a recognized hearsay exception; in all likelihood, it will normally be satisfied when the declaration is treated as an exemption from the hearsay rule—as is the case with party admissions (including statements of employees) and declarations of coconspirators.[58a] Of course, when a statement is not offered for its truth, confrontation is of little or no value and neither the hearsay rule nor the confrontation clause applies.[59]

Perhaps, in the final analysis, the history and jurisprudence of the confrontation clause will roughly parallel those of the due process clause: fact-specific invocations that rest upon broad principles of accuracy in factfinding, fairness to the accused, and the proper allocation of procedural burdens between the government and the accused. Indeed, the decided cases can be explained on no other basis.

57. See Barber v. Page, 390 U.S. 719 (1968). But see Mancusi v. Stubbs, 408 U.S. 204 (1972), also n. 5 of *Inadi,* 475 U.S. at ___, 106 S.Ct. at 1125–1126.

58. United States v. Inadi, 475 U.S. 387, ___, 106 S.Ct. 1121, 1124 n. 5 (1986), on remand, 790 F.2d 383 (3d Cir.1986).

58a. Very recently, the Supreme Court decided that statements of coconspirators do not require an independent inquiry into reliability. Bourjaily v. United States, 55 U.S.L.W. 4962 (U.S. June 23, 1987).

59. See Tennessee v. Street, 471 U.S. 409, 414 (1985).

Chapter VIII

IMPEACHMENT

---

§ 8.1 In General

The term "impeachment" is used loosely by the courts, but generally it refers to the introduction of evidence aimed at discrediting the testimony of a witness. In its broadest use, the term encompasses all evidence intended to cast doubt upon a witness's testimony, including evidence that calls into question the accuracy of his observation, his recollection, or the truthfulness of his testimony.[1] The cross-examiner may, for example, try to get a witness to concede that he was poorly situated to observe the event in question, that his memory has dimmed, or that he was under the influence of an intoxicating substance. The examiner is usually allowed to call other witnesses for the purpose of raising doubts about the credibility of the principal witness. These subsequent witnesses might testify, for example, that visibility at the time in question precluded observation of the event, that the witness has made prior statements inconsistent with his present testimony or that his character, as shown by conduct or reputation, casts doubt on his veracity. The examiner also may seek to show that the witness is biased. Perhaps, during cross-examination (or through other witnesses) the examiner can reveal that the witness is hostile toward one of the parties or that he has a financial interest in the outcome of the case. Finally, in its broadest use, "impeachment" includes the *contradiction* by one witness of another's testimony—that is, the use of a subsequent witness to give a contradictory account of the event about which the principal witness has testified.

§ 8.1

1. Note that attacks on a witness's first-hand knowledge of an event or his ability to perceive, remember and relate can raise questions concerning his competence to testify at all. See § 4.2.

A more limited and technical use of the word "impeachment" refers to certain specific techniques designed to impugn a witness's credibility by revealing his tendency to distort or falsify his testimonial account of the facts. The suggestion is that the *witness* has a defect, not simply that the circumstances surrounding the event—such as poor visibility—prevent accurate reconstruction. Impeachment in this narrow sense includes only discrediting evidence that aims primarily at "showing flaws in the witness," [2] not evidence merely demonstrating some uncalculated flaw or inaccuracy in his testimony. Although the technique of impeachment by psychiatric evidence is generally included within this limited usage, opportunities to invoke this mode of impeachment are relatively infrequent.[3] The most commonly used techniques fall into three categories: (1) a revelation of bad character or dishonesty (shown by producing evidence of (a) a criminal conviction, (b) a prior dishonest act, or (c) bad character for truthfulness); (2) a showing of bias (by adducing evidence of hostility or favoritism); and (3) a demonstration of self-contradiction (by introducing evidence that the witness had made prior statements inconsistent with his present testimony). There is also the possibility of discrediting a witness by calling other witnesses to contradict some portion of his testimony—in other words, by having other witnesses testify to one or more "facts" that conflict with those recited by the witness who is, at least indirectly, being impeached. This contradiction by other witnesses is generally considered a form of impeachment, but it is not always easy to distinguish this impeachment from variant accounts by different witnesses to the same event. We shall consider "contradiction by others" near the end of the chapter, for it poses some special problems.

§ 8.2 Impeachment of One's Own Witness

Determining who is permitted to impeach a witness presents a preliminary problem. For many years a rule has existed, until recently subject only to limited exceptions, that a party may not impeach his own witness. The origins of this prohibition remain uncertain, but it may have gained favor in the late 17th Century when adversary procedures began to replace inquisitorial methods

2. Lempert & Saltzburg at 282.

3. The best known early case is United States v. Hiss, 88 F.Supp. 559 (S.D.N.Y.1950). See United States v. Jackson, 576 F.2d 46, 48–49 (5th Cir. 1978); United States v. Barnard, 490 F.2d 907 (9th Cir.1973), cert. denied, 416 U.S. 959 (1976).

of factfinding.[1] The right to call a witness was viewed as a special privilege, not to be abused by putting forth a witness and then attacking his credibility.[2] The rule against impeachment is embodied in the proposition, often repeated in the cases, that a party "vouches for" the testimony of his own witness.[3]

In modern lawsuits, where litigants have compulsory process and often must subpoena as a witness a stranger or hostile person, there is no justification for a rule forbidding impeachment of one's own witnesses. A party calls a particular witness because the latter has knowledge of relevant facts—not because he has an alliance or partnership with the party. Accordingly, the prohibition against impeaching one's own witness has largely been abandoned. Since the mid-nineteen-seventies, a substantial number of jurisdictions have, by statute or court rule, abandoned altogether this restriction.[4] Furthermore, as we shall see, the rule against impeachment gradually lost much of its sting because of the creation of various exceptions. The invocation of one of these

§ 8.2

1. See Ladd, Impeachment of One's Own Witness—New Developments, 4 U.Chi.L.Rev. 69, 70–74 (1936). But as noted in Weinstein & Mansfield, et al. at 446, this hypothesis is speculative.

2. Weinstein & Mansfield, et al. at 446. Another possible explanation for the origin of the rule against impeaching one's own witness is that it stems from the early ecclesiastical and English practice known variously as wager of law, oath swearing or compurgation. This involved purging or clearing the defendant by having witnesses testify that they believed he was telling the truth. Ibid. Here, of course, there was a strong identification between the defendant and his witness.

3. Lempert & Saltzburg at 282. Although normally this means that impeachment is forbidden, the notion of a party's vouching for his witnesses encompassed a complementary rule that had some support in the early cases: if a party presented a witness whose testimony was *unfavorable*, the points established in the testimony were conclusive against—i.e. "bound"—the proponent unless he could produce other witnesses whose testimony on these points was more favorable. Although the rule against impeachment of one's own witness survives in a shrinking number of jurisdictions, the rule binding a party by his witness's testimony has been broadly rejected. For an illustration of the application of the rule that one is bound by his own witness, see Murray v. New York Central Railroad, 332 Mich. 159, 165, 50 N.W.2d 748, 749 (1952). Fleegar v. Consumers' Power Union, 262 Mich. 537, 540–541, 247 N.W. 741, 742 (1933).

4. Federal Rule 607 abandons entirely the rule against impeaching one's own witness. See text at nn. 17–19 infra. Over half the states have adopted this rule verbatim or with minor changes. Others have adopted rules to the same effect. See, e.g., West's Ann. Cal.Evid.Code § 785; Kan.Stat.Ann. 60–420; McCormick, § 38, at 83–84. The U.S. Supreme Court has held that in some situations to deny a criminal defendant the right to impeach his own witness would interfere with his constitutional right to "confront and cross-examine witnesses and to call witnesses in his own behalf." Chambers v. Mississippi, 410 U.S. 284 (1973).

exceptions may, even today, be necessary in those minority jurisdictions retaining the rule against impeachment. Note, however, that when the *court* calls a witness, which it will sometimes do upon request of counsel, either party is usually free to impeach.[5]

A long-standing exception to the prohibition against impeaching one's own witness arises when the law *requires* a party to call a particular witness.[6] For example, a statute or judicial rule might provide that a party must call the person who attested a will or other document in order to establish due execution.[7] Here, at least, the courts recognized that a party should be able to contest the credibility of a witness whom he was legally compelled to present. Practical as well as legal compulsion also should suspend the rule against impeachment, but only a few cases adopted this broader approach.[8] However, many jurisdictions have adopted (by court rule or statute) a second exception: when a party calls his adversary, some form of impeachment is allowable.[9]

A third exception to the historical prohibition is the "surprise doctrine," invoked when a party calling a witness is surprised by the latter's testimony; unexpected testimony entitles the party to impeach his witness by showing that the latter has made prior inconsistent statements. The theory is that the sponsoring party was deceived and should therefore be allowed to impeach the turncoat witness in an effort to lessen the damage to his case. The doctrine has been applied with varying degrees of strictness. A first requirement for its application is that the proponent demonstrate a basis for having believed that the witness would give favorable testimony. If the witness has given indications of unreliability or has not induced counsel reasonably to expect favorable testimony, the judge may find that the party calling the witness was forewarned and hence not genuinely surprised.[10] Further, under the traditional view, the witness's testimony must affirmatively be damaging: he must make a positive assertion

5. Lempert & Saltzburg at 283; Morgan & Weinstein at 63–64.

6. Morgan & Weinstein at 63; Lempert & Saltzburg at 283; IIIA Wigmore § 917 (Chadbourn).

7. IIIA Wigmore § 917, IV Wigmore § 1288 (Chadbourn). In a criminal case, the prosecution may be required by statute or rule to call all witnesses who endorse the indictment. See People v. Connor, 295 Mich. 1, 294 N.W. 74 (1940); see also People v. Favors, 121 Mich.App. 98, 328 N.W.2d 585 (1982).

8. Morgan & Weinstein at 63.

9. See 111A Wigmore § 916 (Chadbourn); Ladd, Impeachment of One's Own Witness—New Developments, 4 U.Chi.L.Rev. 69, 77–78 (1936); Mich.R. Evid. 607(2)(B).

10. See IIIA Wigmore § 904 (Chadbourn).

adverse to a material part of the proponent's case.[11] Testimony that the witness cannot remember usually will not justify impeachment.[12] But many courts, while not abandoning these requirements, have given the benefit of the doubt to the proponent on the question of whether he genuinely was surprised,[13] and have taken a realistic, practical view of what constitutes affirmative damage.[14]

Without resorting to any of these foregoing exceptions to the rule against impeachment, counsel may by skillful examination of his own witness secure the desired testimony without crossing the forbidden line of impeachment. If the witness displays hostility or has an apparent lapse of memory, counsel usually may use leading questions. He also may ask about prior inconsistent statements if he fairly can characterize his questions as an attempt to refresh his witness's recollection or to prompt the latter to correct an error in his testimony.[15] Finally, the examiner may use a prior writing (or other object) to "refresh" the witness's recollection. None of these techniques is considered "impeachment" in the stricter sense in which that term is used.

11. See Taylor v. Baltimore & Ohio R.R., 344 F.2d 281 (2d Cir.1965), cert. denied 382 U.S. 831 (1965); State v. Matlock, 65 Wash.2d 107, 396 P.2d 164 (1964).

12. McCormick, § 38, at 83; IIIA Wigmore, § 1043, at 1059–61 (Chadbourn). "The maximum legitimate effect of the impeaching testimony can never be more than the cancellation of the adverse answer by which the party is surprised." Kuhn v. United States, 24 F.2d 910, 913 (9th Cir.1928), cert. denied sub nom. Lee v. United States, 278 U.S. 605 (1928). The fear here, of course, is that when the witness is impeached by a prior inconsistent statement, the trier will use the prior statement as substantive evidence and thus violate the hearsay rule. See § 6.4; Note, Prior Statements of One's Own Witness to Counteract Surprise Testimony: Hearsay and Impeachment Under the "Damage" Test, 62 Yale L.J. 650, 654 (1953).

13. Gaitan v. People, 167 Colo. 395, 447 P.2d 1001 (1969) (proponent knew witness was hostile and had not made inquiries of her that would have forewarned him of unfavorable testimony, but impeachment allowed); People v. Spinosa, 115 Cal.App.2d 659, 669–70, 252 P.2d 409, 415 (1953) (witness gave contradictory versions prior to trial, but proponent entitled to rely on most recent account).

14. United States v. Cunningham, 446 F.2d 194 (2d Cir.1971), cert. denied, 404 U.S. 950 (1971) (witness who said at trial that he had seen defendant in the company of one identified as the robber "maybe [two or] three times" impeached by earlier statement that these two persons "hang around" together); People v. Le Beau, 39 Cal.2d 146, 245 P.2d 302 (1952) (denial of a fact that, if true, would help the state's case, sometimes can leave such a "damaging impression" that impeachment by state is justified).

15. See People v. Michaels, 335 Ill. 590, 167 N.E. 857 (1929); People v. Purtell, 243 N.Y. 273, 280–81, 153 N.E. 72, 74–75 (1926); Morgan & Weinstein at 64.

In recent years, most jurisdictions either have granted the judge discretionary power to allow impeachment of a hostile witness, or in increasing numbers, have abandoned altogether the proscription against impeaching one's own witness.[16] Notably, the Federal Rules of Evidence provide:

> *Who May Impeach.* The credibility of a witness may be attacked by any party, including the party calling him.[17]

In the commentary accompanying this provision, the Advisory Committee notes the unreality of the assumption that a party has unfettered liberty in selecting his witnesses.[18] The Federal Rule thus broadly nullifies the historical prohibition by allowing the calling party to impeach his witness, by any of the techniques discussed in the next section.[19] Other reform statutes have not gone this far; they allow impeachment of one's own witness only by prior inconsistent statements.[20]

The reluctance of some jurisdictions to permit a party routinely to use the usual techniques to impeach his own witness apparently stems from a fear that this unlimited freedom might be abused.[21] Impropriety might occur, for example, when the primary motivation for calling a witness identified with the opposing party is not to secure significant testimony, but rather to impeach by a method (such as showing a prior conviction) that directly reveals bad character or dishonesty.[22] Apprehension concerning this abuse probably is unwarranted. Aside from the fact that a party who undertakes this stratagem risks alienating the trier of fact, the judge should have ample discretionary power to prevent improper impeachment.[23] Furthermore, if the witness's testimony

16. See, e.g., West's Ann.Cal.Evid. Code § 785 (complete abrogation); Va. Code 1950, § 8.01–403 (judge's discretion). Do not assume that abandonment or modification of the rule against impeachment of one's own witness renders all forms of impeachment permissible. There could be a limitation, such as Virginia's, that the only allowable form of impeachment is showing prior inconsistent statements. The Virginia statute expressly disallows use of evidence of bad character. See Smith v. Lohr, 204 Va. 331, 130 S.E.2d 433 (1963).

17. Fed.R.Evid. 607.

18. Adv.Comm.Note to Fed.R.Evid. 607.

19. A troubling question is how far this approach allows the prosecution to go in criminal trials. See § 8.3.

20. See, e.g., Va.Code 1950, § 8.01–403; see supra n. 16. McCormick, § 38, at 83, describes the English statutory precedents.

21. See Ladd, Impeachment of One's Own Witness: New Developments, 4 U.Chi.L.Rev. 69, 80–86 (1936).

22. Impeachment by prior inconsistent statement does not necessarily impugn character.

23. See Fed.R.Evid. 611(a).

is important to the outcome of the case, the opponent (or the court) probably will call him, in which event the cross-examiner can impeach by any of the orthodox techniques described below.

§ 8.3 Techniques of Impeachment: Character Traits Reflecting Mendacity

A. *Conviction of a Crime.* As an exception to the general prohibition against the circumstantial use of character,[1] the credibility of a witness may be challenged by showing that he has been convicted of a crime.[2] The desired inference is that a person who commits a criminal offense is likely—or at least more likely than one who has not committed such an act—to give false testimony. Disagreement, however, often occurs over what types of crimes indicate a propensity to falsify. Does a conviction for manslaughter, for example, have probative force regarding credibility? Some convictions, such as those for perjury[3] or fraud, yield strong circumstantial inferences relating to truth-telling. Other offenses, however, such as manslaughter or reckless driving, have a tenuous link with credibility.[4] Some courts have tried to solve this problem by resorting to amorphous verbal formulae.[5] The most common are: crimes involving moral turpitude,[6] "crimen falsi,"[7] and

§ 8.3

1. See generally §§ 5.2–5.8. The law always has displayed a special concern for the truth of courtroom testimony. Conditioning devices, such as the oath and cross-examination, are designed to expose false statements. A witness may be attacked by showing that he has a bad character for truth and veracity. See § 8.3C. Note that when prior convictions (§ 8.3A) and prior bad acts, (§ 8.3B) are used to show a propensity to falsify, the relevant character trait is being shown by specific acts. This means of proof usually is disallowed when character is used circumstantially.

2. At common law, convictions of a felony or of a misdemeanor involving dishonesty (*crimen falsi*) rendered the convicted person incompetent as a witness. McCormick, § 43, at 93. Statutes negating the common-law prohibition typically provide that a conviction that would have rendered the witness incompetent may be shown to affect his credibility. See, e.g., Conn.Gen.Stat. Ann. § 52–145.

3. See Comment, 31 Ford.L.Rev. 797 (1963).

4. See, e.g., McIntosh v. Pittsburg R. Co., 432 Pa. 123, 247 A.2d 467 (1968) (pandering); State v. Russ, 122 Vt. 236, 167 A.2d 528 (1961) (traffic misdemeanor). See also Annot., 88 A.L.R.3rd 74 (1978).

5. See McCormick, § 43, at 93–94, where statutes containing various formulae are set out and cases are cited. Id. at n. 5. See also IIIA Wigmore § 980 (Chadbourn); Slough, Impeachment of Witnesses: Common Law Principles and Modern Trends, 34 Ind.L.J. 1, 22 (1958); Note, Admissibility of Prior Crimes Evidence to Impeach in Florida, 15 U.Fla.L.Rev. 220 (1962).

6. See, e.g., State v. Jenness, 143 Me. 380, 62 A.2d 867 (1948); McGee v. State, 207 Tenn. 431, 332 S.W.2d 507 (1960).

infamous crimes.[8] Other courts, however, by decision or statute make a more practical accommodation: any conviction for a felony may be used to impeach, but a conviction for a misdemeanor may be used only if the illegal act involved dishonesty or a false statement.[9] Some jurisdictions modify this approach by restricting impeachment to felonies; [10] others have allowed proof of any conviction, no matter what its grade.[11] There also is lack of uniformity regarding the admissibility of juvenile adjudications [12] and the effect of probation or of the passage of a long period of time since the conviction was rendered.[13] It now is settled, however, that the Constitution forbids the use of a prior conviction obtained in violation of the right to counsel.[14]

The Federal Rule governing impeachment by prior conviction permits the use of any conviction—misdemeanor or felony—involving "dishonesty or a false statement." [15] Other convictions, however, may be used only if the underlying offense "was punishable by death or imprisonment in excess of one year . . . and the court determines that the probative value of admitting this evidence outweighs its prejudicial effect to the defendant." [16] Thus a crime of "dishonesty or false statement" is always admissible; no balancing by the Court is necessary. Misdemeanors not involving dishonesty or false statement are inadmissible for impeachment purposes. But felony-grade convictions, (those potentially punishable by imprisonment for more than one year) not involving

7. See, e.g., Commonwealth v. Kostan, 349 Pa. 560, 37 A.2d 606 (1944).

8. See Weinstein & Mansfield, et al. at 477 n. 3. See generally IIIA Wigmore § 980 (Chadbourn).

9. See, e.g., D.C.Code 1981, § 14–305.

10. West's Ann.Cal.Evid.Code § 788.

11. 12 Okla.Stat.Ann. § 381. Repealed 1978. See 12 Okla.Stat.Ann. § 2609. The new statute follows the Federal Rule. See Sullivan v. State, 333 P.2d 591 (Okla.Cr.1958). See also State v. Hurt, 49 N.J. 114, 228 A.2d 673 (1967).

12. Fed.R.Evid. 609(d) admits evidence of a juvenile conviction in a criminal case where (1) the juvenile witness is not the accused; (2) the offense would be admissible to attack the credibility of an adult; and (3) "the court is satisfied that admission in evidence is necessary for a fair determination of the issue of guilt or innocence." Most states totally bar evidence of a juvenile proceeding from other proceedings. I Wigmore § 196(3) contains an extensive list of such statutes.

13. Fed.R.Evid. 609(b) sets a 10-year period from the date of conviction or release from prison. After this period evidence of the conviction is admissible only if its probative value "substantially outweighs" its prejudicial effect, and the proponent provides advance written notice of his intent to use the evidence. See infra n. 18.

14. Loper v. Beto, 405 U.S. 473 (1972).

15. Fed.R.Evid. 609(a).

16. Fed.R.Evid. 609(a). The rule apparently reflects a special concern for "defendants" in a criminal context.

dishonesty or a false statement are admissible if the judge determines that probative force is sufficient to overcome any resulting prejudice to the accused.[17] Thus Rule 609 has its own balancing test, and the only party entitled to protection is the accused. We shall return to this topic below. Other features of Rule 609 include a specific provision governing the age of the conviction as a bar to admissibility [18] and particular provisions dealing with the effects of a pardon [19] and the admissibility of juvenile adjudications.[20]

There is nearly general agreement concerning the evidentiary means that may be used to prove a conviction: under the Federal Rules and in most states, counsel may adduce the evidence during cross-examination by asking the witness to admit the fact of the conviction, or he may introduce a certified or exemplified copy of the prior criminal judgment.[21] Neither of these means of proof consumes much time, and the use of evidence of previous convictions usually poses only the problems of what kinds of convictions are admissible and whether probative worth is outweighed by prejudice. Courts usually disallow detailed descriptions of the previous offense, confining counsel to such essentials as the name of the crime, the time and place of prosecution, and the punishment imposed.[22] Nor will courts allow the impeached witness to

17. See infra text accompanying n. 35.

18. Fed.R.Evid. 609(b). Generally, a conviction is "not admissible if a period of more than ten years has elapsed since the date of the conviction or the release of the witness from confinement, . . . whichever is the later date. . . ." Id. Thus, if the witness were not imprisoned for the prior offense, the ten-year period would begin to run on the date of the conviction. The ten-year rule, however, is not absolute. If more than ten years has elapsed since the conviction or release, the judge may nonetheless admit the conviction "in the interests of justice" if probative value substantially outweighs prejudice. A party who proffers a conviction outside the usual ten-year time limit must give his opponent advance written notice so that the latter can muster his arguments against admissibility. Id.

19. Fed.R.Evid. 609(c). In general, a pardon, annulment, or certificate of rehabilitation will render the conviction inadmissible if the forgiving act was based either on a finding of innocence or rehabilitation. Id.

20. Fed.R.Evid. 609(d). In general, juvenile adjudications are not admissible. In criminal cases, the trial judge can make an exception if "necessary for a fair determination" of guilt or innocence and if the witness impeached is not the accused. Id. See also supra n. 12.

21. See Fed.R.Evid. 609(a). McCormick, § 43, at 97. In a few jurisdictions proof is limited to a copy of the criminal judgment. See Gaskill v. Grauman, 255 Iowa 891, 124 N.W.2d 533 (1963); IV Wigmore, § 1270, 657–64 (Chadbourn).

22. McCormick, § 43, at 98. For an example of a federal decision interpreting Federal Rule 609 as limiting the prosecutor's showing to the fact and

give an extended explanation or time-consuming presentation of facts in mitigation of the conviction, although many courts permit a brief ameliorative explanation.[23]

We have already seen that a criminal defendant has the privilege of declining to testify.[24] A principal concern of an accused who contemplates taking the witness stand is whether he can be impeached by a prior conviction. Often he will seek (by a motion "in limine")[25] an early ruling on the admissibility of prior conviction(s) affecting his credibility. An in limine ruling, which may be provided by the judge as an exercise of his authority to manage the trial,[26] is subject to revision, at least until the accused actually testifies. Indeed, only after the content and tenor of the accused's trial testimony is revealed to the trial judge is the latter able to make an informed contextual determination of the admissibility of a prior conviction to impeach. Thus in limine rulings, in contrast to those made when the accused actually takes the stand, are not reviewable on appeal, at least in the federal courts.[27] This means, for example, that if the judge's in limine ruling favors admissibility of prior convictions to impeach and the defendant then chooses not to testify, there will be no appellate review of this preliminary ruling.[28] Of course if the defendant elects to take the stand, he generally is subject to the usual rules governing the examination of witnesses, including the rules that allow the cross examiner to engage in various kinds of impeachment. This opens the possibility that a testifying defendant may be impeached by evidence that he has been convicted previously of crimes that reflect upon credibility. In theory this evidence is admitted solely

date of the conviction and the nature of the offense see United States v. Tumblin, 551 F.2d 1001 (5th Cir.1977).

23. McCormick, § 43, at 98–99; IV Wigmore, § 1117, at 251 (Chadbourn).

24. See § 4.11; see also § 9.11.

25. This is "a written motion which is usually made before or near the beginning of a jury trial for a protective order against prejudicial questions and statements." Robinson v. State, 309 N.E.2d 833, 854 (Ind.App.1974), modified on other grounds, 311 N.E.2d 461. The term "in limine" has been defined as "on or at the threshold; at the very beginning; preliminarily." Black's Law Dictionary 708 (5th ed. 1979). See Note at the conclusion of Ch. XI.

26. See Luce v. United States, 469 U.S. 38, 41 n. 4 (1984). See also Fed.R. Evid. 611(a); see, e.g., Fed.R.Evid. 103(c); cf. Fed.R.Crim.P. 12(e).

27. Luce v. United States, 469 U.S. 38 (1984). In Luce the Supreme Court held that if the accused, in light of an in limine ruling admitting prior convictions for impeachment purposes, chooses not to take the stand he waives his right to challenge the in limine ruling on appeal. Id. at 43.

28. Id. at 43. For a critical analysis of the *Luce* decision, see Martin, Appealability of 609(a) In Limine Rulings, 193 N.Y.L.Jour. 26 (Feb. 7, 1985).

to impugn the accused's testimony; it is not to be used to support the prejudicial inference that an accused-witness who has committed one or more previous crimes is more likely to be guilty of the offense with which he is presently charged.

Upon request, the judge will instruct the jury concerning the limited purpose for which the impeaching evidence may be considered. Nonetheless, the risk that such evidence may prejudice the jury has caused many jurisdictions to formulate protective rules when an accused takes the stand.[29] Over the years this practice has taken various forms. One approach, tried for a period of time in the District of Columbia, allows the trial judge broad discretion to reject evidence of prior convictions when he determines that its probative force is outweighed by the risk of prejudice or by the desirability of hearing the defendant's story free of the distraction of past crimes.[30] However, this balancing process creates uncertainty, disparity of practice among trial judges, and the encouragement of appeals.[31] Another protective method (applicable to all witnesses, but most helpful to the accused) is to narrow the kinds of convictions that will be allowed for impeachment purposes: only those convictions thought to have a strong bearing upon credibility are sanctioned.[32] A technique embodied in American Law Institute's Model Code of Evidence and an earlier version of the Uniform Rules is for the court to disallow an attack on the accused's credibility unless he first presents evidence supporting

29. McCormick, § 43, at 99: "The accused, who has a 'record' but thinks he has a defense to the present crime, is thus placed in a grievous dilemma. If he stays off the stand, his silence alone will prompt the jury to believe him guilty. If he elects to testify, his 'record' becomes provable to impeach him, and this again is likely to doom his defense."

The risk of prejudice is highest where the prior crimes used to impeach are similar to the offense charged.

30. See Luck v. United States, 348 F.2d 763 (1965) and the attempt to explicate the *Luck* doctrine in Gordon v. United States, 383 F.2d 936 (1967), cert. denied, 390 U.S. 1029 (1968). The applicable statute at the time of these cases was amended in 1970 and now provides for impeachment by evidence that the witness was convicted of an offense "punishable by death or imprisonment in excess of one year . . . or . . . involv[ing] dishonesty or false statement (regardless of punishment)." D.C.Code 1973, § 14–305 codifying Fed. R.Evid. 609(a). It is clear that the *Luck* doctrine did not survive the statutory change. See United States v. Lipscomb, 702 F.2d 1049 (D.C.Cir.1973). However, Federal Rule 609(a) embodies a discretionary approach similar to that announced in *Luck*. See United States v. Mehrmanesh, 689 F.2d 822, 833 n. 13 (9th Cir.1982); United States v. Crawford, 613 F.2d 1045, 1050 (1979); see also People v. Montgomery, 47 Ill.2d 510, 516, 268 N.E.2d 695, 698 (1971).

31. These and other criticisms are set forth in Ladd & Carlson at 224–225.

32. See IIIA Wigmore § 980 (Chadbourn).

his truthfulness.[33] This is an unusual provision because it contravenes the traditional rule disallowing evidence in support of credibility unless the opponent (that is, the prosecutor) first has presented impeaching evidence.[34] For various reasons, none of these protective measures, particularly the last, has attracted a wide following.

The Federal Rules of Evidence give the trial judge discretionary power to reject evidence of a prior conviction where he determines "that the probative value of admitting this evidence outweighs its prejudicial effect to the defendant." [35] As noted above, however, this discretion is available only if the prior conviction was not for a crime involving dishonesty or a false statement. Convictions for the latter classes of crime are unconditionally admissible to impeach. The approach is to place limits on the kinds of convictions that are unconditionally admissible and to incorporate a balancing process with respect to other convictions of a felony grade. Several aspects of the Rule cause difficulty. For example, what crimes involve "dishonesty" and thus come within the class of cases where the judge has no discretionary power—at least under Rule 609—to reject the evidence of conviction? The legislative history suggests strongly that the trial judge's discretion extends to all crimes except those in the nature of "crimen falsi," that is, those involving deceit, falsification, or untruthfulness.[36] To illustrate: the courts have held that the trial judge must admit evidence of a conviction for such crimes as: mail fraud,[37] forgery,[38] false pretense,[39] counterfeiting,[40] and bribery.[41]

33. Model Code of Evidence 106(3) (1943); Uniform Rules of Evidence 21 (1953). See Kan.Stat.Ann. § 60–421. The new Uniform Rule follows Federal Rule 609. See 13A Uniform Rules of Evidence 609 (1986). For a case applying the Model Code approach, see State v. Cantrell, 201 Kan. 182, 440 P.2d 580 (1968), cert. denied, 393 U.S. 944 (1968). For a due process approach with a similar result, see State v. Santiago, 53 Hawaii 254, 492 P.2d 657 (1971), appeal after remand; 55 Hawaii 162, 516 P.2d 1256 (1973). See also the discussion in United States v. Palumbo, 401 F.2d 270, 272–73 (2d Cir.1968), cert. denied, 394 U.S. 947 (1969).

34. See § 8.7.

35. Fed.R.Evid. 609(a).

36. See the extensive opinion in United States v. Smith, 551 F.2d 348 (D.C.Cir.1976). In United States v. Brashier, 548 F.2d 1315 (9th Cir.1976), cert. denied, 429 U.S. 1111 (1977), the court held that mail fraud was a crime involving "dishonesty, or false statement" within the meaning of Fed.R. Evid. 609(a). Other courts have given a broader meaning to the word "dishonesty." See, e.g., United States v. George, 752 F.2d 749 (1st Cir.1985) (manufacture and distribution of amphetamines); United States v. Hall, 588 F.2d 613 (8th Cir.1978) (possession and distribution of narcotics).

37. United States v. McClintock, 748 F.2d 1278, 1288 (9th Cir.1984), cert. denied ___ U.S. ___ (1985); United States

Tax evasion and larceny by trick should also fall within the category of crimen falsi. Nonetheless "crimes of dishonesty or false statement" constitute a "fairly narrow subset of criminal activity."[42] This conclusion is also supported by the legislative history of 609.[43] The difficulty lies in discerning what treatment should be given to offenses whose underlying facts reflect dishonesty, but which do not clearly fall within the crimen falsi category. Crimes like robbery or petty larceny have received varied treatment in different cases.[44] Perhaps this is unavoidable since some offenses which do not clearly fall within the crimen falsi class are "more veracity related" than others.[45] One solution—at least where the information is available—is for the trial judge to review the underlying facts of a particular conviction and to make a determination of probative worth in light of these facts.[46] The alternative approach of simply labelling specified crimes as either within or without the dishonesty classification may lead to arbitra-

v. Kuecker, 740 F.2d 496, 501 (7th Cir. 1984).

38. United States v. Hans, 738 F.2d 88, 94 (3d Cir.1984); United States v. Bay, 762 F.2d 1314, 1317–1318 (9th Cir. 1984).

39. Shingleton v. Armor Velvet Corp., 621 F.2d 180, 183 (5th Cir.1980).

40. United States v. Noble, 754 F.2d 1324, 1331–1332 (7th Cir.1985), cert. denied, 106 S.Ct. 63 (1985).

41. United States v. Williams, 642 F.2d 136, 140 (5th Cir.1981).

42. United States v. Smith, 551 F.2d at 362. See also United States v. Fearwell, 595 F.2d 771 (D.C.Cir.1978).

43. H.R. Conf.Rep. No. 93–1597, 93rd Cong., 2d Sess. 9 (1974); S.Rep. No. 93–1277, 93rd Cong., 2d Sess. 14 (1974). For a discussion of the narrow construction endorsed in the congressional committee reports concerning the rule, see 3 Louisell & Mueller, § 317, at 333–35.

44. Compare United States v. Givens, 767 F.2d 574, 579 n. 1 (9th Cir. 1985), cert. denied, ___ U.S. ___ (1985) and Linskey v. Hecker, 753 F.2d 199, 201 (1st Cir.1985), holding that larceny, burglary and armed robbery are not crimes involving "dishonesty or false statement," with United States v. Del Toro Soto, 676 F.2d 13, 18 (1st Cir.1982), appeal after remand, 728 F.2d 44 (1st Cir.1984) and United States v. Brown, 603 F.2d 1022, 1027–29 (1st Cir.1979), holding that grand larceny, petty larceny and burglary do involve these traits.

45. See McCormick, § 43, at 94 n. 9; see, e.g., 3 Louisell & Mueller (Supp. 1986 at 163–170).

46. A few cases indicate that it is inappropriate for the trial judge to examine the particular facts of a prior conviction. See, e.g., United States v. Lewis, 626 F.2d 940, 946 (D.C.Cir.1980): narcotics prosecution in which the court stated in dicta that "contrary to the Government's construction, we do not perceive that it is the manner in which the offense is committed that determines admissibility. Rather we interpret Rule 609(a) to require that the crime 'involved dishonesty or false statement as an element of the statutory offense.'" Id. at 946; see also United States v. Fearwell, 595 F.2d 771 (D.C. Cir.1978) (rejecting scrutiny of underlying facts); United States v. Millings, 535 F.2d 121, 123 (D.C.Cir.1976) (carrying a pistol without a license, and possession of narcotics convictions excluded under 609(a)(2), since "intent to deceive or defraud is not an element of either offense").

ry discriminations that in the particular context of the conviction offered are inaccurate.

In any event, once it is determined that a crime does not involve "dishonesty or false statement" the trial judge must balance the probative force of a prior conviction against its prejudicial effect. Appellate reversal of this determination is unlikely, since appellate courts—both state and federal—have accorded wide discretion to the trial judge in making this determination. However, the judge must in fact balance the probative value against prejudice and articulate for the record the reasoning of his decision to either admit or exclude the proffered conviction.[47] In exercising this discretion, he may take account of such factors as: the age of the conviction, the character of the prior offense, the subsequent history of the witness sought to be impeached, the similarity of the past crime with the crime charged in the case of a defendant witness, and the centrality of the credibility issue to the witness's proffered testimony.[48] With so many relevant variables, it is not surprising that disparate results in essentially similar cases are common.[49]

Additional difficulties arise because Rule 609 contains a particularized balancing process. It weighs probative value against prejudice differently from Rule 403.[50] The latter rule, on its face, applies to all evidence and excludes only such evidence as is "substantially outweighed" by prejudice or some other countervailing consideration. In contrast, the language of Rule 609 demands exclusion if the scales are slightly tipped toward prejudice, for it omits the qualifying word "substantially." The issue is simply whether the probative value outweighs prejudice (which allows admission) or whether prejudice is the weightier concern (which dictates exclusion). More importantly, Rule 609 expressly singles out prejudice *to the defendant.* This formulation

47. For a concise and topically organized review of recent state cases see 13 Uniform Rules of Evidence 415–418 (1986). A similar review of federal cases appears in 3 Louisell & Mueller § 316. See also id., § 320, at 354–58.

48. See United States v. Acosta, 763 F.2d 671, 659 n. 30 (5th Cir.1985), cert. denied, ___ U.S. ___, 106 S.Ct. 179 (1985); see also Vaughn v. Love, 347 N.W.2d 818 (Minn.App.1984); State v. Henderson, 116 Ariz. 310, 569 P.2d 252 (1977). See 3 Louisell & Mueller § 316.

49. For example, decisions may be found that reach conflicting results on the admissibility of such crimes as robbery, larceny, etc. See supra nn. 47–48.

50. Fed.R.Evid. 403 provides in pertinent part:

Although relevant, evidence may be excluded if its probative value is substantially outweighed by the danger of unfair prejudice, confusion of the issues, or misleading the jury. . . .

is broad enough to include the occasional case where impeachment of a defense witness other than the accused may unduly prejudice the latter. However, the extent to which prior impeaching convictions can be excluded because of prejudice to the government or to a party in a civil case is unclear. The federal circuits have split on the question whether the generally applicable balancing standard of Rule 403 applies to the use of convictions that may prejudice some party other than a criminal accused.[51] Both logic and proper statutory (or "rules") construction suggest that Rule 403 ought to be available. Rule 609 offers special protection to the accused by singling him out and applying to him a balancing test that is more favorable to the exclusion of a prior conviction than is Rule 403. However, neither the language of the applicable Rules, nor fairness, justifies a practice that gives special protection to the accused but affords no protection to other parties.[52]

The debate over Rule 609 is not likely to subside. Indeed, no resolution of the tension between the need to reveal to the trier information relevant to assessing credibility, on the one hand, and the risk of misuse of this information, on the other, has ever drawn unchallenged support. Arbitrary rules cannot by their nature take account of the contextual variations from case to case. A rule of discretion or balancing also has disadvantages. The question whether the probative value of a prior conviction outweighs prejudicial effect often is difficult to resolve. There are many variables and different judges are likely to assess these differently. Thus, the conferral upon the trial judge of discretion to reject evidence of a prior conviction creates inconsistencies in the administration of an important evidentiary rule. Of course some observers favor a rule that disallows the use of any prior conviction to impeach an accused. An absolute prohibition has not found acceptance, however, because of an unwillingness among courts and legislators to allow the accused to appear as if his record were unblemished when his record of convictions, if made known to the jury, would cast serious doubt on his testimony. Thus, the tension between providing the jury with a full

51. See Diggs v. Lyons, 471 U.S. 1078 (1986), Justices White, Brennan and Marshall, dissenting from denial of certiorari, noting the discordant decisions of the various circuits. Compare Czajka v. Hickman, 703 F.2d 317 (8th Cir.1983) and Shows v. M/V Red Eagle, 695 F.2d 114 (5th Cir.1983) with Furtado v. Bishop, 604 F.2d 80 (1st Cir. 1979), cert. denied, 444 U.S. 1039 (1980).

52. The competing constructions, applicable policies, and legislative history are carefully and persuasively reviewed in Saltzburg & Redden at 520–521.

context for determining credibility and the consequent risk of undue prejudice remains the subject of a lively policy debate.

B. *Prior Bad Acts.* Suppose a witness has committed an act that reflects unfavorably upon his truthfulness. We have seen that if his prior conduct led to a criminal conviction, that conviction often may be shown to impeach his credibility.[53] But if there were no conviction,[54] can the act itself be proved? The courts divide on this question, but a majority now authorize impeachment by "prior bad acts."

Two difficulties attend this method of impeachment. First, there may be an issue of relevance because not all "bad" acts cast doubt on credibility. This, of course, is a familiar problem, the solution to which turns upon the general principle of relevance. Filing false statements on an application for a retail license clearly involves deceit. But engaging in drunken or disorderly conduct does not, and probably does not adversely reflect upon one's willingness to testify truthfully. A second problem—growing out of the practical aspects of trial administration—arises from the concern, generally shared by courts, that trials be neither unduly prolonged nor so conducted that the trier's attention is diverted from the principal issues in the case. In short, courts resist conducting a trial within a trial—that is, adjudicating the existence and circumstances of some distant act, which has relevance only because it brings into question the credibility of a witness.[55]

These considerations of relevance and distraction have caused some courts to prohibit any impeachment by prior bad acts.[56] Most jurisdictions, however, compromise by allowing impeachment

53. See § 8.3A.

54. In most instances, there will have been no prosecution for the prior act. Suppose, however, there has been a prosecution resulting in acquittal. May the prior act still be used to impeach? A trial judge exercising his discretion sometimes should disallow this inquiry, especially when the witness consistently has denied involvement in the prior act. See Lee v. United States, 368 F.2d 834, 836–37 (D.C.Cir.1966). On the other hand, where a witness's statements are contradicted either by his contentions at the prior trial or by those aspects of the prior act that were shown clearly or uncontested, it would seem that inquiry about the prior act should be allowed. See Walder v. United States, 347 U.S. 62 (1954). Note, also, that the use of a prior bad act to impeach does not depend upon a showing of the act beyond a reasonable doubt. The standard is whether the cross-examiner in good faith believes the prior incident took place. See United States v. Burch, 490 F.2d 1300 (8th Cir.1974), cert. denied, 416 U.S. 990 (1974). See also n. 60 infra.

55. See the discussion below of the collateral matter doctrine, § 8.6. See also § 5.7.

56. McCormick, § 42, at 90–92.

by prior bad acts, but requiring that the examiner settle for such admissions or concessions as he can adduce during cross-examination.[57] He cannot prove the prior bad act by additional or "extrinsic" evidence.[58] In theory, and usually in practice, the examiner may inquire only about acts that reflect upon credibility. Some courts, however, have taken a broad view of this requirement, permitting questions about acts such as assault with a weapon and performance of illegal abortions.[59] Of course, the examiner's cross-questions would be improper unless asked in good faith, based upon his reasonable belief that the witness had committed the prior act in question.[60] Federal Rule of Evidence 608(b) provides in part:

> *Specific Instances of Conduct.* Specific instances of conduct of a witness, for the purpose of attacking or supporting his credibility, other than conviction of crime . . . [which generally is allowed by Rule 609], may not be proved by extrinsic evidence. They may, however, in the discretion of the court, if probative of truthfulness or untruthfulness, be inquired into on cross-examination of the witness (1) concerning his character for truthfulness or untruthfulness, or (2) concerning the character for truthfulness or untruthfulness of another witness as to which character the witness being cross-examined has testified.[61]

57. Id. at 92. This statement implies that the cross-examiner is the counsel trying to impeach. In many instances, however, the attorney who called the witness is allowed to impeach. See § 8.2. But the principle of settling for the witness's answer would still apply.

58. See, e.g., United States v. Cluck, 544 F.2d 195 (5th Cir.1976) (applying Fed.R.Evid. 608(b)); People v. McCormick, 303 N.Y. 403, 103 N.E.2d 529 (1952); McCormick, § 42, at 92. § 8.6 deals in more detail with the use of extrinsic evidence.

59. See People v. Sorge, 301 N.Y. 198, 93 N.E.2d 637 (1950) and cases cited therein. But see People v. Sandoval, 34 N.Y.2d 371, 357 N.Y.S.2d 849, 314 N.E.2d 413 (1974) which sets limits to the cross-examination permitted under *Sorge,* preventing cross-examination when prejudicial effect far outweighs probative worth on the issue of credibility. See also People v. Ocasio, 47 N.Y.2d 55, 416 N.Y.S.2d 581, 389 N.E.2d 1101 (1979), holding that the protection afforded by *Sandoval* is available only to criminal-defendant-witnesses. For discussion of this line of decisions, see Weinstein & Mansfield, et al. at 491. See also Wright v. State, 243 Ark. 221, 419 S.W.2d 320 (1967), where the charge was rape and the prior bad acts consisted of making indecent proposals to women.

60. Compare People v. Alamo, 23 N.Y.2d 630, 298 N.Y.S.2d 681, 246 N.E.2d 496 (1969), cert. denied, 396 U.S. 879 (1969) with State v. Phillips, 240 N.C. 516, 82 S.E.2d 762 (1954). See also People v. Sorge, 301 N.Y. 198, 93 N.E.2d 637 (1950).

61. Fed.R.Evid. 608(b).

This Rule generally accords with the precedents in those jurisdictions that permit impeachment by prior bad acts.[62] It emphasizes discretionary control by the trial judge, as do many of the decided cases.[63] Typically, such prior incidents as false statements on employment or credit applications or on various government forms such as tax return or license applications are fair game for the cross-examiner;[64] so, too, are such acts as fraud and deception.[65] There is less uniformity where an act—such as theft—bears directly upon dishonesty but may or may not meet the "untruthfulness" standard of Rule 608(b).[66] Common observation probably supports the conclusion that a thief's veracity is somewhat suspect. At least, admissibility presents a close enough question so that the trial judge's decision should not be overturned on appeal.

The final clause of Rule 608(b) addresses the situation where one witness (the "principal" witness) is later followed by another witness in support (or derogation) of the former's character for truthfulness. In the limited instances in which this kind of evidence is permitted,[67] the character witness may be asked about acts of the principal witness that the character witness should have taken into consideration.

62. For discussion and a collection of the authorities, see IIIA Wigmore §§ 977–79 (Chadbourn).

63. See, e.g., Lehr v. Rogers, 16 Mich.App. 585, 168 N.W.2d 636 (1969); People v. Sorge, 301 N.Y. 198, 93 N.E.2d 637 (1950). Professor (now Judge) Weinstein asserts that "in the United States the great majority of state court decisions make the discretion of the trial judge determinative." Morgan & Weinstein at 67. Note that Fed.R.Evid. 611(a) allows the court reasonable control over the interrogation of a witness. One objective of such control is to protect against "harassment or undue embarrassment."

64. See representative cases collected in 3 Louisell & Mueller, § 305 (Supp. 1986), at 85–87.

65. 3 Louisell & Mueller, § 305, at 229.

66. The types of prior conduct properly bearing upon untruthfulness has been the subject of disagreement among commentators on the Rule. For a discussion of the differing positions of Wigmore, favoring a narrow construction, and Ladd, who believed that dishonesty as reflected by such prior conduct as theft should be admissible to impeach, see 3 Louisell & Mueller, § 305, at 225–230 and cases collected therein. There seems to be agreement however that cross-examination about such prior matters as sexual relationships, the legitimacy of children, or the use of drugs or alcohol, while bearing on a witness's morality, are not sufficiently probative of veracity to overcome the prohibition of impeachment evidence which serves merely to degrade or embarrass a witness. Id. at 233. See Fed.R.Evid. 412. Cross-examination regarding prior violent conduct has also been disapproved. See United States v. Fountain, 768 F.2d 790, 795 (7th Cir.1985) (cross-examination concerning a witness's "peaceable character" not probative of truthfulness); Cf. United States v. Martino, 648 F.2d 367, 392–93 (5th Cir.1981).

67. See § 8.7, §§ 5.5–5.7.

It sometimes happens that a cross-question concerning a prior bad act calls for an answer that would violate the witness' privilege against self-incrimination.[68] This may occur with an ordinary witness or when the witness is the accused. It seems clear that in either instance the privilege is available. Indeed, the last paragraph in Rule 608(b) provides that:

> The giving of testimony, whether by an accused or by any other witness, does not operate as a waiver of his privilege against self-incrimination when examined with respect to matters which relate only to credibility.[69]

Of course, should the witness neglect to claim the privilege, his answer disclosing the prior bad act may be freely used to assess his credibility.

C. *Bad Character Regarding Truth and Veracity.* As elsewhere indicated,[70] courts usually are reluctant to admit evidence of a party's character to support the inference that on a specific occasion he acted in accordance with the character traits shown. The credibility of witnesses, however, traditionally has been a subject of special concern for the courts; the outcome of many—if not most—trials is determined by which of the conflicting lines of testimony the trier believes. We already have observed that most courts admit evidence of prior conduct that reflects adversely upon a witness's honesty.[71] All courts agree that a witness may be impeached by evidence which speaks even more directly to his present character for truth and veracity: the impeaching party may offer witnesses who assert that based upon their knowledge of the principal witness, derived either from their familiarity with his reputation or (in many jurisdictions) their observations of his conduct, he has a bad character for truth and veracity. Traditionally, the courts have tried to provide the trier with a useful insight into the witness's character for truthfulness, while also attempting to minimize the burdens of delay and distraction caused by the

68. See McCormick, § 42, at 90–92; Coil v. United States, 343 F.2d 573 (8th Cir.1965), cert. denied, 382 U.S. 821 (1965), mere act of testifying does not act as a waiver of privilege with respect to inquiry into prior criminal activities for the purpose of attacking credibility. For analysis of this accused-witness's privilege see Griffin v. California, 380 U.S. 609 (1965), rehearing denied, 381 U.S. 957 (1965); Ferguson v. Georgia, 365 U.S. 570 (1961).

69. Fed.R.Evid. 608(b).

70. §§ 5.2–5.6.

71. The use of evidence of prior convictions and of prior bad acts also constitutes proof through character, although the opinions often do not make this clear. The prior conduct is used to infer a trait or propensity to falsify which is then used to infer that the witness gave false testimony.

introduction of secondary issues. Thus, the common law usually limits the type of evidence that may be provided by impeaching witnesses. Those who take the stand for the purpose of impugning the character of the principal witness are restricted to giving evidence of the latter's *bad reputation* for truth and veracity. Delay is minimized by limiting the evidence to conclusory statements about the witness's reputation and, concomitantly, by prohibiting proof of the underlying events that may have produced this disrepute.[72] Under this approach, if a witness, *W*, testifies for the plaintiff, defense counsel can impeach *W* by calling another witness, *X*, to testify that *W* has a bad reputation for truth and veracity. As a predicate for his testimony, *X* must provide evidence that he is in a position to know about *W*'s bad reputation. Hence, it usually is necessary that *X* testify he has resided or otherwise been present in the community in which *W* lives. In recent years, the courts have tended to receive testimony from an impeaching witness (X) who, by reason of employment or some other circumstance, is likely to be acquainted with the reputation of the principal witness (W). The assumption is that knowledge of *W*'s bad reputation for truth and veracity is acquired from others who speak disparagingly about *W*. The intended inferences from this kind of evidence are clear: from *W*'s unfavorable reputation, the trier can infer the existence of a mendacious trait, and then can infer that *W* is giving untruthful testimony.

In a mobile, urban society, the assumptions underlying impeachment by reputation are dubious at best. It may be doubted, for example, whether many persons who live and work in large urban centers have an established community reputation for traits of truth and veracity. Reacting to this problem, many jurisdictions have adjusted the traditional restrictions. Even some early cases permit the impeaching witness, whatever the basis of his familiarity with the principal witness's reputation, to conclude his direct testimony by stating whether, based upon the reputation to which he has testified, he would believe the principal witness under oath.[73] Surely, this is thinly disguised opinion evidence.

72. See §§ 5.4–5.7.

73. See, e.g., United States v. Walker, 313 F.2d 236, 239–41 (6th Cir.1963), cert. denied, 374 U.S. 807 (1963); Morgan & Weinstein at 66. Wigmore points out the inconsistency of purporting to restrict evidence to reputation yet allowing what amounts to a personal opinion of the impeaching witness. VII Wigmore, § 1982, at 212–13 (Chadbourn). For a case rejecting the question about belief under oath in circumstances where it was clear that the answer was based in part on personal opinion, see People v. Lehner, 326 Ill. 216, 157 N.E. 211 (1927).

Further, as noted above, a growing number of jurisdictions allow impeachment by reputation if the impeaching witness has been present in an association or setting (such as a work environment) in which the principal witness may have established a reputation for truthfulness.[74]

Increasingly, the mechanical repetition of a set formula by the reputation witness has been seen for what it usually is—a thinly veiled form of personal opinion. Consequently, in recent years there has been a decided shift toward permitting the impeaching witness straightforwardly to give his personal opinion of the veracity of the principal witness. The Federal Rules of Evidence state:

> *Opinion and reputation evidence of character.* The credibility of a witness may be attacked or supported by evidence in the form of opinion or reputation, but subject to these limitations: (1) the evidence may refer only to character for truthfulness or untruthfulness, and (2) evidence of truthful character is admissible only after the character of the witness for truthfulness has been attacked by opinion or reputation evidence or otherwise.[75]

This provision loosens the traditional restrictions, but does not go so far as to permit the impeaching witness to describe, during *direct* examination, specific instances of conduct that reflect adversely upon the truth and veracity of the principal witness. The cross-examiner, however, may probe the basis of the opinion (or reputation) by inquiring about these specific events.[76]

§ 8.4 Techniques of Impeachment: Bias

The term "bias" denotes a variety of mental attitudes that may cause a witness to give false or misleading testimony.[1] In general, it signifies a witness's interest in the outcome of the case, including a friendly or hostile association with one of the parties that could induce him to color, distort, or falsify his testimony. The cross-examiner can expose any potential bias by showing the

74. See McCormick, § 44, at 102–103; Morgan & Weinstein at 66–67.

75. Fed.R.Evid. 608(a). See also Fed.R.Evid. 405(a).

76. Fed.R.Evid. 405(a). The form of the inquiry about specific events is discussed in § 5.7.

§ 8.4

1. See Weinstein & Mansfield, et al. at 464–469, which contains summaries of illustrative cases. See also Annot., 74 A.L.R. 1157 (1931).

witness's relationship to the case, his financial interest in the outcome, or his association with one of the parties. For instance, the interrogator can attempt to demonstrate that a witness is related by blood or marriage to a party, employed by a party, has an economic stake in the outcome of the litigation, has a strong identification with an interest (such as nuclear development) involved in the litigation, or that he was promised immunity from prosecution or favored treatment in return for his testimony.[2] These are simply illustrations; the sources of a witness's potential bias are practically infinite.

Courts generally permit the impeaching party to prove bias either through cross-questions or by adducing extrinsic evidence, either from witnesses or documents.[3] However, if the cross-questions and answers adequately expose the basis of the bias, the judge can limit or prohibit further evidence.[4] Many jurisdictions require that as a prerequisite to the introduction of extrinsic evidence, counsel first must ask the witness about the circumstances underlying the alleged bias.[5] The federal decisions are not uniform, but generally do not impose such a requirement unless prior inconsistent statements are used for the purpose of showing bias.[6] In these instances, the courts usually require the founda-

2. For a collection of illustrative cases, see IIIA Wigmore § 949 (Chadbourn).

3. See, e.g., United States v. Brown, 547 F.2d 438 (8th Cir.1977), cert. denied 430 U.S. 937 (1977); Kidd v. People, 97 Colo. 480, 51 P.2d 1020 (1935); Vassar v. Chicago, B. & O. R. R., 121 Neb. 140, 236 N.W. 189 (1931); Morgan & Weinstein at 70.

4. People v. Wilson, 254 Cal.App.2d 489, 62 Cal.Rptr. 240 (1967); State v. Roybal, 33 N.M. 540, 273 P. 919 (1928). Thornton v. Vonallmon, 456 S.W.2d 795, 798 (Mo.App.1970): "[w]here interest or bias is denied by the witness it may be shown by the testimony of others, and even when it is admitted the extent of the witness' bias and prejudice may be shown, though the trial court has considerable discretion as to how far the inquiry may be pursued in detail." See § 8.6 discussing the collateral matter doctrine and use of extrinsic evidence, and see § 8.5, n. 1.

5. United States v. Hayutin, 398 F.2d 944 (2d Cir.1968), cert. denied, 393 U.S. 961 (1968); Taylor v. State, 249 Ind. 238, 231 N.E.2d 507 (1967); People v. Payton, 72 Ill.App.2d 240, 218 N.E.2d 518 (1966). McCormick implies that a majority of courts require this foundation. See McCormick, § 40, at 87–88; IIIA Wigmore § 953 (Chadbourn).

6. See United States v. Leslie, 759 F.2d 366, 379–380 (5th Cir.1985), reh'r en banc 783 F.2d 541 (5th Cir.1985) (applying Fed.R.Evid. 613). Foundation requirements apply to extrinsic evidence offered to impeach a witness by showing bias; United States v. Dinapoli, 557 F.2d 962, 964–965 (2d Cir.), cert. denied, 434 U.S. 858 (1977) (proper to disallow extrinsic evidence of bias because cross-examiner had laid no foundation for bias during cross-examination). See generally Annot., Necessity and Sufficiency of Foundation For Discrediting Evidence Showing Bias or Prejudice of Adverse Witness, 87 A.L.R. 2d 407 (1963). See also § 8.5, n. 1.

tion that, as more fully explained in the next section, is generally essential to impeachment by prior inconsistent statements. At common law, it is necessary, before the introduction of extrinsic evidence, to ask the witness about his prior inconsistent statement. This requirement is justified on the grounds of fairness to the witness and efficient trial administration. In the present context, if this requirement is applied to prior statements disclosing bias, there are some practical advantages. The witness to be impeached has the first opportunity to give evidence regarding bias; furthermore, as noted above, his answers to cross-questions may be sufficiently complete to render extrinsic evidence unnecessary. However, the requirement of a foundation should be applied with flexibility so that in appropriate cases the judge may waive it and simply allow the impeached witness to return to the stand (after the introduction of extrinsic evidence of bias) and attempt to rebut the evidence that he is partial. These alternatives are consistent with modern federal practice respecting prior inconsistent statements.

No federal rule of evidence specifically governs impeachment by evidence of bias. Nonetheless, the federal courts have uniformly allowed such impeachment. The admissibility of evidence of bias was strongly affirmed by the United States Supreme Court in United States v. Abel.[7] In that case, a bank robbery prosecution, the government called witness *A,* who had earlier entered a guilty plea to the same robbery with which Abel was now charged as a coparticipant. Later in the trial, Abel called witness *B* in an effort to counter *A*'s damaging testimony: *B* testified that *A* had once admitted to him that he (*A*) intended to falsely implicate Abel, so that *A* would receive lenient treatment from the government. The prosecution was now faced with the task of rebutting *B*'s testimony. On cross, the prosecutor unsuccessfully attempted to secure an acknowledgment from *B* that he and Abel were members of a secret organization. Subsequently, the government recalled *A,* who testified in rebuttal that Abel, *A* and *B* had previously been members of a secret prison gang. According to *A,* membership in that gang required that each member deny the existence of the organization and " 'lie, cheat, steal [and] kill' to protect each other."[8] Thus, *A* stated, it would have been "suicide" for him to have told *B* that he (*A*) intended to falsely implicate Abel. Note that the probative force of *A*'s testimony

7. 469 U.S. 45 (1984).

8. Id. at 48.

supports both the unlikelihood that he would have disclosed a plan to falsely implicate Abel and, more importantly, the likelihood that *B*'s testimony supporting Abel was biased.

Ultimately, the United States Supreme Court approved the trial judge's admission of *A*'s rebuttal testimony. It found the probative force of this testimony on the issue of *B*'s possible bias favoring Abel was sufficient to justify its reception. In short, the Court held that the trial judge did not abuse its discretion when he concluded that the probative force of the evidence on the issue of bias was not substantially outweighed by possible prejudice to Abel. It was first noted that relevant evidence is admissible unless blocked by some rule of exclusion, and that evidence suggesting bias clearly met the test of relevance: the evidence diminished somewhat the likelihood that the facts to which the biased witness testified were true.[9] Here, the membership of *B* and Abel in an organization embracing secrecy and falsehood "supported the inference that . . . [*B*'s] testimony was slanted or perhaps fabricated in . . . [Abel's] favor." [10] Furthermore, said the Court, the jury was entitled to hear evidence of the type of organization (e.g. closely knit, secret, sworn to perjury and mutual protection) to which *B* and Abel belonged. Knowledge of that organization and its tenets allowed the jury to identify the source of *B*'s possible bias and also to assess the strength of his bias.

Note that *B*'s membership in the secret prison gang might be viewed as a prior bad act bearing on truthfulness and hence governed by the restriction that forbids extrinsic evidence. As we have seen, when impeachment is by evidence of prior acts of misconduct, the cross-examiner must settle for the answers he adduces during cross-examination.[11] However, the evidence of *B*'s membership also disclosed his possible bias. In *Abel* the Supreme Court found it unnecessary to rule on whether *B*'s membership was a prior bad act bearing on credibility and, as such, confined to disclosure during cross-examination. Whether membership in the secret organization is an admissible prior bad act [12] lost its importance when the Court found that the evidence was relevant to

9. For a more detailed treatment of the test of relevance, see §§ 2.1–2.4.

10. 469 U.S. at 52.

11. See § 8.3B and Fed.R.Evid. 608(b).

12. The probative force of the evidence, in the present context, at least, suggests that it should qualify as a prior bad act. The Supreme Court faintly implies that it would. 469 U.S. at 56. The court of appeals strongly suggests that it would not. Abel v. United States, 707 F.2d 1013, 1016 (9th Cir. 1983), cert. granted, 465 U.S. 1098 (1984).

show bias. On the issue of bias, an examiner need not settle for testimony he adduces during cross-examination; extrinsic evidence (i.e. *A*'s rebuttal testimony) is generally admissible. Thus, the Court relied on the familiar principle that evidence admissible for the purpose offered is not rendered inadmissible simply because if offered for some other purpose it would fall within a rule of exclusion.[13]

§ 8.5 Techniques of Impeachment: Prior Inconsistent Statements

A widely-recognized technique of impeachment consists of showing that the witness has made prior statements inconsistent with his testimony at trial. A party entitled to impeach may show the prior oral or written inconsistencies, but in presenting his impeaching evidence he must take account of certain qualifications and restrictions. As we shall see, courts usually allow impeaching counsel to *interrogate* a witness about a prior inconsistent statement even if the inconsistency relates only to an incidental or "collateral" matter. The theory in allowing these inquiries is that if the witness has rendered inconsistent statements about comparatively unimportant matters, his testimony about more important events should be evaluated with special care. But if the prior statement concerns only a collateral topic, the interrogator must settle for such admissions of the prior inconsistency as he is able to adduce during cross-examination. If the witness refuses to concede the existence of the earlier contradictory assertions, the court will not permit resort to extrinsic evidence.[1] The presentation of extrinsic evidence is thought to be too costly in terms of time consumption and distraction. On the other hand, if the prior statement involves a matter material to the elements of a claim or defense, the statement is not considered collateral and extrinsic evidence may be introduced.

Care must be taken to comply with the rules requiring a foundation for impeachment by prior inconsistent statements. The jurisdictions vary somewhat in the strictness of their demands regarding an appropriate foundation. Considerations of fairness to the witness and expedition of trials have led many courts to

13. 469 U.S. at 56. See § 6.2.

§ 8.5

1. See § 8.6 on the collateral matter doctrine. Sometimes, however, a prior inconsistent statement may show bias. In such a case, extrinsic evidence should be permitted. See United States v. Harvey, 547 F.2d 720 (2d Cir.1976) (extrinsic evidence proper if foundation adequate).

require counsel first to ask the witness about the prior inconsistent statement and then to give him the opportunity to deny, affirm, or explain the earlier statement.[2] The witness presumably knows about the statement and can explain the earlier assertion. It seems fair that he should be given an early opportunity to respond to the examiner's charge of inconsistency, and his answers to cross-questions may eliminate the need for additional, extrinsic evidence. The courts demand that impeaching counsel's questions contain enough detail as to the circumstances surrounding the prior statement to enable the witness to identify the occasion and explain or deny the alleged inconsistency.[3] This requirement usually imposes upon counsel—often the cross-examiner—the duty of identifying the subject matter of the statement, the time and place of its utterance, and the person to whom it was made.

A scattering of jurisdictions retain the Rule of Queen's [Caroline's] case[4] and impose an especially strict foundation requirement where the prior inconsistent statement is contained in a writing: the *first* step in laying the foundation for impeachment by a contradictory writing is presentation of the writing to the witness for his examination. Because this presentation precedes any question to the witness regarding whether he has made the writing or any statement within it, this preliminary procedure usually negates any chance of exposing a deceitful witness who otherwise might deny making an inconsistent statement. This early disclosure also affords the witness time to gather his thoughts and, sometimes, to explain away the inconsistency or lessen its effect.[5]

Even where the Rule of Queen's case has been abrogated, some courts display a penchant for excessive technicality when

2. A few jurisdictions, led by Massachusetts, do not require such a foundation. See Tucker v. Welsh, 17 Mass. 160 (1821); IIIA Wigmore § 1028 (Chadbourn). Another approach is to invest the trial judge with discretion to waive the foundation. See Giles v. Valentic, 355 Pa. 108, 49 A.2d 384 (1946) and cases cited therein.

3. See Mead v. Scott, 256 Iowa 1285, 130 N.W.2d 641 (1964); Nichols v. Sefcik, 66 N.M. 449, 349 P.2d 678 (1960). The requirement is defended in Osborne v. McEwan, 194 F.Supp. 117, 118–119 (D.D.C.1961) (pre-Rules case).

4. 2 Br. & B. 284, 129 Eng.Rep. 976 (C.P.1820). The doctrine of Queen's case is discussed in Ladd, Some Observations on Credibility: Impeachment of Witnesses, 52 Cornell L.Q. 239, 245–249 (1967). Many jurisdictions have negated the rule, usually by legislation. See, e.g., West's Cal.Evid.Code § 768 (1966); Va.Code Ann. § 8.01–404 (1977); McCormick, § 28, at 56–57.

5. See McCormick, § 28, at 61: "While reading the [document or] letter the witness will be warned by what he sees not to deny it and can quickly weave a new web of explanation."

assessing the adequacy of the foundation required with respect to any prior statement, whether written or oral.[6] They seemingly lose sight of the modest objectives that the rule requiring a foundation is designed to secure, namely, warning the witness that counsel has evidence of a prior contradictory assertion and giving the witness a fair opportunity to respond. To satisfy this purpose, mere specification of the subject matter of the prior inconsistency should be held sufficient if it enables the witness to identify and respond to the alleged inconsistent statement. Strict adherence to a particular formula is not needed because, as Wigmore notes, the identification of such circumstances as time, place, and persons present when the statement was made are means to the end of fairly apprising the witness.[7] As another example of rigid technicality, some courts impose the usual foundation requirement when the witness to be impeached has not taken the stand, but is the source of admissible evidence because his deposition is introduced, his former testimony contained in transcript from another trial is admitted, or his admissible hearsay declarations are received.[8] If the rule requiring a foundation were unremittingly applied, the declarant whose "testimony" is now offered in some form that substitutes for live testimony, could not be impeached by self contradiction unless he had been afforded a prior opportunity to respond to the prior inconsistency. Although fine distinctions can be drawn [9] among these situations where the "witness" is absent, at least it can be said that no foundation should be necessary where the individual sought to be impeached (1) never has been interrogated in a judicial setting (as usually is the case with the hearsay declarant [10]) or (2) even if subjected to some form of previous judicial interrogation, was not asked about the prior inconsistencies, either because they were unknown to the interrogator or because the inconsistencies were uttered after the interrogation.[11]

6. IIIA Wigmore §§ 1025–1029 (Chadbourn) contains an incisive discussion of the foundation requirement and also collects a host of examples.

7. See IIIA Wigmore, § 1029, at 1029 (Chadbourn).

8. See IIIA Wigmore §§ 1030–1035 (Chadbourn).

9. McCormick, § 37, at 80–81 presents a discriminating analysis.

10. The better cases support this view. See McCormick, § 37, at 80 and cases cited.

11. The authorities yield mixed results as to this proposition, but it appears sound. The admission of the inconsistency is desirable because it gives the trier a basis for careful evaluation of testimony that otherwise would stand unimpeached. For cases dealing with this problem, see IIIA Wigmore §§ 1031–33 (Chadbourn).

The usual foundation for a prior contradictory statement is not necessary when a *party* made the earlier inconsistent statement. Because the party admissions exception to the hearsay rule applies, the extra-judicial statement has independent value as substantive evidence of the facts asserted.[12] Thus, the statement is admissible even if the uttering party does not take the stand. This independent source of admissibility dispenses with the necessity of meeting the special foundation requirements that normally attend the use of prior inconsistent statements.[13]

In those cases where a witness to be impeached is entitled to an opportunity to deny or explain a prior inconsistency, the controlling considerations are fairness to the witness and to the litigants. Usually, efficient trial administration is served by affording the witness an opportunity during his adverse examination—before extrinsic evidence of the prior inconsistency is introduced—to answer the allegation that he has made a prior contradictory statement. His responses to cross-questions may render unnecessary the subsequent introduction of additional evidence. But while it generally is desirable that impeaching counsel inquire about alleged prior inconsistencies before introducing extrinsic evidence, little harm is done if evidence of the prior inconsistency is received and the witness is recalled to give his explanation. In some instances where interrogation of the witness concerning the prior declaration is inconvenient or impossible, the earlier statement usually should be admitted unless special circumstances, such as a deliberate omission of the required foundation, justify a discretionary exclusion. That is, there may be instances in which the introduction of a prior inconsistent statement is justified even though the impeached witness has no opportunity to respond. It is significant that Rule 613(b) of the Federal Rules of Evidence incorporates a flexible approach to the foundation requirement:

> *Extrinsic evidence of prior inconsistent statement of witness.* Extrinsic evidence of a prior inconsistent statement by a witness is not admissible unless the witness is afforded an opportunity to explain or deny the same and the opposite party is afforded an opportunity to interrogate him thereon,

12. See § 7.1.

13. State v. Mays, 65 Wash.2d 58, 395 P.2d 758 (1964), cert. denied, 380 U.S. 953 (1965); Tuthill v. Alden, 239 Iowa 181, 30 N.W.2d 726 (1948); McCormick, § 37, at 81.

> or the interests of justice otherwise require. This provision does not apply to admissions of a party-opponent. . . .[14]

Note particularly that the rule is satisfied if either before or after the introduction of extrinsic evidence the impeached witness is afforded an opportunity to deny, explain, or otherwise rebut it.

Technicalities in addition to those associated with laying a proper foundation can impede the use of evidence of a prior inconsistency. All courts agree that if a prior statement is received in evidence *to impeach,* it in fact must be *at variance* with the testimony of the witness. Some courts, however, extend this requirement beyond its common-sense purpose. In an Illinois case, for example, a witness to an automobile accident stated at trial that he saw several boys "crossing or attempting to cross" the road. Earlier, the witness had asserted that the boys were "trying to beat the traffic across" the highway. The court rejected a cross-question concerning this prior statement, holding that the two statements were not inconsistent.[15] A problem of determining inconsistency arises when the prior statement omits a significant point included in the trial testimony. Does this omission render the prior statement inconsistent? The cases yield conflicting results.[16] Here, however, the controlling principle should be relevance: the judge should base his ruling upon whether a reasonable jury could find the prior statement sufficiently at variance to cast doubt on the present testimony. If the judge answers this question affirmatively, he should admit the earlier assertion, leaving to the jury the decision whether to discredit the witness.[17] Typically, a prior inconsistent statement consists of a witness's previous statement of relevant facts that is at variance with his testimony at trial. However, a previous statement by a witness that he cannot remember an event (or certain facts surrounding it) is inconsistent with trial testimony in which he relates the event (or facts).[18]

14. Fed.R.Evid. 613(b). Rule 613(a) dispenses with the Rule of Queen's Case. See text supra at n. 4. Indeed, it goes further by stating that the witness need not be apprised of the contents of a prior *oral* statement before he is asked if he made it.

15. See Rogall v. Kischer, 1 Ill.App. 3d 227, 273 N.E.2d 681 (1971).

16. See IIIA Wigmore § 1042 (Chadbourn).

17. McCormick, § 34, at 75, states: "Seemingly the test should be, could the jury reasonably find that a witness who believed the truth of the facts testified to would have been unlikely to make a prior statement of this tenor?" See Morgan v. Washington Trust Co., 105 R.I. 13, 249 A.2d 48 (1969).

18. See, e.g., United States v. Dennis, 625 F.2d 782, 796 (8th Cir.1980); see 3 Louisell & Mueller at 551–553 (1977) and at 296 (Supp.1986).

Another technical obstacle is the rule, applied by some courts, that a prior inconsistency in the form of an opinion cannot be used to contradict testimonial "facts" given at trial. Under this view, if a witness recites at trial that the driver stopped at the intersection (or if he gives other "facts" demonstrating careful conduct), it would be improper to impeach the witness by showing that previously he said "it was all the driver's fault." [19] The commentators, especially Wigmore and McCormick,[20] have argued convincingly against this misapplication of the opinion rule. That rule is inappropriate when applied to an out-of-court statement which, unlike trial testimony, is in final form and cannot be rephrased. Hence, the opinion rule should not be raised as an artificial and obstructive limitation to the use of a prior inconsistent statement. Most recent cases have rejected the rule that prohibits contradiction by prior statements in opinion form.[21]

The foregoing discussion has focused upon the use of prior inconsistent statements to impeach a witness. But it will be recalled from an earlier chapter [22] that under the orthodox view any statement not made from the stand in the present proceeding is hearsay if offered for its truth. Under this approach, a prior inconsistent statement is hearsay and cannot be used for the truth of its assertion, unless, of course, it fits within a hearsay exception.[23] When no exception is applicable, the judge will instruct the jury that the prior inconsistent statement may be used solely for the limited purpose of evaluating the witness's trial testimony. This means that the trier may consider evidence that the witness has given more than one version of the same event, but only for the purpose of assessing the witness's credibility. The arguments for and against this traditional restriction are set out elsewhere in

19. See Wolfe v. Madison Ave. Coach Co., 171 Misc. 707, 710, 13 N.Y.S.2d 741, 744 (1939) where the court acknowledges confusion in the cases but reasons that the impeaching evidence, despite its opinion form, still serves to discredit the witness and thus should be received. Cases are collected in Annot., 158 A.L.R. 820 (1945).

20. See IIIA Wigmore § 1041 (Chadbourn); McCormick, § 35, at 76.

21. See, e.g., Atlantic Greyhound Corp. v. Eddins, 177 F.2d 954 (4th Cir. 1949); Tigh v. College Park Realty Co., 149 Mont. 358, 427 P.2d 57 (1967). A very good discussion may be found in Crawford v. Commonwealth, 235 Ky. 368, 31 S.W.2d 618 (1930).

22. §§ 6.1, 6.4.

23. The exception for party admissions often applies because parties frequently take the stand. The application of any hearsay exception permits a prior statement to be used not only to impeach but also as proof of the point asserted in the earlier statement. See §§ 7.1–7.2.

this text.[24] Suffice it to say that some jurisdictions, recognizing that many rules of evidence represent a practical accommodation of competing interests, have begun to permit the substantive use of a prior inconsistent statement.[25] Inasmuch as the witness who made the prior inconsistent assertion is on the stand and can be interrogated respecting both his present testimony and his prior statements, the hearsay dangers associated with the prior statement are significantly lessened. Despite the force of this argument, the Federal Rules do not allow the substantive use of a prior inconsistent statement unless it is made "under oath subject to the penalty of perjury at a trial, hearing, or other proceeding, or in a deposition. . . ."[26] The rules thus strike a middle ground between unrestricted substantive use and disallowance of any use except impeachment. The position taken in the Federal Rules has at least one advantage: there is considerable assurance that the prior statement was actually made and that there was reason for the declarant to seriously consider its content.

§ 8.6 Techniques of Impeachment: Extrinsic Evidence to Contradict and the Restriction Applicable to Collateral Matters

In the section dealing with prior bad acts,[1] we saw that in most jurisdictions impeaching counsel can inquire about past incidents casting doubt upon a witness's credibility, but must "settle" for such admissions as he can elicit during cross-examination. If the witness denies the past dishonest act, the examiner may not pursue the matter further by introducing extrinsic evidence to demonstrate the existence of the prior misdeed.

The prohibition against extrinsic evidence is not limited to impeachment by prior bad acts. It extends to any attempt to contradict testimony (including contradiction by a prior inconsistent statement) on an immaterial or "collateral" matter.[2] Al-

24. § 6.4.

25. The jurisdiction taking the lead in this reform is California. See West's Cal.Evid.Code § 1235; Gibbons v. State, 248 Ga. 858, 286 S.E.2d 717 (1982). The Federal Rules of Evidence permit such substantive use only where the prior statement was made in an earlier trial or proceeding and the declarant spoke under oath and subject to the penalty of perjury. Fed.R.Evid. 801(d)(1)(A).

26. Id.

§ 8.6

1. § 8.3B.

2. The collateral matter doctrine applies to areas other than impeachment, but most often is applied there. The Federal Rules of Evidence contain no general endorsement of the doctrine, but they do expressly apply it in particular rules. See, e.g., Fed.R.Evid. 608(b) (no extrinsic evidence to show prior bad acts).

though the cross-examiner has wide latitude in probing any point that may demonstrate a weakness or inaccuracy in the witness's testimony, he cannot resort to extrinsic evidence which serves the sole purpose of contradicting the witness on a collateral point. Thus, even though one form of impeachment consists of producing witnesses for the specific purpose of giving an account of one or more facts that contradict facts related by the witness assailed, this type of impeachment is restricted. Suppose, for example, a witness to an accident involving a corporate employee states that he is an officer of the corporation: the truth of this assertion may be probed on cross-examination, but under most of the cases the examiner may not show by extrinsic evidence that the witness holds a position of lower rank.[3]

This limitation applies unless the witness's position is material (consequential) to a claim or defense, as it might be, for example, in a case where the issue is the authority of the witness to speak or act for the corporation. In this latter instance, proof that the witness held a position of lesser authority would be admissible as substantive evidence, although it also would have an impeaching effect. Even in the case where the sole purpose of extrinsic evidence showing the witness's subordinate position is to contradict his assertion from the stand, there is a plausible argument supporting admissibility: if the examiner could introduce extrinsic evidence that the witness is only, say, the office manager, the jury reasonably might conclude that one who misrepresents his employment status may be giving false testimony concerning the principal matter under consideration. But the argument "falsus in uno, falsus in omnibus" (false in one, false in all) has generally been rejected by the courts. On balance, they have held that considerations of time and distraction militate against production of additional evidence on factual propositions which have no direct or circumstantial bearing on any element of a claim or defense.[4]

The rejection of extrinsic evidence pertaining to collateral topics usually is defensible. Even in the foregoing example, the application of the rule may be warranted. But the factual pat-

3. Cf. United States v. Rovetuso, 768 F.2d 809 (7th Cir.1985), cert. denied, ___ U.S. ___, 106 S.Ct. 838 (1985) (cannot use extrinsic evidence to contradict witness's statement elicited during cross-examination, that he had once been a Panamanian police officer).

4. It also is argued that the rule against collateral evidence serves to protect the witness from an unfair attack because he may not be prepared to present rebuttal extrinsic evidence on a remote point. See IIIA Wigmore, § 1002, at 960–61 (Chadbourn).

terns with which the courts must deal seldom are clear cut, and determining what topics are collateral is not always easy.[5] The issue of what constitutes collateral evidence often surfaces in cases where counsel seeks to impeach a witness with extrinsic evidence that the witness has made a prior inconsistent statement. It also can arise when counsel seeks to demonstrate the inaccuracy of a seemingly incidental part of a witness's testimony by producing another witness (or documentary evidence) intended to establish facts contradicting those to which the witness has testified. And, as we have seen, the rule against extrinsic evidence on collateral matters absolutely prohibits extrinsic evidence of prior bad acts.[6] Thus, the general prohibition against receiving extrinsic evidence on collateral matters affects admissibility frequently enough that counsel planning trial strategy must take account of this restriction and identify those evidentiary matters that are collateral.

The cases often say that a matter is collateral unless it could be shown in evidence for some purpose other than impeachment by contradiction.[7] Of course, with certain of the impeachment techniques, the courts freely admit extrinsic evidence even though its sole probative value is to discredit the witness. In any event, the general rule for determining what matters are collateral can serve only as a broad guide; often the difference between a matter being material (consequential), as distinguished from being collateral, is one of degree and not kind. Evidence proffered to contradict a testimonial assertion (and hence offered primarily for impeachment) may have at least weak probative value on some consequential proposition.[8] A case decided by the Washington Supreme Court illustrates the extent to which the competing considerations involved in determining collateralness defy any mechanical test.[9] That case involved a prosecution for robbery that allegedly took place in Seattle on July 14, 1961. The defense was alibi, and the supporting witness, a restaurateur, testified that the accused, a regular patron, was in the witness's restaurant in Portland, Ore-

5. Of course, the term itself gives little guidance and, as with many labels, sometimes serves as a substitute for careful analysis.

6. See § 8.3B. When the only purpose of showing the prior bad act is to impeach the witness, extrinsic evidence is forbidden. But if the act has another probative purpose which is consequential—as, for example, to show an element of the offense charged in the present trial—it is not within the rule forbidding extrinsic evidence.

7. See State v. Oswalt, 62 Wash.2d 118, 381 P.2d 617 (1963); Morgan, Basic Problems of Evidence, 76–77 (1963).

8. Ladd, Some Observations on Credibility; Impeachment of Witnesses, 52 Cornell L.Q. 239, 253 (1967).

9. State v. Oswalt, 62 Wash.2d 118, 381 P.2d 617 (1963).

gon on the night of the crime. On cross-examination, the witness stated, in response to a prosecution question, that he thought the accused had been in the Portland restaurant every day for the two months preceding the robbery. The prosecutor then sought to rebut this assertion with extrinsic evidence provided by a police officer that the accused was in Seattle on June 12, 1961 (one month before the alleged robbery) and for several days before that.

On appeal, the defendant contended that this rebuttal evidence was improper because it constituted impeachment by extrinsic evidence on a collateral point. The Washington Supreme Court agreed, holding that the challenged evidence had no purpose aside from the contradiction of the restaurateur because it failed to show that the accused was in Seattle on or near the date of the offense. The justices rejected as speculative the state's contention that evidence placing the accused in Seattle on June 12 had an independent purpose because his presence there gave rise to an inference that he was planning and preparing the crime that occurred a month later.[10]

Clearly the state could have tried to establish the defendant's presence in Seattle on the day of the offense. Probably the government could have shown his presence in that city a few days prior to the crime; certainly it could have done so had there been evidence of preparatory steps such as the acquisition of weapons or instrumentalities used in the offense. In the absence of evidence of planning and preparation, however, the case for admissibility grows weaker in proportion to the passage of time between the accused's presence in Seattle and the offense.

A different line of argument, however, could support admission of the evidence of the defendant's presence in Seattle on June 12. The alibi was the major issue at trial, and the testimony of the restaurateur was critical. Arguably, any evidence that reflected upon the accuracy of his observation and memory is

10. The only evidence of preparation was that the accused had spent several days in Seattle and had purchased a roll of adhesive tape. Although evidence of planning or preparation is admissible, it still must meet the general test of relevance, and its probative force must outweigh practical reasons for exclusion. Even assuming adhesive tape was used in the commission of the offense, the commonplace act of buying a roll of tape a month prior to the commission of the crime has only weak probative value to show preparation. The purchased article was one that most persons buy from time to time; further, absent additional evidence, it is erroneous to infer preparation from mere presence in the city where the offense took place, especially when that presence antedates the offense by a month and transportation facilities permit travel to the city in question in a short period of time.

justified—at least the trial judge should have been given discretion to receive it. Unless there were some particular circumstance associated with July 14 (the day of the offense) that would cause the witness to remember the accused's presence on that date,[11] it may be contended that the trier should have been allowed to evaluate the testimony concerning the critical day in light of evidence that the witness erred in his assertion that the defendant had been in his restaurant continuously for several months. This argument, of course, calls for a flexible application of the collateral evidence rule, suspending its prohibition in instances when the witness's testimony is very important to the outcome.

The essential point here is that shades of difference often are significant in a determination of what is collateral; rigid formulas are ineffective. Of course, even under the usual practice, a demonstration that the proffered evidence has relevance aside from its impeachment value always justifies admission. If the extrinsic evidence is independently relevant to some element of a claim or defense, the fact that it also contradicts a witness simply means that it has a dual value; it is freely admissable during rebuttal. In close cases, however, it is important to consider whether the challenged evidence casts sufficient doubt—albeit indirectly—upon important testimony that goes to a central issue in the case. If it does, the case for admitting extrinsic evidence is stronger—at least where the matter falls in the shadowy area between what clearly is collateral and what clearly is consequential. Another factor that should be considered is whether or not the witness to be impeached asserts in unequivocal terms the fact to be contradicted; if so, the jury may find the contradictory evidence especially useful in evaluating his testimony. Finally, it may be significant whether the (possibly) collateral point was raised first on direct or cross-examination. Where the direct examiner obtains the testimony upon which the "collateral" evidence casts doubt, it may be unfair to prohibit the cross-examiner from contradicting it,[12] at least where the direct examiner deliberately elicited the testimony that is the subject of the contradiction.

11. In fact, the witness did testify that he specifically recalled the defendant's presence in the restaurant on the night of the robbery because the latter had been in the company of a restaurant employee, had assisted with work in the restaurant, and had escorted the employee home. State v. Oswalt, 62 Wash.2d 118, 119, 381 P.2d 617, 618 (1963).

12. It may not be unfair, however, where the cross-examiner had ample opportunity to object to the testimony as irrelevant and could successfully do so without causing the jury to react adversely.

These variables do not lend themselves to mathematical precision. The trial judge must make a contextual judgment and appellate courts should—but sometimes do not—allow him adequate discretion. After all, his decision is in reality simply an assessment of probative value (on the issue of credibility) that is weighed against factors counselling against admission such as "unfair prejudice, confusion of the issues, . . . misleading the jury" or wasting time.[13] Thus, if a testifying witness confidently recites a "collateral" fact "that if he were really there [at the place claimed] and saw what he claims to have seen"[14] the chances of mistake (on the collateral point) are remote, then contradiction by extrinsic evidence should be allowed. Suppose, for example, a plaintiff-witness in a suit for personal injuries sustained at sea, testifies that he was now and had always been employed as a seaman. Should it be error for the trial judge to permit the defense to show by extrinsic evidence that in fact the plaintiff had been employed in other capacities?[15] The plaintiff, we assume, is a key witness and certainly should know the positions he has held. The better approach would be to sustain the trial judge's discretion if he decides to admit contradictory extrinsic evidence. But many courts would hold the reception of extrinsic evidence improper, since (as we are assuming) its only value was to impeach the witness on a point that is not consequential to a claim or defense.

It is noteworthy that, except for prior bad acts, the courts generally have admitted extrinsic evidence even though its sole purpose is to impeach. That is, some techniques of impeachment—the favored ones—are not restricted by the bar against extrinsic evidence. Extrinsic evidence is routinely admitted to show bias, bad character for truth and veracity, or to prove conviction of a crime. But extrinsic evidence of a prior inconsistent statement is permitted only if the subject matter of the inconsistency is consequential for reasons other than contradiction. It is not easy to reconcile these varying results. Perhaps evidence of a prior bad act or of a prior inconsistency relating to

13. See Fed.R.Evid. 403; 3 Weinstein & Berger, ¶ 607(05), at 67–68, noting that rule 403 should provide the test.

14. McCormick, § 47, at 111.

15. See O'Connor v. Venore Transp. Co., 353 F.2d 324 (1st Cir.1965). The case pre-dates the promulgation of the Federal Rules of Evidence and the trial was to the judge—not a jury. But the decision *ought* to have continuing validity, even in a jury trial under the Federal Rules. See generally McCormick, § 47, at 111–112; 2 Louisell & Mueller, § 129, at 91–92.

an incidental point lacks the probative force of the other impeachment techniques and thus fails to justify the delay and distraction associated with extrinsic evidence.

It also may be asked why courts always exclude extrinsic evidence of prior bad acts, but uniformly lift the ban when the bad act has resulted in a conviction. The explanation appears to be that a conviction provides the assurance that a high standard of proof was applied in determining that the bad act occurred. Further, because the only extrinsic evidence that can be introduced to establish the conviction is a certified copy of the judgment of the convicting court, a relatively brief time is spent in proving the impeaching fact.

In any event, the particular technique of impeachment may dictate the admissibility of extrinsic evidence. Thus, one should not overlook the possibility that a specific item of evidence may potentially fall within two or more forms of impeachment—for example, a prior inconsistent statement (or prior bad act) may also reflect bias.[16] It may be advantageous, therefore, to proffer the impeaching evidence for the purpose that offers the most evidentiary possibilities for or poses the fewest obstacles to admission.

§ 8.7 Accrediting the Witness (Rehabilitation)

The starting point for this discussion is the general principle that the credibility of a witness may not be supported in the absence of an impeaching attack. The justification for this restriction is in the assumption that most witnesses are conscientious and honest,[1] so that no reason exists for prolonging the trial by allowing supporting evidence of credibility when truthfulness is not called into question.[2] Further, admission of certain types of accrediting evidence, such as prior consistent statements, could

16. United States v. Harvey, 547 F.2d 720, 722–24 (2d Cir.1976) (prior inconsistent statements show bias); United States v. Robinson, 530 F.2d 1076, 1079–80 (D.C.Cir.1976) (prior drug dealings show bias). See generally IIIA Wigmore, § 1022, at 1015 (Chadbourn).

§ 8.7

1. Fed.R.Evid. 608(a) expressly prohibits evidence of truthful character unless the witness's character has been attacked. See also United States v. Leggett, 312 F.2d 566 (4th Cir.1962); Bryant v. State, 233 Ind. 274, 118 N.E. 2d 894 (1954); Johnson v. State, 129 Wis. 146, 108 N.W. 55 (1906). The courts probably are endorsing a rule designed to keep evidence concerning credibility within manageable bounds. After all, it probably is the case that even those individuals who frequently engage in deceit or falsehood are truthful in the vast majority of instances.

2. Under the prevailing view credibility is not called into question simply because another witness gives contradictory testimony. See United States v. Leggett, 312 F.2d 566 (4th Cir.1962).

motivate parties and witnesses to create favorable evidence, for example, by making a number of consistent pretrial statements.

The general rule against bolstering or accrediting, however, is not violated by incidental background information about a witness's employment or profession, even though this disclosure may carry the inference that the witness, because of his position of trust or responsibility, is probably honest and credible.[3] And even though the rule against bolstering usually operates to exclude prior consistent assertions,[4] many courts have admitted such statements in limited situations.[5] For example, on the theory that a prior out-of-court identification is at least as reliable as one subsequently made in the courtroom, a growing number of jurisdictions admit evidence of an earlier identification when the identifying witness is in the courtroom and available for cross-examination.[6] The admissibility of this evidence usually is analyzed under the hearsay rule, but its admission incidentally results in bolstering the credibility of the identifying witness[7]—at least where he is able to make an in-court identification. Also, a sizable number of jurisdictions now receive evidence of a "fresh complaint" by a victim made promptly after the perpetration of a crime apt to be known only to the victim and offender. The most frequent instance in which this evidence is approved is a rape case.[8] Some authorities extend the exception for prompt complaints to other offenses such as robbery or larceny.[9] There is a

3. See, e.g., Elam v. State, 518 S.W.2d 367 (Tex.Cr.App.1975).

4. State v. Herrera, 236 Or. 1, 386 P.2d 448 (1963). See IV Wigmore § 1124 (Chadbourn).

5. The statements may also violate the hearsay rule. See § 6.4.

6. Cases pro and con are collected in Annot., 46 A.L.R.4th 403 (1986). See § 6.4. See also note 3 at the conclusion of Ch. VI.

7. It is not always clear whether the admission of a prior identification constitutes substantive evidence that the person identified committed the act in question, or whether the court is admitting the evidence not for the "truth" of the prior identification but only to add assurances that the in-court identification is accurate. If the first use is allowed, the prior identification comes in as an exception to the hearsay rule or, under modern codes of evidence, as specially defined nonhearsay. See Fed.R.Evid. 801(d)(1)(C). The second use purports to limit the evidence to an assessment of credibility, but it is doubtful the trier of fact can confine the evidence to such a restricted use. Of course, if only the second use is allowed and if the courtroom identification is so uncertain as to be insufficient to support a finding, the rule restricting the use of the prior identification to credibility has a determinative effect. See § 6.4.

8. See McCormick, § 50, at 120; IV Wigmore §§ 1134–1140 (Chadbourn).

9. See IV Wigmore § 1142 (Chadbourn); State v. Slocinski, 89 N.H. 262, 197 A. 560 (1938) (witness reveals threats of arson).

difference of opinion as to whether only the fact that a complaint was made can be shown or whether the details contained in the complaint also may be revealed.[10] Of course where the complaint is within a hearsay exception such as the one for excited utterances, the dominant purpose of the complaint is to prove the truth of the out-of-court assertion. The evidence is freely admissible on this theory even though an incidental effect of admission is to bolster the credibility of the complaining witness.

Attempts to accredit the witness most often occur after the witness has been impeached by one of the standard techniques discussed in this chapter. This process of supporting the witness following an attack on his credibility sometimes is referred to as rehabilitation. There is occasionally an issue of whether a witness has been impeached so that the right to support credibility is triggered. Most cases hold, for example, that a witness has not been impeached, at least in the sense that permits his subsequent accreditation, when the party opposing the witness merely calls other witnesses who give contradictory testimony.[11] But the determination of whether the witness has been sufficiently impugned to justify rehabilitation is a contextual one, and the trial judge's discretion should be sustained.[12]

A frequent problem attending accreditation involves a determination of what kind of accrediting evidence rebuts the impeaching evidence. Note that evidence designed to rebut impeaching evidence can be directed either at *the impeaching facts themselves* or at *the inference of untruthfulness* that arises from the impeaching facts. Suppose, for example, that the impeaching evidence consists of evidence of a bad reputation for truth and veracity. Rebuttal evidence could consist of a showing that the principal witness enjoys a good reputation for these character traits.[13] The principal thrust of this rebuttal is directed toward the impeaching fact, that is, the witness's allegedly bad reputation. Assume, however, that the impeaching attack consists of evidence of a prior conviction and that in an effort to rehabilitate the witness, counsel offers evidence demonstrating that the witness has a good reputation for truth and

10. See McCormick, § 49, at 120; IV Wigmore §§ 1134–1140 (Chadbourn).

11. McCormick, § 49 at 117; 3 Louisell & Mueller, § 308, at 253.

12. McCormick, § 49, at 117 n. 12. Cf. Adv.Comm.Note to Fed.R.Evid. 608(a).

13. See IV Wigmore § 1105 (Chadbourn). Of course, it also would be possible to impeach the impeaching witness thereby weakening or destroying the impeaching facts. See Morgan & Weinstein at 73–74.

veracity.[14] This rebuttal strikes not at the impeaching fact, but rather at the inference that the witness is untruthful.[15]

This second type of rebuttal, countering the inferences derived from the impeaching evidence, often generates issues of relevance.[16] If, for example, impeachment is by evidence of bad reputation for truthfulness, a rebuttal showing that the witness had made prior statements consistent with his testimony would have little or no probative force. The courts would reject it on the ground that since the witness also may have made false prior assertions, evidence of earlier consistencies has little value to rebut the inferences of untruthful testimony. A similar result should ensue where the witness is impeached on the basis of bias and the opponent seeks to accredit the witness with evidence of prior consistent statements. Unless these statements predate the alleged inception of the bias, they do not negate the impeaching evidence. On the other hand, if the evidence demonstrating bias involves a corrupt or dishonest act, evidence supporting good character (such as opinion or reputation evidence) is probably warranted.[17]

A difficult case is presented when impeachment is by prior inconsistent statements and the accrediting evidence consists of a showing of prior consistent statements—that is, out-of-court statements in accord with the testimony of the impeached witness. Here the courts split,[18] with the majority of decisions denying admissibility by reasoning that even if evidence of the prior

14. Wigmore discusses this particular situation in some detail. IV Wigmore § 1106 (Chadbourn). See also Gertz v. Fitchburg, R. R., 137 Mass. 77 (1884); McCormick, § 49, at 116–118.

15. Where the witness is impeached by a showing of bias, a demonstration of good reputation often is not received, especially where the bias does not flow from a questionable or corrupt motive but is rooted instead in family relationship or affection. See McCormick, § 49, at 117. The courts also divide on the issue of support by good reputation when impeachment has been by prior inconsistent statement. Id. See also IV Wigmore § 1108 (Chadbourn). It would appear that an especially strong argument can be made for rehabilitation evidence when the witness denies ever having made the prior inconsistent statement.

16. See McCormick, § 49, at 117.

17. See supra n. 15.

18. Compare Coltrane v. United States, 418 F.2d 1131 (D.C.Cir.1969), and Wofford Beach Hotel, Inc. v. Glass, 170 So.2d 62 (Fla.App.1964), with Clere v. Commonwealth, 212 Va. 472, 184 S.E.2d 820 (1971). Fine distinctions and qualifications are drawn by some courts. For example, there are holdings that admissibility of the prior consistency is justified when the witness denies uttering the alleged earlier inconsistency and the supporting counsel has evidence of a prior consistency near in time to the alleged self-contradiction. McCormick, § 49, at 119. The theory,

consistencies were received, the trier still would be left with inconsistent versions of the witness's story. Hence, the accrediting evidence fails to dissipate either the impeaching fact or its associated inference. An exception to the majority result is made where impeaching counsel directly or indirectly has charged the witness with recently fabricating his story or with falsifying or distorting his testimony because of some motive such as a financial interest in the outcome of the case or a promise of special leniency from the prosecutor. In these circumstances, a prior consistent statement *that predates* the alleged recent fabrication or the motive to falsify has sufficient probative value to be admitted because it tends to rebut the cross-examiner's charge of recent contrivance.[19] For example, where a prosecution witness is impeached by a prior inconsistent statement, the government may show that he made a prior consistent statement before he entered into plea-bargaining discussions with the prosecution.[20] And even if impeachment does not take the form of a prior inconsistency, an express or implied charge of improper motive or recent fabrication should open the door to an earlier consistent statement.

Notes

1. *Prior Conviction to Impeach.* Assume that in a prosecution for burglary, the accused takes the stand. The government then seeks to impeach him with evidence that he was convicted of illegal possession of intoxicating liquor. Admissible? Would a conviction for illegal sale of intoxicating liquor be treated differently? See State v. Jenness, 143 Me. 380, 62 A.2d 867 (1948). The principal problem, of course, is one of relevance. But recall that the provisions of Fed.R.Evid. 609(a) draw distinctions between felonies and misdemeanors and between crimes (in general) and crimes involving dishonesty or a false statement.

2. *Plea Bargaining and the Plea of Nolo Contendere.* Rule 410 of the Federal Rules renders inadmissible certain statements and

of course, is that the prior consistency makes it less likely that the inconsistency was uttered.

19. People v. Coleman, 71 Cal.2d 1159, 80 Cal.Rptr. 920, 459 P.2d 248 (1969); People v. Singer, 300 N.Y. 120, 89 N.E.2d 710 (1949); Morgan & Weinstein at 74; IV Wigmore § 1128 (Chadbourn). See Fed.R.Evid. 801(d)(1) (B). See also People v. Gardineer, 2 Mich.App. 337, 139 N.W.2d 890 (1966) (consistent statement rejected because made after the bias existed).

20. United States v. Sampol, 636 F.2d 621 (D.C.Cir.1980). In *Sampol* it was also significant that the prior consistent statement was not made to United States law enforcement officials, but rather to Chilean authorities who had released him from custody.

pleas that are made in the course of plea bargaining. These protected declarations are inadmissible against the accused in any criminal or civil proceeding. The thrust of the Rule is to promote the plea bargaining process by freeing the accused from the apprehension that his declarations may be used to his detriment in the pending criminal trial or in subsequent litigation. For example, statements made to the prosecuting attorney are inadmissible *unless* they actually result in a guilty plea that disposes of the case—that is, a guilty plea that is not withdrawn. A plea of guilty and statements associated with it are not protected by Rule 410. The defendant has admitted his guilt and must suffer the direct and collateral consequences.

A plea of nolo contendere (as well as a *withdrawn* guilty plea) is given protection by Rule 410. Neither the plea, nor any statement associated with its negotiation or entry, is admissible in a subsequent civil or criminal action to which the accused is a party. The theory is that, officially at least, the accused has admitted nothing. It appears, however, that the criminal conviction that rests on the nolo contendere plea can be used in subsequent litigation to impeach the pleader. See 2 Louisell & Mueller, § 188, at 560. Furthermore, Rule 410 does not protect an accused when his role in subsequent litigation is not that of a party, but simply that of a witness. Id. at 559–60.

3. *Scientific and Medical Evidence of Credibility.* As noted in the text, one mode of impeachment is by the introduction of psychiatric evidence that the witness whose credibility is attacked suffers from a mental disease or disability that increases the likelihood of false statements. Such an impeachment technique was used by the defense in the prosecution of Alger Hiss. See United States v. Hiss, 88 F.Supp. 559 (S.D.N.Y.1950). Although psychiatric evidence bearing upon credibility generally is admissible, certain circumstances may justify the trial judge's rejection of this type of evidence. Some factors bearing upon admissibility are (1) the time involved in receiving the testimony; (2) the importance of the principal witness's testimony; (3) the nexus, according to medical authorities, between the mental condition alleged to exist and testimonial accuracy or truthfulness; (4) the adequacy of the opportunity for the expert to observe, treat, or evaluate the witness; and (5) whether there is reliable evidence corroborating the principal witness's testimony. Cases are collected in Weinstein & Mansfield, et al. at 510–511.

Science some day may provide us with a test of credibility that invariably detects conscious deception by the witness. The lie detector (polygraph) frequently is used by private persons (such as employers) and in criminal investigations, at least where the subject freely consents. But courts generally have rejected evidence of polygraph results. A typical case is People v. Leone, 25 N.Y.2d 511, 307 N.Y.S.2d 430, 255 N.E.2d 696 (1969). But see United States v. Ridling, 350 F.Supp. 90 (E.D.Mich.1972) (expert opinion based on polygraph admissible in perjury prosecution). Some courts admit evidence of lie detector tests where the parties have stipulated in advance that such evidence would be admissible. State v. Valdez, 91 Ariz. 274, 371 P.2d 894 (1962); Herman v. Eagle Star Ins. Co., 283 F.Supp. 33 (C.D.Cal.1966), aff'd, 396 F.2d 427 (9th Cir.1968). See McCormick, § 206, at 628–29, noting that a few jurisdictions give the trial judge discretion to admit polygraph results even in the absence of stipulation.

Normally, the results of the polygraph examination will be presented by the examiner who qualifies as an expert witness. By any measure, the test and its results have probative value to show sincerity or insincerity. Resistance of the courts probably is rooted in the apprehension that the trier will be strongly inclined to accept the results of the test even if it is made clear that the accuracy rate is considerably short of perfect—probably around 80%. See Horvath & Reid, The Reliability of Polygraph Examiner Diagnosis of Truth and Deception, 62 J.Crim.L.C. & P.S. 276 (1971). There is, however, some disagreement over the accuracy rate. Citations to the experiments, statistics and argument are collected in McCormick, § 206, at 626–627. Much depends upon the skill and experience of the operator.

Various drugs have the effect of weakening or nullifying one's capacity to suppress his thoughts or to fabricate. These "truth serums," such as sodium pentothal and sodium amytal, have been given a cool reception by the courts. Statements made while under the influence of these drugs usually have been rejected. See, e.g., People v. Myers, 35 Ill.2d 311, 331–33, 220 N.E.2d 297, 309–10 (1966), cert. denied, 385 U.S. 1019 (1967). While there is serious doubt whether the results of so-called narco-interrogation are reliable enough to justify admission for the purpose of showing the truth of the subject's statements, a somewhat different issue is raised when a psychiatrist gives an expert opinion on such matters as sanity or the accused's state of mind and the opinion is based in whole or in part upon responses elicited during a drug-induced state. Here, again, the courts have shown resistance. See, e.g., Commonwealth v. Butler, 213 Pa.Super. 388, 247 A.2d 794 (1968); People v. Hiser, 267 Cal.App.2d 47, 72 Cal.Rptr. 906 (1968). These and other authorities and commentary may be found in Weinstein & Mansfield, et al. at 535–537. Hypnosis has been treated similarly to truth serum. See McCormick, § 206, at 631–34. But see State v. Jorgensen, 8 Or.App. 1, 492 P.2d 312 (1971), where the trier is advised that the witness, who had suffered a memory loss, had been successfully treated with a truth drug and hypnosis. Finally, it should be noted that an *absolute* bar to hypnotically refreshed testimony, when applied in a criminal case, intrudes impermissibly on an accused's constitutional right to testify. Rock v. Arkansas, 55 U.S.L.W. 4925 (U.S. June 22, 1987).

4. *Impeachment of a Hearsay Declarant.* The materials in this chapter have dealt with impeaching a witness who appears in the courtroom and gives testimony. But we have seen that evidence often takes the form of an out-of-court declaration that fits an exception to the hearsay rule or, perhaps, that is defined as nonhearsay under modern evidence codes. See Fed.R.Evid. 803, 804, and 801(d)(2), especially subsections (C), (D), and (E). The question arises whether a party who wishes to discredit hearsay evidence may impeach the declarant. Fed.R.Evid. 806 allows the credibility of a hearsay declarant to be attacked by the same techniques that would be available had the declarant appeared as a witness. If the declarant is impeached by one party, the other party may offer evidence supporting credibility.

5. Consider the following exchange (Tex.B.J. 1292–93, Nov. 1985) between counsel and witness, giving particular attention to what counsel should say (or do) after the witness's answer.

The defense attorney, representing a woman charged with murdering her husband, was questioning a character witness:

"Q. What can you tell us about the truthfulness and veracity of this defendant?

"A. Oh, she will tell the truth. She said she'd kill that son of a bitch—and she did."

Chapter IX

PRIVILEGE

§ 9.1 Rationale and Characteristics

Privileged communications enjoy protection for a unique reason. As we have seen, the law of evidence generally seeks accuracy in factfinding by receiving relevant evidence thought to be reliable, while rejecting that thought to be insufficiently probative or trustworthy. But privileged communications, which by usual evidentiary standards may be highly probative as well as trustworthy, are excluded because their disclosure is inimical to a principle or relationship (predominately nonevidentiary in nature) that society deems worthy of preserving and fostering. For example, the law confers upon the individual the constitutional privilege of not incriminating himself; it also accords a privileged status to confidential communications between attorney and client, husband and wife and between certain other communicants in special, private relationships.

The cost of evidentiary privileges is apparent in the courtroom; probative and otherwise admissible evidence is suppressed, requiring the trier to decide factual issues without its benefit. Thus, the application of an evidentiary privilege obviously increases the probability that judicial disputes will be decided erroneously. In fact, when recognition of a privilege threatens to deprive a criminal defendant of evidence critical to his defense, the compulsory process and confrontation clauses of the Constitution may require that the privilege be denied.[1] The benefits thought to be provided are less tangible: conferral of a privilege is prompted by the assumption that its recognition significantly advances an interest, relationship, or principle which society val-

§ 9.1

1. McCormick, § 74.2.

ues highly. But whether recognition of a privilege actually advances the protected interest is always open to question. That is, even if certain relationships, such as those of husband-wife or attorney-client, are worthy of the law's special protection, the privilege may not significantly foster the favored interest. There might, for example, be substantial agreement that the law should promote the stability of marriage, yet whether the conferral of a privilege covering confidential communications between spouses serves to encourage or stabilize marital ties remains uncertain.

Nor are such questions readily subject to empirical proof.[2] More fundamentally, defenders of privileges are increasingly arguing that to require pragmatic justifications is to view the role of privileges too narrowly. Justifications might instead be found in moral principle or social policy. A privilege may protect certain intimate or private relationships (husband and wife; attorney and client) against governmental intrusion simply to preserve an element of individual privacy, or to avoid forcing the communicants to breach their trust.[3]

A unique characteristic of privilege is that the right to assert the privilege, and thus cause the exclusion of privileged evidence, belongs to the person (or persons) vested with the interest or relationship protected by the privilege—the holder(s). The holder may be a party to litigation and thus conveniently situated to claim his privilege if he so wishes. But sometimes neither party-litigant is a holder; in this case, neither party has standing, in his own right, to object to the introduction of privileged evidence. The privilege thus is reserved for the holder, who may or may not wish to exercise it. Sometimes, however, a party or some other person is permitted to claim the privilege in a representative capacity on behalf of the absent holder. Such is always the case where express authorization to make the claim has been given by the holder; the same is true where authorization, if not express, may clearly be implied, as where a lawyer, acting on behalf of a holder-client, invokes the attorney-client privilege. There also is authority in some jurisdictions that allows the judge, in the exercise of his discretion, to assert a privilege on behalf of an absent holder.[4]

2. See McCormick § 75, at 180.

3. See Louisell, Confidentiality, Conformity and Confusion: Privileges in Federal Court Today, 31 Tul.L.Rev. 101, 109–15 (1956).

4. McCormick §§ 73, 73.1, 83, 92.

Interesting standing and appealability problems sometimes arise when information subject to a claim of privilege is offered at trial. If a party is the holder, the privilege can be waived if the holder-party himself offers the privileged evidence, or if an opposing party offers it against him and he fails to object.[5] Of course, if he does make a timely objection and the judge erroneously overrules it, the holder-objector may complain on appeal. Suppose, however, that the holder is not a party, and that evidence subject to a claim of privilege is erroneously admitted[6] against an objecting party. Can the party against whom the evidence was admitted successfully complain on appeal? His appellate posture is not favorable: the evidence presumably is relevant and trustworthy, and the person whose rights have been violated by the incorrect ruling is not a party to the litigation but the holder of the privilege. Furthermore, even if the nonparty-holder deserves some remedy, it is doubtful that reversal of the trial judgment is appropriate because that aids only the appellant. Consequently, the majority of the cases hold that a nonholder-party who has sustained an adverse trial judgment based in part upon evidence that properly was subject to someone else's claim of privilege cannot prevail on appeal.[7] This result must be contrasted with a related, but distinct, appellate disposition. If the trial judge erroneously determines that proffered evidence is subject to a privilege (and thus excludes it), the party offering the evidence *may* complain.[8] It is of no consequence that the purported holder is an outsider: the offering party erroneously was denied the use of relevant evidence not entitled to the special protection of privilege. His right to complain on appeal should not be foreclosed.

5. Markwell v. Sykes, 173 Cal.App. 2d 642, 343 P.2d 769 (1959); Pendleton v. Pendleton, 103 Ohio App. 345, 145 N.E.2d 485 (1957). See Tillotson v. Boughner, 350 F.2d 663 (7th Cir.1965).

6. This could occur when the nonparty-holder, or someone on his behalf, invokes his claim of privilege, but the court wrongly determines that the evidence is not within the ambit of privilege. For example, suppose a witness's testimony is properly subject to the claim of husband-wife privilege, but the holder is not a party to the action in which the witness takes the stand. Assume the holder—who might be the witness or his spouse—invokes the privilege, but the court erroneously determines that the privilege is inapplicable. As the text indicates, the losing party cannot use this ruling as a basis for gaining a reversal. Note, however, that if the holder refuses to divulge the privileged information and is cited for contempt, he can appeal this citation.

7. McCormick, § 73.1, at 174.

8. Id. at 173–74.

In the sections that follow, three privileged relationships are singled out for general discussion—those between attorney and client, between husband and wife, and between physician and patient.[9] There follows an introductory discussion of the privilege against compulsory self-incrimination; additional privileges are mentioned in the notes at the end of the chapter. A general word of caution: care must be taken to examine statutory materials whenever a question of privilege is raised. Most privileges now are embodied in statutory provisions, although the spousal privilege covering confidential communications [10] and the attorney-client [11] privilege have long been recognized at common law. Also, it is important to recognize that privileges fostering confidential relationships prevent only the introduction of evidence designed to disclose *what a communicant said.* A litigant always is free to establish the facts discussed in the protected communication if he can do so by evidence independent of the privileged communication. For example, even though a husband's confidential statement to his wife that he negligently caused an automobile accident may be privileged, his culpability can be shown by other independent evidence, such as testimony from witnesses who observed the accident. Indeed, the husband may be called to the stand and examined fully about the accident; he cannot, however, be made to disclose what he said to his wife—assuming, of course, that it comes within the husband-wife privilege. It will thus be seen that the law's protection of privileged communication goes no further than to allow the privileged communicant to make protected disclosures without thereby harming his case by creating adverse, admissible evidence.

§ 9.2 Privilege Under the Federal Rules of Evidence

When the Proposed Federal Rules of Evidence were considered and amended in Congress, the detailed provisions setting forth the various privileges were deleted. Congress replaced them with Rule 501, which provides that, unless there is a federal enactment to the contrary, privilege in the federal courts is to "be governed by the principles of the common law as they may be interpreted by the courts of the United States in the light of reason and experience." In civil actions where state law governs

9. This selective treatment in part is a concession to limited space, but most of the problems common to other privileges are encountered in studying these three.

10. McCormick, § 78, at 188–90.

11. Id., § 87, at 204.

a claim or defense, as in diversity cases, the law of privilege in connection therewith is to be determined "in accordance with state law.[1]" These two provisions of Rule 501 were intended to affirm the application and content of such federal common law as existed, while permitting future development and evolution through the judicial process.[2]

Although the specific, proposed federal rules for privilege were deleted, many courts have treated them as persuasive evidence as to the content of the federal common law interpreted in light of "reason and experience."[3] This is sensible, especially because the United States Supreme Court had approved the proposed rules and transmitted them to Congress. Furthermore, the proposed rules governing the substantive law of privilege were for the most part not radical departures from existing law, but rather distillations from existing statutory provisions and judicial decisions.[4]

The proposed rules have also influenced state privilege law. For example, the 1974 Uniform Rules governing privilege largely duplicate the corresponding portions of the proposed rules. However, states adopting evidence codes derived from the Federal or Uniform Rules have proved particularly willing to tinker with the privilege provisions.[5] Accordingly, there is less uniformity in this area than in most parts of the law of evidence. Nevertheless, the basic principles of privilege law are reasonably consistent across the jurisdictions.

§ 9.2

1. Fed.R.Evid. 501. Students of civil procedure may wish to ask whether Erie Railroad Co. v. Tompkins, 304 U.S. 64 (1938), mandate conformed to, 98 F.2d 49 (2d Cir.1938), cert. denied, 305 U.S. 637 (1938), reh. denied, 305 U.S. 673 (1938) and its progeny require that in diversity cases the federal courts must observe the state-created law of privilege.

2. 2 Louisell & Mueller, at 626 (Report of the House Committee on the Judiciary), § 203, at 692 (continued applicability of state privilege law).

3. See, e.g., United States v. Mackey, 405 F.Supp. 854, 857 (E.D.N.Y.1975) (Weinstein, J.). See also Waltz, The New Federal Rules of Evidence 47 (2d ed. 1975). The thirteen rules on privilege submitted to Congress are discussed in detail in 2 Weinstein & Berger ¶¶ 501–513.

4. Those looking to the proposed rules for guidance, however, should not lose sight of the fact that in a few instances the proposed rules differed significantly from the common law. Notably, as discussed below, the proposed rules do not recognize the privilege for confidential communications between husband and wife. Yet this privilege is recognized by the common law, see Saltzburg & Redden, at 334, and continues to be recognized by the Supreme Court. Trammel v. United States, 445 U.S. 40, 51 (1980).

5. See generally 2 Weinstein & Berger ¶¶ 501–513.

§ 9.3 Spousal Privilege for Confidential Communications

This privilege protects confidential communications between spouses. It most often is justified on the ground that it promotes marital harmony. The theory usually invoked by courts is that the privilege encourages marital partners to share their most closely-guarded secrets and thoughts, thus adding an additional measure of intimacy and mutual support to the marriage. Serious doubt can be raised as to whether the evidentiary protection produces the desired effect. To begin with, it may be safe to assume that many marital partners are unaware of the existence of the privilege. Generally, when a privilege is conferred, a professional advisor (such as an attorney, doctor, or clergyman) is a party to the protected relationship. Such a person, of course, is likely to be aware of any privileges available to himself or the person with whom he is conferring, and can advise his confidant accordingly. But no professional or other person knowledgeable about privileged communications is a party to the protected husband-wife relationship. Furthermore, even assuming the marriage partners know about the privilege, one may ask whether its existence materially affects the flow of information between husband and wife. If there were no privilege and if the communicating spouses were aware of the absence of such protection, would marital communications be inhibited? Perhaps only in unusual circumstances, such as where a courtroom appearance was anticipated, would any chilling effect be found.[1]

Justification of the privilege, however, may be put on a different footing. There is much to be said for the notion that certain aspects of one's private life should be free from public disclosure.[2] This especially is true in light of recent history, which has witnessed both diminished privacy in general and increased use of sophisticated electronic devices to collect and

§ 9.3

1. McCormick, § 86, at 202; Hines, Privileged Testimony of Husband and Wife in California, 19 Calif.L.Rev. 390 (1931); Hutchins and Slesinger, Some Observations on the Law of Evidence: Family Relations, 13 Minn.L.Rev. 675 (1929). There might be a chilling effect in circumstances where the government focuses on a group or organization—such as draft resisters or the Communist party—even though no litigation is pending.

2. See *Boyd v. United States,* 116 U.S. 616 (1886) (Fifth amendment prohibits use of defendant's private papers against him), and more modern cases in a similar vein. See § 9.11 at n. 27. While the Supreme Court has recently rejected privacy as value triggering fifth amendment protection, *id.*, modern courts continue to share the underlying concern for privacy which motivated the *Boyd* court.

store information. The invasion of private marital communications is an indelicate and distasteful undertaking that should not be sanctioned unless society's interest in disclosure is compelling.

McCormick argues that the marital privilege for confidential communications should yield "where there is a need for otherwise unobtainable evidence critical to the ascertainment of significant legal rights."[3] Although this may accommodate fairly the competing interests involved, most legislatures and courts—perhaps doubting that such discretion would be wisely and evenly exercised—have made the privilege absolute.

The privilege for marital communications extends to any *confidential* statement made *between spouses* during the existence of a legal marriage.[4] The widely accepted rule is that the "quality" of the marriage will not be inquired into; communications intended to be confidential are privileged unless and until a divorce decree has been entered.[5] A substantial number of recent cases remove from the privilege those communications made in furtherance of an ongoing crime or tort,[6] though many jurisdictions do not recognize this "joint participants" exception.[7]

In some jurisdictions, although not under federal law,[8] a broader construction of the privilege gives protection to the actions of one spouse in the presence of the other, at least where it reasonably can be inferred that the actor-spouse did not want his activity revealed.[9] Finally, there is scattered, older authority that

3. McCormick, § 86, at 202.

4. Common-law marriages, where not legally recognized, and other nontraditional "marriage equivalents" will not give rise to a confidential communication privilege. See 2 Louisell & Mueller, § 219, at 894–95.

5. McCormick, § 81; 2 Louisell & Mueller, § 219, at 895. At least one recent appellate decision has held otherwise, denying the privilege to communications between "permanently separated couples," finding the rationale for the privilege inapplicable in such cases. United States v. Byrd, 750 F.2d 585 (7th Cir.1984). But any less-than-rigid rule will invite protracted litigation over the "closeness" of the marriage in many cases in which the privilege is claimed.

6. 2 Louisell & Mueller, § 219, at 909–10.

7. See, e.g., Coleman v. State, 281 Md. 538, 380 A.2d 49, 54 (1977) and cases cited therein. In Trammel v. United States, 445 U.S. 40, 46 n. 7 (1980), the Supreme Court did not include the "joint participants" exception in a list of recognized exceptions, but neither has it overturned appellate rulings which have recognized the exception.

8. 2 Louisell & Mueller, § 219, at 901.

9. See People v. Sullivan, 42 Misc.2d 1014, 249 N.Y.S.2d 589 (1964); People v. Daghita, 299 N.Y. 194, 86 N.E.2d 172 (1949); Menefee v. Commonwealth, 189 Va. 900, 55 S.E.2d 9 (1949). A different result should obtain where one spouse observes the other without the latter's knowledge. See People v. Sullivan, supra; Morgan & Weinstein at 98.

the privilege attaches to facts or information that one spouse discovers, if it reasonably can be said that the discovery would not have been made except for the marital relationship.[10] Only in unusual circumstances will extending the privilege to the latter instance encourage communications, though it will serve the general interest of protecting marital privacy. If a privilege in this context is to be recognized at all, it should be left to the discretion of the trial judge, who can balance such factors as the importance of the testimony and the degree to which testimony would invade the marital privilege.

Although legislatures and courts differ somewhat on the scope of the privilege—that is, as to whether it extends beyond written or verbal communications—most authorities hold that the known presence of a third party when the spousal communication is made renders the privilege inapplicable for lack of confidentiality. This limiting principle recognizes the cost of conferring a privilege (namely, the suppression of relevant evidence) and indicates an unwillingness to extend protection beyond the private husband-wife relationship.[11] Thus, even where the third party is a family member or is brought intentionally into the confidences of the spouses, the privilege generally does not apply.[12] It also should be emphasized that the privilege does not attach unless the court finds from all of the surrounding circumstances that the statements were intended to be imparted in confidence. While courts probably tend to resolve doubts in favor of confidentiality, at least where the subject matter of the conversation is not apt to be widely shared outside the marriage, this inclination usually does

10. See McCormick, § 79, at 192; Morgan & Weinstein at 97–98. But see United States v. Smith, 533 F.2d 1077, 1079 (8th Cir.1976): "It is well settled that the communications to which the privilege applies have been limited to utterances or expressions intended by one spouse to convey a message to the other."

11. Arguably, other close family relationships should be equally entitled to the protection of a privilege, and at least one federal court has recognized a parent-child privilege both for confidential communications, and to refuse to give adverse testimony. In re Agosto, 553 F.Supp. 1298 (D.Nev.1983), disapproved in United States v. Davies, 768 F.2d 893, 897–900 (7th Cir.1985). However, tradition and the almost-unanimous voice of modern authority have singled out the marriage relationship as the only family relationship deserving this special protection. Thus, if a husband admits privately to his wife that he committed the offense of shoplifting, the communication is privileged. A similar admission by a son to his mother is not. Can these disparate results be justified?

12. 2 Louisell & Mueller, § 219, at 896–99; Wolfle v. United States, 291 U.S. 7 (1934); Gutridge v. State, 236 Md. 514, 204 A.2d 557 (1964); Morgan & Weinstein at 98–99.

not extend to statements relating to matters likely to be openly discussed, or to situations in which the privilege would facilitate a fraud by one spouse upon the other.[13] Furthermore, subsequent revelations by one of the spouses may be influential in causing the judge to find that no confidentiality was ever intended. If, however, the court concludes that the statements were intended to be confidential, a wrongful disclosure amounting to a betrayal or breach of faith (as opposed to confirmation that no confidence ever existed) does not destroy the privilege.[14] Whether the privilege exists is a question for the judge.[15]

Several aspects of the privilege have disquieted the commentators. Most jurisdictions hold that the privilege survives the termination of the marriage either by death or divorce.[16] While the goal of encouraging trust in marriages might require the protection of marital confidences after divorce (particularly as divorce becomes increasingly common), to extend this protection even beyond the death of the communicant appears to exceed the fulfillment of any reasonable policy underlying the privilege and to represent an unwarranted obstacle to reliable factfinding. In contrast, there is coexisting authority that when a communication intended to be private is overheard or intercepted by a third person, that person can give testimony revealing what was said by the marital partners.[17] Although seemingly prompted by a desire to minimize the suppression of relevant evidence, this latter result is questionable—at least in those instances in which spouses have taken reasonable precautions to preserve confidentiality. While perhaps adequate to the purpose of preserving marital trust and harmony, this rule does not square with the emerging notion that a zone of marital privacy ought to be protected. And indeed, recent authority suggests that placing the full burden of maintaining secrecy on the spouses is too great a demand, especially in light of modern communication devices (often involving other parties in the process of transmission) and technological advances

13. McCormick, § 80, at 194–95.

14. McCormick, § 82, at 196. The spouse who breached the confidence, of course, could no longer claim the privilege.

15. Fed.R.Evid. 104(a); § 10.4 infra.

16. McCormick, § 85, at 200.

17. 2 Louisell & Mueller, § 219, at 900; McCormick, § 82, at 196. The common law permitted eavesdroppers to testify as to the content of confidential communication based on two justifications: privileges should be strictly construed because they suppress relevant evidence and an individual truly concerned with confidentiality should take precautions to prevent eavesdroppers. VIII Wigmore §§ 2326, 2339 (McNaughton).

in eavesdropping.[18] If the privilege is worth maintaining, it should not fail where the spouses have taken reasonable steps to ensure privacy.[19]

The question often arises whether only the communicating spouse is the holder of the privilege. Wigmore felt that because the privilege was designed to foster marital communication, only the communicating spouse need be the holder.[20] This is the law in some jurisdictions.[21] In others, however, a statute or judicial decision makes both spouses holders.[22] This means that the party seeking to introduce a privileged statement must secure a waiver from both spouses or, in the case of a holder's death, from the successor in interest (usually the executor or administrator) of the deceased. In some situations the law will intercede and terminate the privilege; this occurs, for example, when one spouse is prosecuted for an offense against the other (or the children of either) or in certain civil actions, such as divorce, where the marital partners have assumed an antagonistic posture.[23]

§ 9.4 Spousal Privilege to Prevent Adverse Testimony in a Criminal Trial

At common law, the spouse of a criminal[1] defendant was disqualified from testifying either for or against the defendant.

18. See Adv.Comm. Note to Proposed Fed.R.Evid. 503(b).

19. See generally 2 Louisell & Mueller, § 219, at 900; McCormick, § 82, at 196–97. While many jurisdictions still follow the traditional rule, California has statutorily extended the privilege to prevent testimony by eavesdroppers about confidential marital communications. West's Cal.Evid.Code § 980.

20. VIII Wigmore § 2340(1) (McNaughton). McCormick endorses Wigmore's view, McCormick, § 83, while Louisell & Mueller disagree. 2 Louisell & Mueller, § 219, at 893–94.

21. McCormick, § 83, at 169; see also United States v. Figueroa-Paz, 468 F.2d 1055 (9th Cir.1972); Taylor v. Commonwealth, 302 S.W.2d 378 (Ky.1957); Louisell and Crippin, Evidentiary Privileges, 40 Minn.L.Rev. 413, 417 (1956).

22. Morgan & Weinstein at 101. See West's Ann.Cal.Evid.Code § 980; Martin v. State, 203 Miss. 187, 194, 33 So.2d 825, 827 (1948) (Griffith, J., specially concurring); People v. Sullivan, 42 Misc.2d 1014, 249 N.Y.S.2d 589 (1964).

23. VIII Wigmore § 2338(9) (McNaughton) The privilege also is lifted where one spouse is tried for a criminal offense and a confidential communication would tend to exonerate him or at least reduce the grade of the offense. McCormick, § 84, at 200. There is also some authority denying the privilege when both spouses were participants in illegal activity that is the subject of the trial. See Saltzburg & Redden at 351.

§ 9.4

1. McCormick § 66 (noting that early rule applied in both civil and criminal proceedings). A few jurisdictions still follow the older rule, barring adverse testimony by a spouse even in civil trials. See, e.g., West's Ann.Cal. Evid. Code § 971.

The rule has been universally softened to permit testimony for the defendant. Further, most jurisdictions have transformed the automatic disqualification into a privilege claimable by one or both of the spouses when adverse testimony is sought.[2] Traditionally, where the bar on adverse testimony was not absolute, the accused was a holder, and was thus able to prevent his spouse from testifying. This remains the rule in many jurisdictions. The trend, however, has been to abolish the privilege entirely, or to make the witness the only holder, leaving the accused without the power to object to his spouse's voluntary adverse testimony. A majority of states now follow one of these two rules.[3] In the leading federal case on this privilege, Trammel v. United States, the Supreme Court adopted the latter rule, making the witness-spouse the sole holder. This decision overturned a sizeable body of federal precedent, and rejected the approach of Proposed Rule 505, which made the defendant the only holder.[4] The rationale and possible problems of the *Trammel* decision are discussed at the end of this section.

In grand jury proceedings, in which there is no defendant, the witness should be able to claim the privilege if the spouse is a "target" or likely to be indicted as a result of the grand jury investigation.[5] In jurisdictions in which the witness is not a holder, he or she should nevertheless be entitled to assert to privilege before a grand jury, based on implied authorization from the absent spouse.[6]

No jurisdiction permits the accused to assert the privilege when the crime charged is against the spouse or a child of one or both of the spouses.[7] And of course, testimony by a spouse called

2. Several states still retain the absolute disqualification. See Trammel v. United States, 445 U.S. 40, 48 n. 9 (1980).

3. Trammel, 445 U.S. at 48 n. 9, categorizes the relevant state laws, indicating who holds the privilege, if any.

4. See 2 Louisell & Mueller, § 218, at 872–73. Trammel v. United States, 445 U.S. 40 (1980), is discussed infra at notes 12–15.

5. Appeal of Malfitano, 633 F.2d 276 (3d Cir.1980). See 2 Louisell & Mueller, § 218, at 880–82.

6. See Proposed Fed.R.Evid. 505(b) and Adv.Comm.Note.

7. McCormick, § 66, at 162. See N.C.Gen.Stat. § 8–57 (1969); 22 Okla. Stat.Ann. § 702. For an extensive analysis, see State v. Briley, 53 N.J. 498, 251 A.2d 442 (1969). Suppose the witness-spouse is a holder and the trial is for an offense against the holder-spouse. May he or she invoke the "incompetency privilege" and decline to testify? The usual result is to deny application of the privilege and compel the witness to take the stand. Denial of the privilege probably is justified by the possibility that the accused spouse may exert coercive pressure upon the witness-spouse not to testify. Furthermore, once the government decides to go forward with the prosecution of an

as a witness by the defense is unaffected by the privilege.[8] Further, once the testifying spouse takes the stand for the accused, the government can cross-examine him or her and, so it would seem, the scope of cross-examination will be in accordance with the usual rule for the jurisdiction.[9] The witness, however, may still be entitled to invoke selectively the confidential communications privilege—at least the mere act of taking the stand does not waive this privilege.

The marital privilege against adverse testimony must be clearly distinguished from the privilege protecting confidential marital communications which blocks testimony about private communications made between spouses during marriage, regardless of subsequent divorce. The latter applies in both civil and criminal cases. The privilege allowing a witness-spouse to decline to testify (or a defendant-spouse to block testimony) against the accused is concerned not with the source, but with the effect of the information; it usually blocks adverse testimony based on knowledge gained in any way, at any time, even if it is common knowledge,[10] if the accused and the proposed witness are married at the time of trial.[11] The confidential communications privilege

offense between spouses, it has determined that the disruptive effect of the prosecution upon the marriage is not the dominant consideration. Arguably, the additional disruption caused by compelling the spousal testimony should not be determinative. For a case suggesting that in trials for some offenses against the testifying spouse, he or she could invoke the incompetency privilege even though the accused spouse could not, see Wyatt v. United States, 362 U.S. 525 (1960) (In this Mann Act prosecution, however, the Court relied on the legislative history of the Act to deny the witness-wife the right to invoke the privilege).

8. See Funk v. United States, 290 U.S. 371 (1933); N.C.Gen.Stat. § 8–57; 2 Louisell & Mueller, § 218, at 876.

9. VIII Wigmore, § 2242, at 258 (McNaughton); N.C.Gen.Stat. § 8–57; 22 Okla.Stat.Ann. § 702. See Ch. IV, §§ 30–31.

10. 2 Louisell & Mueller, § 218, at 873–74. But cf. Proposed Fed.R.Evid. 505(c)(2), denying the privilege where testimony concerns events which preceded the marriage. The Seventh Circuit has adopted this "pre-marital acts" exception. United States v. Clark, 712 F.2d 299 (7th Cir.1983); United States v. Van Drunen, 501 F.2d 1393 (7th Cir. 1974), cert. denied, 419 U.S. 1091 (1974). The exception confuses the adverse testimony and confidential communications privileges, and ignores the rationale of the former. Damning testimony from the witness-spouse is liable to destroy the marriage, regardless of the subject matter of the testimony.

A few jurisdictions have also created a "joint participants" exception, denying the privilege altogether when both spouses participated in a crime. 2 Louisell & Mueller, § 218, at 884–85.

11. Should the incompetency privilege be defeated if it appears that the marriage was a ploy to prevent testimony? It often is held that the privilege still exists. See VIII Wigmore, § 2230, at 224 (McNaughton). Recently, federal courts seemed to have abandoned this view. See, e.g., United States v.

must be invoked selectively, while the adverse testimony privilege can keep the spouse off the witness stand entirely. Unfortunately, both courts and legislatures have on occasion failed to distinguish the two privileges.[12]

The adverse testimony privilege, sometimes called the "incapacity privilege," serves an entirely different purpose from the confidential communication privilege. It does not encourage trust and openness in marriages generally (all information gained through marital confidences being more fully protected by the confidential communications privilege); nor is it designed to protect the privacy of the couple before the court. Rather, it is based on an aversion to using judicial compulsion in a criminal trial to place spouses in an opposing posture that may weaken or destroy their marriage.[13] The traditional rule making the accused spouse a holder has been criticized as going beyond the rationale; if one spouse is willing to testify against the other, it is argued, the marriage is probably beyond repair.[14] Thus, if the privilege is to be given at all, only the witness need be a holder. And indeed, the Supreme Court accepted this view in Trammel v. United States.

Mathis, 559 F.2d 294 (5th Cir.1977); United States v. Apodaca, 522 F.2d 568 (10th Cir.1975). And no privilege exists if the marriage is a "sham" which the parties never intended to consummate, and which they entered into for fraudulent purposes. See Lutwak v. United States, 344 U.S. 604 (1953), reh. denied, 345 U.S. 919 (1953), ignoring the validity of the marriage where the sole purpose of the spouses was to gain entry to the United States. The proposed Federal Rule 505(c)(2) would have resolved the difficulty of expedient marriages by limiting the incompetency privilege to matters occurring after the marriage. See 2 Weinstein & Berger ¶ 505[01]. For a case that endorses this approach, see United States v. Clark, 712 F.2d 299 (7th Cir.1983).

12. See, e.g., State of North Carolina v. Freeman, 302 N.C. 591, 276 S.E.2d 450 (1981), and Maryland statute cited in Coleman v. State, 281 Md. 538, 380 A.2d 49, 54 (1977).

13. Since *Trammel,* discussed supra at note 4 and above, a new justification for the spousal privilege in the hands of the witness, closely akin to one justification for the privilege against self-incrimination, has been increasingly offered. Under this view, it is a violation of personal dignity to force upon the witness spouse the "cruel trilemma" of perjury, contempt, or betrayal of the accused spouse. 2 Louisell & Mueller, § 218, at 871–72; In re Agosto, 553 F.Supp. 1298, 1306, 1309, 1331 (D.Nev. 1983). But this justification, if accepted, might prove difficult to contain, as compelled testimony against any close relative may present a similar dilemma. See In re Agosto, recognizing a privilege on the part of children (even adult children) not to testify against their parents, and vice versa. The *Agosto* holding was critized and rejected in United States v. Davies, 768 F.2d 893 (7th Cir.1985), cert. denied ___ U.S. ___, 106 S.Ct. 533 (1985).

14. The counterargument is that the willingness to testify may be a response to temporary marital strife that is not irreconcilable, but that would become so if adverse testimony were permitted in a criminal proceeding. See Hawkins v. United States, 358 U.S. 74, 77–78 (1958).

On the other hand, the *Trammel* ruling may give inadequate protection when both spouses are implicated in a crime. The government can then offer one spouse lenient treatment in exchange for testimony against the other, thereby extracting "voluntary" testimony, while probably destroying a marriage which might have been sound before the choice of imprisonment or testimony was offered.[15] Under some federal case law, however, the witness-spouse is not given a choice: the incapacity privilege is not available when both spouses participated in the underlying offense.[16]

§ 9.5 Attorney-Client Privilege: Introduction and Overview

We have seen that privileges rest uneasily in an adversarial system because they generally promote values unrelated to a central goal of adjudication: resolution of disputes on the basis of all reliable evidence. And doubts are often raised whether a particular privilege produces the desirable end of full disclosure that is asserted as its justification. Yet our system allows certain privileges—such as that for husband and wife, physician and patient—in part because values like privacy and personal autonomy have independent significance in a free society. The weight of these values is cast on the side of sustaining some privileges that may not be essential for full and frank disclosure between the parties to the privilege. In contrast, the privilege protecting communications between attorney and client may rest on firmer footing than many of the other privileges. While the present privilege reflects privacy concerns, it also may promote just legal outcomes. Clients might be inclined to hold back information if forced to discuss their legal problems on a nonprivileged basis. After all, in the legal counselling context the possibility of a judicial proceeding, if not imminent, is at least likely to be something of which the parties to the privilege are aware. The privilege could thus improve the quality of legal representation—and therefore the integrity of the adversarial process—by encouraging clients to inform their lawyers of all facts that might be relevant.

Yet demarking the proper bounds of the attorney-client privilege is not simple. The fundamental tension between full disclosure of facts and the desire to protect communications requires

15. 2 Louisell & Mueller, § 218, at 873, 889–90. The *Trammel* case is found at 445 U.S. 40 (1980).

16. United States v. Clark, 712 F.2d 299 (7th Cir.1983). Contra, Appeal of Malfitano, 633 F.2d 276 (3d Cir.1980).

that difficult lines be drawn between statements of the client and observations of counsel. There is also the risk that clients will improperly use the privilege to conceal evidence or to prevent the incriminating disclosure of basic facts like identity of the client or his whereabouts that are usually unimportant to the real concerns of the privilege. In addition, lawyers and clients necessarily interact with a wide range of third parties—investigators, doctors, accountants, and consulting attorneys—in the normal course of representation. Thorny problems emerge in the efforts of courts to determine whether communications involving such supplemental actors should be within the boundaries of the attorney-client privilege. And numbers alone magnify the difficulty of marking the appropriate bounds of the privilege when the holder is a corporation that necessarily speaks through many agents and employees. Special problems also exist when shareholders sue management on behalf of the corporation, an increasingly common practice in American business life. Other difficulties arise when one lawyer represents several clients on a common matter, or when separately represented clients pool their resources in common defense.

As a general rule, the proper response to these various difficulties begins with the recognition that the privilege *protects only the narrow right of a client to communicate confidentially with his lawyer about a legal problem.* The remainder of our discussion will explore the meaning that courts have poured into the italicized words.

As noted before, the principal Federal Rule addressing privileges simply instructs the courts to apply the principles of common law in "the light of reason and experience."[1] This approach stands in sharp contrast to the detailed Attorney-Client Rule proposed by the Supreme Court but rejected by Congress.[2] This Supreme Court "Standard" lists the requirements of the privilege and provides some guidance on the problems of joint representation, common defense, and third party protection. It also clearly spells out the situations where an otherwise valid claim of privilege will be rejected by the courts. Although not law, the Supreme Court Standard is cited with approval throughout the federal system. Most of the states that have adopted the Federal Rules of Evidence have patterned their Attorney-Client Rule on

§ 9.5

1. Fed.R.Evid. 501.

2. Proposed Fed.R.Evid. 503.

the detailed Standard.[3] Although common-law differences are still part of the full story of attorney-client privilege, the state and federal systems are moving toward greater uniformity in this area.

§ 9.6 Attorney-Client Privilege: Basic Requirements, Scope, and Duration

The privilege prevents testimonial disclosure, discovery, or seizure by subpoena of confidential communications between an attorney and his client, unless the client waives the privilege. Courts mark the temporal boundaries of the protected relationship expansively. The privilege attaches when a prospective client first consults a lawyer about representing him. These preliminary discussions remain privileged even if the attorney is not retained. The privilege applies during any representation that follows and persists after the attorney-client relationship ends. The rules could not easily be otherwise. Attorneys often refuse cases after initial consultation. Clients might communicate less freely if this development could dissolve the privilege. They might also hesitate to speak freely if the privilege did not survive the conclusion of the matter upon which advice is sought.

By contrast, the goals of the privilege do not necessarily require that confidences survive the client's death. Nonetheless, the courts have generally held that the privilege subsists after death and may be claimed by the estate representative (or sometimes, by the next of kin). But in some postdeath contexts the courts refuse to honor the privilege. Notably, in disputes between persons claiming property or an entitlement through the decedent—in other words, disputes among "insiders"—privilege claims are rejected. Thus, in a dispute among beneficiaries about the terms of the decedent-client's will, or in a dispute between persons taking under his will and persons claiming his property by intestacy, the privilege as to relevant communications between the client and attorney is terminated. The Proposed Federal Rule follows this approach.[1] On the other hand, the estate representative can usually invoke the privilege against creditors ("outsiders") claiming against the estate. Simply put, insiders cannot invoke the deceased's privilege against one another, but they often can claim against the outside world. Some modern authority finds this rule a sensible proxy for the waiver decisions the deceased himself

3. 2 Weinstein & Berger, § 503[03], at 76–81 (1986 & Supp.1986).

§ 9.6

1. Proposed Fed.R.Evid. 503(d)(2).

probably would have made. On balance, however, the basic proposition that the privilege should generally survive the death of the holder is of dubious wisdom. Its apparent justification in the attorney-client context is that successor-holders should have the right to claim the privilege against outsiders, thus favoring family members. Yet it is not clear that the law should favor these litigants. Since it is highly doubtful that a different rule—one forbidding the privilege after the client's death—would actually chill free discourse between attorneys and clients, the privilege probably should not survive the holder's death in any context.[2] But this rule has not generally prevailed.

At its core, the privilege only attaches when a client communicates confidentially with his *lawyer about a legal matter.* The italicized words properly narrow the scope of the privilege in three ways. *First,* a lawyer who witnesses a document that his client executes may testify, not only to the fact of execution, but also to his client's mental condition and capacity at the time of execution. Courts everywhere acknowledge that a lawyer/attesting witness is acting more like a witness than a lawyer for the purposes of these limited inquiries.[3] *Second,* the privilege does not arise when a client speaks with a lawyer in the latter's capacity as a business associate, business advisor, or friend, even if legal matters are discussed. Even these guidelines, however, often fail to clearly delineate the reach of the privilege. Problems frequently arise because of the difficulty in identifying the motives of one who speaks with a lawyer; furthermore, several motives may operate simultaneously—a mixture, for example, of business and legal motives. Most authorities hold that the privilege applies only if the desire to acquire legal advice or services predominates over other reasons for making the communication. This solution is compatible with the purpose of the privilege which, as we have seen, is to encourage confidences pertaining to legal matters. To accomplish this purpose, the privilege need not, and should not, be raised with regard to statements that would have been made regardless of the (subordinate) desire to obtain legal services. *Third,* it is well settled that the legal services sought by the client must rise above the "mere scrivening" that results when a lawyer is hired for his mechanical skills as, for example, when a lawyer is asked to draft a document, but not to advise on its terms or

2. McCormick, § 94, at 227–29.

3. 2 Louisell & Mueller, § 213, at 831–32.

consequences.[4] Less settled is the impact of the scrivening exception on tax law. For some courts, the preparation of a tax return is mere accounting; they require an independent showing that the lawyer advised on tax matters before they will allow the privilege to attach. For other courts, preparation itself constitutes legal advice.[5] If preparation is understood as a lawyering activity (hence affording some protection), the *extent* of the privilege involves a straightforward application of the confidentiality requirement: all client information intended for inclusion in the tax return should be unprotected.

The attorney-client privilege is at risk when third parties learn of the communication in question, because courts are likely to infer that confidentiality was not really intended. Mere assertions of confidential intent will not save the privilege in the face of behavior that belies such a purpose. However, as we shall see in the next section, rather wide disclosure is permitted when the client cannot effectively communicate without it. In circumstances where the client needs a third person—for example, a physician—to facilitate the communication of specialized knowledge, the privilege is fully applicable. We shall also see that agents and representatives of the lawyer—such as investigators—whose services are needed in order to render legal services may sometimes come within the circle of protected communicants. The privilege is lost, however, when the client inadvertently and carelessly discloses communications, as when he telephones his lawyer within the hearing of policemen or other bystanders.[6]

But what if a telephone operator eavesdropped on the conversation? Until recently, courts treated the second disclosure like the first. The traditional rule[7] that removed the privilege from all inadvertent disclosures—even those resulting from outside eavesdropping and theft—made sense only on the assumption that all such disclosures were fairly traceable to the negligence or inattention of the client. The reasoning of the cases was that the barrier of privilege should fall from any inadvertent disclosure because a careful client would have prevented the revelation.

4. McCormick, § 88, at 209–10.

5. See, e.g., United States v. Lawless, 709 F.2d 485, 487–88 (7th Cir.1983) (tax preparation is not protected); In re Grand Jury Subpoena Duces Tecum, 697 F.2d 277, 280 (10th Cir.1983) (tax preparation can be protected if all other elements of privilege are satisfied).

6. See, e.g., United States v. Gann, 732 F.2d 714, 723 (9th Cir.1984), cert. denied, 469 U.S. 1034 (1984).

7. See, e.g., Clark v. State, 159 Tex. Crim.R. 187, 261 S.W.2d 339, 342 (1953), cert. denied, 346 U.S. 855 (1953), reh. denied, 346 U.S. 905 (1953).

This exacting standard was more defensible in a technologically simpler time than it is today. Even in an earlier time, some instances of inadvertent disclosure (such as theft) should not, perhaps, have resulted in a loss of the privilege.

Generally speaking, the law of privilege has kept pace with technological change and aligned itself more with realistic notions of fault. The Advisory Committee Notes to the Proposed Federal Rules of Evidence explicitly abandon the older standard that assimilates eavesdropping and theft to negligence, and advise courts to refuse eavesdropping testimony and to exclude stolen documents from evidence.[8] Modern courts have usually followed this path, but with some reservations. Practically speaking, the recent cases have replaced what had become an unfair "strict waiver" rule with a demanding, but fair, negligence rule. It requires that clients take all reasonable precautions to keep the information in question confidential; if this is done, the privilege will survive an unintended disclosure to third persons.[9]

We have said that the privilege protects "communications." It is important to remember that only the confidential communication itself is protected, not the events that are its subject matter. Thus, while the privilege prevents the client from being asked what he told his lawyer about a given matter, the client can properly be asked, in a deposition or at trial, *what he knows about that matter*. The privilege simply allows the client to communicate with his lawyer without the fear that his communication itself will be used adversely against him.

Note that protected communications can take the form of verbal statements, written communications, and even physical acts (conduct). The basic protection accorded oral and written communications sensibly extends to conduct intended as communication. An affirmative nod of the head is a straightforward example. But how should the courts treat a nonverbal disclosure of a physical item or characteristic, such as a gun or a scar? Showing a lawyer a gun in a drawer or exhibiting a scarred leg or needle-pocked arm is no different from telling a lawyer about these things; thus, both forms of communication are generally protected. By contrast, a client's clothes, grooming, fatigue, or

8. Proposed Fed.R.Evid. 503(a)(4) and (b) and Adv.Comm.Note.

9. See In re Grand Jury Proceedings Involving Berkley & Co., 466 F.Supp. 863, 869 (D.Minn.1979); Suburban Sew 'N Sweep, Inc. v. Swiss-Bernina, Inc., 91 F.R.D. 254, 259–60 (N.D.Ill.1981).

palpable fear are usually unprotected communications on the theory that demeanor is outwardly visible to anyone.[10]

Although privileged communications can take many forms, the attorney-client privilege does not properly apply to items such as documents, letters, or other inscribed objects *that existed prior to the attorney-client relationship*. The privilege applies to communications between attorney and client made after the formation of that relationship, for only then does the privilege discharge its function of encouraging frank disclosure for the purpose of legal representation. Furthermore, the privilege does not apply to physical objects—like clothing, a weapon, or stolen goods—because these objects are not "communications" from the client. Of course *discussions* between the lawyer and the client *about any physical items* (whether inscribed or not) *are privileged*. This seems simple enough: preexisting documents are not privileged; neither are "noncommunicative" items, like physical objects that contain no statement. These preexisting documents or noncommunicative things can be freely seized, by any appropriate legal means, from either the client or the lawyer. It is possible, however, that a document in the client's hands would be protected from seizure or discovery because it is within the protection of a privilege. For example, it is conceivable, but unlikely as a practical matter, that a client has possession of his own written statement which was improperly coerced by law enforcement authorities and, thus, within the protection of the Fifth Amendment. It is also possible, and somewhat more likely, that a client has possession of a document that contains communications intended for his lawyer, pertinent to the lawyer's legal advice, and prepared after the formation of the attorney-client relationship. As to this document, the client could invoke the attorney-client privilege and prevent seizure or disclosure.

Let us now suppose that the client transfers to the lawyer a document that in the client's hands was subject to a valid claim of privilege. Is the document accorded a similar protection after it is

10. A close question is raised whether a lawyer can be compelled to testify about a client's responsiveness and coherence during their conversation, or about the client's probable competence to stand trial. At issue is whether a lawyer's assessment of his client's competence can plausibly be based solely on unprotected, publicly observable traits. Since it is quite likely that such assessments derive at least in part from confidential revelations, such testimony could arguably fall within a claim of privilege. Yet some courts allow this kind of testimony, perhaps because it does not involve disclosure of the contents of the clients' communication.

in the lawyer's possession? In Fisher v. United States,[11] the Supreme Court recognized that the attorney-client privilege protects a physical thing in the lawyer's hands if it was entitled to the protection of a privilege while in the client's possession *and* if it was transferred to the lawyer for the purpose of obtaining legal advice. The rule could not logically be otherwise. If, for example, a document that was protected while in the custody of the client were freely compellable from the lawyer after transfer, the client could secure his protection from disclosure only by retaining the document. This retention could impair his ability to freely communicate with his attorney. Thus, the law properly clothes the document transferred to the lawyer (for purposes of legal advice) with the same protection it was accorded while in the custody of the client. If it could not be seized from the client (for example, by a police search) or otherwise disclosed (for example, by discovery), it is similarly immunized when in the lawyer's possession.

Suppose, however, the item is simply an uninscribed physical object or a preexisting writing—that is, one predating the attorney-client relationship. Such an item in the custody of the client could be seized in the course of a lawful search. Further, it could usually be obtained through the use of a subpoena or some other discovery procedure, such as a request to produce documents. But observe that sometimes the client's *act of producing an item* is itself testimonial if it "can be used by the government to show the existence, possession, or authenticity" of the object.[12] If, for example, the client had denied possession of a writing, his production of it in response to a subpoena or discovery request is a form of communication that acknowledges possession; likewise if the client is directed to produce a document said to be authored by him, his production of the item may be viewed as a communicative act acknowledging his authorship.[13] In the comparatively rare case where the existence, possession, or authentication of an object is in issue, the client is protected by the Fifth Amendment against any compelled disclosure that establishes these facts—assuming, of course, that they are incriminating.

This privilege against self-incrimination belongs only to the client; it is his personal privilege not to acknowledge possession or

11. 425 U.S. 391 (1976).

12. In re Grand Jury Proceedings on Feb. 4, 1982, 759 F.2d 1418, 1421 (9th Cir.1985).

13. See, e.g., United States v. Doe, 465 U.S. 605, 612 (1984) ("Although the contents of a document may not be privileged, the act of producing the document may be.")

other links with the object. How is the client's protection altered, if at all, when the object is transferred to the attorney? Suppose, for example, a subpoena issues to the attorney commanding him to produce a writing or other physical object that was thought to be formerly in the client's possession. Delivery of the object sought could be an important step in establishing a link (possession, authentication, and the like) between client and the item. In essence, then, the question is whether the lawyer should be compelled to disclose that he received an object from his client. On the one hand, the client probably intended the transfer of the item to be a confidential communication within the attorney-client privilege because revelation of the transfer implicates the client. The client's narrow "acknowledgment" privilege against self-incrimination (a personal privilege applicable only when the object was in the client's hands) and the attorney-client privilege (arguably applicable to shield the "communicative" fact of transfer) might combine to protect any disclosure that links the client to the object.

The difficulty with shielding the fact of transfer is that by removing the item from his own custody, the client has impaired or blocked the efforts of law enforcement officers to seize the item pursuant to a valid search—a technique of appropriation that need not involve any compelled self-incrimination ("acknowledgment") by the client. As to the close question [14] whether the fact of transfer from the client is within the attorney-client privilege, the authority is scant [15] and the commentators do not speak with a single voice.[16] Observe, however, that no solution can leave the client indifferent to transfer. If the lawyer can be compelled to disclose the transfer, the client might curtail his communications and keep possession of the document or other physical thing in

14. Fortunately, the question is not usually posed. In most cases, issues of the authentication, possession, or existence of a physical thing either do not arise or, if they do, can be resolved without implicating the client's narrow fifth amendment privilege protecting him from a compulsory acknowledgement that affiliates him with a physical thing.

15. See State ex rel. Sowers v. Olwell, 64 Wash.2d 828, 394 P.2d 681, 685 (1964) (courts should preserve client's privilege by "refusing the prosecution an opportunity to disclose the source of the evidence"); Hughes v. Meade, 453 S.W.2d 538, 542 (Ky.1970) (attorney must reveal identity of transferor-client when attorney returns stolen property to the police).

16. Saltzburg, Communications Falling Within the Attorney Client Privilege, 66 Iowa L.Rev. 811, 837–39 (1981) (opposes the privilege in this context); Note, Ethics, Law and Loyalty: The Attorney's Duty to Turn Over Incriminating Physical Evidence, 32 Stan.L.Rev. 977 (1980) (favors the privilege in this context if the identity of the transferor-client is incriminating).

order to preserve his Fifth Amendment right to shield from disclosure (either directly or by production) his connection with the object. Thus a rule requiring compelled disclosure possibly disadvantages the client. But if the lawyer cannot be compelled to disclose the transfer, the client might effectively deprive the other side—typically the police in this context—of the opportunity to establish possessory links through valid searches and other methods that do not require any forbidden communication from the client. In short, a rule denying disclosure possibly advantages the client.

The issue is a close one, but courts should probably adopt the rule that the attorney-client privilege does not apply to protect acknowledgment of the transfer of any writing or physical object from the client. This solution places decisive weight on the proposition that the client should not be allowed to use the privilege to deprive the police of an opportunity to connect him to a document or object by appropriate means that do not infringe the Fifth Amendment. Compelling disclosure of the transfer is fully compatible with the best-reasoned cases dealing with a closely related matter. Suppose the client merely tells his lawyer about an object, such as a gun or a stolen item, and where it is located. Such knowledge is privileged so long as the lawyer does not remove or tamper with the evidence. But if the lawyer disturbs the evidence, he must make a full disclosure to authorities because he has deprived them of an opportunity to view the evidence in pristine form. That is, if the attorney removes the object, some authority holds that he must turn it over to prosecution authorities and reveal its original location; further, if the object was damaged or altered during the lawyer's possession, he must describe its original condition.[17]

Several other aspects of the attorney-client privilege deserve mention. *First,* lawyers can be asked both to confirm the existence of an attorney-client relationship, and to describe its scope and objectives. *Second,* courts generally hold that lawyers can be compelled to disclose the client's identity and such "identifying facts" as address, occupation, and fee arrangements.[18] These "basic facts," as we shall call them, should not be privileged, courts typically reason, because they are not made in confidence

17. See, e.g., Clutchette v. Rushen, 770 F.2d 1469 (9th Cir.1985), cert. denied ___ U.S. ___, 106 S.Ct. 1474 (1986); People v. Meredith, 29 Cal.3d 682, 175 Cal.Rptr. 612, 631 P.2d 46, 54 (1981).

18. McCormick, § 90, at 215–16.

or to secure legal advice.[19] Sometimes, however, this judicial reasoning is inadequate, because the expressed rationale does not resolve those situations where the privilege is denied despite the fact *that the client fully intended* that his identity or some other basic information remain confidential. In such cases courts will sometimes uphold the privilege, but they always require more than confidential intent before they will recognize its application. Perhaps, as one authority speculates, "the real reason [that courts are reluctant to grant the privilege] . . . is the strong aroma of suspicion which emerges from attempts to hide what is normally such innocent data." [20] This notion perhaps explains why courts will readily protect the identity of an *innocent* client who seeks legal advice—but fears that the revelation of his name will result in illegal acts of retaliation against him. At any rate, while "basic" information (such as the client's name, address, and occupation) is generally unprivileged, there are several exceptions to this general rule. The first is not controversial: courts properly protect basic facts if disclosure would also reveal other protected information. In short, basic facts are always protected when they cannot be separated from independently privileged communications. The other two exceptions, though widely upheld, are more problematic. We can label these the "wrongdoer exceptions." Many courts protect a basic fact (e.g., identity or occupation) if its disclosure would implicate the client in the very activity which prompted him to hire a lawyer in the first place. A typical setting is where a client makes anonymous restitution for wrongdoing through his attorney, often for tax violations.[21] Finally, some courts also protect identity and similar basic facts if disclosure would provide the last link in an already existing chain of evidence against the client.[22] Observe the curious anomaly between the general rule of disclosure of basic facts and these last two instances in which courts often recognize the attorney-client privilege. The privilege is usually denied because innocent people have no need for it and the basic facts seem innocuous; yet in these last two circumstances the privilege is often recognized when the basic facts point an incriminating finger at the client. The recognition of privilege in this context might perhaps be

19. Saltzburg & Redden at 348.

20. 2 Louisell & Mueller, § 210, at 776.

21. 2 Louisell & Mueller, § 210, at 778–79.

22. See, e.g., In re Grand Jury Proceedings, 689 F.2d 1351, 1352–53 (11th Cir.1982).

better explained by Fifth Amendment concerns than by the attorney-client privilege. Some courts sense this anomaly—recognize that the attorney-client privilege and the Fifth Amendment address different concerns—and therefore only allow the attorney-client privilege when the basic fact cannot be separated from other properly privileged attorney-client communications.[23] Occasionally, however, the "wrongdoer" exceptions stand on firm footing, at least as regards the overall costs and benefits to the administration of justice. A number of courts protect anonymity when wrongdoing (or, of course, innocent) clients, fearful of incrimination, might not otherwise expose offenses committed by third persons more deeply implicated than themselves.[24]

A final problem should be addressed. Does the privilege protect the lawyer's communications to the client, or is the road to privilege a one-way street? Theoretically, the privilege applies only to the client's statements and not to those of his attorney. But revelation of the attorney's statements, in the context of the case, might shed considerable light on the client's communications. Responding to this practical reality, the courts, generally speaking, grant privileged status to the statements of both client and attorney in order to fully protect the client's statements. There are some variations in approach. Many courts protect lawyers' statements only if they rest "*in part at least*" on a client's statements;[25] most federal courts go even further and broadly hold that a lawyer's legal advice should be confidential regardless of its source.[26] Even though the narrower rule is consonant with the purpose of the attorney-client privilege—protecting the client's communications—its adoption adds some uncertainty to the application of the privilege. In contrast, the broad rule is certain and easy to administer. The modern trend in the states is toward using the broader approach.[27]

§ 9.7 Attorney-Client Privilege: Special Problems of Sharing and Dissemination of Privileged Information

The privilege belongs only to the client, and therefore the lawyer may not claim the privilege when the client waives it, nor

23. In re Osterhoudt, 722 F.2d 591, 593–94 (9th Cir.1983).

24. 2 Weinstein & Berger, ¶ 503(a)(4)[02], at 35.

25. In re Sealed Case, 737 F.2d 94, 99 (D.C.Cir.1984).

26. See, e.g., United States v. Amerada Hess Corp., 619 F.2d 980, 986 (3d Cir.1980).

27. McCormick, § 89, at 212.

waive the privilege without the client's consent. Furthermore, the client need not be a party to the proceeding in order to invoke the privilege; he may also invoke it as a witness or bystander, either himself or through an agent (e.g., his attorney). Generally speaking, invocation of the privilege prevents all who have made or heard privileged communications during the course of the representation from revealing them.[1] Clearly this includes the statements of the client and the lawyer. But who else can be silenced by the invocation of the privilege? In short, which third parties are typically allowed to stand under the umbrella of protection? This is an important question because of its potential impact on the close balance of competing considerations between confidentiality and open factfinding.

There is general recognition that the nature of the attorney-client relationship makes it necessary to extend the privilege beyond statements made between attorney and client to include statements made to and by certain third parties. The Proposed Federal Rule specifically endorses this extension for third parties who, in a "reasonably necessary manner," help clients communicate with lawyers, or who help lawyers provide legal services.[2] Although these purposes overlap, the first derives from the core of the privilege itself, which is communication, and can therefore be fully justified with reference to the privilege itself. The second purpose—covering those persons who help the lawyer provide legal services—is more distantly related to the privilege, and hence more problematic. Yet both extensions generally prevail in the cases, although, as we shall see, with some limitations.

Third persons facilitate lawyer-client communications in two overlapping ways. First, because of practical concerns like time pressures and geographic distance, lawyers and clients often find it convenient, and sometimes necessary, to communicate through agents, assistants, or representatives. Where a client, for example, gives a message to a clerk to relay to the attorney, courts understandably treat the situation as if the client made the communication directly to the attorney. The clerk is within the circle of privilege and cannot disclose the communication without the client's permission. The protected relationship, then, includes representatives of the client; it also embraces typical employees of

§ 9.7

1. See generally Marcus, The Perils of Privilege: Waiver and the Litigator, 84 Mich.L.Rev. 1605 (1986).

2. Proposed Fed.R.Evid. 503(a)(4).

the modern law firm such as clerks, paralegals, and secretaries.[3] And as one might predict, it includes the other lawyers in the firm. The client-protected circle generally embraces employees, agents, family, and friends so long as their involvement is necessary or at least reasonably useful.[4] Most of these examples illustrate what might be called an efficiency-based rationale for the extension of the privilege to third parties. Such persons are not inherently necessary to the communication between client and lawyer; rather they have become a practical necessity because of the complex organization of both modern law firms and modern business entities. Even in a simple setting involving one lawyer and a single client, a stenographer may be practically necessary on the ground of convenience. Beyond this, a third party may *be required* to facilitate adequate communication between client and lawyer: a language barrier, for example, may dictate the need for a translator; a physical injury or disease may require that a physician be present to explain the nature and extent of the disability. In short, both individual and business clients often possess specialized information that either the client cannot impart or the lawyer cannot understand without the help of one or more third parties. Thus, a third party is often necessary to facilitate communication—to allow it to take place (the translator) or to improve its quality or accuracy (the physician). These various justifications depart considerably from the rationale of older cases which often viewed a permissible third party as a conduit who simply related the client's communication to the attorney.[5] Yet, at least for certain kinds of intermediaries, it is well settled that *improvement of communication* is a legitimate goal that warrants the extension of the privilege to a third party.

Accountants, doctors, and psychiatrists are the typical kinds of intermediaries that provide such help.[6] The analogy to the translator is useful here. A disturbed client who may have a valid psychiatric defense to a criminal charge is usually unable to communicate the nature and severity of his mental or emotional problem. Instead he typically imparts only symptoms and glimpses of the underlying reality, and even those might be missed or misunderstood by even the most capable lawyer. A trained

3. 2 Louisell & Mueller, § 209, at 754.

4. McCormick, § 91, at 218–19.

5. United States ex rel. Edney v. Smith, 425 F.Supp. 1038, 1047 (E.D.N.Y. 1976).

6. 2 Louisell & Mueller, § 209, at 751–52.

doctor is invaluable in this situation, and the communications between the client and the doctor, and the doctor and the lawyer, should be privileged. The courts so hold.[7]

Although the extension of the privilege to accountants and medical practitioners is noncontroversial so long as the other requirements of the privilege are satisfied, courts can be unsympathetic to innovative analogies intended to include within the group of protected communicants non-legal personnel who traditionally have not been included. To illustrate: one court rejected the claim of privilege for the statements of members of a "Think Tank" (The Stanford Research Institute), noting that such consulting reports "lie at an outer and indistinct boundary of the law of attorney-client privilege."[8] And even when a communication comes from a third party who is normally within the circle of privilege, the courts usually hold that the privilege is inapplicable if the prospective client communicates with the third party before he seeks a lawyer. In addition, there is a clear risk that the privilege will not apply to a client's statements made to a third party whose participation in the case was not authorized by the lawyer.[9] Finally, the privilege does not apply if the lawyer involves the third party for purposes other than facilitating legal advice.[10]

These broad generalities, however, should not obscure careful distinctions concerning the applicability of the attorney-client privilege to communications through third-party representatives. Often the representative communicates his own independent opinion based only in part (or perhaps not at all) upon the client's communications. A psychiatrist, for example, may listen to the client's communications and make a diagnostic communication to the attorney that was formed, probably in large part, by the doctor's independent knowledge and judgment. Even more clearly, a physician who conducts a physical examination, makes tests, and so forth, may base his communication to the lawyer on these things, and not to any significant extent on what the client has said. Indeed, it is at least arguable that the psychiatrist's and doctor's statements in the foregoing instances constitute ordinary expert opinion and not a *communication by the client* in any

7. The leading case is City and County of San Francisco v. Superior Court, 37 Cal.2d 227, 231 P.2d 26 (1951).

8. Federal Trade Comm'n v. TRW, Inc., 628 F.2d 207, 213 (D.C.Cir.1980).

9. 2 Louisell & Mueller, § 209, at 745–46.

10. In re John Doe Corp., 675 F.2d 482, 488 (2d Cir.1982).

meaningful sense.[11] Most courts have held, however, that such intermediary's communication is within the privilege because the representative is making a communication of a technical or specialized nature that the client, lacking the necessary expertise, cannot make himself.[12] Some of these holdings are theoretically at odds with the prevailing notion, at least among commentators, that the privilege is applicable to the expert's statements only if they are derived from the client's communications, and thus the privilege is inapplicable to those statements based on the expert's own knowledge or any other source.[13] Nonetheless, some courts have tended to give the privilege a broad application; they appear to take the position that both the testimony and written reports of an expert are privileged, even when they draw extensively on the expert's personal knowledge [14] or substantially derive from sources other than the client's communication.[15] The problem, of course, is the practical one of separating threads that are "inextricably intertwined." Courts are sometimes loathe to disadvantage clients by drawing fine distinctions that are difficult to forecast accurately.[16] However, extension of the privilege beyond matters that are within or closely allied with communications of the client loses sight of its purpose—communication—and expands its protection into an area which might better be managed by application of the work-product rule. The difficulty arises because the attorney-client privilege is absolute and cannot be abrogated based on

11. See Friedenthal, Discovery and Use of Adverse Party's Expert Information, 14 Stan.L.Rev. 455, 462–69 (1962).

12. 2 Weinstein & Berger ¶ 503(a)(3)[01]; People v. Lines, 13 Cal.3d 500, 119 Cal.Rptr. 225, 531 P.2d 793 (1975). The point was well made in Lindsay v. Lipson: "Had [the client] possessed the requisite training and skill to make an accurate appraisal of her physical condition and to draw reasonable conclusions therefrom as to probable future developments any communication by her to her attorney of such appraisal and diagnosis would without question have been privileged." 367 Mich. 1, 116 N.W.2d 60, 62 (1962).

13. "[T]he expert's observations, conclusions, and information derived from sources other than the client's communication constitute the expert's knowledge, which, like the client's knowledge and the attorney's knowledge, is not privileged." 2 Weinstein & Berger, ¶ 503(a)(3) [01], at 28. See also Saltzburg, Communications Falling Within the Attorney-Client Privilege, 66 Iowa L.Rev. 811 (1981).

14. People v. Hilliker, 29 Mich.App. 543, 185 N.W.2d 831 (1971) (psychiatrist's evaluation of defendant within privilege). Cf. United States v. Kovel, 296 F.2d 918, 921 (2d Cir.1961) (accountant is closely analogous to translator, at least when receiving client's communications).

15. State v. 62.96247 Acres of Land, 193 A.2d 799 (Del.Super.1963) (real estate appraiser engaged by attorney is within privilege). Contra Levitsky v. Prince George's County, 50 Md.App. 484, 439 A.2d 600 (1982).

16. See United States v. Pipkins, 528 F.2d 559, 564 (5th Cir.1976), cert. denied, 426 U.S. 952 (1976).

balancing by the court. In contrast to the work-product rule[17] (which gives a large measure of protection to the work of an expert conducted in anticipation of litigation), the privilege cannot be overridden by a showing of substantial need or even exceptional circumstances. Suppose, for example, an attorney engages an accountant to examine and analyze a client's preexisting records, or hires a chemist to analyze a bloodstain on an article of clothing belonging to the client. In the usual course of events, the statements and evaluations of these experts are not, in any realistic sense, communications of the client. They are within the protection of the work-product rule. Since the work-product immunity operates to *shield conditionally* these communications, application of the unconditional attorney-client privilege appears unnecessary. Overly broad applications of the privilege seem at variance both with the purpose of the privilege and a sensible balance between confidentiality and disclosure. The attorney-client privilege should, ideally, be restricted to only such parts of the communication as reveal the client's communicative disclosures made in pursuit of legal services.[18] This narrow reading of the privilege is especially appealing when the lawyer engages the third party not really to facilitate a communication from the client, but to assist the lawyer in delivering legal services to the client. A narrow application of the privilege would not unduly burden clients because the work-product rule embodied in Federal Rules of Civil Procedure permits discovery of non-testifying experts only when the denial of such discovery poses substantial hardships to the other side.[19] The close balance between shielding confidences, on the one hand, and open factfinding, on the other, seems better served by a flexible rule that makes discovery of the non-testifying experts who assist counsel difficult, but not impossible.

It should be observed that the attorney-client privilege does not apply when the attorney retains an expert to testify at trial. Under these circumstances, any information that the expert derived from conversations with either the lawyer or the client is

17. See Fed.R.Civ.Proc. 26(b)(3)–(4). As used in the text "work product" refers to both (b)(3) and (b)(4) of Rule 26 and similar provisions in state codes and rules of court.

18. See generally Sachs v. Aluminum Co. of America, 167 F.2d 570 (6th Cir.1948).

19. 2 Weinstein & Berger, ¶ 503(a)(4)[01], at 28–29.

unprotected, and furthermore, is subject to discovery in accordance with the terms[20] of the Federal Rules of Civil Procedure.

Other contexts place a strain upon the reach of the privilege: the limits of the privilege must be defined when the principals to the relationship—the lawyer and the client—grow numerous. One lawyer often represents several clients on a matter of joint or common interest—a real estate transaction, for example, or an insurance policy covering both the insurer and the insured. The rule in such situations protects the statements of both the clients and the lawyer, and allows *any of the clients* to invoke the privilege against outsiders. The privilege is lost, however, in subsequent disputes between the clients themselves. The Proposed Federal Rule explicitly endorses this approach.[21] Thus in the insurance case, for example, either the insured or the insurance carrier could invoke the privilege against the victim of the insured's negligence, but the insured could not invoke the privilege if the carrier subsequently sued him for breaching a term of the policy.[22]

This approach sensibly balances confidence and factfinding. First, the absence of separate representation strongly suggests that joint clients typically do not intend confidentiality between themselves. Second, the privilege is properly lost when, as in this context, preserving it does not plausibly improve candor between clients and lawyers. Joint clients are unlikely to hold back information since none of them can know if compelled disclosure in a subsequent dispute will (or will not) be to their advantage.[23]

The rule is significantly different when parties with their own lawyers pool or share information because they have some interests in common. The Advisory Committee's notes to Proposed Federal Rule 503 (often used by courts as a standard) indicate that such information should remain privileged if and when disputes arise between any of the pooling parties.[24] The cases are generally in accord.[25] This protective rule sensibly acknowledges that

20. 2 Louisell & Mueller, § 209, at 752–53.

21. Proposed Fed.R.Evid. 503(d)(5).

22. 2 Louisell & Mueller, § 210, at 791.

23. McCormick, § 91, at 219.

24. Proposed Fed.R.Evid. 503(b); 2 Weinstein & Berger, ¶ 503(b) [06], at 59–62.

25. The leading pre-Rules case that makes the point is Hunydee v. United States, 355 F.2d 183, 184–85 (9th Cir. 1965). For more recent authority see United States v. McPartlin, 595 F.2d 1321, 1335–37 (7th Cir.1979), cert. denied, 444 U.S. 833 (1979).

some adverseness must already exist between persons who insist on separate representation, and that clients and their attorneys might not communicate freely with their coparties if their statements could be disclosed in subsequent litigation. In short, the law recognizes that separately represented parties who are potentially or actually adverse can still benefit from a common defense strategy. They are allowed to pool their resources without forfeiting their individual attorney-client privilege in subsequent litigation between the affiliated clients.

§ 9.8 Attorney-Client Privilege: Corporate Context

Suppose that the client is a corporation and that the communication is made by a corporate employee to the attorney for the corporation. Because the corporation can speak only through individuals, the question may arise whether *the corporation* is making a communication. Depending on the context and one's view of the proper scope of the privilege, the statements of the employee could be either (1) communications from the corporate client and within the corporation's privilege, or (2) statements by an employee not authorized to speak for the corporate client (thus, essentially those of a witness) and not within the privilege. The first choice, depending on the number of managers and workers the corporation employs, can threaten the integrity of judicial outcomes by depriving factfinders of too much information. If the privilege extends far down into the corporate organization—to middle management or even below—the reach of the privilege may stifle the efforts of an opponent to support his claim or defense. The informational loss occasioned by increasing the number of corporate spokesmen is obvious though difficult to measure precisely. The potential information loss to the adversary may also be assessed by comparing the corporate client to the individual client.[1] In the individual setting, the opposing party may depose the client or call him as an adverse witness at trial and often secure valuable information. But the corporate entity's knowledge of pertinent facts often cannot be easily traced to only one or two individuals within the corporate structure. Personal knowledge of the pertinent facts often is fragmented; a significant number of corporate officials and employees may each have some pertinent information. Yet knowledge of the composite facts may

§ 9.8

1. 2 Weinstein & Berger, ¶ 503(b) [04], at 41–44 draws the comparisons.

reside with only a few persons—typically high officials in the corporate order—who themselves may have little or no first-hand knowledge of the events in question. Typically, the composite facts are embodied in a document. If that document is protected by the attorney-client privilege, the adversary must learn the facts by interviewing, or more likely, by subjecting to discovery a number of persons within the corporate organization, each of whom knows only a portion of the relevant facts. It is true, of course, that the corporate entity must disclose (for example, by answers to written interrogatories) what it "knows" or has learned of the facts, including any information reasonably available to it.[2] The corporation must also disclose to the adversary what persons within the corporation have knowledge of pertinent facts.[3] But gathering facts from a large corporate adversary can be a formidable task. The task of effective discovery is made harder if documents within the corporate organization are shielded from production by the attorney-client privilege.

The application of the protection in the corporate setting often strains some of the basic doctrines of privilege law.[4] The requirement of confidentiality, for example, poorly meshes with the layered structure of the typical corporation, where statements are often passed through many hands before they reach the lawyer. In addition, the indistinct boundary between legal and business advice in large corporations dulls the "legal purpose" requirement that is the heart of the privilege. On the other hand, the modern corporation could simply not realize the full potential of needed legal advice without some application of the privilege.[5] The problem, therefore, becomes one of drawing a line that sensibly balances the corporation's need for confidentiality in its relationship with counsel and the opponent's need to secure the facts necessary to support its claim or defense. The problem is now a familiar one, but its resolution is particularly difficult in the corporate context. The extremes are easily managed. Clearly protected is a communication from the corporate president to the attorney, in which the former seeks legal advice for the corpora-

2. Fed.R.Civ.Proc. 33(a); C. Wright, The Law of Federal Courts, 386, at 578–79.

3. Fed.R.Civ.Proc. 30(b)(6), 33(b); C. Wright, supra n. 2 at 576.

4. 2 Louisell & Mueller, § 211, at 794–97.

5. Only one federal court ever held that the attorney-client privilege did not apply to corporations, and that decision was reversed on appeal. Radiant Burners, Inc. v. American Gas Ass'n, 207 F.Supp. 771 (N.D.Ill.1962), rev'd, 320 F.2d 314 (7th Cir.1963), cert. denied, 375 U.S. 929 (1963).

tion. Clearly unprotected would be a routinely prepared statement by a lower-level employee, made in the normal course of business, but revealing facts about an occurrence pertinent to the matter being litigated. The difficulties lie between these two extremes.

The Supreme Court addressed the scope of the attorney-client privilege in the corporate context in Upjohn Co. v. United States, decided in 1981.[6] Prior to *Upjohn,* two different approaches prevailed. Some courts used a "control-group" test that upheld the privilege only if the individual speaking to the attorney was vested by the corporation with authority both to seek legal advice and to participate significantly in the corporation's response to the advice.[7] The analogy was to the individual client, who could seek legal advice and then, if he wished, tailor his conduct in response to advice given. The problem with this approach is its heavy reliance on formal designations of authority. If the person who spoke with the attorney was an officer whose position was within the upper tiers of management, he probably "spoke for the corporation." At least he spoke in a "corporate capacity" if he was in a position to significantly participate in the corporate entity's response to the attorney's legal advice. But very often this high-level spokesman was not the person with the most information about the matter in question. Nonetheless, application of the control group test made him and other high-level officials the only corporate voices protected by the attorney-client privilege. Lower-level employees, not themselves in a position to influence directly the corporation's response to counsel's advice, could not speak for the corporation. Their statements to the corporation's lawyers were not within the corporation's attorney-client privilege and thus fell outside its absolute protection. If these communications were protected at all, they were shielded by the work-product rule. The control group test was thus subject to the criticism that it often failed to confer the corporate attorney-client privilege upon those corporate spokesmen who had the most knowledge and who should be directly communicating with the attorney.[8] It is not surprising that other approaches would soon develop. The most

6. Upjohn Co. v. United States, 449 U.S. 383 (1981).

7. The test was first announced in City of Philadelphia v. Westinghouse Electric Corp., 210 F.Supp. 483, 484–86 (E.D.Pa.1962).

8. 2 Weinstein & Berger, ¶ 503(b)[04], at 46–46.1; 2 Louisell & Mueller, § 211, at 796–801.

notable alternative, which was basically a subject matter test, extended considerably the boundaries of the privilege. The privilege was allowed to embrace any communication by any employee involving his corporate duties and made at the direction of his corporate supervisor. This later test, usually identified with Harper & Row Publishers v. Decker,[9] yielded possibilities for unduly extending the wall of privilege, especially since careful planning by counsel and corporate officials could increase the number of communications that stayed within the protected area.

In Upjohn Co. v. United States, the Supreme Court addressed the problem of the attorney-client privilege in the corporate context. The facts of the case are relatively simple. Upjohn, through its general counsel, coordinated an investigation into possibly illegal payments made by the corporation to foreign governments. Subsequently, the Internal Revenue Service issued a summons demanding production of files pertaining to the investigation, including questionnaires prepared for counsel and answered by various corporate managers. The Court noted the following facts about the questionnaires: in a letter that accompanied them the Chairman of the Board noted that the investigation was under the direction of counsel, that responses were highly confidential, and that the completed questionnaires should be returned to counsel. In addition to these completed questionnaires, the IRS demanded files containing records of interviews between counsel and some of the Upjohn managers.

The Court began its analysis by considering, generally, the approach that should guide the federal courts in determining the scope of the attorney-client privilege. It then rejected as too restrictive the control group test, in part because of its focus on formal corporate authority. Although the Court did not announce "a broad rule" to supplant the test it rejected, it did clarify privilege law in the corporate context in several respects. Essentially the Court embraced, but tightened, the *Harper & Row* test.[10] In brief, the *Upjohn* approach would allow the privilege if the facts showed that: (1) the communication was part of a corporate purpose to obtain legal advice; (2) the communication "concerned matters within the scope of the employee's corporate duties"; (3) the employee knew that he was making a confidential statement as part of a corporate purpose to secure legal advice; and (4) the

9. 423 F.2d 487 (7th Cir.1970), judgment aff'd, 400 U.S. 348 (1971), reh. denied, 401 U.S. 950 (1971).

10. 2 Louisell & Mueller, § 211, at 803.

statements were kept confidential, or disclosed in a manner consistent with the privilege.[11] The last requirement can arise in two contexts: disclosure *within* or *outside* the firm. Since corporations depend heavily upon information, there is a practical need that at least most corporate records and files be accessible to managers and employees. Yet it is difficult to predict how much disclosure *within* the firm will destroy the privilege. Privileged communicants should be allowed to keep file copies and to circulate them to superiors and to persons generally competent in the subject matter of the communication. There is also authority for the proposition that corporations should be allowed to keep privileged documents in the general filing system, so long as adequate precautions are taken. Close questions should be resolved with reference to normal business practices and the internal need for sharing the privileged information.[12] Courts are generally less sympathetic regarding voluntary disclosure *outside* the firm. Corporations cannot selectively reveal documents when it is to their advantage with—for example, a regulatory agency [13] or an auditing firm [14]—and expect to preserve the privilege. Of course, privileged statements made by a current employee should remain protected after the communicant leaves the firm. The termination or departure of an employee should not impair the protected relationship between the corporation and its counsel. There is, however, only scant authority protecting post-employment statements by a former employee.[15] Also, whether a parent corporation, with the clear status of a client, can invoke the privilege as to the employees of a subsidiary remains an open question.[16] It should be remembered, of course, that the *Upjohn* case is controlling only within the federal system, although state courts may find its reasoning persuasive. It should be noted, further, that *Upjohn* did not hold that all of the factors cited in that case invariably must be present for the corporate privilege to exist. The Court resolved only the case before it.

Several of the remaining issues of corporate privilege deserve brief mention. First, the privilege belongs to the corporate entity,

11. Upjohn Co., 449 U.S. at 394–95.

12. 2 Louisell & Mueller, § 211, at 809–11.

13. See, e.g., In re Subpoenas Duces Tecum, 738 F.2d 1367, 1369–70 (D.C.Cir. 1984).

14. See, e.g., In re John Doe Corp., 675 F.2d 482, 488 (2d Cir.1982).

15. In re Potts & Co., 30 B.R. 708, 710 (Bkrtcy.E.D.Pa.1983). But the *Upjohn* Court expressly left this question open. See Upjohn v. United States, 449 U.S. 383, 394 n. 3 (1981).

16. 2 Weinstein & Berger, ¶ 503(b)[04], at 55.

and it generally can only be waived by management, typically by the board of directors. Second, the power to waive always rests with the present board, regardless of when the communications were made. Third, when a corporation becomes insolvent, control of the attorney-client privilege passes to the trustee regarding pre-bankruptcy statements.[17] Finally, as we shall see, on a proper factual showing, the board can lose control of the privilege to the shareholders themselves.

Shareholder suits ("derivative suits") are becoming prevalent in American business life. In such actions the shareholders sue the managers on behalf of the corporation, typically for self-dealing or breach of fiduciary duty. Who should control the privilege in this situation is a difficult question. If the board maintains control, their corporate decisions will remain largely impervious to shareholder suits. But well-intentioned managers will communicate less freely if they believe that the privilege might evaporate on the mere launching of a shareholder suit. Clearly, if the corporate communication furthered a continuing fraud or crime, the privilege should give way. Beyond this, the best-reasoned cases discourage frivolous suits, but allow the shareholders to defeat the privilege on a showing of need, especially when their charges are serious and colorable, and when the plaintiffs represent a significant percentage of outstanding stock.[18]

§ 9.9 Attorney-Client Privilege: Nonapplicability and Waiver

Judicial systems in free societies endorse the principle that wrongdoers are entitled to their day in court, adequately represented by counsel. As a consequence, communications about past crimes are necessarily shielded to allow lawyers and clients to plan legitimate defenses. Yet the system is subverted, and the privilege properly lost, when the communications advance criminal or fraudulent activity. The standards in this context are demanding: the client forfeits the privilege when he seeks legal advice to advance an objective that he knew, or should have known, was criminal or fraudulent. The Proposed Federal Rule (standard) would also deny the privilege if the client, intent aside, "obtained" legal services that "enabled anyone" to commit what

17. Commodity Futures Trading Comm'n v. Weintraub, 471 U.S. 343, 348–49, 354 (1985), on remand, 776 F.2d 1049 (7th Cir.1985).

18. Garner v. Wolfinbarger, 430 F.2d 1093, 1103–04 (5th Cir.1970), cert. denied, 401 U.S. 974 (1971).

the client knew, or should have known, was a fraudulent act.[1] Drawing a line between past and ongoing crimes (e.g., concealment) is sometimes a difficult problem, especially when the client turns over evidence to his attorney.[2] Some of these problems are discussed in an earlier section.[3] There is recent authority suggesting that the "crime or fraud exception" is itself too narrow, and that the privilege should also be lost when the relationship assists ongoing torts or other wrongful behavior.[4]

Certain relational problems between the lawyer and client can deprive the client of the privilege. When a client sues his lawyer for malpractice, for example, the lawyer can use confidential statements to defend himself against the charge. Similarly, if a client refuses to pay his attorney, the lawyer can support his financial claims with confidential information. In both situations, the client necessarily waives his privilege when he willingly becomes adverse to his lawyer.[5]

Finally, as we noted earlier, the privilege is not recognized in suits between persons claiming some right or entitlement through a deceased client.[6] The same rule of termination usually prevails in suits between one who claims by reason of an inter vivos transaction and one who claims by will or intestacy.[7] And we have seen that the privilege is also lost when two clients jointly represented by an attorney subsequently become adversaries. It would be unfair, in this setting, to protect the statements of one and not the other; and it is equally unsatisfactory to protect the statements of both. The information they openly shared with their common representative ought to remain the "common property" of the clients, available to either in a suit between them. Arrangements in which several clients, each represented by counsel, pool their information, stand on a different footing. In subsequent suits between the clients, their individual privileges are usually preserved.

§ 9.9

1. Proposed Fed.R.Evid. 503(d)(1) and Adv.Comm. Note; 2 Louisell & Mueller, § 213, at 822.

2. 2 Louisell & Mueller, § 213, at 824–29.

3. See supra § 9.6 at notes 11–17.

4. See e.g. Diamond v. Stratton, 95 F.R.D. 503, 505 (S.D.N.Y.1982) (loss of privilege should apply to intentional torts). See also Commodity Futures Trading Comm. v. Weintraub, 471 U.S. 343, at 354. (Although not the holding of the case, the Supreme Court referred to the loss of privilege for "communications relating to the planning or commission of ongoing fraud, crimes, and ordinary torts").

5. 2 Louisell & Mueller, § 213, at 832–33.

6. See supra § 9.6.

7. Proposed Fed.R.Evid. 503(d)(2).

§ 9.10 Physician-Patient Privilege

This privilege, a creature of statute, is recognized in a majority of the states. But there are significant variations among the statutes, thus making hazardous any description that purports to be both general and accurate. The privilege is usually justified on the now familiar ground that it is needed to insure that the patient will speak candidly to his physician. Such candor, it is said, is essential to the physician's diagnosis and the patient's effective treatment. Whether a patient seeking treatment from his doctor, presumably concerned about his health, would withhold information without the assurance of a judicial privilege is highly debatable.[1] Thus, some commentators justify the privilege on a different, essentially privacy, basis: its recognition rests on society's belief that the intimate, personal nature of communications about one's bodily condition justifies the law's assurance of confidentiality.[2]

The essence of the physician-patient privilege is this: it applies when the patient is seeking *treatment* and it usually embraces not only pertinent information that he shares with his doctor, but also information secured by the doctor through examination and tests. Notice that a consultation for the purpose of securing a medical evaluation unrelated to treatment is usually outside the privilege. Thus an examination to secure life insurance,[3] a court-ordered examination,[4] and an examination solely for the purpose of litigation are typically unprivileged.[5] And since

§ 9.10

1. For trenchant criticism of the present exception see VIII Wigmore § 2380a (Chadbourn).

2. McCormick, § 105, at 259; Black, Marital and Physician Privileges—A Reprint of a Letter to a Congressman, 1975 Duke L.J. 45, 50 ("but evaluation of . . . this [privilege] entails not only a guess as to what conduct it will motivate, but also an estimate of its intrinsic decency. . . ."). See Whalen v. Roe, 429 U.S. 589, 598 (1977); In re Zuniga, 714 F.2d 632 (6th Cir.1983), cert. denied, 464 U.S. 983 (1983) (indicating the privacy interest can be overcome by the need for disclosure). Cases suggesting the possibility of a constitutionally based privacy foundation, at least for the psychotherapist privilege, are collected in 2 Louisell & Mueller, § 216, at 863–64. See also Weinstein & Mansfield, et al. at 1489–95.

3. McGinty v. Brotherhood of Railway Trainmen, 166 Wis. 83, 164 N.W. 249 (1917). See generally Annot. 107 A.L.R. 1495 (1937).

4. State v. Cole, 295 N.W.2d 29 (Iowa 1980); Henson v. State, 239 Ark. 727, 393 S.W.2d 856 (1965), appeal after remand, 255 Ark. 600, 501 S.W.2d 619 (1973).

5. McCormick § 99; VIII Wigmore (McNaughton) § 2383. See City and County of San Francisco v. Superior Court, 37 Cal.2d 227, 231 P.2d 26 (1951) (no physician patient privilege covers physicians consulted in preparation for litigation); Lindsay v. Lipson, 367 Mich. 1, 116 N.W.2d 60 (1962) (examination of plaintiff at instigation of plaintiff's

the privilege rests upon either a policy of encouraging full disclosure or the protection of privacy, courts ordinarily require that the information subject to the privilege be confidential—or at least so intended by the patient. However, these courts are reasonable in their allowance of what persons may share the presumably privileged information without destroying its confidential status. Most cases hold that nurses and other medical personnel associated with the physician may share the information.[6] Even a close family member or confidant, present at the consultation in a supportive role will probably not break the "circle of confidence." [7] But a casual sharing of the information with third parties who are present at the consultation, but have no "need to know" probably goes too far, and the privilege will not arise.[8]

It is odd, and probably unwise, that most jurisdictions allow the physician-patient privilege to survive the death of the patient-holder. The privilege can then be claimed by his executor or administrator, (or perhaps the next of kin) acting on behalf of the patient who, during his life, was the sole holder. Surely the right to claim the privilege after the death of the patient is not ordinarily essential to realizing the objectives of the privilege. But the potentially harmful consequences of allowing the privilege to survive death (and thus to needlessly foreclose relevant information) are often avoided by statutory provisions or judicial constructions that permit post-mortem disclosure. In actions by the estate or next of kin to recover money or property from third persons (as, for example, a wrongful death claim or a suit to recover the decedent's goods), the after-death holder may waive the privilege.[9] Indeed, in most jurisdictions, if the holder files a suit based upon the physical or mental condition of the decedent-patient, the privilege is waived.[10] Further, in suits where both litigants are claiming an entitlement or inheritance through the decedent (as, for example, in a will contest), the privilege does not apply.[11] The

counsel not within physician-patient privilege). But see § 9.7, supra.

6. McCormick, § 101, at 250. Shultz v. State, 417 N.E.2d 1127 (Ind. App.1981), reh. denied, 421 N.E.2d 22 (1981); Ostrowski v. Mockridge, 242 Minn. 265, 65 N.W.2d 185 (1954). See also Annot., 47 A.L.R.2d 742 (1956).

7. Denaro v. Prudential Ins. Co. of America, 154 App.Div. 840, 139 N.Y.S. 758, 761 (1913). See Annot. 96 A.L.R. 1419 (1935).

8. Horowitz v. Sacks, 89 Cal.App. 336, 265 P. 281 (1928) ("unnecessary" family members). But see *Denaro,* supra note 7.

9. VIII Wigmore § 2391 (McNaughton).

10. West's Ann.Cal.Evid.Code § 996; Annot., 21 A.L.R.3d 912.

11. Lembke v. Unke, 171 N.W.2d 837 (N.D.1969); McCormick, § 102, at 253.

assumption is that the decedent would want the suit resolved in the light of a full evidentiary development so that the deserving claimant will prevail.

Thus far, the discussion has assumed that the privilege applies to a patient's consultation for treatment with any qualified physician, no matter what the latter's medical specialty. The privilege thus appropriately applies to the psychiatrist-patient relationship. But note the special and compelling reasons that counsel recognition of the privilege when the patient visits a psychiatrist or, more broadly, any licensed psychotherapist. Here the physician's diagnosis and treatment is likely to depend heavily upon the patient's willingness to speak freely about a wide array of intimate subjects. It seems especially important to the work of the psychiatrist and, more cogently, to the eventual well-being of the patient, that full disclosure be encouraged.[12] This encouragement is likely to come, in part at least, from the law's conferral of a privilege that protects the patient's confidences. At the first consultation, the psychiatrist will be able to tell the patient about the privilege, thus adding to the likelihood that the patient will speak fully and frankly.

It is thus not surprising that some jurisdictions which decline to recognize a general physician patient-privilege, nonetheless confer a psychiatrist-patient privilege. This latter privilege may be limited to psychiatrists or may take a broader form in order to embrace other licensed therapists, notably clinical psychologists. Indeed, as originally proposed, the Federal Rules included a "psychotherapist-patient" privilege that embraced both psychiatrists and "a person licensed or certified as a psychologist under the laws of any state or nation while . . . [so] engaged." [13] This proposed rule did not, however, survive Congressional action and, as we have seen,[14] Rule 501 directs the federal courts to develop

12. For a valuable discussion of the policies underlying psychotherapist patient privilege see 2 Louisell & Mueller, § 216, at 849–53, 863–65.

13. Proposed but rejected Federal Rule 504(a)(2)(B), 56 Fed.R.D. 183, 240–241 (1972). For a recent federal case upholding the privilege see In re Zuniga, 714 F.2d 632, 637 (6th Cir.1983), cert. denied, 464 U.S. 983 (1983) asserting that Congress' decision not to adopt Fed.R.Evid. 504 "does not preclude recognition of psychiatrist-patient privilege . . ." But see note 16 infra. It should not be forgotten, of course, that the privilege still belongs to the patient; any claim by the doctor or therapist is made not in his own right, but as an agent or surrogate of the patient-holder. See Lora v. Board of Education, 74 Fed.R.D. 565, 585–586 (E.D.N.Y.1977); In re Lifschutz, 2 Cal.3d 415, 85 Cal. Rptr. 829, 838, 467 P.2d 557, 566 (1970). See Proposed Fed.R.Evid. 504(b), (c).

14. See § 9.2.

privileges in accordance with "the principles of the common law as they may be interpreted . . . in the light of reason and experience." [15] The reported federal cases are mixed, but there is some judicial recognition of the psychotherapist-patient privilege.[16] In contrast, the general physician-patient privilege has not gained judicial recognition as part of the federal common law.[17]

The one point that can confidently be made about the physician-patient privilege (in its variant forms) is that student and practitioner must study this privilege with particular care and attention. First, the statutes vary significantly from state to state. Often, the privilege will be withdrawn from criminal proceedings, from specified types of civil proceedings such as workman's compensation, sanity hearings, or from will contests.[18] Second, the privilege may be overridden by a statute that requires a physician to report certain conditions or findings such as a gunshot wound or venereal disease, at least in the sense that the privilege gives way sufficiently to allow the doctor to make the report to the persons or agencies *designated in the statute.*[19] Third, certain conduct by the patient may be deemed a waiver of the privilege as, for example, when he files a suit to collect damages based upon his physical (or mental) condition, testifies about the condition described in the privileged communication, or calls the treating physician to the stand.[20] Fourth, in some jurisdictions, the trial judge may negate the privilege, wholly or partially, when in his judgment the interest of justice so requires.[21] Finally, it is to be recalled that the attorney-client privilege is usually extended to agents, consultants, and others whose services

15. Fed.R.Evid. 501. The rule instructs the courts to apply state privilege law "with respect to an element of a claim or defense as to which state law supplies the rule of decision . . ." Id.

16. In re Zuniga, 714 F.2d 632, 636–639 (6th Cir.1983), cert. denied, 464 U.S. 983 (1983) ("a psychotherapist-patient privilege is mandated by reason and experience" pursuant to Fed.R.Evid. 501). But see United States v. Lindstrom, 698 F.2d 1154 (11th Cir.1983) (indicating that privilege does not exist); United States v. Meagher, 531 F.2d 752, 753 (5th Cir.1976) cert. denied, 429 U.S. 853 (1976) (rejecting privilege in criminal cases).

17. 2 Weinstein & Berger ¶ 504[01]. See United States v. Witt, 542 F.Supp. 696, 698–99 (S.D.N.Y.1982) aff'd, 697 F.2d 301 (2d Cir.1982). Note that a physician can arguably be functioning as a psychotherapist even though psychotherapy is not his specialty.

18. See McCormick, § 104.

19. For a list of many of these statutory provisions in the several states, see VIII Wigmore § 2380 (McNaughton).

20. See VIII Wigmore §§ 2388–90 (McNaughton); McCormick, § 103, at 254–255.

21. See, e.g., Va.Code § 8.01–399; N.C.Gen.Stat. § 8–53.

are reasonably necessary for the rendition of legal services.[22] Thus, when a physician's examination of a patient (client) is part of the process of securing legal services from the patient's lawyer, the privileged status of the resulting communications among doctor, patient, and lawyer should be determined by resort to both the physician-patient privilege and attorney-client privilege. When one fails, the other may still be applicable.[23]

§ 9.11 The Privilege Against Self-Incrimination: Scope, Application, and Waiver

The Fifth Amendment to the United States Constitution[1] provides in part that "No person . . . shall be compelled in any criminal case to be a witness against himself." In Malloy v. Hogan,[2] decided in 1964, this provision was held applicable to the states through the command of the Fourteenth Amendment that a state shall not "deprive any person of life, liberty, or property without due process of law."

As Professors Whitebread and Slobogin have observed, the privilege against self-incrimination is protected by an exclusionary rule, which has five components. The rule "allows (1) natural persons (2) to prohibit the introduction in a criminal proceeding (3) of self-incriminating disclosures (4) that were obtained through 'compulsion' by the state and (5) that are testimonial in nature."[3] Judicial protection of the right against self-incrimination is not limited to after-the-fact exclusion, however; whenever possible, courts will also act to *prevent* state compulsion of self-incriminating testimony.

Although "person" often is given a broad constitutional or statutory construction, in the present context it is more narrowly read: the privilege against self-incrimination is conferred only upon individuals. It is not available to a corporation, and it also is denied to an unincorporated entity, such as a labor union or a partnership, if the enterprise in question represents group interests as opposed to private or personal ones.[4] The constitutional

22. See § 9.7.

23. See, e.g., City and County of San Francisco v. Superior Court of San Francisco, supra note 5 (physician-patient privilege inapplicable, but attorney-client privilege applies).

§ **9.11**

1. For the history and policies behind the Fifth Amendment, see generally L. Levy, Origins of the Fifth Amendment (1968); VIII Wigmore §§ 2250–51 (McNaughton).

2. 378 U.S. 1 (1964).

3. C. Whitebread & C. Slobogin, Criminal Procedure, § 15.01, at 324 (2d ed. 1986).

4. Hale v. Henkel, 201 U.S. 43 (1906) (corporation); United States v. White, 322 U.S. 694 (1944) (labor union); Bellis

proscription is designed to shield natural persons from sovereign compulsion to give testimony that might subject them to criminal liability;[5] this purpose generally can be achieved without extending the privilege to artificial entities that cannot, as such, be subjected to the same indignities or suffering as an individual.[6] A difficult case is presented when governmental compulsion is exerted to obtain incriminating communications that are attributable to a business group or entity, but the compulsion is resisted by an officer or agent of the enterprise on the ground that the group communications tend to incriminate him personally. Although an individual cannot be compelled to give testimony concerning his activity undertaken for the group when that activity would incriminate him,[7] he cannot bring within the privilege those communications of the entity (usually in the form of business records) that contain assertions or disclosures that incriminate him.[8] To hold otherwise would negate, as a practical matter, the principle that the privilege does not apply to collective enterprises,[9] for usually some individual within the association would claim that the entity's communications incriminate him personally.

The privilege does *not* permit the defense in a criminal trial to withhold all evidence or testimony which might incriminate the defendant; only testimonial communications made by the defendant himself are shielded. Thus, the defense may be compelled to produce damaging real evidence, investigative reports, or third-party statements elicited by the defense, without raising Fifth Amendment problems.[10]

v. United States, 417 U.S. 85 (1974) (partnership).

5. Compulsion need not consist of a direct, apparently enforceable order to speak, but can take a different form, such as a threat of job forfeiture, if Fifth Amendment rights are claimed. See Garrity v. New Jersey, 385 U.S. 493 (1967); Lefkowitz v. Turley, 414 U.S. 70 (1973). For a discussion of the policies and values underlying the privilege, see McCormick § 118. See also supra note 62.

6. McCormick, § 128, at 311. It has also been noted that a corporation derives its rights from the state that creates it, and states almost always reserve the right to inspect the corporate records. Id. Interestingly, this same argument has been squarely rejected in the context of corporate free-speech rights. First National Bank of Boston v. Bellotti, 435 U.S. 765 (1978), reh. denied, 438 U.S. 907 (1978).

7. Curcio v. United States, 354 U.S. 118 (1957).

8. United States v. White, 322 U.S. 694, 699–700 (1944). The sole proprietor, who is not a "representative" in any meaningful sense, is an exception; he cannot be compelled to turn over business records of the sole proprietorship which might incriminate him. See Bellis v. United States, 417 U.S. 85, 88 (1974).

9. Bellis v. United States, 417 U.S. 85, 89, (1974).

10. United States v. Nobles, 422 U.S. 225, 233–34 (1975) on remand, 522 F.2d

Read literally, the constitutional language conferring the privilege against self-incrimination would apply only in criminal proceedings against the holder and, further, might be construed as protecting only incriminating statements that the government sought to elicit from the accused after he was sworn as a witness. But as we shall see, the language has received a sympathetic reading, consistent with its underlying purpose of preventing the government from compelling an individual to make statements that contain incriminating assertions. To begin with, the privilege of the *accused* not to be a witness against himself has been construed to confer a right to remain off the witness stand—that is, the accused cannot be called or sworn as a witness if he claims his privilege.[11] He thus is able completely to avoid interrogation in a criminal trial in which he is a named defendant. Furthermore, the prosecutor cannot emasculate the privilege by forcing the accused to claim it in the jury's presence [12] or by commenting to the jury that the defendant refused to testify (thus inviting them to draw adverse inferences from his silence).[13]

Even this liberal judicial construction of the accused's privilege might not fulfill the broad purpose of the Fifth Amendment. If the privilege were confined to criminal trials where the claimant was the accused, individuals would have no protection against forced disclosure in other settings, such as a legislative investigation, a grand jury proceeding, or a civil trial. Coerced disclosures in any kind of proceeding might be used as evidence in a subsequent criminal prosecution to convict the person forced to speak, even though at this later trial he was not compelled to testify. To prevent this result, the privilege against self-incrimination has a second branch: not only does the accused enjoy a right not to be called to the stand in criminal proceedings against him, but *any witness* in a federal or state civil or criminal proceeding may

1274 (9th Cir.1975). However, some of the evidence developed in the course of preparing the defense may be protected from compelled disclosure by the attorney work-product doctrine. See Note 1 at the conclusion of Chapter IX.

11. See VIII Wigmore, § 2268, at 406 (McNaughton) and cases cited.

12. See, e.g., United States v. Housing Found. of America, 176 F.2d 665, 666 (3d Cir.1949); cf. San Fratello v. United States, 340 F.2d 560 (5th Cir.1965), reh. denied, 343 F.2d 711 (1965) (accused's wife forced to claim privilege in presence of jury).

13. Griffin v. California, 380 U.S. 609 (1965), reh. denied, 381 U.S. 957 (1965). Neither can the judge instruct the jury that adverse inferences are permissible. Ibid. See Grunewald v. United States, 353 U.S. 391 (1957) (improper to receive evidence that accused, who testified at trial, had invoked the Fifth Amendment before the grand jury).

decline to answer any question that raises an appreciable danger of incriminating him. In sum, the Fifth Amendment may be selectively invoked. When the privilege is thus claimed, a judge must decide, on the basis of the interrogator's question and all the surrounding circumstances, whether the answer would tend to incriminate the witness-claimant.[14] The fact that there is other inculpatory evidence against the witness is immaterial; the question is whether the witness's response is apt to be incriminating in nature. It is sufficient to sustain the privilege that the expected answer, though not incriminating on its face, appears to form part of the circumstantial evidence potentially available to convict the witness or that the response may lead to incriminating evidence.[15]

Certain points should be emphasized. *First,* the privilege is only available when there is a risk that any disclosures may be used against the declarant in a *criminal* proceeding. In determining the nature of the future proceeding (to which the presently sought testimony would relate), the legislative classification, as well as the nature of the attending penalties, is often helpful. But the Supreme Court has the final word with regard to what proceedings are criminal for purposes of applying the Fifth Amendment. For many years it was thought that any proceeding which threatened loss of liberty was "criminal" for Fifth Amendment purposes.[16] However, this view was firmly rejected in *Allen v. Illinois,* which declared that the only criterion is the extent to which the proceedings are punitive in *purpose.* The possibility of confinement (resulting, for example, from a finding of mental impairment) does not necessarily mean that a proceeding is criminal.[17]

14. McCormick § 139.

15. Blau v. United States, 340 U.S. 159, 161 (1950); Hashagen v. United States, 283 F.2d 345, 348 (9th Cir.1960); McCormick, § 138, at 340. See also Malloy v. Hogan, 378 U.S. 1, 11 (1964): "The privilege afforded not only extends to answers that would in themselves support a conviction . . . but likewise embraces those which would furnish a link in the chain of evidence needed to prosecute." Observe the difficulty of the judge's decision: he can not compel the witness to reveal his answer even for the limited purpose of making a ruling.

16. See In re Gault, 387 U.S. 1 (1967).

17. Allen v. Illinois, ___ U.S. ___, 106 S.Ct. 2988 (1986). Allen v. Illinois concerned a state "civil" commitment procedure for "sexually dangerous" sexual offenders. While the statute mandated treatment, and release once a "patient" was found no longer dangerous, commitment required the full criminal "proof beyond a reasonable doubt," and resulted in imprisonment in the state prison system. Nevertheless, the Court found these proceedings "civil," and thus outside the reach of the fifth amendment privilege. See C. White-

Second, the privilege only protects persons from compelled *communicative* activity; it is not available where official compulsion is used to obtain blood samples or fingerprints, or to have the accused engage in other noncommunicative activity such as participating in a lineup or wearing certain items of apparel.[18] A defendant can be compelled to speak for the purpose of voice identification or to provide a handwriting exemplar [19] so long as what is compelled is not a statement that is an incriminating assertion. For similar reasons, the Court has held that one involved in an accident may be required to give his name, since a name, like a fingerprint, provides mere identification, not "evidence of a testimonial or communicative nature." [20]

Third, pre-existing records, especially those of a business nature, may usually be obtained by the government without violating the privilege against self-incrimination. As noted earlier, corporations and similar entities cannot claim the privilege. Furthermore, the government can obtain the production of an individual's business records if these are required to be maintained in connection with a regulated activity and the government seeks the records as an integral part of regulatory enforcement.[21]

bread & C. Slobogin, Criminal Procedure, § 15.03, at 327–28 (2d ed.1986).

18. The principal case is Schmerber v. California, 384 U.S. 757 (1966) (blood sample). See also United States v. Wade, 388 U.S. 218, 221–23 (1967) (lineup); Holt v. United States, 218 U.S. 245 (1910) (apparel); State v. Stuard, 104 Ariz. 305, 452 P.2d 98 (1969) (fingerprints).

19. United States v. Chibbaro, 361 F.2d 365 (3d Cir.1966) (ordered to speak during lineup); Vigil v. People, 134 Colo. 126, 300 P.2d 545 (1956) (handwriting exemplars); State v. McKenna, 94 N.J.Super. 71, 226 A.2d 757 (1967) (D directed to submit to tape recording). See also Gilbert v. California, 388 U.S. 263, 266–67 (1967); 1 Louisell & Mueller, § 106, at 834–35.

20. California v. Byers, 402 U.S. 424, 431–33 (1971) (Burger, C.J., for the plurality). See Whitebread & Slobogin, supra note 17, at § 15.06. The result in this case was alternatively justified under the required records doctrine. See infra n. 21.

21. Grosso v. United States, 390 U.S. 62, 67–68 (1968). In a leading case, Shapiro v. United States, 335 U.S. 1 (1948), reh. denied, 335 U.S. 836 (1948), the government sought and obtained records maintained in connection with the Emergency Price Control Act of 1942. However, the *Shapiro* "required records" doctrine does not apply if the regulatory system seems targeted at a group inherently suspected of criminal activity, and deals with an area of the law "permeated with criminal statutes." Albertson v. Subversive Activities Control Board, 382 U.S. 70 (1965). See Whitebread & Slobogin, supra note 17, § 15.05, at 340–41. Accordingly, governmental attempts to compel disclosure under the federal wagering tax laws and the laws regulating firearms have been unsuccessful. See Marchetti v. United States, 390 U.S. 39 (1968); Haynes v. United States, 390 U.S. 85 (1968). But see California v. Byers, 402 U.S. 424 (1971) holding that the self-incrimination privilege is not offended by a state statute requiring a driver involved in an accident to stop and give

Even ordinary business records may be seized pursuant to a valid search warrant because such a seizure does not involve any incriminating assertion by the owner of the records.[22] A more difficult case is presented where officials issue a subpoena to an individual, directing him to produce specified business records. Does his act of compliance fall within the protection of the Fifth Amendment because obedience amounts to an implied assertion by the respondent that the records produced are those called for in the subpoena? The very act of producing the records could be an implied statement, that they are the papers sought, and this statement could be incriminating—for example by linking the producer with the records. In the vast majority of cases, the Supreme Court has said, the existence and authenticity of the documents subpoenaed is a "foregone conclusion," [23] so that the act of gathering and submitting to the government those documents requested will have no significant testimonial value, and thus receives no Fifth Amendment protection. The respondent is not called upon to verify the truth of any incriminating *contents* that may be within the records produced; he only produces specified documents that were voluntarily prepared at an earlier time. When, however, the existence or authenticity of the documents requested is not a foregone conclusion, but remains an open question, compulsory production may indeed violate the self-incrimination privilege.[24] Even in this circumstance, however, the *contents* of the documents remain unprivileged, and may be used if the documents are otherwise obtained.[25]

Another longstanding question relating to pre-existing documents has been whether the Fifth Amendment protects the

his name and address. The Supreme Court found that the statute in question was essentially regulatory, was directed at the driving public at large, and that disclosing identity was a neutral act that, itself, posed an insubstantial risk of self-incrimination.

22. Andresen v. Maryland, 427 U.S. 463 (1976).

23. Fisher v. United States, 425 U.S. 391, 411 (1976).

24. United States v. Doe, 465 U.S. 605 (1984). It is likely, however, that a subpoena that is so general in its description of the documents desired that it runs afoul of the fifth amendment will commonly lack the necessary specificity required by the fourth amendment.

25. Probably, the government can get access to the contents of such documents by granting use immunity for the "communicative" aspects of only the act of production, and then compelling production. See United States v. Doe, 465 U.S., at 617 n. 17. This tactic will not work, however, if the *existence* of the document is in question: in that event, use immunity would effectively mean the suppression of the document and all its fruits. See Mosteller, Simplifying Subpoena Law: Taking the Fifth Amendment Seriously, 73 Va.L.Rev. 1, 43–49 (1987).

seizure of intimate private papers (such as a diary) even though the means of obtaining the material involves no element of prohibited compulsion. While the argument can be made that there is a zone of privacy into which governmental intrusion will not be tolerated,[26] this contention does not fit comfortably within the modern Fifth Amendment framework. In recent years, the Supreme Court has broken away from the notion that the Fifth Amendment serves a privacy interest in addition to its prohibition against compulsion, and has resolved Fifth Amendment issues by asking whether coercive means were used to extract an incriminating communication.[27] The fact that a preexisting, noncoerced communication is private in nature is probably no longer a legitimate claim for protection, so long as the communication can be obtained and presented at trial without compelling the individual resisting disclosure to make incriminating statements.[28]

The *fourth* situation in which the Fifth Amendment privilege is unavailable is the instance in which the danger of new criminal liability has been removed, as, for example, where the claimant has already been convicted (or acquitted) of the act to be disclosed or where the prosecutor grants immunity from prosecution.[29] In Minnesota v. Murphy,[30] the Court held that a probation hearing is not a "separate criminal proceeding," and that criminal liability is

26. Early Supreme Court cases, starting with Boyd v. United States, 116 U.S. 616 (1886), pronounced that the fifth amendment shielded a person's private papers from seizure or production through either a search warrant or a subpoena. Subsequent cases have departed sharply from *Boyd* and have emasculated, if not in effect overruled, it. The cases are carefully reviewed in Note, Formalism, Legal Realism and Constitutionally Protected Privacy Under the Fourth and Fifth Amendments, 90 Harv.L.Rev. 945 (1977).

27. See Andresen v. Maryland, 427 U.S. 463 (1976); Fisher v. United States, 425 U.S. 391, 399, 401 (1976); United States v. Doe, 465 U.S. 605, 610 n. 8 (1984).

28. Despite the clear import of *Fisher,* supra note 27, a number of lower courts have continued to find in the fifth amendment a special protection for private papers. See, e.g., United States v. Davis, 636 F.2d 1028, 1042 (5th Cir.1981), cert. denied, 454 U.S. 862 (1981); United States v. Schlansky, 709 F.2d 1079, 1083 (6th Cir.1983), cert. denied, 465 U.S. 1099 (1984) (*Boyd* may still protect private diary); see cases collected in Mosteller, Simplifying Subpoena Law: Taking the Fifth Amendment Seriously, 73 Va.L.Rev. 1, 5 n. 10 (1987). The Supreme Court's yet clearer rejection of the privacy principle in *Doe,* supra note 27, may finally lay the *Boyd* privacy rationale to rest.

29. See McCormick, § 143, at 354. Statutory authority empowering the prosecutor to act is considered necessary in some jurisdictions. The federal immunity statute is found at 18 U.S. C.A. §§ 6001–6005. Other circumstances in which the privilege does not apply because there is no possibility of criminal liability include the expiration of the applicable statute of limitations and the pardon of the witness.

30. 465 U.S. 420 (1984), reh. denied, 466 U.S. 945 (1984).

not at issue. Consequently, provided the statements sought pose "no realistic threat" of new criminal liability, statements contrary to the prisoner's interests may be compelled in a probation hearing. Similarly, the privilege is not available to a defendant in a postconviction sentencing hearing,[31] except in capital sentencing proceedings. This last context, the Court has held, involves a new decision and a possible consequence at least as grave as the initial finding of guilt, so Fifth Amendment protections continue in force.[32]

Grants of immunity sometimes are employed in criminal investigations and prosecutions. Although prosecutors often grant immunity from prosecution for the *transaction* to which the compelled testimony relates (transactional immunity), the Constitution demands no broader immunity than a prohibition against *using the incriminating statements themselves* (use immunity), including any evidence derived therefrom, in a future prosecution.[33] Thus, under the latter, more narrow grant of immunity, the person ordered to give incriminating testimony is not necessarily free of prosecution for the transaction to which his statements relate. The government still could initiate a criminal prosecution if sufficient evidence could be obtained without the use of the incriminating statements or evidentiary "fruits" derived therefrom.

Immunized testimony generally may not be used at a subsequent trial to impeach the declarant, even if his later testimony is inconsistent with the earlier, immunized testimony.[34] This rule follows from the principle that, if testimony is to be compelled, the immunity given must be broad enough so that the declarant is not injured by his own compelled testimony. However, an exception is made if the declarant is subsequently prosecuted for perjuring himself in the course of giving the immunized testimony. In this context, the prosecutor may introduce into evidence not only the immunized statements alleged to be false, but as much of the testimony as is relevant to the charge of perjury.[35] The Supreme

31. Whitebread & Slobogin, supra note 17, § 15.03, at 328.

32. Estelle v. Smith, 451 U.S. 454 (1981).

33. Kastigar v. United States, 406 U.S. 441 (1972), reh. denied, 408 U.S. 931 (1972). See Whitebread & Slobogin, supra note 17, § 15.04, at 333–34.

34. New Jersey v. Portash, 440 U.S. 450 (1979).

35. United States v. Apfelbaum, 445 U.S. 115 (1980), on remand, 621 F.2d 62 (3d Cir.1980). The language of the majority suggests that immunized testimony could also be introduced to show that *later* testimony by the declarant was perjured, but there has been no

Court has explained that, absent such a "perjury exception" to immunity, an immunized witness could lie with complete impunity.

Immunity granted by one sovereign within the United States (for example, a state) must be respected by another sovereign therein (for example, the federal government or another state), at least to the extent of prohibiting any use or derivative use ("fruits") of the incriminating statement by the nongranting jurisdiction.[36] The leading case of Murphy v. Waterfront Commission [37] held that a witness given a state grant of immunity may not refuse to testify on the ground that no federal immunity has been granted. The witness is protected against federal prosecutorial use of the state testimony by the Fifth Amendment. Dictum in *Murphy* indicates that a similar constitutional prohibition would apply where the federal government confers immunity and a state thereafter seeks to prosecute.[38] Presumably, the same result would obtain between two states.[39]

Waiver, a doctrine common to all privileges, sometimes operates to defeat one's claim to a right to remain silent. While waiver commonly is defined as the intentional relinquishment of a known right, we have seen (in the context of other privileges) that a waiver also may occur by implication even when it is doubtful that the holder intended to forfeit a right or privilege. In short, considerations of fairness or some other policy may influence a court's decision concerning what actions constitute an implied waiver.

The extent of the waiver of the privilege against self-incrimination when the accused takes the stand and testifies provides a good example of the influence of these policies. Does the accused-witness have a right either to limit generally the scope of adverse interrogation or, as to particular questions, to claim the privilege

holding on this point. See id., at 133 (Brennan, J., concurring).

36. If transactional immunity granted by one sovereign—say a state—were fully binding on nongranting jurisdictions, a severe strain upon intergovernmental relations might result. For example, a state grant of immunity would prohibit any federal prosecutions concerning the transaction to which the compelled testimony related, even if the federal government had ample evidence to prosecute without reliance upon the compelled testimony. Accordingly, courts have recognized that a grant of transactional immunity by one jurisdiction binds other jurisdictions only to accord use immunity to the testimony compelled. See Agrella v. Rivkind, 404 So.2d 1113 (Fla.App.1981); McCormick, § 143, at 356 n. 19.

37. 378 U.S. 52 (1964).

38. Id. at 78. See Reina v. United States, 364 U.S. 507 (1960).

39. Lempert & Saltzburg at 719.

of an ordinary witness? Obviously, the accused's election to become a witness waives that branch of the privilege that shields him from giving any testimony. Beyond this, at a minimum the accused may be compelled to respond to cross-examination that tests the accuracy and truthfulness of his direct testimony. In short, he cannot put forward favorable testimony and expect to successfully resist cross-questions that challenge that testimony or call for the disclosure of closely-related incriminating facts. Furthermore, support can be found for declaring a constitutional waiver of broader scope: when the accused testifies concerning the offense for which he is on trial, he forfeits the privilege as to all facts relevant to that offense.[40] Some cases go beyond even this proposition and permit cross-examination concerning other offenses (in a multiple-count indictment) for which the accused is on trial, even though these other offenses were not the subject of his direct testimony.[41] Under either of these broader views, incriminating testimony can be compelled even if it does not relate to the direct testimony of the accused. The test is the relevance of the testimony to the present offense(s), and the fact that compelled testimony may have the effect of incriminating the accused as to the offense(s) charged, or even as to some other related offense, is not determinative.[42] This broad waiver may prevent the accused from electing to testify, and arguably exact too severe a penalty. But declaring a waiver only as to the particular subject of the accused's direct testimony allows him the perhaps unwarranted advantage of tailoring his testimony so as to unduly curtail adequate cross-examination—as where the accused testifies solely on the subject of alibi and (under the most limited view of waiver) waives his constitutional privilege only as to this subject.

Most cases, however, resolve the issue of the extent of the accused's waiver by holding that the testifying-accused waives the privilege against self-incrimination to a degree coextensive with the allowable scope of cross-examination.[43] An accused who takes the stand in a jurisdiction that follows the federal rule in limiting the scope of cross-examination to matters probed on direct exami-

40. McCormick, § 132, at 323–24.

41. Id. at 325 discussing People v. Perez, 65 Cal.2d 615, 55 Cal.Rptr. 909, 422 P.2d 597 (1967), writ dismissed, 395 U.S. 208 (1969).

42. However, the accused may still claim the privilege regarding an act for which he is not on trial when the prosecutor seeks to interrogate him as to this act for the purpose of impeaching the accused's testimony. McCormick, § 42, at 92. See also § 81.3B.

43. Brown v. United States, 356 U.S. 148, 154–55 (1958), reh. denied, 356 U.S. 948 (1958); see McCormick, § 132, at 323 n. 4.

nation[44] waives his Fifth Amendment privilege only to the extent of the testimonial "coverage" normally permitted by the application of the rule governing permissible scope.[45] Some jurisdictions, of course, employ the rule of wide-open cross-examination that permits adverse interrogation on any relevant subject about which the witness has knowledge. In these jurisdictions an accused's waiver of Fifth-Amendment rights has its broadest reach, and cross-examination may extend to any subject relevant to the offense for which the accused is on trial.[46]

The waiver rule that depends upon the allowable scope of cross-examination in each jurisdiction has the appeal of symmetry with the non-constitutional rule governing the scope of cross-examination. It raises troublesome questions, however, in the wake of Malloy v. Hogan,[47] which purported to impose a federal standard governing the privilege against self-incrimination. A uniform standard for determining the extent of the waiver imposed by the accused's testimony seems called for by the logic of *Malloy,* but the Supreme Court has not, in the decades since *Malloy,* shown any inclination to restrict state discretion in this area.[48] Uniformity is further impaired by the traditional rule which gives the trial judge broad discretion in governing the scope

44. See Fed.R.Evid. 611(b); Ch. IV, § 4.10.

45. 2 C. Wright & A. Miller, Federal Practice and Procedure, Criminal, § 407, at 451 (2d ed. 1982).

46. Even in a jurisdiction that limits the scope of cross to that of direct, a broad direct examination results in an equally sweeping forfeiture of the privilege. See Johnson v. United States, 318 U.S. 189 (1943), reh. denied, 318 U.S. 801 (1943). But even sweeping testimony on direct does not waive the privilege regarding misconduct not mentioned during direct, the sole purpose of which is to impeach the testimony of the accused. Fed.R.Evid. 608(b); McCormick, § 42, at 90.

47. 378 U.S. 1 (1964).

48. The cases leave the extent of the accused's waiver upon taking the stand somewhat in doubt. Johnson v. United States, 318 U.S. 189, 195–96 (1943), reh. denied, 318 U.S. 801 (1943), stated that the prosecutor could question the accused about matters relevant to the crime charged. Justice Frankfurter later said the accused waives his privilege against self-incrimination to the extent of the rule as to scope of cross-examination. Brown v. United States, 356 U.S. 148 (1958), reh. denied, 356 U.S. 948 (1958). Still again, the Court recently has said that the defendant waives the privilege as to "matters reasonably related to the subject of his direct examination," McGautha v. California, 402 U.S. 183, 215 (1971), reh. denied, 406 U.S. 978 (1972). However, this new formula does not seem to have narrowed the scope of the waiver in practice. See McCormick, § 132, at 324. See also, United States v. Nobles, 422 U.S. 225, 240 (1975), on remand, 522 F.2d 1274 (9th Cir.1975). See generally, 2 C. Wright & A. Miller, Federal Practice and Procedure, Criminal, § 407, at 451–52 (2d ed. 1982).

of cross-examination.[49] Such discretion is consistent with the purpose of the "scope rule" (which accommodates trial efficiency), but is not a proper means of governing a constitutional principle responsive to an entirely different set of values. McCormick advances the possibility of extending the waiver no further than necessary to provide a fair testing through cross-examination of the truth of the testimony given on direct.[50] Arguably, the government has no justification for a claim that the waiver should be more extensive than is necessary to enable the prosecutor to conduct a full and fair cross-examination of the accused's testimony.

This solution, however, is not without difficulties. It permits the accused to take the stand and, if he chooses, to confine his testimony to those portions of the case that cannot be weakened or destroyed by cross-examination. Because he does not (under this practice) forfeit Fifth Amendment protection as to those points not addressed in his direct testimony,[51] he insulates himself from cross-examination upon them. Presumably, he also can get an instruction that no adverse inferences may be drawn from his election to testify only as to part of the case.[52] Whether these consequences accommodate the interests of both the government and the accused raises difficult questions about the values served by the privilege. Regardless of how this particular balance is struck, it is hoped that courts will begin to determine the extent of waiver by reference to constitutional principles, rather than relying on the housekeeping rule that normally governs the scope of cross-examination.

The waiver doctrines applicable to the ordinary witness necessarily differ from those applicable to the accused. A witness compelled to take the stand and testify may invoke the Fifth Amendment selectively, declining to answer questions that require an incriminating response. If he does not claim his privilege, but

49. McCormick, § 132, at 280 (2d ed. 1972); 2 C. Wright & A. Miller, Federal Practice and Procedure, Criminal, § 416, at 539 (2d ed. 1982). See Fed.R.Evid. 611(b) (court has discretion to allow "inquiry into additional matters as if on direct examination," *i.e.* usually without leading questions).

50. McCormick, § 132, at 325.

51. This statement assumes that fair testing of the direct testimony can be had without probing those other parts of the case.

52. The argument supporting this instruction would be that the accused who gives limited testimony should not be disadvantaged when compared with the accused who wholly declines to take the stand; in neither instance should a penalty attach to the exercise of a fifth amendment right.

rather gives an incriminating answer, he waives the privilege for that response. Theoretically, this waiver, like other effective waivers of Fifth Amendment privileges, must be "voluntary and intelligent." But, quite unlike the rule in the custodial interrogation setting,[53] a trial witness is not entitled to be warned of his Fifth Amendment rights and, unless the privilege is affirmatively asserted, a valid waiver is *conclusively* presumed.[54] Further, once such a waiver occurs, the interrogator may be able to force disclosure of additional details or closely related information. The test appears to be whether further revelation significantly would add to the risk of prosecution. In a leading case, Rogers v. United States,[55] the witness voluntarily testified that, as an officer of the Communist Party, she once had possession of membership lists and party books. Claiming her Fifth Amendment privilege, she then declined to name the person to whom she had transferred these materials. The privilege was held unavailable: disclosure of her successor's identity posed no risk to her of incrimination beyond the information already revealed.[56]

Two aspects of waiver apply uniformly to the accused and the ordinary witness. First, in jurisdictions that permit the cross-examiner to impeach a witness by inquiring into prior "bad acts"—incidents that cast doubt on credibility but that have not been the subject of a conviction[57]—it is settled that as to these acts the privilege against self-incrimination is not waived by the act of testifying.[58] The second aspect of waiver common to the accused and an ordinary witness is the extent to which a waiver survives the proceeding in which it was given and operates to forfeit the privilege in a later inquiry. In general, the courts have rejected the extreme notions, on the one hand, of a permanent

53. See § 9.12.

54. See United States v. Kordel, 397 U.S. 1 (1970); Whitebread & Slobogin, supra note 17, § 15.05, at 337–38.

55. 340 U.S. 367 (1951).

56. See also Shendal v. United States, 312 F.2d 564, 566 (9th Cir.1963), finding the privilege still available for any new details which "might provide a link not already provided" in a case against the witness.

57. See Ch. VIII, § 8.3B.

58. As to the ordinary witness, there is no basis upon which to conclude a waiver has occurred. But where the accused elects to take the stand, it has been argued that he forfeits protection from questions designed to test credibility. Wisely, the courts have rejected this argument, favoring instead the right of the accused to testify regarding the crime charged without the penalty of forced incriminations regarding separate events. See Coil v. United States, 343 F.2d 573 (8th Cir.1965), cert. denied 382 U.S. 821 (1965); Fed.R.Evid. 608(b); McCormick, § 42, at 92.

waiver applying to any subsequent proceeding and, on the other, a waiver applying only to the examination in which it occurs.

Normally, a waiver operates for the entire trial or other proceeding in which it was rendered.[59] However, the clear majority rule is that waiver of the privilege in a *pretrial* proceeding does not preclude the witness from reasserting his privilege in a later trial concerning the same charge,[60] but at least one court has partially broken away from this traditional position. In Ellis v. United States [61] the United States Court of Appeals for the District of Columbia ruled that a *non-indicted* witness voluntarily testifying to incriminating matter before a grand jury may not invoke the privilege to avoid a second disclosure at a criminal trial following the grand jury's indictment of other persons. Among other reasons advanced in support of the holding, the court suggested that the trial testimony did not substantially raise the risk of prosecution so long as the witness was not compelled to disclose incriminating matters that were unknown to the government. Because the government obviously had access to the grand jury testimony, the compelled trial testimony posed little or no danger of additional incriminating matter.[62]

§ 9.12 The Privilege Against Self-Incrimination: Special Application in Custodial Interrogation

Among the recurring constitutional issues before the Supreme Court, few surpass in importance or frequency the question of what protections should surround a criminal defendant's out-of-court admission or confession to police or other investigatory officials. Generally, "confession" means an admission of guilt, including details of the accused's perpetration of the crime in question, while "admission" denotes an inculpatory statement which falls short of a complete acknowledgment of guilt. The

59. McCormick, § 132, at 326.

60. Whitebread & Slobogin, supra note 17, § 15.05, at 351; McCormick, § 140, at 348.

61. 135 U.S.App.D.C. 35, 416 F.2d 791 (D.C.Cir.1969).

62. Commentators are in disagreement as to whether *Ellis* was an unfortunate aberration, or a sign of an emerging trend. The second edition of McCormick took strong issue with the *Ellis* opinion, rebutting it point by point, McCormick, § 140, at 298–99 (2d ed. 1972), while the third edition deleted most of this discussion and dismissed *Ellis* as contrary to the "overwhelming weight of authority." McCormick, § 140, at 348. By contrast, Whitebread and Slobogin, writing even more recently, believe that a more expansive view of the effect of a pre-trial waiver, along the lines suggested by *Ellis,* "seems to be developing." Whitebread & Slobogin, supra note 17, § 15.05, at 351.

difference is unimportant in the present context, and the terms will be used interchangeably. Preliminarily, recall that the hearsay rule does not forbid the evidentiary use of the accused's extrajudicial inculpatory statements, because such remarks constitute party admissions and as such are admitted into evidence either as an exception to the hearsay rule or, under the Federal Rules of Evidence, as nonhearsay. But the constitutional inquiry implicates other concerns, e.g., the guarantees of due process, the right to counsel,[1] and most importantly for our purposes, the prohibition against compelled self-incrimination. This constitutional analysis usually is pursued in texts and courses devoted to criminal procedure or constitutional law. Consequently, what follows should be considered either a brief reminder or a bare introduction to a complex subject.

The judicial approach regarding the constitutional requirements governing criminal confessions initially developed along two lines: one based on the Supreme Court's review of confessions admitted in state criminal trials and the other based on the Court's review of confessions received in federal prosecutions. The differences in the Court's responses are now largely a matter of history, except for the enduring distinction that within the federal system the Supreme Court exercises an appellate supervisory power over lower federal courts and, by virtue of its place atop the national judicial hierarchy, may prescribe procedural rules and standards that govern federal proceedings.[2] To the

§ **9.12**

1. Miranda v. Arizona, 384 U.S. 436 (1966), reh. denied, 385 U.S. 890 (1966); Escobedo v. Illinois, 378 U.S. 478 (1964). See generally McCormick §§ 147, 150–55. See also Id. at § 144 where the author raises doubts about placing a confession within the traditional explanation of a party admission.

2. In McNabb v. United States, 318 U.S. 332 (1943), reh. denied, 319 U.S. 784 (1943), the Court, citing a federal statute that entitled an arrested person to be brought before a judicial officer, held inadmissible statements obtained by federal agents during a period of unnecessary delay before presenting the suspect to a magistrate. This judicial officer performs such functions as advising the arrestee of his rights, inquiring into the need for a preliminary hearing, and setting bail. Later, in Mallory v. United States, 354 U.S. 449 (1957), the Court made it clear that a delay for *purposes of interrogation* was "unnecessary" within the meaning of Rule 5(a) of the Federal Rules of Criminal Procedure which, like the statute in *McNabb,* called for presentation without unnecessary delay. The so-called *McNabb-Mallory* Rule operated within the federal system and resulted in excluding statements obtained during the forbidden period of delay. In 1968 Congress intervened and prescribed that statements made within six hours of arrest should not be excluded on the sole ground of delay in bringing the arrestee before a judicial officer. See Title II of the Omnibus Crime Control and Safe Streets Act of 1968, 18 U.S.C.A. § 3501(c). Statements made after the six-hour pe-

extent these rules are not constitutionally required, they are not binding upon the states. By contrast, the constitutional standards presently governing the admissibility of confessions in federal and state proceedings are uniform. For example, the incorporation of the Fifth Amendment privilege against self-incrimination into the Fourteenth Amendment in 1964 [3] makes the privilege directly applicable to the states and provides a single constitutional standard for the national and state sovereignties. The evolution of this standard is a fascinating chapter in constitutional history, the final pages of which are yet to be written by the United States Supreme Court.

In Brown v. Mississippi,[4] decided in 1936, the Supreme Court overturned, for the first time, a state conviction based upon an involuntary confession which had been obtained after police had severely beaten the accused. Decided almost thirty years before the incorporation of the Fifth Amendment privilege into the Fourteenth, the Court based its holding on the due process clause of the Fourteenth Amendment.[5] This clause was read as prohibiting state courts from basing a conviction upon evidence procured by state authorities through coercion.[6] The court's ruling was narrow, covering only the situation where physical abuse produced an involuntary confession of doubtful reliability that constituted the *sole* evidence of guilt. But subsequent rulings made it clear that coerced confessions would not be tolerated even where there was other evidence of guilt,[7] where coercion took a subtle form such as psychological pressure,[8] or where promises of favored treatment were given in return for a confession.[9] These post-*Brown* cases stressed that the probable unreliability of a coerced confession was not the only basis for its exclusion; other bases

riod may also be admissible if the delay in presentation was reasonable. Id.

3. Malloy v. Hogan, 378 U.S. 1 (1964).

4. 297 U.S. 278 (1936).

5. The Court stated that the privilege against self-incrimination was not at issue in its holding. 297 U.S. at 285.

6. Id. at 286.

7. Payne v. Arkansas, 356 U.S. 560 (1958).

8. Ashcraft v. Tennessee, 322 U.S. 143 (1944) (sustained interrogation over thirty-six hour period); see also Haynes v. Washington, 373 U.S. 503 (1963) (threat of continued incommunicado detention); Rogers v. Richmond, 365 U.S. 534 (1961) (police tell suspect his ill wife has been arrested for questioning).

9. See, e.g., Lynumn v. Illinois, 372 U.S. 528 (1963) (promise that cooperation would mean easier treatment coupled with threat that failure to comply would mean that conviction would result in loss of children). McCormick notes inconsistent results in cases where promises have been made. See McCormick, § 148, at 376–81.

included the Court's unwillingness to tolerate improper police practices, its view that tactics designed to produce self-incrimination were incompatible with the Anglo-American adversarial system, and its desire to protect the values underlying the Fifth Amendment.[10] Thus the policies and values thought to underlie the Fifth Amendment privilege against self-incrimination greatly influenced the Court's determination of when activity by state—and for that matter federal—officials resulted in a violation of due process.[11]

Brown and its progeny required that a court determine the voluntariness of a confession, and thus its admissibility, by assessing all of the circumstances that attended the rendering of the confession. This "totality-of-the-circumstances" test took account of such variables as physical abuse, psychological pressures generated by substantial questioning or incommunicado detention, police artifice, the age and experience of the suspect, whether he had been advised of his right to remain silent, and whether he had been accorded a prompt hearing before a magistrate or other judicial officer.[12] Imprecision necessarily attended assessment of these and other variables, and the test predictably produced uncertainty and conflict among lower courts. It was not uncommon to find disagreement between state and federal judges reviewing the same confession, or between federal judges themselves.[13] Even the

10. See Blackburn v. Alabama, 361 U.S. 199 (1960); McCormick, § 147, at 373–74.

11. Until Malloy v. Hogan, 378 U.S. 1 (1964), the use of pre-trial confessions in federal cases was governed only by the due process clause of the fifth amendment. The existence of coercion was determined by assessing the same factors considered by the Supreme Court when reviewing state cases under the fourteenth amendment—although the federal courts may have been held to a higher standard. But in *Malloy,* the Court, citing the long-neglected case of Bram v. United States, 168 U.S. 532 (1897), declared that the federal standard was in fact based on the self-incrimination clause. *Malloy,* supra at 7. Because *Malloy* also "incorporated" the self-incrimination clause into the fourteenth amendment due process requirements, see supra text at notes 7–10, it both shifted the basis of the law of confessions, and made the new standard uniformly applicable to both state and federal courts.

12. C. Whitebread & C. Slobogin, Criminal Procedure § 16.02 (1986); McCormick, §§ 147–149.

13. A case in point is Davis v. North Carolina, 384 U.S. 737 (1966). After Davis was convicted in the state trial court, he initiated appellate proceedings within the state system, where evidentiary admission of his admission was sustained. See State v. Davis, 253 N.C. 86, 116 S.E.2d 365 (1960), cert. denied, 365 U.S. 855 (1961). Subsequently, Davis brought a collateral attack by filing a petition for habeas corpus in a federal district court. The use of the challenged confession was approved by the district court, 221 F.Supp. 494 (E.D.N.C. 1963) and by a split court of appeals, 339 F.2d 770 (4th Cir.1964), but the

Supreme Court varied its inquiry, scrutinizing each of the circumstances in some cases,[14] while in others pronouncing the circumstances "inherently coercive" without undertaking any inquiry into the effect of each separate pressure upon the subject.[15]

Despite the vicissitudes of the totality-of-circumstances test, the cases decided by the Court kept moving toward more rigorous control of state police and judicial practices.[16] In other areas of criminal procedure, the Court complemented this trend by ordering the states to exclude evidence derived from unlawful searches [17] and increasing its emphasis upon the accused's right to counsel.[18] The right to counsel was extended to pre-trial events (such as arraignment and pleading) whenever these events constituted a "critical stage" [19] in the criminal process. In one notable decision, Escobedo v. Illinois,[20] the court appeared to be edging toward a right to counsel during police interrogation. A divided court held that where a police investigation

> is no longer a general inquiry into an unsolved crime but has begun to focus on a particular suspect, the suspect has been taken into police custody, the police carry out a process of interrogations that lends itself to eliciting incriminating statements, the suspect has requested and been denied an opportunity to consult with his lawyer, and the police have not effectively warned him of his absolute constitutional right to

Supreme Court reversed. Davis v. North Carolina, supra.

14. See, e.g., Greenwald v. Wisconsin, 390 U.S. 519 (1968); Lynumn v. Illinois, 372 U.S. 528 (1963).

15. See Haynes v. Washington, 373 U.S. 503 (1963); Ashcraft v. Tennessee, 322 U.S. 143 (1944).

16. Compare, e.g., Brown v. Mississippi, 297 U.S. 278 (1936), with Haynes v. Washington, 373 U.S. 503 (1963).

17. Mapp v. Ohio, 367 U.S. 643 (1961), reh. denied, 368 U.S. 871 (1961). The reach of *Mapp* was limited by United States v. Leon, 468 U.S. 897 (1984) and Massachusetts v. Sheppard, 468 U.S. 981 (1984) (evidence admissible if seized on basis of objective good faith belief).

18. Gideon v. Wainwright, 372 U.S. 335 (1963), on remand, 153 So.2d 299 (Fla.1963) (right to appointed counsel at trial of indigents in all serious cases); Douglas v. California, 372 U.S. 353 (1963), reh. denied, 373 U.S. 905 (1963) (right to appointed counsel exists through the first appeal of right).

19. See White v. Maryland, 373 U.S. 59 (1963) (initial appearance before judicial officer is critical when accused must enter plea and adverse effects flow from his election of plea); Hamilton v. Alabama, 368 U.S. 52 (1961), on remand, 273 Ala. 504, 142 So.2d 868 (1962) (arraignment is critical stage when certain defenses are lost if not raised during this procedure). The Court has subsequently characterized certain post-trial procedures as critical. See, e.g., Mempa v. Rhay, 389 U.S. 128 (1968) (probation revocation critical when this proceeding includes sentencing).

20. 378 U.S. 478 (1964).

> remain silent, the accused has been denied "the Assistance of Counsel" in violation of the Sixth Amendment to the Constitution as "made obligatory upon the States by the Fourteenth Amendment" . . . and that no statement elicited by police during the interrogation may be used against him at a criminal trial.[21]

Thus, pre-trial interrogation became a point of confluence where important rights, derived from several parts of the Constitution, merged to restrict police practices. *Escobedo* suggested the possibility that the right to counsel during interrogation would emerge in a future case as the most significant constitutional principle governing confessions.

That case turned out to be Miranda v. Arizona,[22] regarded as one of the most significant cases decided by the Supreme Court during this century. In *Miranda,* the Court abandoned the totality-of-circumstances test and set out specific procedural steps for all custodial interrogations. Relying primarily upon the Fifth Amendment right not to incriminate oneself, the Court found that, absent a waiver, the assistance of counsel during interrogation was necessary to vindicate this right. Nor would such waivers be readily implied: when a suspect "in custody . . . or otherwise deprived of his freedom of action in any significant way," [23] makes an inculpatory statement in the absence of an attorney, said the Court, "a heavy burden rests on the government to demonstrate that the defendant knowingly and intelligently waived his privilege against self-incrimination and his right to retained or appointed counsel." [24] Then, in an unusual technique of constitutional adjudication, the Court prescribed an elaborate set of procedural rules which establish *minimum* standards for custodial interrogation. If these were not followed, there arose an irrebuttable presumption that there was no adequate waiver of the right to have counsel present, and consequently, that any statements made must be excluded. Specifically, the Court provided:

> 1. Before questioning begins, the suspect must be clearly advised of his right to remain silent and he must be warned that anything he says can be used against him in court.

21. Id. at 490–91.

22. 384 U.S. 436 (1966), reh. denied, 384 U.S. 436 (1966).

23. Miranda v. Arizona, 384 U.S. 436, 478 (1966), reh. denied, 384 U.S. 436 (1966).

24. Id. at 475.

2. The suspect also must be told, prior to questioning, that he has the right to a lawyer's assistance before and during interrogation and that a lawyer will be appointed to assist him if he cannot afford to retain one.

3. The suspect may exercise his right to remain silent or to engage counsel at any time prior to or during interrogation. If the suspect indicates that he wishes to remain silent, there can be no interrogation; if interrogation is in progress when he manifests his desire to remain silent, questioning must cease. Similarly, if the suspect indicates that he wants an attorney, there can be no further questioning until an attorney is present.

4. Unless the suspect is expressly and fully warned of his rights to silence and counsel and there is compliance with his decision, then no statement given by him can be used at trial to establish his guilt.

Satisfaction of these requirements avoids *per se* inadmissibility, but does not, without more, establish admissibility. An effective waiver cannot be implied from the bare fact that a suspect made a statement after receiving his warnings; the prosecution must make at least some further showing that a knowing, intelligent, and voluntary waiver was in fact made.[25] Still, an *express* waiver is not required,[26] and where warnings have been given, lower courts commonly imply a waiver based on only a modest additional showing.[27] However, where coercion, deception, or overly manipulative interrogation tactics negate the voluntariness of the waiver, or where low intelligence, intoxication, or some other factor indicates that the waiver was not "knowing and intelligent," even an express waiver will not be effective.[28]

Subsequent cases have addressed important questions left unanswered by *Miranda.* It is now settled that *Miranda* applies even where the detention is for a minor offense.[29] By contrast, *Miranda* does not apply at all when the interrogation is by private persons, such as private security guards.[30] Rejecting arguments

25. *Miranda,* 384 U.S. at 475; Tague v. Louisiana, 444 U.S. 469 (1980), on remand, 381 So.2d 507 (La.1980).

26. North Carolina v. Butler, 441 U.S. 369 (1979).

27. See, e.g., United States v. Pheaster, 544 F.2d 353, 368 (9th Cir. 1976), cert. denied, 429 U.S. 1099 (1977).

28. McCormick, § 153, at 398–403; *Miranda,* 384 U.S. at 475.

29. Berkemer v. McCarty, 468 U.S. 420 (1984); Whitebread & Slobogin, supra note 12, § 16.05, at 391.

30. Whitebread & Slobogin, supra note 12, § 16.06, at 391–92; McCormick, § 151, at 390.

that the information is necessary for the suspect to make a "knowing and informed" decision as to whether to waive his rights, the Supreme Court has held that the suspect need not be told the nature of the charges about which the police intend to question him.[31] While interrogation must cease if the suspect indicates that he wants an attorney present, it will not be *presumed* that the suspect wishes to exercise this right; interrogation may continue unless the suspect gives some indication that he desires an attorney.[32] Further, unless the defendant has requested the presence of an attorney, the fact that the police have blocked efforts by the defendant's attorney to contact the defendant does not violate the Fifth Amendment, or render statements made by the defendant inadmissible.[33] The reason this obstructive conduct is not unconstitutional is that the Fifth and Sixth Amendment rights implicated in the right to have counsel present during questioning are strictly personal rights, claimable only by the defendant.

A suspect who has asked to have an attorney present during any further questioning may of course change his mind. Cautious lest police improperly induce such changes of heart, the Supreme Court announced in Edwards v. Arizona[34] that statements given in the absence of counsel, but after counsel has been requested, are admissible only if 1) the suspect initiated the renewed discussion with the police, and 2) there is some further showing that the suspect knowingly and voluntarily chose to waive his right to have counsel present.

The *Miranda* opinion touched off a heated debate that continues today. Critics of the decision argue that it unnecessarily impedes law enforcement; proponents assert that the protective steps mandated by the Court are necessary to protect fundamental rights. Two years after *Miranda*, Congress reacted by passing a statute that applies to the federal courts and purports to negate the *Miranda* ruling that proper warnings are prerequisites to

31. Colorado v. Spring, ___ U.S. ___, 107 S.Ct. 851 (1987).

32. Smith v. Illinois, 469 U.S. 91 (1984); Whitebread & Slobogin, supra note 12, § 16.05, at 384. However, ambiguities as to whether any such "indication" was given will generally be resolved in favor of the defendant.

33. Moran v. Burbine, 475 U.S. 412, (1986); Whitebread & Slobogin, supra note 12, § 16.05, at 385.

34. 451 U.S. 477 (1981), reh. denied, 452 U.S. 973 (1981); Whitebread & Slobogin, supra note 12, § 16.05, at 383–84.

admissibility.[35] Under the statutory approach, which reinstates a totality-of-circumstances test, a confession is admissible if voluntary. Failure of the police to warn the defendant of his rights or the absence of counsel during questioning are merely circumstances to be considered in determining voluntariness. Even though the *Miranda* court did leave the way open for Congress or the states to devise alternative means of protecting the custodial rights of the accused, it is difficult to read the *Miranda* opinion as sanctioning a return to the uncertain protection of the indefinite "totality" approach. And in fact, perhaps because its constitutionality is so widely doubted,[36] the statute has not significantly affected the practices of the federal authorities, and has therefore received little attention in the courts.

Although the early legislative attempt to vitiate *Miranda* was ineffective, the Supreme Court, reflecting the views of a changing membership,[37] has since qualified *Miranda* in significant ways. The Court has emphasized that unwarned questioning does not necessarily mean that any statement given is *actually* coerced, involuntary, and therefore unconstitutionally obtained; *Miranda* merely created a presumption to that effect, to deter improper police interrogation techniques.[38] If such a statement is offered as evidence in the case in chief against the declarant, the presumption is irrebuttable; the statement cannot come in. In other contexts, however, the trial court may enquire behind the presumption, essentially returning to a due process totality of the circumstances test for coercion. For instance, statements obtained in violation of *Miranda* or *Edwards* may be used at trial to impeach a defendant whose testimony is inconsistent with the earlier statement.[39] In approving this collateral use, the Court distinguished *Miranda* on the ground that in that case the state-

35. Omnibus Crime Control and Safe Streets Act of 1968, 18 U.S.C.A. § 3501.

36. See, e.g., McCormick, § 154, at 405; Whitebread & Slobogin, supra note 12, § 16.08, at 410.

37. Of the nine justices presently composing the Court, only Justices Brennan and White participated in the *Miranda* decision; Justice White dissented.

38. Michigan v. Tucker, 417 U.S. 433, 446 (1974); Oregon v. Elstad, 470 U.S. 298, 308 (1985), on remand, 78 Or. App. 362, 717 P.2d 174 (1986), review denied, 302 Or. 36, 726 P.2d 935 (1986).

39. Harris v. New York, 401 U.S. 222 (1971); Oregon v. Hass, 420 U.S. 714 (1975); Whitebread & Slobogin, supra note 12, § 16.05, at 392–94. Some states, relying on state grounds, do not recognize an impeachment exception to the *Miranda* rule. See, e.g., People v. Disbrow, 16 Cal.3d 101, 127 Cal.Rptr. 360, 545 P.2d 272 (1976); McCormick, § 162, at 438. The *Disbrow* case was nullified by the adoption of Cal.Const. art. 1, § 28. See People v. McCarthy,

ments had been used by the state to establish guilt.[40] Ascribing to *Miranda* a primary purpose of preventing improper police conduct, the majority concluded that the *Miranda* rules had a sufficient deterrent effect on proscribed activity if tainted statements offered to establish guilt were excluded. To apply *Miranda* to evidence used to impeach credibility would unnecessarily allow perjurious testimony to go unchallenged because of improper investigatory procedures.[41] However, a statement that was "involuntary" under the due process, totality-of-circumstances criteria cannot be used for *any* purpose.[42]

Again on the grounds that a narrow exclusionary rule provides adequate deterrence to improper police interrogation, the Court has declined to extend the "fruit of the poisonous tree" concept to exclude evidence gained as a result of a statement obtained in violation of *Miranda* or *Edwards.*[43] As in the impeachment context, statements obtained through coercion violative of due process are more strongly condemned, and any evidence gained as a result of such a statement *will* be excluded.[44]

In New York v. Quarles,[45] the Supreme Court created a major exception to the bright-line *Miranda* rule that warnings must precede custodial interrogation. When the *public safety* reasonably requires the speedy discovery of information probably known to the suspect, ("Where did you put the bomb?"), *Miranda* warnings need not be recited. The Court reasoned that the warnings might dissuade the suspect from giving the needed information, and that, in such emergency situations, "the public safety outweighs the need for the prophylactic rule protecting the Fifth Amendment's privilege against self-incrimination."[46] However, statements made in response to *Quarles* interrogation, and evi-

182 Cal.App.3d 822, 227 Cal.Rptr. 457 (1986).

40. *Harris,* 401 U.S. at 224–25. The controlling precedent was found to be Walder v. United States, 347 U.S. 62 (1954), a case in which the Court approved impeaching questions about a heroin capsule that had been illegally seized in connection with a narcotics offense other than the one charged. The government was seeking to impeach Walder's assertion, made during his direct examination, that he never in his life handled narcotics.

41. 401 U.S. at 225–26.

42. Mincey v. Arizona, 437 U.S. 385, 398 (1978).

43. Oregon v. Elstad, 470 U.S. 298 (1985), on remand, 78 Or.App. 362, 717 P.2d 174 (1986), review denied, 302 Or. 36, 726 P.2d 935 (1986).

44. Whitebread & Slobogin, supra note 12, § 16.06, at 396.

45. 467 U.S. 649 (1984), on remand, 63 N.Y.2d 923, 483 N.Y.S.2d 678, 473 N.E.2d 30 (1984).

46. *Quarles,* 467 U.S. at 657.

dence discovered as a result of such statements, are not automatically admissible against the declarant. The *Quarles* public safety exception eliminates only the *Miranda* presumption of inadmissibility; traditional due process voluntariness requirements must still be met, or the statement and its fruits are inadmissible.[47]

The passage of two decades since the *Miranda* ruling, and the creation of several important exceptions to its *per se* exclusionary rule, have reduced the chance that *Miranda* itself will ever be reversed. However, important and controversial questions concerning the proper reach of the *Miranda* principle remain to be settled, and are certain to demand continuing attention from the Supreme Court. Particularly difficult issues include the question of what constitutes an adequate request for counsel so that interrogation must stop under *Edwards,*[48] and what will suffice as a suspect-initiated waiver of *Miranda* rights, after those rights have once been claimed.[49] The same difficult questions arise under the Sixth Amendment right to counsel, so that statements that were obtained voluntarily and in compliance with *Miranda* and *Edwards* may nevertheless be found inadmissible under the Sixth Amendment.[50] These issues continue to divide the Supreme Court, so their future treatment may depend to a considerable extent on personnel changes on the Court, rather than on more predictable doctrinal evolution.

Notes

1. *Attorney-Client Privilege: Related Rules and Doctrines.* The attorney-client privilege gives absolute protection to communications that meet the requisite criteria. As we have seen, the privilege belongs to the client who alone has the right to invoke or waive it—although he may make or relinquish his claim through an agent. The core of the privilege is the protection of certain confidential communications. Several related doctrines also protect communications made in the context of legal consultation or representation.

47. *Quarles,* 467 U.S. at 655 n. 5.

48. Compare Smith v. Illinois, 469 U.S. 91 (1984) (ambiguous statements by suspect held sufficient to trigger *Edwards*), with Connecticut v. Barrett, ___ U.S. ___, 107 S.Ct. 828 (1987) (suspect's statement that he would not make a written statement without an attorney present held not to foreclose continued oral interrogation by police).

49. See generally Brewer v. Williams, 430 U.S. 387, 401–03, 405–06 (1977), reh. denied 431 U.S. 925 (1977).

50. See, e.g., Maine v. Moulton, 474 U.S. 159 (1985) (surreptitious post-indictment questioning by undercover informant held to violate right to counsel).

Both the Code of Professional Responsibility (and the more recent Model Rules of Professional Conduct) impose on attorneys the obligation of preserving their clients' confidences and secrets. See Model Code of Professional Responsibility DR 4–101. This obligation is independent of the attorney-client privilege and includes communications outside its ambit. An improper disclosure by the attorney can result in disciplinary action by appropriate authorities within the bar or court system in which the offending attorney has membership.

The work-product doctrine is usually traced to the case of Hickman v. Taylor, 329 U.S. 495 (1947). In recent years, the central features of the doctrine typically are found in a rule of court or statute. Federal Rule of Civil Procedure 26(b)(3) sets forth the basic rules of work product; subsection (b)(4) extends the work-product doctrine (or at least its rationale) to include experts engaged by a party to assist in trial preparation. Generally speaking, the work-product doctrine extends *conditional immunity* from discovery or disclosure to written materials prepared in "anticipation of litigation." Typically, the protected materials are prepared by the lawyer, but materials prepared by others—such as an agent, consultant, or the party himself—are also conditionally immune. The court may order discovery if the party seeking the materials shows substantial need for them or, in the case of an expert who will not be called as a witness, exceptional need. The requisite showing of need varies with the particular context and is affected by the party's ability to secure unprotected evidence that is the substantial equivalent of that sought.

Note the major differences between the protection afforded by the attorney-client privilege and that given by the work-product doctrine. First, the attorney-client privilege belongs to the client; work-product protection, on the other hand, can only be invoked by the lawyer. Second, the attorney-client privilege attaches when the client first consults the lawyer, even if no litigation is planned or pending. By contrast, work-product protection only attaches to materials prepared in "anticipation of litigation, or for trial." (Fed.R.Civ.Proc. 26(b)(3)). Third, work-product protection applies principally to written materials and tangible things; the definition of communication in the law of attorney-client privilege is, as we have seen, far more expansive. Finally, the attorney-client privilege is absolute and cannot be overridden by the court; by contrast, a court can defeat work-product immunity if the circumstances justify the disclosure. For an analysis of the privilege and the doctrine, see Cohn, The Work-Product Doctrine: Protection, Not Privilege, 71 Georgetown L.J. 917 (1983).

The Sixth Amendment, by conferring the right to effective counsel, adds a possible constitutional dimension to the attorney-client privilege in criminal cases. The relationship between the amendment and the privilege is carefully summarized in Weinstein & Mansfield, et al., at 1475–77.

2. *Priest-Penitent Privilege.* A vast majority of states recognize a clergyman-penitent privilege shielding confidential statements made to a clergyman in his religious office. VIII Wigmore § 2395 (McNaughton). The lay communicant is the only holder of the privilege, though the clergyman is presumptively entitled to assert the privilege on the absent layman's behalf. Note that this privilege has never been held to be constitutionally required, though it does seem to be recognized as a matter of federal common law under Fed.R.Evid. 501. See 2 Louisell & Mueller, § 214, at 834. The limits of the privilege vary among the jurisdictions. A few states adhere to the pattern of Rule 29 of the 1953 Uniform Rules of Evidence, limiting the privilege to statements that are the outgrowth of "enjoined religious discipline." Proposed Federal Rule 506, however, extended the privilege to cover any confidential communication made "to a clergyman in his professional character as a spiritual advisor," and most states have now adopted a wider privilege along this line. See 2 Weinstein & Berger, § 506[04]; Unif.R.Evid. 505 (1974); Prop. Fed.R.Evid. 506.

3. *Journalist's Privilege.* A novel but increasingly accepted privilege is one protecting confidential relationships between a journalist and his source. A substantial number of states have enacted "shield laws" which, though they vary in detail, provide the newsman with qualified immunity from forced disclosure of the identity of his source. See statutes listed in Caldero v. Tribune Publishing Co., 98 Idaho 288, 562 P.2d 791, 794 n. 1 (1977), cert. denied, 434 U.S. 930 (1977). The journalist, not his source, is the holder of this privilege. The privilege is not absolute; it may be overridden if an adequate showing of necessity is made. While the Supreme Court has rejected the notion that the First Amendment places journalists' secrets beyond the reach of government enquiry, Branzburg v. Hayes, 408 U.S. 665 (1972), and although no journalist's privilege was included in the Proposed Rules, a qualified privilege protecting not only the identity of sources, but unpublished information gained in the course of journalistic investigation is now widely accepted as part of the federal common law under Rule 501. See cases collected in 2 Louisell & Mueller § 238.

The privilege is motivated by concern that forced disclosure of sources would make potential informants much less willing to talk to newsgatherers, and would thus deprive the public of important information. The privilege is less than absolute because it seems unacceptable that reporters should be entirely excused from the general duty to give whatever evidence one has to aid the state in the pursuit of justice and the suppression of crime. The privilege is accorded less respect in criminal prosecutions, where the cost of withholding evidence seems higher than in the civil context, 2 Louisell & Mueller, § 238, at 1120–21, and is least likely to succeed when a journalist's evidence is sought by a criminal defendant. See generally McCormick, § 76.2, at 184–85.

4. *State Secrets.* The federal government is entitled to prevent the disclosure of military or state secrets if it can demonstrate a reasonable likelihood of danger to national security or of injury to international relations. This privilege is recognized in the leading case of United States v. Reynolds, 345 U.S. 1 (1953), where the Supreme Court considered, among other things, the kind of showing the government must make to invoke the privilege and the question of which governmental official should make this showing. Drawing on English and American precedents, the Court found the existence of the privilege in no doubt and went on to declare that the claim to privilege should be advanced by the governmental department head who had responsibility for the matter in question. The governmental officer must give the matter his "actual personal consideration," thereby assuring that the privilege will not be lightly invoked. See generally 2 Louisell & Mueller § 226.

Once the privilege is claimed, the judge "must determine whether the circumstances are appropriate for the claim of privilege, and yet do so without forcing a disclosure of the very thing the privilege is designed to protect." 345 U.S. 1 at 7–8. The *Reynolds* Court thought that the judge's role in resolving a claim to the privilege against self-incrimination provided a helpful analogy. In many cases the attending circumstances, including the statement of the department head, will indicate that exposure of the evidence in question poses a reasonable likelihood of danger to national interests. In such instances, the judge need not, and in particularly sensitive cases should not, order an *in camera* examination. The Court, however, left open the possibility of inspection of the disputed evidence by the judge, and courts have shown an increasing willingness to adopt this procedure since Congress in 1974 amended the Freedom of Information Act so as to heighten judicial scrutiny of claims of privilege for government documents. See 2 Louisell & Mueller, § 227, at 977–86. While the privilege is absolute where it applies, the judge's inquiry to make certain the privilege is properly invoked should increase in rigor in proportion to the degree of necessity demonstrated by the party seeking the evidence. See generally, 2 Louisell & Mueller § 227. See also Prop.Fed.R.Evid. 509. For an analogous state statute, see West's Ann.Cal.Evid. Code § 1040. See also VIII Wigmore § 2378 (McNaughton).

Suppose an appropriate governmental unit, resisting the disclosure of evidence, makes a convincing showing of necessity so that the privilege clearly applies. If the government is a party to the action in which it invokes the privilege, may the judge take steps (such as striking a witness's testimony or finding certain facts against the government) to counterbalance the disadvantage suffered by the adverse party through loss of the privileged evidence? Clearly, strict measures, extending as far as dismissal, can be applied where the government invokes a claim of privilege in a criminal action in which it is the prosecuting party. Compensatory measures in civil cases also are appropriate where the government is a party and invokes the privilege, thereby denying the adversary access to relevant evidence. See McCormick, § 109, at 268. In a civil case, what difference, if any, does it make whether the government is a plaintiff or a defendant?

5. *Executive Privilege.* In the wake of the Watergate scandal and the case of United States v. Nixon, 418 U.S. 683 (1974), the privilege of the President to withhold evidence concerning high-level communications within the Executive Department attracted a great deal of scholarly attention. Nevertheless, because the issue has been litigated on only a few occasions in American history, the features of the privilege cannot be sketched with much detail or confidence. That the privilege exists is undoubted; it is considered essential to ensure free and open discussion among persons responsible for executive decisions, and is also believed to follow from the principle of separation of powers. On the other hand, it is clear from *Nixon* that the privilege is not absolute; it must give way in criminal cases when a showing of necessity is made that outweighs the need for executive privacy concerning the information sought. The *Nixon* court cautiously declined to specify how this balancing is to be carried out, and it is unlikely that claims of executive privilege will ever be litigated with sufficient frequency, or under sufficiently apolitical circumstances, for a coherent standard to emerge.

Claims of executive privilege are accorded less deference than assertions of privilege based on national security considerations, as is evidenced by the fact that *in camera* review and redaction of the assertedly privileged material seems to be the regular procedure in executive privilege cases once the party seeking the evidence makes an adequate showing of need. *Nixon,* 418 U.S. at 714–16. Though the "free discussion" rationale supporting executive privilege would seem to call for privacy extending well beyond the term of an administration—perhaps as long as anyone quoted in the sought materials remains active in public affairs—it may be that the privilege will be accorded less weight when asserted by an ex-president. Nixon v. Administrator of General Services, 408 F.Supp. 321, 357 n. 50 (D.D.C.1976), aff'd, 433 U.S. 425 (1977). A recent holding indicates that the privilege is not absolute even in civil cases. Dellums v. Powell, 561 F.2d 242 (D.C.Cir.1977), cert. denied, 434 U.S. 880 (1977). See generally McCormick, § 108, at 263–66; 2 Louisell & Mueller § 234.

A broader version of executive privilege, justified on closely analogous grounds, shields from forced disclosure confidential communications made in the course of policy formulation, by or within a governmental agency—unless an adequate showing of need is made. McCormick, § 108, at 266–67. However, litigants seeking governmental information should not overlook the Freedom of Information Act, 5 U.S.C.A. § 552, which provides that "any person" may request and obtain agency records covered by the Act. Where applicable, this act limits the availability of the traditional common-law privileges permitting governmental secrecy. If necessary, the person seeking information may file a complaint in the federal district court and compel the agency to comply with the Act.

6. *Informer's Identity.* Both the federal and state governments often protect the source of informers' information about criminal activity. This source would "dry up" if there were not some protection against disclosure of the names of the individuals supplying the information. The privilege not to disclose has several important exceptions, including one that applies when the informer's testimony is important to the accused in presenting his defense. See Roviaro v. United States, 353 U.S. 53 (1957). For discussions of the privilege of national and state governments to refuse to name an informant, see 2 Louisell & Mueller, §§ 235–37; McCormick § 111.

Chapter X

THE ROLE OF JUDGE AND JURY: A SUMMARY

§ 10.1 Factual Determinations Made by the Judge and Jury: In General

The allocation of function between judge and jury, as we have observed elsewhere,[1] cannot be dismissed with the generalization that the jury decides questions of fact and the judge decides questions of law. An irregular line, drawn in light of historical judgments of each participant's particular strengths, divides the roles of these principals in the litigation process.

Despite his role as the principal arbiter of laws, the judge must make a variety of factual determinations regarding both the evidence as a whole and individual offers of proof. Different situations require him to apply dissimilar standards in these determinations, and, in turn, his factual determinations have varying effects on the jury's role as the principal arbiter of factual questions. We already have encountered numerous instances in which the complementary roles of judge and jury were brought into clear relief: [2] Although the jury generally decides historic or adjudicative facts from the evidence as a whole, the judge first must determine whether the total evidence is *sufficient* to permit a reasonable jury to decide for either party; if a rational jury could reach but one conclusion, the judge directs a verdict.[3] Individual offers of proof place the judge in a different role. When proffered evidence is challenged as irrelevant he must determine

§ 10.1

1. See § 1.6.

2. See, e.g., §§ 1.6; 2.2; 2.6; 3.1; 3.6; 4.2; 7.3; 7.4; 7.5; Note 2 at the conclusion of Ch. VII, Part B; §§ 7.21; 9.11, text at nn. 14–15. See also Note 3 at the conclusion of Ch. II.

3. See § 3.1.

whether, if believed by the jury, the evidence could increase the likelihood of a consequential factual proposition. This role may be complicated by problems of conditional relevance. For example, if evidence tends to show that *X* made certain representations in the sale of *D*'s boat that are relevant (consequential) only if *X* were acting as *D*'s agent, the judge must decide[4] whether there is sufficient evidence of the agency relationship (the conditioning fact) to permit a reasonable jury to find that the relation existed at the time *X* made the statements. The jury, however, makes the final decision as to whether the relation did exist, and it then assesses the probative force of *what X said.*

Distinctly different problems are encountered where the judge's ruling upon the application of a technical, exclusionary rule of evidence depends on the existence of certain preliminary facts:[5] a witness offered for the purpose of giving expert testimony is competent only if he has the requisite training or experience; a copy of a document offered to establish its terms is admissible only if the original is not available; an excited utterance is admissible as an exception to the hearsay rule only if the declarant spoke with the requisite mental state; a communication is privileged only if confidentiality was intended and the communication was between persons entitled to the privilege. In these and similar instances, the judge normally determines the existence of disputed facts that control the applicability of an exclusionary rule; furthermore he usually makes the *final decision* as to the existence of such preliminary facts, precluding any subsequent inquiry by the jury.

The judge's role as the exclusive factfinder is grounded in (1) a recognition of his expertise pertaining to evidentiary rules and his awareness of the policies underlying them; (2) the comparative limitations of a lay jury's ability to deal with complex factual questions that interface with technical legal rules; and (3) the need to avoid the frequent disruptions of the trial that would result from putting these preliminary factual questions to the jury. In the following sections, we shall assess in detail the roles of judge and jury in dealing with questions of fact.[6]

4. See § 2.6.

5. See McCormick § 53; Morgan & Weinstein at 40–45; Note 3 at the conclusion of Ch. II.

6. For a full discussion of the role of judge and jury, see generally Kaplan, Of Mabrus and Zorgs—An Essay in Honor of David Louisell, 66 Calif.L.Rev. 987, 987–93 (1978).

§ 10.2. The Judge's Role in Evaluating the Evidence as a Whole

At the close of the plaintiff's case and, later, at the close of all the evidence, the judge must determine whether the evidence *as a whole* justifies sending the case to the jury. The question before him is whether the jury reasonably could find for *either* of the contending parties (put otherwise, whether the evidence favoring either party, if believed by the jury, would justify its verdict for that party). If the evidence reasonably could lead to but one controlling factual conclusion, there is no role for the jury: its function is confined to the resolution of matters that *reasonably* are disputed. It follows that the party with the burden of persuasion—usually the plaintiff [1]—can place his case before the jury only if the evidence, taken as a whole, in support of his position, justifies a finding in his favor by a preponderance of the evidence (or by whatever standard of proof is applicable). If the evidence is insufficient to justify this finding, the judge should direct a verdict for the defendant. Similarly, if the plaintiff's evidence is so convincing that no reasonable jury could find against him, the judge should direct a verdict in his favor.

Note that in administering the test for sufficiency, the judge prescribes only the outer limits of permissible jury action. Within its appropriate sphere of authority, the jury is empowered to make its own determination, finding only such facts as it believes exist. In sending a case to the jury for resolution, the judge leaves the jury free to evaluate any and all of the evidence before it.[2] Thus, even though the evidence supporting the plaintiff may be sufficient—*if believed and if accorded favorable inferences*—to justify a plaintiff's verdict, the jury is entitled to disbelieve the evidence or to decline to draw the possible inferences from it.

§ 10.3. The Judge's Factual Determinations Regarding Individual Offers of Proof of Fact

In making a relevance determination after objection to a particular offer of proof, the judge must assess the proffered

§ 10.2

1. Sometimes, of course, the defendant bears the burden of persuasion as, for example, with affirmative defenses. See § 3.1. The prosecutor in a criminal case must establish the elements of the charged offense beyond a reasonable doubt and there can be no directed verdict in his favor. §§ 3.1, 3.2, 3.5.

2. The jury also has a second function in many cases: it characterizes the facts it chooses to believe in accordance with the controlling rule of substantive law. For example, in an action based upon negligence, the jury decides not only what the defendant did (i.e. his conduct) but also whether the defendant's action should be characterized as negligent. See § 1.6.

evidence and the proposition to which it is directed. The test of relevance, of course, is whether the proffered evidence tends to make the existence of a consequential proposition more probable than that proposition would be without the evidence.[1] If the judge finds that the proffered evidence could add to the likelihood of a consequential fact, he admits it (assuming it otherwise is not objectionable), but he leaves to the jury the final evaluation of that evidence. As we have seen, the jury is free to find the evidence false or discount it as being of little or no help in establishing the proposition it supports.

While the relevancy test applies to each proffered item of evidence, the more stringent sufficiency test applies only to certain offers of evidence.[2] Such offers occur when the relevance of proffered evidence is dependent upon the existence of a conditioning fact. Without the existence of the fact upon which relevance is conditioned, the proffered evidence is of no consequence in the case. Thus, Federal Rule of Evidence 104(b) provides that evidence conditioned upon the existence of an underlying fact shall be admitted only "upon, or subject to, the introduction of evidence sufficient to support" the conditioning fact. To draw upon an earlier illustration, suppose that in a suit for breach of contract for sale of goods the plaintiff claims that *X*, as agent for the defendant (*D*), made certain representations warranting the quality of the goods. *D* denies both the representations and the agency of *X*. In an effort to prove the representations, the plaintiff offers witnesses *A*, *B*, and *C* who will testify that *X* made similar representations of warranty to them regarding the goods. This evidence passes the simple test of relevance: it tends to increase the probability that such representations also were made to the plaintiff—and thus to support this *apparently* consequential proposition. But close observation reveals that the relevance (or, strictly speaking, the consequentialness or materiality)[3] of this evidence is conditioned upon a preliminary factual finding that *X* was acting as *D*'s agent, because (we assume) the defendant cannot be held liable for the representations of a person not its agent. Thus, the plaintiff's use of evidence of *X*'s representations depends upon his establishing the conditioning (or allied) fact that *X* was

§ 10.3

1. § 2.2. But see United States v. Flores, 679 F.2d 173, 178 (9th Cir.1982), cert. denied, 459 U.S. 1148 (1983) ("substantial evidence" of agency (the conditioning fact) satisfies the requirement).

2. § 2.6.

3. Materiality deals with whether a factual proposition has any legal significance or, in the modern language of the Federal Rules, is "of consequence." See § 2.1.

acting as *D*'s agent. Other examples of conditional relevance are provided elsewhere.[4]

In situations involving conditional relevance, proper use of the proffered evidence depends upon the jury's finding of the existence of the conditioning fact upon which relevancy is premised. Therefore, in order to admit the conditionally relevant evidence the judge must determine only that there is *sufficient* evidence of the allied or conditioning fact to permit a reasonable jury to find its existence.[5] The judge does *not make* a *conclusive* determination; the final responsibility for determining the existence of the conditioning fact is left to the jury.[6] So, in the above example, if the judge finds the evidence sufficient to support a reasonable belief that *X* was *D*'s agent, he should admit the evidence of *X*'s representations to *A, B,* and *C.*[7] The jury then should be instructed that if it finds that *X* was not defendant's agent, it should disregard the evidence of *X*'s representations to others. This procedure should create no difficulty or confusion, because the jury readily can understand that if *X* was not acting for the defendant, the latter should not be liable for *X*'s representations. It is apparent, of course, that since evidence of the conditioning fact and the evidence based upon it cannot be offered simultaneously, the proponent must choose which evidence to offer first. Although the final decision concerning the order of evidentiary presentation is made by the judge[8] (at least where there is an objection), he usually will approve the proponent's choice, provided the latter assures the judge that the "connecting evidence" will be forthcoming.

The judge also applies the sufficiency test in another situation. A general rule of evidence requires that a witness have first-hand knowledge of the matter about which he testifies.[9] Usually

4. § 2.6.

5. Fed.R.Evid. 104(b) provides: "*Relevancy Conditioned on Fact.* When the relevancy of evidence depends upon the fulfillment of a condition of fact, the court shall admit it upon, or subject to, the introduction of evidence sufficient to support a finding of the fulfillment of the condition."

6. Morgan & Weinstein at 39–40.

7. But see § 2.5.

8. See Fed.R.Evid. 104(b) and 611(a). Note that when documents are relevant only if authenticated, authentication is required *before* the document will be admitted. See § 13.6.

9. See Fed.R.Evid. 602: "A witness may not testify as to a matter unless evidence is introduced sufficient to support a finding that he has personal knowledge. . . ." This rule, however, does not render inadmissible a party admission made by a party without personal knowledge of the event or condition about which he speaks. See Note 3 at the conclusion of Ch. VII, Part B.

it is apparent from the witness's testimony that he has personal knowledge of the facts he is recounting, although, as we have seen, the opponent frequently challenges the accuracy of the account. Occasionally, however, an opponent objects that since the witness did not observe or hear the matter about which he testifies, his testimony should be either struck (if already given) or disallowed. Although the role of the judge in responding to this objection has not often been discussed, the preferable procedure is for the judge to admit the testimony if he finds that there is sufficient evidence for the jury reasonably to conclude that the witness has first-hand knowledge.[10] Again it is assumed that the jury can perform its proper role without difficulty. If the jury concludes that the witness did not have first-hand knowledge, it should—and presumably will—disregard his testimony.

If the witness purports to be reporting what another person (the declarant) has said, the witness need have first-hand knowledge *only that the statements were made,* as opposed to first-hand knowledge of the events described in the statements. As to whether the absent declarant has first-hand knowledge of the events, the judge must determine from all of the circumstances whether the jury reasonably could find the declarant had an opportunity to observe them. The problem of whether the declarant lacked first-hand knowledge usually is confronted after the evidence surmounts the barrier posed by the hearsay rule: absent an exception, this rule generally precludes evidence of the declarant's statement if offered to prove the truth of its content.[11] If an exception is applicable, the judge still must determine whether there is a reasonable basis for believing that the declarant had first-hand knowledge of the events described in his out-of-court declaration.

§ 10.4 The Judge's Role in Determining Competence and Applying Technical Exclusionary Rules

The law of evidence consists largely of a complex of rules that protect the integrity of the trial process or that otherwise serve policies that a jury of laymen is unlikely to understand or appreciate. Application of many of these rules turns upon the existence of certain facts. An example is provided by the rule that a witness's competence depends upon his ability to observe, remember, relate,

10. McCormick, § 10, at 24.

11. See §§ 6.1, 6.2.

and to appreciate his obligation to speak truthfully.[1] A witness may lack competence if he is very young or if he suffers from an extremely disabling mental defect. Arguably, the jury should make the final determination of competence, for presumably it could discount the witness's testimony in accordance with the disabilities that it concludes exist. Present authority, however, favors a conclusive resolution by the judge: [2] if he makes a negative determination, the testimony of the witness is disallowed, even if a reasonable jury could have believed the testimony. Likewise, the judge makes a conclusive determination when the qualifications of a proffered expert witness are challenged.[3] The explanation for this placement of final responsibility in the judge may be that his training and experience enable him to make a more discriminating decision than can a lay jury. Courts also may be apprehensive that the jury would be unable to ignore the testimony of the challenged witness, even if, acting under instructions from the judge, it agreed that he technically was incompetent or unqualified.[4] Of course, once the judge rules that a witness is qualified, it is the jury's task to decide issues of credibility, i.e., whether to believe (wholly or in part) the witness's testimony.

The judge's role in the application of the technical exclusionary rules, such as those governing hearsay or privilege, remains to be considered. Suppose, for example, as to certain testimony a party or witness invokes the privilege for confidential communications between husband and wife; the opponent asserts that the couple was not married at the time of the communication. If this assertion is accurate, no privilege attaches. (The person who claims a privilege must show that the privilege is applicable.) Assuming the evidence regarding marriage at the time of the communication is conflicting, the judge resolves the conflict. If this factual question were allocated to the jury, several difficulties would arise. First, the judge would have to instruct the jury that if it believed the marriage existed at the time of the private communication, it should disregard the privileged statement. Such an instruction would place a difficult burden on the jury,

§ 10.4

1. § 4.2.

2. See McCormick, § 53, at 135–36, § 70, at 167–68; Morgan & Weinstein at 41–42 points out some inconsistencies in the cases. Fed.R.Evid. 104(a) makes it clear that the judge determines "the qualifications of a person to be a witness. . . ."

3. McCormick, § 53, at 136 n. 6. Fed.R.Evid. 104(a). See also McCormick, § 13, at 33–34.

4. Of course, if the judge finds the witness competent, opposing counsel still may assert (in closing argument) that the testimony was weak or unreliable because of extreme youth, mental infirmity, lack of expertise, etc. As

especially if it had to perform a similar function with regard to every disputed fact pertaining to a technical exclusionary rule. Second, it is doubtful whether a lay jury would be capable or desirous of ignoring a relevant communication simply because it passed between husband and wife. As McCormick notes, the exclusionary rules often are based upon long-term policies in which the jury has little or no interest.[5] Understandably, it would seem to a lay juror much more important to reach a "correct" verdict than to obey an exclusionary rule that forbids the use of probative evidence.

For these reasons, preliminary questions of fact governing the application of an exclusionary rule (other than relevancy or first-hand knowledge) normally are determined exclusively by the judge. Federal Rule 104(a) makes this clear; it provides that "[p]reliminary questions concerning . . . the existence of a privilege, or the admissibility of evidence shall be determined by the court. . . ." The judge's decision is final and is not subject to a contrary determination by the jury. Note that the judge not only decides factual issues surrounding the existence of a privilege, but also resolves factual questions that determine the applicability of any technical evidentiary rules. He decides, for example, if a dying declarant had a sense of impending death,[6] if an entry was made promptly in the regular course of business,[7] if there was the necessary state of excitement to qualify a declaration as an excited utterance,[8] if a witness is unavailable (where unavailability is essential to the application of a hearsay exception),[9] or if an original document is unavailable so as to justify the admission of a copy under the best evidence rule.[10] Furthermore, in making these determinations the judge is "not bound by the rules of

with other admitted evidence, the jury decides the degree of belief to which it is entitled.

5. McCormick, § 53, at 135.

6. See, e.g., Soles v. State, 97 Fla. 61, 119 So. 791 (1929); People v. Davis, 93 Ill.App.3d 217, 48 Ill.Dec. 675, 416 N.E.2d 1197 (1981).

7. See, e.g., O'Malley v. United States Fid. & Guar. Co., 776 F.2d 494, 500 (5th Cir.1985); Eubanks v. Winn, 469 S.W.2d 292 (Tex.Civ.App.1971).

8. See, e.g., Wright v. Swann, 261 Or. 440, 493 P.2d 148 (1972).

9. See, e.g., Jackson v. State, 133 Neb. 786, 277 N.W. 92 (1938); State v. Fondren, 11 Kan.App.2d 309, 721 P.2d 284 (1986).

10. See, e.g., United States v. O'Connor, 433 F.2d 752 (1st Cir.1970), cert. denied, 401 U.S. 911 (1971). The best evidence rule is discussed in § 13.9. Basically, it imposes upon the party who wishes to prove the terms of a writing, the obligation of producing the original writing (if it is available), instead of proving the contents of the document by secondary evidence such as a copy or through oral testimony. See also Fed.R.Evid. 1008 (role of judge and jury as to documents); Saltzburg & Redden at 1078–80.

evidence except those with respect to privileges." [11] This authority to escape the exclusionary rules does not mean that the judge will routinely rely upon "inadmissible" evidence in determining a preliminary fact. The extent to which he considers such evidence should depend upon its probable reliability, the need for it, and the extent to which the party opposing the establishment of the preliminary facts appears to simply be insisting that the proponent be "put to his proof."

We noted above that even though the judge makes a final determination concerning admissibility, the jury still determines how much, if any, probative value or "weight" to accord to the admitted evidence. Opposing counsel can argue that the evidence should be given little weight, but he may not argue to the jury that the nonexistence of one of the facts conditioning admissibility should preclude entirely the jury's consideration of the evidence. The judge already has made a conclusive determination as to the existence of these preliminary facts. Thus, in the context of one of the foregoing examples, it would be improper for counsel to contend before the jury that they should not even consider evidence of an excited utterance because they should find that it was not made under the influence of excitement or stress. Counsel had the opportunity to press this argument when the judge (usually out of the jury's hearing) was deciding the contested preliminary fact; having lost, he should not be allowed to resurrect this contention. He can, of course, argue to the jury that they should disbelieve the utterance or give it little weight because it was made under conditions of stress which might have impaired the witness's ability to observe accurately.

§ 10.5 Factual Determinations Necessary for the Application of an Evidentiary Rule: Special Situations

Several special circumstances qualify the foregoing discussion of the respective roles of judge and jury. In certain instances, a few jurisdictions vary the normal rule that gives to the judge

11. Fed.R.Evid. 104(a); McCormick, § 53, at 136 n. 8. At least this is the dominant and wiser view. McCormick, § 53, at 136 n. 8. The assumption is that the judge, experienced in the evaluation of evidence and aware of possible evidential infirmities, can properly weigh evidence that under the exclusionary rules would be inadmissible. Furthermore, in some situations practical necessity dictates that the judge consider "inadmissible" evidence. See Adv.Comm.Note to Fed.R.Evid. 104(a). For example, the judge cannot determine if a proffered excited utterance relates to the excited event unless he hears the possibly inadmissible utterance.

exclusive responsibility for factual determinations that attend the application of an exclusionary rule. For example, although it now is settled that the judge determines for purposes of admissibility whether a confession is voluntary [1] (including whether the warnings required by Miranda v. Arizona [2] were given), several jurisdictions permit the jury to make a second determination as to whether a lack of voluntariness should preclude consideration of the confession. In these jurisdictions, the judge, who already has passed on the voluntariness question, instructs the jury that if they find that the confession was not voluntary, they should disregard it altogether. This instruction allows the jury to reject the same evidence that satisfied the judge and permits counsel to argue to the jury that they should find the confession involuntary and hence exclude it entirely from their consideration.[3] As noted below, it is doubtful whether this second determination operates, as a practical matter, to give any additional protection to the accused.

Another variation from the prevailing practice exists in some jurisdictions with regard to the dying declarations of a homicide victim. The principal preliminary fact governing the admissibility of a dying declaration is that the declarant spoke under the influence of a sense of impending death. Most jurisdictions make the judge responsible for resolving conclusively any factual dispute as to the declarant's state of mind. Under the majority view, this ends the matter insofar as argument about *admissibility* is concerned. The jury need only decide what weight to give the dying declaration. But some jurisdictions preserve for the jury a factfinding function with regard to admissibility. The judge instructs the jury that should they find that the dying declaration

§ 10.5

1. In Jackson v. Denno, 378 U.S. 368 (1964), the Supreme Court held that a procedure that left to the jury the *sole* responsibility for determining voluntariness (in cases where a reasonable dispute existed) was a violation of the due process clause of the Fourteenth Amendment because this procedure did not adequately protect the substantive right of the accused not to be convicted on the basis of an involuntary confession.

2. 384 U.S. 436 (1966), rehearing denied, 385 U.S. 890 (1966). See § 9.12.

3. Because the jury always can consider the weight to be given a particular confession, it is appropriate in a case involving a contested confession for counsel to point to certain factors that might contribute to involuntariness (such as the youth of the accused) and to argue that these reduce the weight that should be accorded the confession. This generally accepted practice, however, is different from that of a few jurisdictions which permit the jury to find facts contrary to those found by the judge and to completely disregard the confession, thereby, in effect, applying an exclusionary rule of evidence.

was made without the required "settled, hopeless expectation of death," they should entirely disregard it.[4] Thus, despite the fact that the judge has determined that the requisite state of mind existed, counsel may urge the jury to find that it did not. A few jurisdictions appear to ignore altogether the orthodox view and hold that the judge makes only a sufficiency finding—that is, he determines only whether the evidence would support a reasonable dispute as to expected death. If the evidence is sufficient, the jury makes a final determination of the preliminary fact.[5]

None of these variant approaches merits continued support. The orthodox rule that assigns to the judge sole responsibility for ruling on preliminary facts governing an exclusionary rule is practical and expeditious. Further, it does not embroil the jury in the administration of evidentiary rules—a task it is ill-equipped to perform. It is even doubtful whether the minority rule that allows both the judge and the jury to rule on the exclusion of a confession or a dying declaration (presumably to give the accused the benefit of a second decision) results in any additional protection for the accused. In a close case of admissibility, the judge may be inclined to rule against the accused, knowing that the latter has a second chance to urge the inadmissibility of the contested evidence. Yet it is unlikely that the jury will be receptive to such an argument; presumably they are more interested in learning the facts than they are in securing the values that underlie the Fifth Amendment or the hearsay concerns that attend dying declarations. Furthermore, however conscientious the jury, it will be hard for its members to disregard evidence they have already heard.

Aside from these minority deviations from the practice of the vast majority of courts, there are diverse practices of more widespread consequence. These diverse approaches result from special circumstances that call into question the usual procedure of conclusively assigning preliminary questions to the judge. The difficulties arise when a preliminary question of fact governing the application of an exclusionary rule coincides with an ultimate issue in the case. The point can be made in several contexts, but a case involving the spousal incompetency privilege not to testify against an accused spouse is illustrative. Suppose that the ac-

4. McCormick, § 53, at 138 n. 12; Morgan & Weinstein at 269.

5. This position presumably is prejudicial to the defendant because the jury is exposed to evidence that might be inadmissible. McCormick, § 53, at 138; Morgan & Weinstein at 269.

cused is prosecuted for bigamy resulting from a common-law marriage to *X*, followed by a ceremonial marriage to *Y*. The accused contends he was never married to *X*. When the state calls *Y* as a witness, she objects, invoking a statute that excuses a "spouse" from being called in a criminal proceeding to testify against a marital partner. Such a statute would be interpreted so that *Y* would not be considered a spouse if the accused already was married to *X* when he purported to marry *Y*. But whether the accused was married to *X* is an ultimate issue in the case; ordinarily this issue would be resolved by the jury. How should the judge discharge his function as the preliminary factfinder when the fact conditioning an exclusionary rule coincides with a disputed ultimate fact? At least two possibilities exist, each with some judicial support.

First, the judge could follow the usual practice and make a final determination of the preliminary evidentiary question. Federal Rule 104(a), for example, states that the judge shall determine "the qualification of a person to be a witness, [and] the existence of a privilege. . . ." If he decides by a preponderance of the evidence that the accused never married *X*, he would sustain *Y*'s objection and presumably would thereafter grant the accused's motion for acquittal.[6] If he determines by a preponderance of the evidence that the accused was married to *X*, he then would order *Y* to testify, but he would not disclose to the jury that he has found a preexisting common-law marriage between the accused and *X*. Counsel for the defendant would be free to argue to the jury that the accused should not be found guilty because he was never married to *X*.[7] The judge's undisclosed evidentiary ruling that the accused and *X* were married would not foreclose argument on the ultimate issue, which properly is within the jury's province. Note also that the judge's ruling is made on the basis of a preponderance of the evidence,[8] but that the jury, in order to

6. If the judge, using a more-probable-than-not standard, determines that the defendant and *X* never were married, it would be inconsistent to allow a jury finding, based upon a reasonable doubt standard, that the accused was guilty of bigamy because he first married *X*, and then purported to marry *Y*.

7. Should the judge instruct the jury completely to disregard the evidence if the preliminary fact (the marriage of *X* and the accused) was not established? This would be confusing and unnecessary. If the jury found that the accused had not been married, then they would acquit the defendant.

8. Preliminary questions of fact are ordinarily resolved in both criminal and civil trials by using a preponderance standard. This practice has been challenged when applied to confessions, but in Lego v. Twomey, 404 U.S. 477 (1972), a split Supreme Court sustained the use of the preponderance test. See general-

convict, must find beyond a reasonable doubt that the accused and *X* were married. In sum, many courts find that the usual practice of allocating preliminary questions to the judge operates satisfactorily in most instances [9] when the preliminary fact coincides with an ultimate fact. It is essential, however, that the judge not disclose to the jury his resolution of the preliminary fact when his determination is adverse to the accused.

A second practice limits the judge to a finding of sufficiency.[10] If the proponent (the prosecutor in the foregoing illustration) provides sufficient evidence to enable a reasonable jury using a preponderance-of-the-evidence standard to find the preliminary fact (that the accused and *X* were married), then the contested evidence is admitted. Insufficient evidence of this preliminary fact not only would result in excluding *Y*'s testimony, but also would result in granting the defendant's motion for acquittal. As will be noted in the following discussion, this approach is subject to the criticism that it offers insufficient protection for the accused.

Enormous confusion and diversity of practice have surrounded the introduction into evidence of a coconspirator's party admission in a case in which the substantive offense of conspiracy is charged. Before the coconspirator's statement can be admitted against the other alleged conspirators, there must be preliminary evidence (which may include, the Supreme Court has recently held, the statement itself) [11] that there was a conspiracy in which the declarant and the opponent(s) of the evidence were participants. There must also be preliminary evidence indicating that the declaration in question was made in furtherance of the alleged conspiracy.[12] It

ly Saltzburg, Standards of Proof and Preliminary Questions of Fact, 27 Stan. L.Rev. 271 (1975).

9. For a variant practice under the Federal Rules, see Fed.R.Evid. 1008 (Best Evidence Rule). See also Note 1 at the end of this chapter.

10. See the discussion in I Wigmore § 17 n. 20 (Tillers).

11. Most, but not all, circuits had required that the judge consider only evidence of conspiracy that was independent of the statement in question in making the preliminary finding that conditions the admissibility of the statement. See 1 Weinstein & Berger, ¶104[05], at 44–80; Saltzburg & Redden at 735. But see United States v. Vinson, 606 F.2d 149 (6th Cir.1979), cert. denied, 444 U.S. 1074 (1980), rehearing denied, 445 U.S. 972 (1980). In Bourjaily v. United States, 55 U.S.L.W. 4962 (U.S. June 23, 1987), the Supreme Court held that it was appropriate, under Fed.R.Evid. 104(a), for the judge to consider the contested statement.

12. See § 7.5. In determining whether the statement was made in furtherance of the conspiracy, it is clearly appropriate for the judge to consider the statement itself. See Graham, Handbook of Federal Evidence, § 801.25, at

will be seen that the resolution of the preliminary factual question of the existence of a conspiracy and its membership requires that the judge reach ultimate issues in the case.

It is not surprising that the courts developed different approaches as to both the standard of probative force to be applied in assessing the independent evidence and the function of the judge in making the necessary factual determination.[13] One line of cases requires only a finding by the judge that the proponent has produced "prima facie" evidence of a conspiracy. Within this group of cases, the opinions are not always clear as to what measure of proof is prescribed by the term "prima facie." [14] What usually is meant is evidence sufficient to sustain a finding of conspiracy by a preponderance-of-the-evidence standard.[15] In any event, the judge *screens* the independent evidence (drawing all reasonable inferences in the government's favor) to ensure its sufficiency. Sometimes he goes further by instructing the jury that they should not consider the statement of the coconspirator unless they first find from independent evidence that a conspiracy existed.[16]

Another line of cases, which has recently drawn the approval of the Supreme Court, requires that the judge make a factual determination that there was a conspiracy.[17] Here the judge does not, as under the first approach, *simply screen* the independent evidence to ensure that it is sufficient to justify a finding of conspiracy; the judge himself makes a determination whether the

783. Considering the contents of the statement is a practical necessity. As noted, it is even permissible to use the statement in the finding of conspiracy and membership, supra n. 11.

13. Differing approaches are identified and thoughtfully discussed in Saltzburg & Redden at 729–37.

14. Id. at 729–30.

15. See, e.g., United States v. King, 552 F.2d 833 (9th Cir.1976), cert. denied, 430 U.S. 966 (1977); Carbo v. United States, 314 F.2d 718 (9th Cir.1963), cert. denied, 377 U.S. 953 (1964), rehearing denied, 377 U.S. 1010 (1964).

16. This instruction is very difficult for the jury to understand and follow. To complicate matters, some courts erroneously charge the jury not to consider the coconspirator's statement unless they first find from the independent evidence that beyond a reasonable doubt there was a conspiracy. Saltzburg & Redden at 730–32. If the jury makes this finding, the subsequent use of the declaration is unnecessary.

17. See Bourjaily v. United States, 55 U.S.L.W. 4962 (U.S. June 23, 1987). At least, the Court characterized the problem of admissibility as one requiring a *determination* under Rule 104(a). See also United States v. Mastropieri, 685 F.2d 776 (2d Cir.1982), cert. denied, 459 U.S. 945 (1982); United States v. Stanchich, 550 F.2d 1294 (2d Cir.1977) (judge must find conspiracy from a "preponderance" of the independent evidence). *Bourjaily* also affects the independent evidence requirement. See supra n. 11.

preliminary fact of a conspiracy exists. Under this approved practice, the judge employs the usual measure of proof for resolving preliminary questions of fact: the preponderance-of-the-evidence standard.[18] Further, he gives no instruction to the jury to make a preliminary factual determination before considering the coconspirator's declaration. The judge simply instructs the jury that in order to convict the accused they must find beyond a reasonable doubt that a conspiracy existed and that the accused was a participant in it.

Although this area has seen much debate,[19] both policy and sound practice suggest that the judge should determine the preliminary fact using a preponderance standard. This provides more protection for the accused than mere screening to ensure that prima facie evidence of the conspiracy exists. The preponderance rule operates in practice to produce a more stringent test of admissibility and thereby protects the accused where only weak evidence of a conspiracy exists. Further, this approach also protects the accused by avoiding the confusion that has been produced in some courts when the jury was instructed to make a preliminary finding of conspiracy before considering the coconspirator's declarations. Because it is unlikely that a jury could either understand or follow such an instruction, it is equally unlikely that jury determination of a preliminary fact can afford significant protection against the improper use of evidence.

Notes

1. *Concurrence of Preliminary and Ultimate Facts.* The coincidence of preliminary and ultimate fact can occur in various factual patterns in both criminal and civil settings. Suppose plaintiff sues defendant on the ground that the latter issued a surety bond that obligated him to guarantee the payment of debts of a certain third party who has defaulted. Plaintiff starts to testify as to the terms of the bond, whereupon defendant objects on the grounds of the best evidence rule. As discussed in § 13.9, in cases where the terms of a contested writing are to be proved, this rule requires the production of

18. Bourjaily v. United States, 55 U.S.L.W 4962 (U.S. June 23, 1987). Some judges may have been applying a higher standard of proof, but not confining the evidence they considered to the independent evidence. For a careful analysis, see Saltzburg & Redden at 732–35. For an argument supporting a higher standard, see 1 Weinstein & Berger ¶ 104[05], at 43.

19. See, e.g., Bergman, The Coconspirator's Exception: Defining the Standard of the Independent Evidence Test Under the New Federal Rules of Evidence, 5 Hofstra L.Rev. 99 (1976).

the original writing if it is available. The plaintiff contends that the bond was lost; defendant asserts that it never existed. Only if the original is unavailable is oral testimony acceptable. Availability normally is a preliminary question for the judge. But if the judge decides the question of loss, he also must resolve the question whether the bond existed, which is an ultimate issue in the case. That is, the document could not be lost unless it originally existed, and in determining the question of loss the judge must necessarily decide whether or not the document ever existed. Should he rule that the bond never existed and hence that secondary evidence was inadmissible, the plaintiff's case would terminate. Yet, whether or not the document ever existed—the basic issue in the case—is usually a question for the jury. Under the preferred practice the judge determines whether there is sufficient evidence to support a finding that the surety bond existed; that is, he screens the evidence. He then assumes (regardless of his personal belief) that the bond existed and goes on to determine whether under this assumption it is more probable than not that the bond was lost. If he determines that it is lost (or, for that matter, is unavailable for some other reason) he will allow secondary evidence of the terms of the bond. The issue of whether the bond ever existed will be resolved by the jury, as, of course, will be any issues regarding its terms. See Fed.R.Evid. 1008. The judge uses a similiar approach (screening) when there is a dispute over which of several variant documents is the true original. Id.

2. *Privileges and Preliminary Factfinding.* Note that Fed.R.Evid. 104(a) states that in making determinations of preliminary facts, the judge "is not bound by the rules of evidence except those with respect to privileges." Yet whether a privilege is applicable (e.g., the attorney-client privilege) usually depends on one or more preliminary facts (e.g., was legal advice sought in connection with a future crime or fraud?). It would appear that, as a practical matter, the judge must learn about the content of the communications between attorney and client before he can rule intelligently on the question of whether the privilege applies. Yet Rule 104(a) would, on its face at least, appear to forbid this revelation. Most judges reach a practical accommodation by holding an in-chambers inquiry that probes far enough into the communication to allow an informed ruling.

3. *Judge's Role: A Problem.* Assume that plaintiff sues defendant on the basis of fraudulent representations made with reference to certain timberland. The plaintiff testifies as to the alleged representations but on cross-examination is confronted with a letter, purportedly written by him, inconsistent with his testimony. A witness's prior inconsistent statements normally are admissible to impeach his

testimony. In this case the statements, if made by the plaintiff, also constitute a party admission. The second page of the letter, containing the signature, is missing. Plaintiff denies ever having written or seen the letter and objects to its contents being revealed to the jury. How should the judge proceed in resolving the problem of whether the evidence is admissible?

Chapter XI

OFFER OF PROOF AND OBJECTIONS

§ 11.1 The Offer, Objection, and Motion to Strike: In General

In a broad sense, every document proffered as evidence and every statement solicited from a witness on the stand is an offer of proof. But the term "offer of proof" is generally used to refer to the dual showing a proponent must make when the admissibility of his evidence is challenged. The offer includes (1) a presentation or description of the evidence he wishes to introduce and (2) a statement of what he proposes to prove. Both the evidence proffered and the intended line of proof may be apparent in the context of the trial; if so, clarifying statements are unnecessary. But when evidence is challenged by an opponent's objection (or, as occasionally happens, by a question or objection from the judge [1]), the proponent often must specify the nature and purpose of his evidence. In short, the adequacy of an offer of proof is judged within the particular trial context in which it is made. The requirement of an offer of proof is simply to inform the judge and the adversary about forthcoming evidence that is (or is likely to be) challenged by objection.

A question to the witness will suffice as an offer of proof if both the response sought and its intended purpose are clear. But if there is any doubt regarding the content or purpose of the evidence

§ 11.1

1. Failure of the opponent to object "does not of itself preclude the trial judge from excluding the [objectionable] evidence on his own motion if the witness is disqualified for want of capacity or the evidence is incompetent, and . . . [the judge] considers that the interests of justice require the exclusion of the testimony." McCormick, § 55, at 143–144.

sought, the proponent should specify, as part of the trial record, exactly what evidence he seeks to adduce and the proposition to which it is directed. This he may accomplish either by summarizing the expected evidence himself or by questioning the witness (out of the jury's presence) and having the reporter record the answers. If the proponent offers a document or tangible object, he should explain for the record its purpose and ensure that the object—or at least an adequate description of it—becomes a part of the record. It will be seen that the steps necessary to complete an offer of proof are dictated by the particular setting. And although the offer often is made out of the presence of the jury (and before only the judge, the court reporter, and opposing counsel), it is sometimes made in the regular course of interrogating a witness. Furthermore, the proponent can often state for the record what he proposes to prove without any significant risk of wrongly influencing the jury, thus eliminating the need for excusing the jury or making the offer at the judge's bench, out of the jury's hearing.

By indicating the nature and purpose of the evidence, an offer of proof serves three related purposes. First, it enables the opponent to withdraw, refine, or restate his objection. Second, it allows the judge to make an intelligent, informed ruling on the admissibility of the evidence. Finally, it allows an appellate court to conduct an adequate, informed review of the trial court's ruling on admissibility, for the record will reveal what the proponent sought to prove and the evidence with which he intended to prove it.

The objection, like its counterpart the offer, should inform the adversary, the trial judge, and the appellate tribunal about the evidence being contested. Hence, it should indicate the basis of the objector's challenge to the proffered evidence. Sound trial administration and fairness to the proponent dictate that the objection should be made as soon as the alleged defect in the proffered evidence is perceived. Ideally, the objection will be made as soon as the question calling for improper evidence is asked (or as soon as an objectionable item is offered). But sometimes there is insufficient time to object, as when a witness answers quickly or gives an answer that is not responsive to the question. In circumstances where the evidentiary defect is not apparent until after the testimony has been received, a motion to strike the evidence is the proper remedy.[2]

2. Such a motion is appropriate, for instance, when evidence is admitted conditionally and it later becomes apparent the required conditions have not been fulfilled. See § 2.6. The motion to strike, sometimes called an "after-

Because offers and objections serve important informational functions, it is not surprising that the rules governing these devices encourage the offeror and objector to state their respective positions as specifically as is reasonably possible. This demand for specificity reflects the assumptions that counsel are familiar with the forthcoming evidence—presumably having had an opportunity to develop and study the available evidence—and that the judge, who does not have equal familiarity, is entitled to expect informed and clearly stated offers and objections. As we shall see, the specific rules governing offers and objections adversely affect the proponent or opponent who fails to take timely action that makes clear his position with regard to proffered evidence. Furthermore, these rules favor the trial judge by giving him "the benefit of the doubt" when his evidentiary rulings are brought into question before an appellate court.

§ 11.2 Offer of Proof: Proponent's Responsibilities

The requirement that an offeror make a showing of what evidence he seeks to adduce and what he intends to prove by this evidence not only advises the judge and opposing counsel of the proponent's claim of relevance, but also reveals whether the evidence is being offered for an admissible purpose. There are many instances, of course, where evidence offered for an admissible purpose would be inadmissible if offered for another purpose, and vice versa.[1]

The burden of selecting the purpose of the evidence falls, as it should, upon the proponent: if he chooses an improper purpose, he cannot prevail on appeal by showing some other basis for admissibility.[2] The offer was accepted on its terms by the opponent and the judge ruled accordingly. The proponent bears a similar responsibility when he offers evidence, such as documents or conversations, of which only a part is admissible. If he fails to offer only the admissible portions, he cannot prevail on appeal after the judge has rejected the entire offer.[3] It is not the duty of the judge

objection," usually includes a request that the jury be instructed to disregard the inadmissible evidence.

§ 11.2

1. See §§ 2.3, 6.2.

2. See, e.g., United States v. Grapp, 653 F.2d 189 (5th Cir.1981); I Wigmore, § 17, at 789 (Tillers). See also 1 Weinstein & Berger, ¶ 103(03), at 36.

3. See Hawkinson Tread Tire Co. v. Walker, 715 S.W.2d 335 (Mo.App.1986). Cf. Mucci v. LeMonte, 157 Conn. 566, 254 A.2d 879 (1969). See McCormick, § 51, at 125: "If counsel offers both good and bad together and the judge rejects the entire offer, the offeror may not complain on appeal." See also I Wigmore, § 17, at 787 (Tillers).

to screen the proposed evidence and discriminate between the good and the bad, although in the give-and-take of trial, the judge may, and probably should, reveal his reason for rejecting the evidence so that the proponent might cure the defect by offering only the admissible portion.

§ 11.3 Objection: Waiver and Appellate Review

If a party intending to complain about evidence admitted against him fails to enter a timely objection, he waives his right to protest [1]—save to urge an appellate court to deem the admission of the evidence so egregious that it constitutes plain error and justifies granting relief notwithstanding his failure to object.[2] Invocation of the plain error doctrine is often urged, but appellate courts are seldom obliging. It should be noted that in a few jurisdictions, the failure to take "exception" to the judge's adverse ruling on an objection also waives the right of appellate review of the judge's ruling. Recent thinking, however, rejects the ritual of "taking exception" as unnecessary and counterproductive,[3] and this requirement is being abandoned. Waiver also can occur where, after a party's objection to opposing evidence is sustained, he introduces through his own witness similar evidence of the same facts or transactions.[4] Note, however, that evidence admit-

§ 11.3

1. Fed.R.Evid. 103(a). See United States v. Blackshear, 568 F.2d 1120, 1121–22 (5th Cir.1978); United States v. Jamerson, 549 F.2d 1263, 1266–67 (9th Cir.1977).

2. See United States v. Musgrave, 444 F.2d 755 (5th Cir.1971), appeal after remand 483 F.2d 327 (5th Cir.1973), cert. denied 414 U.S. 1023 (judge's prejudicial comments to jury); McCormick, § 52, at 134. Fed.R.Evid. 103, which requires offers and objection, nonetheless specifies that the court will consider plain errors. Fed.R.Evid. 103(d). See also 1 Weinstein & Berger ¶ 103(07). Cf. People v. Humphreys, 24 Mich. App. 411, 180 N.W.2d 328 (1970) (alleged error in admitting pistol waived because no objection; however, prosecutor's improper remarks to jury would not have been cured by objection, so failure to object did not bar appellate consideration).

3. The objection itself makes it known that the objector believes the evidence inadmissible. Little is accomplished by the added expression "I take exception." Counsel, having made known his objection, should be permitted to wait until the full trial transcript is available for his review before deciding whether to appeal the point. Further, the accidental failure to take exception, which easily can occur in the heat of trial, will preclude appellate review of a meritorious point. See State v. Abbott, 36 N.J. 63, 75–79, 174 A.2d 881, 887–90 (1961).

4. See, e.g., United States v. Silvers, 374 F.2d 828 (7th Cir.1967), cert. denied 389 U.S. 888 (1967), where defense counsel objected to evidence that the accused had been in prison, but then made extensive use of the accused's prison background in an attempt to prove insanity. See also McCormick, § 55, at 143. The reported cases vary on the propriety of waiver. See I Wig-

ted after an objection is *overruled* may be rebutted or explained without waiving the right to challenge the court's ruling on appeal.[5]

Crucial at both trial and appellate levels is the specificity of the objection itself. Here again the responsibility is that of the moving party: his statement must be sufficiently specific for the judge and opposing counsel to know which of the many rules of evidence is being invoked. If counsel simply states "I object"—a so-called general objection—it is difficult for the trial judge to make an informed ruling. Accordingly, as we shall see, any ruling he does make will likely be upheld on appeal, unless no possible ground supports his decision.[6] The rationale for favoring the judge at the expense of the objecting attorney is that the latter has had an opportunity to examine the available evidence through investigation and discovery procedures and to anticipate problems associated with the evidence; the trial judge, it is assumed, has had no comparable opportunity to familiarize himself with the evidence. A specific objection also is fair to the proponent of the evidence, for it gives him the opportunity to restate his offer or to cure the deficiency in his proof by resort to other evidence. It can be seen that effective advocacy by the objector is important, not only in securing a favorable ruling from the trial judge, but also in preserving the objector's appellate rights should the judge rule against him. Because the argument accompanying the objection becomes part of the record which the appellate court will review, it may help to support a claim of error or to bolster the trial judge's ruling if favorable to the objector.

The familiar litany that evidence is "irrelevant, incompetent and immaterial" hardly focuses the objection. There are many reasons why evidence might be incompetent (as when made so by rules of privilege, hearsay, or a dead man's statute). By adding the words "irrelevant" and "immaterial," the objector at most has suggested that the evidence is not probative of the proposition to which it is directed or that it is directed toward a proposition that

more, § 18, at 836–37 (Tillers). Perhaps the waiver doctrine is a convenient device in cases where the trial judgment clearly appears correct. An alternative appellate disposition is to hold that the evidence adduced by the objector rendered the error of overruling his objection harmless.

5. See § 11.5.

6. Morgan & Weinstein at 47. An objection general in form ("I object") can function as a specific objection if it is clear that the judge and opposing counsel knew the specific (but unarticulated) ground upon which the objection was made. McCormick, § 52, at 129.

is not consequential. Thus the objector's trilogy can be viewed as no more educative of the court and the opponent than the general interjection "I object." McCormick suggests that the "three i's" do specify an objection based on the lack of probative force or materiality.[7] Many of the decided cases, however, support the view that this overworked rhetoric lodges only a general objection equivalent to "I object."

The specific rules governing a general objection are these: If a general objection *is overruled,* the objector rarely prevails on appeal. The appellate court will attribute to the trial judge a proper motive if any can be credited. There is an element of fair play in this attribution because the objector's failure to be specific has resulted in admission of the evidence and, at the same time, has failed to apprise the proponent of the specific defect. Thus, the latter has had no meaningful opportunity or incentive to cure the infirmity or supply other evidence. Additionally, it is sometimes said to be unfair to upset the ruling below on an argument presented for the first time on appeal. In any event, the general objector who suffers an unfavorable ruling from the trial judge is also likely to receive an unfavorable appellate disposition. Only if there is no purpose or theory of admissibility to support the trial judge's ruling will it be overturned. It needs no emphasis that this is hardly the kind of appellate posture upon which careful counsel chooses to rely.

If the general objection *is sustained,* the protective appellate attitude toward the trial judge favors the objector. By charitably assuming that the judge had in mind all conceivable proper grounds for rejecting the evidence, the appellate court will uphold the ruling unless there is no basis for it whatsoever. Note that here the party appealing the judge's ruling will be the proponent of the evidence. He can increase his chances for success on appeal by making a careful offer of proof at trial. In the offer he should indicate clearly the purposes for which the evidence is offered, especially if it might be inadmissible for some purposes but not others. He also should request that the reason for the trial judge's ruling be indicated on the record, thereby perhaps exposing a specific erroneous basis underlying the judge's decision.

Specific objections are governed by the following rules. The appellate disposition of the trial court's ruling on an opponent's

7. McCormick, § 52, at 130. See also 1 Weinstein & Berger, ¶ 103(02), at 23 (1986). Compare I Wigmore, § 18, at 826 (Tillers).

specific objection—that is, where the opponent points out particular grounds—favors the judge only where the objector is wrong in his contention. If the opponent's specific objection *correctly* indicates the defect in the proffered evidence, but the judge *erroneously overrules* his objection, the merits of the ruling will be reviewed on appeal. But the situation is different if the opponent of the evidence states an *erroneous* specific objection—that is, one based upon an untenable ground—which is (correctly) *overruled.* Here, even if another ground would have called for exclusion of the evidence (for example, if the objector based his objection on a claim of marital privilege, but the evidence actually was hearsay), the objector's posture on appeal is unfavorable.[8] The objector presented the trial judge with an invalid ground for excluding the evidence—an alleged defect that did not exist. Counsel's objection will be accepted on its terms on appeal, just as it was at trial: the appellate court will hold the trial judge acted correctly in overruling the erroneous objection—at least if there is any conceivable ground supporting admission. This result is consistent with the notion of party responsibility, and protects the trial judge who presumably recognized that the objection was without merit.

A more difficult question arises when the specific objector names an untenable ground and the judge *wrongly sustains* the objection, although there is a valid, unnamed ground for exclusion. When the proponent of the evidence appeals, some appellate courts sustain the ruling of the trial judge on the theory that, although the reason was wrong, the result was correct.[9] There would seem to be little reason to retry the case merely to enter the proper reason for exclusion. But arguably this result is unfair to the proponent: if the proper basis for exclusion had been revealed, he might have been able to cure the defect[10] or present other, admissible evidence. For this reason, some courts, with the gener-

8. See McCormick, § 52, at 131; I Wigmore, § 18, at 828 (Tillers).

9. See I Wigmore, § 18, at 831–32 n. 26 (Tillers). The leading case is Kansas City So. R.R. v. Jones, 241 U.S. 181 (1916). See also Eschbach v. Hurtt, 47 Md. 61, 65 (1877): the court "must determine . . . whether the testimony offered was admissible, and not whether a right or wrong reason was assigned for its rejection." Note that it is difficult to reconcile this language with the rule that if a specific objection based upon the wrong ground is *overruled,* the judge will be sustained on appeal even if a proper specific objection would have resulted in exclusion.

10. Suppose, for example, the true basis for exclusion were the best evidence rule. If this were known, the proponent perhaps could lay the foundation for introducing a copy. See § 13.9.

al approval of the commentators, reverse the ruling of the trial judge.[11]

Of course, one must study all of the foregoing rules with an awareness that evidentiary rulings, though erroneous, may be comparatively insignificant in their ultimate effect on the final judgment. In such circumstances, the appellate court may deem the error harmless. An appellate court will not reverse a judgment below unless—to use a phrase from the Federal Rules—an erroneous ruling on a question of evidence affected "a substantial right" of the appealing party.[12]

§ 11.4 Offers of Proof and Objections Under the Federal Rules of Evidence

Offers and objections are governed by Rule 103 of the Federal Rules of Evidence.[1] The Rule is, generally speaking, consistent with the common law. In order to predicate error upon a ruling of the trial judge admitting evidence, the party opposing the evidence ordinarily must make a timely objection (or motion to strike) and set out his supporting ground.[2] A parallel requirement applies to a party who predicates error upon a ruling excluding evidence: he must ordinarily make an adequate offer of proof in order to preserve his right to an appellate review on the merits. In either situation, the Rule allows the context of the situation to provide the required specificity; sound practice, however, usually dictates that the party against whom a trial ruling is made state clearly for the record the pertinent information regarding the admitted or excluded evidence.

Rule 103 also expressly vests the trial judge with discretion to manage the flow of information pertaining to the offer and objec-

11. See Bloodgood v. Lynch, 293 N.Y. 308, 56 N.E.2d 718 (1944); Larson v. Dougherty, 72 S.D. 43, 29 N.W.2d 383 (1947); Arcola v. Wilkinson, 233 Ill. 250, 84 N.E. 264 (1908); I Wigmore, § 18, at 831–32 n. 26 (Tillers); Morgan & Weinstein at 48.

12. Fed.R.Evid. 103(a). See 21 C. Wright & K. Graham, Federal Practice and Procedure, Evidence § 5035 (1977).

§ 11.4

1. Fed.R.Evid. 103 provides in part:

> (a) *Effect of Erroneous Ruling.* Error may not be predicated upon a ruling which admits or excludes evidence unless a substantial right of the party is affected, and . . . (1) in case the ruling is one admitting the evidence, a timely objection or motion to strike appears of record, stating the specific ground of objection, if the specific ground was not apparent from the context; or (2) . . . in case the ruling is one excluding evidence, the substance of the evidence was made known to the court by offer or was apparent from the context within which the questions were asked.

2. Note 1, supra. See e.g., United States v. Jamerson, 549 F.2d 1263 (9th Cir.1977).

tion. The Rule states that the court may direct that the offer be made in question and answer form. The court is also empowered to add statements pertaining to the character of the evidence, the form in which it is offered, the objections raised, and its ruling on the evidence.[3] The Rule makes clear that to the extent practicable, the court should take steps to prevent suggesting to the jury the content of inadmissible evidence. Normally the trial judge will implement this directive by using a side-bar conference or by excusing the jury.[4] In general, the Federal Rule reflects the prevailing principle that the parties are primarily responsible for controlling the presentation and exclusion of evidence.

§ 11.5 Curative Admissibility ("Open Door" Theory)

Should one party's introduction of improper evidence (that is, evidence violative of an exclusionary rule) justify a counterattack with improper evidence by the other party? The counterattack could take place either during the other party's cross-examination or, later, when as a direct examiner, the opponent offers inadmissible evidence of his own. Two limiting propositions should be stated at the outset. First, the use of improper evidence of a particular excludable *class* (for example, hearsay evidence or privileged evidence) does not justify the opponent's introduction, generally, of evidence from the same class: that is, hearsay evidence on point A does not warrant the opponent's introduction of hearsay evidence on point B. The issue is whether the use of improper evidence on point A justifies the opponent's use of improper rebuttal evidence (regardless of class) *relevant to the same point.* Second, regardless of whether the opponent is entitled to introduce "inadmissible" evidence of his own, he always is entitled to attack by cross-examination the accuracy or reliability of his adversary's improper evidence. The problem involving a counterattack arises only when the party rebutting the improper evidence seeks to *introduce additional improper evidence,* not when he merely attempts by cross-examination or through the use of admissible evidence to reduce the probative force of the improper evidence that his opponent has produced.

3. Fed.R.Evid. 103(b).

4. Fed.R.Evid. 103(c) directs that "to the extent practicable" inadmissible evidence shall be kept from the jury. For an extensive treatment of Rule 103, see 1 Louisell & Mueller, §§ 6–23. For more concise coverage, see Saltzburg & Redden at 15–34.

Wigmore identified three views of the so-called doctrine of curative admissibility.[1] The first rejects the improper rebuttal evidence, the second admits it, and the third (probably the majority) makes the result turn upon whether the rebuttal evidence is needed to remove prejudice caused by the initial incompetent evidence. In Wigmore's view, the variations in the cases largely are explained by the fact that whatever rule was chosen on appeal resulted in upholding the ruling of the trial judge.[2] McCormick, noting variations in the announced rules, offers valuable statements of what he believes are, or should be, controlling principles.[3] It should be added that direct or inferential case support probably can be found for any reasonable solution in this difficult and confused area.[4]

Suppose the proponent introduces evidence that violates the hearsay rule and the opponent *enters a correct specific objection* which the trial judge erroneously overrules. In theory, the opponent is protected because he can appeal the ruling. But appeals are expensive, and there is a risk the appellate court will view the error as harmless. Further, a litigant wants to win at trial not only to improve his posture on appeal but also to gain an advantage in any post-trial negotiations to compromise or settle the suit and avoid an appeal. For these reasons, then, a litigant should be afforded an opportunity at trial[5] to counterbalance inadmissible evidence used against him.

If the rebuttal evidence is of the same class and origin as the admitted evidence, the rebuttal evidence is likely to be admitted because the judge, consistently with his earlier ruling, will believe the rebuttal evidence proper. But what is the impact of this rebuttal evidence on the initial objection? One view results in a waiver of the rebutting party's earlier objection to this specific line of evidence: if he loses the verdict, he may not successfully

§ 11.5

1. I Wigmore § 15 (Tillers).

2. I Wigmore, § 15, at 746 (Tillers). The author indicates that if the opponent duly objected, there was no need to admit improper rebuttal evidence because the opponent had a right to appeal the erroneous ruling. Thus, Wigmore would choose among the three rules only when there has been no objection. Id. at 731. As noted later in the present text, a mere objection does not give sufficient protection; the objector wants to win the case at trial.

3. McCormick, § 57, at 147–148.

4. A multitude of cases are collected in I Wigmore § 15 (Tillers); see also McCormick, § 57, at 147–148.

5. See Dolan, Rule 403: The Prejudice Rule in Evidence, 49 S.Cal.L.Rev. 220, 276–77 (1976). Cf. McCormick, § 58, at 148.

complain on appeal. A preferable view is that the "improper" rebuttal does not effect a waiver because the rebuttal was necessitated by the original admission. Under this view, however, the rebuttal evidence may make the original error harmless—a point which the trial judge can bear in mind when considering a motion for new trial and which the appellate court also can consider.[6]

Additional difficulties may be introduced when the rebuttal evidence violates a different exclusionary rule than that violated by the original proponent. If the original proponent objects to the rebuttal evidence, but the trial judge does *not exclude it,* the original proponent will complain on appeal. The appellate question should be whether the original improper evidence rendered the rebuttal evidence harmless error. A less desirable approach routinely estops the original proponent from complaining because he started the sequence of erroneous admissions by "opening the door."[7] The harmless error approach has the flexibility that allows the reviewing court to weigh the respective prejudicial effects of the initial evidence and the rebuttal evidence. However, if the objection to rebuttal evidence which violates a different exclusionary rule than the original evidence *is sustained,* the rebutting party may be relegated to an appellate argument that the initial inadmissible evidence should not have come in over his objection. However, the appellate court should be receptive to his argument that it is immaterial that his evidence violated a different exclusionary rule; he was entitled to offset the *effect* of the initial proponent's evidence.

When the initial proponent introduces improper evidence to which the opponent does not object, but subsequently the opponent offers improper rebuttal evidence to which the original proponent objects, does the action of the original proponent preclude him from complaining about the rebuttal evidence?[8] The equities are close: the original proponent initiated the improper evidentiary course, but his opponent either chose not to object (even though, presumably, he could have blocked the improper evidence) or

6. See I Wigmore, § 15, at 746–48 (Tillers) and cases cited for a discussion of the scope of judicial discretion at trial and on appeal.

7. See 1 Louisell & Mueller, § 11, at 45–52.

8. State v. Witham, 72 Me. 531, 535 (1881), appears to foreclose appeal by an original offeror whose improper evidence, admitted without objection, subsequently is rebutted by equally improper evidence. See also Meyers v. United States, 147 F.2d 663 (9th Cir. 1945). The case results vary.

failed to see that the evidence was defective. This situation is best resolved by giving the trial judge discretion to admit or reject the evidence according to the impact or degree of prejudice caused by the first improper evidence.[9] In most cases the decision of the trial court will not be disturbed on appeal. If one were to generalize, it can probably be stated, with support from the authorities,[10] that the introduction (even without objection) of inadmissible evidence usually entitles the opponent to fairly meet that evidence with "inadmissible" evidence of his own. But the courts should take special care in sanctioning this practice since its effect is to circumvent the usual exclusionary rules. Even though in theory the parties are generally "masters of their own cases," a device that gives a party the option of not objecting, secure in the notion that he can then introduce his own inadmissible evidence, must be cautiously employed.

Notes

1. *No Necessity for Offer of Proof During Cross-Examination.* The requirements that normally attend an offer of proof usually are relaxed during cross-examination. McCormick, § 51, at 124. Presumably, the cross-examiner does not know what answer the witness will give. It would appear, however, that the cross-examiner could be required to show what he intends to prove by his question(s) if this is not apparent. However, this requirement has to be balanced against the disadvantage that might be caused the cross-examiner if he has to disclose his plan of attack or rebuttal. See generally Note, Appeal and Error—Excluded Evidence on Cross-examination—Reservation for Appeal, 33 N.C.L.Rev. 476 (1955).

2. *Pretrial Objections to Evidence.* In certain instances, especially in criminal cases in which it is claimed that evidence was obtained in violation of a constitutional principle (such as the prohibition against illegal searches and seizures or the ban against involuntary confessions), it is proper to object to the challenged evidence prior to trial. The procedural device for raising the objection is a motion to suppress the evidence or a "motion in limine," as it is often

9. This solution generally accords with that of Wigmore who maintains that the results in most of the decided cases support the action of the trial judge. See I Wigmore, § 15, at 746 (Tillers).

10. See, e.g., United States v. Johnson, 730 F.2d 683, 691 (11th Cir.1984), cert. denied, 469 U.S. 857 (1984); United States v. Helina, 549 F.2d 713 (9th Cir.1977); for a case limiting the principle see United States v. Winston, 447 F.2d 1236, 1240 (D.C.Cir.1971). For a discussion of curative admissibility see Graham, Handbook of Federal Evidence, § 103.4, at 17–22 (2d ed. 1986).

called. Such motions have been used with increasing frequency in recent years, and the practice of obtaining a pre-trial ruling has also found favor in civil cases. The judge has discretion whether or not to give an early ruling. He may decline to rule on the motion in limine, and probably should do so, if the evidentiary issue is relatively unimportant or it is not certain exactly what form the evidence will take or in what context it might be offered. On the other hand, an early ruling permits the parties to plan for trial with more certainty about the course of the evidence. A ruling "in limine" is not invariably final; technically, the ruling is advisory, and it can thus be altered at trial in the light of actual circumstances. This power to modify or reverse the in-limine ruling means that a party who objects to the pretrial ruling must usually enter an objection at trial if he is to preserve his point for appeal. See Hale v. Firestone Tire & Rubber Co., 756 F.2d 1322, 1333 (8th Cir.1985) ("a motion in limine does not preserve error for appellate review. A party whose motion in limine has been overruled must object when the error the party sought to prevent with the motion is about to occur at trial"). Some recent authority holds that when it is clear that the trial judge's pretrial ruling is definitive and will not be reconsidered, no further objection is necessary. See, e.g., Sprynczynatyk v. General Motors Corp., 771 F.2d 1112 (8th Cir.1985), cert. denied 106 S.Ct. 1263 (1986). Motions in limine are discussed in 1 Weinstein & Berger, ¶ 103(02), at 17–20 (1986).

3. *Waiver of Objection.* Suppose inadmissible evidence is offered by *P,* but *D* does not object and the evidence is admitted. Subsequently, for unrelated reasons, there is a new trial on the same cause of action. *P* again offers the improper evidence, but this time *D* objects. Did *D*'s failure to object at the first trial operate as a waiver in the second trial? See I Wigmore, § 18, at 814 (Tillers), indicating that, except as to privileged communications and evidence excludable under a dead man's statute, there is usually not a waiver.

4. *Objections: Tactical Considerations.* Knowing when to object is sometimes as important as knowing the correct ground. Often, for tactical reasons, counsel will withhold an objection that could have been made. A constant objector does not make a favorable impression upon the jury. Additionally, counsel may withhold an objection where admissibility is questionable because he thinks the topic introduced by his opponent's questions is one that he would like to pursue. Cf. § 11.5. See generally R. Keeton, Trial Tactics and Methods, Ch. IV, especially § 4.2.

5. The following advice appears in G. Keeton, Harris's Hints on Advocacy (18 ed. 1943) at 264:

But you must narrowly watch *and* object if counsel for the prosecution propose to read any letter or document, or state any conversation which, when the proper time comes, may not be admissible. It is useless after the mischief has been done, and the impression made on the minds of the jury, for the Judge to say, "I shall tell the jury that that document or that conversation is not evidence, and that they are to dismiss it from their minds." They cannot dismiss it from their minds, and it *is* evidence, no matter whether you call it so or not, when once before them, and will in all human probability have an influence on their judgment. It is like the village lawyer telling the man that they could not put him in the stocks; the irrefutable answer was "But I *am* here."

Chapter XII

EXPERT TESTIMONY AND SCIENTIFIC EVIDENCE

§ 12.1 Role and Qualification of the Expert Witness

In an earlier chapter[1] we observed that there is a general restriction against receiving in evidence the opinion of a lay witness—at least, in circumstances where the opinion is not helpful to the trier of fact. By definition, however, an expert witness possesses knowledge and skill that distinguish him from ordinary witnesses. Presumably, he is in a position superior to the other trial participants, including the jury, to draw inferences and reach conclusions within his field of expertise. It follows that a witness who qualifies as an expert should be entitled to render opinions and conclusions within the area of his specialty. If he were always forbidden to express his opinion, his testimony might not assist the trier, for his only role would be to facilitate the admission of specialized information (facts and data) which was largely outside the grasp of the jury and from which they would be unable to draw rational inferences. This is not to suggest that an expert can never be helpful unless he expresses an opinion. He can sometimes serve a useful role by simply helping the trier understand or evaluate technical evidence.[2]

When one of the parties presents a witness to testify as an expert, the judge[3] must determine whether the proffered individual has the necessary qualifications. But there is a preliminary issue for resolution by the judge: he must decide whether the

§ 12.1

1. See § 4.9.

2. See United States v. Stifel, 433 F.2d 431, 435–441 (6th Cir.1970), cert. denied 401 U.S. 994 (1971) (expert testimony admitted as to neutron activation analysis).

3. § 10.4.

subject matter about which the expert will testify is sufficiently removed from common experience so that the trier will benefit from the assistance of a specialist.[4] The older cases often required that the subject matter in question be outside the reach of the trier of fact, thus emphasizing the technical or specialized nature of the subject. Modern courts are less demanding, and require only that the expert's testimony be helpful to the trier in the latter's task of finding and evaluating facts. Of course, when the subject concerns a technical aspect of such specialized fields as medicine, science, banking, or photography, there is little question that expert opinion is appropriate.[5] But such subjects as burglars' tools [6] and the effect on livestock of drinking salt water [7] have also been deemed appropriate subjects for expert testimony.

The Federal Rules of Evidence simply state:

> If scientific, technical, or other specialized knowledge will assist the trier of fact to understand the evidence or to determine a fact in issue, a witness qualified as an expert . . . may testify thereto in the form of an opinion or otherwise.[8]

The test is one of helpfulness.[9] The federal courts have approved expert testimony regarding such subjects as carpentry, plumbing, and bricklaying.[10] However, these courts have excluded expert testimony when it would not assist the trier.[11] For example, expert testimony by psychologists on the reliability of eyewitness testimony has, in the past at least, often been rejected. This

4. See McCormick, § 13, at 33; II Wigmore §§ 559–560 (Chadbourn). For a case finding the subject matter sufficiently within the grasp of lay persons, see United States v. Booth, 669 F.2d 1231, 1240 (9th Cir.1981), appeal after remand, 692 F.2d 584 (9th Cir.1982) (expert not permitted to testify that the reason no fingerprints were on the getaway vehicle was because the occupants "had either used gloves or wiped the fingerprints from the vehicle"). See also Skelton v. Sinclair Refining Co., 375 P.2d 948 (Okl.1962) (testimony by architect as to safety of restroom design excluded).

5. For a general discussion containing various examples, see Graham, Handbook of Federal Evidence, § 702.4 (2d ed. 1986); II Wigmore, §§ 556–61, 564–71 (Chadbourn).

6. State v. Oertel, 280 Mo. 129, 217 S.W. 64 (1919); but see Central Mutual Ins. Co. v. D. & B., Inc., 340 S.W.2d 525 (Tex.Civ.App.1960), rejecting testimony by an experienced burglar concerning how a professional outlaw would rob a safe.

7. Manhattan Oil Co. v. Mosby, 72 F.2d 840 (8th Cir.1934).

8. Fed.R.Evid. 702. See Fernandez v. Chios Shipping Co., Ltd., 542 F.2d 145 (2d Cir.1976).

9. See VII Wigmore, § 1923, at 29–32 (Chadbourn).

10. These and other examples are collected in Graham, Handbook of Evidence, § 702.2, at 611–612 n. 7 and n. 9.

11. E.g., United States v. Affleck, 776 F.2d 1451 (10th Cir.1985) (memory expert in fraud case).

exclusion is based on the premise that questions of accuracy of perception and memory "can be adequately addressed in cross-examination and that the jury can adequately weigh . . . [these factors] through common-sense evaluation." [12] Recent opinions in the Third and Sixth Circuits question this assumption, however, and hold that an accused in a criminal case may present expert testimony concerning the reliability of eyewitness identifications if there are scientifically verified principles that apply to the particular identification in question.[13]

In determining *if the person proffered* has the necessary expertise to deal with the specialized subject matter, the judge considers education and experience. Either of these factors alone may suffice to qualify the witness, but typically both qualifications are present to some degree.[14] The determination is made with primary emphasis upon the qualifications the witness possesses when compared to lay or untrained persons. Hence, a general practitioner of medicine can qualify as an expert on a specialty within medicine (such as neurology or orthopedics) even though there are specialists who presumably are more knowledgeable within the restricted field.[15] Furthermore, formal education—advanced degrees and similar credentials—is not an essential characteristic of the expert witness. Practical training or experience will suffice, and such persons as stone masons, mechanics, or photographers may be found to have the necessary expertise.[16] It should be emphasized that considerable latitude is given to the trial judge in making his decision regarding expertise [17] and appellate reversals are infrequent.

§ 12.2 The Expert Witness: Direct Examination

The factfinder, of course, is always faced with the problems of determining what evidence to believe and what inferences to draw

12. United States v. Thevis, 665 F.2d 616, 641 (5th Cir.1982), reh'g denied, 671 F.2d 1379 (5th Cir.1982), and cases cited therein.

13. See United States v. Downing, 753 F.2d 1224 (3d Cir.1985), on remand, 609 F.Supp. 784 (E.D.Pa.1985), affirmed, 780 F.2d 1017 (3d Cir.1985) (reversing district court's exclusion of such expert testimony); United States v. Smith, 736 F.2d 1103, 1106 (6th Cir.1984), cert. denied 469 U.S. 868 (1984). See also Graham, supra note 10, § 702.4, at 614–616.

14. McCormick, § 13, at 33–34. Fed.R.Evid. 702 allows the witness to qualify by "knowledge, skill, experience, training, or education. . . ."

15. Parker v. Gunther, 122 Vt. 68, 164 A.2d 152 (1960); see generally II Wigmore § 569 (Chadbourn).

16. Graham, supra note 10, § 702.2.

17. II Wigmore § 561 (Chadbourn). Wigmore favors a rule that absolutely precludes appellate review. Id.

from the evidence. But the use and evaluation of expert testimony raises special difficulties. The first is determining exactly what facts underlie the expert opinion, and the second is deciding which, if any, of the specialized inferences or conclusions drawn by the expert should be accepted as true. The trier's task is made more difficult because the expert usually gives his testimony in an atmosphere of disputed facts and conflicting contentions. He testifies prior to the trier's deliberation and factfinding, and usually before all of the evidence in the case is in. His opinion is necessarily based upon an underlying set of assumed facts, but these "facts" might be rejected by the trier as false or unproven. If the assumed underlying facts are ultimately rejected by the trier, the opinion of the expert is weakened or destroyed. Therefore, it is essential that there be some means by which the trier can identify what factual assumptions underlie the expert's opinion.

A simple example illustrates this point: A physician gives an opinion that his patient has a certain disease or injury. Three symptoms of the condition in question are persistent headaches, dizziness, and frequent nausea. The patient testifies that he has had these ill effects, but the opposing party offers conflicting evidence that challenges these assertions. It is important for the trier to know that the doctor's opinion was based at least in part upon the assumption that the patient experienced the symptoms. If the trier rejects all or part of the testimony of the patient, it will take this into account in determining the validity of the physician's opinion. Of course, the trier must still grapple with the question whether the doctor's conclusion might be valid despite the absence of some of the underlying facts; we shall take up this difficulty shortly.[1]

Notice the various means by which the expert may gain knowledge of the facts that pertain to his opinion. He may have conducted a personal examination prior to trial as, for example, when a doctor examines the patient whose condition is in question; he may have learned the facts prior to trial through a briefing provided by another person as, for example, when another physician shares the patient's medical files with the expert and elaborates upon the case history; he may learn the facts during courtroom proceedings by observing and hearing the pertinent

§ 12.2

1. See § 12.3.

evidence as it is introduced; finally, he may become aware of the facts when he takes the witness stand and is asked a question that is preceded by a recitation of the assumed facts as, for example, when counsel states, "Assuming, Doctor, that during the four weeks before the patient was hospitalized, and while he was working in close proximity to liquid known as benzene, he experienced persistent headaches, dizziness, and frequent nausea, do you have an opinion. . . ." This kind of question, called by lawyers and judges a hypothetical question, not only informs (or reminds) the witness of the underlying facts, it also *identifies the assumed facts* upon which the expert is to base his opinion. It is one of several means by which the underlying facts can be identified for the trier. Consider another possibility: suppose one or even several of the witnesses who preceded the expert give all of the evidence upon which the expert bases his opinion. Counsel conducting direct examination of the expert can simply ask his witness to assume, for purposes of giving his opinion, that all of the facts to which the preceding witness(es) testified are true. When the preceding testimony has not been long or involved, the trier is adequately informed concerning the assumed facts underlying the opinion; the relative importance of these various facts is usually clarified during cross-examination. A similar convenience is realized where the expert himself supplies evidence of all of the underlying facts.[2] Complications arise, however, when evidence of the facts that underlie the opinion can be traced to numerous witnesses and documents or when the one or two witnesses who supply the underlying facts give extensive testimony or appear to alter, qualify, or change their testimony during cross-examination. It then becomes necessary to use some other technique to identify the supporting facts. The traditional technique for accomplishing this end is the use of a hypothetical question,[3] the essence of which we noted above. The relevant assumed facts are simply summed up in the interrogator's question, and the expert is asked to state his opinion if he is able to reach a conclusion within a reasonable degree of professional certainty.[4] The central idea is to incorpo-

2. In this situation, some courts using the older or traditional approach will permit the expert to express his opinion on the basis of personal knowledge of the facts without first setting out the facts. Development of the underlying facts occurs during the remainder of direct examination and on cross-examination. However, considerations of tactics usually dictate that the expert first give the underlying facts; by so doing his opinion is usually more persuasive.

3. McCormick, § 14, at 35.

4. For a complete example of a hypothetical question, see 6 Am.Jur.Proof of Facts 159–85 (1960).

rate into the question the assumed, underlying facts so that the trier can understand the basis of the opinion. Yet, despite the apparent utility of the hypothetical question, it has been the subject of extensive discussion and, in recent years, growing dissatisfaction.[5]

One objection to the hypothetical question is that it is encumbered with technical requirements that ensnare the unwary and lead to excessive appeals.[6] Many of the older cases require that every fact in evidence that is relevant to the expert's opinion be included within the hypothetical. There is an ancillary requirement, strictly imposed by some courts, that every fact alluded to must be supported by evidence in the record—that is, evidence actually introduced at trial. Reliance upon a presumably accurate hospital record that was not formally received into evidence would be improper even if it could have been introduced as a business entry. If any part of the opinion was based upon inadmissible hearsay, which of course cannot be received into evidence over objection, then this improper basis invalidates the hypothetical.

These technical demands, coupled with counsel's desire to phrase his hypothetical so as to broadly expose and emphasize his most favorable evidence, often lead to lengthy, slanted questions that are difficult for the jury to follow and understand. Furthermore, these burdensome inquiries frequently demand of the expert an artificial exactitude and definitiveness foreign to his accustomed training and methodology. The matter becomes increasingly complicated when sharp conflicts in the evidence make it necessary either on direct or cross-examination for the expert to render an opinion on various hypothetical factual groupings ("Would your opinion be the same if there were no headaches, but a low-grade fever?"). This series of varying factual assumptions increases the chance of jury misunderstanding and exaggerates even more the required precision with which the expert is required to respond—for in most jurisdictions he must affirm that his opinion is within the bounds of reasonable professional (e.g. medical) certainty.

5. See McCormick § 16; II Wigmore § 686 (Chadbourn).

6. For a case illustrating the pitfalls of the hypothetical question, see Ingram v. McCuiston, 261 N.C. 392, 134 S.E.2d 705 (1964). For a thoughtful article on expert testimony, see Ladd, Expert Testimony, 5 Vand.L.Rev. 414 (1952). See also Annot., 71 A.L.R.2d 6 (1960).

There is a growing movement away from the judicial rigidity associated with expert testimony and the strict requirements surrounding the hypothetical question. The recent trend, found in the federal courts and elsewhere, is toward a flexible procedure that gives the expert freedom to testify other than in "opinion form," makes optional the hypothetical question, and abandons the exacting requirements that traditionally have called for admissibility of all of the underlying facts.

The Federal Rules of Evidence carry forward the reform momentum that began in some of the states.[7] Significantly, Rule 702 provides that an expert "may testify . . . in the form of an opinion or otherwise." This provision enables the expert to share his knowledge without the necessity of disclosing it in the form of an opinion. The purpose is to encourage the use of experts to explain scientific or other principles relevant to the case so that, in appropriate circumstances, the trier may apply them to the facts. In Rule 705, the federal draftsmen have made it clear that the use of the hypothetical question usually is optional. That Rule specifies that an "expert may testify in terms of opinion or inference and give his reasons therefor without prior disclosure of the underlying facts or data, unless the court requires otherwise." Usually it is not necessary to bridle the expert (and the jury) with a long and detailed recitation of all of the assumed facts. These can be explored on cross-examination.[8] In another important reform provision, Rule 703, the federal rulemakers state:

> *Bases of Opinion Testimony by Experts.* The facts or data in the particular case upon which an expert bases an opinion or inference may be those perceived by or made known to him at or before the hearing. If of a type reasonably relied upon by experts in the particular field in forming opinions or inferences upon the subject, the facts or data need not be admissible in evidence.[9]

As we have noted, the courts traditionally required that the expert's factual source be supported by admissible evidence. Each assumed fact underlying the expert's opinion had to rest upon admissible evidence that had actually been introduced at trial.

7. See McCormick § 17. Professor McCormick's careful and trenchant criticism of the hypothetical question has been an influential factor in effecting change. See Rabata v. Dohner, 45 Wis. 2d 111, 172 N.W.2d 409 (1969).

8. Fed.R.Evid. 705: "The expert may in any event be required to disclose the underlying facts or data on cross-examination."

9. Fed.R.Evid. 703.

The quoted provision abandons this restriction by sanctioning two significant innovations. The Rule makes it clear that it suffices if the facts or data underlying the opinion (or inference) of the expert be "made known to him at or before the hearing." Further, the Rule specifies that such "facts or data need not be admissible in evidence" if they are "of a type reasonably relied upon by experts in the particular field in forming opinions. . . ." This means that the expert is permitted to learn the facts prior to trial by a variety of means such as personal examination, firsthand investigation, files, reports of other specialists, or the reports or comments of professional observers. The only requirement is that the sources be reliable in the sense that they are normally relied on in the expert's field, even though these materials may not qualify for admission into evidence.

Finally, another significant provision of the Federal Rules negates a rule still found in some common-law jurisdictions.[10] The Federal Rules [11] make it clear that in most instances an expert (and a lay witness, as well) is free to give his opinion on an ultimate issue in the case. Of course, the opinion must assist the factfinder; the provision in the Rules does not clear the way for unnecessary expressions as to an ultimate matter that is beyond the expert's special competence.[12] There is only one area in which an expert is still forbidden to give his opinion on the ultimate issue: in criminal cases, he may not give his "opinion or inference as to whether the defendant did or did not have the mental state or condition constituting an element of the crime charged or the defense thereto." [13] The purpose of this restriction is to confine the expert—usually a psychiatrist—to his field of expertise, namely, the nature of the mental disease in question, its characteristics, and its manifestations. The issue of whether the accused's mental condition provides a partial or complete legal excuse for his conduct is left to the trier.

Thus, the Federal Rules allow the expert to acquire his knowledge by various means, to testify on the basis of assumed

10. See McCormick, § 12, at 30–31. But many recent cases reject the "ultimate issue" rule, particularly where the challenged opinion comes from an expert as opposed to a lay witness.

11. See Fed.R.Evid. 704.

12. "The promulgation of Rule 704 [negating the ultimate issue rule] does not mean that witnesses will now be able to give testimony that involves nothing more than choosing up sides." J. Waltz, The New Federal Rules of Evidence 112 (2d ed. 1975).

13. Fed.R.Evid. 704(b).

facts that are not supported by admissible evidence, to testify with or without giving his opinion, to testify with or without the use of a hypothetical question, and, generally, to give an opinion on the ultimate issue. The guiding principle is that of "helpfulness" to the trier of fact.

§ 12.3 The Expert Witness: Cross-Examination and Impeachment

The technique of cross-examining the expert differs somewhat depending upon which of the modes of direct examination discussed in the preceding section is used. For example, if the direct examiner does not ask a hypothetical question, the cross-examiner may need to identify more definitely the factual assumptions underlying the opinion; if the expert himself has supplied evidence of the underlying facts, the cross-examiner may wish to probe the accuracy of the expert's observation or memory.[1] There are several additional possibilities for testing or weakening the expert's opinion. The cross-examiner may ask the expert to assume different facts than those assumed during direct examination, and to state whether these new factual assumptions would alter his opinion. The interrogator may also probe the expert's education or experience, attempting to expose weaknesses that might discredit the soundness of the latter's opinion.[2]

Like other witnesses, the expert is subject to impeachment by any of the usual methods such as prior inconsistent statements, bad reputation for truthfulness, and so forth.[3] A commonly employed impeachment technique is to show that the expert is biased. For instance, the cross-examiner may prove that the expert is receiving a large fee to testify or that he always aligns himself with a particular point of view or with a particular kind of litigant (such as the plaintiff in a personal injury suit). Further-

§ 12.3

1. Sometimes, of course, the safest path for the adverse examiner is to waive his right of cross-examination. Since the expert is usually considerably more knowledgeable about his subject than the cross-examiner, he can sometimes embarrass his questioner or at least add strength to the opinion expressed during direct.

2. In an extreme case, it might be possible to elicit facts that would render the witness unqualified as an expert. However, in the usual case, a challenge to the expert's qualification would take place before he had rendered his opinion.

3. See §§ 8.3–8.5. See, e.g., Scott v. Spanjer Bros., Inc., 298 F.2d 928 (2d Cir. 1962) (bias); Young v. Group Health Co-op of Puget Sound, 85 Wash.2d 332, 534 P.2d 1349 (1975) (prior inconsistent statement). See generally LeMere v. Goren, 233 Cal.App.2d 799, 43 Cal.Rptr. 898 (1965).

more, in many jurisdictions, the examiner may confront the expert witness with a text or other reference and, after extracting a concession that the work is recognized as a standard authority, point to passages that contradict the expert's opinion.[4] For example, if the expert has testified on direct that a "whiplash" injury is always manifested within several hours after the accident purportedly causing it, the examiner may impeach the expert by having the latter read from a learned treatise a passage that states that such manifestations can occur as long as a year after the accident.[5] As a tactical matter, however, the cross-examiner must be cautious lest the expert persuasively state why the passage is inapplicable to the present case or why its correctness is rejected by current professional thinking.

Note that although the text or other publication is ostensibly being used to discredit the expert witness, it is possible in many jurisdictions to use the text as affirmative proof of its quoted content. This means of proof is available in those jurisdictions recognizing a hearsay exception for learned treatises. Federal Rule 803(18) is illustrative of this exception:

> *Learned Treatises.* To the extent called to the attention of an expert witness upon cross-examination or relied upon by him in direct examination, statements contained in published treatises, periodicals, or pamphlets on a subject of history, medicine, or other science or art, established as a reliable authority by the testimony or admission of the witness or by other expert testimony or by judicial notice [are not excluded by the hearsay rule]. . . .

This exception to the hearsay rule assumes that the reliability of a standard work is likely to be high. Not only is the professional author's reputation at stake, but also his work is scrutinized and used by other professionals in the field.[6] Note the dual requirements of the Rule: either through testimony of an expert witness or by invocation of judicial notice, the court must find that the work in question is a reliable authority; and the work must come to the attention of the expert witness being questioned either

4. A few jurisdictions restrict this form of impeachment to circumstances in which the expert has conceded that he relied upon the treatise. See Adv. Comm.Note to Fed.R.Evid. 803(18); Annot., 60 A.L.R.2d 77, 83–87 (1958); Annot. 64 A.L.R. Fed. 971 (1983).

5. See Ruth v. Fenchel, 21 N.J. 171, 121 A.2d 373 (1956).

6. See Adv.Comm.Note to Fed.R. Evid. 803(18).

by calling it to his attention or through his own reliance upon it during direct examination. This latter requirement allows the witness to comment on the written authority and indicate why he agrees or disagrees with it. Finally, note that the exception for learned treatises is not limited to the context of impeachment, although it is most often invoked in this setting.

§ 12.4 Scientific Proof: General Principles

No attempt is made in this comparatively brief section to discuss comprehensively the various kinds of proof that might be termed "scientific." Instead, selected illustrations are provided and the general principles governing scientific proof are set forth. The adjective "scientific," as we broadly use it here, refers to evidence that draws its convincing force from some principle of science, mathematics, or the like. Typically, scientific evidence is presented by an expert witness who can explain data or test results and, if necessary, explain the scientific principles that are said to give the evidence its reliability.[1]

A difficult question is how well established a scientific principle or process must be before it is acceptable as judicial evidence. The issue arises frequently. To illustrate: (1) the results of a radar speedometer are offered to show that the defendant was driving at a speed of 75 miles per hour; (2) a scientist offers to give his opinion, based on "carbon dating," that an archaeological specimen is 1.6 million years old; (3) the operator of a lie detector, who administered tests to the plaintiff, offers to testify that the plaintiff lied about events upon which suit is now brought. Whenever a scientific principle is used at trial to prove or disprove disputed facts, a question may be raised concerning the validity of that principle. There also is a kindred issue regarding the *validity or accuracy* of the *particular application* of the principle to the subject under judicial investigation. It may be conceded, for example, that there are certain identifiable characteristics of human hair that show variations from individual to individual, yet it might be doubted whether these characteristics are a valid basis for diagnosing a certain disease. Likewise, it may be conceded

§ 12.4

1. As to expert testimony, see §§ 12.1–12.2. See also § 12.3. For a comprehensive treatment of scientific evidence, see P. Giannelli & E. Imwinkleried, Scientific Evidence (1986). Where the underlying scientific principles are well established, and hence subject to judicial notice, the witness need only be qualified to interpret accurately the evidence as, for example, where a police officer testifies to the results of using radar to detect the subject's vehicular speed.

that radar can accurately measure the speed of an object, yet it might be doubted whether a particular application produced an accurate reading. Perhaps there was interference from other moving objects or some other condition that impaired validity. In short, questions often arise regarding the validity of a scientific principle *and* the particular technique that applies the principle. The courts need a standard governing the required reliability of scientific evidence—that is, a standard that prescribes the minimum degree of recognition or acceptance by professionals that gives a principle or a process sufficient reliability to allow its use as evidence.

An early federal case, *Frye v. United States,*[2] addressed the issue of reliability:

> Just when a scientific principle or discovery crosses the line between the experimental and demonstrable stages is difficult to define. Somewhere in this twilight zone the evidential force of the principle must be recognized and while the courts will go a long way in admitting expert testimony deduced from a well-recognized scientific principle or discovery, the thing from which the deduction is made must be sufficiently established to have gained general acceptance in the particular field to which it belongs.

It is probably a fair comment to say that over the years the *Frye* standard has been warmly embraced, emphatically rejected, occasionally ignored, openly modified, and the subject of both criticism and praise by the commentators. Generally speaking, it has been the dominant standard, especially in the older cases, but in recent years it has come under increasing attack. Even the *Frye* test is ambiguous, for by its terms it speaks only to the standard of the scientific principle and does not specifically embrace the implementation (use or process) of the principle. The cases using the *Frye* standard are not uniform, but the tendency is to apply the standard to the validity of the scientific principle and the validity of the scientific hypothesis that supports the particular application of the principle to the problem before the court.[3]

2. 293 F. 1013, 1014 (D.C.Cir.1923).

3. See United States v. Brown, 557 F.2d 541, 557–59 (6th Cir.1977). There is less agreement about the standard to be applied where the principle and the process are valid, but human error (mistakes by an operator or technician) may have led to erroneous conclusions. Id. See generally United States v. Baller, 519 F.2d 463, 466 (4th Cir.), cert. denied 423 U.S. 1019 (1975); State v. Cavallo, 88 N.J. 508, 443 A.2d 1020 (1982); A. Moenssens, F. Inbau, J. Starrs, Scientif-

Those courts that have adhered to it argue that the *Frye* standard is appropriate because it allows disputes about scientific validity to be resolved by the relevant scientific community, spares the courts the time-consuming, difficult tasks of assessing scientific developments, and protects the trier—especially the jury—from its likely inclination to find all "matters of science" accurate and reliable.[4] Conversely, critics of *Frye*,[5] including many courts,[6] find that its standard is difficult to apply. More importantly, they note that its demand for "general acceptance" usually requires a protracted waiting period during which a newly discovered principle or technique awaits acceptance throughout the scientific community.[7] In the interim, judicial tribunals are deprived of useful scientific evidence, even though reliable professional specialists will vouch for the validity of the principle or process in question. It is not surprising that there is continuing disagreement about *Frye*, even among judges within the federal court system. The modern trend, particularly in civil cases, is toward modifying or abandoning the *Frye* standard. A few courts assess the admissibility of scientific evidence by using the familiar test of relevance and asking if the probative value of the evidence is substantially outweighed by its tendency to mislead the jury or embroil the court in a time-consuming dispute about scientific reliability.[8] Other courts, probably a growing minority, simply relax the strict demands of the *Frye* test: they require only that the scientific principle or process in question be shown to have gained "substantial acceptance" as opposed to "general acceptance" within the relevant scientific community.[9] This test would be met if significant numbers of

ic Evidence in Criminal Cases § 1.04 (3d ed. 1986).

4. See Graham, Handbook of Federal Evidence, § 703.2, at 632 (1986).

5. See McCormick, § 203, at 607–609.

6. E.g., United States v. Downing, 753 F.2d 1224 (3d Cir.1985), on remand, 609 F.Supp. 784 (E.D.Pa.1985), judgment affirmed, 780 F.2d 1017 (3d Cir.1985); United States v. Williams, 583 F.2d 1194 (2d Cir.1978), cert. denied, 439 U.S. 1117 (1978).

7. For a thorough and comprehensive discussion of this and other difficulties with *Frye*, and some potential alternatives, see Giannelli, The Admissibility of Novel Scientific Evidence: Frye v. United States, a Half-Century Later, 80 Colum.L.Rev. 1197 (1980).

8. See State v. Catanese, 368 So.2d 975 (La.1979); State v. Walstad, 119 Wis.2d 483, 351 N.W.2d 469 (1984); and cases collected in 3 Louisell & Mueller, § 382, at 359–362 (1986 Supp.).

9. See United States v. Gould, 741 F.2d 45 (4th Cir.1984); cf. United States v. Downing, 753 F.2d 1224 (3d Cir.1985) (degree of acceptance by scientific community is one factor to be used by court in assessing reliability of evidence). See also United States v. Baller, 519 F.2d 463 (4th Cir.1975), cert. denied, 423 U.S. 1019 (1975).

scientists—especially those who are highly specialized in the field in question—affirm the validity of the principle or process in question.

In the pages that follow, two issues are explored, largely through illustrations from the cases. The first is whether the proffered scientific evidence is admissible; the second is what probative force should be accorded scientific evidence that is admitted.

§ 12.5 Scientific Proof: Illustrations

Occasionally, scientific evidence will establish conclusively the proposition to which it is directed, with the result that the factfinder will be prohibited from making a contrary finding. This conclusiveness is assured by instructing the trier to accept the scientifically established proposition as true or, in cases where the proposition is dispositive of the action, by concluding the trial through the use of a directed verdict or some other appropriate procedure. Often, however, the scientific evidence will not be conclusive, but will serve only to increase the likelihood of the proposition toward which it is directed. Here the courts struggle with the question of whether to admit the evidence for its probative worth or simply to exclude it. There is often a risk that the trier will exaggerate the reliability of scientific proof, and in some cases the courts wisely have rejected evidence that has some probative force, yet might be misleading.

In People v. Collins,[1] a case arising in California, the main issue was whether the accused couple, a Negro man and a Caucasian woman, were the persons who had committed the robbery in question. The couple was apprehended after the offense, at a place away from the scene of the crime. A witness for the state testified that a woman with blond hair and a ponytail ran from the scene and entered a yellow car driven by a black male. He was described as having a beard and a mustache.

A mathematician then was called to the stand and asked to support the hypothesis that the defendants were the assailants by applying the product rule of probability theory to the evidence of identification. Use of the product rule involves assessing the separate probability (expressed as a fraction) of the occurrence of

§ 12.5

1. 68 Cal.2d 319, 66 Cal.Rptr. 497, 438 P.2d 33 (1968).

each of a number of independent events and, then, because these events allegedly concurred, multiplying these individual probabilities. The product represents the probability of the *joint* occurrence of these separate events or characteristics. Thus, if the probability were 1 in 10 that a given automobile were yellow and 1 in 500 that an interracial couple were in the same car, the odds of such a couple being in a yellow car would be 1 in 5,000 ($\frac{1}{10} \times \frac{1}{500}$). This result indicates that the couple apprehended was the same couple that committed the offense because of the comparatively remote chance that a similar couple was riding in a yellow car.

Already, a difficulty is apparent. How is it known that 1 out of 10 automobiles is yellow? Perhaps this statistic is available, but it would not be easy to obtain it. Furthermore, it is highly doubtful that there is a reliable statistic representing the chance that a car will be occupied by an interracial couple. Perhaps the chance of this separate event is as probable as 1 in 500 or as remote as 1 in 10,000. The point is that without a reliable probability, obtained by random sample or otherwise, for the happening of each of the component events represented in the product formula, the final product cannot accurately reflect the actual chance of the joint occurrence. It is true that one can make arbitrary but conservative assignments of probability [2] to each separate event and arrive at a product that supposedly understates the probability of all events simultaneously concurring. Thus, conservatively, it might be assumed that the chance of a yellow car should be placed at $\frac{1}{3}$ and that of an interracial couple occupying a car at $\frac{1}{3}$ so that the chance of fortuitous concurrence is $\frac{1}{9}$, or 1 in 9. But these assumptions are outside the province of reasonable certainty, and making calculations on the basis of such suppositions amounts to little more than simply taking a common-sense observation (it is unlikely that a given car will be yellow *and* contain an interracial couple) and giving it a mathematical expression.

There is yet another cautionary note to be sounded in the use of simple probability theory. The validity of the final product depends upon the *independence* of the separate events or charac-

2. People v. Collins, supra n. 1, involved a "conservative" estimate of probabilities; see also State v. Sneed, 76 N.M. 349, 414 P.2d 858 (1966), appeal after remand, 78 N.M. 615, 435 P.2d 768 (1967), in which an expert attempted to show by the product rule that the suspect was the same person as the one who entered name, address, and physical description in a sales register.

teristics. Suppose in the *Collins* case the following characteristics are said to have the probability noted:

	Probability
Interracial couple	1/500
Male with beard	1/10
Male with mustache	1/4

Arguably, these last two events are not independent because many, perhaps even most, men with beards also have mustaches. The danger lies in postulating as independent events those which in fact are related or dependent. By way of further example, suppose a murder weapon is known to be a .38 caliber handgun with five lands and grooves (ridges and depressions in the barrel). It might be a mistake to treat the number of lands and grooves as an independent factor. Even though, say, only one-fourth of all pistols have five lands and grooves, a high proportion of .38 caliber pistols may have this number.[3] If this is true, either the number of lands and grooves must be discarded as dependent or some adjustment in the mathematical formula must be made in order to take account of the dependency.

A final observation: The probability of the congruence of multiple, independent events *is built upon the assumption* that the independent events or characteristics exist. Suppose, for example, the separate events (or characteristics) in *Collins* were independent and suppose further that it were possible to assign an accurate probability to each event. A fatal defect in the accuracy of the conclusion based upon probability theory may still exist because there was a faulty observation of one or more of the separate events or characteristics. The woman assailant in fact may have had red hair instead of blonde; the man identified as Negro may have been an Indian, and so forth. Of these possibilities of mistaken perception (or faulty memory) the probability rule takes no account. To take an extreme example, suppose the eyewitness in *Collins* gave false testimony; in fact, the offense was committed by two Caucasian males. Obviously, the probability rule is of no help in reconstructing the historical facts, and it may endanger reliable factfinding. The tendency of the trier might be to focus upon the superficially persuasive mathematical odds and to lose sight of the significant point that the factual assumptions

3. See Louisell, Kaplan & Waltz, Cases and Materials on Evidence, 70–72 (3rd ed. 1976) (where the problem is posed by excerpts from a closing argument).

underlying the probabilities might be false or inaccurate. The Supreme Court of California stressed this danger in the *Collins* case, but it also rejected the statistical proof on other grounds: there was no showing that the probability factors assigned to the separate characteristics were accurate and no showing that these characteristics were mutually independent.

It is important to note that the *Collins* case did not broadly reject all evidentiary uses of probability theory.[4] The principle of relevance, which lies at the core of the law of evidence, rests, after all, upon estimates of probability. What *Collins* condemns is a "scientific" calculation of probability that does not comport with sound statistical practices and that is very likely to mislead the trier. In appropriate circumstances, the courts admit statistical data or mathematical computations that reveal the estimated probability of an event or circumstance.[5]

An accepted means of proof using statistics and principles of biology is the allowance of blood tests to establish identity. This technique can be useful in a variety of contexts. In its simplest form, it may only involve a showing that blood taken from clothing or elsewhere is the same type as, say, the defendant's blood. Since under one traditional classification (ABO) there are four major blood groups (O, A, B, and AB) and the approximate percentage of persons falling within each group is well established,[6] similarity of type can add force to the argument that the blood in question came from the person alleged to be the source. This contention is especially cogent where the group is comparatively rare: type AB is a good example for it is found in only 4% of

4. People v. Collins, 68 Cal.2d 319, 332, 66 Cal.Rptr. 497, 505, 438 P.2d 33, 41 (1968).

5. See, e.g., Castaneda v. Partida, 430 U.S. 482 (1977) (statistics established prima facie case of discrimination in grand jury selection); Contemporary Missions Inc. v. Famous Music Corp., 557 F.2d 918 (2d Cir.1977) (record industry sales used to project possible success of plaintiff's record). But see Moultrie v. Martin, 690 F.2d 1078 (4th Cir.1982) (rejecting statistical evidence for "mathematically incorrect methodology" in failure to apply standard deviation analysis).

6. In the United States,

O—45% of the population
A—41% of the population
B—10% of the population
AB—4% of the population

See State v. Rolls, 389 A.2d 824 (Me. 1978); Shanks v. State, 185 Md. 437, 45 A.2d 85 (1945); for a detailed explanation, see Race & Sanger, Blood Groups in Man (6th ed. 1975). There are many other systems of grouping. These have resulted from subsequent discoveries of additional characteristics of human blood. The availability of multiple systems yields additional opportunities to discriminate among blood groups.

the population.[7] Thus, if the victim (with, say, type O blood) injures his assailant (AB blood) and the blood found at the scene of the crime matches the blood of the accused assailant, probative value is high.[8] Even where a more commonly found blood group is involved—for example O, which is found in 45% of the population—similarity of blood type has probative value and is usually admitted into evidence for the purpose of establishing identity.[9] This result is proper, especially since the trier should have no difficulty in understanding the evidence or in assigning to it an appropriate weight.

Recent medical research and sophisticated techniques of analysis now permit scientists to make fine discriminations that distinguish the blood of one person from that of another. Potentially, at least, the end result of these scientific advances will be to demonstrate that each person's blood has unique characteristics which, like fingerprints, can be a means of positive identification.[10] For the present, it should be acknowledged that new blood-typing procedures allow serologists to identify genetically controlled substances, such as specific proteins and enzymes, that typically vary from person to person. The group of persons with particular combinations of characteristics may be quite small. The "new science" of blood identification is beginning to find its way into the courtroom, sometimes as an adjunct to the traditional blood-typing results [11] and other times as a new source of proof.[12]

7. Again, see State v. Rolls, 389 A.2d 824 (Me.1978) (various blood-typing techniques place victim in 5% of population possessing particular combination of characteristics).

8. See supra n. 6. The reader is reminded that other classifications exist. Ibid.

9. A leading American case is Shanks v. State, 185 Md. 437, 45 A.2d 85 (1945); see also United States v. Kearney, 420 F.2d 170 (D.C.Cir.1960); People v. Mountain, 66 N.Y.2d 197, 495 N.Y.S.2d 944, 486 N.E.2d 802 (1985); Parson v. State, 222 A.2d 326 (Del.Supr. 1966), cert. denied 386 U.S. 935 (1966). For an English case where similarity of blood was apparently routinely admitted as increasing the probability of the asserted identity, see Mawaz Khan v. The Queen, 3 Weekly Law Reports 1275 (Privy Council, 1966).

10. See Diamond, The Story of Our Blood Groups, in Wintrobe, ed., Blood Pure and Eloquent 691 (1980). The traditional system of blood-typing, called the ABO classification, distinguishes among the major four blood groups on the basis of antigens. Modern science continues to discover new blood components and it is quite possible that "each person is uniquely identifiable" by the particular combinations of substances found in his blood. McCormick, § 205, at 618.

11. State v. Rolls, 389 A.2d 824 (Me. 1978).

12. See State v. Washington, 229 Kan. 47, 622 P.2d 986 (1981). However, the courts split on the admissibility of the new blood-typing techniques. Authorities pro and con are reviewed in People v. Brown, 401 Cal.2d 512, 220 Cal.Rptr. 637, 709 P.2d 440 (1986).

Evidence of blood group is also useful in resolving an issue of paternity. It is scientifically established that certain parental blood group combinations create an impossibility that the offspring can have blood of certain specified types. When the blood group(s) of the parents is known, these biological laws of heredity can be applied to limit the range of blood types that it is possible to find in an offspring. The most frequent use of these hereditary principles is in making determinations about whether a particular person (usually the putative father) is, or could be, the parent of the child in question. Information about the blood type of the child and that of one parent permits reliable conclusions about the possible blood type of the father. If, for example, the child's blood group is A and the mother's group is O, the father must be either A or AB; he cannot be either B or O.[13]

It readily can be seen that it is scientifically possible to separate and exclude absolutely certain persons from those individuals who may be suspected of being the parent of the child in question. It is not surprising that evidence of blood grouping tests is always admissible when the results *preclude* the possibility that the defendant (or some other named person) is in fact the unknown parent. The principles of blood grouping are so widely recognized that it is not even necessary that an expert provide proof of the validity of the underlying principles; these can be the subject of judicial notice.[14] The expert can, if he wishes, briefly state the scientific principles and provide and interpret the test results. Is this evidence given a conclusive effect, or could there still be a civil or criminal judgment against the person who, under biological laws, could not be the parent? The better view, overwhelmingly adopted in recent years, is that evidence establishing nonpaternity is conclusive if the blood-grouping tests were properly conducted. Any jury finding to the contrary cannot stand.[15]

13. See McCormick, § 205(B), at 620. For a discussion of current and highly specific blood-antigen testing, see Reisner & Bolk, A Layman's Guide to the Use of Blood Group Analysis in Paternity Testing, 20 J.Fam.L. 657 (1981–82).

14. See § 1.8.

15. See Commonwealth v. D'Avella, 339 Mass. 642, 162 N.E.2d 19 (1959); Jordan v. Mace, 144 Me. 351, 69 A.2d 670 (1949); Commissioner of Welfare v. Costonie, 277 App.Div. 90, 97 N.Y.S.2d 804 (1st Dept.1950); Steiger v. Gray, 145 N.E.2d 162 (Ohio Juv.Ct.1957). A famous early case to the contrary involved the actor Charles Chaplin; see Berry v. Chaplin, 74 Cal.App.2d 652, 169 P.2d 442 (1950). A more recent case awarding child support despite blood test evidence excluding the defendant father is State v. Camp, 286 N.C. 148, 152–153, 209 S.E.2d 754, 756–757 (1974). But see N.C.Gen.Stat. § 8–50.1(a)(1) (enacted in response to State v. Camp) making conclusive a blood test excluding paternity. As suggested in

A difficulty arises when the test results do not exclude the alleged parent. May the party seeking to prove parentage introduce the results into evidence? The argument for admission is that since the putative parent is not within the excludable groups, his inclusion within one or more of the blood groups that could account for the child's blood type is probative that he is the parent. This contention is quite consistent with the general principle of relevance, which holds that evidence is relevant if it makes the proposition to which it is directed more likely than it would be in the absence of the evidence. The fact that the alleged parent is not within the excluded group adds to the probabilities that he is the father. In cases where the excluded blood groups constitute a high proportion of the general population, yet the putative parent is not excluded, probative force is significantly increased. But we have repeatedly observed that relevant evidence can be rejected if its probative value is substantially outweighed by such factors as unfair prejudice or misleading the jury. Nonetheless, it seems that the jury can properly assess the evidence that the charged party is within a group that could have produced the offspring. The danger of misleading the trier is reduced by revealing the percentages of the various blood groups within the total population. Thus, it is curious, and seemingly indefensible, that until recently a vast majority of cases [16] exclud-

the text, the courts usually accord a conclusive effect by taking judicial notice of the undisputed validity of blood-grouping tests.

A more difficult question is presented in cases where a child is born in wedlock, but the husband seeks to show that he is not the father. The law favors legitimacy and often raises a presumption that the husband is the father. Should this presumption be overcome by evidence of blood-test results that establish that the husband could not have been the father? See Kusior v. Silver, 54 Cal.2d 603, 354 P.2d 657 (1960).

16. See the cases collected in Annot., 43 A.L.R. 4th 579, 615 (1986). Rejection of this evidence sometimes is justified as a matter of statutory interpretation. In many states, admission of test results that *exclude* paternity is provided for by statute (although it appears that a court would have inherent power to admit this evidence). It is thus possible to conclude that when a statute only grants admissibility to results that preclude the possibility of paternity, results that do not exclude the charged party are inadmissible. Whether the legislature intended this result is a matter that can be pursued in the legislative history of the particular statute in question. Arguably, only a clear demonstration of the intended rejection of results showing the possibility of parenthood should overcome the usual judicial prerogative to admit relevant evidence that appears to fall within the area of admissibility. In any event, the recent trend is toward admitting the results of a blood test that indicates possible paternity. See text accompanying n. 17 infra.

ed test evidence that showed the alleged parent was within a blood group that made his (or her) parentage possible.

This traditional view is losing ground. As new research increases the capacity of the forensic serologists to differentiate among genetic traits found in the blood and either to exclude the putative father or place him within a statistically small group of possible fathers, the probative force of blood-typing is almost irresistible. Recent cases, often spurred by statutory changes, reflect a new receptivity to evidence that places the putative father within a group whose blood type is consistent with parentage.[17]

The foregoing description of the use and admissibility of blood tests as evidence illustrates several points of general application in the field of scientific evidence. Whenever scientific evidence (as we broadly use that term here) is offered, the first inquiry is whether it adds to the likelihood of the proposition to which it is directed. This, of course, is the simple test of relevance. But with evidence of a technical nature, there is special concern: the trier might give undue weight to this evidence since it may appear to lend the certainty of an exact discipline to problematic factfinding. This concern is manifested in at least two cautionary judicial principles.

First, as we have seen, courts require at least substantial recognition by the scientific community of both the scientific principles that underlie the evidence and the application of those principles to the issue before the court. Second, the courts require foundation evidence showing that the procedures used in adducing the results were carefully performed in accordance with accepted standards. Of course, in cases where the scientific principle and its application are well established, judicial notice is appropriate.

Observe, then, the various possibilities for rejecting scientific evidence. The evidence might be refused because it is irrelevant, because probative value is overcome by a substantial possibility of jury confusion or misuse, because it was developed without following proper test procedures, or finally, because the underlying scientific principle (or its application to the problem at hand) has not received sufficient acknowledgement by those in the relevant scientific community. At one point, the courts required accept-

17. See, e.g., State v. Unterseher, 255 N.W.2d 882 (N.D.1977). See also McCormick, § 205, at 621–622, noting the increasing acceptance of this evidence in the courts and under statutes.

ance by those within the general field from which the evidence was derived. However, in recent years as highly developed specialties have burgeoned, it is sufficient in many jurisdictions if experts in the particular narrow field of endeavor would accord validity to the scientific basis of the evidence.[18] Recall that if the evidence is admitted it can be given either of two distinct effects: It could be considered conclusive as to the proposition to which it is directed or it could be given only such probative effect as the trier deems appropriate. The important factor in determining whether the evidence should be conclusive is the extent to which those in the field accept as irrefutable the scientific conclusion in question. Here the courts wisely await the development of a consensus within the general scientific community before denying to the trier the authority to reach a contrary conclusion. Obviously, the greater impact of conclusiveness justifies a caution beyond that necessary when the evidence is admitted only for such probative effect as the trier determines to give it.

The use of radar for speed detection involves the application of several of the general rules governing the acceptability and use of scientific evidence. It is now undisputed, and hence can be judicially noticed, that the principles underlying radar are valid.[19] Thus, it is unnecessary to offer proof that a radio wave which strikes a moving object changes frequency in proportion to the speed of the object.[20] The application of radar to detect the speed of automobiles (i.e. the technique or process) is also subject to judicial notice. Of course, an officer or some other person must still provide a foundation covering such matters as the condition of the equipment, operating and record-keeping procedures, and identity of the offender's vehicle.[21] If this foundation testimony is not challenged, is the result of the radar test conclusive as to the driver's speed? This question is most frequently posed in criminal prosecutions for speeding where, by tradition if not by constitu-

18. Commonwealth v. Lykus, 367 Mass. 191, 327 N.E.2d 671 (1975). Cf. 1 Louisell & Mueller, § 105, at 824–825.

19. See, e.g., People v. Magri, 3 N.Y.2d 562, 170 N.Y.S.2d 335, 147 N.E.2d 728 (1958); State v. Dantonio, 18 N.J. 570, 115 A.2d 35 (1955). For a treatment of judicial notice, see § 1.8. See generally McCormick §§ 328 et seq. McCormick elsewhere makes the point that state statutes may provide for judicial notice of the scientific principles underlying radar. McCormick, § 204, at 613.

20. For a description of the principle and operation of a radar unit, see J. Waltz, Introduction to Criminal Evidence 430–31 (2d Ed.1983); McCarter, Legal Aspects of Police Radar, 16 Clev.-Mar.L.Rev. 455 (1966).

21. See Waltz, supra n. 20; Russell, Radar Speedometers in Court, 6 ABA Law Notes 69 (1970).

tional force, a verdict is not directed against the person charged.[22] Thus, the results of the radar measurement are not conclusive against the accused. In civil cases, however, it should be the rule that in the absence of a challenge to the foundation testimony, the test results are conclusive.

Even this concise treatment of scientific evidence would be truncated without some reference to comparatively new techniques and devices that are currently being proffered for judicial acceptance. Neutron activation analysis (NAA) is a technique for the analysis, identification, and comparison of physical evidence. Almost any substance can be subjected to this elaborate and sophisticated process which can isolate and measure minute traces of an endless variety of materials such as gunpowder, narcotics, hair, alcohol, soil, rubber, etc.[23] The identification and quantitative analysis of the material in question are accomplished by measuring the gamma rays emitted after the sample has been irradiated by bombardment with neutrons in a nuclear reactor.[24] Although neutron activation analysis is expensive and requires complicated nuclear equipment, it appears exceedingly accurate in revealing most substances[25] and has yet another advantage: the material analyzed normally is not damaged and consequently can be preserved for other purposes such as courtroom exhibition.

In recent years courts have given careful consideration to NAA; generally their attitude has been receptive.[26] In most cases at least, a party intending to use NAA results as evidence should

22. But the cases hold that the trier can find guilt beyond a reasonable doubt on the basis of the results of radar detection. See McCormick, § 204, at 614.

23. Good descriptions of neutron activation analysis may be found in 1 Louisell & Mueller, § 106, at 846–849; Waltz, supra n. 20, at 390–91. See also Note, Evidence—Admissibility of the Neutron Activation Analysis Test, 18 St. Louis U.L.J. 235 (1973).

24. Waltz, supra n. 20, at 390. For more details, consult Moenssens, Inbau & Starrs, Scientific Evidence in Criminal Cases 528 et seq. (3d ed.1986).

25. Difficulty is encountered in comparing blood samples. See State v. Stout, 478 S.W.2d 368 (Mo.1972); Waltz, supra n. 20, at 392.

26. A leading case is United States v. Stifel, 433 F.2d 431 (6th Cir.1970), cert. denied 401 U.S. 994 (1970); see also State v. Coolidge, 109 N.H. 403, 260 A.2d 547 (1969), rev'd on other grounds, 403 U.S. 443 (1971). See generally Karjala, Evidentiary Uses of Neutron Activation Analysis, 59 Calif.L.Rev. 997 (1971). But see State v. Stout, 478 S.W.2d 368 (Mo.1972), holding that NAA, although generally valid, is not sufficiently reliable to justify admission when employed to compare blood samples. Blood presents special problems, one of which is that certain trace elements in blood produce a disproportionate emission. See Waltz, supra n. 20, at 392.

be prepared to offer one or more experts who will testify as to the validity of the process.[27] In short, judicial notice may not be applicable, with the result that the proponent will have to present evidence relating to the scientific validity of NAA. Further, it is advisable, and apparently mandatory in a criminal case, to give the other party or the accused pretrial notice of the intended use of NAA test results.[28]

Another technique that has recently gained the attention of courts and commentators is that of achieving voice identification through the use of an electromagnetic instrument called a spectrograph. This device is capable of producing graphic impressions ("voiceprints") of the human voice, taking account of such variables as frequency, volume, and time intervals. If an identified voice sample is available, a voiceprint is made and it is then compared with the voiceprint of the unknown voice. The favored method of comparison is to obtain an identified sample containing exactly the same words as the unidentified sample—as, for example, when a suspect is asked to repeat the message of an anonymous bomb threat that the police have taped. If this is not possible, certain frequently used words (such as "and," "the," "I," and "you") sometimes serve as the basis of the comparative analysis. The theory underlying this means of identification is that human voices differ because of the number of variables involved in voice production. Speech involves the use of the various parts of the vocal cavities (throat, mouth, nose, and sinuses) which will vary in size and relationship from person to person. Voice production also utilizes the so-called "articulators" (soft palate, jaws, tongue, teeth, and lips) which will be used differently among speakers.[29] The combination of differing physical characteristics and varying use of the articulators is said to make it highly unlikely that any two voices are actually the same.[30]

The validity of the spectrographic technique of voice identification is subject to considerable dispute within the scientific community. Hence, it is not surprising that cases considering the

27. See, e.g., State v. Smith, 637 S.W.2d 232 (Mo.App.1982).

28. Compare United States v. Kelly, 420 F.2d 26 (2d Cir.1969), with United States v. Stifel, 433 F.2d 431 (6th Cir. 1970), cert. denied, 401 U.S. 994 (1970). *Stifel* indicates that the government must not only give notice, but must also give the financial assistance necessary to enable the accused to conduct his own tests.

29. See Moenssens et al., supra note 24, at 654–62; Waltz, supra n. 20, at 408–09.

30. See Waltz, supra n. 20, at 409.

admissibility of voiceprints reflect varying judicial attitudes. Many cases reject spectrographic evidence, usually on the ground that the principles underlying this form of proof are not sufficiently accepted by the scientific community.[31] But there are cases to the contrary. The courts receiving this evidence do not claim that there is a general scientific consensus about the validity and accuracy of spectrographic techniques. But they find significant scientific support and seem to take comfort in those studies that (contrary to other investigations) find a favorable accuracy rate.[32] If voiceprints are received only after comprehensive foundation evidence and the jury is instructed that there is disagreement as to the reliability of this evidence, it would appear that spectrographic results can make a positive contribution to factfinding.

Notes

1. *Fingerprints.* The use of fingerprints for the purpose of identification has long been accepted by the courts. The underlying biological principle is that the friction skin ridges, which make up the fingerprint pattern, begin to form during fetal life and remain unchanged until the skin decomposes after death. These patterns are never duplicated in their minute details, not even on the fingers of a single individual. Perspiration and bodily oils coat the skin ridges and leave an impression of the pattern whenever a smooth surface is touched. It is this impression that is analyzed and used to match a person with the print. The scientific principles underlying fingerprinting are judicially noticed. See generally II Wigmore § 414. For the history of fingerprinting, see Hoover, The Role of Identification in Law Enforcement: An Historical Adventure, 46 St.John's L.Rev. 613 (1972). For a detailed discussion, see Moenssens, Starrs & Inbau, Scientific Evidence in Criminal Cases Ch. 7 (3d ed.1986).

31. See State v. Gortarez, 141 Ariz. 254, 686 P.2d 1224 (1984); Reed v. State, 283 Md. 374, 391 A.2d 364 (1978); United States v. Addison, 498 F.2d 741 (D.C. Cir.1974) ("[T]echniques of speaker identification by spectrogram comparison have not attained the general acceptance of the scientific community to the degree required in this jurisdiction by *Frye*. Whatever its promise may be for the future, voiceprint identification is not now sufficiently accepted by the scientific community as a whole to form a basis for a jury's determination of guilt or innocence."). See McCormick, § 207, at 639–641.

32. United States v. Williams, 583 F.2d 1194 (2d Cir.1978), cert. denied 439 U.S. 1117 (1979); United States v. Baller, 519 F.2d 463 (4th Cir.1975), cert. denied 423 U.S. 1019 (1975) (evidence proper where competent witnesses testified on both sides of the question of reliability of the spectrogram and jury was allowed to make its own aural comparisons); State v. Wheeler, 496 A.2d 1382 (R.I.1985). For a discussion of the debate over spectrographic evidence, see 1 Louisell & Mueller, § 106, at 849–853. For case authority pro and con, see Saltzburg & Redden at 665–66.

2. *Ballistics.* The scientific analysis of projectiles that are fired from various kinds of arms yields important and admissible evidence about the firearm used. See Annot., 26 A.L.R.2d 892 (1952). Variations in rifling, firing pins and even shell ejector mechanisms make possible fine discriminations.

3. *Detection of Intoxication.* There are now several devices used to determine, by chemical means, the subject's level of intoxication. Measurements of the breath (by use of a "breathalyzer") and of the blood or urine can be used to indicate the approximate amount of alcohol that has reached the brain. The legislatures have given extensive attention to this kind of evidence. Typically, the statutes permit evidence of test results and prescribe what presumptions, if any, shall arise from the findings. For example, a level of 0.05 percent (or less) of blood alcohol usually raises a presumption that the subject was not under the influence of alcohol. On the other hand, a finding of 0.10 percent (or more) usually creates a presumption of intoxication. McCormick, § 205, at 617. See generally Erwin, Defending Drunk Driving Cases, §§ 14.01–28.06 (3d ed. Rev.1982); see also Annot., 16 A.L.R.3d 748 (1986 Supp.).

4. *Detection of Narcotics Use.* The drug Nalline can be used to detect the recent use of narcotics. When the drug is administered, the eye pupils of a recent user dilate. The courts have been receptive to "Nalline tests." See People v. Zavala, 239 Cal.App.2d 732, 49 Cal. Rptr. 129 (1966). The results of Enzyme Multiple Immunoassay testing of subjects' urine are also widely accepted. See generally Spence v. Farrier, 807 F.2d 753 (8th Cir.1986).

5. *Detection of Lying.* Both scientists and lawyers have long been intrigued with the possibility that scientific techniques can accurately reveal when a person is lying. Perhaps the best known device for detecting false statements is the polygraph or "lie detector." Generally speaking, the courts have rejected the results of polygraph examinations, although some courts will receive the results if the parties so stipulate prior to the examination. See Brown v. Darcy, 783 F.2d 1389, 1394–95 (9th Cir.1986). A few appellate decisions give the trial judge discretion to admit the results even in the absence of a stipulation. See McCormick, § 206, at 628–29. See also note 3 at the conclusion of Chapter VIII.

6. *Compelling Testimony from an Expert.* In a typical trial involving scientific or other technical matters, the opposing parties, acting through their attorneys, will each engage one or more experts to assist in the preparation for trial. Of course, the parties often want these experts to testify at trial. Arrangements between party and expert for assistance (including trial testimony) are ordinarily

consensual and nearly always include provisions for payment of the expert's fees and expenses.

Suppose, however, a party wishes to compel an expert to give testimony either at a deposition hearing or at trial. If the expert has been engaged by the opposing party, the extent of discovery, including the taking of a deposition, is regulated by Fed.R.Civ.Proc. 26(b)(4) and, as to matters falling outside of that provision, by Fed.R.Civ.Proc. 30 and 45. The balance struck is between a party's need to rely on an expert and the adversary's need to prepare adequately for trial.

Whether one may call his adversary's expert as a trial witness does not frequently arise. If the *adversary* calls the expert witness, cross-examination is routinely available; if he does not, there may be a tactical risk for the potential cross-examiner who calls an opposing expert. In any event, some cases support the right of a party to call an opponent's expert, at least where the trial judge determines that there is a need for the testimony of the particular expert in question. See Anderson v. Florence, 288 Minn. 351, 181 N.W.2d 873 (1970) (expert opinion by defendant physician); Annot., 77 A.L.R.2d 1182, 1191 (1961).

An important and often debated question is whether a party may simply subpoena an expert not engaged by either adversary and compel his testimony either by deposition or at trial. Two circumstances must be carefully distinguished. Sometimes an expert observes the event in question as, for example, an engineer who, while attending an athletic event, sees a portion of the stadium collapse. He can be called to testify as to his observations, and many courts also hold that he may be required to give any opinion he has already formed (assuming, of course, there is an adequate basis for it). But the courts will not compel the "occurrence expert," as he is sometimes called, to undertake any special preparation in order to equip himself to render a judicially acceptable opinion. See generally Maurer, *Compelling the Expert Witness: Fairness and Utility Under the Federal Rules of Civil Procedure,* 19 Ga.L.Rev. 71, esp. 82–83 (1984).

A different context is found when the expert did not observe the event in question. Suppose a party, by subpoena, tries to compel the expert's testimony because of the latter's expertise in a subject pertinent to the issues litigated. Traditionally, many courts declined to require his testimony either at trial or by deposition. See, e.g., Ondis v. Pion, 497 A.2d 13, 18 (R.I.1985) ("compelling expert testimony would in essence involve a form of involuntary servitude"). Some courts have viewed the expert's knowledge as a form of property and have been apprehensive that if he could be forced to testify, he might be subjected to continual demands. See Mason v. Robinson, 340 N.W.2d 236 (Iowa 1983) (compelling necessity is required before expert can be forced to testify). In recent years, these justifications have been questioned and an increasing number of courts have been willing to decide the issue of compulsion in the particular circumstances of each case. A leading federal decision is Kaufman v. Edelstein, 539 F.2d 811 (2d Cir.1976), which (a) rejects the notion that an expert enjoys a "privilege not to testify"; (b) supports the court's right to compel this testimony if good cause is shown; and (c) indicates that his testimony may properly include his factual knowledge about the relevant area, previously formed opinions, and "in rare cases, a freshly formed opinion." Id. at 821. But the courts stop short of compelling the expert to expend his labors preparing his testimony and, where special compensation is appropriate, they direct the payment of appropriate professional fees. Mason v. Robinson, 340 N.W.2d at 242–43.

Note that under Fed.R.Evid. 706 the court may appoint an expert to aid it in the resolution of technical issues. The expert so appointed is expected to study carefully the case at hand and render unbiased assistance, usually including a professional opinion. Since the expert must prepare extensively, the Rule properly provides that he must consent to his appointment and, further, that he is entitled to reasonable compensation.

Chapter XIII

REAL EVIDENCE AND WRITINGS

§ 13.1 Real and Demonstrative Evidence: In General

The term "real evidence" generally refers to animate or inanimate physical things exhibited to the jury. Often, however, the term is used narrowly to refer only to tangible items (such as a weapon or a damaged mechanical part) originally involved in the litigated occurrence. The term "demonstrative evidence" is then employed to indicate those tangible items (such as maps, diagrams, or models) not directly involved in the litigated occurrence, but subsequently constructed or obtained by the parties to illustrate or demonstrate their factual contentions or to help the jury understand the case. It has been suggested that although real evidence, in the narrow sense, itself has probative value, demonstrative evidence has none, being a mere visual or artificial aid designed to assist the trier in understanding the probative testimony or contentions of the parties.[1] The validity of this distinction is doubtful, at least if the term "probative value" denotes the tendency of evidence to make the existence of a fact more probable to the trier than it would be in the absence of the evidence.[2] In any event, this distinction often is ignored by the appellate opinions and, as we shall see, the use of both real and demonstrative evidence is

§ 13.1

1. See Smith v. Ohio Oil Co., 10 Ill. App.2d 67, 75, 134 N.E.2d 526, 530 (1956).

2. Whatever the technical limits of demonstrative evidence, practicing lawyers regard it as having probative force. See Belli, Demonstrative Evidence and the Adequate Award, 22 Miss.L.J. 284 (1951). See also III Wigmore, § 791, at 227 (Chadbourn), which states that a map or diagram used as part of a witness's testimony "*is evidence* like any other part of the witness' utterance."

conditioned upon criteria that reduce the risk that the evidence will improperly influence the trier.

In the following discussion, the term "real evidence," unless otherwise indicated, is used in its broadest sense to include any tangible thing ("res") exhibited to the jury. However, there is an important distinction regarding the proper evidentiary foundation: when the exhibited item allegedly was involved in the occurrence or controversy in question (*original* real evidence), its admission is conditioned upon a showing by the proponent that the thing displayed is the *same* thing that originally was involved.[3] But when the real evidence is used only demonstratively—that is, to illustrate or clarify—its origin is not important.[4] What matters is whether the properties or characteristics of the item (map, model, or so forth) are sufficiently clear and accurate to assist, without misleading, the trier in understanding some aspect of the case.

When a party presents real evidence, its perceptible qualities can be sensed by the trier without reliance on the testimonial capacities (observation, memory, and sincerity) of others.[5] Nonetheless, the use of real evidence also involves some reliance upon foundation testimony that establishes the origin or nature of the evidence. If the proponent fails to persuade the jury of the authenticity or accuracy of his real evidence, they may disregard it. In any event, the jury must assess the credibility of testimony relating to the imperceptible aspects of real evidence.

Finally, real evidence, like other forms of proof, can be used directly or circumstantially.[6] If an ultimate issue in a case rests on whether a certain antique is chipped and discolored, display of the item provides direct evidence of the defects.[7] But if the issue is the cause of the damage, the item is mere circumstantial proof, generating an inference as to the cause of the defect. Likewise, the perceptible characteristics of a child (color of eyes, skin, or hair, for example) are direct evidence of these features, but cir-

3. See Higginbotham v. State, 262 Ala. 236, 240, 78 So.2d 637, 640 (1955); Isaacs v. National Bank of Commerce of Seattle, 50 Wash.2d 548, 551, 313 P.2d 684, 686 (1957); McCormick, § 212, at 667.

4. McCormick, § 212, at 668.

5. Morgan & Weinstein at 171. A leading article on the theoretical basis of real proof is Michael & Adler, Real Proof, 5 Vand.L.Rev. 344 (1952).

6. McCormick, § 212, at 665.

7. Cf. Woodward & Lothrop v. Heed, 44 A.2d 369 (D.C.Mun.Ct.App.1945) (condition of fur coat in action for breach of warranty).

cumstantial evidence that *X*, who has similar characteristics, is the father.[8]

§ 13.2 Real and Demonstrative Evidence: Conditions of Admissibility and Required Foundation

To be admissible, tangible evidence must provide the trier of fact with some knowledge or understanding it lacked before viewing the thing presented.[1] Further, the insights thus gained must be consequential (material) to the controversy being tried. This is a familiar theme. Relevant evidence makes the consequential proposition to which it is directed more likely than it would be without the evidence; often, however, courts relax even this undemanding standard when dealing with real evidence. Although real evidence sometimes can have very high probative force—as, for example, when it is used as direct proof of an ultimate issue[2]—it also may serve only to illustrate or explain testimony directed to the background or setting of the litigated transaction. In this latter circumstance, the probative force of the real evidence is marginal at best, but courts nonetheless admit it unless it has a potential for causing confusion or delay. Perhaps it may be generalized that courts consider real evidence "relevant" if it either increases the probability of a consequential proposition *or* assists the trier in understanding the case.

All evidence, of course, is subject to the objection that its probative value is substantially outweighed by prejudice, distraction, confusion, or undue delay. With real evidence this balancing test most often is required when the proffered item likely will inspire a sharp emotional response such as pity or repugnance. Nonetheless, when the evidence displays a condition that is in issue, the courts almost always will admit it.[3] And even when

8. See Glascock v. Anderson, 83 N.M. 725, 497 P.2d 727 (1972); McCormick, § 212, at 666.

§ 13.2

1. See McAndrews v. Leonard, 99 Vt. 512, 134 A. 710 (1926), where one question presented on appeal was whether the trier could gain useful knowledge from touching a depression (caused by a fracture) in the plaintiff's skull. This case and other pertinent cases and comments may be found in Weinstein & Mansfield, et al. at 64–83.

2. If there were an issue whether a person were scarred or dismembered and that person were presented to the trier, the probative force would be obvious. See McCormick, § 212, at 665.

3. Lanford v. People, 159 Colo. 36, 409 P.2d 829 (1966) (motion picture of allegedly intoxicated driver); Darling v. Charleston Comm. Mem. Hosp., 50 Ill. App.2d 253, 200 N.E.2d 149 (1964) (stump of amputated leg); Olson v. Tyner, 219 Iowa 251, 257 N.W. 538 (1934) (shriveled arm). See McCormick, § 212, at 665–66, especially nn. 15 and

probative force is comparatively weak, the tendency still is toward admission: such things as a plaintiff's preserved knee cap,[4] decedent's blood-stained clothing,[5] and pictures of a deceased victim of a crime[6] all have been admitted. Because the trial judge has considerable discretion in balancing the worth of real evidence against its negative aspects, reversals of his rulings are relatively rare.[7]

The proponent of real evidence must provide a proper foundation, a process referred to as identification or authentication. This generally consists of having one or more witnesses describe the item, supply information about its origin, and, if needed, provide such additional testimony as is required to show that the item is relevant. When the evidence is "original" in the sense that it played a part in the controversy, identification entails a showing that the thing offered is the *same item* that was involved in the litigated transaction[8]—for example that the proffered rifle is the weapon used by the defendant or the proffered ring is the one that was falsely claimed to be a diamond. It will be seen immediately that this requirement that the origin of the thing be shown is a function of the principle of relevance—more specifically of conditional relevance.[9] The weapon or the ring is not helpful unless it is the one involved in the parties' conduct. Observe,

22. See also Slattery v. Marra Bros., 186 F.2d 134, 138 (2d Cir.1951), cert. denied, 341 U.S. 915 (1951).

4. Russell v. Coffman, 237 Ark. 778, 376 S.W.2d 269 (1964) (physician used severed knee cap to demonstrate nature of injury and reason for surgery). But see Harper v. Bolton, 239 S.C. 541, 124 S.E.2d 54 (1962) (admission of removed eye was error because it was conceded plaintiff lost her eye in the accident).

5. Wilson v. State, 247 Ind. 680, 221 N.E.2d 347 (1966); see also Wimberley v. Patterson, 75 N.J.Super. 584, 183 A.2d 691 (1962) (wrongful death action based on shooting; while refusing to hold that the trial court abused its discretion in rejecting the clothing, the court noted that the apparel might have assisted the jury in determining the decedent's visibility).

6. Washington v. Commonwealth, 228 Va. 535, 323 S.E.2d 577 (1984), cert. denied, 471 U.S. 1111 (1985); People v. Mireles, 79 Ill.App.3d 173, 34 Ill.Dec. 475, 398 N.E.2d 150 (1979), cert. denied, 449 U.S. 860 (1980); IV Wigmore, § 1157, at 340–50 n. 3. But see State v. Banks, 564 S.W.2d 947 (Tenn.1978). In Commonwealth v. Chacko, 480 Pa. 504, 391 A.2d 999 (1978), the court held that the trial judge abused his discretion in admitting photographs of deceased taken after a grisly murder; probative value, in the court's view, was low or nonexistent and the potential for prejudice quite high.

7. See, e.g., United States v. McRae, 593 F.2d 700 (5th Cir.1979), reh'g denied, 597 F.2d 283 (5th Cir.1979); Hillman v. Funderburk, 504 A.2d 596 (D.C. App.1986); Masters v. Dewey, 109 Idaho 576, 709 P.2d 149 (App.1985). See also discussion infra at n. 26.

8. See supra § 13.1, n. 3.

9. See § 2.6; Adv.Comm.Note to Fed.R.Evid. 901.

however, that when the evidence is only demonstrative, authentication involves having a witness identify the proffered item—for example, as the map of a certain region or a model of the human skeleton—or provide such brief additional explanation as is necessary for the trier to understand what is exhibited. The origin of the res is not important.

An additional requirement—again based upon relevance—must be satisfied during identification, and it too varies with whether or not the real evidence is original. With original evidence, the proponent should elicit testimony that the relevant quality or condition of the proffered thing *has not changed substantially* since the time of its involvement in the controversy.[10] The basic principle of relevance, which demands probative force but weighs it against countervailing practical considerations, requires this showing.[11] If the material features of the item have been substantially altered, its probative value is reduced or negated and it may mislead or confuse the jury. On the other hand, if the proffered thing is not original, but rather is demonstrative, the proponent need show only that the proffered item is a fair representation of what it purports to show.[12] For example, if a map or a model is used, it should be sufficiently accurate in all pertinent respects so as not to mislead the trier of fact.

There is occasional uncertainty about the proper role of the judge in determinations of authenticity or identification. In most instances he performs only a screening function: if a reasonable jury could find that the object is what its proponent claims, the real evidence will be admitted. But real evidence, which appeals directly to the senses, can sometimes have a telling probative impact upon the jury.[13] This usually calls only for a careful weighing by the judge of probative force against such practical concerns as prejudice and confusion. But in certain instances where there is a danger that the jury might be misled, the judge may himself determine if authentication is satisfactory. In such cases, he is treating the real evidence as raising an issue of competence and not as simply raising an issue of conditional

10. Cheek v. Avco Lycoming Div., 56 Ill.App.3d 217, 13 Ill.Dec. 902, 371 N.E.2d 994 (1977); McCormick, § 212, at 667.

11. See §§ 2.3–2.5.

12. See III Wigmore, § 793, at 239 (Chadbourn); McCormick, § 213, at 670.

13. 5 Weinstein & Berger, ¶ 901(a)[01], at 19: "Real proof often has enormous apparent probative force because the lay trier may lose sight of the fact that its connection to a party may depend upon the credibility of an authenticating witness."

relevance. Although the governing rules in some jurisdictions are not always clear, the judge sometimes—at least under the common law—assumes a factfinding role when scientific evidence is offered or, as we shall see shortly, when there is a question involving a chain of custody.[14] In these instances he is demanding more than simply a prima facie evidentiary foundation that, *if believed by the jury*, would entitle it reasonably to find the elements of identification (authentication).

In any event, when the foundation is complete, the proffered thing should be formally introduced into evidence. This invariably is the practice with original evidence, but some jurisdictions do not require that demonstrative evidence be introduced into the record.[15] This relaxation of the usual requirement of having a complete trial record seems ill-advised because it leads to uncertainty at the appellate review stage.[16]

As the foregoing suggests, the general principles governing the introduction of real evidence are relatively simple. Practical complications, however, often arise in the case of original real evidence when the proffered res has no distinguishing characteristic, or when, even though such a characteristic exists, the witness is unable to recall having observed this characteristic. The practical problem posed is this: how can the proponent fulfill the requirement of identification that demands foundation evidence to show that the proffered item is the same one involved in the controversy? The difficulty can arise with any kind of original evidence—for example, a weapon, a bottle, or a piece of rope. The resolution is found in establishing a *chain of custody,* through the testimony of successive custodians, that substantially eliminates the possibility the proffered item is not the original res. Identification through a chain of custody is also necessary when a sample (such as blood, semen, or clothing particles) is collected and subjected to scientific tests. Typically, the specimen passes through the custody of several persons: the police, for example, give the sample to a technician, who delivers it to an expert who, after conducting tests, places the sample in the prosecutor's safekeeping. Absent a stipulation as to authenticity, the evidentiary foundation must show that the original item was the thing tested, that it is the same as the thing now offered, and that the test

14. See infra n. 23 and accompanying text.

15. McCormick, § 213, at 669.

16. Id. See Crocker v. Lee, 261 Ala. 439, 74 So.2d 429 (1954); Radetsky v. Leonard, 145 Colo. 358, 358 P.2d 1014 (1961).

results reported in court were derived from analysis of the original sample.[17] Again, the solution lies in the testimony of the various custodians,[18] perhaps supplemented by business entries [19] that help to substantiate authenticity.

There is some variation in the degree of certainty required when a chain of custody is used to fulfill the requirement of identification. If tracing an item by its chain of custody is tested by the principle of conditional relevance, the chain adequately should be forged if the evidence accounting for the item is *sufficient* to allow a reasonable jury to conclude that the offered res is the original.[20] Presumably, if the trier concluded that an item other than the original had been introduced, it would ignore the evidence because it readily would see that a false or substituted thing had no probative force.[21] Yet some cases, most commonly criminal ones, appear to require that the evidence of custody render it *reasonably certain* that the original evidence has been traced accurately.[22] This more rigorous requirement arguably is justified by the seriousness of a criminal proceeding and by the obligation of the government to adopt standard, trustworthy procedures for safeguarding evidence.

17. See Brewer v. United States, 353 F.2d 260 (8th Cir.1965). It is customary to introduce the sample into evidence. Introduction of the sample, however, would not appear essential, at least if the evidence shows that the original item was analyzed and the results produced in court were derived from that test. Even when such evidence is offered at trial, breaks in the chain of custody *after* testing arguably are irrelevant to the authenticity of the evidence. See Giannelli, Chain of Custody and the Handling of Real Evidence, 20 Am.Crim.L.Rev. 527 (1983). If, however, loss or destruction of the sample prevented the other party from challenging the test because of his inability to conduct his own analysis, a more difficult problem arises. The resolution should turn upon whether there is a reasonable possibility that further testing and testimony would produce different results.

18. See, e.g., Eisentrager v. State, 79 Nev. 38, 45, 378 P.2d 526, 530–531 (1963). See also Lestico v. Kuehner, 204 Minn. 125, 283 N.W. 122 (1938) (no chain of custody necessary when a witness can identify the object).

19. See Wheeler v. United States, 211 F.2d 19 (D.C.Cir.1953), cert. denied, 347 U.S. 1019 (1954), reh'g denied, 348 U.S. 852 (1954).

20. Fed.R.Evid. 901 appears to have adopted this standard. See text and discussion infra at n. 25.

21. This statement assumes that the proponent did not provide an alternative foundation by supplying evidence that, even if the proffered item were not the original, it had the same relevant characteristic.

22. See Eisentrager v. State, 79 Nev. 38, 45, 378 P.2d 526, 530–531 (1963). McCormick states that the chain must "render it improbable that the original item has either been exchanged with another or been contaminated or tampered with." McCormick, § 212, at 668.

Application of this higher standard takes two forms. Under both, the jury must find with reasonable certainty that an adequate chain of custody has been established. It is the judge's role that varies: he may screen the evidence for sufficiency and then instruct the jury as to the reasonable certainty standard, or he may himself apply the standard preliminarily, keeping the evidence from the jury unless he is satisfied that authenticity is reasonably certain. In this latter instance, the judge departs from his usual role of screening the foundation for simple sufficiency.[23]

The possibility that false or altered evidence may be produced by the prosecution under circumstances not easily exposed by a defendant may justify the policy described above. Yet against these considerations must be weighed the jury's probable competence to deal with an issue of authenticity. It should also be noted that the recorded cases contain many examples of unnecessarily formalistic application of the "reasonably certain" standard, resulting in the exclusion of evidence that in all likelihood was reliable.[24] Lowering these barriers, Federal Rule of Evidence 901(a) provides that authentication or identification requires only a showing *sufficient* to support a jury finding that the item offered is what it purports to be.[25] It states:

> The requirement of authentication or identification as a condition precedent to admissibility is satisfied by evidence sufficient to support a finding that the matter in question is what its proponent claims.

Once the proponent supplies evidence sufficient to support a finding of genuineness, the question of proper identification always becomes a jury issue. This accords with existing common law with regard to most items of real evidence. However, courts applying Rule 901 continue to be concerned with establishing a chain of custody, particularly in criminal cases. Many judges use an indeterminate standard that is somewhat stricter than the simple sufficiency standard applied to other real evidence.[26] Of

23. The usual rule of conditional relevancy requires simply that the judge pass upon whether the jury could reasonably find that the evidence is what the proponent claims it is. See §§ 2.6, 10.3; infra § 13.6.

24. See, e.g., Robinson v. Commonwealth, 212 Va. 136, 183 S.E.2d 179 (1971).

25. 5 Weinstein & Berger, ¶ 901(a)[01], at 17. But see Saltzburg & Redden at 1005–10.

26. Giannelli, supra note 17, at 554–55. See United States v. Howard-Arias, 679 F.2d 363 (4th Cir.1982), cert. denied, 459 U.S. 874 (1982) (chain of custody must be "sufficiently complete so as to convince the court that it is improbable that the original item had been ex-

course, the trial judge still has power under Rule 403 to exclude probative evidence that raises substantial dangers of prejudice or of misleading the jury. Indeed, a judge may apply the Rule 403 balancing test more stringently when real evidence, with its heightened power of persuasion and thus increased danger of misleading, is involved.[27] The use of Rule 403 is an appropriate means of resolving the present difficulty.

§ 13.3 Pictorial Evidence: Photographs, X-rays, and Motion Pictures

Accuracy of reproduction usually is important when pictorial evidence is presented to the trier. It always is required that the proponent of photographic evidence establish that the pertinent parts of the picture are a reasonably accurate representation of the subject pictured. This general requirement may be satisfied in various ways, depending upon the particular kind of photographic evidence. Identification of a still picture or snapshot is complete if a witness (not necessarily the photographer) has observed the subject and testifies that the picture is an accurate reproduction.[1] This same means of identification usually suffices in cases where a moving picture is offered.[2]

Sometimes photographic evidence may be authenticated by reliance upon basic principles of photography strengthened by assurances that the equipment used and the procedures followed were proper.[3] This always is the case with x-rays, and is also the case with photographs or motion pictures in circumstances in which no witness can verify the accuracy of the depiction of the

changed with another or otherwise tampered with," but court can so find despite "missing link"), and other cases described in Saltzburg & Redden at 1011–13.

27. 5 Weinstein & Berger, ¶ 901(a)[ol][01], at 19.

§ 13.3

1. United States v. Valdes, 417 F.2d 335, 338 (2d Cir.1969), cert. denied, 399 U.S. 912 (1970); State ex rel. State Highway Commission v. Eilers, 406 S.W.2d 567, 570 (Mo.1966); McCormick, § 214, at 671.

2. The more recent cases so hold. See United States v. Richardson, 562 F.2d 476 (7th Cir.1977), cert. denied, 434 U.S. 1021 (1978); McCormick, § 214, at 673–74. Some cases—particularly older ones—require a more elaborate method of identification, including testimony about the conditions and technical aspects of taking, processing, and showing the film. McCormick, § 214, at 673.

3. See, e.g., Ferguson v. Commonwealth, 212 Va. 745, 187 S.E.2d 189 (1972), cert. denied, 409 U.S. 861 (1972), reh'g denied, 409 U.S. 1050 (1972) ("Regiscope" pictures of accused's bad check and identification papers); Sisk v. State, 236 Md. 589, 204 A.2d 684 (1964) (same). See Fed.R.Evid. 901(b)(9); McCormick, § 214, at 672.

subject.[4] X-rays, for example, may be introduced upon an evidentiary foundation establishing that the x-ray equipment was an acceptable type, in proper working order, that a qualified operator using correct procedures took the picture, and that the x-ray film (plate) offered depicts the subject in question.[5] In addition, because most x-ray photographs require interpretation in order to be understood by the trier, it usually becomes necessary to show that the individual "reading" the x-ray is a qualified expert. In practice, however, a lengthy process of identification during trial proceedings often is unnecessary; issues of authentication usually are settled at pre-trial conference or by stipulation. Furthermore, unless there is reason to doubt the accuracy of the x-ray picture, the testifying expert usually assumes that the written record on the plate is accurate and proceeds to interpret the picture.[6]

The better-reasoned decisions support the proposition that photographs are "substantive evidence" in the sense that photographic evidence alone can support a finding by the trier. Surprisingly, contrary authority can be found to the effect that photographs are merely illustrative of a witness's testimony and, as such, have no independent probative effect.[7] McCormick correctly describes this limitation as groundless, and given contemporary society's increasing use of photographic techniques in a wide variety of areas, it is difficult to believe that this restriction will persist.[8]

§ 13.4 Experiments

The result of a carefully conducted experiment often can assist the factfinder. For example, an experiment may demonstrate the unlikelihood or impossibility that certain testimonial

4. See supra note 3.

5. See Waltz, Introduction to Criminal Evidence 384 (2d ed. 1983). Case authorities are collected in Annot., 5 A.L.R.3d 303 (1966).

6. See Weinstein & Mansfield et al. at 129 n. 1; Fed.R.Evid. 703 (allowing expert to base his opinion on facts "of a type reasonably relied upon by experts in the particular field . . .") Cf. Fed. R.Evid. 901(b)(9), indicating by way of illustration that the requirement of identification can be satisfied by describing a process or system that produces an accurate result. See also §§ 12.2–12.3.

7. McCormick, § 214, at 671–72.

8. Id. Suppose an accused, while burglarizing a commercial establishment at night, is photographed by an automatic camera. If there is no eyewitness, would the prosecution fail even if the pictures showed beyond a reasonable doubt that the accused had perpetrated the act? See supra n. 3.

assertions are true [1] or that the factual hypothesis of one of the parties is invalid.[2] Conversely, of course, experimental evidence can help establish the correctness of testimonial assertions or of a factual hypothesis.[3]

The principal requirement for admissibility is that the experiment be conducted under conditions substantially similar to those existing when the contested event occurred.[4] This requirement follows from considerations of relevance; therefore, as with other problems of relevance, the counterweights to admissibility (such as distraction, delay, and prejudice) must be considered. Predictably, the trial judge's decision whether to admit the experimental evidence is likely to be upheld on appeal.[5]

Occasionally, the thrusts and parries of the adversaries will permit relaxation of the usual requirement that an experiment must be performed under substantially similar conditions. This is not to suggest that an irrelevant experiment is permitted, but only that the nature of the parties' assertions may make the exact duplication of conditions unnecessary. Thus, where one party asserted that it was impossible for a driver to control an automobile with a disabled suspension system, it was held proper to demonstrate otherwise, even though the experiment involved another driver who traversed different terrain in another automobile equipped with the same type of suspension system.[6]

§ 13.4

1. E.g., Brown v. State, 74 Tex.Cr.R. 356, 169 S.W. 437 (1913) (experiment to show that murderer's position could not have been where accused claimed it was).

2. Cheetham v. Union R.R. Co., 26 R.I. 279, 58 A. 881 (1904) (demonstration that speed was not cause of derailment of electric car); Davis v. State, 51 Neb. 301, 70 N.W. 984 (1897) (experiment demonstrates, contrary to defendant's contention, that it was possible to remove certain part of railroad track in a short time).

3. People v. Spencer, 58 Cal.App. 197, 208 P. 380 (1922) (test conducted to show scream was audible at place witness said he heard it). See McCormick, §§ 202 and 215, where cases are collected that demonstrate the varying uses of experimental evidence. In one interesting case, described in Comment, Experimental Evidence, 34 Ill.Law Rev. 206, 210–211 (1939), a magician was used to show that a money bag used by banking institutions could be opened and resealed without leaving traces of the tampering. Because of the time required for this feat, it was possible to ascertain who the custodian was at the time of the loss.

4. Ramseyer v. General Motors Corp., 417 F.2d 859, 864 (8th Cir.1969); Thomas v. Chicago Transit Authority, 115 Ill.App.2d 476, 253 N.E.2d 492 (1969).

5. E.g., Ramseyer v. General Motors Corp., 417 F.2d 859, 864 (8th Cir.1969).

6. Chambers v. Silver, 103 Cal.App. 2d 633, 230 P.2d 146 (1951). See McCormick, § 202, at 602, citing *Chambers* and other cases; Comment, Experimental Evidence, 34 Ill.L.Rev. 206, 207–208 (1939).

Courts have approved experiments conducted both in and out of the courtroom.[7] When the experiment is conducted as part of the trial proceedings, the factors of delay and distraction from the principal issues take on added proportions.[8] On the other hand, an out-of-court experiment, even though it takes less judicial time, often involves more difficulty in ensuring that the test was fairly conducted. This problem becomes most acute where the adversary is unaware of the experiment until presentation of the results at trial. If lack of notice has denied the opposing party an opportunity to ensure the fairness and validity of the experiment, exclusion from evidence of the test results seems appropriate.[9]

§ 13.5 Writings and Other Recordations: In General

Writings are subject to the general requirement of identification or authentication; traditionally, the latter term has been the one used most frequently when discussing writings. Because writings, unlike most chattels, directly display recorded information, the process of authentication is slightly different. Generally, the relevance of a writing depends upon its authorship, so that the proponent of the writing must, *as a condition preceding admission,* provide an evidentiary basis sufficient for the trier to conclude that the writing came from the source claimed. For example, when a document is signed, the proponent usually must provide evidence sufficient for a reasonable trier to conclude that the writing in fact was signed by the person whose name appears on the document. Of course, written materials are not always signed; in these instances, the proponent must offer preliminary evidence that allows the factfinder to conclude that the document came from the source claimed. The justification for the requirement of authentication, and in particular the requirement that proof of authorship always precede the introduction of the writing, will be

7. Cases are collected in Weinstein & Mansfield et al. 111–22.

8. McCormick, § 215, at 677.

9. See McCormick, § 202, at 604. He notes that the present law does not impose as a condition of admissibility the giving of notice and the opportunity of the adversary to be present. Perhaps this is because a careful and thorough cross-examination often can expose any unfairness in the conduct of the experiment. One difficulty with a routine requirement that the adversary be present at the experiment is that the proponent may hesitate to attempt the test if he is uncertain of the results. One possible solution is to require the proponent of test results to give notice to his adversary after the experiment, but prior to trial. This notice should give the pertinent details of the experiment and should be served in ample time to allow the opponent to draft interrogatories asking about the experiment or to conduct his own test.

discussed in the next section. Suffice it to say that the law of evidence always has treated writings with special care.

A second instance of such careful treatment is the so-called "best evidence" or "original documents" rule. Frequently, a litigated issue turns upon the contents or terms of a writing, making it important that the evidence of the writing be reliable. It could be maintained that writings should be treated like other evidence, leaving to the parties the free choice of what material they produce to prove the content or terms of a writing. Under such an approach, a party who relied only on testimony to prove the contents of a writing, when there was no apparent reason why he could not produce the writing itself, would presumably suffer in his efforts to persuade the jury. Nonetheless, for reasons explained later, the law of evidence imposes a rule of preference: the original document is preferred whenever a party seeks to prove the terms of a writing; secondary evidence (such as copies or testimony) generally is inadmissible if the original is available. The best evidence rule originally applied exclusively to writings. In recent years, however, there has been a tendency to extend it to other kinds of permanent recordation such as electronic recordings and, in certain instances, photographs. In its modern form—illustrated by Federal Rules of Evidence 1002 and 1003—the best evidence rule is modified to give due recognition to the accuracy of modern means of producing copies.

It should be stressed that the obstacles encountered in satisfying the requirements of authentication and best evidence often are more apparent than real. By means of requests for admissions, stipulations, or other agreements reached before or during trial, the opposing lawyers often reach practical accommodations that obviate the need for courtroom compliance with the evidentiary requirements pertaining to documentary evidence.

§ 13.6 Authentication: In General

The requirement of authentication can be viewed simply as a function of the principle of relevance: a writing must be linked to its source by sufficient evidence whenever the relevance of the written matter depends upon its source. Evidence of a written contractual acceptance, for example, will be irrelevant unless it came from the defendant now charged with breach; an acceptance not traceable to the defendant will not support his liability. In most other circumstances where (as in this example) there is a problem of conditional relevance—that is, the relevance of proffered evidence depends upon the existence of some preliminary fact—the judge can, in his discretion, admit the proffered evidence. His admission is conditioned upon a subsequent presentation of evidence of the allied or conditioning fact, so as to make it reasonable for the jury to find this underlying fact.[1] This option regarding the order of presentation is not usually available with writings (or other tangible evidence). The general practice in all jurisdictions is to require that *before* a writing is admitted, there must be sufficient evidence of authorship to enable a reasonable factfinder to conclude that the writing is genuine or, put otherwise, that it is what the proponent claims it to be. Note, however, that in jury trials, the judge need not decide himself that the writing is genuine, but he must, as a condition of admission, conclude that the evidence of authenticity is sufficient for the jury so to find. However, even if the proponent meets this preliminary condition of admissibility (authentication), the final determination of authenticity rests with the jury. If the jury finds that the document did not come from the source claimed, it should disregard the writing.

Authentication may thus be properly seen as a logical application of the general principle of conditional relevance. If it were only this, however, and no more, the exacting demands of some of the cases would be unexplainable. Additional purposes of authentication are said to be the prevention of fraud and of mistaken attribution of a writing to one who, by coincidence, has the same name as the author.[2] Whether authentication effectively serves either of these purposes is doubtful, but the belief that it does accounts for the stringent standard applied, especially in the older cases, when courts are asked to determine whether evidence of authorship is sufficient to link the writing with its purported source. This standard is based upon the premise that the mere appearance on the face of a document, for example, of a signature or letterhead, standing alone, is not sufficient evidence of authorship. Thus, in order to satisfy the judge that there exists sufficient evidence of authorship to permit a jury finding, the proponent of a writing usually must offer some evidence *in addition* to the appearance of a signature or other written recital of the source. Thus, subject to certain exceptions (found especially in

§ 13.6

1. See §§ 2.6, 10.3.

2. See McCormick, § 218, at 687.

modern evidence codes), he usually needs evidence that is extrinsic to the document itself.

The net effect of this requirement is to make the standard of sufficiency rather demanding when applied to writings.[3] Indeed, some of the earlier cases carried the concept of sufficiency to aberrant extremes.[4] Although recent cases and evidence codes maintain the basic principle that authentication requires evidence in addition to a mere recital of source within the writing, this requirement is not applied to some types of writings such as newspapers, government publications, documents from a public depository and certain kinds of commercial paper. Even when the principle applies, there is an increasingly liberal attitude concerning what evidence beyond a recital on the face of the proffered document is sufficient to establish genuineness. As we shall see, such additional evidence, standing alone, need not meet high standards of probativeness. Remember, also, that we are presently addressing only the requirement of admissibility; the ultimate determination of whether a document or other recordation is genuine is made by the trier of fact.

§ 13.7 Authentication by Evidence Extrinsic to the Writing

The requirement of authentication can be satisfied by producing either direct or circumstantial evidence extrinsic to the proffered document. Direct evidence of genuineness can consist of testimony by the author or by a witness who saw the proffered writing made or signed.[1] A witness familiar with the handwriting in question also can testify that the proffered document, or the

3. Supra n. 2. As McCormick points out, in both business and social affairs, it is customary and seemingly quite reasonable to rely upon the writing itself as accurately divulging its source. McCormick, § 218, at 686.

4. The cases most frequently cited are Mancari v. Frank P. Smith, Inc., 114 F.2d 834 (D.C.Cir.1940), holding that a newspaper advertising circular containing defendant's name and advertising the shoes he sold did not provide a sufficient basis to attribute the writing to defendant, and Keegan v. Green Giant Co., 150 Me. 283, 110 A.2d 599 (1954), holding the label on a can of peas insufficient to support a finding that the writing (the label) was published by the defendant, Green Giant. Without this evidence, the plaintiff could not establish that the peas came from the defendant and hence a directed verdict was entered in favor of Green Giant. These cases are usually reprinted or summarized in the leading casebooks. See, e.g., Weinstein & Mansfield et al. at 146–151. The holding in *Green Giant* is rejected by Fed.R. Evid. 902(7). *Mancari*, too, appears to have been cast aside by the rulemakers. See Fed.R.Evid. 901(b)(4), 902(6); 5 Weinstein & Berger, ¶ 902(6)[01], at 36.

§ 13.7

1. Fed.R.Evid. 901(b)(1); McCormick, § 219, at 687.

signature on it, is genuine.[2] The reliability of the latter mode of authentication is suspect [3] and the leniency of the courts in routinely approving it cannot be reconciled with other circumstances in which courts, purportedly applying the normal standard for authentication, make greater demands of the proponent.[4]

Circumstantial evidence of genuineness also can take a variety of forms. For example, the handwriting of the proffered document may be compared by the jury (or by an expert) to exemplars that are supported by evidence of genuineness [5] or distinctive characteristics of the appearance or contents of a document may be shown in support of a finding that the signature or recital of authorship is authentic.[6] Authentication by reference to *communicative content* occurs when the document or other recordation in question reveals information likely to be known only to the purported author.[7] Similarly, the proponent may authenticate by showing that the questioned writing is a *reply* to

2. Fed.R.Evid. 901(b)(2) (lay opinion "based upon familiarity not acquired for purposes of litigation"); Apple v. Commonwealth, 296 S.W.2d 717 (Ky. 1956); Hershberger v. Hershberger, 345 Pa. 439, 443, 29 A.2d 95, 98 (1942); McCormick, § 221, at 689–90. One could view the form of proof as circumstantial because the witness is comparing what he sees with what he remembers and infers from the similarities that the proffered writing is genuine. Nonetheless, the trier is not required to make inferences. See § 2.7.

3. Very limited familiarity often is held to qualify the witness to assert that the writing is genuine. E.g., State v. Bond, 12 Idaho 424, 86 P. 43 (1906) (witness had seen person write "several" times). See McCormick, § 221, at 690. Professor Inbau has conducted an experiment strongly indicating that authentication by one familiar with the handwriting in question is unreliable. See Inbau, Lay Witness Identification of Handwriting (An Experiment), 34 Ill.L. Rev. 433 (1939).

4. See supra § 13.6, n. 4.

5. This is an area in which the competence of a lay jury overlaps that of an expert. Although a handwriting expert is entitled to give his professional opinion, based upon a comparison of the sample with the contested writing, the jury also is held competent to compare genuine exhibits with the one in dispute. See Tracy, The Introduction of Documentary Evidence, 24 Iowa L.Rev. 436, 445 (1939). Some courts require the judge to make a final determination that the specimens used for comparison themselves are genuine. See, e.g., University of Illinois v. Spalding, 71 N.H. 163, 51 A. 731 (1901). The Federal Rules, however, require only that there be sufficient evidence that the samples are genuine. See Fed.R.Evid. 901(b)(3). Thus the jury must find first that the samples are genuine and then, circumstantially, that the writing offered in evidence is authentic.

6. McFarland v. McFarland, 176 Pa. Super. 342, 345, 107 A.2d 615, 616 (1954) (writing style of author); Fed.R. Evid. 901(b)(4).

7. People v. Adams, 162 Mich. 371, 127 N.W. 354 (1910) (letter discloses knowledge of a conversation and was mailed in city where purported writer said he would be); Abbott v. McAloon, 70 Me. 98 (1879) (knowledge of oral agreement concerning sale of certain goods).

an earlier writing addressed to the purported author. For example, if *A* writes to *B* inquiring about a loan and *B*'s reply directly or indirectly makes reference to *A*'s letter, *B*'s writing can be authenticated by first introducing acceptable proof of the content of *A*'s letter and then showing the responsive terms of the document allegedly written by *B*.[8] Another means of providing circumstantial evidence of authentication is to introduce evidence of the process or system that produced the questioned writing and then to show the accuracy of that system. A writing produced by a computer, for example, could be authenticated by this means. Finally, to this nonexhaustive list can be added the ancient documents rule: a document that is sufficiently aged (usually 20 or more years),[9] regular on its face, and found in a place (or in a person's custody) where it likely would be located were it genuine, can be admitted without further authentication. These requirements for admitting old documents perhaps provide a modest check against fraud because (1) the circumstances raise no suspicions, (2) it is rather unlikely that a fraudulent document will go undetected for such a long period, and (3) it is unlikely that someone would falsify a document if the erroneous entries would not have an operative effect for many years thereafter. Whatever the validity of these assumptions, however, the ancient documents rule practically accommodates the recognized difficulty of finding authenticating witnesses after the passage of many years. It should be emphasized that the ancient documents rule here discussed is a means of proving authorship or authenticity. Introducing documentary assertions often raises a hearsay difficulty,[10] although many jurisdictions have created an exception to the hearsay rule for ancient documents.[11]

§ 13.8 Self-Authentication

The preceding section focused upon accepted methods of meeting the requirement of authentication by producing evidence ex-

8. Fed.R.Evid. 901(b)(4). See Anstine v. McWilliams, 24 Wash.2d 230, 163 P.2d 816 (1945). It may be presumed that *B* received *A*'s initiating letter. Id. See §§ 3.2–3.3.

9. The common-law rule required that the document be 30 or more years old. McCormick, § 223, at 692. The Federal Rules of Evidence reduce the minimum to 20 years. Fed.R.Evid. 901(b)(8).

10. This difficulty arises when the assertions in the document are offered for their truth. See §§ 6.1–6.2. Proof of the contents of a document also may raise problems associated with privileged communications. See Ch. IX.

11. See, e.g., Fed.R.Evid. 803(16) (twenty-year standard).

trinsic to the proffered writing. In a number of situations, usually specified by statute or rule,[1] a document can be authenticated from within its four corners; that is, in specified instances, the face of the document contains sufficient proof of authenticity to justify its admission. Documents so classified often are said to be "self-authenticating" or "prima facie genuine" and, as such, entitled to admission into evidence. Any dispute as to the authenticity of these documents, of course, will be resolved by the trier.

Analytically, the process of self-authentication normally involves an assertion on the face of the document that it is genuine,[2] coupled with an indication (such as an official seal or stamp) that the asserter is the official duly authorized to certify authenticity. Typically, the official will be a notary public or the public custodian of the writing in question. Acknowledged bills of exchange or instruments of conveyance frequently are authenticated on their face. Documents in the custody of a public official, such as tax returns, wills, licenses, and court judgments, usually are admitted on the basis of a written certification executed by the public custodian. Many states have passed laws that permit legislative enactments to be admitted into evidence if the printed material containing the statutes purports to have been printed or published by a sovereign.[3] Finally, the Federal Rules of Evidence extend the concept of self-authentication beyond its traditional boundaries to include such writings as newspapers and trade inscriptions.[4]

This expansion reflects a recognition by the drafters that the possibility of "unauthenticity" in such items is so small as to obviate the necessity of authenticating evidence. If the opponent challenges genuineness, the proponent will, as a practical matter, provide for the trier's consideration the evidence that the Rule does not require him to supply in order to gain admissibility.[5]

§ 13.8

1. See Fed.R.Evid. 902. There also is a common-law rule providing for the "self-authentication" of public documents. See Lembeck v. United States Shipping Board Emergency Fleet Corp., 9 F.2d 558, 559 (2d Cir.1925). See also Annot., 70 A.L.R.2d 1227 (1960).

2. This assertion, which is accepted for its truth, constitutes an exception to the hearsay rule. See V Wigmore § 1677 (Chadbourn).

3. See V Wigmore, § 1684 (Chadbourn); McCormick, § 228, at 700.

4. See Fed.R.Evid. 902.

5. See Adv.Comm.Note to Fed.R. Evid. 902. With regard to trade inscriptions and the like, trademark laws provide safeguards comparable to those attending seals, notarizations, and so forth on official documents. Id.

§ 13.9 The Best Evidence Rule

We have noted that the rule requiring the production of the original document applies only when the proponent is attempting to prove the contents or terms of a writing. The original is preferred because its use eliminates the risk of mistranscriptions or testimonial misstatements of what the document said; inspection of the original also reduces somewhat the chance of undetected tampering.[1] Note that sometimes a writing recites or records a perceivable event or condition such as a marriage (marriage certificate), payment of money (receipt), or the utterance of certain words (transcript). Here, the proponent wishing to prove the underlying event may proceed in either of two ways: he may (1) offer the testimony of an observer, or (2) offer the writing that records or recites the event. The first approach does not involve the best evidence rule because the proponent is not attempting to prove the terms of a writing, but merely is presenting evidence of an event perceived by a witness with first-hand knowledge. It makes no difference that the occurrence of the event is recited in a writing that was made subsequent to its occurrence, for the writing does not, so far as legal rules of proof are concerned, "erase" or supplant the preceding event. Of course, if the proponent chooses to make his proof by use of a writing, the best evidence rule must be satisfied. There are, moreover, some instances where the law prescribes that a writing has the effect of subsuming, so to speak, any prior events or, otherwise put, the transaction in dispute takes the form of a writing. In these situations, illustrated by a deed, a written contract, or a judgment, the law regards the transaction as "essentially written" and the proponent must make his proof by the writing if it is available.[2]

The courts are in general accord with the foregoing analysis, although there has been some tendency in criminal cases to prefer a written, signed confession over the testimony of a person claiming to have heard an oral confession.[3] Perhaps this preference can be justified as a protective measure, but analytically the proponent does not seek to prove the terms of a writing; therefore his choice should affect only the weight of his evidence.

§ 13.9

1. McCormick, § 231, at 704.

2. McCormick, § 233, at 704.

3. Id. at 709. The leading case to the contrary is Meyers v. United States, 171 F.2d 800 (D.C.Cir.1948), cert. denied, 336 U.S. 912 (1949), where a split Court of Appeals held that in a trial for subornation of perjury, the prior transcribed testimony of a witness could be proved by oral testimony of one who overheard it.

Where there are several writings, application of the best evidence rule requires a determination of which one (or ones) is an original. Preliminarily, it should be noted that parties can create *multiple* originals. The question is: What did they intend? For example, if copies (such as carbons or photostatic reproductions) of a contract, will, or other agreement are duly executed (signed), the parties have manifested their intention to accord equal status to all of the identical writings regardless of their mechanical characteristics. Other circumstances might suggest the creation of several originals as, for example, where one sales receipt is given to the customer and the other (usually a carbon copy) is retained by the seller. Beyond this, reference to the substantive law is often necessary to determine what constitutes an "original" for purposes of the best evidence rule. Suppose, for example, a defendant types an original of a libelous document; he then makes a photostatic copy, but he publishes only the latter. The copy is the operative document under the substantive law and, as such, constitutes the original with respect to the best evidence rule. A similar analysis should be employed with regard to telegrams. If *D* writes out a contractual offer at the telegraph office and the terms of the offer then are embodied in a telegram, the telegram is the original—assuming the telegraph company is acting as *D*'s agent. This result turns not upon which writing was created first, but rather upon which document has an operative legal effect.[4] In addition to the problems created by certain substantive legal doctrines, modern technology often blurs the line between an original and a copy. For instance, data can be entered and stored in a computer or similar device and then, upon command, returned in printed form. All such printouts should be considered originals, and this characterization appears to have been accepted by the courts,[5] as well as by the drafters of the Federal Rules.[6] The term "duplicate original" or "multiple original" often is used to describe these documents of equal evidentiary status.

Once an original has been identified, it should be produced, if feasible, assuming the proponent seeks to prove its terms. Unexecuted photographic copies of the original are (in the absence of evidence that the parties intended to treat it as an original) considered secondary evidence and, quite obviously, oral testimony

4. See McCormick § 235.

5. McCormick, § 236, at 714. See also Federal Union Surety Co. v. Indiana Lumber & Mfg. Co., 176 Ind. 328, 95 N.E. 1104 (1911) (three printed slips made by a device called an autographic register are held triplicate originals).

6. Fed.R.Evid. 1001(3).

purporting to give the terms of the original falls into the same category. Unexecuted carbon copies probably should stand on the same footing as photographic copies, but some authorities treat a carbon as a duplicate original.[7]

It might be asked whether there is any longer a need for the best evidence rule, given the reliability of modern means of reproduction. Because of technological accuracy, it is difficult to base one's choice between the original and a copy (as opposed to one's choice between the original and verbal testimony) on the ground that the copy lacks reliability because it more likely contains accidental inaccuracies or omissions. Perhaps the rule preferring the original can be justified on the ground that as between the original and a copy, the former is more likely to yield clues to tampering or fraud.[8]

The Federal Rules of Evidence strike a balance that preserves a preference for the original and, at the same time, gives due recognition to the accuracy of copies produced by modern means. Rule 1002 provides that "To prove the content of a writing, recording, or photograph, the original . . . is required, except as otherwise provided. . . ." Rule 1003, however, states that a duplicate—that is, a counterpart not qualifing as an original—is "admissible to the same extent as an original unless (1) a genuine question is raised as to the authenticity of the original or (2) in the circumstances it would be unfair to admit the duplicate in lieu of the original."[9] Thus, the federal drafters adopted a middle ground between rejection of the best evidence principle and adherence to its traditional formulation. Another feature of the Federal Rules is noteworthy: the application of the best evidence rule extends beyond writings to include sound recordings and photographs.[10] This enlargement of the rule can be traced to similar

7. See, e.g., Davis, Agent v. Williams Brothers Const. Co., 207 Ky. 404, 269 S.W. 289 (1925); Annot., 65 A.L.R.2d 342 (1959). Under the Federal Rules, an unsigned carbon would be an original only if the carbon was "intended to have the same effect [as the original] by the party issuing it." Fed.R.Evid. 1001(3). It could be argued that carbon copies are more reliable than photographic copies because tampering can be more easily detected in the former.

8. McCormick, § 231, at 704. See supra n. 7.

9. As an example of a circumstance of unfairness, consider a situation where the copy reveals only a portion of the original and there is a reasonable possibility that the remainder would modify the duplicated excerpts or provide other relevant information. See 5 Weinstein & Berger ¶ 1003[03] where this and other examples of unfairness are cited.

10. Fed.R.Evid. 1002.

extensions in several of the states,[11] and it should not be viewed as a far-reaching change.

The original of a sound recording usually is the initial recording, and the original of a photograph is the "negative or any print therefrom." [12] In most cases, the proponent would offer these "originals" even without the force of a rule.[13] With regard to still and moving pictures, proof of the photographic contents is not necessary very often. Commonly, photographic evidence is admitted as a graphic representation of a scene or subject that a testifying witness has observed. This illustrative use of photographic evidence does not involve proving the contents of the picture, but rather is an attempt to establish the scene itself by testimony.[14] But if no witness has observed the pictured scene or event (as in the case of an x-ray or where an automatic camera photographs a litigated event), or a photograph is alleged to be libelous, obscene, violative of a copyright or of one's privacy, the photographic contents are in issue and the best evidence rule applies.[15]

Federal or state statutory provisions sometimes modify the usual application of the best evidence rule. Congress, for example, has enacted a statute allowing photographic reproduction of tax returns and certain Treasury documents.[16] State and federal statutes permitting copies of public records are common,[17] as are provisions that apply to regularly kept business records.[18] If no exception to the best evidence rule can be discovered, then care

11. People v. King, 101 Cal.App.2d 500, 225 P.2d 950 (1950) (recording); Cellamare v. Third Ave. Transit Corp., 273 App.Div. 260, 77 N.Y.S.2d 91 (1948) (x-rays); Annot., 62 A.L.R.2d 686, 689; West's Ann.Cal.Evid.Code § 250.

12. Fed.R.Evid. 1001(3).

13. For a case in which a "copy" of a tape was admitted along with the original (which contained excessive background noise), see United States v. Madda, 345 F.2d 400 (7th Cir.1965); see also McGuire v. State, 200 Md. 601, 92 A.2d 582 (1952), cert. denied, 344 U.S. 928 (1953) (written transcript of tape admitted because accurate playback of tape not practical).

14. See Paradis, The Celluloid Witness, 37 U.Colo.L.Rev. 235, 249–251 (1965).

15. See Saltzburg & Redden, at 1049; Adv.Comm.Note to Fed.R.Evid. 1002.

16. 26 U.S.C.A. § 7513.

17. See McCormick, § 240; Fed.R.Evid. 1005. There also is a common-law rule allowing copies of public documents. McCormick at 720, n. 2.

18. The Uniform Photographic Copies of Business and Public Records as Evidence Act has been adopted by a large number of states. See 9A U.L.A. 117 (1967 Supp.). A federal statute has similar provisions. See 28 U.S.C.A. § 1732.

should be taken to determine what circumstances will excuse production of the original.

If the original is lost or destroyed (excepting bad faith destruction by the proponent himself) production is excused.[19] Records are often destroyed in the ordinary course of business; showing that destruction was a business practice should suffice to show absence of bad faith by the proponent.[20] The same result occurs when the original cannot be obtained by judicial process,[21] or where the original is in the hands of the opponent and, after due notice, he fails to produce it.[22]

Finally, the careful practitioner should ascertain if the jurisdiction in question prefers a particular kind of *secondary* evidence. Some courts extend the principle of the best evidence rule and thus give it an operative effect even after production of the original has been excused. The most common extension of the rule to secondary evidence is to require a copy (when available) in lieu of oral testimony purporting to give the terms of the original.[23] The Federal Rules of Evidence, however, contain no provision for "classes" of secondary evidence. If the proponent, under the operation of Fed.R.Evid. 1002 and 1003, is required to produce the original, but production of the original is excused under the provisions of Fed.R.Evid. 1004, then any probative secondary evidence may be used.[24] Usually, the self-interest of the proponent will operate to place before the trier the most reliable secondary evidence.

Notes

1. *Ease of authentication under the Federal Rules.* The approach of the Federal Rules to the authentication of real evidence maintains the "careful skepticism" of the common law while liberalizing admissibility so that possible nonauthenticity becomes a matter for the trier. 5 Louisell & Mueller, § 506, at 16–17. The effect of the authentication Rules, consistently with the approach of the Federal

19. McCormick, § 237, at 715–16; Fed.R.Evid. 1004(1).

20. IV Wigmore, § 1198, at 457–60.

21. Fed.R.Evid. 1004(2); McCormick, § 238, at 716–17.

22. McCormick, § 239, at 717–18; Fed.R.Evid. 1004(3). If the proponent wants the original, he should use an appropriate discovery device, such as a request to produce documents or a subpoena *duces tecum*, to obtain it.

23. See Baroda State Bank v. Peck, 235 Mich. 542, 209 N.W. 827 (1926); McCormick § 241.

24. See Adv.Comm.Note to Fed.R. Evid. 1004.

Rules in general, is thus to increase the frequency with which issues of authenticity are resolved by the jury.

Rule 901(b)(4) exemplifies the common-sense approach of the Rules: the "[a]ppearance, contents, substance, internal patterns, or other distinctive characteristics" of the matter in question may suffice to lay the foundation for admissibility. The judge must find features of the evidence sufficiently distinctive to enable the trier reasonably to find that an item is what its proponent claims. This provision does not open the door, however, to all items with self-identifying characteristics. For instance, the Federal Rule, like the common law, does not allow a signature, standing alone, to show authorship. 5 Louisell & Mueller, § 512, at 55.

Consider the following pre-Rules case. A telegram was sent by *X* who gave his address as the *Y* Hotel; the fact that *X* was registered at the *Y* Hotel, coupled with evidence that he had dispatched a wire on the day in question, provided sufficient evidence of authentication. See Ford v. United States, 10 F.2d 339, 350 (9th Cir.1926). Suppose that the question arose today under the Federal Rules. Suppose further that the only evidence of authentication was that *X* resided at the *Y* Hotel on the day in question.

Is this sufficient evidence to allow the jury to resolve the issue of authenticity?

2. *Jury's Use of Real Evidence.* By force of tradition, or in some instances statute, the jury usually is permitted to take to the jury room tangible exhibits (including writings) admitted into evidence. This general practice, however, is subject to the trial judge's discretionary modification unless a court rule or statute provides otherwise. When a writing serves as a substitute for testimony, as in the case of depositions and recorded recollection, the prevailing practice is to disallow inspection in the jury room. The reason is that the "written testimony" may be given undue emphasis in relation to the oral testimony presented during trial. Should the written confession of an accused be withheld from jury-room inspection? McCormick notes in § 217, at 681, that such confessions, even though testimonial in nature, usually are made available to the jury during their deliberations. What, if anything, justifies this practice?

3. *Authentication of Telephone Calls.* Telephonic communications, although obviously not a writing or tangible thing, present a problem of authentication similar to that presented by written evidence. If a witness testifies that he recognized the voice of the speaker, the requirement of authentication is fulfilled. Even in the absence of voice recognition, the witness can authenticate the speaker's voice by showing that he (the witness) called the number assigned

to the speaker by the telephone company and that during the conversation the speaker identified himself. See Fed.R.Evid. 901(b)(6). Cf. Benson v. Commonwealth, 190 Va. 744, 750, 58 S.E.2d 312, 314 (1950). Calls to a business entity may be authenticated by showing that the number dialed was that which the telephone company assigned to the business and that the conversation related to the entity's line of business. Fed.R.Evid. 901(b)(6). Furthermore, if the number is a business number and the answering speaker purports to act for the company called, it will be presumed that the speaker was "clothed with authority to transact the business conducted." Korch v. Indemnity Ins. Co., 329 Ill.App. 96, 102, 67 N.E.2d 298, 301 (1946).

In the absence of voice recognition, a difficult problem can arise when the speaker calls the witness and then identifies himself. This identification, standing alone, is insufficient to authenticate the speaker's voice. Other clues, however, such as the revelation of facts likely to be known only to the speaker, may supply the needed link. See Sunray Sanitation, Inc. v. Pet, Inc., 249 Ark. 703, 461 S.W.2d 110 (1970); McCormick, § 226, at 697.

4. *Judge's Role.* The reader is reminded that with regard to authentication of writings, the judge usually ensures only that the evidence is sufficient for a jury finding of authenticity. However, preliminary factual questions attending the application of the best evidence rule—such as whether the original has been lost—normally are resolved with finality by the judge. See §§ 10.3–10.4 and note 1 at the conclusion of Ch. X.

Appendix

RULES OF EVIDENCE FOR UNITED STATES COURTS AND MAGISTRATES

Effective July 1, 1975

*Including Amendments * Effective October 1, 1987, absent contrary Congressional action*

Table of Rules

ARTICLE I. GENERAL PROVISIONS

Rule

101. Scope.
102. Purpose and Construction.
103. Rulings on Evidence.
   (a) Effect of Erroneous Ruling.
      (1) Ojection.
      (2) Offer of Proof.
   (b) Record of Offer and Ruling.
   (c) Hearing of Jury.
   (d) Plain Error.
104. Preliminary Questions.
   (a) Questions of Admissibility Generally.
   (b) Relevancy Conditioned on Fact.
   (c) Hearing of Jury.
   (d) Testimony by Accused.
   (e) Weight and Credibility.

* Excerpts from the Federal Rules appearing in the text do not include the 1987 amendments. These amendments are technical only; they do not affect the substance of any of the Rules quoted.

Rule
105. Limited Admissibility.
106. Remainder of or Related Writings or Recorded Statements.

ARTICLE II. JUDICIAL NOTICE

201. Judicial Notice of Adjudicative Facts.
    (a) Scope of Rule.
    (b) Kinds of Facts.
    (c) When Discretionary.
    (d) When Mandatory.
    (e) Opportunity to Be Heard.
    (f) Time of Taking Notice.
    (g) Instructing Jury.

ARTICLE III. PRESUMPTIONS IN CIVIL ACTIONS AND PROCEEDINGS

301. Presumptions in General in Civil Actions and Proceedings.
302. Applicability of State Law in Civil Actions and Proceedings.

ARTICLE IV. RELEVANCY AND ITS LIMITS

401. Definition of "Relevant Evidence".
402. Relevant Evidence Generally Admissible; Irrelevant Evidence Inadmissible.
403. Exclusion of Relevant Evidence on Grounds of Prejudice, Confusion, or Waste of Time.
404. Character Evidence Not Admissible to Prove Conduct; Exceptions; Other Crimes.
    (a) Character Evidence Generally.
        (1) Character of Accused.
        (2) Character of Victim.
        (3) Character of Witness.
    (b) Other Crimes, Wrongs, or Acts.
405. Methods of Proving Character.
    (a) Reputation or Opinion.
    (b) Specific Instances of Conduct.
406. Habit; Routine Practice.
407. Subsequent Remedial Measures.
408. Compromise and Offers to Compromise.
409. Payment of Medical and Similar Expenses.
410. Inadmissibility of Pleas, Plea Discussions, and Related Statements.
411. Liability Insurance.

Rule
412. Rape Cases; Relevance of Victim's Past Behavior.

ARTICLE V. PRIVILEGES

501. General Rule.

ARTICLE VI. WITNESSES

601. General Rule of Competency.
602. Lack of Personal Knowledge.
603. Oath or Affirmation.
604. Interpreters.
605. Competency of Judge as Witness.
606. Competency of Juror as Witness.
(a) At the Trial.
(b) Inquiry Into Validity of Verdict or Indictment.
607. Who May Impeach.
608. Evidence of Character and Conduct of Witness.
(a) Opinion and Reputation Evidence of Character.
(b) Specific Instances of Conduct.
609. Impeachment by Evidence of Conviction of Crime.
(a) General Rule.
(b) Time Limit.
(c) Effect of Pardon, Annulment, or Certificate of Rehabilitation.
(d) Juvenile Adjudications.
(e) Pendency of Appeal.
610. Religious Beliefs or Opinions.
611. Mode and Order of Interrogation and Presentation.
(a) Control by Court.
(b) Scope of Cross-Examination.
(c) Leading Questions.
612. Writing Used to Refresh Memory.
613. Prior Statements of Witnesses.
(a) Examining Witness Concerning Prior Statement.
(b) Extrinsic Evidence of Prior Inconsistent Statement of Witness.
614. Calling and Interrogation of Witnesses by Court.
(a) Calling by Court.
(b) Interrogation by Court.
(c) Objections.
615. Exclusion of Witnesses.

ARTICLE VII. OPINIONS AND EXPERT TESTIMONY

Rule
701. Opinion Testimony by Lay Witnesses.
702. Testimony by Experts.
703. Bases of Opinion Testimony by Experts.
704. Opinion on Ultimate Issue.
705. Disclosure of Facts or Data Underlying Expert Opinion.
706. Court Appointed Experts.
(a) Appointment.
(b) Compensation.
(c) Disclosure of Appointment.
(d) Parties' Experts of Own Selection.

ARTICLE VIII. HEARSAY

801. Definitions.
(a) Statement.
(b) Declarant.
(c) Hearsay.
(d) Statements Which Are Not Hearsay.
(1) Prior Statement by Witness.
(2) Admission by Party-Opponent.
802. Hearsay Rule.
803. Hearsay Exceptions; Availability of Declarant Immaterial.
(1) Present Sense Impression.
(2) Excited Utterance.
(3) Then Existing Mental, Emotional, or Physical Condition.
(4) Statements for Purposes of Medical Diagnosis or Treatment.
(5) Recorded Recollection.
(6) Records of Regularly Conducted Activity.
(7) Absence of Entry in Records Kept in Accordance With the Provisions of Paragraph (6).
(8) Public Records and Reports.
(9) Records of Vital Statistics.
(10) Absence of Public Record or Entry.
(11) Records of Religious Organizations.
(12) Marriage, Baptismal, and Similar Certificates.
(13) Family Records.
(14) Records of Documents Affecting an Interest in Property.
(15) Statements in Documents Affecting an Interest in Property.
(16) Statements in Ancient Documents.
(17) Market Reports, Commercial Publications.
(18) Learned Treatises.
(19) Reputation Concerning Personal or Family History.

Rule

803. Hearsay Exceptions; Availability of Declarant Immaterial—Continued
    - (20) Reputation Concerning Boundaries or General History.
    - (21) Reputation as to Character.
    - (22) Judgment of Previous Conviction.
    - (23) Judgment as to Personal, Family, or General History, or Boundaries.
    - (24) Other Exceptions.

804. Hearsay Exceptions; Declarant Unavailable.
    - (a) Definition of Unavailability.
    - (b) Hearsay Exceptions.
        - (1) Former Testimony.
        - (2) Statement Under Belief of Impending Death.
        - (3) Statement Against Interest.
        - (4) Statement of Personal or Family History.
        - (5) Other Exceptions.

805. Hearsay Within Hearsay.

806. Attacking and Supporting Credibility of Declarant.

ARTICLE IX. AUTHENTICATION AND IDENTIFICATION

901. Requirement of Authentication or Identification.
    - (a) General Provision.
    - (b) Illustrations.
        - (1) Testimony of Witness With Knowledge.
        - (2) Nonexpert Opinion on Handwriting.
        - (3) Comparison by Trier or Expert Witness.
        - (4) Distinctive Characteristics and the Like.
        - (5) Voice Identification.
        - (6) Telephone Conversations.
        - (7) Public Records or Reports.
        - (8) Ancient Documents or Data Compilation.
        - (9) Process or System.
        - (10) Methods Provided by Statute or Rule.

902. Self-Authentication.
    - (1) Domestic Public Documents Under Seal.
    - (2) Domestic Public Documents Not Under Seal.
    - (3) Foreign Public Documents.
    - (4) Certified Copies of Public Records.
    - (5) Official Publications.
    - (6) Newspapers and Periodicals.
    - (7) Trade Inscriptions and the Like.
    - (8) Acknowledged Documents.
    - (9) Commercial Paper and Related Documents.
    - (10) Presumptions Under Acts of Congress.

Rule
903. Subscribing Witness' Testimony Unnecessary.

ARTICLE X. CONTENTS OF WRITINGS, RECORDINGS, AND PHOTOGRAPHS

1001. Definitions.
  (1) Writings and Recordings.
  (2) Photographs.
  (3) Original.
  (4) Duplicate.
1002. Requirement of Original.
1003. Admissibility of Duplicates.
1004. Admissibility of Other Evidence of Contents.
  (1) Originals Lost or Destroyed.
  (2) Original Not Obtainable.
  (3) Original in Possession of Opponent.
  (4) Collateral Matters.
1005. Public Records.
1006. Summaries.
1007. Testimony or Written Admission of Party.
1008. Functions of Court and Jury.

ARTICLE XI. MISCELLANEOUS RULES

1101. Applicability of Rules.
  (a) Courts and Magistrates.
  (b) Proceedings Generally.
  (c) Rule of Privilege.
  (d) Rules Inapplicable.
    (1) Preliminary Questions of Fact.
    (2) Grand Jury.
    (3) Miscellaneous Proceedings.
  (e) Rules Applicable in Part.
1102. Amendments.
1103. Title.

INDEX

ARTICLE I. GENERAL PROVISIONS

RULE 101. SCOPE

These rules govern proceedings in the courts of the United States and before United States bankruptcy judges and United

States magistrates, to the extent and with the exceptions stated in Rule 1101.

[Amended effective October 1, 1987.]

RULE 102. PURPOSE AND CONSTRUCTION

These rules shall be construed to secure fairness in administration, elimination of unjustifiable expense and delay, and promotion of growth and development of the law of evidence to the end that the truth may be ascertained and proceedings justly determined.

RULE 103. RULINGS ON EVIDENCE

(a) **Effect of Erroneous Ruling.** Error may not be predicated upon a ruling which admits or excludes evidence unless a substantial right of the party is affected, and

(1) *Objection.* In case the ruling is one admitting evidence, a timely objection or motion to strike appears of record, stating the specific ground of objection, if the specific ground was not apparent from the context; or

(2) *Offer of Proof.* In case the ruling is one excluding evidence, the substance of the evidence was made known to the court by offer or was apparent from the context within which questions were asked.

(b) **Record of Offer and Ruling.** The court may add any other or further statement which shows the character of the evidence, the form in which it was offered, the objection made, and the ruling thereon. It may direct the making of an offer in question and answer form.

(c) **Hearing of Jury.** In jury cases, proceedings shall be conducted, to the extent practicable, so as to prevent inadmissible evidence from being suggested to the jury by any means, such as making statements or offers of proof or asking questions in the hearing of the jury.

(d) **Plain Error.** Nothing in this rule precludes taking notice of plain errors affecting substantial rights although they were not brought to the attention of the court.

RULE 104. PRELIMINARY QUESTIONS

(a) **Questions of Admissibility Generally.** Preliminary questions concerning the qualification of a person to be a witness, the existence of a privilege, or the admissibility of evidence shall be determined by the court, subject to the provisions of subdivision (b). In making its determination it is not bound by the rules of evidence except those with respect to privileges.

(b) **Relevancy Conditioned on Fact.** When the relevancy of evidence depends upon the fulfillment of a condition of fact, the court shall admit it upon, or subject to, the introduction of evidence sufficient to support a finding of the fulfillment of the condition.

(c) **Hearing of Jury.** Hearings on the admissibility of confessions shall in all cases be conducted out of the hearing of the jury. Hearings on other preliminary matters shall be so conducted when the interests of justice require, or when an accused is a witness and so requests.

(d) **Testimony by Accused.** The accused does not, by testifying upon a preliminary matter, become subject to cross-examination as to other issues in the case.

(e) **Weight and Credibility.** This rule does not limit the right of a party to introduce before the jury evidence relevant to weight or credibility.

[Amended effective October 1, 1987.]

RULE 105. LIMITED ADMISSIBILITY

When evidence which is admissible as to one party or for one purpose but not admissible as to another party or for another purpose is admitted, the court, upon request, shall restrict the evidence to its proper scope and instruct the jury accordingly.

RULE 106. REMAINDER OF OR RELATED WRITINGS OR RECORDED STATEMENTS

When a writing or recorded statement or part thereof is introduced by a party, an adverse party may require the introduction at that time of any other part or any other writing or recorded statement which ought in fairness to be considered contemporaneously with it.

[Amended effective October 1, 1987.]

ARTICLE II. JUDICIAL NOTICE

RULE 201. JUDICIAL NOTICE OF ADJUDICATIVE FACTS

(a) Scope of Rule. This rule governs only judicial notice of adjudicative facts.

(b) Kinds of Facts. A judicially noticed fact must be one not subject to reasonable dispute in that it is either (1) generally known within the territorial jurisdiction of the trial court or (2) capable of accurate and ready determination by resort to sources whose accuracy cannot reasonably be questioned.

(c) When Discretionary. A court may take judicial notice, whether requested or not.

(d) When Mandatory. A court shall take judicial notice if requested by a party and supplied with the necessary information.

(e) Opportunity to Be Heard. A party is entitled upon timely request to an opportunity to be heard as to the propriety of taking judicial notice and the tenor of the matter noticed. In the absence of prior notification, the request may be made after judicial notice has been taken.

(f) Time of Taking Notice. Judicial notice may be taken at any stage of the proceeding.

(g) Instructing Jury. In a civil action or proceeding, the court shall instruct the jury to accept as conclusive any fact judicially noticed. In a criminal case, the court shall instruct the jury that it may, but is not required to, accept as conclusive any fact judicially noticed.

ARTICLE III. PRESUMPTIONS IN CIVIL ACTIONS AND PROCEEDINGS

RULE 301. PRESUMPTIONS IN GENERAL IN CIVIL ACTIONS AND PROCEEDINGS

In all civil actions and proceedings not otherwise provided for by Act of Congress or by these rules, a presumption imposes on the party against whom it is directed the burden of going forward with evidence to rebut or meet the presumption, but does not shift to such party the burden of proof in the sense of the risk of nonpersuasion, which remains throughout the trial upon the party on whom it was originally cast.

RULE 302. APPLICABILITY OF STATE LAW IN CIVIL ACTIONS AND PROCEEDINGS

In civil actions and proceedings, the effect of a presumption respecting a fact which is an element of a claim or defense as to which State law supplies the rule of decision is determined in accordance with State law.

ARTICLE IV. RELEVANCY AND ITS LIMITS

RULE 401. DEFINITION OF "RELEVANT EVIDENCE"

"Relevant evidence" means evidence having any tendency to make the existence of any fact that is of consequence to the determination of the action more probable or less probable than it would be without the evidence.

RULE 402. RELEVANT EVIDENCE GENERALLY ADMISSIBLE; IRRELEVANT EVIDENCE INADMISSIBLE

All relevant evidence is admissible, except as otherwise provided by the Constitution of the United States, by Act of Congress, by these rules, or by other rules prescribed by the Supreme Court pursuant to statutory authority. Evidence which is not relevant is not admissible.

RULE 403. EXCLUSION OF RELEVANT EVIDENCE ON GROUNDS OF PREJUDICE, CONFUSION, OR WASTE OF TIME

Although relevant, evidence may be excluded if its probative value is substantially outweighed by the danger of unfair prejudice, confusion of the issues, or misleading the jury, or by considerations of undue delay, waste of time, or needless presentation of cumulative evidence.

RULE 404. CHARACTER EVIDENCE NOT ADMISSIBLE TO PROVE CONDUCT; EXCEPTIONS; OTHER CRIMES

(a) Character Evidence Generally. Evidence of a person's character or a trait of character is not admissible for the purpose of proving action in conformity therewith on a particular occasion, except:

(1) *Character of Accused.* Evidence of a pertinent trait of character offered by an accused, or by the prosecution to rebut the same;

(2) *Character of Victim.* Evidence of a pertinent trait of character of the victim of the crime offered by an accused, or by the prosecution to rebut the same, or evidence of a character trait of peacefulness of the victim offered by the prosecution in a homicide case to rebut evidence that the victim was the first aggressor;

(3) *Character of Witness.* Evidence of the character of a witness, as provided in rules 607, 608, and 609.

(b) Other Crimes, Wrongs, or Acts. Evidence of other crimes, wrongs, or acts is not admissible to prove the character of a person in order to show action in conformity therewith. It may, however, be admissible for other purposes, such as proof of motive, opportunity, intent, preparation, plan, knowledge, identity, or absence of mistake or accident.

[Amended effective October 1, 1987.]

RULE 405. METHODS OF PROVING CHARACTER

(a) Reputation or Opinion. In all cases in which evidence of character or a trait of character of a person is admissible, proof may be made by testimony as to reputation or by testimony in the form of an opinion. On cross-examination inquiry is allowable into relevant specific instances of conduct.

(b) Specific Instances of Conduct. In cases in which character or a trait of character of a person is an essential element of a charge, claim, or defense, proof may also be made of specific instances of that person's conduct.

[Amended effective October 1, 1987.]

RULE 406. HABIT; ROUTINE PRACTICE

Evidence of the habit of a person or of the routine practice of an organization, whether corroborated or not and regardless of the presence of eyewitnesses, is relevant to prove that the conduct of the person or organization on a particular occasion was in conformity with the habit or routine practice.

RULE 407. SUBSEQUENT REMEDIAL MEASURES

When, after an event, measures are taken which, if taken previously, would have made the event less likely to occur, evidence of the subsequent measures is not admissible to prove negligence or culpable conduct in connection with the event. This rule does not require the exclusion of evidence of subsequent measures when offered for another purpose, such as proving ownership, control, or feasibility of precautionary measures, if controverted, or impeachment.

RULE 408. COMPROMISE AND OFFERS TO COMPROMISE

Evidence of (1) furnishing or offering or promising to furnish, or (2) accepting or offering or promising to accept, a valuable consideration in compromising or attempting to compromise a claim which was disputed as to either validity or amount, is not admissible to prove liability for or invalidity of the claim or its amount. Evidence of conduct or statements made in compromise negotiations is likewise not admissible. This rule does not require the exclusion of any evidence otherwise discoverable merely because it is presented in the course of compromise negotiations. This rule also does not require exclusion when the evidence is offered for another purpose, such as proving bias or prejudice of a witness, negativing a contention of undue delay, or proving an effort to obstruct a criminal investigation or prosecution.

RULE 409. PAYMENT OF MEDICAL AND SIMILAR EXPENSES

Evidence of furnishing or offering or promising to pay medical, hospital, or similar expenses occasioned by an injury is not admissible to prove liability for the injury.

RULE 410. INADMISSIBILITY OF PLEAS, PLEA DISCUSSIONS, AND RELATED STATEMENTS

Except as otherwise provided in this rule, evidence of the following is not, in any civil or criminal proceeding, admissible against the defendant who made the plea or was a participant in the plea discussions:

(1) a plea of guilty which was later withdrawn;

(2) a plea of nolo contendere;

(3) any statement made in the course of any proceedings under Rule 11 of the Federal Rules of Criminal Procedure or comparable state procedure regarding either of the foregoing pleas; or

(4) any statement made in the course of plea discussions with an attorney for the prosecuting authority which do not result in a plea of guilty or which result in a plea of guilty later withdrawn.

However, such a statement is admissible (i) in any proceeding wherein another statement made in the course of the same plea or plea discussions has been introduced and the statement ought in fairness be considered contemporaneously with it, or (ii) in a criminal proceeding for perjury or false statement if the statement was made by the defendant under oath, on the record and in the presence of counsel.

[Amended December 12, 1975; April 30, 1979, effective December 1, 1980.]

RULE 411. LIABILITY INSURANCE

Evidence that a person was or was not insured against liability is not admissible upon the issue whether the person acted negligently or otherwise wrongfully. This rule does not require the exclusion of evidence of insurance against liability when offered for another purpose, such as proof of agency, ownership, or control, or bias or prejudice of a witness.

[Amended effective October 1, 1987.]

RULE 412. RAPE CASES; RELEVANCE OF VICTIM'S PAST BEHAVIOR

(a) Notwithstanding any other provision of law, in a criminal case in which a person is accused of rape or of assault with intent to commit rape, reputation or opinion evidence of the past sexual behavior of an alleged victim of such rape or assault is not admissible.

(b) Notwithstanding any other provision of law, in a criminal case in which a person is accused of rape or of assault with intent to commit rape, evidence of a victim's past sexual behavior other than reputation or opinion evidence is also not admissible, unless such evidence other than reputation or opinion evidence is—

(1) admitted in accordance with subdivisions (c)(1) and (c)(2) and is constitutionally required to be admitted; or

(2) admitted in accordance with subdivision (c) and is evidence of—

(A) past sexual behavior with persons other than the accused, offered by the accused upon the issue of whether the accused was or was not, with respect to the alleged victim, the source of semen or injury; or

(B) past sexual behavior with the accused and is offered by the accused upon the issue of whether the alleged victim consented to the sexual behavior with respect to which rape or assault is alleged.

(c)(1) If the person accused of committing rape or assault with intent to commit rape intends to offer under subdivision (b) evidence of specific instances of the alleged victim's past sexual behavior, the accused shall make a written motion to offer such evidence not later than fifteen days before the date on which the trial in which such evidence is to be offered is scheduled to begin, except that the court may allow the motion to be made at a later date, including during trial, if the court determines either that the evidence is newly discovered and could not have been obtained earlier through the exercise of due diligence or that the issue to which such evidence relates has newly arisen in the case. Any motion made under this paragraph shall be served on all other parties and on the alleged victim.

(2) The motion described in paragraph (1) shall be accompanied by a written offer of proof. If the court determines that the offer of proof contains evidence described in subdivision (b), the court shall order a hearing in chambers to determine if such evidence is admissible. At such hearing the parties may call witnesses, including the alleged victim, and offer relevant evidence. Notwithstanding subdivision (b) of rule 104, if the relevan-

cy of the evidence which the accused seeks to offer in the trial depends upon the fulfillment of a condition of fact, the court, at the hearing in chambers or at a subsequent hearing in chambers scheduled for such purpose, shall accept evidence on the issue of whether such condition of fact is fulfilled and shall determine such issue.

(3) If the court determines on the basis of the hearing described in paragraph (2) that the evidence which the accused seeks to offer is relevant and that the probative value of such evidence outweighs the danger of unfair prejudice, such evidence shall be admissible in the trial to the extent an order made by the court specifies evidence which may be offered and areas with respect to which the alleged victim may be examined or cross-examined.

(d) For purposes of this rule, the term "past sexual behavior" means sexual behavior other than the sexual behavior with respect to which rape or assault with intent to commit rape is alleged.

[Added October 28, 1978.]

ARTICLE V. PRIVILEGES

RULE 501. GENERAL RULE

Except as otherwise required by the Constitution of the United States or provided by Act of Congress or in rules prescribed by the Supreme Court pursuant to statutory authority, the privilege of a witness, person, government, State, or political subdivision thereof shall be governed by the principles of the common law as they may be interpreted by the courts of the United States in the light of reason and experience. However, in civil actions and proceedings, with respect to an element of a claim or defense as to which State law supplies the rule of decision, the privilege of a witness, person, government, State, or political subdivision thereof shall be determined in accordance with State law.

ARTICLE VI. WITNESSES

RULE 601. GENERAL RULE OF COMPETENCY

Every person is competent to be a witness except as otherwise provided in these rules. However, in civil actions and proceedings, with respect to an element of a claim or defense as to which

State law supplies the rule of decision, the competency of a witness shall be determined in accordance with State law.

RULE 602. LACK OF PERSONAL KNOWLEDGE

A witness may not testify to a matter unless evidence is introduced sufficient to support a finding that the witness has personal knowledge of the matter. Evidence to prove personal knowledge may, but need not, consist of the witness' own testimony. This rule is subject to the provisions of Rule 703, relating to opinion testimony by expert witnesses.

[Amended effective October 1, 1987.]

RULE 603. OATH OR AFFIRMATION

Before testifying, every witness shall be required to declare that the witness will testify truthfully, by oath or affirmation administered in a form calculated to awaken the witness' conscience and impress the witness' mind with the duty to do so.

[Amended effective October 1, 1987.]

RULE 604. INTERPRETERS

An interpreter is subject to the provisions of these rules relating to qualification as an expert and the administration of an oath or affirmation to make a true translation.

[Amended effective October 1, 1987.]

RULE 605. COMPETENCY OF JUDGE AS WITNESS

The judge presiding at the trial may not testify in that trial as a witness. No objection need be made in order to preserve the point.

RULE 606. COMPETENCY OF JUROR AS WITNESS

A member of the jury may not testify as a witness before that jury in the trial of the case in which the juror is sitting. If the juror is called so to testify, the opposing party shall be afforded an opportunity to object out of the presence of the jury.

(b) Inquiry into Validity of Verdict or Indictment. Upon an inquiry into the validity of a verdict or indictment, a juror may not testify as to any matter or statement occurring during the course of the jury's deliberations or to the effect of anything upon that or any other juror's mind or emotions as influencing the juror to assent to or dissent from the verdict or indictment or concerning the juror's mental processes in connection therewith, except that a juror may testify on the question whether extraneous prejudicial information was improperly brought to the jury's attention or whether any outside influence was improperly brought to bear upon any juror. Nor may a juror's affidavit or evidence of any statement by the juror concerning a matter about which the juror would be precluded from testifying be received for these purposes.

[Amended December 12, 1975; amended effective October 1, 1987.]

RULE 607. WHO MAY IMPEACH

The credibility of a witness may be attacked by any party, including the party calling the witness.

[Amended effective October 1, 1987.]

RULE 608. EVIDENCE OF CHARACTER AND CONDUCT OF WITNESS

(a) Opinion and Reputation Evidence of Character. The credibility of a witness may be attacked or supported by evidence in the form of opinion or reputation, but subject to these limitations: (1) the evidence may refer only to character for truthfulness or untruthfulness, and (2) evidence of truthful character is admissible only after the character of the witness for truthfulness has been attacked by opinion or reputation evidence or otherwise.

(b) Specific Instances of Conduct. Specific instances of the conduct of a witness, for the purpose of attacking or supporting the witness' credibility, other than conviction of crime as provided in Rule 609, may not be proved by extrinsic evidence. They may, however, in the discretion of the court, if probative of truthfulness or untruthfulness, be inquired into on cross-examination of the witness (1) concerning the witness' character for truthfulness or untruthfulness, or (2) concerning the character for truthfulness or untruthfulness of another witness as to which character the witness being cross-examined has testified.

The giving of testimony, whether by an accused or by any other witness, does not operate as a waiver of the accused's or the witness' privilege against self-incrimination when examined with respect to matters which relate only to credibility.

[Amended effective October 1, 1987.]

RULE 609. IMPEACHMENT BY EVIDENCE OF CONVICTION OF CRIME

(a) **General Rule.** For the purpose of attacking the credibility of a witness, evidence that the witness has been convicted of a crime shall be admitted if elicited from the witness or established by public record during cross-examination but only if the crime (1) was punishable by death or imprisonment in excess of one year under the law under which the witness was convicted, and the court determines that the probative value of admitting this evidence outweighs its prejudicial effect to the defendant, or (2) involved dishonesty or false statement, regardless of the punishment.

(b) **Time Limit.** Evidence of a conviction under this rule is not admissible if a period of more than ten years has elapsed since the date of the conviction or of the release of the witness from the confinement imposed for that conviction, whichever is the later date, unless the court determines, in the interests of justice, that the probative value of the conviction supported by specific facts and circumstances substantially outweighs its prejudicial effect. However, evidence of a conviction more than 10 years old as calculated herein, is not admissible unless the proponent gives to the adverse party sufficient advance written notice of intent to use such evidence to provide the adverse party with a fair opportunity to contest the use of such evidence.

(c) **Effect of Pardon, Annulment, or Certificate of Rehabilitation.** Evidence of a conviction is not admissible under this rule if (1) the conviction has been the subject of a pardon, annulment, certificate of rehabilitation, or other equivalent procedure based on a finding of the rehabilitation of the person convicted, and that person has not been convicted of a subsequent crime which was punishable by death or imprisonment in excess of one year, or (2) the conviction has been the subject of a pardon, annulment, or other equivalent procedure based on a finding of innocence.

(d) **Juvenile Adjudications.** Evidence of juvenile adjudications is generally not admissible under this rule. The court may, however, in a criminal case allow evidence of a juvenile adjudication of a witness other than the accused if conviction of the offense would be admissible to attack the credibility of an adult and the court is satisfied that admission in evidence is necessary for a fair determination of the issue of guilt or innocence.

(e) Pendency of Appeal. The pendency of an appeal therefrom does not render evidence of a conviction inadmissible. Evidence of the pendency of an appeal is admissible.

[Amended effective October 1, 1987.]

RULE 610. RELIGIOUS BELIEFS OR OPINIONS

Evidence of the beliefs or opinions of a witness on matters of religion is not admissible for the purpose of showing that by reason of their nature the witness' credibility is impaired or enhanced.

[Amended effective October 1, 1987.]

RULE 611. MODE AND ORDER OF INTERROGATION AND PRESENTATION

(a) Control by Court. The court shall exercise reasonable control over the mode and order of interrogating witnesses and presenting evidence so as to (1) make the interrogation and presentation effective for the ascertainment of the truth, (2) avoid needless consumption of time, and (3) protect witnesses from harassment or undue embarrassment.

(b) Scope of Cross-Examination. Cross-examination should be limited to the subject matter of the direct examination and matters affecting the credibility of the witness. The court may, in the exercise of discretion, permit inquiry into additional matters as if on direct examination.

(c) Leading Questions. Leading questions should not be used on the direct examination of a witness except as may be necessary to develop the witness' testimony. Ordinarily leading questions should be permitted on cross-examination. When a party calls a hostile witness, an adverse party, or a witness identified with an adverse party, interrogation may be by leading questions.

[Amended effective October 1, 1987.]

RULE 612. WRITING USED TO REFRESH MEMORY

Except as otherwise provided in criminal proceedings by section 3500 of title 18, United States Code, if a witness uses a writing to refresh memory for the purpose of testifying, either—

(1) while testifying, or

(2) before testifying, if the court in its discretion determines it is necessary in the interests of justice,

an adverse party is entitled to have the writing produced at the hearing, to inspect it, to cross-examine the witness thereon, and to introduce in evidence those portions which relate to the testimony of the witness. If it is claimed that the writing contains matters not related to the subject matter of the testimony the court shall examine the writing in camera, excise any portions not so related, and order delivery of the remainder to the party entitled thereto. Any portion withheld over objections shall be preserved and made available to the appellate court in the event of an appeal. If a writing is not produced or delivered pursuant to order under this rule, the court shall make any order justice requires, except that in criminal cases when the prosecution elects not to comply, the order shall be one striking the testimony or, if the court in its discretion determines that the interests of justice so require, declaring a mistrial.

[Amended effective October 1, 1987.]

RULE 613. PRIOR STATEMENTS OF WITNESSES

(a) Examining Witness Concerning Prior Statement. In examining a witness concerning a prior statement made by the witness, whether written or not, the statement need not be shown nor its contents disclosed to the witness at that time, but on request the same shall be shown or disclosed to opposing counsel.

(b) Extrinsic Evidence of Prior Inconsistent Statement of Witness. Extrinsic evidence of a prior inconsistent statement by a witness is not admissible unless the witness is afforded an opportunity to explain or deny the same and the opposite party is afforded an opportunity to interrogate the witness thereon, or the interests of justice otherwise require. This provision does not apply to admissions of a party-opponent as defined in Rule 801(d)(2).

[Amended effective October 1, 1987.]

RULE 614. CALLING AND INTERROGATION OF WITNESSES BY COURT

(a) **Calling by Court.** The court may, on its own motion or at the suggestion of a party, call witnesses, and all parties are entitled to cross-examine witnesses thus called.

(b) **Interrogation by Court.** The court may interrogate witnesses, whether called by itself or by a party.

(c) **Objections.** Objections to the calling of witnesses by the court or to interrogation by it may be made at the time or at the next available opportunity when the jury is not present.

RULE 615. EXCLUSION OF WITNESSES

At the request of a party the court shall order witnesses excluded so that they cannot hear the testimony of other witnesses, and it may make the order of its own motion. This rule does not authorize exclusion of (1) a party who is a natural person, or (2) an officer or employee of [a] party which is not a natural person designated as its representative by its attorney, or (3) a person whose presence is shown by a party to be essential to the presentation of the party's cause.

[Amended effective October 1, 1987.]

ARTICLE VII. OPINIONS AND EXPERT TESTIMONY

RULE 701. OPINION TESTIMONY BY LAY WITNESSES

If the witness is not testifying as an expert, the witness' testimony in the form of opinions or inferences is limited to those opinions or inferences which are (a) rationally based on the perception of the witness and (b) helpful to a clear understanding of the witness' testimony or the determination of a fact in issue.

[Amended effective October 1, 1987.]

RULE 702. TESTIMONY BY EXPERTS

If scientific, technical, or other specialized knowledge will assist the trier of fact to understand the evidence or to determine a fact in issue, a witness qualified as an expert by knowledge, skill, experience, training, or education, may testify thereto in the form of an opinion or otherwise.

RULE 703. BASES OF OPINION TESTIMONY BY EXPERTS

The facts or data in the particular case upon which an expert bases an opinion or inference may be those perceived by or made known to the expert at or before the hearing. If of a type reasonably relied upon by experts in the particular field in forming opinions or inferences upon the subject, the facts or data need not be admissible in evidence.

[Amended effective October 1, 1987.]

RULE 704. OPINION ON ULTIMATE ISSUE

(a) Except as provided in subdivision (b), testimony in the form of an opinion or inference otherwise admissible is not objectionable because it embraces an ultimate issue to be decided by the trier of fact.

(b) No expert witness testifying with respect to the mental state or condition of a defendant in a criminal case may state an opinion or inference as to whether the defendant did or did not have the mental state or condition constituting an element of the crime charged or of a defense thereto. Such ultimate issues are matters for the trier of fact alone.

[Amended effective October 12, 1984.]

RULE 705. DISCLOSURE OF FACTS OR DATA UNDERLYING EXPERT OPINION

The expert may testify in terms of opinion or inference and gives reasons therefor without prior disclosure of the underlying facts or data, unless the court requires otherwise. The expert may in any event be required to disclose the underlying facts or data on cross-examination.

[Amended effective October 1, 1987.]

RULE 706. COURT APPOINTED EXPERTS

(a) Appointment. The court may on its own motion or on the motion of any party enter an order to show cause why expert witnesses should not be appointed, and may request the parties to submit nominations. The court may appoint any expert witnesses agreed upon by the parties, and may appoint expert witnesses of its own selection. An expert witness shall not be appointed by the court unless the witness consents to act. A witness so appointed shall be informed of the witness' duties by the court in writing, a copy of which shall be filed with the clerk, or at a conference in which the parties shall have opportunity to participate. A witness so appointed shall advise the parties of the witness' findings, if any; the witness' deposition may be taken by any party; and the witness may be called to testify by the court or any party. The witness shall be subject to cross-examination by each party, including a party calling the witness.

(b) Compensation. Expert witnesses so appointed are entitled to reasonable compensation in whatever sum the court may allow. The compensation thus fixed is payable from funds which may be provided by law in criminal cases and civil actions and proceedings involving just compensation under the fifth amendment. In other civil actions and proceedings the compensation shall be paid by the parties in such proportion and at such time as the court directs, and thereafter charged in like manner as other costs.

(c) Disclosure of Appointment. In the exercise of its discretion, the court may authorize disclosure to the jury of the fact that the court appointed the expert witness.

(d) Parties' Experts of Own Selection. Nothing in this rule limits the parties in calling expert witnesses of their own selection.

[Amended effective October 1, 1987.]

ARTICLE VIII. HEARSAY

RULE 801. DEFINITIONS

The following definitions apply under this article:

(a) Statement. A "statement" is (1) an oral or written assertion or (2) nonverbal conduct of a person, if it is intended by the person as an assertion.

(b) Declarant. A "declarant" is a person who makes a statement.

(c) **Hearsay.** "Hearsay" is a statement, other than one made by the declarant while testifying at the trial or hearing, offered in evidence to prove the truth of the matter asserted.

(d) **Statements Which Are Not Hearsay.** A statement is not hearsay if—

(1) *Prior Statement by Witness.* The declarant testifies at the trial or hearing and is subject to cross-examination concerning the statement, and the statement is (A) inconsistent with the declarant's testimony, and was given under oath subject to the penalty of perjury at a trial, hearing, or other proceeding, or in a deposition, or (B) consistent with the declarant's testimony and is offered to rebut an express or implied charge against the declarant of recent fabrication or improper influence or motive, or (C) one of identification of a person made after perceiving the person; or

(2) *Admission by Party-Opponent.* The statement is offered against a party and is (A) the party's own statement in either an individual or a representative capacity or (B) a statement of which the party has manifested an adoption or belief in its truth, or (C) a statement by a person authorized by the party to make a statement concerning the subject, or (D) a statement by the party's agent or servant concerning a matter within the scope of the agency or employment, made during the existence of the relationship, or (E) a statement by a coconspirator of a party during the course and in furtherance of the conspiracy.

[Amended October 16, 1975; amended effective October 1, 1987.]

RULE 802. HEARSAY RULE

Hearsay is not admissible except as provided by these rules or by other rules prescribed by the Supreme Court pursuant to statutory authority or by Act of Congress.

RULE 803. HEARSAY EXCEPTIONS; AVAILABILITY OF DECLARANT IMMATERIAL

The following are not excluded by the hearsay rule, even though the declarant is available as a witness:

(1) **Present Sense Impression.** A statement describing or explaining an event or condition made while the declarant was perceiving the event or condition, or immediately thereafter.

(2) Excited Utterance. A statement relating to a startling event or condition made while the declarant was under the stress of excitement caused by the event or condition.

(3) Then Existing Mental, Emotional, or Physical Condition. A statement of the declarant's then existing state of mind, emotion, sensation, or physical condition (such as intent, plan, motive, design, mental feeling, pain, and bodily health), but not including a statement of memory or belief to prove the fact remembered or believed unless it relates to the execution, revocation, identification, or terms of declarant's will.

(4) Statements for Purposes of Medical Diagnosis or Treatment. Statements made for purposes of medical diagnosis or treatment and describing medical history, or past or present symptoms, pain, or sensations, or the inception or general character of the cause or external source thereof insofar as reasonably pertinent to diagnosis or treatment.

(5) Recorded Recollection. A memorandum or record concerning a matter about which a witness once had knowledge but now has insufficient recollection to enable the witness to testify fully and accurately, shown to have been made or adopted by the witness when the matter was fresh in the witness' memory and to reflect that knowledge correctly. If admitted, the memorandum or record may be read into evidence but may not itself be received as an exhibit unless offered by an adverse party.

(6) Records of Regularly Conducted Activity. A memorandum, report, record, or data compilation, in any form, of acts, events, conditions, opinions, or diagnoses, made at or near the time by, or from information transmitted by, a person with knowledge, if kept in the course of a regularly conducted business activity, and if it was the regular practice of that business activity to make the memorandum, report, record, or data compilation, all as shown by the testimony of the custodian or other qualified witness, unless the source of information or the method or circumstances of preparation indicate lack of trustworthiness. The term "business" as used in this paragraph includes business, institution, association, profession, occupation, and calling of every kind, whether or not conducted for profit.

(7) Absence of Entry in Records Kept in Accordance With the Provisions of Paragraph (6). Evidence that a matter is not included in the memoranda reports, records, or data compilations, in any form, kept in accordance with the provisions of paragraph (6), to prove the nonoccurrence or nonexistence of the matter, if the matter was of a kind of which a memorandum, report, record, or data compilation was regularly made and preserved, unless the sources of information or other circumstances indicate lack of trustworthiness.

(8) **Public Records and Reports.** Records, reports, statements, or data compilations, in any form, of public offices or agencies, setting forth (A) the activities of the office or agency, or (B) matters observed pursuant to duty imposed by law as to which matters there was a duty to report, excluding, however, in criminal cases matters observed by police officers and other law enforcement personnel, or (C) in civil actions and proceedings and against the Government in criminal cases, factual findings resulting from an investigation made pursuant to authority granted by law, unless the sources of information or other circumstances indicate lack of trustworthiness.

(9) **Records of Vital Statistics.** Records or data compilations, in any form, of births, fetal deaths, deaths, or marriages, if the report thereof was made to a public office pursuant to requirements of law.

(10) **Absence of Public Record or Entry.** To prove the absence of a record, report, statement, or data compilation, in any form, or the nonoccurrence or nonexistence of a matter of which a record, report, statement, or data compilation, in any form, was regularly made and preserved by a public office or agency, evidence in the form of a certification in accordance with rule 902, or testimony, that diligent search failed to disclose the record, report, statement, or data compilation, or entry.

(11) **Records of Religious Organizations.** Statements of births, marriages, divorces, deaths, legitimacy, ancestry, relationship by blood or marriage, or other similar facts of personal or family history, contained in a regularly kept record of a religious organization.

(12) **Marriage, Baptismal, and Similar Certificates.** Statements of fact contained in a certificate that the maker performed a marriage or other ceremony or administered a sacrament, made by a clergyman, public official, or other person authorized by the rules or practices of a religious organization or by law to perform the act certified, and purporting to have been issued at the time of the act or within a reasonable time thereafter.

(13) Family Records. Statements of fact concerning personal or family history contained in family Bibles, genealogies, charts, engravings on rings, inscriptions on family portraits, engravings on urns, crypts, or tombstones, or the like.

(14) Records of Documents Affecting an Interest in Property. The record of a document purporting to establish or affect an interest in property, as proof of the content of the original recorded document and its execution and delivery by each person by whom it purports to have been executed, if the record is a record of a public office and an applicable statute authorizes the recording of documents of that kind in that office.

(15) Statements in Documents Affecting an Interest in Property. A statement contained in a document purporting to establish or affect an interest in property if the matter stated was relevant to the purpose of the document, unless dealings with the property since the document was made have been inconsistent with the truth of the statement or the purport of the document.

(16) Statements in Ancient Documents. Statements in a document in existence twenty years or more the authenticity of which is established.

(17) Market Reports, Commercial Publications. Market quotations, tabulations, lists, directories, or other published compilations, generally used and relied upon by the public or by persons in particular occupations.

(18) Learned Treatises. To the extent called to the attention of an expert witness upon cross-examination or relied upon by the expert witness in direct examination, statements contained in published treatises, periodicals, or pamphlets on a subject of history, medicine, or other science or art, established as a reliable authority by the testimony or admission of the witness or by other expert testimony or by judicial notice. If admitted, the statements may be read into evidence but may not be received as exhibits.

(19) Reputation Concerning Personal or Family History. Reputation among members of a person's family by blood, adoption, or marriage, or among a person's associates, or in the community, concerning a person's birth, adoption, marriage, divorce, death, legitimacy, relationship by blood, adoption, or marriage, ancestry, or other similar fact of personal or family history.

(20) Reputation Concerning Boundaries or General History. Reputation in a community, arising before the controversy, as to boundaries of or customs affecting lands in the community, and reputation as to events of general history important to the community or State or nation in which located.

(21) **Reputation as to Character.** Reputation of a person's character among associates or in the community.

(22) **Judgment of Previous Conviction.** Evidence of a final judgment, entered after a trial or upon a plea of guilty (but not upon a plea of nolo contendere), adjudging a person guilty of a crime punishable by death or imprisonment in excess of one year, to prove any fact essential to sustain the judgment, but not including, when offered by the Government in a criminal prosecution for purposes other than impeachment, judgments against persons other than the accused. The pendency of an appeal may be shown but does not affect admissibility.

(23) **Judgment as to Personal, Family, or General History, or Boundaries.** Judgments as proof of matters of personal, family or general history, or boundaries, essential to the judgment, if the same would be provable by evidence of reputation.

(24) **Other Exceptions.** A statement not specifically covered by any of the foregoing exceptions but having equivalent circumstantial guarantees of trustworthiness, if the court determines that (A) the statement is offered as evidence of a material fact; (B) the statement is more probative on the point for which it is offered than any other evidence which the proponent can procure through reasonable efforts; and (C) the general purposes of these rules and the interests of justice will best be served by admission of the statement into evidence. However, a statement may not be admitted under this exception unless the proponent of it makes known to the adverse party sufficiently in advance of the trial or hearing to provide the adverse party with a fair opportunity to prepare to meet it, the proponent's intention to offer the statement and the particulars of it, including the name and address of the declarant.

[Amended December 12, 1975; amended effective October 1, 1987.]

RULE 804. HEARSAY EXCEPTIONS; DECLARANT UNAVAILABLE

(a) **Definition of Unavailability.** "Unavailability as a witness" includes situations in which the declarant—

(1) is exempted by ruling of the court on the ground of privilege from testifying concerning the subject matter of the declarant's statement; or

(2) persists in refusing to testify concerning the subject matter of the declarant's statement despite an order of the court to do so; or

(3) testifies to a lack of memory of the subject matter of the declarant's statement; or

(4) is unable to be present or to testify at the hearing because of death or then existing physical or mental illness or infirmity; or

(5) is absent from the hearing and the proponent of a statement has been unable to procure the declarant's attendance (or in the case of a hearsay exception under subdivisions (b)(2), (3), or (4), the declarant's attendance or testimony) by process or other reasonable means.

A declarant is not unavailable as a witness if exemption, refusal, claim of lack of memory, inability, or absence is due to the procurement or wrongdoing of the proponent of a statement for the purpose of preventing the witness from attending or testifying.

(b) Hearsay Exceptions. The following are not excluded by the hearsay rule if the declarant is unavailable as a witness:

(1) *Former Testimony.* Testimony given as a witness at another hearing of the same or a different proceeding, or in a deposition taken in compliance with law in the course of the same or another proceeding, if the party against whom the testimony is now offered, or, in a civil action or proceeding, a predecessor in interest, had an opportunity and similar motive to develop the testimony by direct, cross, or redirect examination.

(2) *Statement Under Belief of Impending Death.* In a prosecution for homicide or in a civil action or proceeding, a statement made by a declarant while believing that the declarant's death was imminent, concerning the cause or circumstances of what the declarant believed to be impending death.

(3) *Statement Against Interest.* A statement which was at the time of its making so far contrary to the declarant's pecuniary or proprietary interest, or so far tended to subject the declarant to civil or criminal liability, or to render invalid a claim by the declarant against another, that a reasonable person in the declarant's position would not have made the statement unless believing

it to be true. A statement tending to expose the declarant to criminal liability and offered to exculpate the accused is not admissible unless corroborating circumstances clearly indicate the trustworthiness of the statement.

(4) *Statement of Personal or Family History.* (A) A statement concerning the declarant's own birth, adoption, marriage, divorce, legitimacy, relationship by blood, adoption, or marriage, ancestry, or other similar fact of personal or family history, even though declarant had no means of acquiring personal knowledge of the matter stated; or (B) a statement concerning the foregoing matters, and death also, of another person, if the declarant was related to the other by blood, adoption, or marriage or was so intimately associated with the other's family as to be likely to have accurate information concerning the matter declared.

(5) *Other Exceptions.* A statement not specifically covered by any of the foregoing exceptions but having equivalent circumstantial guarantees of trustworthiness, if the court determines that (A) the statement is offered as evidence of a material fact; (B) the statement is more probative on the point for which it is offered than any other evidence which the proponent can procure through reasonable efforts; and (C) the general purposes of these rules and the interests of justice will best be served by admission of the statement into evidence. However, a statement may not be admitted under this exception unless the proponent of it makes known to the adverse party sufficiently in advance of the trial or hearing to provide the adverse party with a fair opportunity to prepare to meet it, the proponent's intention to offer the statement and the particulars of it, including the name and address of the declarant.

[Amended December 12, 1975; amended effective October 1, 1987.]

RULE 805. HEARSAY WITHIN HEARSAY

Hearsay included within hearsay is not excluded under the hearsay rule if each part of the combined statements conforms with an exception to the hearsay rule provided in these rules.

RULE 806. ATTACKING AND SUPPORTING CREDIBILITY OF DECLARANT

When a hearsay statement, or a statement defined in Rule 801(d)(2), (C), (D), or (E), has been admitted in evidence, the credibility of the declarant may be attacked, and if attacked may be supported, by any evidence which would be admissible for those purposes if declarant had testified as a witness. Evidence of a statement or conduct by the declarant at any time, inconsistent with the declarant's hearsay statement, is not subject to any requirement that the declarant may have been afforded an opportunity to deny or explain. If the party against whom a hearsay statement has been admitted calls the declarant as a witness, the party is entitled to examine the declarant on the statment as if under cross-examination.

[Amended effective October 1, 1987.]

ARTICLE IX. AUTHENTICATION AND IDENTIFICATION

RULE 901. REQUIREMENT OF AUTHENTICATION OR IDENTIFICATION

(a) General Provision. The requirement of authentication or identification as a condition precedent to admissibility is satisfied by evidence sufficient to support a finding that the matter in question is what its proponent claims.

(b) Illustrations. By way of illustration only, and not by way of limitation, the following are examples of authentication or identification conforming with the requirements of this rule:

(1) *Testimony of Witness With Knowledge.* Testimony that a matter is what it is claimed to be.

(2) *Nonexpert Opinion on Handwriting.* Nonexpert opinion as to the genuineness of handwriting, based upon familiarity not acquired for purposes of the litigation.

(3) *Comparison by Trier or Expert Witness.* Comparison by the trier of fact or by expert witnesses with specimens which have been authenticated.

(4) *Distinctive Characteristics and the Like.* Appearance, contents, substance, internal patterns, or other distinctive characteristics, taken in conjunction with circumstances.

(5) *Voice Identification.* Identification of a voice, whether heard firsthand or through mechanical or electronic transmission or recording, by opinion based upon hearing the voice at any time under circumstances connecting it with the alleged speaker.

(6) *Telephone Conversations.* Telephone conversations, by evidence that a call was made to the number assigned at the time by

the telephone company to a particular person or business, if (A) in the case of a person, circumstances, including self-identification, show the person answering to be the one called, or (B) in the case of a business, the call was made to a place of business and the conversation related to business reasonably transacted over the telephone.

(7) *Public Records or Reports.* Evidence that a writing authorized by law to be recorded or filed and in fact recorded or filed in a public office, or a purported public record, report, statement, or data compilation, in any form, is from the public office where items of this nature are kept.

(8) *Ancient Documents or Data Compilation.* Evidence that a document or data compilation, in any form, (A) is in such condition as to create no suspicion concerning its authenticity, (B) was in a place where it, if authentic, would likely be, and (C) has been in existence 20 years or more at the time it is offered.

(9) *Process or System.* Evidence describing a process or system used to produce a result and showing that the process or system produces an accurate result.

(10) *Methods Provided by Statute or Rule.* Any method of authentication or identification provided by Act of Congress or by other rules prescribed by the Supreme Court pursuant to statutory authority.

RULE 902. SELF-AUTHENTICATION

Extrinsic evidence of authenticity as a condition precedent to admissibility is not required with respect to the following:

(1) **Domestic Public Documents Under Seal.** A document bearing a seal purporting to be that of the United States, or of any State, district, Commonwealth, territory, or insular possession thereof, or the Panama Canal Zone, or the Trust Territory of the Pacific Islands, or of a political subdivision, department, officer, or agency thereof, and a signature purporting to be an attestation or execution.

(2) **Domestic Public Documents Not Under Seal.** A document purporting to bear the signature in the official capacity of an officer or employee of any entity included in paragraph (1) hereof, having no seal, if a public officer having a seal and having official duties in the district or political subdivision of the officer or employee certifies under seal that the signer has the official capacity and that the signature is genuine.

(3) **Foreign Public Documents.** A document purporting to be executed or attested in an official capacity by a person authoriz-

ed by the laws of a foreign country to make the execution or attestation, and accompanied by a final certification as to the genuineness of the signature and official position (A) of the executing or attesting person, or (B) of any foreign official whose certificate of genuineness of signature and official position relates to the execution or attestation or is in a chain of certificates of genuineness of signature and official position relating to the execution or attestation.

A final certification may be made by a secretary of embassy or legation, consul general, consul, vice consul, or consular agent of the United States, or a diplomatic or consular official of the foreign country assigned or accredited to the United States. If reasonable opportunity has been given to all parties to investigate the authenticity and accuracy of official documents, the court may for good cause shown order that they be treated as presumptively authentic without final certification or permit them to be evidenced by an attested summary with or without final certification.

(4) **Certified Copies of Public Records.** A copy of an official record or report or entry therein, or of a document authorized by law to be recorded or filed and actually recorded or filed in a public office, including data compilations in any form, certified as correct by the custodian or other person authorized to make the certification, by certificate complying with paragraph (1), (2), or (3) of this rule or complying with any Act of Congress or rule prescribed by the Supreme Court pursuant to statutory authority.

(5) **Official Publications.** Books, pamphlets, or other publications purporting to be issued by public authority.

(6) **Newspapers and Periodicals.** Printed materials purporting to be newspapers or periodicals.

(7) **Trade Inscriptions and the Like.** Inscriptions, signs, tags, or labels purporting to have been affixed in the course of business and indicating ownership, control, or origin.

(8) **Acknowledged Documents.** Documents accompanied by a certificate of acknowledgment executed in the manner provided by law by a notary public or other officer authorized by law to take acknowledgments.

(9) **Commercial Paper and Related Documents.** Commercial paper, signatures thereon, and documents relating thereto to the extent provided by general commercial law.

(10) **Presumptions Under Acts of Congress.** Any signature, document, or other matter declared by Act of Congress to be presumptively or prima facie genuine or authentic.

[Amended effective October 1, 1987.]

RULE 903. SUBSCRIBING WITNESS' TESTIMONY UNNECESSARY

The testimony of a subscribing witness is not necessary to authenticate a writing unless required by the laws of the jurisdiction whose laws govern the validity of the writing.

ARTICLE X. CONTENTS OF WRITINGS, RECORDINGS, AND PHOTOGRAPHS

RULE 1001. DEFINITIONS

For purposes of this article the following definitions are applicable:

(1) **Writings and Recordings.** "Writings" and "recordings" consist of letters, words, or numbers, or their equivalent, set down by handwriting, typewriting, printing, photostating, photographing, magnetic impulse, mechanical or electronic recording, or other form of data compilation.

(2) **Photographs.** "Photographs" include still photographs, X-ray films, video tapes, and motion pictures.

(3) **Original.** An "original" of a writing or recording is the writing or recording itself or any counterpart intended to have the same effect by a person executing or issuing it. An "original" of a photograph includes the negative or any print therefrom. If data are stored in a computer or similar device, any printout or other output readable by sight, shown to reflect the data accurately, is an "original".

(4) **Duplicate.** A "duplicate" is a counterpart produced by the same impression as the original, or from the same matrix, or by means of photography, including enlargements and miniatures, or by mechanical or electronic re-recording, or by chemical reproduction, or by other equivalent techniques which accurately reproduces the original.

RULE 1002. REQUIREMENT OF ORIGINAL

To prove the content of a writing, recording, or photograph, the original writing, recording, or photograph is required, except as otherwise provided in these rules or by Act of Congress.

RULE 1003. ADMISSIBILITY OF DUPLICATES

A duplicate is admissible to the same extent as an original unless (1) a genuine question is raised as to the authenticity of the original or (2) in the circumstances it would be unfair to admit the duplicate in lieu of the original.

RULE 1004. ADMISSIBILITY OF OTHER EVIDENCE OF CONTENTS

The original is not required, and other evidence of the contents of a writing, recording, or photograph is admissible if—

(1) **Originals Lost or Destroyed.** All originals are lost or have been destroyed, unless the proponent lost or destroyed them in bad faith; or

(2) **Original Not Obtainable.** No original can be obtained by any available judicial process or procedure; or

(3) **Original in Possession of Opponent.** At a time when an original was under the control of the party against whom offered, that party was put on notice, by the pleadings or otherwise, that the contents would be a subject of proof at the hearing, and that party does not produce the original at the hearing; or

(4) **Collateral Matters.** The writing, recording, or photograph is not closely related to a controlling issue.

[Amended effective October 1, 1987.]

RULE 1005. PUBLIC RECORDS

The contents of an official record, or of a document authorized to be recorded or filed and actually recorded or filed, including data compilations in any form, if otherwise admissible, may be proved by copy, certified as correct in accordance with rule 902 or testified to be correct by a witness who has compared it with the original. If a copy which complies with the foregoing cannot be obtained by the exercise of reasonable diligence, then other evidence of the contents may be given.

RULE 1006. SUMMARIES

The contents of voluminous writings, records, or photographs which cannot conveniently be examined in court may be presented in the form of a chart, summary, or calculation. The originals, or duplicates, shall be made available for examination or copying, or both, by other parties at a reasonable time and place. The court may order that they be produced in court.

RULE 1007. TESTIMONY OR WRITTEN ADMISSION OF PARTY

Contents of writings, recordings, or photographs may be proved by the testimony or deposition of the party against whom offered or by that party's written admission, without accounting for the nonproduction of the original.

[Amended effective October 1, 1987.]

RULE 1008. FUNCTIONS OF COURT AND JURY

When the admissibility of other evidence of contents of writings, recordings, or photographs under these rules depends upon the fulfillment of a condition of fact, the question whether the condition has been fulfilled is ordinarily for the court to determine in accordance with the provisions of rule 104. However, when an issue is raised (a) whether the asserted writing ever existed, or (b) whether another writing, recording, or photograph produced at the trial is the original, or (c) whether other evidence of contents correctly reflects the contents, the issue is for the trier of fact to determine as in the case of other issues of fact.

ARTICLE XI. MISCELLANEOUS RULES

RULE 1101. APPLICABILITY OF RULES

(a) **Courts and Magistrates.** These Rules apply to the United States district courts, the District Court of Guam, the District Court of the Virgin Islands, the District Court for the Northern Mariana Islands, the United States Courts of Appeals, the United States Claims Court, and to United States bankruptcy judges and United States magistrates, in the actions, cases, and proceedings and to the extent hereinafter set forth. The terms "judge" and "court" in these rules include United States bankruptcy judges and United States magistrates.

(b) **Proceedings Generally.** These rules apply generally to civil actions and proceedings, including admiralty and maritime cases, to criminal cases and proceedings, to contempt proceedings except those in which the court may act summarily, and to proceedings and cases under title 11, United States Code.

(c) **Rule of Privilege.** The rule with respect to privileges applies at all stages of all actions, cases, and proceedings.

(d) **Rules Inapplicable.** The rules (other than with respect to privileges) do not apply in the following situations:

(1) *Preliminary Questions of Fact.* The determination of questions of fact preliminary to admissibility of evidence when the issue is to be determined by the court under rule 104.

(2) *Grand Jury.* Proceedings before grand juries.

(3) *Miscellaneous Proceedings.* Proceedings for extradition or rendition; preliminary examinations in criminal cases; sentencing, or granting or revoking probation; issuance of warrants for arrest, criminal summonses, and search warrants; and proceedings with respect to release on bail or otherwise.

(e) **Rules Applicable in Part.** In the following proceedings these rules apply to the extent that matters of evidence are not provided for in the statutes which govern procedure therein or in other rules prescribed by the Supreme Court pursuant to statutory authority: the trial of minor and petty offenses by United States magistrates; review of agency actions when the facts are subject to trial de novo under section 706(2)(F) of title 5, United States Code; review of orders of the Secretary of Agriculture under section 2 of the Act entitled "An Act to authorize association of producers of agricultural products" approved February 18, 1922 (7 U.S.C. 292), and under sections 6 and 7(c) of the Perishable Agricultural Commodities Act, 1930 (7 U.S.C. 499f, 499g(c)); naturalization and revocation of naturalization under sections 310–318 of the Immigration and Nationality Act (8 U.S.C. 1421–1429); prize proceedings in admiralty under sections 7651–7681 of title 10, United States Code; review of orders of the Secretary of the Interior under section 2 of the Act entitled "An Act authorizing associations of producers of aquatic products" approved June 25, 1934 (15 U.S.C. 522); review of orders of petroleum control boards under section 5 of the Act entitled "An Act to regulate interstate and foreign commerce in petroleum and its products by prohibiting the shipment in such commerce of petroleum and its products produced in violation of State law, and for other purposes", approved February 22, 1935 (15 U.S.C. 715d); actions for fines, penalties, or forfeitures under part V of title IV of the Tariff Act of 1930 (19 U.S.C. 1581–1624), or under the Anti-Smuggling Act

(19 U.S.C. 1701–1711); criminal libel for condemnation, exclusion of imports, or other proceedings under the Federal Food, Drug, and Cosmetic Act (21 U.S.C. 301–392); disputes between seamen under sections 4079, 4080, and 4081 of the Revised Statutes (22 U.S.C. 256–258); habeas corpus under sections 2241–2254 of title 28 United States Code; motions to vacate, set aside or correct sentence under section 2255 of title 28, United States Code; actions for penalties for refusal to transport destitute seamen under section 4578 of the Revised Statutes (46 U.S.C. 679); actions against the United States under the Act entitled "An Act authorizing suits against the United States in admiralty for damage caused by and salvage service rendered to public vessels belonging to the United States, and for other purposes", approved March 3, 1925 (46 U.S.C. 781–790), as implemented by section 7730 of title 10, United States Code.

[Amended December 12, 1975; amended effective October 1, 1982; April 1, 1984; October 1, 1987.]

RULE 1102. AMENDMENTS

Amendments to the Federal Rules of Evidence may be made as provided in section 2076 of title 28 of the United States Code.

RULE 1103. TITLE

These rules may be known and cited as the Federal Rules of Evidence.

*

INDEX

References are to Pages

ACCIDENTS
Other accidental occurrences, 168–71
Remedial steps following, 172–75
Trait of carelessness, 127–28

ADMISSIONS OF PARTY OPPONENT
See also, Hearsay Exceptions, Party admissions
Generally, 218–36
Adoption of another's statement, 224
Agent's statements, 224–29
By conduct and implication, 221–23
Coconspirator's statement, 232–33
Effect on factfinding, 219–20
Federal Rule, 233–35
Guilty plea in another action, 235–36
Illustration, 220–21
Nature of, 219–20
Personal knowledge not required, 236
Privity, 229–31
Rationale for, 209–10, 218
Silence, 222
Vicarious or representative, 223–31

ADVERSARY SYSTEM
Characteristics, 3–4
Civil law system compared, 19–22
Complex litigation, 9–13

ANCIENT DOCUMENT
Authentication, 527
Hearsay exception, 304 n. 2–305

ARGUMENT TO JURY
Admissions by party, 219–20
Closing argument, 118–19
Opening statement, 90

ATTORNEY–CLIENT PRIVILEGE
See Privileges

AUTHENTICATION
See also, Writings and Other Recordations
Ease of satisfaction under Federal Rules, 533–34
General nature, 514–15, 522–23
Judge's role, 515–19, 523–24

BEST EVIDENCE (ORIGINAL DOCUMENTS) RULE
See also, Writings and Other Recordations
Applicability to classes of secondary evidence, 533
Application and illustrations, 529
Basis for, 529, 531
Duplicates, 531
Federal Rules, 531–33
General nature, 523, 529
Identifying the original, 530
Multiple originals, 530

BIAS
See Impeachment

BLOOD TESTS
To establish identity, 499–500
To establish paternity, 501–03

BODILY CONDITION, STATEMENT OF
See Hearsay Exceptions, Physical condition, statements of

BREATH TEST
For intoxication, 508

BURDEN OF PERSUASION (PROOF)
Generally, 47–55, 59–62
Affirmative defenses, 50, 66–67
Criminal cases, 66
Criteria for allocating, 48
Directed verdict, 50–51

References are to Pages

BURDEN OF PERSUASION (PROOF)—Cont'd
Effect on instructions, 51–54
Nature of, 47–51
Presumption, effect of, 59–65
Production of evidence to meet, 51–53
Standard of persuasion, 48–49, 66
When decisive, 54

BURDEN OF PRODUCING EVIDENCE
Consequences of, 50–55
Illustrations, 51–55
Nature of, 50–51
Presumption, effect of, 55–57, 59–65

BUSINESS RECORDS
See Hearsay Exceptions, Records of business and related enterprises

CHAIN OF CUSTODY
To authenticate, 516–19

CHARACTER
Circumstantial use defined, 127
Civil cases, 127–30
Countervailing dangers, 124–25
Criminal cases, 130–34
Essential element of suit, 125–26
Examination of "character" witness, 134–38
Federal Rules, 129, 132–33, 140, 141
Non-party, 138–42
Probative value generally, 122–25
Types of evidence to prove, 124–25, 132–34
Victim, 138–42

CIRCUMSTANTIAL EVIDENCE
Character used circumstantially, 123–24, 127–34, 138–39
Compromises, 175–76
Distinguished from direct, 43
Habit, 146–48
Mental state as evidence of conduct, 248
Other criminal acts, 148–49, 153–61
Payment of medical expenses of injured party, 176
Probative force, 27–33
Rape victim's conduct, 142–44
Similar incidents in civil cases, 168–71
Subsequent remedial action, 172–75

CIVIL LAW SYSTEM
Compared with adversary system, 19–22
Criminal trials, 21
Judge's role, 20

CIVIL LAW SYSTEM—Cont'd
Variations within, 20

CLERGY PRIVILEGE
See Privileges, Priest-penitent

CLOSING ARGUMENT
See Opening Statement and Closing Argument

COCONSPIRATOR'S DECLARATIONS
Hearsay exception, 232–33
Judge's role, 232–33, 464–66

COLLATERAL MATTERS
Extrinsic evidence, 367–73
Nature of, 369–72

COMMENT
On evidence by judge, 9–10
Privilege, claim of, 425

COMPETENCY
Early impairments, 85
Effect of dead man's statutes, 87–89
Evidence, 85
Judge and jury, 86
Relation to impeachment, 86
Relation to privilege, 85
Witnesses generally, 85–87

COMPROMISE AND OFFERS OF COMPROMISE
Protected (inadmissible) statements, 175–76

CONDITIONAL RELEVANCE
See Relevance

CONDUCT
As hearsay, 193–98

CONFESSIONS
Generally, 436–46
History, 436–42
Judge's role, 460–61
Miranda case, 441–42
Miranda rule, modern application, 442–46
Nature of, 436

CONFRONTATION
Generally, 311–36
Early constructions, 319–24
Effect on availability of declarant requirement, 334–36

References are to Pages

CONFRONTATION—Cont'd
Effect on reliability of declaration requirement, 336
History, 311–19
Recent interpretations,
Inadi case, 333–36
Roberts case, 325–33
Relation to hearsay rule, 312–19

CONFUSION OF TRIER
As basis for excluding evidence, 34–35

CONVICTION OF CRIME
See Impeachment; Other Crimes

CREDIBILITY
See Impeachment

CROSS-EXAMINATION
See also, Examination of Witnesses
Accused, 115–18, 121
Effect of "scope rule" on privilege, 114
Exceeding direct, effects, 113
Federal Rule, 113
Impeachment, 112–13
Party who calls himself, 121
Scope, 110–114
Waiver, 91–92

CURATIVE ADMISSIBILITY ("OPENING THE DOOR")
Generally, 477–80
Explanation of doctrine, 477
Trial judge's discretion, 480

CUSTOM AND HABIT
Evidence to support, 145–48

DEAD MAN'S STATUTES
Generally, 87–90
Reform, 88–89

DEATH CERTIFICATE
Restrictions on admissibility, 277–78

DECLARATIONS AGAINST INTEREST
See Hearsay Exceptions

DEMONSTRATIVE AND REAL EVIDENCE
See Real and Demonstrative Evidence

DIRECT EXAMINATION
See also, Examination of Witnesses
Generally, 91–98
Character witness, 134, 138

DIRECT EXAMINATION—Cont'd
Forgetful witness, 95
Infant, 95
Leading questions, 93–95

DIRECTED VERDICT
Basis, 7, 50–52
Judge's responsibility, 50–53
Presumptions, 59–60

DRUNKENNESS
Detection of, 508
Opinion as to, 106–08

DYING DECLARATIONS
See Hearsay Exceptions

EVIDENCE
Bases for restricting, 3–4, 19
Definition, 2
Legal perspective, 2
Responsibility for admission, exclusion, use of, 4–6

EXAMINATION OF WITNESSES
See also, Cross-examination, Direct Examination, Expert Witness
Federal Rule, 96, 109
Judge's control, 91, 96
Leading, misleading, and argumentative questions, 93–98
Opinion rule (lay witness), 105–10
Refreshing recollection, 98–104
Scope of cross-examination, 110–14

EXCEPTIONS
See Objections

EXCITED UTTERANCE
See Hearsay Exceptions

EXPERIMENTS
Conditions of admissibility, 521–22
Use of, 520–21

EXPERT WITNESS
Basis for opinion, 486–89
Compelling testimony, 508–10
Cross-examination and impeachment, 491–93
Direct examination, 485–91
Federal Rules, 484, 489–90, 492, 510
Hypothetical question, 487–89
Learned treatises, use of, 492–93
Role and qualifications, 483–85
Subjects of testimony, 483–85

References are to Pages

EXPERT WITNESS—Cont'd
Training necessary, 485
Ultimate issue, 490

FACTS
See also, particular topics, especially Judge-Jury Roles
Adjudicative, 13–14, 16–17
Decisive in litigation, 1
Judicially noticed, 13–19
Legislative, 14–16

FAMILY RECORDS (PEDIGREE)
See Hearsay Exceptions

FIFTH AMENDMENT
See Privileges, Self-incrimination

FIRSTHAND (PERSONAL) KNOWLEDGE
Death certificates, 277–78
General requirement, 236, 456–57
Hearsay declarant, 457
Judge's role, 456–57
Party admissions, 236
Pedigree and family history, 305–06

FORM OF QUESTIONS
Argumentative, 97
Control by court, 91, 96
Cross-examination, 92, 95–97
Direct examination, 91–96
Federal Rule, 96
Hypothetical, 487–89, 491
Leading, 93–97
Misleading, 97–98

FORMER TESTIMONY
See Hearsay Exceptions

GUILTY PLEA
As party admission, 178, 280–81
Conclusive effect, 178
Withdrawn, 176

HABIT AND CUSTOM
Generally, 145–48
Character distinguished, 146
Federal Rule, 147

HEARSAY EXCEPTIONS
See also, Admissions of Party Opponent
Declarations against interest,
Generally, 296–304

HEARSAY EXCEPTIONS—Cont'd
Confrontation concerns, 327–30, 335–36
Corroboration, 300–02
Distinguished from party admissions, 296
Due process concerns, 303
Federal Rule, 301–02
Illustrations, 297–99
Kinds of interests, 297, 299–300, 302
Partially neutral or self-serving, 303
Rationale, 297
Dying declarations,
Generally, 292–96
Confrontation clause, 296, 319 n. 1
Federal Rule, 294–95
First-hand knowledge, 295–96
Offered by defense, 295
Rationale, 292–93
Religious belief as affecting admissibility, 295
Requirements, 295–96
Excited utterance,
Federal Rule, 239
Judge's role, 240, 242
Rationale, 239, 240–41
Requirements, 239–42
Res gestae, 243
Sex offenses, 243
Family records (pedigree), 305–06
Former testimony,
Generally, 285–92
Federal Rule, 287–89
Hearsay nature, 287
Illustrations, 285–86, 290
Predecessor's (privy's) earlier examination, 288–89, 290–91
Rationale, 285–86
Requirements, 286–90
Waiver of objections, 291
Identifications prior to trial, 207–08
Judgment of criminal conviction,
Generally, 278–83
Against person other than accused, 282–83
Federal Rule, 281
Illustrations, 278–79, 282–83
Issue preclusion, 278–81
Learned treatises, 492–93
Mental condition (state of mind), statements of,
As evidence of conduct, 248
Bearing on sanity, 259

References are to Pages

HEARSAY EXCEPTIONS—Cont'd
Federal Rule, 244, 258
Hillmon case, 250–52
Rationale, 249
Relevance in lawsuits, 247–48
Requirements, 249–59
Shepard case, 255–58
Will and intestate succession, 258–59
Party admissions,
Generally, 218–36
As nonhearsay, 209–10
Distinguished from declaration against interest, 296–97
Linked with other exceptions, 267
Physical condition, statements of,
Federal Rules, 244, 246
Made to medical personnel, 246
Requirements, 245–47
Revealing cause of injury, 247
Present sense impression,
Federal Rule, 237
Rationale, 238
Requirements, 237–39
Public records,
Double hearsay problem, 272
Federal Rule, 273–76, 278
Investigative findings, 275–76
Observations by law enforcement personnel, 274
Rationale, 271
Relation to business entries, 270–71, 276–77
Requirements, 272–73
Vital statistics, 277–78
Recorded recollection (past recollection recorded),
Federal Rule, 261
Rationale and application, 260–63
Refreshing recollection distinguished, 104–05, 259–60
Several persons involved, 263
Records of business and related enterprises,
Generally, 263–271
Absence of business duty, 266–67
Absence of entry, 270
Exclusion when entry suspect, 268–69
Federal Rules, 265, 270
Foundation required, 265–66
Medical diagnoses, 269
Rationale, 264
Showing cause of injury, 269–70
Res gestae, 243

HEARSAY EXCEPTIONS—Cont'd
Residual (catch-all) exceptions,
Generally, 308–11
Federal Rules, 308–10
Precedential value, 310
Unavailability of declarant, effect of,
Generally, 283–85
Confrontation clause, 328–31, 333–35
Federal Rule, 284–85

HEARSAY RULE
Bridges case, 213–14
Conduct, 193–98
Federal Rules, 208–212
Illustrative applications, 189–93
Non-assertive conduct, 194–98, 212
Polls and surveys, 216–17
Principle and rationale, 180–83
Prior identifications, 213
Prior statements of witness, 198–208, 212
Risks of inaccuracies, 182
Statements affecting another's mental state, 186–88
Statements having independent legal significance, 183–86
Statements revealing state of mind of speaker, 191–93
Statements showing knowledge, 188–89
Tribe triangle, 214–16
Verbal acts, 186
Written declarations, 193

HOSPITAL RECORDS
See Hearsay Exceptions, Records of business and related enterprises

HUSBAND-WIFE
See Privileges, Spousal

HYPNOSIS
General approach to admissibility, 379
Per se rule of exclusion, 380

HYPOTHETICAL QUESTION
See Expert Witness

IDENTIFICATION
See Hearsay Exceptions, Identifications prior to trial

IMPEACHMENT
See also, Rehabilitation (Accrediting or Bolstering) of Witness
Generally, 337–80

References are to Pages

IMPEACHMENT—Cont'd
Accrediting (rehabilitation), 373–77
Bad character (truth and veracity), 355–57
Bias, 357–61
Collateral matters, 367–73
Conviction of a crime, 343–52, 377
Extrinsic evidence, 345, 352–53, 358–59, 361–65, 367–73
Federal Rules, 342, 344–45, 348–52, 353–55, 357, 364–65, 377–78, 380
In limine ruling, 346
Meaning, 337–38
Means of proving conviction, 345
Of hearsay declarant, 380
One's own witness, 338–43
Pleas and plea bargaining, 377–78
Prior bad acts, 352–55
Prior inconsistent statements, 361–67
Protecting accused, 347–52
Scientific and medical evidence, 378–79
Surprise doctrine, 340–41
Witness called by court, 340
Witness required by law, 340

IMPLIED ASSERTIONS
See Hearsay Rule, Conduct

INSANITY
Affirmative defense, 66–67
Expert opinion, 490

INSTITUTIONAL LITIGATION
See Judge

INSTRUCTIONS TO JURY
Confessions, 461
Dying declarations, 461
Judge's duty, 6
Limiting use of evidence, 6, 189–90, 347
Preliminary fact, 458–59, 465–66
Presumptions, 59, 63–64, 78–80
Taking issues from jury, 51, 53
Types of instructions, 6
When given, 119

INTOXICATION
Tests to determine, 508

INVESTIGATIONS
See Hearsay Exceptions, Public records

JENCKS ACT
Application to refreshing recollection, 100–04

JOURNALIST
See Privileges, Journalist's source

JUDGE
See also, Judge-Jury Roles
Comment on evidence, 9–10
Control of trial proceedings, 96
Evidentiary issues, 45
Role in complex and institutional litigation, 9–13
Role in trial, 7–9

JUDGE–JURY ROLES
Generally, 452–68
Coconspirator's statements, 232–33, 464–66
Coincidence of preliminary and ultimate issues, 462–64, 466–67
Competence and technical exclusionary rules, 457–60
Confessions, 460–61
Evaluating evidence as a whole, 454
Hypothetical problem, 467–68
Individual offers of proof, 454–57
Overview, 7–9
Screening and factfinding, 452–53
Special situations, 460–68

JUDICIAL NOTICE
Adjudicative fact, 13–14, 17, 19
Conclusive effect, 13–14
Federal Rule, 16–17
Law, 18
Legislative fact, 14–17, 19
Responsibility for, 13

LEADING QUESTIONS
See Form of Questions

LIE DETECTOR (POLYGRAPH) TEST
Admissibility of results, 378–79

MAPS AND MODELS
Uses and requirements, 511–12

MARITAL COMMUNICATIONS
See Privileges, Spousal, Confidential communications

MATHEMATICAL PROBABILITIES
See Scientific Evidence (Proof), Probability evidence

MEDICAL EXPENSES
Paid by potential defendant, 176

MEMORY
Competency, 86
Recorded past recollection, 104–05, 259–62
Refreshing, 95, 98–104
Role in hearsay rule, 214–16
Tested by cross-examination, 182

MENTAL STATE
See Hearsay Exceptions, Mental condition; Hearsay Rule, Statements revealing state of mind of speaker

MILITARY AND STATE SECRETS
See Privileges, State secrets

MISLEADING QUESTION
See Form of Questions

MOTION IN LIMINE
Generally, 346, 480–81

MOTION PICTURES
Authentication, 519–20
Best evidence (original), 532

MOTION TO STRIKE
Function, 470

MULTIPLE PROBATIVE VALUE
Basic principle, 32–33, 148–49
Illustrations (selected), 32–33, 137, 174–75, 176–77, 184–93

NEWSMEN
See Privileges, Journalist's source

NOLO CONTENDERE
Inadmissible in subsequent suit, 176

NOTICE
To introduce prior conduct of rape victim, 144
To produce best evidence, 533 n. 22
To use old conviction to impeach, 344 n. 13

OATH OR AFFIRMATION
As bearing on witness's competency, 86
Effect on prior statement of witness, 210–11

OBJECTIONS
Curative admissibility, 477–80
Exceptions, 472
Federal Rule, 476–77
Former testimony, 291–92

OBJECTIONS—Cont'd
Function, 470
Motion in limine, 480–81
Tactical considerations, 481–82
Waiver and appellate review, 472–76, 481

OFFER OF PROOF
Cross-examination, 480
Federal Rule, 476–77
Meaning and purposes, 469–70
Motion in limine, 480–81
Proponent's responsibilities, 471–72

OFFICIAL WRITTEN STATEMENTS
See Hearsay Exceptions, Public records

OPENING STATEMENT AND CLOSING ARGUMENT
Closing argument, 118–19
Opening statement, 90
Order of argument, 119
Order, effect on jury, 120
Restrictions, 118

"OPENING THE DOOR"
See Curative Admissibility

OPINIONS
See also, Expert Witness
Basis for allowing, 106, 110
Basis of rule forbidding, 106
Federal Rule, 109
Lay witness, 105–110
Nature of, 105–06, 121
Ultimate issue, 108–09
Use as evidence, 109

ORDER OF PRESENTATION
Generally, 90–93, 96, 118–19
Conditionally relevant evidence, 42–43
Federal Rule, 96
Judge's control, 96

ORIGINAL WRITING RULE
See Best Evidence Rule

OTHER CLAIMS
By civil plaintiff, 177–78

OTHER CRIMES
See also, Impeachment
Generally, 148–67
Balancing competing considerations, 161–67
Certainty of commission, 150–53

OTHER CRIMES—Cont'd
Federal Rule, 155
Illustrations, 155–61
Offered by accused, 178
Possibilities for admitting, 177
"Quasi-crimes" offered in civil cases, 168, 171
Test of admissibility, 149, 153–54

OWN WITNESS
Examination of, 93–97
Impeachment of, 338–43

PARTY ADMISSIONS
See Admissions of Party Opponent; Hearsay Exceptions, Party admissions

PAST RECOLLECTION RECORDED
See also, Hearsay Exceptions, Recorded recollection
Distinguished from present recollection refreshed, 104–05

PATERNITY
See Blood Tests

PEDIGREE
See Hearsay Exceptions, Family records (pedigree)

PHOTOGRAPHS
Authentication, 519–20
Best evidence (original), 532

PHYSICIAN–PATIENT PRIVILEGE
See Privileges

PLAIN ERROR
As basis for appellate reversal, 472

PLEA BARGAINING
Protected statements, 377–78

POLICE REPORTS
See Hearsay Exceptions, Records of business and related enterprises; Public records

POLLS AND SURVEYS
Hearsay character, 216–17

PREJUDICE
See also, particular topics
As basis for excluding evidence, 34–40
Character evidence, 124–25, 130–31, 137, 141, 148

PREJUDICE—Cont'd
Evidence of other crimes, 149–50, 161–65
Impeachment by criminal convictions, 344–52
Meaning of, 44–45
Probability evidence, 496–99
Statements revealing declarant's state of mind, 257

PRELIMINARY QUESTIONS OF FACT
See also, Judge; Judge-Jury Roles
Nature of, 8–9, 457–58
Role of judge, 8–9, 457–60
Special situations, 460–67

PRESUMPTIONS
Generally, civil, 55–65
Generally, criminal, 65–78
Against burdened party, 82–83
Basic facts, 55
Conclusive, 57
Conflicting, 83
Constitutionality, 65–78
Disparate approaches, 60, 64–65
Factors or policies underlying, 58, 61
Federal Rules, 80–82
Impact on opponent, 59–64
Inference distinguished, 56–57
Instructing jury, 78–80
Mandatory, 67
Morgan view, 59–62
Nature and effect, 55–57
Permissive, 67
Rebuttal evidence, 59–64
Samples, 57–58
Special concerns in criminal cases, 66, 78
Strength of probative force, 65–66, 71–75
Thayer view, 59–65

PRIEST–PENITENT
See Privileges

PRIMA FACIE EVIDENCE
Coconspirator's statements, 465

PRIOR CONSISTENT STATEMENTS
Hearsay nature, 205–06
When admissible, 206–08, 277

PRIOR INCONSISTENT STATEMENTS
Extrinsic evidence, 361–65, 367
Federal Rule, 364–65
Foundation, 361–65

PRIOR INCONSISTENT STATEMENTS—Cont'd
Hearsay nature, 198–205, 366–67
Rule in Queen's case, 367
To impeach, 361–67

PRIVILEGES
Generally, 381–451
Attorney-client, 394–418
Agents and employees, 406–07
Corporate context, 412–17
Documents and objects, 399–403
Duration, 396–97
Eavesdroppers, 398–99
Experts, 407–11
Extended to third persons, 406–12
Holder, 405–06
Joint clients, 411
Overview, 394–96
Rationale, 394, 399
Requirements, 396–98
Scope, 399, 403–05, 408–09
Shared or "pooled" representation, 411–12
Upjohn case, 415–16
Waiver and nonapplicability, 417–18
Work product rule, 410
Executive, 450–51
Federal Rules, 384–85
Informer's identity, 451
Journalist's source, 448–49
Physician-patient,
Generally, 419–23
Duration, 420–21
Psychotherapist, 421–22
Rationale, 419
Preliminary factfinding, 467
Priest-penitent, 448
Rationale and characteristics, 381–84
Self-incrimination,
Generally, 423–46
Custodial interrogation, 436–46
History, 436–42
Miranda case, 441–46
Immunity, 430–31
Scope (generally), 423–30
Waiver, 431–36
Spousal, 386–94
Confidential communications, 386–90
Prevent adverse testimony, 390–94
State secrets, 449–50
Work-product doctrine, 447

PROBABILITY THEORY
See Scientific Evidence (Proof)

PROBATIVE VALUE
See Multiple Probative Value; Relevance

PSYCHOTHERAPISTS
See Privileges, Physician-patient

PUBLIC RECORDS
See Hearsay Exceptions

RADAR
See Scientific Evidence (Proof)

RAPE
Federal Rule, 142–44
Modern reform, 142
Promiscuous behavior of victim, 142
Shield laws, 142, 178–79

REAL AND DEMONSTRATIVE EVIDENCE
Admissibility and foundation, 513–19
Authentication (identification), 514–17
Chain of custody, 516–19
Change in condition, 515, 518
Counterweights to admission, 513–14
Experiments, 520–22
General nature, 511–13
Judge's discretion to admit, 514
Jury's use, 534
Photographs, X-rays, and motion pictures, 519–20
Probative value, 513

RECORDED PAST RECOLLECTION
See Hearsay Exceptions

REDIRECT EXAMINATION
Order and scope, 92

REFRESHING RECOLLECTION
Devices and techniques, 98
Federal Rule, 100
Judge's role, 99, 101
Leading questions allowed, 95, 98
Object used not evidence, 99, 120
Opponents' inspection and use of object, 99–104
Past recollection recorded distinguished, 104–05, 259–60
Writings, 98–104

REHABILITATION (ACCREDITING OR BOLSTERING) OF WITNESS
Generally, 373–77
"Fresh" complaints, 374–75

References are to Pages

REHABILITATION (ACCREDITING OR BOLSTERING) OF WITNESS—Cont'd
Prior consistent statements, 376–77
Probative force of accrediting evidence, 375–77
When allowed, 375

RELEVANCE
Assessing, 30–33
Assumptive admissibility, 33–34
Basic concepts, 23–26
Circumstantial and direct evidence, 43–44
Conditional, 40–43, 46
Credibility of witnesses, 26
Evidence restricted to relevant, 23–24
Federal Rules, 26, 40, 42, 144
Judge's role, 45
Legal relevance, 46
Meaning, 23
Offset by other considerations (counterweights), 33–40
Prejudice as counterweight, 44
Safety measures after accident, 172
Sexual conduct of rape victim, 142–44
Test of, 27–28
Time consumption as counterweight, 44
Underlying premises, 29–30

REMEDIAL MEASURES
See Safety Measures After Accident

REPUTATION
Affecting damage award, 177
Effect on defendant's state of mind, 144–45
Rape victim, 142–43
Used to show character, 124–26, 132
Witness's examination, 134–38

RES GESTAE
Meaning, 243

SAFETY MEASURES AFTER ACCIDENT
Generally, 172–75
Federal Rule, 174
Policy underlying exclusion, 172–73
Relevance of, 172
Strict liability cases, 174

SCIENTIFIC EVIDENCE (PROOF)
Generally, 493–510
Ballistics, 508

SCIENTIFIC EVIDENCE (PROOF)—Cont'd
Basic principles, 493–96, 503
Blood tests and typing, 499–503
Conclusive nature, 496, 501
Detection of intoxication, 508
Detection of lying, 378–80, 508
Detection of narcotics use, 508
Fingerprints, 507
Frye test, 494–96
Neutron activation analysis, 505–06
Probability evidence, 496–99
Radar, 504–05
Rejection of scientific evidence, 503–04
Spectrograph ("voiceprints"), 506–07

SELF-INCRIMINATION
See Privileges

SHOPBOOK RULE
History and nature, 264 n. 2

SIMILAR HAPPENINGS
See also, Habit and Custom; Other Crimes
Absence of, 168–69, 170
Civil actions generally, 168–71
Fraudulent and deceitful acts, 171
Probative force and counterweights, 168–69

SIXTH AMENDMENT
See Confrontation

SOUND RECORDINGS
Best evidence rule, 531–32

SPEED
Determination by radar, 493, 504–05
Opinion as to, 108

SPONTANEOUS DECLARATIONS
See Hearsay Exceptions; Excited utterance; Present sense impression

SPOUSES
See Privileges, Spousal

SUBSEQUENT REMEDIAL MEASURES
See Safety Measures After Accident

SUPPORT OF WITNESS
See Rehabilitation (Accrediting or Bolstering) of Witness

SURPRISE
As basis for exclusion of evidence, 34, 40

TELEPHONE CALLS
Authentication of, 534–35

THREATS
As affecting listener's state of mind, 145
As evidence of conduct of speaker, 145, 249–50

TIME CONSUMPTION
As basis of exclusion of evidence, 34, 36, 39

TREATISES
See Hearsay Exceptions, Learned treatises; Expert Witness, Learned treatises

TRIALS
Characteristics, 3–4
Civil law, 19–22
Components of, 90–93
Modern, complex litigation, 9–13
Order of proof, 90–91, 93
Role of judge and jury, 7–9

ULTIMATE ISSUE
See Opinions

UNAVAILABILITY
See Hearsay Exceptions, Unavailability of declarant, effect of

WAIVER
See particular topics, especially Objections; Privileges

WITNESS
See Competency; Form of Questions; Impeachment

WORK PRODUCT
Generally, 446–47
Applicable to expert's communications, 410

WRITINGS AND OTHER RECORDATIONS
See also, Authentication; Best Evidence Rule
Authentication,
Ancient document, 527
As general requirement, 522
Extrinsic evidence, 525–27
Federal Rules, 533–34
Judge's role, 535
Nature of, 523–25
Reply doctrine, 526–27
Self-authentication, 527–28
Telephone calls, 534–35
Best evidence (original documents) rule,
Basis for, 529, 531
Escapes from, 533
Federal Rules, 531–33
General nature, 523, 529
Photographs, 532
Sound recordings, 531–32
Telegrams, 530
When applicable, 529–33

X-RAYS
Foundation for admissibility, 519–520

†